EARLY JUDAISM
AND ITS MODERN INTERPRETERS

EARLY JUDAISM
AND ITS MODERN INTERPRETERS

SECOND EDITION

Edited by

Matthias Henze and Rodney A. Werline

SBL PRESS

Atlanta

Copyright © 2020 by SBL Press

All rights reserved. No part of this work may be reproduced or transmitted in any form or by any means, electronic or mechanical, including photocopying and recording, or by means of any information storage or retrieval system, except as may be expressly permitted by the 1976 Copyright Act or in writing from the publisher. Requests for permission should be addressed in writing to the Rights and Permissions Office, SBL Press, 825 Houston Mill Road, Atlanta, GA 30329 USA.

Library of Congress Control Number: 2020950497

Contents

Acknowledgments ix
Chronology xi
Abbreviations xiii

Introduction: The Modern Study of Early Judaism
    Matthias Henze and Rodney A. Werline................................. 1

Part 1. Historical and Social Settings

1. Jewish History from Alexander to Hadrian
   Chris Seeman 21

2. The Social World of Early Judaism
   Philip F. Esler 45

3. Judaism in the Diaspora
   Erich S. Gruen 69

4. Gender in Early Jewish Literature
   Françoise Mirguet 93

Part 2. Methods, Manuscripts, and Materials

5. New Methodologies
   Rodney A. Werline..117

6. The Dead Sea Scrolls
   Alison Schofield 147

7. Early Jewish Epigraphy
   Pieter W. van der Horst 183

8. Documentary Papyri
   Robert Kugler 205

9. The Archaeology of Early Judaism
   Eric M. Meyers 217

10. Early Judaism and Modern Technology
    Todd R. Hanneken 239

Part 3. Early Jewish Literatures

11. The Literature of Early Judaism
    Timothy H. Lim 257

12. Alexandrian Judaism
    Maren R. Niehoff 281

13. Thinking about Scripture in Second Temple Times
    James Kugel 305

14. Testaments
    Robert Kugler 329

15. Narrative Literature
    Sylvie Honigman 353

16. Jewish Historiography
    Steve Mason 379

17. Apocalyptic Literature
    Matthias Henze 405

18. Wisdom Literature
    Benjamin G. Wright III 437

19. Early Jewish Prayer
    Daniel K. Falk and Angela Kim Harkins 461

Part 4. The Afterlife of Early Judaism

20. Early Judaism and Rabbinic Judaism
    Ishay Rosen-Zvi 489

21. Early Judaism and Mysticism
    Andrea Lieber 519

22. Early Judaism and Early Christianity
    Lutz Doering 541

23. The Transmission History of the Apocrypha
    and Pseudepigrapha
    Liv Ingeborg Lied 567

Appendix 597
Contributors..611
Ancient Sources Index..613
Modern Scholars Index 630

Acknowledgments

We wish to thank our teachers, friends, and colleagues who kindly helped us with the production of this book. We express our sincere appreciation to Robert A. Kraft and George W. E. Nickelsburg, editors of the first edition of *Early Judaism and Its Modern Interpreters* some thirty-five years ago, a time when early Judaism had not yet become a recognizable field of study. The book soon became a classic, and many of us used it in our early days of study with great benefit. The idea of producing a second edition came from George W. E. Nickelsburg, who approached Bob Buller at SBL Press. Both of them offered their help throughout the process of producing this book, for which we owe them our gratitude. We have benefited immensely from our conversations with our colleagues Kelley Coblentz Bautch, Judith H. Newman, and Benjamin G. Wright III, who read parts of the manuscript and who gave us sage advice. Rodney Werline wishes to thank the Barton College Library for the many interlibrary loans and the Duke University Divinity School Library for allowing him access to their collection. At the SBL Press, Bob Buller, Heather McMurray, Nicole Tilford, and Lindsay Lingo saw the book through its production with characteristic professionalism. We remain grateful to all of them.

Matthias Henze
Rodney A. Werline

Chronology

BCE

539	Persian rule of Judea begins
515	Jerusalem temple rebuilt
332	Greek rule under Alexander begins
322–301	Wars between Diadochi
301–198	Ptolemies rule Judea
198–142	Seleucids rule Judea
177–164	Antiochus IV rules Seleucid Empire
167	Antiochus IV desecrates Jerusalem temple Hasmonean revolt begins
164	Rededication of the Jerusalem temple Antiochus IV dies
160	Judas dies in battle; Jonathan becomes leader
152	Jonathan becomes high priest
142	Jonathan dies; Simon becomes leader
140	Simon becomes high priest, commander, ethnarch
134	Simon dies; John Hyrcanus I becomes leader
129	Judea becomes independent
104–103	Aristobulus I is high priest and king
103–76	Alexander Jannaeus is high priest and king
76–67	Salome Alexandra rules
67–66	Dispute between Hyrcanus II and Aristobulus II; Aristobulus II emerges as victor
63	Pompey captures Jerusalem; Roman rule of Judea begins
42	Phasael and Herod appointed tetrarchs
37	Herod the Great becomes king of Judea
4	Herod the Great dies
4 BCE–6 CE	Archelaus rules Judea, Idumea, and Samaria Antipas rules Galilee and Perea Herod Philip II rules territory northwest of Galilee until 34 CE
6–41	Judea is Roman province governed by prefects

26–36	Pontius Pilate is prefect of Judea
41–44	Agrippa I rules most of Palestine
44–66	Roman procurators govern most of Palestine
66–70	Jewish revolt against Rome
70	Jerusalem temple destroyed by Titus
73/74	Masada falls to Romans
115–117	Jews revolt in Egypt, Cyprus, and Cyrene
132–135	Bar Kokhba Revolt
ca. 200	Codification of Mishnah

Abbreviations

Primary Sources

1 En.	1 Enoch
2 En.	2 Enoch
Abr.	Philo, *De Abrahamo*
Aem.	Plutarch, *Aemilius Paullus*
A.J.	Josephus, *Antiquitates judaicae*
Alex.	Plutarch, *Alexander*
Ann.	Tacitus, *Annales*
Att.	Cicero, *Epistulae ad Atticum*
b.	Babylonian Talmud
B. Bat.	Bava Batra
b. Qam.	Bava Qamma
Barn.	Barnabas
Bell. Cat.	Plutarch, *Bellum catalinae*
Bell. Jug.	Plutarch, *Bellum jugurthinum*
Ber.	Berakhot
Bib. hist.	Diodorus Siculus, *Bibliotheca historica*
B.J.	Josephus, *Bellum judaicum*
C. Ap.	Josephus, *Contra Apionem*
Cher.	Philo, *De cherubim*
Civ.	Augustine, *De civitate Dei*
Claud.	Suetonius, *Divus Claudius*
Comm. Matt.	Origen, *Commentarium in evangelium Matthaei*
Congr.	Philo, *De congressu eruditionis gratia*
Conf.	Philo, *De confusione linguarum*
Contempl.	Philo, *De vita contemplativa*
Decal.	Philo, *De decalogo*
Dem.	Plutarch, *Demosthenes*
De or.	Cicero, *De oratore*
Fact.	Valerius Maximus, *Factorum ac dictorum memorabilium libri IX*

Fam.	Cicero, *Epistulae ad familiares*
Flac.	Cicero, *Pro Flacco*
Flacc.	Philo, *In Flaccum*
Fug.	Philo, *De fuga et invention*
Git.	Gittin
Gramm.	Suetonius, *De garmmaticis*
Haer.	Irenaeus, *Adversus haereses*
Hag.	Hagigah
Hist.	Herodotus, *Historiae*; Polybius, *Historiae*; Tacitus, *Historiae*
Hist. eccl.	Eusebius, *Historia ecclesiastica*; Gelasius, *Historia ecclesiastica*
Hist. rom.	Cassius Dio, *Historia romana*
Hypoth.	Philo, *Hypothetica*
Inst.	Quintilian, *Institutio oratoria*
Jub.	Jubilees
Kip.	Kippurim
LAB	Liber antiquitatum biblicarum
LAE	Life of Adam and Eve
Leg.	Philo, *Legum allegoriae*
Legat.	Philo, *Legatio ad Gaium*
Let. Aris.	Letter of Aristeas
Luc.	Plutarch, *Lucullus*
m.	Mishnah
Math.	Sextus Empiricus, *Adversus mathematicos*
Meg.	Megillah
Menah.	Menahot
Migr.	Philo, *De migratione Abrahami*
Mos.	Philo, *De vita Mosis*
Nat.	Pliny, *Naturalis historia*
Nid.	Niddah
Oct.	Minucius Felix, *Octavius*
Pat.	Tertullian, *De patientia*
Praep. ev.	Eusebius, *Praeparatio evangelica*
P.W.	Thucydides, *History of the Peloponnesian War*
QE	Philo, *Quaestiones et solutiones in Exodum*
QG	Philo, *Quaestiones et solutiones in Genesin*
Quaest. conviv.	Plutarch, *Quaestiones convivialum libri IX*

Rhet	Suetonius, *De rhetoribus*
Sacr.	Philo, *De sacrificiis Abelis et Caini*
Sanh.	Sanhedrin
Sat.	Horace, *Satirae*; Juvenal, *Satirae*; Macrobius, *Saturnalia*
Somn.	Philo, *De somniis*
Spec.	Philo, *De specialibus legibus*
Sull.	Plutarch, *Sulla*
t.	Tosefta
Taʿan.	Taʿanit
Thes.	Plutarch, *Theseus*
Thuc.	Dionysius, *De Thucydide*
Tib.	Suetonius, *Tiberius*
T. Jos.	Testament of Joseph
T. Jud.	Testament of Judah
T. Levi	Testament of Levi
T. Naph.	Testament of Naphtali
T. Reu.	Testament of Reuben
Usu part.	Galen, *De Usu partium corporis humani*
Vir. ill.	Jerome, *De viris illustribus*
y.	Jerusalem
Yad.	Yadayim

Secondary Sources

AAAbo.H	Acta Academiae Aboensis Ser. A, Humaniora
AB	Anchor (Yale) Bible
ABRL	Anchor (Yale) Bible Reference Library
AbrN	*Abr Nahrain*
AcBib	Academia Biblica
ADPV	Abhandlungen des Deutschen Palästina-Vereins
AGJU	Arbeiten zur Geschichte des antiken Judentums und des Urchristentums
AJEC	Ancient Judaism and Early Christianity
AJSR	*Association for Jewish Studies Review*

ALGHJ	Arbeiten zur Literatur und Geschichte des hellenistischen Judentums
AmUStTR	American University Studies, Theology and Religion
ANEM	Ancient Near East Monographs
ANRW	*Aufstieg und Niedergang der römischen Welt: Geschichte und Kultur Roms im Spiegel der neueren Forschung. Part 2, Principat.* Edited by Hildegard Temporini and Wolfgang Haase. Berlin: de Gruyter, 1972–.
ANYAS	Annals of the New York Academy of Sciences
AOS	American Oriental Series
BAC	Bible in Ancient Christianity
BAR	*Biblical Archaeology Review*
BARIS	BAR International Series
BASOR	*Bulletin of the American Schools of Oriental Research*
BCAW	Blackwell Companions to the Ancient World
BEATAJ	Beiträge zur Erforschung des Alten Testaments und des antiken Judentums
BETL	Bibliotheca Ephemeridum Theologicarum Lovaniensium
BGBE	Beiträge zur Geschichte der biblischen Exegese
BibInt	*Biblical Interpretation*
BibInt	Biblical Interpretation Series
BibSem	Biblical Seminary
BIOSCS	*Bulletin of the International Organization for Septuagint and Cognate Studies*
BISNEL	Bar Ilan Studies in Near Eastern Languages and Culture
BJS	Brown Judaic Studies
BJSUCSD	Biblical and Judaic Studies from the University of California, San Diego
BLS	Bible and Literature Series
BMI	Bible and Its Modern Interpreters
BO	*Bibliotheca Orientalis*
BRLJ	Brill Reference Library of Judaism
BS	Mazar, Benjamin, Moshe Schwabe, Baruch Lifshitz, Nahman Avigad. *Beth She'arim I–III.* 3 vols. Jerusalem: Massada; New Brunswick: Rutgers University Press, 1973–1976.
BSJS	Brill's Series in Jewish Studies
BTAVO	Beihefte zum Tübinger Atlas des Vorderen Orients

BTB	*Biblical Theology Bulletin*
BThSt	Biblisch-theologische Studien
BW	Bible and Women
BWANT	Beiträge zur Wissenschaft vom Alten und Neuen Testament
BZAW	Beihefte zur Zeitschrift für die alttestamentliche Wissenschaft
BZNW	Beihefte zur Zeitschrift für die neutestamentliche Wissenschaft
CahRB	Cahiers de la revue biblique
CBET	Contributions to Biblical Exegesis and Theology
CBQMS	Catholic Biblical Quarterly Monographs Series
CCO	*Collectanea Christiana Orientalia*
CCS	Cambridge Classical Studies
CCSA	Corpus Christianorum: Series Apocryphorum
CEJL	Commentaries on Early Jewish Literature
CHANE	Culture and History of the Ancient Near East
CHJ	Cambridge History of Judaism
CIIP I	Cotton, Hannah M., et al. *Corpus Inscriptionum Iudaeae/Palaestinae, Volume I: Jerusalem; 1–1120*. 2 vols. Berlin: de Gruyter, 2010–2012.
CIIP II	Ameling, Walter, et al. *Corpus Inscriptionum Iudaeae/Palaestinae, Volume II: Caesarea and the Middle Coast; 1121–2160*. Berlin: de Gruyter, 2011.
CIIP III	Ameling, Walter, et al. *Corpus Inscriptionum Iudaeae/Palaestinae, Volume III: The South Coast; 2161–2648*. Berlin: de Gruyter, 2014.
CIIP IV	Ameling, Walter, et al. *Corpus Inscriptionum Iudaeae / Palaestinae, Volume IV: Iudaea/Idumaea; 2649–3978*. 2 vols. Berlin: de Gruyter, 2018.
CIJ	Frey, Jean-Baptiste. *Corpus Inscriptionum Judaicarum: Recueil des inscriptions juives qui vont du IIIe siècle avant Jésus-Christ au VIIe siècle de notre ère*. 2 vols. Rome: Pontificio Istituto di Archeologia Cristiana, 1936–1952. Vol. 1 repr., New York: Ktav, 1975.
CJAn	Christianity and Judaism in Antiquity
ClAnt	*Classical Antiquity*
ConBNT	Coniectanea Biblica New Testament

CPJ 1–3	*Corpus Papyrorum Judaicarum*. Edited by Victor A. Tcherikover and Alexander Fuks. 3 vols. Cambridge: Harvard University Press, 1957–1960.
CPJ 4	*Corpus Papyrorum Judaicarum*. Edited by Tal Ilan and Noah Hacham. Berlin: de Gruyter, 2020.
CPR	Corpus Papyrorum Raineri
CQS	Companion to the Qumran Scrolls
CRINT	Compendia Rerum Iudaicarum ad Novum Testamentum
CSHJ	Chicago Studies in the History of Judaism
CurBR	*Currents in Biblical Research*
CurBS	*Currents in Research: Biblical Studies*
CW	Classical World
DCLS	Deuterocanonical and Cognate Literature Studies
DCLY	*Deuterocanonical and Cognate Literature Yearbook*
DJD	Discoveries in the Judaean Desert
DMOA	Documenta et Monumenta Orientis Antiqui
DSD	*Dead Sea Discoveries*
EANEC	Explorations in Ancient Near Eastern Civilizations
ECDSS	Eerdmans Commentaries on the Dead Sea Scrolls
ECL	Early Christianity and Its Literature
EJL	Early Judaism and Its Literature
EPRO	Etudes préliminaires aux religions orientales dans l'empire romain
ErIsr	*Eretz Israel*
ET	English Translation/Text
ETR	*Études théologiques et religieuses*
ExpTim	*Expository Times*
FBBS	Facet Books, Biblical Series
FCB	Feminist Companion to the Bible
frag(s).	fragment(s)
FSBP	Fontes et Subsidia ad Bibliam Pertinentes
HBM	Hebrew Bible Monographs
HBS	Herders biblische Studien
HCS	Hellenistic Culture and Society
HdO	Handbuch der Orientalistik
HDR	Harvard Dissertations in Religion
HeBAI	*Hebrew Bible and Ancient Israel*
Hen	*Henoch*

Hesperia	*Hesperia: The Journal of the American School of Classical Studies at Athens*
HSCP	*Harvard Studies in Classical Philology*
HSM	Harvard Semitic Monographs
HSS	Harvard Semitic Studies
HTS	*Harvard Theological Studies*
HUCA	*Hebrew Union College Annual*
HUCM	Monographs of the Hebrew Union College
HvTSt	*Hervormde teologiese studies*
IECOT	International Exegetical Commentary on the Old Testament
IEJ	*Israel Exploration Journal*
IJO 1	Noy, David, Alexander Panayotov, and Hans-Wulf Bloedhorn. *Inscriptiones Judaicae Orientis I: Eastern Europe.* TSAJ 101. Tübingen: Mohr Siebeck, 2004.
IJO 2	Ameling, Walter. *Inscriptiones Judaicae Orientis II: Kleinasien.* TSAJ 99. Tübingen: Mohr Siebeck, 2004.
IJO 3	Noy, David, and Hans-Wulf Bloedhorn. *Inscriptiones Judaicae Orientis III: Syria and Cyprus.* TSAJ 102. Tübingen: Mohr Siebeck, 2004.
ISBL	Indiana Studies in Biblical Literature
JAAR	*Journal of the American Academy of Religion*
JAH	*Journal of Ancient History*
JAJ	*Journal of Ancient Judaism*
JAJSup	Journal of Ancient Judaism Supplements
JBL	*Journal of Biblical Literature*
JBR	*Journal of Bible and Religion*
JBS	Jerusalem Biblical Studies
JBTh	*Jahrbuch für biblische Theologie*
JDS	Judean Desert Studies
JECS	*Journal of Early Christian Studies*
JHebS	*Journal of Hebrew Scriptures*
JIGRE	Horbury, William, and David Noy. *Jewish Inscriptions of Graeco-Roman Egypt.* Cambridge: Cambridge University Press, 1992.
JIWE 1	Noy, David. *Jewish Inscriptions of Western Europe I: Italy (Excluding the City of Rome), Spain and Gaul.* Cambridge: Cambridge University Press, 1993.

JIWE 2	Noy, David. *Jewish Inscriptions of Western Europe II: The City of Rome*. Cambridge: Cambridge University Press, 1995.
JJS	*Journal of Jewish Studies*
JJSSup	Journal of Jewish Studies Supplement Series
JJTP	*Journal of Jewish Thought and Philosophy*
JJTPSup	Supplements to the Journal of Jewish Thought and Philosophy
JQR	*Jewish Quarterly Review*
JR	*Journal of Religion*
JRA	*Journal of Roman Archaeology*
JRASup	Journal of Roman Archaeology Supplement Series
JRS	*Journal of Roman Studies*
JSem	*Journal of Semitics*
JSHRZ	Jüdische Schriften aus hellenistisch-römischer Zeit
JSJ	*Journal for the Study of Judaism*
JSJSup	Supplements to the Journal for the Study of Judaism
JSNT	*Journal for the Study of the New Testament*
JSNTSup	Journal for the Study of the New Testament Supplement Series
JSocS	*Jewish Social Studies* NS
JSPSup	Journal for the Study of the Pseudepigrapha Supplement Series
JSQ	*Jewish Studies Quarterly*
JSRC	Jerusalem Studies in Religion and Culture
JTS	*Journal of Theological Studies*
LAI	Library of Ancient Israel
LCBI	Literary Currents in Biblical Interpretation
LHBOTS	Library of Hebrew Bible/Old Testament
LSTS	Library of Second Temple Studies
MEP	Meiron Excavation Project
MJSt	Münsteraner Judaistische Studien
MnS	Mnemosyne Supplementum
MS	manuscript
MScRel	*Mélanges de science religieuse*
MT	Masoretic Text
NEAEHL	Stern, Ephraim, ed. *The New Encyclopedia of Archaeological Excavations in the Holy Land*. 5 vols. Jerusalem: Israel Exploration Society, 1993, 2008.

NedTT	*Nederlands theologisch tijdschrift*
NHMS	Nag Hammadi and Manichaean Studies
NovT	*Novum Testamentum*
NovTSup	Supplements to Novum Testamentum
NS	new series
NTOA	Novum Testamentum et Orbis Antiquus
NTOA.SA	Novum Testamentum et Orbis Antiquus, Series Archaeologica
NTS	*New Testament Studies*
NTTS	New Testament Tools and Studies
ÖBS	Österreichische biblische Studien
OBT	Overtures to Biblical Theology
OLA	Orientalia Lovaniensia Analecta
OTE	*Old Testament Essays*
OTM	Oxford Theological Monographs
OTP	Charlesworth, James H., ed. *Old Testament Pseudepigrapha*. 2 vols. New York: Doubleday, 1983–1985.
OTS	Old Testament Studies
OTWSA	*Oud Testamentiese Werkgemeenschap in Suid-Afrika*
par.	parallel
P.Count	Clarysse, Willy, and Dorothy Thompson, eds. *Counting the People in Hellenistic Egypt*. CCS. 2 vols. Cambridge: Cambridge University Press, 2006.
P.Polit.Iud.	Maresch, Klaus and James M. S. Cowey, eds. *Urkunden des Politeuma der Juden von Herakleopolis (144/3, 133/2 v. Chr.)*. Papyrologica Coloniensia 29. Wiesbaden: Westdeutscher, 2001.
P.Murabbaʿât	Benoit, P., J. T. Milik, and R. de Vaux. *Les grottes de Murabbaʿât*. Oxford: Clarendon, 1961.
P.Yadin 2	Yadin, Y., J. C. Greenfield, A. Yardeni, and and B. A. Levine, eds. *Hebrew, Aramaic and Nabataean—Aramaic Papyri*. Vol. 2 of *The Documents from the Bar Kochba Period in the Cave of Letters*. Jerusalem: Israel exploration Society, 2002.
PSBF	Pubblicazioni dello Studium Biblicum Franciscanum
PTSDSSP	Princeton Theological Seminary Dead Sea Scrolls Project.
PVTG	Pseudepigrapha Veteris Testamenti Graece
RAC	Klauser, Theodor, et al., eds. *Reallexikon für Antike und Christentum*. Stuttgart: Hiersemann, 1950–.

RB	*Revue Biblique*
REJ	*Revue des études juives*
RelSoc	Religion and Society
RevQ	*Revue de Qumran*
RGRW	Religions in the Graeco-Roman World
RHPR	*Revue d'histoire et de philosophie religieuses*
RHR	*Revue de l'histoire des religions*
RMP	*Rheinisches Museum für Philologie* NS
RRJ	*Review of Rabbinic Judaism*
RSR	*Religious Studies Review*
RVV	Religionsgeschichtliche Versuche und Vorarbeiten
SBLDS	Society of Biblical Literature Dissertation Series
SBLMS	Society of Biblical Literature Monograph Series
SBLSP	Society of Biblical Literature Seminar Papers
SBLTT	Society of Biblical Literature Texts and Translations
SBS	Stuttgarter Bibelstudien
SBT	Studies in Biblical Theology
SBTS	Sources for Biblical and Theological Study
SC	Sources Chrétiennes
SCI	*Scripta Classica Israelica*
SCJud	Studies in Christianity and Judaism
Scr	*Scriptura*
SCS	Septuagint and Cognate Studies
SDSS	Studies in the Dead Sea Scrolls and Related Literature
SEÅ	*Svensk exegetisk årsbok*
SemeiaSt	Semeia Studies
SFSHJ	South Florida Studies in the History of Judaism
sg.	singular
SIJD	Schriften des Institutum Judaicum Delitzschianum
SJ	Studia Judaica
SJLA	Studies in Judaism in Late Antiquity
SJOT	*Scandinavian Journal of the Old Testament*
SNTSMS	Society for New Testament Studies Monograph Series
SPhiloA	*Studia Philonica Annual*
ST	Studia Theologica
STAC	Studien und Texte zu Antike und Christentum
STDJ	Studies on the Texts of the Desert of Judah
StPB	Studia Post-biblica
SUNT	Studien zur Umwelt des Neuen Testaments

SVTP	Studia in Veteris Testamenti Pseudepigrapha
SymS	Symposium Series
TANZ	Texte und Arbeiten zum neutestamentlichen Zeitalter
TBN	Themes in Biblical Narrative
TBT	*The Bible Today*
Text	*Textus*
TLZ	*Theologische Literaturzeitung*
Transeu	*Transeuphratène*
TSAJ	Texts and Studies in Ancient Judaism
TUGAL	Texte und Untersuchungen zur Geschichte der altchristlichen Literatur
UBS.MS	United Bible Societies Monograph Series
VC	*Vigiliae Christianae*
VCSup	Supplements to Vigiliae Christianae
VTSup	Supplements to Vetus Testamentum
WGRW	Writings from the Greco-Roman World
WLAW	Wisdom Literature of the Ancient World
WMANT	Wissenschaftliche Monographien zum Alten und Neuen Testament
WUNT	Wissenschaftliche Untersuchungen zum Neuen Testament
ZAC	*Zeitschrift für Antikes Christentum/Journal of Ancient Christianity*
ZPE	*Zeitschrift für Papyrologie und Epigraphik*
ZTK	*Zeitschrift für Theologie und Kirche*

Introduction:
The Modern Study of Early Judaism

MATTHIAS HENZE AND RODNEY A. WERLINE

The First Edition of *Early Judaism and Its Modern Interpreters*

The first edition of *Early Judaism and Its Modern Interpreters*, edited by Robert A. Kraft and George W. E. Nickelsburg, was published in 1986 as part of a trilogy of volumes. The other two volumes in the series focus on the Hebrew Bible (Knight and Tucker 1985) and the New Testament (Epp and McRae 1989), and together they are part of the 1980 centennial celebration of the Society of Biblical Literature. Douglas K. Knight, who served as the trilogy's editor, summarized the task and goal of the series in the following manner: "The three volumes that make up The Bible and Its Modern Interpreters encompass the international range of research on, respectively, the Hebrew Bible, Early Judaism, and the New Testament. Structured according to the usual subdisciplines and subject matter, each sets for itself the task of describing the course of scholarship since ca. 1945. The essays are intended as critical reviews, appraising the current state of affairs in each area of study and calling attention to the issues that scholars should face in the years ahead" (Kraft and Nickelsburg 1986, "Preface to the Series").

This revised edition of *Early Judaism and Its Modern Interpreters* intends to honor the spirit of the earlier volume and the trilogy. The idea of producing this second edition originated with George Nickelsburg, who approached Bob Buller at SBL Press about the project. The press secured the two of us, Matthias Henze and Rodney Werline, to serve as editors of the volume. Both Nickelsburg, and Buller encouraged us to follow the same approach as the first edition. There are emerging ideas about producing second editions of the other two volumes of the original trilogy, but much of the initial planning for those volumes remains.

The first edition reviewed, analyzed, and assessed scholarship in the field from 1945 to 1980, though the volume was not in print until 1986. The reviews in prominent journals were nearly always positive. The volume's essays, several written by newly established scholars, often revealed the mistakes, oversimplifications, and anti-Jewish tendencies of the previous generations (see, e.g., the reviews by Greenspoon 1988; Janowitz 1989; VanderKam 1989). By contrast, the new and emerging scholarship portrayed a Judaism of the period that was varied, complex, and dynamic. Informal and anecdotal reviews rang just as positive. Several contributors to this new edition, as well as other colleagues who learned about this current project, recalled how the first edition helped them navigate their doctoral programs by assisting in preparations for comprehensive exams and revealing possible dissertation topics.

The Study of Early Judaism since the First Edition of *Early Judaism and Its Modern Interpreters*

Commenting on the forty years in between the end of World War II and the publication of the first edition of *Early Judaism and Its Modern Interpreters*, Kraft and Nickelsburg noted the dramatic increase in interest in early Judaism: "This explosion of interest in the history and literatures of early Judaism is one of the most remarkable developments in biblical studies in the past forty years, for it has involved the rebirth and rapid growth of an entire subdiscipline" (1986, 3). Over the last forty years since then, we have seen an even more dramatic increase in scholarly activities, and the subdiscipline of which Kraft and Nickelsburg write has grown and matured into a discipline of its own. One of the most significant changes in the study of early Judaism has been the increased availability of, and ready access to, the ancient texts themselves, both to the texts in their English translations and to their manuscripts. As more and more texts have become readily available to the modern reader, a host of new tools has also appeared, designed to make the world of early Judaism accessible to specialists and nonspecialists alike. Together, these publications have completely transformed the modern study of early Judaism and have led to a remarkable shift in perception.

The advances in the publication of texts and new data are nowhere more evident than in the case of the Dead Sea Scrolls. As many of the essays in this volume repeat, when the first edition of *Early Judaism and Its*

Modern Interpreters was in preparation, not all the Dead Sea Scrolls were in print. In fact, by 1980, only volumes 1–6 of Discoveries in the Judaean Desert had been published. Soon the pace of scrolls projects picked up, and the volumes in the series began to appear regularly. Oxford University Press has recently announced that the series, which began in 1951, is now complete with forty volumes, which means that since 1980 thirty-four volumes have been published. Unsurprisingly, perhaps no other phenomenon in early Jewish studies over the past four decades has had an impact that matches that of the scrolls. Nearly every contribution in this volume refers to them. While Alison Schofield's essay rehearses the implications of scroll studies, their contribution to the understanding of early Jewish groups and sects and the production and transmission of texts have had far-ranging consequences across the disciplines. One can add to this their value for providing a fuller picture of Jewish thought, ideas, uses of scriptural traditions, literary genres, religious practices, and much more. The availability and accessibility of the scrolls steadily drew a greater number of scholars committed to their interpretation.

The scrolls are not the only texts that have become available. In 1980, James H. Charlesworth's *The Old Testament Pseudepigrapha* (*OTP*) was in the works but not yet in print. However, a few essays in the first edition of *Early Judaism and Its Modern Interpreters* list both of Charlesworth's edited volumes in their bibliographies, and the list of abbreviations in the front matter and in the appendix contains both volumes. Since then, Charlesworth's edition of the Pseudepigrapha has become the most widely used English translation. More recently, Richard Bauckham, James R. Davila, and Alexander Panayotov (2013) have published more Old Testament pseudepigraphic texts, with yet another volume forthcoming.

We have also seen a staggering increase in secondary literature since the first edition. This includes several new monograph series and journals. For example, The Journal for the Study of the Pseudepigrapha Supplement Series was launched in 1988. In the 1990s, SBL Press consolidated earlier series into Early Judaism and Its Literature. The first volume, *Women Like This: New Perspectives on Jewish Women in the Greco-Roman World*, was edited in 1991 by Amy-Jill Levine. In 1996, Brill replaced the Studia Post Biblica monograph series with the Journal for the Study of Judaism Supplement Series, which has yielded volumes 49–193. In addition, new journals were created, such as the *Journal for the Study of the Pseudepigrapha* (1987), *Dead Sea Discoveries* (1994), and the *Journal of Ancient Judaism* (2010).

A number of critical commentaries have appeared on early Jewish writings. The most significant series in which these works are included are Hermeneia (Fortress), Commentaries on Early Jewish Literature (de Gruyter), and the Oxford Commentary on the Dead Sea Scrolls (Oxford). Eerdmans also commissioned and began to publish commentaries on the Dead Sea Scrolls. Besides these, several handbooks, dictionaries, and encyclopedias have been produced in the past decade, such as *The Oxford Handbook of the Dead Sea Scrolls* (Lim and Collins 2010), *The Eerdmans Dictionary of Early Judaism* (Collins and Harlow 2010), *The Oxford Handbook of Apocalyptic Literature* (Collins 2014), *T&T Clark Companion to the Dead Sea Scrolls* (Brooke and Hempel 2019), and the *T&T Clark Encyclopedia of Second Temple Judaism* (Stuckenbruck and Gurtner 2019). Further, several software companies, like Accordance and the now-shutdown BibleWorks (as of 2018), offer packages that include the Dead Sea Scrolls, some Greek Pseudepigrapha, the LXX, Josephus, and Philo. As the essay by Todd Hanneken, "Early Judaism and Modern Technology," in this volume explains, online databases continue to emerge and expand. This volume's appendix records a much fuller list of the most relevant titles.

Abiding Challenges with Our Terminology and Categories

Like the first volume, this new edition of *Early Judaism and Its Modern Interpreters* provides a snapshot of the field, which includes and, ideally, exposes the stresses and strains on some of our current working categories. Contributors also anticipate where their subdisciplines may be headed. This latter assignment includes what should be addressed in our scholarship and what should be avoided or discarded.

As tempting as it is to play the role of the iconoclast, discard problematic categories, and create new ones, this volume does not take up that mission. The central reason for this is that, while there is broad recognition of the problems with our current vocabulary and classifications, no consensus on new terminology and categories has yet emerged. This volume delineates problems and raises concerns, but it does not seek to forge a new consensus. For the moment, we continue to operate with the categories and terms that we see in the field while fully recognizing the deficiencies and limitations of many of these matters. Hopefully, these acknowledgements will hedge against mischaracterizations and misunderstandings in the presentations here included. To paraphrase Randall Chesnutt's (2019) assessment at the celebration of fifty years of the Pseudepigrapha Group at the 2019 Annual Meeting of the Society of Biblical Literature in San Diego, our designations and categories offer only limited heuristic value, which assumes full recognition of their faults and limitations. With that recognition, then, they must be applied with caution.

A review of a few key and more general problems is required. The place to begin is with the terms related to the title of this volume: *Judaism* and *early*. Commonly used modern definitions and categorizations of Jews and Judaism do not adequately account for the meanings of the terms in the Greco-Roman period (see, e.g., Collins 2017; Mason 2007, 2014; Reed 2014; Reinhartz 2014; Boyarin 2019). Steve Mason has argued that *Ioudaios* in the Greco-Roman period referred to people associated with the territory of Judea and the customs of those people and that the beginnings of a category "Judaism" can be traced to the ascendency of Christianity in the third–fifth centuries CE (Mason 2007, 2014; but cf. the nuances offered by Reed). Shaye Cohen charts the transformation of the term Jew (*Ioudaios*) beginning in the Second Temple period "from membership in a people to citizenship in a state to adherence to a religion, to membership in an enthnoreligion" (Cohen 1999, 348). Cohen asserts that

> all occurrences of the term *Ioudaios* before the middle or end of the second century B.C.E. should be translated not as "Jew," a religious term, but as "Judean," an ethnic-geographic term. In the second half of the second century B.C.E. the term *Ioudaios* for the first time is applied to people who are not ethnic or geographic Judeans but who either have come to believe in the God of the Judeans (i.e., they have become "Jews") or have joined the Judean state as citizens (i.e., they have become "Judeans" in a political sense). (71)

Within Cohen's schema, then, up to the mid-second century BCE the designation *Ioudaios* functioned in the same way as Syrians, Greeks, or Egyptians (cf. Cohen 1999, 77–78). However, even after this date the term still might connote the geographic origins of a person. In regards to this volume, then, if Cohen is correct, the term Jew is in flux in the historical period under investigation, and accounting for that is not always simple. As Loren Stuckenbruck (2019, 3) notes in his discussion of the problems of terminology, a couple of sources from the era use the designation Judaism (*Ioudaïsmos*; see 2 Macc 2:21, 8:1, 14:38; cf. 4 Macc 4:26).

When we consider Second Temple Judaism or early Judaism from the perspective of a religion, further difficulties emerge. Jonathan Z. Smith (1988, 234–35) alerted scholars that religion as a category is a modern scholarly invention: "It is the study of religion that created the category, it is the study of religion that invented 'religion'.... Religion is solely the creation of the scholar's study. It is created for the scholar's analytical purposes by his [sic] imaginative acts of comparison and generalization. Religion has no independent existence apart from the academy." Thus, religion is not a distinct category in the mind of the people who lived in this era. The term is etic, not emic.

Also problematic is the term *early* when attached to Judaism. Kraft and Nickelsburg (1986, 2) recognized the weaknesses of this qualifier. *Early* apparently accepts the continuity between Judaism that arises about the time of Ezra, through the Second Temple, to the classical Judaism of the Mishnah and Talmuds. Thus, while they complain that "'early Judaism' is not a particularly precise term," they adopt the designation "by default for its simplicity and relative comprehensiveness." They go on to explain the category in this manner: "By 'early Judaism' we intend to refer to the phenomena collectively designated 'Judaism' in the period bounded approximately by Alexander the Great (330 B.C.E.) on the one end and the Roman Emperor Hadrian (138 C.E.) on the other" (2). While generally not a problem for the study of this era (though see Klawans 2006), assuming that the contours of the era roll directly into rabbinic Judaism, classical Judaism can convey a false sense of inevitability that would have obviously not been recognized by the people living at that time. Further, this can sometimes determine or delimit questions and perspectives that one might have about texts in this era and thus skew their interpretation (see Klawans 2006; cf. Najman and Garrison 2019, 334–35). A corollary to this problem is the way in which anachronistic canonical assumptions can creep into interpretation. As discussed below, canonical assumptions bedevil our categories for modern constructions of collected texts, like apocrypha and pseudepigrapha.

The other possible designation for the era is the Second Temple period. This has the advantage of pushing the *terminus a quo* into the Persian era, to 515 BCE. However, the *terminus ad quem* becomes a problem because the Second Temple is destroyed in 70 CE. If strictly applied, this would exclude several important texts from consideration, such as 4 Ezra and 2 Baruch. Kraft and Nickelsburg knew that they were setting the chronological boundaries in a somewhat arbitrary manner, but they needed to make some decision on the limits of their period. However, one wonders to what degree the *terminus a quo* of the first edition was externally determined by the first volume in the series, *The Hebrew Bible and Its Modern Interpret-*

ers. That volume continued past 515 BCE, the time of the completion of the Second Temple, in order to discuss aspects of the Persian period. The struggle to define the era is also apparent in Nickelsburg's title for his introduction to the literature of the era—*Jewish Literature between the Bible and the Mishnah: A Historical and Literary Introduction* (2005)—though he examined texts in the Bible and the Apocrypha. Further, some might question if the use of the designation *Bible* in the title of that volume is anachronist and assumes a canonical category that, at the time, simply did not exist.

The point here is not to criticize Kraft's and Nickelsburg's choices or that of other scholars, for that matter, but to highlight the difficulties—which Kraft and Nickelsburg acknowledged—and to recognize that after forty years the problems have not disappeared, nor have satisfactory alternatives arrived. At the moment, there seems to be no clear way out of this array of problems with our categories and designations; certainly no consensus has emerged. Thus, scholars continue to work with these categories, being mindful of their limitations. Consider the ongoing use of some of these terms in titles for journals, monograph series, dictionaries, encyclopedias, and handbooks published over the past decades, and even as recently as 2019 with *T&T Clark Encyclopedia of Second Temple Judaism* (Stuckenbruck and Gurtner). Compare also Collins and Harlow *The Eerdmans Dictionary of Early Judaism* (2010). Constant vigilance about these matters during the interpretive process provides the only security against misinterpretation and misrepresentation.

For this volume, because no path clear of these problems is currently available, we have stayed with the same title as the first edition and have told the contributors to cover the era roughly from the construction of the Second Temple to the codification of the Mishnah—in other words, from ca. 515 BCE to ca. 200 CE. Part 4 of this volume reviews the ties between the literature and movements of this era and the immediately following era and thus extends beyond 200 CE.

The Terms *Apocrypha* and *Pseudepigrapha*

Apart from the problem of how to name and date the era of early Judaism, the terms that are widely used to designate the early Jewish writings are equally problematic. Especially acute are the problems with the terms *apocrypha* and *pseudepigrapha* (Stuckenbruck 2012). One basic problem with them is that both assume the existence of a biblical canon, particularly a Christian (Protestant) canon. This means that the labels are theological and primarily Western constructs (Ahearne-Kroll 2019, 124).

Jerome coined the term apocrypha to designate and set apart books that are not included in the Hebrew Bible (Feder and Henze, 2019–2020). His choice of word was clearly deliberate, to distinguish apocryphal from canonical books. Martin Luther adopted both the term apocrypha and the concept of a textual hierarchy from Jerome and, in his 1532 German translation of the Old Testament, grouped them together and placed them at the end of his Bible translation. The term apocrypha, meaning "hidden, obscure," is intentionally pejorative. It was chosen precisely to denigrate these books and to suggest that they are of inferior status.

The term pseudepigrapha is problematic for its own reasons (Reed 2009). Pseudepigrapha means "having a false title" or "falsely attributed writings." It is often interpreted to imply that the texts are either deceitfully produced or wrongly attributed to a well-known ancient author, typically of the biblical past. Understood that way, the term carries negative connotations that suggest forgery and deceit. While this negative understanding of the term pseudepigrapha is still prevalent today, several scholars have begun to redefine it, seeking a more positive understanding. Instead of thinking of pseudepigraphy as an act of forgery, they argue that it should be understood "as a reading practice that is fundamentally interpretative." The case has been made most compellingly by Hindy Najman and Irene Peirano Garrison (2019, 331, 351): "In reframing pseudepigraphy as an act of interpretation or as a generative mechanism that enables growth of a tradition, we can study these texts not as intruders or interlopers into the canon but as creative responses to their respective traditions."

There are many problems with the traditional, pejorative understanding of the term pseudepigrapha. The most acute is that all the texts that are labeled pseudepigrapha are automatically classified as false, deceitful, and forgeries. Benjamin Wright (2019, 135–37) recently described how such categorizations push the texts into the shadows—while treating them as oddities and misfits. As a result, much of Second Temple Judaism becomes marginalized, is turned into the background or foil for New Testament studies, and continues the struggle to be studied on its own terms.

Another problem with the term pseudepigrapha is that it can leave the erroneous impression that the literary device of pseudepigraphy is only found outside the Bible and that the Bible does not include pseudepigraphic texts (see Ahearne-Kroll 2019, 104–5), when, in fact, the Bible contains several pseudepigraphic texts. The prophet Isaiah did not write the sixty-six chapters of the book named after him, David did not write all the psalms that bear his name in the superscriptions, and Daniel did not write the book of Daniel. Only theological prejudice and preconceived notions about the primacy of canonical authority could cause interpreters to see the biblical texts differently from texts now classified as pseudepigrapha (see Najman and Garrison 2019, 348–51).

With few exceptions, the documents labeled *Old Testament Pseudepigrapha* were preserved and transmitted by Christians, even those that are not of Christian origin. That means that these texts survive because Christians have adopted, translated, used, and transmitted them. For several generations, debates have continued about whether the Old Testament Pseudepigrapha should be considered Jewish or Christian and how to make that distinction, if it is possible at all (Kraft 2009).

From the perspective of modern materiality, the collection of the Pseudepigrapha into one volume is certainly handy. And yet, the danger arises that in subtle ways one can begin to think of them as a collection of texts. That collection, though, results from modern scholarly projects, and, of course, did not exist in early Judaism.

Other terms face their own problems. Obviously, *Bible* invokes canonical status. Thus the label *rewritten Bible* for texts such as Jubilees, the Genesis Apocryphon, and Pseudo-Philo, which not long ago was used by Second Temple scholars, has now widely, and properly, fallen out of use (Bernstein 2005). The designation also assumes a canonical perspective. The term *Scripture* enjoys the advantage of not necessarily implying a canonical status. However, the term is somewhat vague, and interpreters seem to use it to indicate that a text has a special degree of authority, even if describing that status is difficult. Thus, texts that eventually achieve canonical status are usually called Scriptures by modern interpreters, while other texts, such as 1 Enoch, rarely receive that designation (despite its status in Ethiopic Christianity). The term seems acceptable to many precisely because of its ambiguity. The distinction between texts that are "scriptural" as opposed to "authoritative" remains somewhat unclear.

Just as the designations early Judaism and Second Temple Judaism are still widely in use, despite their proven limitations, so scholars have not been able to avoid using the terms apocrypha, pseudepigrapha, Scripture, and [authoritative] tradition. A new set of terms has yet to be determined.

Conceptual and Methodological Changes

Much has changed in the area of methodology since 1986. For the most part, scholars of Second Temple Judaism have adopted historical-critical methodologies from biblical studies without much hesitation. But with these methodologies also came the limitations and sometimes the problems of these approaches (see Werline's essay in this volume). Clearly, form, redaction, and tradition criticism held sway in the 1980s. As a result, there was a tendency to rely on genre analysis as a primary way to categorize and characterize texts. Given that nearly no text exhibits a pure, ideal type, however, many texts have resisted categorization. Moreover, scholars did not always account for the fact that the genres of the Hebrew Bible may not fit early Jewish texts. For example, how should one categorize the Qumran Hodayot when using Hebrew Bible form criticism?

Kraft and Nickelsburg included a section titled "New Approaches" in their introduction (1986, 6–9). These newer approaches did not yet include the more complex methodological and theoretical interpretations currently in use that are informed by religious and interdisciplinary studies. Their comments about treating the texts "as literary wholes" (7), which may signal their awareness of methods such as reader-response criticism, is the closest they come to the new methodologies. Further, they mention that anthropological and sociological assessments of texts and traditions were beginning to appear in 1980. The Society of Biblical Literature Annual Meeting program books from the era reveal the popularity of these methods in biblical studies.

Kraft and Nickelsburg identify rhetorical criticism as a potentially useful tool. At that time, rhetorical analysis was gaining prominence in both Hebrew Bible and New Testament studies, though the character of the approach differed in each. Rhetorical criticism of the Hebrew Bible, following James Muilenburg (1969), tended to analyze artistry, especially in poetic texts, while New Testament scholars generally employed the categories of classical rhetoric (e.g., Betz 1979). Rhetorical criticism on early Jewish texts has now developed under the influence of theorist such as Kenneth Burke, typically in conversation with other ideological and literary theorists (cf. Newsom 2004, 2010)—a significantly different approach from that earlier generation. Moreover, the first edition of *Early Judaism and Its Modern Interpreters* did not include an essay on gender studies. The introduction noted that work has begun in this area but that it lagged behind biblical studies. As Françoise Mirguet's essay in this volume demonstrates, feminist interpretation and gender studies have significantly increased and developed since the first edition.

Often, methodological changes are triggered by a change in our understanding of the text we are interpreting. Close attention to the textual evidence from the Second Temple period has made scholars realize that they needed to overcome the idea of a single canonical text. Earlier generations of exegetes often assumed that the Masoretic Text (MT) presents the true authoritative tradition, an assumption that was then projected back into the Second Temple period. The belief was that the versions other than the MT represented departures from what was considered the more original tradition represented by the MT. The versions were thus seen as aberrations of that textual tradition. However, scholarship especially since the 1990s has emphasized that the understanding of what constituted a text in the Second Temple period needs reconsideration. The traditional conviction, for example, that it is the primary task of textual criticism to reconstruct the original text, was abandoned. Instead, scholars came to realize that texts were significantly more fluid and pluriform and that there was no single, authoritative text. This new perspective on the text has had significant implications for how scholars think about the nature and transmission of texts in early Judaism. For example, the textual tradition behind the Septuagint came to be seen as a product of that fluidity and pluriformity. It used to be common practice to speak of the Additions to Daniel and Additions to Esther in the Septuagint. The underlying assumption is that there was an original text, the MT, to which these traditions were added. A more prudent understanding of the different versions would be that the Septuagint testifies to a separate tradition, a textual tradition used by some Jewish, and later Christian, communities. These kinds of textual issues extend to other texts of the era. For example, textual pluriformity is apparent in the versions of the Community Rule at Qumran (see Metso 2007, 2019). Further, it is also characteristic of many of the texts that now appear among the Pseudepigrapha, for example, 1 Enoch and Joseph and Aseneth (see Liv Ingeborg Lied's essay in this volume; see also Ahearne-Kroll 2020).

Growth at the Annual Meeting of the Society of Biblical Literature

The number of sessions on early Judaism at the Society of Biblical Literature Annual Meeting has grown exponentially since the 1980s. In 1980, the centennial year of the society, there were only a couple of sessions that focused on early Judaism. The Qumran and Pseudepigrapha units were essentially the anchors for the study of early Judaism on its own merits. There was both a Pseudepigrapha Group and Section session, even though in 1980 the Pseudepigrapha Group met for only one session (Henze 2019). The Septuagint and Cognate Studies unit also held a single session. Apparently, the Qumran group did not meet that year, though in celebration of the centennial Yigael Yadin delivered one of the special addresses titled "The Temple Scroll: A Sectarian Document?" There was a session on Qumran within the context of New Testament studies. Compare this to the 2020 list of about sixteen program units related to the study of early Judaism that are planning sessions for the Annual Meeting. Most of the units will hold two or three sessions each, which means that there will be between thirty to forty sessions related to early Judaism.

The Second Edition of
Early Judaism and Its Modern Interpreters

The aim of the second edition of *Early Judaism and Its Modern Interpreters* is not to replace but to build on and complement the first edition, which remains an immensely useful tool. All essays in the present volume have been newly commissioned. Kraft and Nickelsburg (1986, xii) established the year 1980 "as a rough *terminus*" for the first edition. The second edition picks up the history of scholarship from that point forward up to the year 2019. It thus covers a period of about forty years of vibrant scholarship and enormous advances. Only in a few cases did we consider it important to reach back further than 1980. Contributors to the volume were also asked to add a brief assessment of anything omitted from the first edition that should have been included, though there are only a few cases where this seemed necessary.

Of the changes included in the second edition of *Early Judaism and Its Modern Interpreters*, two are particularly noteworthy. First, there are a few essays in the first edition that have either been subsumed under broader categories (e.g., "The Samaritans and Judaism" and "Judaism as Seen by Outsiders" no longer have their own essays) or that have dropped out altogether (e.g., "Jewish Numismatics").

Second, the organization of the second edition departs from the first in an attempt to reflect the shifts that have taken place in the field. The first edition consisted of three parts: "Historical Settings," "Recent Discoveries," and "Literature." We have replaced that organization with four parts: "Historical and Social Settings"; "Methods, Manuscripts, and Materials"; "Early Jewish Literatures"; and "The Afterlife of Early Judaism." Part 1, "Historical and Social Settings," includes essays on the social world of early Judaism and on Judaism in the diaspora. There is also an essay on gender in early Jewish literature that discusses the significant progress made on the issues of gender and the location of women in ancient societies. In Part 2, "Methods, Manuscripts, and Materials," two new essays are particularly emblematic of recent changes in the field. The first article in this section is devoted to recent methodological discussions and surveys the increased attention to methodology, particularly over the last fifteen or so years. The last essay in part 2 investigates how the use of modern technologies has impacted the study of early Judaism. Part 3, "Early Jewish Literatures," preserves several of the topics from the first edition. Structurally, it is one of the more problematic parts of the book. The main problem concerns the division of the ancient Jewish library into distinct literary genres. The pitfalls of dividing texts into genres have often been pointed out. Genres should not be defined too rigorously, since genres by definition are hybrids, and the lines of demarcation between them are not always clear. Texts can belong to more than one genre. Moreover, genre analysis might lead to forgetting that texts were somehow a part of community and part of faith and practice. For all of these and other reasons, some scholars have called for genres to be abandoned altogether. We have chosen to retain this aspect of the basic structure of *Early Judaism and Its Modern Interpreters*, however, and to follow the model of the first edition largely for practical reasons—in order to give the reader a quick orientation concerning which texts and aspects of early Judaism are discussed in which essay. Part 4, "The Afterlife of Early Judaism," finally, is a new addition to *Early Judaism and Its Modern Interpreters* that reflects one of the most exciting changes in the study of early Jewish texts in recent decades: the attention many scholars now devote to the afterlives of the early Jewish texts and traditions, their transmission and use in late antiquity and the early Middle Ages (often by Christians), and their rich manuscript histories. The four essays in this section follow the exceedingly diverse trajectories that begin in early Judaism but extend well beyond it.

The Next Forty Years

Since the publication of the first edition of *Early Judaism and Its Modern Interpreters*, the study of early Judaism has moved from the margins to the center. What used to be a period in Israel's history that was poorly understood and marginalized at best has since emerged as a vibrant, rigorous, and innovative field of study with its own subdisciplines. The Dead Sea Scrolls and the enormous energy the scrolls have brought to the study of early Judaism have been a major factor in this change in attitude. Other factors have been the availability of new data, the publication of more texts, the adoption of new methods, and a general willingness to reconsider misconceived notions about the inferiority of this period and its literatures. And yet, some obstacles remain within our too-siloed disciplines that cast Second Temple Judaism as a postscript to the Hebrew Bible and as prelude or background to the New Testament. Recently, serious questions have arisen about whether New Testament studies has adequately engaged Second Temple texts, at least in a way that matches its interest in Greek and Roman texts and contexts.

Forty years ago, Kraft and Nickelsburg (1986, 9) anticipated that their volume would contribute to "a drastically revised picture of early Judaism," even if they were quick to concede that "the fullness of that picture, with all its details and hues, is not yet in clear focus." As that picture has increasingly come into focus since the publication of the first edition, so have the limitations of the basic frameworks, categories, and vocabularies that have largely remained in place. As the study of early Judaism continues, grows, and becomes increasingly interdisciplinary, an era of redefinition and reconfiguration is certainly on the horizon.

Bibliography

Ahearne-Kroll, Patricia D. 2019. "The History of the Study of the Pseudepigrapha." Pages 103–31 in *The Old Testament Pseudepigrapha: Fifty Years of the Pseudepigrapha Section at the SBL*. Edited by Matthias Henze and Liv Ingeborg Lied. EJL 50. Atlanta: SBL Press.

———. 2020. *Aseneth of Egypt: The Composition of a Jewish Narrative*. EJL 53. Atlanta: SBL Press.

Bauckham, Richard, James R. Davila, and Alexander Panayotov, eds. 2013. *Old Testament Pseudepigrapha: More Noncanonical Scriptures*. Vol. 1. Grand Rapids: Eerdmans.

Bernstein, Moshe J. 2005. "'Rewritten Bible': A Generic Category Which Has Outlived Its Usefulness?" *Text* 22:169–96.

Betz, Hans Dieter. 1979. *Galatians: A Commentary on Paul's Letter to the Churches in Galatia*. Hermeneia. Philadelphia: Fortress.

Boyarin, Daniel. 2019. *Judaism: The Genealogy of a Modern Notion*. New Brunswick, NJ: Rutgers University Press.

Brooke, George J., and Charlotte Hempel, eds. 2019. *T&T Clark Companion to the Dead Sea Scrolls*. London: T&T Clark.

Chesnutt, Randall D. 2019. "*Encomium* or *Apologia*? The Future (?) of the Society of Biblical Literature Pseudepigrapha Section." Pages 383–97 in *The Old Testament Pseudepigrapha: Fifty Years of the Pseudepigrapha Section at the SBL*. Edited by Matthias Henze and Liv Ingeborg Lied. EJL 50. Atlanta: SBL Press.

Cohen, Shaye J. D. 1999. *The Beginnings of Jewishness: Boundaries, Varieties, Uncertainties*. HCS 31. Berkley: University of California Press.

Collins, John J., ed. 2014. *The Oxford Handbook of Apocalyptic Literature*. Oxford: Oxford University Press.

———. 2017. *The Invention of Judaism: Torah and Jewish Identity from Deuteronomy to Paul*. Oakland: University of California Press.

Collins, John J., and Daniel C. Harlow, eds. 2010. *The Eerdmans Dictionary of Early Judaism*. Grand Rapids: Eerdmans.

Epp, Jay, and George W. MacRae, eds. 1989. *The New Testament and Its Modern Interpreters*. BMI 3. Philadelphia: Fortress Press; Atlanta: Scholars Press.

Feder, Frank, and Matthias Henze, eds. 2019–2020. *Textual History of the Bible: The Deuterocanonical Scriptures*. 3 vols. Leiden: Brill.

Greenspoon, Leonard. 1988. Review of *Early Judaism and Its Modern Interpreters*, edited by Robert A. Kraft and George W. E. Nickelsburg. *JR* 68:139–40.

Henze, Matthias. 2019. "The Pseudepigrapha Project at the Society of Biblical Literature, 1969–1971." Pages 11–50 in *The Old Testament Pseudepigrapha: Fifty Years of the Pseudepigrapha Section at the SBL*. Edited by Matthias Henze and Liv Ingeborg Lied. EJL 50. Atlanta: SBL Press.

Janowitz, Naomi. 1989. Review of *Early Judaism and Its Modern Interpreters*, edited by Robert A. Kraft and George W. E. Nickelsburg. *CBQ* 51:392–94.

Klawans, Jonathan. 2006. *Purity, Sacrifice, and the Temple: Symbolism and Supersessionism in the Study of Ancient Judaism*. New York: Oxford University Press.

Knight, Douglas A., and Gene M. Tucker, eds. 1985. *The Hebrew Bible and Its Modern Interpreters*. BMI 1. Philadelphia: Fortress Press; Chico, CA: Scholars Press.

Kraft, Robert A. 2009. *Exploring the Scripturesque: Jewish Texts and Their Christian Contexts*. JSJSup 137. Leiden: Brill.

Kraft, Robert A., and George W. E. Nickelsburg, eds. 1986. *Early Judaism and Its Modern Interpreters*. BMI 2. Philadelphia: Fortress Press; Atlanta: Scholars Press.

Levine, Amy-Jill. 1991. *Women Like This: New Perspectives on Jewish Women in the Greco-Roman World*. EJL 1. Atlanta: Scholars Press.

Lim, Timothy H., and John J. Collins, eds. 2010. *The Oxford Handbook of the Dead Sea Scrolls*. Oxford: Oxford University Press.

Mason, Steve. 2007. "Jews, Judaeans, Judaizing, Judaism: Problems of Categorization in Ancient Judaism." *JSJ* 38:457–512.

———. 2014. "Ancient Jews or Judaeans? Different Questions, Different Answers." *Marginalia*. https://tinyurl.com/SBLPress9027a1.

Metso, Sarianna. 2007. *The Serekh Texts*. LSTS 62. London: T&T Clark.

———. 2019. *The Community Rule: A Critical Edition with Translation*. EJL 51. Atlanta: SBL Press.

Muilenburg, James. 1969. "Form Criticism and Beyond." *JBL* 88:1–18.

Najman, Hindy, and Irene Peirano Garrison. 2019. "Pseudepigraphy as an Interpretive Construct." Pages 331–55 in *The Old Testament Pseudepigrapha: Fifty Years of the Pseudepigrapha Section at the SBL*. Edited by Matthias Henze and Liv Ingeborg Lied. EJL 50. Atlanta: SBL Press.

Newsome, Carol A. 2004. *The Self as Symbolic Space: Constructing Identity and Community at Qumran*. STDJ 52. Leiden: Brill.

———. 2010. "Rhetorical Criticism and the Dead Sea Scrolls." Pages 198–214 in *Rediscovering the Dead Sea Scrolls: An Assessment of Old and New Approaches and Methods*. Edited by Maxine L. Grossman. Grand Rapids: Eerdmans.

Nickelsburg, George W. E. 2005. *Jewish Literature between the Bible and the Mishnah: A Historical and Literary Introduction*. 2nd ed. Minneapolis: Fortress.

Reed, Annette Yoshiko. 2009. "The Modern Invention of 'Old Testament Pseudepigrapha.'" *JTS* 60:403–36.

———. 2014. "Ioudaios before and after 'Religion.'" *Marginalia*. https://tinyurl.com/SBLPress9027a3.

Reinhartz, Adele. 2014. "The Vanishing Jews of Antiquity." *Marginalia*. https://tinyurl.com/SBLPress9027a2.

Smith, Jonathan Z. 1988. "'Religion' and 'Religious Studies': No Difference at All." *Soundings* 71:231–44.

Stuckenbruck, Loren T. 2012. "Apocrypha and Pseudepigrapha." Pages 179–203 in *Early Judaism: A Comprehensive Overview*. Edited by John J. Collins and Daniel C. Harlow. Grand Rapids: Eerdmans.

———. 2019. "What Is Second Temple Judaism?" Pages 1–19 in vol. 1 of *T&T Clark Encyclopedia of Second Temple Judaism*. Edited by Loren T. Stuckenbruck and Daniel M. Gurtner. 2 vols. London: T&T Clark.

Stuckenbruck, Loren T., and Daniel M. Gurtner, eds. 2019. *T&T Clark Encyclopedia of Second Temple Judaism*. 2 vols. London: T&T Clark.

VanderKam, James C. 1989. Review of *Early Judaism and Its Modern Interpreters*, edited by Robert A. Kraft and George W. E. Nickelsburg. *RSR* 15:327–33.

Wright, Benjamin G., III. 2019. "The Pseudepigrapha within and without Biblical Studies." Pages 133–56 in *The Old Testament Pseudepigrapha: Fifty Years of the Pseudepigrapha Section at the SBL*. Edited by Matthias Henze and Liv Ingeborg Lied. EJL 50. Atlanta: SBL Press.

Part 1
Historical and Social Settings

1
Jewish History from Alexander to Hadrian

CHRIS SEEMAN

Alexander the Great's conquest of the Persian Empire (334–324 BCE) and Hadrian's administrative transformation of Judea into Syria Palaestina (ca. 135 CE) are defensible chronological boundaries for the study of early Judaism, though they are ultimately artificial; Jewish history before and after these events was not entirely different from what transpired between them. Obviously, those four hundred years contain a lot of history—more than can be handled in a single essay. What follows, then, is not an overarching survey of historical events; that can be found elsewhere. Nor does it discuss every historiographic problem; that would be impossible within the scope of an essay. Rather, I have selected three topics whose analysis highlights significant directions research in the field has taken and that have perennially attracted the attention of interpreters. Because another essay in this volume is devoted exclusively to the diaspora (see Erich Gruen's contribution), I shall confine my coverage to the Jewish homeland except where comparison of the two settings can help illuminate realities that impinged on both.

First, I discuss the high priesthood, arguably one of the most distinctive institutions of the Second Temple period. The office changed shape at the beginning of Second Temple period and continued to be altered throughout the era. As will become apparent, many assumptions that are made about this office and its incumbents have impacted the way scholars reconstruct the social and political history of early Judaism. It will therefore be a valuable point of entry into broader topics.

In this era, the office functioned as perhaps the point of contact between the Jewish people and their overlords, except, of course, during the period of Hasmonean independence. However, even then the priesthood was a focal point because of the question of whether the Hasmoneans legitimately held the office and properly executed its duties. Through most of this period, then, of central concern was the interaction between Jewish communities and Greco-Roman society. Was the relationship one of conflict and tension or one of harmonious coexistence? Obviously, there is evidence for both; by examining how recent scholarship has approached this evidence in new ways, it will be possible to move beyond simplistic formulations toward a more contextual understanding—especially of signal instances of breakdown like the Antiochene persecution and the Alexandrian pogrom. Finally, I consider key turning points in the political history of Judea in relation to Rome, again with a view to how scholars have rethought longstanding assumptions or questioned existing paradigms through new data or enhanced methodological sophistication.

1. The High Priesthood

The history of the postexilic high priesthood has attracted much scholarly attention over the past three decades. This is due, in part, to the intertwining of this office with virtually every dimension of Judean society during Second Temple times. While the available data concerning the high priesthood have remained more or less unchanged since the 1980s, new assessments of that data have arisen and new questions have been posed.

1.1. Theocracy?

According to Josephus, the traditional Jewish "constitution" (Greek *politeia*) was a theocracy headed by a high priest (*C. Ap.* 2.184–189). In spite of the idealizing, apologetic nature of the work in which it appears, Josephus's claim that the high priest served as secular as well as cultic representative of the people fits comfortably with literary portrayals of high priests throughout the period (except under Herodian rule). Evidence for the conceptual combination of cultic and royal functions has also been adduced in Greek versions of key biblical texts, indicating a normalization of this convergence in the minds of some translators (Van der Kooij 2007). Because this arrangement differed markedly from preexilic times, scholars have attempted to trace the origin and evolution of this reordering of power. How, when, and why did high priests come to exercise political power?

Since the publication of Deborah Rooke's *Zadok's Heirs* in 2000, reconstructions of the postexilic high priesthood have called into question various aspects of the regnant hypothesis that high priests consistently wielded civic power since the Persian restoration (vigorously defended by VanderKam 2004). Rooke (2000, 302) viewed the Seleucid investiture of the Hasmoneans with military and administrative functions as the dramatic politicizing of a hitherto exclusively cultic role. Subsequent studies of Persian Yehud (Fried 2004; Cataldo 2009) have further eroded confidence that the theocratic model was operative during Achaemenid times, while careful analysis of literary sources for the early Hellenistic era renders historical certainty about the high priest's political status during that time difficult to achieve (Brutti 2006).

Most recently, Vasile Babota (2014, 154–58) has argued that the high priesthood that was conferred on the Hasmonean Jonathan in 152 BCE should be understood in the context of the Hellenistic administrative office of *archiereus* attested in Seleucid inscriptions—rather than simply as a calque for Hebrew *hakkohen haggadol*—thus implying a significant departure from Jewish tradition. This thesis has been challenged by Benedikt Eckhardt (2016), who insists upon the distinction between the (native) role of high priest and the (Seleucid) military rank of *strategos*, while acknowledging the innovation that resulted.

The dominant scholarly trend, then, has been to explain the genesis of high priestly political authority in terms of circumstances peculiar to the second century BCE, rather than as an unchanging default position for the postexilic period as a whole. This shift has resulted in greater attention being paid to the ways in which such power was conceptualized and justified through texts, coins, and other media. It has also coincided with challenges to an older assumption that Zadokite lineage was an essential criterion for high priestly legitimacy.

1.2. Hasmoneans versus Zadokites?

Evidence that not all Jews regarded the Hasmonean high priesthood as legitimate is plentiful—not only in sectarian circles but in the sympathetic narrative of 1 Maccabees (e.g., 10:61–65; 11:20–27; 14:14; 15:21). These sources are conspicuously silent as to the underlying *reasons* for this hostility—in contrast to later texts, which are articulate in their criticism of Hasmonean monarchy (e.g., Pss. Sol. 17; Diodorus Siculus, *Bib. hist.* 40.2). One attempt to account for the initial antagonism during the second century BCE centers on the genealogy of the Hasmoneans and that of the high priestly clan whose interrupted tenure they supplanted.

Synthesizing Ezekiel's claim that the sons of Zadok alone would have access to the altar of the restored temple (Ezek 40:46; 43:19) with the Chronicler's revisionist genealogy of the first temple priesthood (1 Chr 6:1–15) and Josephus's high priest list (*A.J.* 20.224–51), earlier scholarship posited an unbroken Zadokite lineage for high priests of the second temple up to the deposition of Jason in 172 BCE. Since the Hasmoneans nowhere styled themselves as Zadokites, it was inferred that they were regarded as illegitimate high priests by many Jews. This premise was reinforced by the positive affiliation of the Qumran community with the sons of Zadok (e.g., CD III, 20–IV, 4; 1QS V, 2, 9; 1Q28a [1QSa] I, 2, 24). This correlation of texts and circumstance spawned the hypothesis that the Dead Sea Scrolls community originated in an exodus of Zadokite priests from Jerusalem who had been disempowered by the Hasmoneans.

Cracks in the Zadokite hypothesis—both as an explanation for anti-Hasmonean sentiment and as a Qumran origin story—have begun to appear. A basic weakness in the appeal to Zadokite lineage is that none of the high priests of the Hellenistic period is actually referred to as a "son of Zadok" (Grabbe 2003), suggesting that this was not as crucial a determinant of legitimacy as being a "son of Aaron" (1 Macc 7:14). Conversely, an argument has been made that the Hasmoneans' descent from the priestly course of Joiarib would not clearly *exclude* them from Zadokite lineage (Schofield and VanderKam 2005). Further doubt on the very existence of the sons of Zadok as an historical group has been cast by Alice Hunt's comprehensive 2006 study of the tradition, raising the possibility that the Qumran references are actually symbolic epithets, either for the Yahad as a whole or for some faction within it.

Whether the sons of Zadok are judged to be a textual mirage or an actual high priestly group, recent analysis of the Hasmoneans' own legitimation strategies reveals the genealogical question to be a red herring. The honorary decree for Simon in 140 BCE (1 Macc 14:27–49), the most important documentary evidence for the justification of Hasmonean rule, is quite uninterested in genealogy of any kind. Instead, it follows the rubrics of Hellenistic benefactor decrees, exalting the recipient's accomplishments on behalf of the sponsors (Van Henten 2001). This emphasis on deeds rather than lineage matches the only genealogical claim the Hasmoneans *do* make: namely, their descent from Aaron's grandson, Phinehas (1 Macc 2:54). To query whether this claim was meant literally or figuratively is beside the point: Phinehas gained eternity for his priesthood not by pedigree but by personal achievement (Num 25:10–13).

The Hasmoneans, of course, stopped short of claiming eternality—"until a trustworthy prophet should arise" (1 Macc 14:41)—indicating a sensitivity to the limits of their own propaganda. But the fact that they felt no need to advertise their ancestry in their own documents suggests that this was not a major flashpoint for opposition prior to their embrace of a dynastic model of rule during the first century BCE (Seeman 2013, 160–61).

1.3. Hasmonean Kingship

The political transformation of the high priesthood reached its zenith with the Hasmoneans' assumption of kingship, a move that became a lightning rod for criticism of the family and that seems to have accelerated the development of messianism (Oegema 1998). Whereas earlier research on Hasmonean monarchy tended to focus on ideological reasons why Jews might have objected to it, recent scholarship has explored the positive side of the equation: the significance of the royal claim itself and how the Hasmoneans related it to their identity as high priests.

Efforts to explain the move to monarchy in terms of hellenization are inadequate. To be sure, the world in which the Hasmoneans asserted their kingship was a Greek world, and their royal claim could be expressed in patently Greek idiom (*A.J.* 13.318). But these forms coexisted with overtly Jewish symbols and traditions without any hint of tension (Gruen 1998, 1–40; Rajak 1996). Tessa Rajak in particular has emphasized that the improvisational nature of Hasmonean monarchy will be missed if it is analyzed purely in terms of established biblical or Hellenic rubrics (Rajak 1996,106–10; cf. Osterloh 2008; Regev 2013).

Improvisation is especially evident in the extant coinage of Alexander Janneus and Mattathias Antigonus, which often juxtaposed Hebrew and Greek inscriptions. With one exception (Meshorer 2001, 38–39), no royal coins combine the titles of "high priest" and "king" on the same inscription, which suggests that these remained conceptually distinct roles, even if they were performed by the same person. Moreover, the high priest inscriptions, where they contain information beyond the monarch's name, consistently associate him with "the community (or council) of the Judeans" (Meshorer 2001, 31–32). The emphasis on people ("Judeans") rather than territory ("Judea") frames Hasmonean authority as something exercised in concert with, rather than at the expense of, the nation (Goodblatt 2006, 157; Regev 2012). This image of consultative leadership, even if pure propaganda, demonstrates the dynasty's attentiveness to the values and expectations of its subjects (cf. 11Q19 [11QTemple] LVII, 11–15).

1.4. Roman Puppets?

The usurpation of Hasmonean rule by Herod the Great in 37 BCE appears to have resulted in a suspension of the high priest's political role. Because Herod was not of priestly origin, he could not occupy the office himself and was unwilling to share power with another. Appointing and deposing high priests at will—and deliberately recruiting these from noninfluential families after having killed off the surviving Hasmonean hopefuls (*A.J.* 20.247)—the monarch maintained an iron grip on the institution.

Because the Romans continued Herod's practice of discretionary appointment, the high priests of the first century CE have often been portrayed as mere figureheads of imperial policy, beholden to the whims of the prefect and lacking in autonomous influence. This image of a politically insecure high priesthood has contributed to explanations for the eventual breakdown of Roman-Judean concord in 66 CE: having been eviscerated by Herod, Judea lacked an effective ruling class. Consequently, when their weakness was exposed and Rome's local representatives offered them no acceptable exit strategy, the high priests along with other members of the endangered aristocracy threw in their lot with the rebels (Goodman 1987).

More recent assessments suggest a different interpretation. While Judea's prefects and procurators obviously controlled who was high priest and how long they served, this need not mean that the office-holders were bereft of agency. In his study of Josephus's accounts of the period, James McLaren (1991, 192–200) emphasized the efficacy of high-priestly initiative in responding to and resolving crises through negotiation. Rather than interpreting the rapid turnover rate of high-priestly appointments as evidence for institutional dysfunctionality, McLaren considered the opportunities this would afford for broader participation by influential priestly families in the governance of Judea (218). McLaren also observed the emergence of the plural *archiereis* ("chief priests") as a recognizable group within Judean society precisely during the first century CE (201–2). Paradoxically, then, one unintended consequence of Herod's strategy of curtailing high-priestly influence through repeated appointment and deposition was to *create* a bloc of high priests, ex-high priests, and their associates who would go on to exercise influence over public affairs.

Paul McKechnie's 2005 study of Judean embassies to Rome during the two decades preceding the first revolt supports this analysis. Disputes (sometimes with Judea's own Roman official) were frequently decided by the emperors in favor of the Jews. Minimally, this indicates that the Jewish ruling class (whether headed by the high priest, the chief priests, the lay notables, or some combination of the above) was quite functional. However, as McKechnie observes, what determined the success or failure of a petition was often not the identity of the petitioners, but which favorites of the emperor—Agrippa II, Poppea, Pallas—happened to be present and were prepared to intervene (355). This wild card, the unpredictably interpersonal nature of imperial judgments, should caution us against evaluations of high priestly influence that reduce the issue to the internal politics of Judea.

2. Integration and Marginalization

In contrast to some portrayals of Second Temple life that see Jewish communities as being under chronic threat from their environment (Kasher 1985; 1990), others have emphasized the ways in which Jews lived harmoniously with and as active participants in Greco-Roman society (Barclay 1996; Collins 2000; Gruen 2002). This presumption of integrability has prompted a reevaluation of the civil and religious rights enjoyed by Jews. It has also resulted in fresh examination of two of the starkest breakdowns of this détente: the Antiochene persecution of 167–165 BCE and the Alexandrian pogrom of 38 CE.

2.1. The Antiochene Persecution

The singularity of Antiochus IV's attempt to unmake Jewish identity in Coele Syria between 167 and 165 BCE continues to exercise the scholarly imagination. The Maccabean narrative does not supply a satisfactory explanation for the Seleucid's unprecedented assault on Judean cult and culture, and Daniel's allusive visions offer few data that can be pressed into the service of historical inquiry without substantial inference on the part of the reader. Consequently, efforts to explain Antiochus's actions resort to reading texts against the grain, searching for some plausible scenario or frame of reference that will account for the anomalous attack.

In 1993, Erich Gruen surveyed five traditional approaches to the problem: Antiochus as Hellenic crusader, Antiochus as political and economic opportunist, Antiochus as creative emulator of Roman domestic policies, Antiochus as madman, and Antiochus as enabler of Jewish hellenizers. Finding all these explanations wanting, he proposed a propagandistic rationale for the king's coercive decree: humiliated by the Romans at Eleusis and eager to reassure the world of his mastery over his own realm, Antiochus sought to deliver an object lesson to his far-flung subjects by showing them that he could compel the Jews to abandon their tenaciously held practices (263–64). While few have concurred with the particulars of this reconstruction (see the response and discussion in Gruen 1993, 264–74), its impulse to seek a solution in the realm of political symbolism has anticipated the direction of more recent scholarship.

Johannes Christian Bernhardt (2017, 166–216) has connected Antiochus's cultic innovations with his overall legitimation needs as a usurper to the throne. Anathea Portier-Young's (2011, 176–216) study of apocalyptic literature contains an extensive analysis of the persecution decree as an ideological tool for re-creating an empire whose efficacy has been called into question. My own research (Seeman 2013, 191–93) has followed a similar line of reasoning but with greater emphasis on the persecution's immediate audience—the Greek citizenries of Coele Syria who were encouraged to participate in the suppression of Jewish practices (2 Macc 6:8–9). These were the populations who had witnessed first-hand Antiochus's humiliating withdrawal from Eleusis. If the king had any anxieties about his hold over this region, victimizing its Jewish communities by rebranding their way of life as rebellious would have been an effective means of identifying loyalty to the regime with *Greek* identity. This would help to explain both the Hellenic idiom of the persecution as well as its extent (not empire-wide, but broader than Judea itself).

A quite different approach has been fielded by Sylvie Honigman (2014). Maintaining that the sources have been misread through historically anachronistic lenses, Honigman draws on Steven Weitzman's 2004 proposal that 1 and 2 Maccabees were modeled on Babylonian cult foundation narratives involving temple desecration by a wicked king. The premise that a text was composed according to a preexisting blueprint does not, by itself, vitiate the possibility that it embeds historical information (so, rightly, Weitzman 2004, 222). What leads Honigman to reject the historicity of the Antiochene persecution is her contention that modern attempts to synthesize the chronologies of the Maccabean accounts with that of Daniel have created the illusion of three distinct sequences of events (of which the persecution is the last). In reality, argues Honigman (229–58), there was only one event—Antiochus's repression of a Jewish tax revolt—that the literary sources have embellished with pious trappings.

Honigman's proposed reversal of cause-and-effect—the Jews rebelled; Antiochus reacted—is not all that different in principle from Victor Tcherikover's (1959, 186–92) classical revolt hypothesis, though her explanation of it flows from an epigraphic discovery unknown to Tcherikover, the so-called Heliodorus Stele (Cotton and Wörrle 2007; Gera 2009). In 178 BCE, Seleucus IV issued a directive to his vizier, Heliodorus, to appoint an officer to supervise the sanctuaries throughout Coele Syria and Phoenicia (which would presumably include the Jerusalem temple). The nature and extent of this official's activities are unknown due to the fragmentary state of the inscription, but historians have been quick to link his mandate with the Heliodorus story in 2 Macc 3 (Rappaport 2011). Be that as it may, the premise that royal interference in Jerusalem's cult precipitated a popular insurgency goes well beyond what the stele itself discloses and is amenable to alternative interpretations (Eckhardt 2016, 63–66).

2.2. Jewish Rights in the Diaspora

Josephus claims to provide evidence that the Roman government consistently guaranteed Jews living outside their homeland the right to live according to their ancestral customs (A.J. 14.185–267; 16.160–178; 19.278–312). At times, this might also include political rights with accompanying communal institutions within Greek cities (A.J. 14.117). For the most part, though, the documents he cites confine their directives to specific communities at specific times: There was no empire-wide charter for the Jews (Rajak 1984; Gruen 2002, 84–104). Nonetheless, this anecdotal testimony supports a broader picture of Jews maintaining their distinctive identity while taking part in the civic life of the Greco-Roman world.

Josephus's overtly apologetic usage of these dossiers, combined with the vagaries of their preservation, has long raised legitimate doubts about their historicity. Since Rajak's (1984) programmatic essay on this problem, substantial progress has been made toward a better understanding of this corpus and the phenomenon it provides testimony for. Foundational to establishing its genuineness was Miriam Pucci Ben Zeev's 1998 analytical commentary. This compendium contextualizes each document and compares its wording with the formulas found in indisputably authentic Roman decrees.

A recent papyrological discovery bearing on the subject has resolved yet another issue relating to Jewish rights, at least as far as Egypt is concerned. In 2001, James Cowey and Klaus Maresch published an archive from a second-century BCE Jewish community in the Fayyum town of Herakleopolis identified as a *politeuma*, a term whose legal ramifications had hitherto been obscure (Lüderitz 1994). The Herakleopolis papyri revealed an association whose members enjoyed autonomy in matters of private law. They did not, however, provide much evidence that the members of this *politeuma* used their prerogatives to adhere to legal norms or procedures different from those of other Egyptians. Precious finds such as this serve as a reminder of the real complexity that underlies the rhetoric of "living according to ancestral laws" that one finds in Josephus and other Jewish apologists of the period.

2.3. The Alexandrian Pogrom

As with the Antiochene persecution, the mob violence suffered by the Jewish community of Alexandria in 38 CE and the measures that were taken to redress it are recounted in multiple, biased, inconsistent ancient sources. As a result, the causality of the event has been obscured and must be reconstructed through both deduction and imagination. While it has become conventional to describe the conflict as a pogrom (Van der Horst 2003), suggesting a meaningful resemblance to modern Jewish experiences of institutionalized violence, scholars disagree over how to categorize it. Much depends on how one assesses the polemical claims and apologetic silences of Philo's two treatises on the subject, *In Flaccum* and *Legatio ad Gaium* (Gambetti 2009, 13–21).

A basic problem is determining the identity of the Jews' assailants. Philo is not always precise in labeling the aggressors. In the past, scholars have been inclined to assume Alexandrian Greeks to be the culprits even when Philo calls them "Egyptians" (*Flacc.* 17, 29); now the pendulum seems to be shifting toward a literal (ethnic Egyptian) understanding (Schäfer 1997, 145; Gruen 2002, 63–65; Van der Horst 2003, 105–6). Koen Goudriaan (2002, 86–94), however, has argued that Philo uses Egyptian as a polemical slur as well as a genuine ethnic descriptor, thus complicating both readings. Decoding Philo's rhetoric is important because it has a bearing on motive. Scholars who understand the attackers to be Greek citizens are likely to read the incident as a Hellenic attempt to exclude Alexandrian Jews from citizen status. Conversely, those who view the enemy as ethnic

Egyptians are apt to analyze the violence as an expression of native frustration at being stripped of status under Roman rule.

Rejecting the assumption that the attack on the Jews was unprovoked, Allen Kerkeslager (2006) has argued that the prefect's decree depriving them of civic status was actually a punitive measure launched in retribution for a perceived insult against the imperial family. Taking his cue from Philo's off-handed remark that Jewish shops at the time of the violence were closed in memory of the emperor's sister, who had recently died (*Flacc.* 56), Kerkeslager infers that the Jews had offended Alexandrian sensibilities by refusing to participate fully in the mourning rites (394).

In this reconstruction, the Alexandrians' call for images to be erected in the Jews' synagogues was part of the mourning rites rather than an intentionally malicious provocation (395–97). On this reading, then, the violence of 38 CE was not caused by some long-standing resentment against Jews; rather, it was this immediate grievance—failure to join their fellow citizens in an expected gesture of loyalty to the imperial household—that resulted in the Jews' marginalization, leading the Alexandrians to view them henceforth as treacherous fifth-columnists in need of removal.

Like Honigman's reinterpretation of the Antiochene persecution, Kerkeslager's revisionist reading of Philo illustrates the challenges inherent in recovering historical events from partisan texts. Andrew Harker (2008) has applied a similar optic to the papyrological counterparts of Philo's treatises, the so-called Acta Alexandrinorum, a collection of documents and literary accounts of embassies to the emperors Gaius and Claudius as told from an anti-Jewish perspective. In Harker's (2008, 33–34) judgment, these papyri tendentiously retell the resolution of the Alexandrian crisis in ways that instructively parallel Philo and therefore enable us to better assess the biases of his treatises. A systematic reappraisal of both corpora in light of this insight seems in order.

3. Rome and Judea

Understanding the changing relationship between the Jewish homeland and Rome's imperium—from friendship and alliance to subjugation and eventual obliteration—remains a basic desideratum of scholarship (Shatzman 1999). One of the banes of historical analysis is the distorting effect of hindsight: Because *we* know how the story of Judea tragically ends, there is a temptation to inflate those events, forces, and actors that precipitated this outcome in our interpretations. Recent research on Roman-Judean relations has sought a more balanced view.

3.1. Hasmonean Diplomacy

The first half-century of contact between Judea and the Roman Republic was diplomatic rather than hegemonic. Documents preserved in 1 Maccabees and Josephus trace these interactions between the Hasmoneans and the distant Senate, opening a window onto Judea's engagement with international power politics (Gera 1998). Because diplomacy is a bilateral process, it needs to be analyzed from the vantage point of both parties. In the Judean case, one must reckon with the protocols of Roman diplomacy as they were applied to the Greek East (a vast and complicated subject in its own right) as well as the shifting objectives of the Hasmoneans who initiated, maintained, and ultimately abandoned their bond with the Roman Republic.

The incomplete state of the documents preserved in 1 Maccabees has been a matter of fierce scholarly contention for more than a century: whether they originate in authentic senatorial decrees, the extent to which the literary sources have accurately transmitted them, and how they are to be classified. The most extensive analysis of the initial embassy, sent to Rome by Judas Maccabee in 162 or 161 BCE (1 Macc 8), is that of Linda Zollschan (2017), who argues that the Senate established *amicitia* ("informal friendship") with the Judean people rather than a *foedus* ("a formal, binding treaty"). This conclusion has been vigorously challenged by Altay Coşkun (2018), who argues the reverse.

The dispute is more than taxonomical. The differing degree of commitment implied by each type of relationship has a bearing on how we interpret the Romans' failure to provide military support to Judas—and later to his brothers—in their struggles against the Seleucids. (The case of Judas is not clear-cut, since he may have died in battle before the Senate could take action.) It also raises the issue of the Senate's motives for consenting to the Hasmonean overtures. The same applies to the Judean side: Given that ties with Rome brought them no discernable military advantage, why did the Hasmoneans invest so much energy in them? Why, finally, does evidence for diplomacy with the Roman Republic cease during the first century BCE? There is as yet no consensus on these questions. (See Coşkun 2019; Dabrowa 2019; Eilers 2012; Rocca 2014; Seeman 2013; Zollschan 2017.)

3.2. The Herodian Dynasty

Because Herod the Great dominates both the textual and material record of first-century BCE Judea, it is not surprising to find a flourishing cottage industry of monographs and articles devoted to him. By far the most important recent synthesis is that of Adam Kolman Marshak (2015), who strives to correct one-sided portrayals of Herod as an oppressive tyrant in order to highlight his multifaceted political persona as Jewish king, Hellenistic benefactor, and Roman ally. Marshak treats Herod's self-presentation not as a static projection but as an evolving response to challenges from different quarters. Similar in approach is Samuel Rocca (2008) who, however, focuses less on Herod himself than on the institutions he developed to govern his kingdom. Rocca and Marshak are able to achieve this holistic assessment of Herod in large part thanks to advances in the study of Herod's coinage (Ariel and Fontanille 2012) and building activity (Burrell and Netzer 1999; Lichtenberger 1999; Roller 1998). Achim Lichtenberger's analysis in particular has been instrumental in exposing how architecture encodes Hellenistic and Roman ideologies of rule.

Ehud Netzer's (2011) claim to have discovered Herod's mausoleum at Herodium has been questioned by fellow archaeologists on account of the lack of epigraphic confirmation. Recent architectural analysis of the monument reveals a blending of Hellenistic, Roman, and Jewish traditions similar to what Marshak has proposed for Herod's kingship as a whole. Its ostentatious plan and decoration suggest the tomb was designed to inter someone of exalted status (Arnould-Béhar 2015). Thus Netzer's conviction, while as yet neither proved nor disproved, remains defensible. Even if it is not Herod's own mausoleum, it may well have been designated for members of the Herodian family, which makes it evidence for the monumentalization of the dynasty.

Study of the dynasty has been facilitated by Nikos Kokkinos's (1998) exhaustive prosopography and by the comprehensive monographs of Morten Hørning Jensen (2006) and Daniel Schwartz (1990) on Antipas and Agrippa I respectively. In the latter, Schwartz (1990, 149–53) posited that Claudius's decision not to appoint Agrippa's son as king following his father's death in 43/44 CE, but instead to reassign Judea to direct Roman administration, reflects an empire-wide policy. This raises the issue of what Judea's pre- and post-Agrippa status actually was.

3.3. Provincia Iudaea?

The death of Herod the Great provoked contention over Judea's future. The king's descendants naturally wished to remain in power; many Jewish notables, on the other hand, advocated the abolition of Herodian rule and the annexation of the region to the Roman province of Syria (Josephus, *B.J.* 2.20–22, 80–91; *A.J.* 17.299–314). Initially, Augustus embraced the Herodian option; but after deposing Archelaus in 6 CE, the emperor removed Judea, Samaria, and Idumea from their control. In *Antiquitates judaicae*, Josephus affirms that Archelaus's territory was absorbed into the Syrian province (17.355; 18.2). In *Bellum judaicum*, by contrast, the former ethnarchy was "delimited for (or into) a province" (*eis eparchian perigrapheises*; 2.117), which could either mean that it was constituted as a separate province or that it was designated for the province of Syria. The imprecision in Josephus's expression, compounded by the absence of unambiguous attestation of the name, *provincia Iudaea*, prior to 70 CE, has impacted the interpretation of Judea's history during the intervening decades.

From an initial preference for annexation, scholarly opinion gradually shifted in favor of the view that Judea became its own province in 6 CE, formally independent of Syria. In recent years, however, the annexation hypothesis has been revived (Cotton 1999, 76–79; Eck 2007, 23–37; Ghiretti 1985; Labbé 2012, 289; Mason 2016, 239–45). At stake in this debate are at least two substantive issues. First, to what degree should Judea's administrative history be regarded as typical or atypical within the empire? An independent *provincia Iudaea* whose prefect was de facto dependent on the legate of Syria would be anomalous and has been used as a basis for arguing that this exacerbated the region's political problems (Goodman 1987, 7–9; see also Eck 2011). Second, how should the relationship between Jerusalem (metropolis of the Judean ethnarchy), Caesarea (headquarters of the prefect), and Antioch (seat of the imperial legate) be understood? According to Josephus, the Judean aristocracy sought annexation to Syria, presumably with the expectation that this arrangement would enhance their own influence. So, on either interpretation of 6 CE, where would the regional balance of power have resided, and how did the presence or absence of a Herodian in Jerusalem (Archelaus, Agrippa) alter that equation?

3.4. The First Revolt

"The war of Judeans against Romans," as Josephus dubbed the rebellion of 66–74 CE, continues to attract scholarly interest—not, as Josephus boasted with Thucydidean zest, because it was "the greatest ever joined" (*B.J.* 1.1), but because it remains the best-documented conflict of its kind under Roman rule. Not only does it have a consummate narrator in Josephus; its outcome was also enthusiastically broadcast by the Flavian dynasty it helped bring to power (Overman 2002). Indeed, the revolt's unique publicity in Rome, and the negative press this created for Jews throughout the empire, seems to have been a major stimulus for Josephus's literary oeuvre. The long-standing conundrum of Josephus's historical reliability has not gone away, but over the past three decades it has been approached with greater sophistication. (Since that issue is dealt with at length in the "Jewish Historiography" essay of this volume, I focus here on the revolt itself: its causes, the motivations and identities of its participants, and its impact on Judea during the years that immediately followed it.)

Josephus's richly detailed backstory to the war has supplied endless material for speculation concerning the long-term causes of the conflict. Rural banditry, urban terrorism, prophetic protest, elite infighting, and provincial misrule all play a symptomatic role in Josephus's drama (McLaren 1998), and they have been productively analyzed many times (e.g., Goodman 1987; Gray 1993; Price 1992). One limitation to this kind of approach to explaining the first revolt is that Josephus himself does not attribute primary causality to any of these factors. Instead, he locates the origin of the chain-reaction in interethnic strife between Judeans and *Greeks* in Caesarea. This has led Steven Mason (2016, 260–80) to question the assumption that the revolt is explicable in terms of long-standing grievances between Judeans and Romans. Taking a different view, Nadav Sharon (2017) reads Josephus's accounts of persistent and widespread Jewish support for the Hasmoneans after 63 BCE as evidence of deeply ingrained opposition to Roman interference in Judean affairs from the beginning.

Josephus takes a cynical view of the revolt's instigators, branding their leaders tyrants and parsing their rhetoric of liberation as pretext for self-aggrandizement. Unfortunately, since Josephus is our sole literary source, it is difficult to evaluate the veracity of his perspective. McLaren (2011) has sought to compensate for this handicap by comparing Josephus's representations with the words and images the rebels themselves produced on coins and documents from Wadi Murabbaʿat to communicate their aims and achievements. The evidence points to the creation of a state called Israel that had functioning institutions and stable practices (an important counterpoint to Josephus's anarchic portrait).

In his influential 1961 monograph, *Die Zeloten*, Martin Hengel posited a unitary ideology underlying the many resistance movements that populate the pages of Josephus. Many scholars today regard this synthetic view as a potentially distorting oversimplification. As a counterbalance, Richard Horsley and John Hanson (1985) offered a sociologically more diverse typology of dissident groups within first-century CE Judea, while Jonathan Price (1992) carefully distinguished the divergent agendas of the warring factions in Jerusalem during the revolt itself. More recently, Mark Andrew Brighton (2009) has undertaken a comprehensive rhetorical analysis of a particular rebel group, the Sicarii, in Josephus's narrative, arguing that they cannot be equated with either the Zealots or the "fourth philosophy."

With the conclusion of Josephus's narrative in 74 CE, our knowledge of the internal history of Judea diminishes considerably (Isaac 1984). Some two-dozen documents attest to a populace actively involving the provincial governor in their domestic legal affairs (Goodman 1991). The absence of any reference to native institutions in these documents raises the issue of whether the Romans recognized any during this period. David Goodblatt (1994, 176–231) infers from a Mishnaic tradition concerning Rabbi Gamaliel II that the Romans invested him with some kind of authority (an antecedent for the later development of a patriarchate), but the speculative nature of this hypothesis renders it unprovable based on current evidence.

3.5. The Bar Kokhba Revolt

Recent archaeological and numismatic evidence has definitively solved a problem concerning the Bar Kokhba revolt. According to Cassius Dio (*Hist. rom.* 69.12), Hadrian founded (or announced his intention to found) Aelia Capitolina on the site of Jerusalem in 129 or 130 CE. Eusebius (*Hist. eccl.* 4.6) contradicts this chronology, asserting that Aelia was founded only after the suppression of the revolt, that is, in 136 CE. The timing is crucial to interpretation: If Aelia's founding preceded the revolt, then the revolt was likely caused by this event; conversely, if the founding postdated the war, the war's causality must be sought elsewhere. Excavation of the Eastern Cardo of Jerusalem indicates that the street was begun in preparation for the founding of Aelia quite early in Hadrian's principate (Weksler-Bdolah

2014; cf. Zissu and Eshel 2016). This indicates that Cassius Dio's is the correct chronology: hence, the emperor's intent to rededicate Jerusalem to Jupiter Capitolium probably provoked the revolt.

Why did Hadrian decide to do this? Circumstantial evidence suggests that there may have been an uprising in Judea just prior to Hadrian's accession in 117 CE (Pucci Ben Zeev 2005, 250–56). During this period, Judea became a consular province and received a second legionary base. During the following decade, a network of military roads was established in the province, enhancing troop mobility in the region. Coinage emphasized pagan motifs, anticipating the founding of Aelia. In other words, not only was Aelia the provocation for the revolt; it was the climax of a sequence of developments which were themselves a response to an earlier revolt (Pucci Ben Zeev 2018).

Judging by the Roman reaction to it (Eck 1999), the Bar Kokhba revolt was a major conflict that exhausted the energies of at least nine legions and inflicted heavy loss of life and property over a three-year period (132–135 CE). Even more so than the refounding of Jerusalem as a pagan city, Emperor Hadrian's decision to change the province's name from *Iudaea* to *Syria Palaestina* highlights the Romans' ultimate aim: to decisively sever the Jews' link to their ancestral homeland. The physical exclusion of Jews from Jerusalem following the war completed this decreation of Jewish space. Henceforth, rabbinic Galilee would become the geographical center of Jewish life and learning in the region.

4. Conclusion

In the first edition of *Early Judaism and Its Modern Interpreters*, Shaye Cohen (1986, 34–37) spoke of a "methodological crisis" overshadowing the study of Jewish history in the Greco-Roman period. Appropriating ancient textual data without due attention to their context or biases, post-1945 research had not fully escaped the legacy of constructs and assumptions inherited from Christian anti-Judaism and from what Cohen saw as a defensive overreaction to it by Israeli scholarship. The way forward, Cohen urged, was to confront, rather than sidestep, the limits of our evidence: "Which sources are reliable? How are the sources to be used? What assumptions can we make? How can we determine which questions are answerable and which unanswerable?" (37).

Investigators of Second Temple Judaism and its protorabbinic aftermath have taken Cohen's questions to heart. As should be evident from the preceding discussion, it is increasingly uncommon to encounter an article or monograph that is *not* sensitive to the problems inherent in reconstructing the past from ancient texts or material remains. Needless to say, heightened methodological rigor does not necessarily result in agreement.

The dual goal of this essay has been to highlight where our understandings have advanced and where disagreements persist over the historical events and forces that shaped early Judaism. It would be premature to speak of an emerging consensus on all the *topics* we have surveyed; the range of scholarly approaches and conclusions remains quite diverse. It may, however, be accurate to speak of an emerging set of *issues* that more and more researchers of the Second Temple period recognize to be deserving of critical inquiry: the interpenetration of native and Greco-Roman idioms in the legitimation of Jewish leaders, the intersection of local, regional, and imperial factors in the analysis of crises as well as normal relations between Jewish communities and the larger world, and the integration of literary with nonliterary sources. These and other questions are likely to remain on the agenda of historians for the foreseeable future.

Bibliography

Ariel, Donald T., and Jean-Philippe Fontanille. 2012. *The Coins of Herod: A Modern Analysis and Die Classification*. AJEC 79. Leiden: Brill.

Arnould-Béhar, Caroline. 2015. "Le 'tombeau d'Hérode' et sa place dans l'architecture funéraire de l'antiquité." *RB* 122:104–18.

Babota, Vasile. 2014. *The Institution of the Hasmonean High Priesthood*. JSJSup 165. Leiden: Brill.

Barclay, John M. G. 1996. *Jews in the Mediterranean Diaspora from Alexander to Trajan (323 BCE–117 CE)*. HCS 33. Berkeley: University of California Press.

Bernhardt, Johannes Christian. 2017. *Die Jüdische Revolution: Untersuchungen zu Ursachen, Verlauf und Folgen der hasmonäischen Erhebung*. Klio 22. Berlin: de Gruyter.

Brighton, Mark Andrew. 2009. *The Sicarii in Josephus' Judean War: Rhetorical Analysis and Historical Observations*. EJL 27. Atlanta: Society of Biblical Literature.

Brutti, Maria. 2006. *The Development of the High Priesthood during the pre-Hasmonean Period: History, Ideology, Theology*. JSJSup 108. Leiden: Brill.

Burrell, Barbara, and Ehud Netzer. 1999. "Herod the Builder." *JRA* 12:705–15.

Cataldo, Jeremiah W. 2009. *A Theocratic Yehud? Issues of Government in a Persian Province*. LHBOTS 498. London: T&T Clark.
Cohen, Shaye J. D. 1986. "The Political and Social History of the Jews in Greco-Roman Antiquity: The State of the Question." Pages 33–56 in *Early Judaism and Its Modern Interpreters*. Edited by Robert A. Kraft and George W. E. Nickelsburg. BMI 2. Philadelphia: Fortress; Atlanta: Scholars Press.
Collins, John J. 2000. *Between Athens and Jerusalem: Jewish Identity in the Hellenistic Diaspora*. 2nd ed. Grand Rapids: Eerdmans.
Coşkun, Altay. 2018. "'Friendship and Alliance' between the Judaeans under Judas Maccabee and the Romans (1 Macc 8: 17–32): A Response to Linda Zollschan's *Rome and Judaea*." *Electrum* 25:85–125.
———. 2019. "Triangular Epistolary Diplomacy with Rome from Judas Maccabee to Aristobulos I." Pages 355–88 in *Rome and the Seleukid East: Selected Papers from Seleukid Study Day V, Brussels, 21–23 August 2015*. Edited by Altay Coşkun and David Engels. Collection Latomus 360. Brussels: Société d'études latines.
Cotton, Hannah M. 1999. "Some Aspects of the Roman Administration of Judaea/Syria-Palestina." Pages 75–91 in *Lokale Autonomie und römische Ordnungsmacht in den kaiserzeitlichen Provinzen vom 1.–3. Jh. Kolloquien des Historischen Kollegs*. Edited by Werner Eck. Munich: Oldenbourg.
Cotton, Hannah, and Michael Wörrle. 2007. "Seleukos IV to Heliodoros: A New Dossier of Royal Correspondence from Israel." *ZPE* 159:191–205.
Cowey, James M. S., and Klaus Maresch. 2001. *Urkunden des Politeuma der Juden von Herakleopolis (144/3–133/2 v. Chr) (P. Polit. Jud.): Papyri aus Sammlungen von Heidelberg, Köln, München und Wien*. Papyrologica Coloniensia 29. Wiesbaden: Westdeutcher.
Dabrowa, Edward D. 2019. "The Seleukids, Rome and the Jews (134–76 BC)." Pages 389–99 in *Rome and the Seleukid East: Selected Papers from Seleukid Study Day V, Brussels, 21–23 August 2015*. Edited by Altay Coşkun and David Engels. Collection Latomus 360. Brussels: Société d'études latines.
Eck, Werner. 1999. "The Bar Kokhba Revolt: The Roman Point of View." *JRS* 89:76–89.
———. 2007. *Rom und Judaea: Fünf Vorträge zur römischen Herrschaft in Palaestina*. Tria Corda 2. Tübingen: Mohr Siebeck.
———. 2011. "Die römischen Repräsentanten in Judaea: Provokateure oder Vertreter der römischen Macht?" Pages 45–68 in *The Jewish*

Revolt Against Rome: Interdisciplinary Perspectives. Edited by Mladen Popović. JSJSup 154. Leiden: Brill.

Eckhardt, Benedikt. 2016. "The Seleucid Administration of Judea, the High Priesthood and the Rise of the Hasmoneans." *JAH* 4:57–87.

Eilers, Claude. 2012. "Diplomacy and the Integration of the Hasmonean State." Pages 155–65 in *Belonging and Isolation in the Hellenistic World*. Edited by Sheila L. Ager and Riemer A. Faber. Phoenix Supplement 51. Toronto: University of Toronto Press.

Fried, Lisbeth. 2004. *The Priest and the Great King: Temple-Palace Relations in the Persian Empire*. BJSUCSD 10. Winona Lake, IN: Eisenbrauns.

Gambetti, Sandra. 2009. *The Alexandrian Riots of 38 C.E. and the Persecution of the Jews: A Historical Reconstruction*. JSJSup 135. Leiden: Brill.

Gera, Dov. 1998. *Judaea and Mediterranean Politics, 219 to 161 B.C.E.* BSJS 8. Leiden: Brill.

———. 2009. "Olympiodoros, Heliodoros and the Temples of Koile Syria and Phoinike." *ZPE* 169:125–55.

Ghiretti, Maurizio. 1985. "Lo 'status' della Giudea dall'età Augustea all'età Claudia." *Latomus* 44:751–66.

Goodblatt, David. 1994. *The Monarchic Principle: Studies in Jewish Self-Government in Antiquity*. TSAJ 38. Tübingen: Mohr Siebeck.

Goodman, Martin. 1987. *The Ruling Class of Judaea: The Origins of the Jewish Revolt against Rome A.D. 66–70*. Cambridge: Cambridge University Press.

———. 1991. "Babatha's Story." *JRS* 81:169–75.

Goudriaan, Koen. 1992. "Ethnical Strategies in Graeco-Roman Egypt." Pages 74–99 in *Ethnicity in Hellenistic Egypt*. Edited by Per Bilde, Troels Engberg-Pedersen, Lise Hannestad, and Jan Zahle. Studies in Hellenistic Civilization 3. Aarhus: Aarhus University Press.

Grabbe, Lester L. 2003. "Were the Pre-Maccabean High Priests 'Zadokites'?" Pages 205–15 in *Reading from Right to Left: Essays on the Hebrew Bible in Honour of David J. A. Clines*. Edited by Cheryl J. Exum and Hugh G. M. Williamson. JSOTSup 373. Sheffield: Sheffield Academic.

Gray, Rebecca. 1993. *Prophetic Figures in Late Second Temple Jewish Palestine: The Evidence from Josephus*. Oxford: Oxford University Press.

Gruen, Erich S. 1993. "Hellenism and Persecution: Antiochus IV and the Jews." Pages 238–74 in *Hellenistic History and Culture*. Edited by Peter Green. HCS 9. Berkeley: University of California Press.

———. 1998. *Heritage and Hellenism: The Reinvention of Jewish Tradition*. HCS 30. Berkeley: University of California Press.

———. 2002. *Diaspora: Jews amidst Greeks and Romans*. Cambridge: Harvard University Press.
Harker, Andrew. 2008. *Loyalty and Dissidence in Roman Egypt: The Case of the Acta Alexandrinorum*. Cambridge: Cambridge University Press.
Hengel, Martin. 1961. *Die Zeloten, Untersuchungen zur jüdischen Freiheitsbewegung in der Zeit von Herodes I. bis 70 n. Chr*. AGJU 1. Leiden: Brill.
Henten, Jan Willem van. 2001. "The Honorary Decree for Simon the Maccabee (1 Macc 14:25–49) in Its Hellenistic Context." Pages 116–45 in *Hellenism in the Land of Israel*. Edited by John J. Collins and Gregory Sterling. CJAn. Notre Dame: University of Notre Dame Press.
Honigman, Sylvie. 2014. *Tales of High Priests and Taxes: The Books of the Maccabees and the Judean Rebellion against Antiochos IV*. HCS 56. Berkeley: University of California Press.
Horsley, Richard A., and John S. Hanson. 1985. *Bandits, Prophets, and Messiahs: Popular Movements at the Time of Jesus*. San Francisco: Harper & Row.
Horst, Pieter W. van der. 2003. *Philo's Flaccus: The First Pogrom*. Leiden: Brill.
Hunt, Alice. 2006. *Missing Priests: The Zadokites in Tradition and History*. LHBOTS 452. New York: T&T Clark.
Isaac, Benjamin. 1984. "Judaea after A.D. 70." *JJS* 35:44–50.
Jensen, Morten Hørning. 2006. *Herod Antipas in Galilee: The Literary and Archaeological Sources on the Reign of Herod Antipas and Its Socio-economic Impact on Galilee*. WUNT 2/215. Tübingen: Mohr Siebeck.
Kasher, Aryeh. 1985. *The Jews in Hellenistic and Roman Egypt: The Struggle for Equal Rights*. TSAJ 7. Tübingen: Mohr Siebeck.
———. 1990. *Jews and Hellenistic Cities in Eretz-Israel: Relations of the Jews in Eretz-Israel with the Hellenistic Cities during the Second Temple Period (332 BCE–70CE)*. TSAJ 21. Tübingen: Mohr Siebeck.
Kerkeslager, Allen. 2006. "Agrippa and the Mourning Rites for Drusilla in Alexandria." *JSJ* 37:367–400.
Kokkinos, Nikos. 1998. *The Herodian Dynasty: Origins, Role in Society and Eclipse*. JSPSup 30. Sheffield: Sheffield Academic.
Kooij, Arie van der. 2007. "The Greek Bible and Jewish Concepts of Royal Priesthood and Priestly Monarchy." Pages 255–64 in *Jewish Perspectives on Hellenistic Rulers*. Edited by Tessa Rajak, Jennifer Dines, Sarah Pearce, and James Aitken. HCS 50. Berkeley: University of California Press.

Labbé, Gilbert. 2012. *L'affirmation de la puissance romaine en Judée (63 avant J.-C.–136 après J.-C.)*. Collection d'études anciennes Série latine 74. Paris: Les Belles lettres.

Lichtenberger, Achim. 1999. *Die Baupolitik Herodes des Grossen*. ADPV 26. Wiesbaden: Harrassowitz.

Lüderitz, Gerd. 1994. "What Is the Politeuma?" Pages 183–225 in *Studies in Early Jewish Epigraphy*. Edited by Jan Willem van Henten and Pieter W. van der Horst. AGJU 21. Leiden: Brill.

Marshak, Adam Kolman. 2015. *The Many Faces of Herod the Great*. Grand Rapids: Eerdmans.

Mason, Steve. 2016. *A History of the Jewish War, A.D. 66–74*. Cambridge: University of Cambridge Press.

McKechnie, Paul. 2005. "Judaean Embassies and Cases before Roman Emperors, AD 44–66." *JTS* 56:339–61.

McLaren, James S. 1991. *Power and Politics in Palestine: The Jews and the Governing of their Land, 100 BC–AD 70*. JSNTSup 63. Sheffield: Sheffield Academic.

———. 1998. *Turbulent Times? Josephus and Scholarship on Judaea in the First Century CE*. JSPSup 29. Sheffield: Sheffield Academic.

———. 2011. "Going to War against Rome: The Motivation of the Jewish Rebels." Pages 129–53 in *The Jewish Revolt against Rome: Interdisciplinary Perspectives*. Edited by Mladen Popović. JSJSup 154. Leiden: Brill.

Meshorer, Ya'akov. 2001. *A Treasury of Jewish Coins: From the Persian Period to Bar Kokhba*. Jerusalem: Yad Ben-Zvi; Nyack: Amphora.

Netzer, Ehud. 2011. "In Search of Herod's Tomb." *BAR* 37/1:37–48, 70.

Oegema, Gerbern S. 1998. *The Anointed and His People: Messianic Expectations from the Maccabees to Bar Kochba*. JSPSup 27. Sheffield: Sheffield Academic.

Osterloh, Kevin Lee. 2008. "Judea, Rome and the Hellenistic 'Oikoumenê': Emulation and the Reinvention of Communal Identity." Pages 168–206 in *Heresy and Identity in Late Antiquity*. Edited by Eduard Iricinschi and Holger M. Zellentin. TSAJ 119. Tübingen: Mohr Siebeck.

Overman, J. Andrew. 2002. "The First Revolt and Flavian Politics." Pages 213–20 in *The First Jewish Revolt: Archaeology, History, and Ideology*. Edited by Andrea A. Berlin and J. Andrew Overman. London: Routledge.

Portier-Young, Anathea E. 2011. *Apocalypse against Empire: Theologies of Resistance in Early Judaism*. Grand Rapids: Eerdmans.

Price, Jonathan J. 1992. *Jerusalem under Siege: The Collapse of the Jewish State 66–70 C.E.* BSJS 3. Leiden: Brill.
Pucci Ben Zeev, Miriam. 1998. *Jewish Rights in the Roman World: The Greek and Roman Documents Quoted by Josephus Flavius.* TSAJ 74. Tübingen: Mohr Siebeck.
———. 2005. *Diaspora Judaism in Turmoil, 116/117 CE: Ancient Sources and Modern Insights.* Interdisciplinary Studies in Ancient Culture and Religion 6. Leuven: Peeters.
———. 2018. "New Insights into Roman Policy in Judea on the Eve of the Bar Kokhba Revolt." *JSJ* 49:84–107.
Rajak, Tessa. 1984. "Was There a Roman Charter for the Jews?" *JRS* 74:107–23.
———. 1996. "Hasmonean Kingship and the Invention of Tradition." Pages 99–115 in *Aspects of Hellenistic Kingship*. Edited by Per Bilde, Troels Engberg-Pedersen, Lise Hannestad, and Jan Zahle. Studies in Hellenistic Civilization 7. Aarhus: Aarhus University Press.
Rappaport, Uriel. 2011. "Did Heliodoros Try to Rob the Treasures of the Jerusalem Temple? Date and Probability of the Story of II Maccabees, 3." *REJ* 170:3–19.
Regev, Eyal. 2012 "Ḥever ha-Yehudim and the Political Ideology of the Hasmoneans" [Hebrew]. *Tarbiz* 80:329–46.
———. 2013. *The Hasmoneans: Ideology, Archaeology, Identity.* JAJSup 10. Göttingen: Vandenhoeck & Ruprecht.
Rocca, Samuel. 2008. *Herod's Judaea: A Mediterranean State in the Classical World.* TSAJ 122. Tübingen: Mohr Siebeck.
———. 2014. "The Hasmonean State and Rome: A New Appraisal." *REJ* 173:263–95.
Roller, Duane W. 1998. *The Building Program of Herod the Great.* Berkeley: University of California Press.
Rooke, Deborah W. 2000. *Zadok's Heirs: The Role and Development of the High Priesthood in Ancient Israel.* OTM. Oxford: Oxford University Press.
Schäfer, Peter. 1997. *Judeophobia: Attitudes toward the Jews in the Ancient World.* Cambridge: Harvard University Press.
Schofield, Alison, and James C. VanderKam. 2005. "Were the Hasmoneans Zadokites?" *JBL* 124:73–87.
Schwartz, Daniel R. 1990. *Agrippa I: The Last King of Judaea.* TSAJ 23. Tübingen: Mohr Siebeck.

Seeman, Chris. 2013. *Rome and Judea in Transition: Hasmonean Relations with the Roman Republic and the Evolution of the High Priesthood.* AMUStTR 325. New York: Lang.

Sharon, Nadav. 2017. *Judea under Roman Domination: The First Generation of Statelessness and Its Legacy.* EJL 46. Atlanta: SBL Press.

Shatzman, Israel. 1999. "The Integration of Judaea into the Roman Empire." *SCI* 18:49–84.

Tcherikover, Victor. 1959. *Hellenistic Civilization and the Jews.* Philadelphia: Jewish Publication Society.

VanderKam, James C. 2004. *From Joshua to Caiaphas: High Priests after the Exile.* Minneapolis: Fortress.

Weitzman, Steven. 2004. "Plotting Antiochus's Persecution." *JBL* 123:219–34.

Weksler-Bdolah, Shlomit. 2014. "The Foundation of Aelia Capitolina in the Light of New Excavations along the Eastern Cardo." *IEJ* 64:38–62.

Zissu, Boaz, and Hanan Eshel. 2016. "Religious Aspects of the Bar Kokhba Revolt: The Founding of Aelia Capitolina on the Ruins of Jerusalem." Pages 387–405 in *The Religious Aspects of War in the Ancient Near East, Greece, and Rome.* Edited by Krzysztof Ulanowski. CHANE 84. Leiden: Brill.

Zollschan, Linda. 2017. *Rome and Judaea: International Law Relations, 162–100 BCE.* Routledge Studies in Ancient History. London: Routledge.

2
THE SOCIAL WORLD OF EARLY JUDAISM

PHILIP F. ESLER

The current chapter updates chapters 2 and 3 in the first edition of *Early Judaism and Its Modern Interpreters* (Kraft and Nickelsburg 1986a). Significant literature that has appeared since 1980 on the topics covered in those chapters will be included here. Nevertheless, given the immense changes in scholarly emphases in the last four decades—changes reflected in this chapter's title—a different, and more inclusive, form of presentation will be adopted. This approach will draw on social-scientific approaches, especially from sociology and anthropology, to inform the framework of the discussion.

Driving the new approach is the need to resolve a tension in the first edition as to what *Judaism* means. For the editors, the focus was on Judaism as a religion (Kraft and Nickelsburg 1986b, xi). This accorded with the then-dominant approach of discussing the ancient *Ioudaioi/Iudaei* as if they were representatives of a religion called Judaism. Scholars of Judaism did this even though they did not treat other groups (e.g., the Romans, Egyptians, and Nabateans), who all had religious beliefs and practices, as representing different religions, but rather as national groups with distinctive religious dimensions. As Shaye Cohen (1986, 46, passim) observed in the first edition, this interest in the theology of ancient Jews reflected the theological interests of the guild; classicists familiar with Greece and Rome looked at the data quite differently.

Yet the editors also rightly recognized that there was more to Jews than their religion. Notwithstanding their emphasis on literary works as evidence for the religion of Judaism, they referred to the introduction of social sciences to the field (Nickelsburg and Kraft 1986b, 4, 8), the role of archaeology (9) and, most revealingly, to the recent concern with "the realia of

Jewish life in Palestine and the Diaspora and with the domestic, social, economic, and legal factors of that life" (10). Later they even asked the key question, "What makes them Jewish" (13), while doubting that Josephus ever thought "in just such terms," even though his *Contra Apionem* suggests he did. Cohen (1986, 46–49) expressly distinguished the religious and economic aspects of being a Jew. Yet he also recognized, probably correctly, "that the Jewish religious scene was unique; no other ancient society was so torn by religious strife" (47–48).

What is needed here, therefore, is a scoping of the field that recognizes Jews as a people whose identity included a strong religious dimension that some will wish to call Judaism. That is to say, we must map the totality of their social world but in a manner that pays proper regard to, and helps us understand, the prominent role religious beliefs and practices played in it. The focus must be Palestine because the diaspora is covered by Erich Gruen elsewhere in this volume. The broad topics to be addressed are these: (1) the broad social system; (2) major socioreligious institutions; (3) minority socioreligious movements; (4) the Samaritans; and (5) recent approach to Jewish/Judean identity.

1. The Broad Social System of Palestine

Many interpreters have interested themselves in the broad social system of Palestine, a word that I am using to refer roughly to the entirety of the area that had been included in the kingdom of Herod the Great. The macrosociology of Gerhard and Jean Lenski provides a suitable starting-point (see Lenski and Nolan 2014). The Lenskis formulated a model of the stages of human development that ran from hunting and gathering, to horticulture using digging sticks, to agrarian where wooden ploughs were employed, to advanced agrarian where the plough was tipped with iron to allow a larger acreage to be covered. The significance of the agrarian and advanced agrarian stages was that only at this point did an individual farmer produce a surplus of food beyond the subsistence needs of his family. This, inevitably, led to the rise of elites, backed by armies, who confiscated this surplus for themselves, erected cities in which to live with the support of numerous retainers, and fostered the introduction of divine cults that served to legitimate the whole process. Social stratification was notably vertical, with a tiny elite supported by a large population of peasants. The Lenski model provides a broad outline of the social system, with the details changing in different places and periods. Yet the picture is visible throughout the history of ancient Israel, from the eighth century BCE (see Chaney 2017) to the first century CE (see below). Early Judaism as a religion was practiced by people living in this system.

The political undergirding of this social pattern was analyzed by John Kautsky in *The Politics of Aristocratic Empires* (1962). Like Lenski and Lenski, he maintained that most aristocratic empires had been established by the conquest of the peasantry and their subsequent exploitation. His central argument was that aristocrats (the top of the social elite), who lived off the labor of the peasantry, performed the primary governmental functions of taxation and warfare. How they performed was conditioned by certain values (e.g., honor) and beliefs, and these influenced how they competed with one another and their arenas of conflict, the totality of which comprises the politics of the aristocracy. This situation could only be changed through commercialization. While this is a general picture that certainly changed over time (including by changes in the governing regime), ancient Palestine was subject to these pressures of aristocratic politics from the Iron Age onward (Chaney 2017). It has been recently argued that the behavior of the angels in 1 En. 1–36, from the third century BCE, reflects the way kings and courtiers conducted themselves in Hellenistic monarchies (Esler 2017b, 35–108). The period when Herod the Great, a client king of the Romans, ruled much of Palestine (37 to 4 BCE) also reflected this situation. Yet, as K. C. Hanson and Douglas Oakman (2008) have shown, even when Rome split up Herod's kingdom among his sons after his death, much the same social, economic, and political patterns (as described by Lenksi and Nolan 2014; and Kautsky 1962) continued in the Tetrarchy and later Province of Judea (comprising Judea, Samaria, and Idumea) and in the Tetrarchies of Galilee and Perea (under Archelaus, 4 BCE–39 CE; see his aristocratic elite in Mark 6:21) and Batanea (under Philip, 4 BCE–34 CE).

Also undergirding the argument of Oakman and Hanson was Mediterranean anthropology, introduced into biblical research by Bruce Malina (1981). Malina's central interests included the prominence of the values of honor and shame, the importance of group rather than individualistic orientation, the notion of limited good, patron and client relations, and the importance of purity. These interests were repeatedly adverted to by Hanson and Oakman (2008), as many other scholars have done, since 1981, as essential in understanding the particular cultural shape of the broad picture that is accessible using the ideas of the Lenskis and Kautsky. Hanson and Oakman rightly focus upon kinship as the dominant social institution, leading them to explore how issues such as descent, gender, marriage, dowry and bridewealth, divorce, and inheritance take particular forms in the patrilineal and patrilocal society of early Judaism, both in the elite and nonelite sectors of society. An examination of theses issues in relation to the thirty-five papyrus documents of the Babatha archive dated 94–132 CE results in a better focus (Lewis 1989; Yadin 2002; Esler 2017a). These cast light on how, among the Jews living in Maoza (in Nabatea and then the Roman province of Arabia) and En-Gedi (in Judea) in the period 94–132 CE, fathers used dowries and marriage gifts to shield their daughters against the effects of patrilineal succession; women lent their dowries to their husbands and were imperiled when the latter died without repaying the loan; how husbands divorcing their wives often stipulated that they could only marry Jewish men; and how men and women used the provincial courts to protect their interests.

The plight of the peasantry in Palestine, particularly Galilee, especially in relation to the amount of taxation and other imposts that they had to pay, what might be called the economic dimensions of their situation (Freyne 1995; Fiensy and Hawkins 2013), has attracted a great deal of attention since 1986. Interpreters basically line up around two positions. The first, sometimes inspired by conflict theory, looks to tension between groups that are the result of power relations in which one group seeks to dominate and manipulate others. In relation to the role of cities and towns, this position tends to appeal to Moses Finley's (1973) ideas concerning "the consumer city," which was largely dependent on the local countryside for what it needed given the prohibitive cost of land transportation. These pressures tended to produce latifundialization in the city's hinterland. Scholars favoring this approach include John Dominic Crossan (1991), Richard Horsley (1996), Douglas Oakman (2014a, 2017), Jonathan Reed (2014), and, most recently, Roland Boer and Christina Petterson (2017).

The second position, sometimes reflecting a structuralist-functionalist approach that looks to society seeking equilibrium among its various parts, takes a more positive view of the position of the peasants and is unwilling to give too much credence to their being grossly oppressed. Some of those advocating this position adopt the critique of Finley developed by Donald Engels (1990) in relation to Corinth, who prefers the model of the "service city," with cities providing services to rural communities and the peasants themselves. Whether Corinth, with its trading links and commercial activities, represents a model capable of effective wider application has been called into doubt. Nevertheless, scholars who tend to take a structuralist-functionalist approach (even if they do not use the term) include Mordechai Aviam (2004), Douglas Edwards (2007), Morten Jensen (2006), Sharon Mattila (2013), and Fabian Udoh (2014). A particular issue that arises in this area is the incidence of taxation, with advocates of the former group arguing for heavy taxation and advocates of the latter suggesting taxation was more moderate (Udoh 2014). For many interpreters the conditions and experience of the Galilean peasantry are critical as providing the context for the ministry and teaching of Jesus (Freyne 2004; Horsley 2014; Oakman 2012, 2014b; and Reed 2000).

One of the most significant developments since 1986 in our knowledge of the social system in which the Jewish people found themselves has come from archaeology. While archaeology in the region had by then been long established and surveys and excavations, including in Jerusalem and Galilee (Meyers and Strange 1981), had begun to yield rich fruit, the three decades since have seen an explosion of discoveries (Magness 2012). From Jerusalem we have well-preserved remains of luxurious houses dated pre-70 CE probably owned by high priests (Avigad 1983). In Galilee the discovery of limestone vessels and mikvaot (steep and stepped, plastered basins for ritual immersion), from the period 100 BCE to 100 CE, strongly points to occupation by Jews with their characteristic purity concerns (Aviam 2004; Chancey 2005; Fiensy and Strange 2015).

2. The Major Socioreligious Institutions

Three institutions were central to the religious life of the Jewish people: the temple in Jerusalem, the synagogue, and the household. All three had social and religious functions, hence the designator socioreligious. In the 1990s Malina (1994, 1996), accurately observing that in the ancient world the phenomena we refer to as religious were not stand-alone entities but were embedded in other dimensions of social reality, usefully distinguished between public, or political, religion and domestic religion. He regarded the temple as the focus of the former and the household as the focus of the latter. This binary arrangement could perhaps be improved with the addition of a mediating category such as community religious practice, which would allow proper scope to be given to the synagogue throughout the towns and villages of ancient Palestine. Synagogues were public but were not subject to the same level of control by the apparatus of the state as was the temple.

2.1. The Temple

The temple was the heart of Jerusalem, the *mētropolis* ("mother-city") of the ethnic homeland of the Jewish people, with the thousands of local and foreign Jews who attended the festivals a testament to its importance. Oakman and Hanson (2008, 123–47) have described the role of the temple within the political religion of the Jewish people. They discuss the sacrificial cult and its personnel (which were absolutely central to the role of the temple as an instrument of individual and group atonement), the social and economic impact of the temple, the views of the nonelite to the institution (which were sometimes negative), but also embracing the pilgrimages, and the attitude of the Jesus movement to the institution. More particularly, Francis Schmidt (2001) has argued for the importance of the temple in maintaining Jewish identity. Using Mary Douglas, he argues for its role, not merely as an edifice, but as establishing and legitimating a system of thought that created a double distinction between the pure and the impure, and the sacred and the profane that extended beyond its architecture to the land of Israel, from the sacrificial altars to daily meals. This view, however, has been criticized as too reliant on Douglas's early functionalist ideas so that, for example, it neglects the extent to which the purity system was relaxed during festivals and largely overlooks the symbolical implications of purity and sacrifice (Klawans 2006). It has also been argued that in the Second Temple period the influence of the temple on Jewish identity was significantly reduced, for example, in relation to the reduction of high priests' power under the Romans (Mendels 1997). How one could prove such an alleged reduction of influence, however, is not at all obvious.

2.2. The Synagogue

Since 1986 there has been an explosion of interest in the ancient synagogue. Archaeological discoveries have been highly significant in this context. Anders Runesson, Donald D. Binder, and Birger Olsson (2008, 7–10), surveying the field, have isolated four major areas of interest: (1) spatial aspects (especially architecture and art); (2) liturgical aspects, in that we know the Torah was read but what else happened? For example, was prayer said, were fasts and festivals observed, was "magic" practiced?; (3) social, or nonliturgical aspects, such as the use of synagogues as council halls, law courts, schools, treasuries, and public archives (see Levine 2000); and (4) institutional aspects, relating to synagogue leadership and operations. One aspect of synagogal leadership involves the role of women (Brooten 1982, 2000). The subject of gender in early Judaism is covered by Françoise Mirguet in this volume.

According to Philo in the *Hypothetica* (quoted by Eusebius in *Praep. ev.* 7.8), Jews were required to assemble on the Sabbath to hear the law read; Pseudo-Philo, probably writing in the first century CE (LAB 11.8), states they had to gather in assembly to praise the Lord (Sanders 1990, 78–79). To similar effect is 2 Macc 8:27. In Egypt and Rome synagogues were referred to as *proseuchai* ("prayer-halls") (for Egypt: Philo, *Legat.* 156–57; for Rome: Juvenal, *Sat.* 3.296 and in one inscription [Esler 2003, 94]). The Sabbath gatherings mentioned by Philo and Pseudo-Philo probably occurred in a synagogue, either a custom-made one or in a house or other building serving as a synagogue. Such evidence rather counts against the view of Heather McKay (1994) that there was no formal synagogue worship in the first century.

The existence of synagogues in Palestine in the first century CE has been doubted by some (Kee 1990; White 2017, 680–81). Yet the archaeological evidence for first century CE synagogues in Gamla, Magdala, Herodium, and Masada is strong. Runesson, Binder, and Olsson (2008) list twenty places where synagogues have been identified in ancient Palestine. The famous Theodotus inscription, found on Mount Ophel in Jerusalem and almost certainly to be dated before 70 CE (Kloppenborg 2000; Runesson, Binder, and Olsson 2008, 52–54), refers to a synagogue in Jerusalem. There is also literary evidence in Josephus and in the Gospels (e.g., Mark 6:1–6). Donald Binder (1999) has argued that the services in the synagogue, its functionaries, and its architecture were based on the Jerusalem temple, but this view has been called into doubt (Levine 2001, 26–28). Synagogue buildings, moreover, were probably also used for community meetings not connected with Sabbath religious practice.

2.3. The Household

Religious beliefs and practices in the family and household have proved to be of more interest to Hebrew Bible scholars than to those interested in Herodian Palestine (see Ackerman 2008; and Albertz and Schmidt 2012). Nevertheless, according to E. P. Sanders (1990, 77), "the home was the most frequent place of worship; it was there that people prayed and observed the sabbath and many other holy occasions." This is accurate, except to the extent that Jewish families also attended a local synagogue on such occasions. Perhaps the major influence on religious belief and practice in the home was the Shema of Deut 6:4–5 (Sanders 1990, 68–69). The torah required Jews to teach these words to their children (Deut 6:7), recite them (Deut 6:7), and bind them on their hands, their foreheads, and the doorposts of their homes and gates (Deut 6:8–9; 11:20). Ongoing concern for teaching the law of Moses appears, for example, in Susanna (v. 3) and Josephus (*C. Ap.* 1.11). (For prayer, see the chapter in this volume by Daniel K. Falk and Angela Kim Harkins.)

Particular religious practices punctuated daily life. Men and women contracted impurity from bodily discharges, which required various types of washing (Lev 15). Ritual purification was available by recourse to mikvaot (see above). From the mid-first-century BCE, mikvaot began to appear in Judea and Galilee and became common, with some three hundred discovered by 2005. In many villages in Judea, mikvaot were situated outside of houses and seem to have been communal (Berlin 2005, 453). The expanding use of stone vessels in houses may also indicate a religious concern with purity (429–34).

Parents were obliged to have their sons circumcised on the eighth day after their birth (Josephus, *A.J.* 1.214; Philo, *QG* 3.49; Lev 12:3). Marriage also reflected Jewish religious practice and belief (Archer 1990). Among the Dead Sea legal papyri are wedding contracts that stipulate that the woman will be the man's wife according to the law of Moses (P.Murabba'ât 20.3) or the law of Moses and the Judeans (P.Yadin 2 10.5). The religious dimension exists here as long as Moses was seen not just as their law-giver from long ago, but as providing laws received from God on Sinai.

Practices concerning death and funerals also manifested religious elements. Jews of the period practiced interment, not cremation, and this may well have been dictated by Gen 3:19: "You are dust, and to dust you shall return." The most common type of tomb in first century CE Palestine was the rock-cut grave (Berlin 2005, 454). The common period of seven days of mourning may have originated with Gen 50:10 (Archer 1990, 252, 260). The discovery of water and cooking vessels near tombs suggests funerary meals were conducted at the graveside (Berlin 2005, 455). One other religious practice that would have characterized the domestic context above all was that of fasting (Sanders 1990, 81–84). Fasting was compulsory on the Day of Atonement (Lev 23:20). Fasting was common during mourning (as with Judith) and during times of need, even for children (Jdt 4:9–11).

3. Minority Socioreligious Movements

3.1. Factions, Reform Movements, and Sects

A notable feature of early Judaism was the proliferation of minority groups within society. Albert Baumgarten (1997) has surveyed the field, attributing the fragmentation to the collision between Judaism and Hellenism and the need for Jews to tighten boundaries against outsiders. The most useful social-scientific approach to this phenomenon has been the sociology of sectarianism. At its most extreme form, a sect represents a socioreligious movement that has either broken away from its mother group, so that membership in both is no longer possible, or has become seriously alienated from the wider society. Bryan Wilson's typology of "sectarian responses to the world" allows close comparative analysis of the latter type of phenomena (Esler 1987, 46–51). Lesser degrees of separation have been referred to as reform movements (51–53) or factions (Elliot 1995).

3.2. Social Dimensions of Apocalyptic Texts

Since Matthias Henze is covering apocalyptic literature elsewhere in this volume, the focus is on the social dimensions of apocalyptic phenomena, using social-scientific ideas to frame the discussion. A notable development since the first edition has been an effort to distinguish apocalypse as a genre (Collins 1979) from various socioreligious phenomena (which used to be routinely situated under the banner of apocalypticism) that are referred to as eschatological from a theological perspective and, very often, millenarian from a social-scientific one. Anthropological and sociological research into millenarian movements in the last two centuries in Africa, the Pacific, and the United States has been used extensively to understand comparable phenomena in biblical texts (as overviewed by Esler 2014, 129–31). Jewish apocalyptic literature has also been treated as resistance literature in the face of ancient empires (Portier-Young 2011), although the approach has been questioned (Esler 2014, 132–39; 2017c, 33–34). Postcolonial perspectives have also been applied to the apocalyptic corpus (Smith-Christopher 2014). In relation to the most important apocalyptic text of all, 1 Enoch, a sociology-based proposal has recently been published arguing that the model for heaven in 1 En. 1–36 is that of an ancient king in his court with his courtiers, not the Jerusalem temple (Esler 2017b).

3.3. Pharisees

On a number of occasions Josephus referred to three *haireseis* ("choices") of philosophy among the Jews: Pharisees, Saducees, and Essenes (*B.J.* 2.119, 162, 164; *A.J.* 13.171; 18.11; *Vita* 10), always in this order, which suggests he regarded the Pharisees as being the most significant. Sometimes he added a fourth, "the fourth philosophy." It is unhelpful to translate *haireseis* as "sects" as that would, if we defer to the main streams in the sociology of sectarianism (probably a preferable course than applying folk psychology), mean that membership of both the *hairesis* in question and the wider Jewish people was impossible or that they were seriously alienated from other Jews, and neither seems to have been the case, at least as far as the Pharisees or the Sadducees were concerned. This is in spite of the possible etymology of *Pharisaioi* from Hebrew *parash* ("separate"). Perhaps these social entities more basically resembled reform movements with a socioreligious nature.

In Gary Porton's (1986) treatment of the Pharisees in the first edition, the most significant of the recent scholarship that he mentioned was that of Jacob Neusner. Central to Neusner's (1973) understanding of the Pharisees was that purity was a central feature of their interests, in relation to the table-fellowship of everyday life especially, and that this set them apart from other people. Porton (1986, 395–412) did not, however, mention (undoubtedly unavailable to him) Sanders's recent discussion of the Pharisees with which James Dunn was to focus his survey of the subject. Sanders (1985) had been especially concerned to dispel notions that the Pharisees had been hostile to Jesus or that they regarded the ordinary people (*am haaretz*) as sinners over whom they had the power to exclude from the social and religious life of Judaism or that they "ran Judaism." He also considered Neusner had exaggerated the role of purity in their identity. Yet Dunn (1990) points out that their very name, "separated ones," is connected with purity, as suggested by the prevalence of mikvaot (mentioned above). Furthermore, according to Dunn (2003, 267–68), Sanders tends to underestimate their influence with the people. Another noteworthy aspect of the Pharisees, as Josephus frequently points out, was their concern with *akribeia* ("exactness," "strictness"), including in relation to their interpretation of the law (Dunn 2003, 269–70).

Drawing upon the broad analysis of agrarian society by Lenksi and Lenski (now in Lenski and Nolan 2014), Anthony Saldarini (1988) argued that the Pharisees belonged to the retainer segment of Jewish society, where retainers served various needs of the elite and were dependent upon them.

Although this is an important idea and remains influential, it has been criticized as being inconsistent with Josephus's portrayal of the Pharisees as popular with the people and as pushing interests such as purity and a strict interpretation of the law (Dunn 2003, 269). In 2006, Hillel Newman analyzed the Pharisees and the other three sectarian movements mentioned by Josephus in relation to their proximity to power. As noted above, the notion that the Pharisees were a sect is open to the objection that this sits awkwardly with aspects of the sociology of sectarianism. Roland Deines (1997, 2010) has argued that the Pharisees sought, successfully, to influence the religious practice of the ordinary people. They did not actively seek to influence officers of the state, but, if asked for a view, were willing to provide it. He argues that they were not a group isolated from wider Israel but instead voluntarily sought to support Israel in performing its obligations in the world.

3.4. Sadducees (and Boethusians)

The Sadducees were the second *hairesis* of Jewish philosophy mentioned by Josephus (see above). They were thought to be connected with the priesthood, did not believe in the resurrection of the dead, and had no truck with an oral law. Their name possibly derives from the priest Zadok, probably the first high priest in Solomon's temple (1 Kgs 2:35). The Boethusians (mentioned in talmudic sources but not in the ancient Greek sources, including Josephus), possibly derived from Boethus, the high priest around 25 BCE, were probably a separate group but tended to become synonymous with them. Porton (1986, 68) ended his treatment of the Sadducees by noting how little we know about them and suggesting that what was needed was "sober and careful study of the picture of the Sadducees in each of the corpora that contain evidence about them." Unfortunately, such a major monograph has yet to appear. Since 1986, however, there have been a number of coverages of ancient Jewish socioreligious movements (usually based on Josephus), including the Sadducees (see Saldarini 1988; Stemberger 2006; Newman 2006). Eyal Regev (2005) has undertaken a fresh exploration of the halakah of the Sadducees and has applied this to understanding the halakic disputes the Sadducees had with the Pharisees (2006).

3.5. The Essenes and Qumran

The Essenes/ Essaeans are known from Philo, Pliny the Elder, and Josephus (Vermès and Goodman 1989), with Josephus mentioning the Essenes twelve times. The discussion of whether the Essenes are to be identified with the people at Qumran rumbles on (Collins 2010, 127). One significant contribution has been Steve Mason's (2000) argument for analyzing the passages in Josephus in accord with the wider patterns of Josephan historiography, for which reasons and others he is skeptical of the alleged connection. John Collins (2010, 122–65) has, however, provided a careful defense of the Essene hypothesis that meets most of Mason's objections.

This is one area that has fed into the lively discussion of the scrolls using the sociology of sectarianism as a new way to comprehend their social and religious meanings. A lively discussion has arisen as to whether it makes sense to view the people by whom and for whom the texts were written as sectarian in a sociological sense. Early intimations of the possibilities (e.g., Esler 1994) have led to major treatments by Eyal Regev (2007) and Jutta Jokiranta (2010, 2013). Jokiranta (2013) has also inaugurated the study of the scrolls from the perspective of social identity theory. That said, it is clear that the scrolls would repay further research using social-scientific ideas and perspectives. Meanwhile, religious themes in the scrolls have continued to attract intense interest (Lim and Collins 2010, 377–513), as have textual and linguistic issues (281–374).

3.6. The Therapeutae

Another group who arguably comprised a reform movement in early Judaism were the Therapeutae, who are known mainly from Philo's *De vita contemplativa*. Major developments in the study of the Therapeutae have come in the publication of a monograph by Joan Taylor in 2003. Noting that Philo locates the Therapeutae on Lake Maerotis just outside Alexandria (*Contempl.* 21-22)—and Taylor persuasively claims to have found the actual location—she argues strongly for their actual existence, against claims that they were imaginary. She observes that authors normally situate utopias far away, not nearby, where they can be examined. This view contrasts favorably with that of Troels Engberg-Pedersen (1999) who argues that they represent a "philosopher's dream." Taylor also proposes that they are to be understood within the context of the bitter conflict between Jews and Greeks in Alexandria. She argues for their sharp distinction from the Essenes by reason of the fact that women played a central role in the movement, indeed they were highly educated philosophers.

Another concern of Taylor's argument is the extent to which Philo sees the Therapeutae as exemplars of the *bios theoretikos* ("the meditative" or "contemplative life"). A similar case has since been mounted by Celia Deutsch (2006), who has argued that for Philo the text is a site of mystical experience with the Therapeutae being a prime example, in that their life involves communal solitude and contemplation.

4. The Samaritans

While only a brief discussion of the Samaritans is possible here, the recent monograph by Reinhard Pummer (2016) covers most recent research in considerable detail. Of utmost importance in understanding the history of the Samaritans has been the extensive excavations carried out on Mount Gerizim (Magen 2008). It is now clear that the first phase of a Samaritan sacred precinct on Mount Gerizim dates to the Persian period (in the fifth century BCE) and not to the time of Alexander the Great, as Josephus asserted (Pummer 2016, 80). In the Hellenistic period, beginning in the late fourth century BCE, a city developed on the mountain around the temple precinct. This city continued to exist even after Alexander the Great's destruction of Samaria (Pummer 2016, 84). Josephus was also wrong in dating the destruction of the temple to 130 BCE (*B.J.* 1.62) or 129 BCE (*A.J.* 13.254), since the archaeology reveals it was destroyed in about 110 BCE (Pummer 2016, 86), by John Hyrcanus I. Pummer considers that it was probably the destruction of the temple on Gerizim by this Judean king that led to the division between Samaritans and Judeans, not the fact of the construction of the temple (89).

As to the origin of the Samaritans, the debate centers largely on whether they represent their own strand of Israelite tradition in the north, an ancient form of Yahwism, or whether they were a break-away group from the Judeans in the south, a process often construed as "a Samaritan sect breaking away from Judaism," the latter being rather close to the view of James Purvis (1986, 91–92) in the first edition. The course of scholarship since 1986, however, tends to favor the former alternative, even if expressions of the latter view are still to be found. Étienne Nodet (2010) represents a strong argument for the Samaritans being the heirs of ancient Israelites and not Jewish dissidents. Recent archaeology has shown the north to be much stronger economically and socially and more populous than has hitherto been realized (Finkelstein 2013). Two recent works on the origins of the Samaritans argue for their being a separate branch of Yahwism, who became separated from the Judeans in the south by the construction of the temple on Gerizim (Kartveit 2009) or by its destruction (Knoppers 2013). In spite of the split, however, some interchange between Samaritans and Judeans continued.

Other subjects concerning the Samaritans can be followed up in the relevant sections of Pummer's (2016) monograph: Samaritan literature (219–56); Samaritan rituals and customs (257–88); and the Samaritans today (216, 289–301).

5. A New Approach:
The Recognition of Jewish/Judean Identity

This final section brings us back to the tensions concerning the meanings of *Judaism*, *Jew*, and *Jewish* that were apparent in the first edition as discussed at the start of this chapter. The major uplift in the discussion of group identities in the last three decades provides an entry-point for considering recent developments and possible future trajectories. The two points of most relevance are the expanding agreement that the identity of the *Ioudaioi* is best described as ethnic and the problematization of religion as an appropriate category for the ancient Mediterranean world.

As to ethnic identity, modern research into the subject was inaugurated by an essay by Fredrik Barth (1969b) who argued for a self-ascriptional and processual approach. A group's sense of itself as a group came first, and it then chose cultural indicia to mark out its boundary from other groups. This was an ongoing process, where the changing patterns of interaction led to different indicia coming into prominence at different times. While Barth (1969b, 13) considered that ethnic identity was presumptively determined by a person's origin and background, a more useful list of indicators of ethnic identity (to be regarded as diagnostic of and not essential for such identity) has been developed by John Hutchinson and Anthony Smith (1996, 6–7): (1) a common name for the group; (2) a myth of shared ancestry; (3) a shared history; (4) a common culture, embracing customs, language, and religious practices and beliefs; (5) a link with a homeland, either by actual occupation or by diaspora longing; and (6) a sense of communal solidarity.

In his *Contra Apionem*, Josephus defends the *Ioudaioi* against attack from the hellenized Egyptian Apion by situating them within the wider setting of Mediterranean peoples (*ethnē*, *genē*, *laoi*), or ethnic groups within the modern understanding, and arguing not that they are some different sort of group, but just an excellent example of such a people (Esler 2003, 59, 63; 2009). Josephus describes both *Ioudaioi* and other peoples as sharing features that are the same as or similar to the indicators of ethnic identity delineated by Hutchinson and Smith. Having reached the view that the *Ioudaioi* were an ethnic group, it is not a big step to translating that word as Judeans, given that every other ethnic group in their world was also named after their homeland (Esler 2003, 63–74; 2009) and that to translate the word as Jews is too exceptionalist as to be historically acceptable.

Proceeding independently, Mason (2007, 2016) reached very similar views, although he is not opposed to retaining Jew and Jewish to translate *Ioudaios*. A recent joint publication by Mason and Philip Esler (2017) has reiterated this position. Many other scholars have now taken to describing the identity of the *Ioudaioi* as ethnic, although many of them continue with the words Jew and Jewish. In 2015, Amy-Jill Levine noted that among the ethnic aspects of Jewish self-definition (in the past and the present) is possession of common ancestors and a connection to a homeland. Paula Fredriksen (2018), moreover, has recently argued that Jews and non-Jewish peoples adopted very similar indicators to express their ethnic identity, while the Jews were unique in claiming cross-ethnic supremacy for their God. It is preferable to follow Fredriksen in viewing Jews as sharing much the same ethnic discourse as non-Jewish peoples—and Josephus to similar effect in the *Contra Apionem* (see above)—than John Barclay's (2006) approach of describing Judean identity in terms of features distinctive to that people.

The second issue, that of religion, draws on the growing recognition that religion as we understand it, especially to the extent we regard it as a stand-alone entity, is a modern phenomenon that did not exist in the ancient Mediterranean world. This view was put forward by William Cantwell Smith as long ago as 1962 (and applied in Esler 2003; Mason 2007), but the case has been made with increasing insistence and a wider evidence base by Brent Nongbri (2015) and Carlin Barton and Daniel Boyarin (2016). If religion cannot be said to exist in antiquity, the continued use of the expression Judaism, given that it almost always means Jewish religion but is inapt in reference to the Judean ethnic group, becomes highly problematic, perhaps even a category error for that period. Yet this does not entail denying that religious beliefs and practices (here essentially meaning beliefs and practices involving what were perceived to be human-divine interactions) were not of great importance to Judean ethnic identity. They were. The importance of religious phenomena for this people was rightly stressed by Cohen in the first edition of this book, as mentioned above.

Changing the frame of reference in this way has huge implications for virtually all the phenomena concerning the Judeans. From a perspective valorizing Judaism, the underlying model for the heavenly architecture and angels in this text is the Jerusalem temple and its priests. But changing focus to ethnic identity leads one in the direction of another model, namely, the court and courtiers of ancient Near Eastern and Hellenistic kings (Esler 2017b).

But to bring this discussion to an end, it will assist to illustrate the shift of thinking this involves from two features of the preceding discussion. First, this new approach renders problematic Andrea Berlin's (2005) proposal that the almost standardized use of similar kitchen pottery, standard containers, stone vessels, and knife pared lamps—with some of these (e.g., stone vessels) being common throughout Judea and Galilee but almost nonexistent in Samaria—indicates a "household Judaism" which "allowed people to incorporate a religious sensibility into their daily lives" (466). The widespread use of such domestic items might rather denote a sense of ethnic pride not necessarily associated with specifically religious views.

Second, another consequence of this change of focus is evident in relation to the Samaritans. Even in his admirably thorough 2016 treatment of the Samaritans, Pummer frames his discussion about their origins around two options: either they were "a sect which separated from its mother religion" (identified as Judaism) or a branch of Yahwistic Israel in the same sense as, but distinct from, the Jews (15–25). Yet, it is reasonably clear that Judeans did not regard the Samaritans as members of a religion. This is not just because our notion of religion did not exist in the ancient world, but because the way they describe Samaritans indicates an identity that is ethnic in character. In Luke 17:18, Jesus refers to a Samaritan as an *allogenēs* (17:16). While this means, broadly, "foreigner," its specific reference is to someone who comes from a different people (*genos*), where *genos* conveys a group defining itself by shared descent (cf. *gennaō*), as many ethnic groups of the time did. *Allogenēs* was also the word used of all those not permitted to pass the wall into the inner part of the temple in Jerusalem; it meant all ethnic groups (including the Samaritans) apart from the Judeans. Josephus refers to the Samaritans as *alloethnēs* (*A.J.* 9.291), a word very close in meaning to *allogenēs*, as is confirmed by his use of *alloethnēs* in relation to the temple ban on non-Judeans mentioned above (*A.J.* 15.417).

It will be interesting to see if, in the years ahead, the change of emphasis advocated here from a focus of examination on Judaism, the religion of the Jews, to that of a Judean ethnic group with a strong religious dimension moves from its current minority position in the field to become that of the majority of scholars.

Bibliography

Ackerman, Susan. 2008. "Household Religion, Family Religion, and Women's Religion in Ancient Israel." Pages 127–158 in *Household and Family Religion in Antiquity*. Edited by John Bodel and Saul M. Olyan. Oxford: Wiley-Blackwell.
Albertz, Rainer, and Rüdiger Schmidt. 2012. *Family and Household Religion in Ancient Israel and the Levant*. Winona Lake, IN: Eisenbrauns.
Archer, Leonie J. 1990. *Her Price Is Beyond Rubies: The Jewish Woman in Graeco-Roman Palestine*. JSOTSup 60. Sheffield: Sheffield Academic.
Aviam, Mordechai. 2004. *Jews, Pagans and Christians in the Galilee: Twenty-Five Years of Archaeological Excavations and Surveys; Hellenistic to Byzantine Periods*. Rochester, NY: University of Rochester Press.
Avigad, Nahman. 1983. *Discovering Jerusalem*. Nashville: Nelson.
Barclay, John M. G. 2006. *Against Apion*. Vol. 10 of *Flavius Josephus: Translation and Commentary*. Leiden: Brill.
Barth, Fredrik, ed. 1969a. *Ethnic Groups and Boundaries: The Social Organization of Culture Difference*. London: Allen & Unwin.
———. 1969b. "Introduction." Pages 9–38 in *Ethnic Groups and Boundaries: The Social Organization of Culture Difference*. Edited by Fredrik Barth. London: Allen & Unwin.
Barton, Carlin A., and Daniel Boyarin. 2016. *Imagine No Religion: How Modern Abstractions Hide Ancient Realities*. New York: Fordham University Press.
Baumgarten, Albert I. 1997 *The Flourishing of Jewish Sects in the Maccabean Era: An Interpretation*. JSJSup 55. Leiden: Brill.
Berlin, Andrea M. 2005. "Jewish Life Before the Revolt: The Archaeological Evidence." *JSJ* 36:417–70.
Binder, Donald. 1999. *Into the Temple Courts: The Place of the Synagogues in the Second Temple Period*. SBLDS 169. Atlanta: Society of Biblical Literature.
Boer, Roland, and Christina Petterson. 2017. *Time of Troubles: A New Economic Framework for Early Christianity*. Minneapolis: Fortress.
Brooten, Bernadette J. 1982. *Women Leaders in the Ancient Synagogue: Inscriptional Evidence and Background Issues*. BJS 36. Chico, CA: Scholars Press.

———. 2000. "Female Leadership in the Ancient Synagogue." Pages 215–23 in *From Dura to Sepphoris: Studies in Jewish Art and Society in Late Antiquity*. Edited by Lee I. Levine and Zeev Weiss. JRASup 40. Portsmouth, RI: Journal of Roman Archaeology.

Chancey, Mark A. 2005. *Greco-Roman Culture and the Galilee of Jesus*. SNTSMS 134. Cambridge: Cambridge University Press.

Chaney, Marvin L. 2017. *Peasants, Prophets, and Political Economy: The Hebrew Bible and Social Analysis*. Eugene, OR: Cascade.

Cohen, Shaye J. D. 1986. "The Political and Social History of the Jews in Graeco-Roman Antiquity: The State of the Question." Pages 33–56 in *Early Judaism and Its Modern Interpreters*. Edited by Robert A. Kraft and George W. E. Nickelsburg. BMI 2. Philadelphia: Fortress; Atlanta: Scholars Press.

Collins, John J. 1979. "Introduction: The Morphology of a Genre." *Semeia* 14:1–20.

———. 2010. *Beyond the Qumran Community: The Sectarian Movement of the Dead Sea Scrolls*. Grand Rapids: Eerdmans.

Crossan, John Dominic. 1991. *The Historical Jesus: The Life of a Mediterranean Jewish Peasant*. San Francisco: HarperSanFrancisco.

Deines, Roland. 1997. *Die Pharisäer: Ihr Verständnis im Spiegel der christlichen und jüdischen Forschung seit Welhausen und Graetz*. WUNT 101. Tübingen: Mohr Siebeck.

———. 2010. "The Social Profile of the Pharisees." Pages 111–32 in *The New Testament and Rabbinic Literature*. Edited by Reimund Bieringer, Florentino García Martínez, Didier Pollefeyt, and Peter Tomson. JSJSup 136. Leiden: Brill.

Deutsch, Celia. 2006. "The Therapeutae, Text Work, Ritual, and Mystical Experience." Pages 287–311 in *Paradise Now: Essays on Early Jewish and Christian Mysticism*. Edited by April DeConick. SymS 11. Atlanta: Society of Biblical Literature.

Dunn, James D. G. 1990. "Pharisees, Sinners, and Jesus." Pages 61–88 in *Jesus, Paul, and the Law: Studies in Mark and Galatians*. Louisville: Westminster John Knox.

———. 2003. *Jesus Remembered*. Christianity in the Making 1. Grand Rapids: Eerdmans.

Edwards, Douglas R. 2007. "Identity and Social Location in Roman Galilean Villages." Pages 357–74 in *Religion, Ethnicity, and Identity in Ancient Galilee: A Region in Transition*. Edited by Jürgen Zangenberg,

Harold W. Attridge, and Dale B. Martin. WUNT 210. Tübingen: Mohr Siebeck.

Elliott, John H. 1995. "The Jewish Messianic Movement: From Faction to Sect." Pages 75–95 in *Modelling Early Christianity: Social-Scientific Studies of the New Testament in Its Context*. Edited by Philip F. Esler. London: Routledge.

Engberg-Pedersen, Troels. 1999. "Philo's *De Vita Contemplativa* as a Philosopher's Dream." *JSJ* 30:40–64.

Engels, Donald. 1990. *Roman Corinth: An Alternative Model for the Classical City*. Chicago: University of Chicago Press.

Esler, Philip F. 1987. *Community and Gospel in Luke-Acts: The Social and Political Motivations of Lucan Theology*. SNTSMS 57. Cambridge: Cambridge University Press.

———. 1994. "Introverted Sectarianism at Qumran and in the Johannine Community." Pages 70–91 in *The First Christians in Their Social Worlds: Social-Scientific Approaches to New Testament Interpretation*. Edited by Philip F. Esler. London: Routledge.

———. 2003. *Conflict and Identity in Rom*ans*: The Social Setting of Paul's Letter*. Minneapolis: Fortress.

———. 2009. "Judean Ethnic Identity in Josephus' *Against Apion*." Pages 73–91 in *A Wandering Galilean: Essays in Honour of Seán Freyne*. Edited by Zuleika Rodgers, Margaret Daly-Denton, and Anne Fitzpatrick-McKinley. JSJSup 132. Leiden: Brill.

———. 2014. "Social-Scientific Approaches to Apocalyptic Literature." Pages 123–44 in *The Oxford Handbook of Apocalyptic Literature*. Edited by John J. Collins. New York: Oxford University Press.

———. 2017a. *Babatha's Orchard: The Yadin Papyri and an Ancient Jewish Family Tale Retold*. Oxford: Oxford University Press.

———. 2017b. *God's Court and Courtiers in the Book of the Watchers: Reinterpreting Heaven in 1 Enoch 1–36*. Eugene, OR: Cascade.

Fiensy, David A., and James Riley Strange, eds. 2015. *The Archaeological Record from Cities, Towns and Villages*. Vol. 2 of *Galilee in the Late Second Temple and Mishnaic Periods*. Minneapolis: Fortress.

Fiensy, David A., and Ralph K. Hawkins, eds. 2013. *The Galilean Economy in the Time of Jesus*. ECL 11. Atlanta: Society of Biblical Literature.

Finkelstein, Israel. 2013. *The Forgotten Kingdom: The Archaeology and History of Northern Israel*. ANEM 5. Atlanta: Society of Biblical Literature.

Finley, Moses. 1973. *The Ancient Economy*. Berkeley: University of California Press.

Fredriksen, Paula. 2018. "How Jewish Is God? Divine Ethnicity in Paul's Theology." *JBL* 137:193–212.
Freyne, Sean. 1995. "Herodian Economics in Galilee: Searching for a Suitable Model." Pages 23–46 in *Modelling Early Christianity: Social-Scientific Studies of the New Testament in Its Context*. Edited by Philip F. Esler. London: Routledge.
———. 2004. *Jesus, A Jewish Galilean: A New Reading of the Jesus-Story*. London: T&T Clark.
Hanson, K. C., and Douglas E. Oakman. 2008. *Palestine in the Time of Jesus: Social Structures and Social Conflicts*. 2nd ed. Minneapolis: Fortress.
Horsley, Richard A. 1996. *Archaeology, History, and Society in Galilee: The Social Context of Jesus and the Rabbis*. Valley Forge, PA: Trinity Press International.
———. 2014. *Jesus and the Politics of Roman Palestine*. Columbia: University of South Carolina Press.
Hutchinson, John, and Anthony D. Smith. 1996. "Introduction." Pages 3–14 in *Ethnicity*. Edited by John Hutchinson and Anthony D. Smith. Oxford: Oxford University Press.
Jensen, Morten Hørning. 2006. *Herod Antipas in Galilee: The Literary and Archaeological Sources on the Reign of Herod Antipas and Its Socio-economic Impact on Galilee*. WUNT 2/215. Tübingen: Mohr Siebeck.
Jokiranta, Jutta. 2010. "Sociological Approaches to Qumran Sectarianism." Pages 200–31 in *The Oxford Handbook of the Dead Sea Scrolls*. Edited by Timothy H. Lim and John J. Collins. Oxford: Oxford University Press.
———. 2013. *Social Identity and Sectarianism in the Qumran Movement*. STDJ 105. Leiden: Brill.
Kartveit, Magnar. 2009. *The Origin of the Samaritans*. VTSup 128. Leiden: Brill.
Kautsky, John H. 1962. *The Politics of Aristocratic Empires*. New Brunswick, NJ: Transaction.
Kee, Howard Clark. 1990. "The Transformation of the Synagogue after 70 C.E." *NTS* 36:1–24.
Klawans, Jonathan. 2006. *Purity, Sacrifice, and the Temple: Symbolism and Supersessionism in the Study of Ancient Judaism*. New York: Oxford University Press.
Kloppenborg, John S. 2000. "Dating Theodotus (CIJ II 1404)." *JJS* 51:243–80.

Knoppers, Gary N. 2013. *Jews and Samaritans: The Origins and History of Their Early Relations*. New York: Oxford University Press.

Kraft, Robert A., and George W. E. Nickelsburg, eds. 1986a. *Early Judaism and Its Modern Interpreters*. BMI 2. Philadelphia: Fortress; Atlanta: Scholars Press.

———. 1986b. "Preface." Pages xi–xiii in *Early Judaism and Its Modern Interpreters*. Edited by Robert A. Kraft and George W. E. Nickelsburg. BMI 2. Philadelphia: Fortress; Atlanta: Scholars Press.

Lenski, Gerhard, and Patrick Nolan. 2014. *Human Societies: An Introduction to Macrosociology*. 12th ed. Oxford: Oxford University Press.

Levine, Amy-Jill. 2015. "*The Gospel and the Land* Revisited: Exegesis, Hermeneutics, and Poltics." Paper presented at the General Meeting of the Society for New Testament Studies. Amsterdam, Netherlands, July 30.

Levine, Lee I. 2000. *The Ancient Synagogue: The First Thousand Years*. New Haven: Yale University Press.

———. 2001. "The First-Century Synagogue: New Perspectives." *STK* 77:22–30.

Lewis, Naphthali. 1989. *The Documents from the Bar Kokhba Period in the Cave of Letters: Greek Papyri*. JDS 2. Jerusalem: Israel Exploration Society.

Lim, Timothy H., and John J. Collins, eds. 2010. *The Oxford Handbook of the Dead Sea Scrolls*. Oxford: Oxford University Press.

Magen, Yitzhak. 2008. *A Temple City*. Vol. 2 of *Mount Gerizim Excavations*. Judea and Samaria Publications 8. Jerusalem: Israel Antiquities Authority.

Magness, Jodi. 2012. *The Archaeology of the Holy Land: From the Destruction of Solomon's Temple to the Muslim Conquest*. Cambridge: Cambridge University Press.

Malina, Bruce J. 1994. "Religion in the Imagined New Testament World: More Social Science Lenses." *Scr* 51:1–26.

———. 1996. "Mediterranean Sacrifice: Dimensions of Domestic and Political Religion." *BTB* 26:26–44.

———. 2001. *The New Testament World: Insights from Cultural Anthropology*. 3rd ed. Louisville: Westminster John Knox.

Mason, Steve. 2000. "What Josephus Says about the Essenes in His *Judean War*." Pages 423–55 in *Text and Artifact in the Religions of Mediterranean Antiquity: Essays in Honour of Peter Richardson*. Edited by Stephen G. Wilson and Michel Desjardins. SCJud 9. Waterloo: Wilfrid Laurier University Press.

———. 2007. "Jews, Judaeans, Judaizing, Judaism: Problems of Categorization in Ancient History." *JSJ* 38:457–512.

———. 2016. *Orientation to the History of Roman Judaea*. Eugene, OR: Cascade.

Mason, Steve, and Philip F. Esler. 2017. "Judaean and Christ-Follower Identities: Grounds for a Distinction." *NTS* 63:493–515.

Mattila, Sharon L. 2013. "Revisiting Jesus' Capernaum: A Village of Only Subsistence-Level Fishers and Farmers?" Pages 75–138 in *The Galilean Economy in the Time of Jesus*. Edited by David A. Fiensy and Ralph K. Hawkins. ECL 11. Atlanta: Society of Biblical Literature.

McKay. Heather. 1994. *Sabbath and Synagogue: The Question of Sabbath Worship in Ancient Judaism*. RGRW 122. Leiden: Brill.

Mendels, Doron. 1997. *The Rise and Fall of Jewish Nationalism*. Grand Rapids: Eerdmans.

Meyers, Eric M., and James L. Strange. 1981. *Archaeology, the Rabbis and Early Christianity*. London: SCM.

Neusner, Jacob. 1973. *From Politics to Piety: The Emergence of Pharisaic Judaism*. Englewood Cliffs, NJ: Prentice Hall.

Newman, Hillel. 2006. *Proximity to Power and Jewish Sectarian Groups of the Ancient Period: A Review of Lifestyle, Values and Halakha in the Pharisees, Sadducees, Essenes and Qumran*. BRLJ 25. Leiden: Brill.

Nickelsburg, George W. E., and Robert A. Kraft. 1986. "Introduction: The Modern Study of Judaism." Pages 1–30 in *Early Judaism and Its Modern Interpreters*. Edited by Robert A. Kraft and George W. E. Nickelsburg. BMI 2. Philadelphia: Fortress; Atlanta: Scholars Press.

Nodet, Étienne. 2010. *Samaritains, Juifs, Temples*. CahRB 74. Paris: Gabalda.

Nongbri, Brent. 2015. *Before Religion: A History of a Modern Concept*. New Haven: Yale University Press.

Oakman, Douglas E. 2012. *The Political Aims of Jesus*. Minneapolis: Fortress.

———. 2014a. "Debate: Was the Galilean Economy Oppressive or Prosperous? A Late Second Temple Galilee; Socio-archaeology and Dimensions of Exploitation in First-Century Palestine." Pages 346–56 in *Life, Culture, and Society*, vol. 1 of *Galilee in the Late Second Temple and Mishnaic Periods*. Edited by David A. Fiensy and James Riley Strange. Minneapolis: Fortress.

———. 2014b. *Jesus, Debt, and the Lord's Prayer: First Century Debt and Jesus' Intentions.* Eugene, OR: Cascade.

———. 2017."The Galilean World of Jesus." Pages 97–120 in *The Early Christian World.* Edited by Philip F. Esler. 2nd ed. London: Routledge.

Portier-Young, Anathea. 2011. *Apocalypse against Empire: Theologies of Resistance in Early Judaism.* Grand Rapids: Eerdmans.

Porton, Gary G. 1986. "Diversity in Postbiblical Judaism." Pages 57–80 in *Early Judaism and Its Modern Interpreters.* Edited by Robert A. Kraft and George W. E. Nickelsburg. BMI 2. Philadelphia: Fortress; Atlanta: Scholars Press.

Pummer, Reinhard. 2016. *The Samaritans: A Profile.* Grand Rapids: Eerdmans.

Purvis, James D. 1986. "The Samaritans and Judaism." Pages 81–98 in *Early Judaism and Its Modern Interpreters.* Edited by Robert A. Kraft and George W. E. Nickelsburg. BMI 2. Philadelphia: Fortress; Atlanta: Scholars Press.

Reed, Jonathan L. 2000. *Archaeology and the Galilean Jesus: A Re-examination of the Evidence.* Harrisburg, PA: Trinity Press International.

———. 2014 "Mortality, Morbidity, and Economics in Jesus' Galilee." Pages 242–52 in *Life, Culture, and Society.* Vol. 1 of *Galilee in the Late Second Temple and Mishnaic Periods.* Edited by David A. Fiensy and James Riley Strange. Minneapolis: Fortress.

Regev, Eyal. 2005. *The Sadducees and Their Halakhah: Religion and Society in the Second Temple Period* [Hebrew]. Jerusalem: Yad ben Zvi.

———. 2006. "The Sadducees, the Pharisees, and the Sacred: Meaning and Ideology in the Halakhic Controversies Between the Sadducees and the Pharisees." *RRJ* 9:126–40.

———. 2007. *Sectarianism in Qumran: A Cross-Cultural Perspective.* RelSoc 45. Berlin: de Gruyter.

Runesson, Anders, Donald D. Binder, and Birger Olsson. 2008. *The Ancient Synagogue from Its Origins to 200 C.E.: A Source Book.* Leiden: Brill.

Saldarini, Anthony J. 1988. *Pharisees, Scribes, and Sadducees in Palestinian Society: A Sociological Approach.* Wilmington, DE: Glazier.

Sanders, E. P. 1985. *Jesus and Judaism.* Philadelphia: Fortress.

———. 1990. *Jewish Law from Jesus to the Mishnah: Five Studies.* London: SCM; Philadelphia: Trinity Press International.

Schmidt, Francis. 2001. *How the Temple Thinks: Identity and Social Cohesion in Ancient Judaism.* BibSem 78. Sheffield: Sheffield Academic.

Smith, William Cantwell. 1962. *The Meaning and End of Religion*. New York: Macmillan.

Smith-Christopher, Daniel L. 2014. "A Postcolonial Reading of Apocalyptic Literature." Pages 180–98 in *The Oxford Handbook of Apocalyptic Literature*. Edited by John J. Collins. Oxford: Oxford University Press.

Stemberger, Günter. 1995. *Jewish Contemporaries of Jesus: Pharisees, Sadducees, Essenes*. Translated by Alan W. Mahnke. Minneapolis: Fortress.

Taylor, Joan E. 2003. *Jewish Women Philosophers of First-Century Alexandria: Philo's "Therapeutae" Reconsidered*. Oxford: Oxford University Press.

Udoh, Fabian E. 2014. "Taxation and Other Sources of Government Income in the Galilee of Herod and Antipas." Pages 366–87 in *Life, Culture, and Society*. Vol. 1 of *Galilee in the Late Second Temple and Mishnaic Periods*. Edited by David A. Fiensy and James Riley Strange. Minneapolis: Fortress.

Vermès, Géza, and Martin D. Goodman, eds. 1989. *The Essenes: According to the Classical Sources*. Oxford Centre Textbooks 1. Sheffield: JSOT Press.

White, L. Michael. 2017. "Early Christian Architecture: The First Five Centuries." Pages 673–716 in *The Early Christian World*. Edited by Philip F. Esler. 2nd ed. London: Routledge.

Yadin, Yigael. 2002. *The Documents from the Bar Kokhba Period in the Cave of Letters: Hebrew, Aramaic and Nabatean-Aramaic Papyri*. JDS 3. Jerusalem: Israel Exploration Society.

3
JUDAISM IN THE DIASPORA

ERICH S. GRUEN

Diaspora has a long history for the Jews of antiquity. Contrary to popular impression that the principal motive for the scattering was the destruction of the temple in 70 CE, Jews had, in fact, dwelled outside of Palestine for centuries before—and in substantial numbers.

1. The Dispersion

Although we lack any reliable figures, there is no doubt that Jews in the diaspora far outnumbered those in Palestine. They lived in the cities, villages, and countryside of all the lands that bordered the Mediterranean and to some extent beyond. Migration or uprooting began at least as early as the Babylonian captivity in the sixth century BCE, and it is likely that most of those who found themselves in that foreign land remained to carve out their own communities on an enduring basis rather than partake in the supposed return. A Jewish military colony at Elephantine in Egypt thrived as a flourishing community in the sixth and fifth centuries BCE under the aegis of the Persian Empire. The spread of Jews beyond Palestine exploded, however, after the conquest of that empire by Alexander the Great in the late fourth century, when dislocation and migration speeded up dramatically. As Greeks and Macedonians created a host of new cities and refounded and refurbished others in Asia Minor and the Levant, Jews too moved to these communities, settling and installing themselves as permanent dwellers. Most of Jewish history from the coming of Alexander to the coming of Hadrian took place in the diaspora, in the cities and lands dominated by Greek language and culture and under the suzerainty of the Roman Empire. Already in the second century BCE, the author of 1 Maccabees maintained that Jews could be found in Mesopotamia, Syria, Egypt, and the Iranian plateau; indeed they had spread to mainland Greece and the islands of the Aegean, Cyprus, Crete, and Cyrene.

This means that diaspora life was no mere aberration, no brief breakaway from Palestine, but the only existence that most Jews knew through much of the Second Temple period and beyond. The temple in Jerusalem still existed and diaspora Jews continued to revere it, but few ever saw it. Their lives were elsewhere.

2. The Debate

The Jewish diaspora has received considerable attention in the last thirty years. The topic spurred a plethora of publications, only a few of which can be registered here. Characterization of Jewish life in the diaspora has generated divergent opinions. Did Jews regard it as a form of exile? Did they adjust readily or with difficulty to the circumstances of leading their lives away from the homeland? Older literature leaned to the negative, conjuring up a picture of yearning for the temple and lamenting an enforced absence from the center, the lachrymose version of Jewish history. This was countered already by Thomas Kraabel in a series of studies in the 1980s, republished by J. Andrew Overman and Robert MacLennan (1992). Kraabel argued on the basis of both literary and archaeological evidence that Jews found themselves entirely at home in Hellenistic communities. Leonard Rutgers (1998), in his collected essays, expresses sympathy for that view, but regards it as going too far and views the Jewish experience as subject to a series of ups and downs rather than a smooth accommodation. The gloomier aspect, however, still retains force in the scholarship. It received powerful expression in a previous generation by a number of studies by Willem Cornelis van Unnik and then revived in an edition of several of his unpublished posthumous papers (1993). The negative image of an exile, rather than a voluntary migration, has been adopted by many, envisioning a Jewish longing for a return, the reacquisition of a lost homeland. Jews who held out that hope may themselves have been operating under an illusion, the whole image of exile and return being a construct, as argued by Jacob Neusner (1987), an idea reinforced by several essays in Lester Grabbe's volume (1998) and in the comparable volume edited by James Scott (1997). Even if it was an invented topos, however, its potent imagery may well have held sway among many diaspora Jews. Lachrymose interpretations did not die easily. A more balanced estimate appears in the work of Isaiah Gafni (1997), who explores various strategies whereby diaspora Jews sought to account for or legitimize their situation. The work of Erich Gruen (2002) leans decidedly to the positive. He sees no inherent contradiction between a successful existence in the diaspora and a continuing allegiance to the homeland, as expressed by gifts to the temple and periodic pilgrimages to Jerusalem.

There was, of course, no uniform pattern of diaspora life. Circumstances in Alexandria would be quite different from those in Cyrenaica or Ephesus or Rome. Although there would doubtless be shared beliefs, practices, and traditions, relations with gentiles and modes of behavior would inevitably diverge and fit no consistent scheme. It would be hard to pin a label on this diversified experience. The substantial study of Louis Feldman (1993) collects an admirable range of material, with carefully organized discussions of contacts between Jewish and pagan societies. But insofar as he treats differences within Jewish communities, they resolve themselves into "orthodoxy" and "deviance." The bifurcation is misleading. One cannot easily identify what would count as orthodox or heterodox in the fluid and multifarious contingencies of life in cities from Syria to Western Europe. The miscellany of mores, in fact, led many scholars to presume the absence of anything that can be labeled Judaism, postulating instead many Judaisms. Neusner (1993 and elsewhere) was a forceful and influential advocate of the idea in his critique of E. P. Sanders's (1992) notion of a common Judaism or covenantal nomism. But the proposition of multiple Judaisms has also faced criticism in turn, as scholars shrank from embracing the concept of a multiplicity without a core. The recent work of Daniel Schwartz (2014) seeks to restore meaning to Judaism as an integral concept. Others have moved in the opposition direction, denying any significance to the term Judaism at all. Steve Mason (2007) made the case in a very influential long article, and it now reappears in a new book by Daniel Boyarin (2019). However this debate plays out, there can be little doubt that Jews in a variety of diaspora situations found a variety of means to adjust themselves to the particular conditions without losing a sense of their distinctiveness or integrity.

3. The Jews of Egypt

Our knowledge of Jewish life in the lands of the Mediterranean and in the society of Greeks and Romans is spotty. The available material brings some glimmers of light in certain places and certain times in Egypt, in various principalities of Asia Minor, and in Rome. The rest of the Jewish world outside Palestine is largely dark with the occasional exception that provides insight and whets desire for more.

The papyri of Egypt do supply some welcome illumination. A wealth of Aramaic papyri from Elephantine include invaluable documentation of the Jewish colony on that island in the Nile, providing testimony on the military garrison, disputes and litigation within the community, legal transactions, the existence of a temple of Yahweh, conflicts with Egyptian priests, negotiations with Persian overlords, evidence for Passover celebrations, and the ultimate destruction of the temple. Many of the letters, family archives, and legal contracts that shed important light on the social history of that diaspora community are newly collected, translated, and commented upon by the preeminent scholar of that subject, Bezalel Porten, and a team of collaborators (2011), making the material more readily accessible to scholars and a wider readership.

The preserved papyri multiply in the Ptolemaic and Roman periods. The great work of Victor Tcherikover and Alexander Fuks two generations ago (1957–1960), assembling the documents related to Jews and supplying extensive historical introductions and commentary, has not been superseded. Yet a most significant recent publication revealed a Jewish *politeuma* in Herakleopolis, a political community hitherto unknown, with an archive of legal documents that provides our fullest information on the governance of a semiautonomous Jewish entity within the broader realm of Ptolemaic Egypt. That publication by James Cowey and Klaus Maresh (2001) supplies unique information on Jewish officials, a *politarches* and *archontes*, their relations with Ptolemaic governance, their judicial and administrative responsibilities, and the procedures for settling legal disputes. The archive, even though many particulars are unclear, affords precious insight into the internal operations of a Jewish community under the aegis of a Hellenistic kingdom.

More information exists on the Jews in Alexandria, much of it concentrated on events leading to the violent upheaval and oppressive actions in 38 CE. Principal evidence resides in a literary text, the *In Flaccum* of Philo, who was himself a contemporary of the events. The turbulent activities, involving clashes between Egyptians and Jews, hostility by Greek leaders in Alexandria, and the repressive decrees of the Roman prefect of Egypt, Flaccus (Philo, *Flacc.* 1–101), have been much discussed in recent years with various interpretations, ascribing diverse responsibilities to Greeks, Jews, Romans, or Egyptians. A survey of the evidence and scholarly controversies can be found in Gruen (2002, 54–83), who argues for the exceptional, rather than the representative, character of that pogrom, a far from typical diaspora experience. Sandra Gambetti (2009) treats in detail and with acuity the highly complex and disputed issues of Jewish civic rights and privileges within Alexandria that featured in the upheaval. Andrew Harker (2008) provides analysis of these events and beyond through exploiting the largely fictitious but quite relevant material in the papyrological texts of the Acta Alexandrinorum (Tcherikover and Fuks 1960, II, nos.154–159). How far the Jews enjoyed rights of citizenship in Alexandria and the degree to which struggles over those rights animated Greeks and Egyptians in the city remain very much in dispute. The whole subject of Jewish civic life and political privileges not only in Alexandria but in the Greek cities of the Mediterranean generally has now been put on a firmer footing by the scrupulous and sweeping study of Bradley Ritter (2015).

4. The Jews of Asia Minor

Vital evidence on the Jews of Asia Minor comes in the text of Josephus. The historian quotes a plethora of edicts, letters, and decrees, mostly stemming from Roman magistrates responding to Jewish complaints about mistreatment in the Hellenic cities of Asia Minor (Josephus, *A.J.* 14.185–246, 256–267; 16.160–178). Extrapolating from these items represents a challenge because Josephus presents them in no systematic order, many are quoted in part rather than in whole, chronology is confused, and there are numerous errors and repetitions. Even their authenticity has been questioned. Roman replies to the complaints were almost uniformly positive, reasserting Jewish privileges and affirming Roman support for them in messages to the officialdom of the Greek cities. This too has prompted suspicion about Josephus's selectivity, manipulation, and possible fabrication of the documents or their content. But those concerns, expressed by an earlier generation of scholars, have largely been dispelled. Parallels for the award of such privileges appear in many other Roman documents preserved on stone, bronze, or papyrus, not subject to literary misrepresentation. Josephus could gain access to informants in the various diaspora cities like Ephesus, Laodicea, Miletus, Sardis, and Halicarnassus, where the Jews had reason to preserve documents that guaranteed the unhindered practice of traditional rites and adherence to ancestral laws. The case for authenticity was made decisively by Miriam Pucci Ben Zeev (1998), whose excellent assemblage of and commentary on each of the documents constitutes a landmark in the field. The very existence of these directives by Roman officials to Greek cities, about thirty in number, mostly clustered in the late first century BCE and early first century CE, has given rise to the conclusion that Jewish life in those diaspora communities was precarious, subject to oppression and eradication of cultic practices and traditional institutions by the governing powers of Greek cities and requiring the protection of Roman intervention. That need not, however, be the case. Investigation of the historical circumstances in which each of the decrees was issued, many of them in the turbulent time of a Roman civil war, indicates that the conditions that called them forth were complex and shifting, contingent upon particular events and personalities, rather than reflecting a general pattern or policy of Greek oppression and Roman championship of Jews. That interpretation can be found in Gruen (2002, 84–104). A fuller survey of testimony, including inscriptions and New Testament sources, appears in the useful monograph of Paul Trebilco (1991) buttressed more recently by the extensive probe into the legal standing and prerogatives of Jews of Asia Minor in the late Republic and Augustan period of Monika Schuol (2007).

5. The Jews of Rome

Jews had established a community or communities in Rome itself at least from the time of the second century BCE. Testimony is fragmented and scattered but revealing. They appear in our texts in the year 139 BCE when, under mysterious circumstances, they were expelled from the city (Valerius Maximus, *Fact.* 1.3.3) but probably not for long. There was a well-established Jewish presence in Rome three quarters of a century later when Cicero attests directly (though not happily) to their vocal involvement in the political process (*Flac.* 66–69). Some Jews may have arrived in Rome initially as war captives, subsequently liberated, but most probably migrated voluntarily for purposes of commerce, employment, the joining of families, and the opportunities presented by the center of power in the Mediterranean. By the later Roman Republic, many of them, at any rate, were Roman citizens. They thrived in the age of Augustus (Philo, *Legat.* 155–157) and, despite brief and temporary expulsions under Tiberius and Claudius (Josephus, *A.J.* 18.65–84; Tacitus, *Ann.* 2.85; Suetonius, *Tib.* 36; *Claud.* 25.4; Acts 18:2; Dio Cassius, *Hist. rom.* 57.18.5a) maintained viable communities throughout the Julio-Claudian era. They were conspicuous in the city and made no secret of their peculiar practices and characteristic customs. Roman writers like Seneca, Quintilian, Juvenal, and Tacitus found reason to mock or scorn the strange customs of the Jews and their penchant for keeping to themselves, but there was no campaign to repress or eradicate them. Jews maintained the Sabbath, dietary laws, circumcision, and the worship of Yahweh with little fear of persecution.

The classic work on the Jews of Rome by Harry Leon (1960) still holds up well. It has the great virtue of exploring the rich epigraphic record contained in the Roman catacombs that provides some sense of the source of migration, range of occupations, marriage practices, economic status, religious observances, and openness to proselytes. The topic has attracted recent attention in the study of Silvia Cappelletti (2006), who teases out evidence on the corporate structure of Jewish governance in the city, sketches the history of Roman Jews from the Republic through the Flavian emperors, and summarizes the evidence from the catacombs. A more ambitious new work issued from the pen of Shlomo Simonsohn (2014), a wide-ranging examination of Jewish settlements in Rome and elsewhere in Italy, their socioeconomic circumstances, legal status, cultural activities, and relations to both paganism and Christianity from the time of their appearance in Rome to the age of Augustine.

6. Jewish Life in the Diaspora

The conduct of Jewish life in diaspora cities is exceedingly hard to document. A useful volume of essays edited by John Bartlett (2002) addressed that topic. But, despite a number of fine essays and several that strayed widely from the subject, the volume only demonstrated how little we know. The testimony from Egypt, mostly papyrological, disclosed that Jews served regularly in the Ptolemaic armies and police forces, reached administrative posts as tax farmers and tax collectors, as bankers and granary officials. They turn up in the papyri as merchants, shippers, farmers, and participants in a myriad of occupations. As we have seen, they had their own governing body in Herakleopolis, a *politeuma*, with its own juridical authority and officialdom. A parallel one is attested in Cyrenaica (Lüderitz 1983, nos. 70–71). And there is no reason to doubt that other Jewish *politeumata* existed in other Egyptian cities where there was a large enough number of Jews. To what degree Jews shared in civic privileges outside their own communities is more difficult to say. But evidence does exist for some role in the political structure of Alexandria.

How far one can extrapolate from the Egyptian experience is difficult to say. Testimony comparable to the papyri does not exist elsewhere. But we know that the Jews in Rome had political influence, could put pressure when needed upon public policy, and had access to the grain distribution, which meant that a significant number enjoyed Roman citizenship (Philo, *Legat.* 158). Among other things, they were eligible for service in the Roman army, for we are told that many sought, and usually received, exemption from recruitment into the military (Josephus, *A.J.* 14.236–240). The precise nature of the civic prerogatives exercised by Jews must have varied considerably from place to place, dependent on location, local regulations, and contingent circumstances. That highly complex topic has now been considerably illuminated by the scrupulous study of Ritter (2015), a major step forward in our understanding.

Among the most important recent developments in the study of the Jewish diaspora in antiquity is the publication of three hefty volumes of Jewish inscriptions, encompassing Greece, Macedonia, the Greek islands, the Roman provinces of Eastern Europe, Asia Minor, the Black Sea region, Syria, and Cyprus. This is a monumental accomplishment in three volumes by David Noy, Alexander Panayotov, Hans-Wulf Bloedhorn (2004), and Walter Ameling (2004). The work represents an admirable assemblage of texts, translations, commentaries, bibliographies, introductory material, and extensive indices for each region. The enterprise is a model of its kind, a major advance in the accessibility of epigraphic documents for understanding the diaspora experience. Earlier collections appeared for other regions, William Horbury and Noy (1992) for Egypt and two volumes by Noy (1993, 1995) on Western Europe. Together with the three more recent publications, they provide an indispensable tool and a trustworthy guide for all subsequent research on the Jewish diaspora.

The epigraphic texts bring to light numerous aspects of Jewish life outside Palestine that expand, reinforce, or complicate what is known from the literary evidence. Among other things, the inscriptions add a vital dimension to our grasp of how Jews related to, integrated into, and adapted the institutions of the gentile societies in which they dwelled. Jews, for instance, did not shy away from support of pagan festivals. An inscription from Iasos in Asia Minor records a donor from Jerusalem who supplied funds for the festival of Dionysos (Ameling 2004, no. 21). At Delphi a Jew manumitted his slave in conventional Hellenic fashion through a fictitious sale to Apollo (Noy, Panayotov, Bloedhorn 2004, Ach44). In a manumission declaration from the Black Sea region, the Jewish manumitter accompanied his deed with a vow to Zeus, Earth, and Sun (Noy, Panayotov, Bloedhorn 2004, BS20). Moschos the Jew even announced that he had been accorded a dream by the Greek deities Amphiaraos and Hygeia when he slept in their temple at Oropos in Boeotia (Noy, Panayotov, Bloedhorn 2004, Ach45). An epitaph from Hierapolis in Asia Minor discloses the accomplishment of a Jew who was a most renowned victor in sacred contests, clear testimony that Jews were participants in the games of the gymnasium (Ameling 2004, no. 189). A remarkable instance of Jewish adaptation of Hellenic practice comes in an inscription from Ionia where the grateful Jewish community honors a benefactress for the building of the synagogue and its courtyard by awarding her a golden crown and a choice seat in the synagogue, honors that closely follow the conventions of Greek cities in showing gratitude to benefactors (Ameling 2004, no. 36). A recently published Phoenician epitaph from Cyprus displays the Hebrew name of the father and the Phoenician name of the son, one of them alluding to Yahweh, the other to Astarte (Noy and Bloedhorn 2004, Cyp7). None of this overlapping and integration meant that Jews abandoned a sense of their distinctive identity. A number of inscriptions put biblical quotations on display. A stone from Nicaea in Asia Minor offers a quotation from the Psalms (Ameling 2004, no. 153). The longest extant quotation drawn from Deuteronomy and written in Hebrew comes from Palmyra (Noy and Bloedhorn 2004, Syr44). Perhaps most telling among the documents are two donor inscriptions from Aphrodisias in western Asia Minor that not only settled the scholarly controversy of whether "Godfearers" constitute an identifiable group of sympathizers with Judaism (they do) but offer priceless data on Jewish onomastics and occupations (Ameling 2004, no. 14).

7. Synagogues

An excellent index of the spread of diaspora Judaism lies in the noteworthy number of synagogues in the cities of the Mediterranean. Some are known to us from literary evidence, others from archaeological findings, and many more doubtless remain to be discovered. Epigraphy helps here too. Intriguing inscriptions disclose the existence of synagogues (*proseuchai*) in Egypt, which Jews dedicated to the Ptolemaic rulers of that land beginning in the mid-third century BCE (Horbury and Noy 1992, nos. 24, 117). Diaspora Jews in Egypt obviously felt comfortable in honoring gentile rulers while constructing houses of worship (perhaps with Ptolemaic help) for Yahweh. These synagogues perhaps paved the way for the erection of an actual temple in Leontopolis founded by a refugee high priest from Jerusalem who had earned the favor and patronage of Ptolemy in the mid-second century (Josephus, *A.J.* 13.62–72). Whether or not this was designed as a rival to the Jerusalem temple remains controversial in the scholarship, a controversy explored anew and thoroughly by Livia Capponi (2007). In any case, the existence of several attested places of worship in Egypt shows the penchant of diaspora Jews (with due deference to the pagan authorities) for establishing roots in the land that had become their own.

Evidence for the ubiquity of the synagogue comes in a variety of forms. For the Jews of Cyrenaica on the North African coast an inscription displays a list of donors who contributed to the repair of a synagogue, a signal example of the civic pride of the community in its sacred institutions (Lüderitz 1983, no. 72). The book of Acts outlines the extensive travels of Paul in the mid-first century CE. His mission took him to a host of cities in Greece, Macedon, and Asia Minor where his first stop was often that of the Jewish synagogue. Jews were far flung in the Aegean as well (Acts 17–19). A letter by a Roman magistrate registered by 1 Maccabees went to Jewish communities in Delos, Samos, Cos, and Rhodes, among other places (1 Macc 15:14–24). One can go still further afield. A treasure trove of inscriptions from the first century CE recording manumissions by Jews dwelling on the shores of the Black Sea reveals that the procedure regularly took place in synagogues, with procedures and formulas that parallel those employed by Greeks elsewhere, thus demonstrating the natural adaptation of pagan practices by Jews dwelling in their midst. An excellent edition of the Black Sea inscriptions by E. Leigh Gibson (1999) remains definitive on that subject.

Additional testimony comes from the spade. The earliest synagogue discovered on the ground may, surprisingly, be one on the sacred isle of Delos, home of the oracular shrine of Apollo. Whether the structure was, in fact, a synagogue is a matter of debate among scholars, but most now concur in the identification. If so, it is particularly striking that Jews should have erected a structure of worship in the heart of a site that held so much religious meaning for the whole Greek world. There could be no better testimony to the comfortable relationship between Jewish and pagan sites of worship. No synagogue has yet been found in Rome, but the presence of Jews in the city in significant numbers would almost demand one. An actual structure turned up at Ostia, the port city of Rome. It is hardly possible that diaspora Jews built a synagogue in Ostia but neglected to put one in Rome. In fact, the catacomb inscriptions from the city provide the names of at least eleven synagogues. Many more have emerged from the ground, most famously at Sardis and Dura-Europos, in the centuries after the destruction of the temple in Jerusalem. Scholarship on the topic has been far from idle. The important work of Donald Binder (1999) on Second Temple synagogues, is often speculative but always insightful. He rightly insists that synagogues of this period represented no substitute for nor opposition to the temple in Jerusalem. They were the alternative structures that served the needs of Jewish communities abroad. The sweeping survey by Lee Levine (2000) takes the subject from its beginnings to the Byzantine period with the balanced judgment and reasonableness characteristic of that scholar. Anders Runesson, Donald Binder, and Birger Olsson (2010) have compiled a most valuable collection of sources on the synagogue that will greatly facilitate further study of the subject.

The synagogue provided services well beyond worship, prayer, and ritual acts. Scattered literary evidence from Philo, Acts, and Josephus indicates that a range of activities could take place there, including instruction and study, communal dining, celebration of festivals, arbitration and adjudication, assemblage to recommend actions by the community, a repository for dedicatory offerings and sacred funds, and an archive for public records (Philo, *Hypoth.* 7.11-13; *Somn.* 2.127; *Legat.* 156; *Mos.* 215-216; Acts 17-19; Josephus, *A.J.* 14.57, 16.43). The synagogue indeed possessed a whole scale of officials with titles and duties to run the establishments. The few glimpses that we get on this score do not allow reconstruction of a uniform system, and it is unlikely that there was such a thing. Individual communities doubtless administered their synagogues to their own taste, with diverse titles, structures, procedures, and activities. But, however varied were the structures and functions, the synagogue clearly provided a center to reinforce the identity of diaspora Jews in their several communities. And the fact that they did not conduct their activities hidden from the gaze of the gentiles who surrounded them is significant. Numerous comments by pagan authors demonstrate their awareness of Jewish observance of the Sabbath, the practice of circumcision, and the rigidity of dietary laws. Diaspora Jews evidently felt confidence in their centers of operation, a means of self-expression within the larger pagan society.

8. Jewish Literature in Greek

Beyond social and religious life was involvement with the cultural world of the Hellenistic Mediterranean. A landmark publication appeared in 1986 and 1987: the third volume, published in two parts, of the monumental revision of Emil Schürer's classic *History of the Jewish People in the Age of Jesus Christ* by Géza Vermès, Fergus Millar, and Martin Goodman devoted nearly half of its one thousand pages to Jewish literature composed in Greek and deriving from the diaspora. The assiduous labors of the editors provided a comprehensive geographic survey of places from Mesopotamia to Germany where Jews were to be found from the fifth century BCE to late antiquity. Their review of Jewish literature in Greek ranges from the Septuagint to Philo and encompasses numerous authors extant only in fragments but who were key voices in the self-expression of Jews dwelling outside Palestine. They produced a growing body of writings in a wide span of genres, like historiography, epic, drama, philosophy, novelistic fiction, and recast biblical narratives. The new Schürer supplies extensive summaries of the works and valuable bibliographies for each of them up to the mid-1980s.

That revised and much expanded edition served as a most beneficial resource and accompanied a wave of scholarly interest in the intellectual products of the Jewish diaspora. Carl Holladay's (1983–1996) superb edition in four volumes of fragments from Hellenistic Jewish authors, with texts, translations, notes, and commentary inspired and facilitated scholarship on a large number of authors previously unfamiliar to most researchers. In these same years James Charlesworth oversaw two large volumes (1983, 1985; *OTP*) of annotated translations of the pseudepigrapha, broadly understood, including texts like the Sibylline Oracles, the Letter of Aristeas, Joseph and Aseneth, 3 and 4 Maccabees, and the Psalms of Solomon, making them widely accessible to scholars and students. One of the earliest examples of this new wave of interest was John Collins's (2000) well-written and influential *Between Athens and Jerusalem,* first published in 1986, a succinct analysis of numerous authors and texts stemming from the Hellenistic diaspora. Collins found in much of this literature an apologetic character, an effort by diaspora Jews to express their own identity and to justify their presence, indeed to assert their superiority in a Hellenic intellectual universe. The argument for apologia as a central element was developed more fully in the important study by Gregory Sterling (1992). That idea was resisted or at least downplayed by John Barclay (1996) and Gruen (1998) thus provoking a rejoinder by Collins (2000) in a new edition of his book. Barclay's innovative study classified the texts and the circumstances they reflected into categories of assimilation, acculturation, and accommodation, going even further to identify levels of high, medium, and low assimilation. The categorization is perhaps too schematic, but it affords an illuminating approach to interpreting a diaspora mentality in relation to its cultural surroundings. Gruen looks at the texts also as expressions of Jewish identity but sees them as primarily positive and self-confident, often light-hearted and entertaining, rather than struggling for a voice in an alien world.

The Hebrew Bible (or, at least, the Pentateuch) was translated into Greek some time in the third century BCE. The famous story of the event in the Letter of Aristeas, which has seventy Jewish sages gathered in Alexandria, commissioned by Ptolemy II to produce the translation, may or may not have much historical validity (Let. Aris. 1–11, 300–321). The excellent recent commentary on the letter by Benjamin Wright (2015) explores all the details with thoroughness and reasoned judgment. Whether or not the event is historical, the setting is plausible, and a Greek version of the Bible, subsequently to become what we know as the Septuagint, did take shape in this period. There is little reason to doubt that diaspora Jews, living for a generation or more in Greek-speaking communities, had lost command of Hebrew. Availability of the scriptures in the lingua franca of the diaspora world spurred an explosion of literary activity by Hellenistic Jews: reframing, refashioning, and rewriting biblical stories in a variety of genres long familiar in Greek tradition and now adapted for Jewish purposes. So, for instance, historians like Demetrius, late third century BCE, who dissected biblical texts to reconcile discrepancies and sort out chronological inconsistencies in Genesis and Exodus, or Eupolemos, probably second century BCE, whose work *On the Kings of Judea*, included freely embellished accounts of the exploits of David and Solomon, reworked biblical narratives and produced new Greek versions. The imaginative and amusing author Artapanus, among other things, recreated the Moses story, turning the lawgiver into a military hero and a world-historical figure who brought hieroglyphics to the Egyptians and circumcision to the Ethiopians. Moses indeed was the subject of a full-blown tragic drama, in the style of classical Greek tragedy, composed by a certain Ezekiel, a work acutely analyzed by Howard Jacobson (1983). Although that is our only extant example, we know that other such plays were produced by Jewish authors on biblical themes.

Jewish intellectuals and writers became conversant with other Hellenic genres as well. They produced epic poetry, philosophy, and even novels or novellas, demonstrating a command of Hellenic traditions and disclosing an audience or readership receptive to a variety of literary creations that brought entertainment and edification. They covered a wide span of diverse writings, most of which we no longer possess. But the surviving fragments, quotations, and references make clear that there was a thriving literary activity among diaspora Jews, certainly in Alexandria and very probably in other sites on which we are not so well informed. Grabbe (2008, 84–110) offers a handy sketch of these authors. The works are newly assembled, with introductions, commentary, and bibliography for each by Folker Siegert (2016). It is noteworthy that, although Jewish writers readily adapted the forms and means employed by their Hellenic models, they had their own stories to tell. They did not recount the myths of Hellas but the tales of the patriarchs and the achievements of the kings and leaders of Judea. In short, however adept the writers were in exploiting the literary forms of Greek tradition, they put them to use in conveying the characteristic stories and values of the Hebrew heritage.

9. The Pagan Perceptions of Jews

How were Jews viewed by the larger society? We get glimpses only, here and there. No full-scale work by a pagan author on the Jews survives, and few indeed were written. Jewish history and institutions were of marginal interest, at best, to Greek and Roman writers. What did capture the attention at least of some were the strange habits of the Jews. Greeks and Romans in general lived comfortably with religious and cultural activities practiced by a wide variety of ethnic groups. But Jews struck them as particularly bizarre, thus prompting some puzzled and often uninformed remarks. Most of the authors did not bother to get their facts straight.

So, for example, the Greek historian Hecataeus of Abdera, writing in the late fourth century BCE, reports that the Jews never had a king, that they chose their high priest for his virtue and his wisdom, and that Moses founded the city of Jerusalem where he installed the temple (Diodorus Siculus, *Bib. hist.* 40.3). In fact, of course the ancient Israelites had many kings, their high priesthood was a hereditary office, and Moses never made it to the holy land. Hecataeus was not here engaging in polemic, and, indeed, what little we know of his writing on the subject included some approving remarks about Moses. But this excerpt gives a sense of how sketchy was pagan knowledge of Jews.

Roman authors, despite having many Jews living in their midst, were not always much better informed. That Jews kept the Sabbath, with its firm restrictions on activity, was widely known, but few gentiles probed much further. Many presumed that the Sabbath was a day of fasting, and others by contrast, like Plutarch (*Quaest. conviv.* 4.6.2) and Tacitus (*Hist.* 5.5.5), debated as to whether it was a form of Dionysian festival, an occasion for drink and revelry. Some went further in their assessment, adjudging observance of the Sabbath as a colossal folly. Seneca quipped that by observing the Sabbath, Jews waste one-seventh of their lives in idleness (Augustine, *Civ.* 6.11). Tacitus (*Hist.* 5.4.3) speculated that the claims of laziness not only induced Jews to while away every seventh day but even prompted them to devote every seventh year to lolling about. Pliny the Elder (*Nat.* 31.24) took it one step further still: he claimed to know of a river in Judea that dries up every Sabbath, thus taking a weekly rest.

The abstention from pork provoked similar cracks. As Augustus famously put it, speaking about the intrigues and murders that took place in the family and court of Herod, "I would feel safer as Herod's pig than as his son" (Macrobius, *Sat.* 2.4.11). Petronius (frag. 37) mocked the Jews as worshiping a pig-god. Finally, Juvenal (*Sat.* 6.159–160) observed that Judea is the one place where pigs can live to a ripe old age.

Circumcision seemed even more baffling and incomprehensible. For gentiles, this was perhaps the most characteristic of Jewish practices. For Horace (*Sat.* 1.9.70) it was a natural expression of the people. Tacitus (*Hist.* 5.5.2) indeed surmised that the Jews adopted the custom precisely in order to make themselves distinct from all other peoples. Not only did Roman satirists like Petronius, Juvenal, and Martial find it a source of amusement, but even the Jewish philosopher Philo (*Spec.* 1.1–2) acknowledged that it prompted ridicule and laughter among many. As is clear, the practice of circumcision gave rise to mockery and parody, a valuable source of material for jokesters.

Remarks of this kind, however one might wish to interpret them, demonstrate that diaspora Jews had no qualms (and no fears) about practicing their conventional customs and underscoring their distinctiveness. Did this really do them any damage? Scholars vary in how much weight they place upon these sarcastic jibes and dismissive utterances. Some in recent years have taken them seriously as reflecting pagan hostility (Feldman 1993, 153–72; Schäfer 1997, 180–95; Isaac 2004, 463–77). Others see them as merely droll and parodic, rather than reflecting deep animosity (Gruen 2002, 41–52; Goodman 2007, 366–76).

The debate touches on the larger question of how far one can discern traces of anti-Semitism or a form of protoracism in pagan attitudes toward Jews. Scholarship on the subject, which began as early as the eighteenth century, featured by luminaries such as Johann Gustav Droysen, Theodor Mommsen, Eduard Meyer, and Elias Bickerman, has labored mightily to identify reasons why gentiles might have found Jews to be odious or menacing. A valuable summary of opinions from the nineteenth through the mid-twentieth centuries can be found in Christhard Hoffman (1988). The most common reasons for pagan animosity toward Jews that have been postulated by researchers are the social nonconformism of the Jews, their supposed shunning of the majority culture in diaspora communities, their isolationism that slid into xenophobia and misanthropy, their monotheism that scorned civic cults, not to mention emperor worship, their religious beliefs that set them apart from the rest of society, their claim to be a chosen people, and their proselytism that threatened the coherence and stability of traditional Greco-Roman values.

Did this amount to anti-Semitism? Did diaspora Jews in antiquity fall under that dark cloud? As is well known, anti-Semitism is a modern expression, not an ancient one. It first surfaces in nineteenth-century Germany, and most recent scholars eschew the terminology. The earlier scholarship is usefully summarized by John Gager (1985, 11–34). Benjamin Isaac's nuanced discussion (2004, 442–46, 481–84) denies the applicability of the term, insofar as it signifies racism, but allows that there was extensive hostility that amounted to ethnic hatred. Volker Herholt (2009, 19–30) explores a distinction between anti-Semitism and anti-Judaism, which does not get us far. The sweeping recent study by David Nirenberg (2013, 13–47) of what he calls "anti-judaism" throughout the Western tradition, treats only Egyptian attitudes toward the Jews in antiquity. If anti-Judaism alludes to animosity toward the religion rather than toward race or ethnicity, its applicability is dubious. Religion as such, whatever that may mean (a matter of considerable dispute) was not suppressed, persecuted, or eradicated. The concept of "Judeophobia" was advanced by Zvi Yavetz (1997) and Peter Schäfer (1997). But the idea of Greek or Roman fear of the Jews carries little credence. What would they be afraid of? Jews, to be sure, had spread widely in the ancient Mediterranean and had gained a substantial number of converts or Godfearers. For some scholars, for example, Feldman (1993, 288–304) and Schäfer (1997, 183–192), this signaled proselytism and may have raised alarm among pagans. In fact, however, there is almost no evidence for proselytism, let alone for any alarm about the numbers of coverts (Gruen 2016, 313–32).

10. Diaspora Jews' Sense of Themselves

It is perhaps time to get beyond the somewhat exhausted question of whether the ancients viewed Jews through racist lenses that either exhibited or presaged anti-Semitism. More to the point is the issue of how far Jews in the diaspora found themselves comfortable in striking a balance between the maintenance of their traditions and adjustment to societies in which they were a minority culture. One might ask, most fundamentally, whether Jews living outside Palestine felt themselves to be in a diaspora at all, a state that needed to be justified, rationalized, or defended. It is noteworthy that none seems to have felt the need to compose a treatise on the subject. The Jews did not theorize diaspora as a topic that required dissection. That alone is suggestive. The term *diaspora*, of course, is a Greek one. It rarely appears as a substantive in Hellenistic Jewish authors. In normal Greek usage, the word carried no negative connotations, and it is nowhere equated with *galut* or *golah* as signifying an enforced exile. The sense that Jews were in a diaspora barely surfaces in the evidence and was certainly not a dominant perception that guided Jewish life. It may well have had some resonance with recent migrants, whether they moved abroad for economic reasons, sought a more stable existence, or joined family members who were already abroad. But the idea of displacement or refuge or instability would hardly have survived a generation or two in which the immigrants set down roots and established a settled presence. And it is well to remember that Jewish communities in the various cities of the Mediterranean endured for many generations. The existence of synagogues, like the magnificent ones in Dura-Europos in Syria, Sardis in Asia Minor, and Stobi in Macedonia, flourishing in the second and third centuries CE, well after the destruction of the temple, are enough to establish that.

The degree of assimilation, accommodation, or adaptation to Greco-Roman society cannot be calculated. It undoubtedly varied widely, dependent upon place, time, and circumstance. But the terms alone are misleading. They imply a continuing effort of diaspora Jews to find ways of fitting in or adjusting themselves to alien locations or conditions. In fact, there is little sign of struggle. The cities of the diaspora were *their* cities, not places of forced exile or temporary sojourn. Much modern conceptualization still imagines the diaspora as a grim existence, a matter of suffering or endurance, as in Arnold Eisen (1986, 3–34) and Van Unnik (1993, passim). But the idea that diaspora Jews spent much of their time lamenting the loss of Jerusalem and longing for the return is simply at odds with most of what we know of their experience.

Jerusalem and the temple, of course, were not abandoned or forgotten. Pilgrimages to the holy land by those who could afford them occurred regularly at major festivals. And Jews held firmly to the practice of sending a tithe to the temple annually from wherever they might be in the diaspora. That practice not only exercised its hold on Jews living in the far-flung lands of the Roman Empire, but also on those outside Rome's reach in Babylon and the satrapies of the Parthian dominion who sent delegations each year to deposit their contributions in the temple (Philo, *Legat.* 155–156, 216; Josephus, *A.J.* 14.110). Homage to Jerusalem was inviolable. But that did not entail a yearning to move back to the fatherland or dissatisfaction with life abroad. Yearly remittance of the tithe implied that diaspora communities had successfully established themselves and were indeed in a position to bolster the homeland. Far from signifying a desire for the return, it rendered the return unnecessary. The same implication holds for annual or periodic pilgrimages (Philo, *Spec.* 1.69; Acts 2:1–11; Josephus, *A.J.* 6.426–427). The pilgrimage by definition represented a temporary stay to pay homage to the heart of Jewish tradition. Jerusalem possessed an irresistible claim on the Jews' sense of themselves, but it required no permanent homecoming. The case for compatibility between diaspora life and allegiance to Jerusalem is made more fully in Gruen (2002, 232–52). The eminent philosopher Philo of Alexandria, thoroughly steeped in Hellenic culture but at the same time a devout Jew who dedicated many years to the explication of the Pentateuch, expressed the point with clarity and deep sincerity. Although he thrived in the diaspora, enjoyed its advantages, and appreciated its Hellenic virtues, he nevertheless found a profound significance in the land of Israel. He interprets the Shavuot festival as a celebration of the ancient Israelites' possession of their own land, a heritage of long standing, and even finds it a means whereby they could cease their wandering (Philo, *Spec.* 2.168). Philo saw no inconsistency or contradiction between those two conceptualizations. Diaspora Jews could enjoy fulfillment and reward in their own communities, feeling no need to depart from them. But they could still honor Judea as a refuge for those who were once displaced and unsettled, and prime legacy of all. The respect and awe laid to the holy land stood in full harmony with a commitment to the local community and allegiance to gentile government.

None of this means that diaspora Jews were altogether secure and unassailable in Greco-Roman cities. The very openness with which they practiced their unique customs and displayed their distinctiveness rendered them conspicuous—and vulnerable. When individual circumstances and contingent events demanded state action, they could serve as useful targets. This occurred when the Roman government felt the need to expel certain marginal groups (not just Jews) temporarily from the city on ostensibly religious grounds or when local conditions in Greek cities of Asia Minor induced the officialdom to curtail Jewish privileges or control their traditional practices and activities. It needs to be emphasized, however, that these episodes, and even the so-called pogrom in Alexandria in 38 CE were hardly regular features of the Jewish experience. Conflicts over Jewish privileges in Greek cities were almost exclusively concentrated in the period of Caesar and Augustus when special circumstances produced unusual tensions. The riots in Alexandria arose from the combustible mix of rivalries of Egyptians, Greeks, and Jews in that city, triggered by the particular situation in which the Roman prefect found himself. These rare outbursts are quite unusual and should not be taken as representative of the diaspora experience.

Nevertheless, it would be hard to deny that even the few disturbing episodes left a mark and that many Jews, however comfortable their setting, lived with a certain wariness and an unspoken sense that it might not last. An interesting paradox lay at the root of it. The more that Jews became an integral part of pagan society, the greater the need they may have felt to maintain their own traditions and observances in order to assert the distinctiveness of their identity. It was a source of pride, to be sure. But it could also be a risk and a hazard. Through much of the time this commitment to singularity provoked nothing worse than amusement or irritation, and the Jews were left untroubled. In periods of crisis, however, whether political upheaval or regional conflict, local tensions become intensified, and cultural differences, usually ignored or just scorned, take on sudden relevance. The outsider then becomes more obvious, an easier object for scapegoating. The Jews' insistence upon their special attributes and mores gave them a firmer sense of self-esteem, but it also meant that, when crises came, they were readily identifiable as prospective victims. Diaspora experience, in short, was predominantly stable, untroubled, and productive. But the aura of potential disruption never fully dissipated.

Bibliography

Ameling, Walter. 2004. *Kleinasien*. Vol. 2 of *Inscriptiones Judaicae Orientis*. TSAJ 99. Tübingen: Mohr Siebeck.

Barclay, John M. G. 1996. *Jews in the Mediterranean Diaspora from Alexander to Trajan (323 BCE–117 CE)*. HCS 33. Berkeley: University of California Press.

Bartlett, John R. 2002. *Jews in the Hellenistic and Roman Cities*. London: Routledge.

Binder, Donald D. 1999. *Into the Temple Courts: The Place of the Synagogues in the Second Temple Period*. SBLDS 169. Atlanta: Society for Biblical Literature.

Boyarin, Daniel. 2019. *Judaism: The Genealogy of a Modern Notion*. New Brunswick, NJ: Rutgers University Press.

Cappelletti, Silvia. 2006. *The Jewish Community of Rome: From the Second Century B.C. to the Third Century C.E.* JSJSup 113. Leiden: Brill.

Capponi, Livia. 2007. *Il tempio di Leontopoli in Egitto: Identità politica e religiosa dei Giudei di Onia (c. 150 a.C–73 d.C.)*. Pubblicazioni della Facoltà di Lettere e Filosofia dell'Università di Pavia 118. Pisa: ETS.

Collins, John J. 2000. *Between Athens and Jerusalem: Jewish Identity in the Hellenistic Diaspora*. 2nd ed. Grand Rapids: Eerdmans.

Cowey, James M. S., and Klaus Maresch. 2001. *Urkunden des Politeuma der Juden von Herakleopolis (144/3–133/2 b. Chr.)*. Papyrologica Coloniensia 29. Wiesbaden: Westdeutscher.

Eisen, Arnold M. 1986. *Galut: Modern Jewish Reflection on Homelessness and Homecoming*. Modern Jewish Experience. Bloomington: Indiana University Press.

Feldman, Louis H. 1993. *Jew and Gentile in the Ancient World: Attitudes and Interactions from Alexander to Justinian*. Princeton: Princeton University Press.

Gafni, Isaiah M. 1997. *Land, Center, and Diaspora: Jewish Constructs in Late Antiquity*. JSPSup 21. Sheffield: Sheffield Academic.

Gager, John G. 1985. *The Origins of Anti-Semitism: Attitudes toward Judaism in Pagan and Christian Antiquity*. Oxford: Oxford University Press.

Gambetti, Sandra. 2009. *The Alexandrian Riots of 38 C.E. and the Persecution of the Jews: A Historical Reconstruction*. JSJSup 135. Leiden: Brill.

Gibson, E. Leigh. 1999. *The Jewish Manumission Inscriptions of the Bosporus Kingdom*. TSAJ 75. Tübingen: Mohr Siebeck.

Goodman, Martin. 2007. *Rome and Jerusalem: The Clash of Ancient Civilizations*. New York: Knopf.

Grabbe, Lester L., ed. 1998. *Leading Captivity Captive: "The Exile" as History and Ideology*. JSOTSup 278. Sheffield: Sheffield Academic.

———. 2008. *The Coming of the Greeks; the Early Hellenistic Period (335–175 BCE)*. Vol. 2 of *A History of the Jews and Judaism in the Second Temple Period*. London: T&T Clark.
Gruen, Erich S. 1998. *Heritage and Hellenism: The Reinvention of Jewish Tradition*. HCS 30. Berkeley: University of California Press.
———. 2002. *Diaspora: Jews amidst Greeks and Romans*. Cambridge: Harvard University Press.
———. 2016. *Constructs of Identity in Hellenistic Judaism: Essays on Early Jewish Literature and History*. DCLS 29. Berlin: de Gruyter.
Harker, Andrew. 2008. *Loyalty and Dissidence in Roman Egypt: The Case of the Acta Alexandrinorum*. Cambridge: Cambridge University Press.
Herholt, Volker. 2009. *Antisemitismus in der Antike: Kontinuitäten und Brüche eines historischen Phänomens*. Pietas 2. Gutenberg: Computus.
Hoffmann, Christhard. 1988. *Juden und Judentum im Werk deutscher Althistoriker des 19. und 20. Jahrhunderts*. Studies in Judaism in Modern Times 9. Leiden: Brill.
Holladay, Carl R. 1983–1996. *Fragments from Hellenistic Jewish Authors*. 4 vols. Chico, CA; Atlanta: Scholars Press.
Horbury, William, and David Noy. 1992. *Jewish Inscriptions of Graeco-Roman Egypt*. Cambridge: Cambridge University Press.
Isaac, Benjamin H. 2004. *The Invention of Racism in Classical Antiquity*. Princeton: Princeton University Press.
Jacobson, Howard. 1983. *The Exagoge of Ezekiel*. Cambridge: Cambridge University Press.
Leon, Harry. 1960. *The Jews of Ancient Rome*. Philadelphia: Jewish Publication Society.
Levine, Lee I. 2000. *The Ancient Synagogue: The First Thousand Years*. New Haven: Yale University Press.
Lüderitz, Gert. 1983. *Corpus jüdischer Zeugnisse aus der Cyrenaika*. BTAVO 53. Wiesbaden: Reichert.
Mason, Steve. 2007. "Jews, Judaeans, Judaizing, Judaism: Problems of Categorization in Ancient History." *JSJ* 38:457–512.
Neusner, Jacob. 1987. *Self-Fulfilling Prophecy: Exile and Return in the History of Judaism*. Boston: Beacon.
———. 1993. *Judaic Law from Moses to the Mishnah: A Systematic Reply to Professor E. P. Sanders*. SFSHJ 84. Atlanta: Scholars Press.
Nirenberg, David. 2013. *Anti-Judaism: The Western Tradition*. New York: Norton.

Noy, David. 1993, 1995. *Jewish Inscriptions of Western Europe*. Vols. 1–2. Cambridge: Cambridge University Press.

Noy, David, and Hans-Wulf Bloedhorn. 2004. *Syria and Cyprus*. Vol. 3 of *Inscriptiones Judaicae Orientis*. TSAJ 102. Tübingen: Mohr Siebeck.

Noy, David, Alexander Panayotov, and Hans-Wulf Bloedhorn. 2004. *Eastern Europe*. Vol. 1 of *Inscriptiones Judaicae Orientis*. TSAJ 101. Tübingen: Mohr Siebeck.

Overman, J. Andrew, and Robert S. MacLennan. 1992. *Diaspora Jews and Judaism: Essays in Honor of, and in Dialogue with, A. Thomas Kraabel*. SFSHJ 41. Atlanta: Scholars Press.

Porten, Bezalel A., ed. 2011. *The Elephantine Papyri in English*. 2nd ed. DMOA 22. Atlanta: Society of Biblical Literature.

Pucci Ben Zeev, Miriam. 1998. *Jewish Rights in the Roman World: The Greek and Roman Documents Quoted by Josephus Flavius*. TSAJ 74. Tübingen: Mohr Siebeck.

Ritter, Bradley. 2015. *Judeans in the Greek Cities of the Roman Empire*. JSJSup 170. Leiden: Brill.

Runesson, Anders, Donald D. Binder, and Birger Olsson. 2010. *The Ancient Synagogue from Its Origins to 200 C.E.: A Source Book*. Leiden: Brill.

Rutgers, Leonard V. 1998. *The Hidden Heritage of Diaspora Judaism*. CBET 20. Leuven: Peeters.

Sanders, E. P. 1992. *Judaism: Practice and Belief, 63 BCE–66 CE*. London: SCM.

Schäfer, Peter. 1997. *Judeophobia: Attitudes toward the Jews in the Ancient World*. Cambridge: Harvard University Press.

Schürer, Emil. 1986–1987. *The History of the Jewish People in the Age of Jesus Christ*. Rev. and ed. by Géza Vermès, Fergus Millar, and Martin Goodman. 3 vols. Edinburgh: T&T Clark.

Schuol, Monika. 2007. *Augustus und die Juden: Rechtsstellung und Interessenpolitik der kleinasiatischen Diaspora*. Studien zur alten Geschichte 6. Frankfurt: Antike.

Schwartz, Daniel R. 2014. *Judeans and Jews: Four Faces of Dichotomy in Ancient Jewish History*. Toronto: University of Toronto Press.

Scott, James M. 1997. *Exile: Old Testament, Jewish, and Christian Conceptions*. JSJSup 56. Leiden: Brill.

Siegert, Folker. 2016. *Einleitung in die hellenistisch-jüdische Literatur: Apokrypha, Pseudepigrapha und Fragmente verlorener Autorenwerke*. Berlin: de Gruyter.

Simonsohn, Shlomo. 2014. *The Jews of Italy: Antiquity*. BSJS 52. Leiden: Brill.
Sterling, Gregory E. 1992. *Historiography and Self-Definition: Josephus, Luke-Acts, and Apologetic Historiography*. VTSup 54. Leiden: Brill.
Tcherikover, Victor A., and Alexander Fuks. 1957–1960. *Corpus Papyrorum Judaicarum*. Vols. 1–2. Cambridge: Harvard University Press.
Trebilco, Paul R. 1991. *Jewish Communities in Asia Minor*. SNTSMS 69. Cambridge: Cambridge University Press.
Unnik, Willem Cornelis van. 1993. *Das Selbstverständnis der jüdischen Diaspora in der hellenistisch-römischen Zeit*. AGJU 17. Leiden: Brill.
Wright, Benjamin G., III. 2015. *The Letter of Aristeas: "Aristeas to Philocrates" or "On the Translation of the Law of the Jews."* CEJL. Berlin: de Gruyter.
Yavetz, Zvi. 1997. *Judenfeindschaft in der Antike*. Munich: Beck.

4
Gender in Early Jewish Literature

FRANÇOISE MIRGUET

Attention to gender in early Jewish literature has followed theoretical discussions in the broader humanities; more specifically, it has drawn upon research on ancient Greek and Roman cultures. I start by briefly outlining some of the most significant works in these two areas of study. I then turn to scholarship on gender in early Judaism and develop three major aspects: (1) what sources suggest about women's and men's experiences and social roles (since most texts deal overwhelmingly with men, studies have often focused on women's lives); (2) the constructions or discourses of gender (i.e., how notions such as femininity and masculinity are construed); and (3) the use of gender to structure other notions, especially as they share similar characteristics, such as hierarchy, scale, and fluidity.

1. Gender in Philosophy and Theory: Some Landmarks

The concept of gender makes its appearance in humanities scholarship in the 1950s and 1960s. It is initially used to designate cultural constructions of sexual difference, in contrast to biological sex. Starting in the late 1960s, feminist scholars turned their attention to gender norms and their possible transgression. Gender is understood as a powerful tool for structuring not only relationships between women and men but also social systems more broadly—especially when they involve relationships of power (Wallach Scott 1986). In *Gender Trouble* (1990), Judith Butler argues that gender is a performance; it is produced through multiple iterative acts that eventually make gender into what we expect it to be, a natural fact or essence. Gender, therefore, is the process by which sexes are produced and established as natural and prediscursive. There is no binary relationship between gender and sex, since the former generates the latter. In the same book, Butler denounces the heterosexuality often assumed in feminist theory and the heteronormative frame that it projects. In *Bodies That Matter* (1993), Butler contends that discourses of power form actual bodies, not just representations. Through readings of texts by Plato, Freud, Lacan, and others, she traces the genealogy of heterosexual discourses and lays bare their instability. The *Timaeus*, in particular, establishes that matter, associated with femininity, preexists language and culture; materiality is thus produced through a "gendered matrix" (Butler 1993, 7). Pierre Bourdieu (1998, 2001) condemns masculine domination as hidden violence, sometimes imperceptible even to its victims. For Bourdieu, the principle of distinction between male and female is arbitrary and contingent but is presented as normative and natural.

One of the most recent trends in the study of gender, often referred to as feminist new materialism, aims to uncover the material conditions under which gender norms are built and imposed. Among a variety of approaches, one tendency is to recognize the formative role of matter: Rather than being merely a passive support to processes of power, the biological or material interacts in complex ways with political and social systems, in modes that range from contribution to resistance (e.g., Grosz 1994; Fausto-Sterling 2000). Biology and culture are coemergent: "They provoke, challenge, and consequently shape one another" (Frost 2011, 77). Scholarship thus evolves to posit more reciprocal and complex—rather than unidirectional and linear—interactions between bodies and cultural discourses.

2. Gender in Scholarship on Ancient Greece and Rome

These theoretical discussions shape, to a large extent, studies on ancient history and literature. Studies on antique women, both prominent and anonymous, as well as their status in their various societies, have been published since the end of the nineteenth century. Starting in the mid-1970s, scholars of ancient Greece, Rome, and other Mediterranean cultures progressively focus their attention on discourses of gender, norms, and politics. Ancient constructions of sexuality, femininity, and masculinity, as well as the use of gender as an organizing structure for other categories, become the subjects of many studies in the 1980s and 1990s. In *Making Sex: Body and Gender from the Greeks to Freud* (1990), the historian Thomas Laqueur argues that, before the eighteenth century, men and women were thought to share the same body; he proposes a one-sex model, with varying gradations of feminine and masculine features (such as the states of being dry/wet or hot/cold). Sexual difference in ancient sources is based less on the physical body than on social and political discourses. Sex is unstable and may change during an individual's life. By contrast, the social roles associated with femininity and masculinity are firmly established and are rarely questioned. As Brooke Holmes (2012) points out, Laqueur is engaged in a critique of the sex/gender binary; his aim is to unearth the processes by which sex—in its anatomical definitions—is culturally constructed and established as authoritative.

Other works (e.g., Halperin, Winkler, Zeitlin 1990; Hallett and Skinner 1997) unfold this view of ancient sex as a continuum; they also emphasize the plurality of experiences related to gender roles, depending especially on social status. The gamut, they note, runs from adult free men, at the pinnacle of masculinity, down through less masculine people, including elderly men, boys, and slaves, to women at the lowest end of the spectrum. A body identified as male, therefore, does not guarantee masculinity. Conversely, women are not thought of as the opposite of men, but rather as incompletely or imperfectly male (e.g., Galen, *Usu part.* 2.630). In *Becoming Female* (2008), Katrina Cawthorn analyzes the manipulations of the body in Greek tragedy; she describes masculinity as an unstable process, since a male may always fall to a state of femininity. Old age and suffering, in particular, cause a loss of masculinity. Conversely, courage (*virtus*) is the hallmark of masculinity: military service institutionalizes Roman manliness. Furthermore, victory reinforces masculinity, while defeat emasculates (McDonnell 2006).

Reflecting on the state of the field, Holmes (2012) reiterates that the opposition between the biological body and its social constructions (as expressed in the sex/gender binary) is typical of modern discourses; it does not fit the antique mindset. Ancient texts present male and female bodies; these bodies display both masculine and feminine traits, which are sometimes fixed and sometimes malleable. There is a basis of either masculinity or femininity, but always with some possibility for fluidity and change. A paradigmatic example is the figure of the *kinaidos* (Greek) or *cinaedus* (Latin), a male person defined by a desire to be penetrated sexually. Such a desire, which is a determining feature of femininity, makes the *kinaidos/cinaedus* into a gender deviant (rather than a sexual deviant; deviance here is not based on sexual acts but on the performance of gender). This social figure—though perhaps nothing more than a rhetorical scarecrow (Winkler 1999)—betrays anxiety about a slippery, fragile masculinity. Classical texts, therefore, offer complex views of sexual difference, which fail to match modern categories. For Holmes, both Butler and Laqueur, despite using classical texts in opposite ways (the former to posit a genealogical continuity and the latter to assert a radical shift), integrate ancient literature in the project to deconstruct a binary (nature/culture) that is simply foreign to them.

Gender is also constructed alongside imperial ideology. Rome presents itself as an embodiment of triumphant masculinity; the emperor and other figures of authority are constructed as male, while conquered nations are feminized and infantilized. Augustan art, in particular, uses women and feminized men to represent submission to the victorious empire, which, in turn, is pictured as a family ruled by the paternal figure of the emperor (Ramsby and Severy-Hoven 2007). Both imperial propaganda and anxieties linked to imperial status contribute to the production of gender stereotypes. For example, the figure of the *tribas*—a Greek word designating a woman who desires to penetrate other women—betrays male elites' anxiety over losing their privileged status (Swancutt 2007). The *tribas*, as an androgynous monster, represents the threat that both Roman matrons (internal or proximate others) and Greeks (ethnic or imperial others) pose to Roman men; letting these others gain control is associated with the spread of this malformation. Gender is thus constructed in parallel with politics.

3. Gender in Scholarship on Early Judaism

This section presents different areas of study where scholarship on early Judaism has discussed gender: (1) status and roles of women, including epistemological questions on the use of texts; (2) constructions of gender; and (3) gender as structuring category, used to organize other discourses, such as textual authority, morality, and politics.

3.1. Status and Roles of Women

Tal Ilan (1995) traces the study of ancient Jewish women back to the late nineteenth century. Publications have generally focused on the status of women, often with an assessment of either its improvement or deterioration. Ilan highlights several biases displayed in these studies. One consists of a romanticization of a particular milieu—whether it be ancient Israel, antique Greece or Rome, or early Christianity. There is also a strong anti-Jewish bias in some studies claiming that Jesus and early Christianity improved women's conditions against an oppressive Jewish context; this prejudice has been denounced in several articles (e.g., Plaskow 1980, 1993; Heschel 1990). Other scholars have posited that the deterioration of female status in the Second Temple and rabbinic periods is due to Hellenism, often understood as a monolithic entity (Archer 1990; Wegner 1991). Ilan points to the influence, in the last three decades of the twentieth century, of theological feminist movements, within both Judaism (first in Reform movements, then in Conservative and Orthodox communities) and Christianity; in general, these studies have focused on canonical texts (e.g., Biale 1984; Schüssler Fiorenza 1994). Jacob Neusner's (1980) work on legal material in the Mishnah has been influential beyond rabbinic literature: a particular source's stance on women is not necessarily representative of its period, but is only indicative of its author's (or authors') views (for an application to Ben Sira, see Trenchard 1982). In concluding her overview, Ilan (1995, 6) expresses her reservations about the categories of "improvement" and "deterioration"; the historian should limit herself to describing developments, without rendering value judgments.

Subsequent to Ilan's overview, scholarship has discussed the presence of women in diverse early Jewish texts. Multiple studies have been devoted to women in the Dead Sea Scrolls (e.g., Schuller 1999, 2011; Crawford 2003; Wassen 2005; Regev 2008; Loader 2009; Ilan 2010, 2011; Bernstein 2013; Heger 2014; Grossman 2004, 2010, 2015). Although later evidence (Philo, Josephus, and Pliny the Elder) suggests that the Essene community was (at least in part) celibate, two sectarian texts include women as members of the sect. The Rule of the Congregation mentions the appropriate age for men to marry, with a stipulation that the wife "shall be received to bear witness about him [her husband]" (1 QSa I, 11); women's testimony is apparently accepted, likely in regard to their husbands' sexuality. The Damascus Document pertains to community members who marry and have children. Cecilia Wassen (2005) distinguishes two layers: an early law code (first part of the second century BCE), nonsectarian in nature, and a later collection of laws (second half of the same century), presupposing a sectarian setting. The early code, while strictly regulating sexuality, does not rule it out; it may even improve the conditions of women vis-à-vis biblical laws. The later legal collection refers to women infrequently; the leaders of the community exert considerable control over private lives (e.g., approval of marriages and divorces). The overall text strikes a strong patriarchal and androcentric pose. The Damascus Document may reveal tensions about gender roles. For example, a text states that "mothers" are denied any authoritative status (4Q270 I, 13–15); the very need to assert this may imply that some authority is, in fact, granted to these mothers (Grossman 2015).

Research has also been devoted to women in Josephus's works, both those in historiographic material (Ilan 1999, 2016; Van Henten 2010; Atkinson 2012; Liebowitz 2015) and in scriptural retelling (below). In general, Josephus's estimation of women is far from positive. In an alleged quotation of scripture (not present in any extant texts), he claims: "A woman is inferior to a man in all respects" (*C. Ap.* 2.201). Josephus mentions several women in the Hasmonean and Herodian courts. Among them, Queen Salome Alexandra (Shelamzion in Hebrew) is particularly significant; her husband, Alexander Jannaeus, confers the throne on her despite his having two sons. Alexandra is the only ruling queen of Judaea (76 to 67 BCE) and also its last independent ruler. In the *Bellum judaicum* (1.107–119), Alexandra is praised for her piety and skillful leadership. In the *Antiquitates judaicae*, however, she is "enraged in her love for power" (13.417); she is also attributed with deviant gender traits: she displays "none of the weaknesses of her sex" but rather "a desire of things that do not fit a woman" (13.430, 431). The difference may be due to a change in Josephus's own social climate, as women's political roles shrink between the Hellenistic and early Roman imperial period (Liebowitz 2015). Alexandra's age (sixty-four when she accedes to the throne) and her widowhood may have contributed to her unusual political involvement, as they freed her—to some extent—from male rule. The portrayal of Mariamme, wife of Herod, is likewise heavily gendered: "She had something both womanly and harsh, out of nature" (*A.J.* 15.219). When reporting her death, however, Josephus praises her as "a woman superior by her self-control and generosity" (*A.J.* 15.237). Josephus may be particularly severe about women's qualities that threaten male leadership (Liebowitz 2015). Salome, Herod's sister, is a dark character, seeking the death of both Mariamme and her two sons; in addition, she is also accused of sexually abusing her nephew, Alexander. Ilan notes that Josephus, surprisingly, does not append a diatribe when he reports Salome's death, perhaps an indication that he personally does not consider her guilty. In general, Ilan (1999, 2016) attributes the sections of Josephus's work devoted to women—especially those with a misogynistic stance—to a source allegedly written by the historian Nicolaus of Damascus. Since none of Nicolaus's works are extant, the hypothesis is hard to confirm.

Josephus's portrayals of biblical women have also been examined (Halpern-Amaru 1988; Brown 1992; Roncace 2000; Tervanotko 2016a; Ilan 2016, 2017). These studies often take the form of an assessment of women's status and its evolution. They tend to point out that Josephus reshapes scriptural women into more submissive figures—whereas Pseudo-Philo (Brown 1992; Tervanotko, 2016a) and Jubilees (Halpern-Amaru 1999) empower female characters. For Ilan (2017), by contrast, Josephus stays in line with the scriptures, deviating only when he is using external sources.

As for Philo, Maren Niehoff (2017) argues that his views of women transform during his three-year stay in Rome, as he heads the Jewish embassy to Gaius Caligula. In Alexandria, Philo is mainly influenced by Platonism, including in his perception of women. For example, in his *Legum allegoriae*, scriptural women are interpreted as allegories of the passive soul receiving the divine sperm. In Rome, Philo interacts with Stoic philosophers and develops more immanentist positions, more in touch with this world. For example, Philo praises Livia, Augustus's wife, who, he states, is superior to other women due to the wisdom that her husband imparted to her—although women's minds, Philo underscores, are weaker than men's (*Legat.* 319–320). Similarly, among scriptural women, Philo commends Sarah for her "most excellent soul" (*Abr.* 93) and her partnership with Abraham (*Abr.* 245–246). Philo is here likely influenced by the Roman ideal of marital friendship, a value that emerges in the early imperial period (Konstan 1994). Philo's perception of women thus evolves in line with his cultural context.

Different female characters in early Jewish literature have been the subjects of literary studies (e.g., Levine 1991; Kraemer 1998; Stocker 1998; Hancock 2013; Calduch-Benages and Maier 2014; Tervanotko 2016a, 2016b; Schuller and Wacker 2017). Different recensions of a given text have also been compared in regard to the roles of women. For example, the short text of Joseph and Aseneth presents a more active depiction of its main female protagonist than the corresponding long version, where Aseneth is portrayed as arrogant and misandrist (Standhartinger 2012).

Multiple studies have examined institutions and norms regulating different aspects of women's lives, such as childhood and education (Lieber 2012), submission to paternal authority (Ilan 1995; Berquist 1998; Balla 2011; Beentjes 2013), marriage (Ilan 1995; Zlotnick 2002, 76–102; D'Angelo 2014), and widowhood (Balla 2011). Rebecca Hancock (2013) argues that it is anachronistic to posit a strict binary relationship between the domestic/private realm, occupied by women, and the political sphere, where men are active. Both men and women gain (or lose) authority through familial relationships. Kinship is "the central metaphor that governed political discourse" (Hancock 2013, 47). The book of Esther, as well as Greek and Persian parallels, calls for a more fluid model of gendered space, where power is negotiated in diverse loci (such as family, occupation, location, and so on).

Archaeology offers invaluable resources on gender—provided that attention is given to the right material (Meyers 2003). Excavations at Qumran, in particular, have yielded evidence suggesting that women likely lived in the settlement; women's and children's bones, as well as some gender-specific objects, have been found at the site (Magness 2004; Galor 2010). Papyri (Ilan 1999, 217–33, 253–62) and epigraphy (Brooten 1982, 2000; Kraemer 2011, 179–241; Lieber 2012) also contribute to illuminating women's social roles. A few inscriptions mention female names together with titles indicating prominence, for example, leader of the synagogue (*archisynagōgos*), member of the council of elders, mother, and donor. Some women who financially contributed to the construction of synagogues were converts. Others may not have been Jewish; a Phrygian inscription (Lifshitz 1967, no. 33), for example, commemorates a certain Julia Severa who was a high priestess of the imperial cult (Lieber 2012).

Ilan warns that sources, as they are mostly produced by and for elite men, do not necessarily give an accurate view of the actual living conditions of women; authors, rather, present and impose their own views. Stereotypes and generalizations are to be expected. Ultimately, however, Ilan maintains confidence that the texts, if correctly interpreted, can provide reliable information on the history of women (Ilan 1995, 41–42; see also Zlotnick 2002; Tervanotko 2016a). For Ross Kraemer (2011, 6), by contrast, texts are "unreliable witnesses": authors promulgate ideas about gender that serve their own interests and only mention women when they are of concern to men. Women's voices are appropriated by male authors and thus are rendered practically inaudible. The most that a historian can do is to write a history of gender—in its different constructions—while using caution not to reproduce dominant discourses.

This debate finds a paradigmatic expression in the study of Philo's portrayal of the Therapeutae, in his *De vita contemplativa*. The Therapeutae are presented as a community of men and women living in seclusion outside of Alexandria and devoting themselves to spiritual and intellectual activities. One strand of scholarship (Taylor 2003, 2017) holds that Philo's account has some historical basis. Since he aims at demonstrating that contemplative life does exist within Judaism, a purely fictional depiction would have defeated his purpose—especially since the location of the community is easily verifiable. The presence of female Therapeutae also goes against Philo's mostly negative perception of women. Other scholars (esp. Kraemer 2011, 57–116; see also Goldberg 2008), however, doubt that Philo's Therapeutae have much to do with historical facts, as no supporting external literary or archaeological evidence has been found. In addition, Philo's description fits his philosophical ideals too closely to be realistic (Engberg-Pedersen 1999). Biblical quotations (Exod 15; Gen 1–3) may also suggest that the Therapeutae represent a form of reconciled humankind, existing before its division into males and females. Rather than providing a window into the lives of ancient Jews, therefore, the text, as it is read here, documents Philo's ideals about gender.

These two views—on one hand, that texts transmit information on women's lives; on the other hand, that they only propagate dominant discourses—rely in fact on a similar opposition between discourses and practices. If gender is a performance, however, then *both* the actual practices of ancient women and the overwhelmingly male voice in texts are iterations of the same discourse. There is no outside to the discourse, and thus no reason to strictly dissociate scripts and experiences. Discourses and practices are engaged in a two-way relationship: discourses, in their pervasiveness, shape every practice; conversely, these discourses only exist through their embodied enactments, whether these are faithful or transgressive.

3.2. Constructions of Gender, Femininities, and Masculinities

Studies have started to explore constructions of gender in early Jewish literature; they aim to better understand ancient authors' conceptions of femininity and masculinity. Scholars tend to accept that Jewish authors from the Hellenistic and Roman periods assume the Greek and Roman model of gender (Burrus 2006; however, Ellis 2013 claims that Ben Sira counters this model).

Although there is no concept of gender per se in Philo (or in contemporaneous literature), femininity and masculinity pervade his work (Baer 1970; Sly 1990; Mattila 1996; Van den Hoek 2000; Conway 2003). Gender is here understood as a spectrum ranging from a perfect and active masculinity to an imperfect and passive femininity (Mattila 1996; Conway 2003; Neutel and Anderson 2014). In this vein, Philo notes that the Passover lamb must be male since "male is more perfect than female—it is said by naturalists that the female is nothing else than an imperfect male" (*QE* 1.7). Superiority of the male is thus naturalized, alongside its capacity for domination (*Spec.* 1.200). For Philo, "female is a non-category apart from its definition as imperfect male" (Conway 2003, 475). Gender, for Philo, is fluid; men's love for other men, for example, causes a "female disease" that makes men androgynous (*Contempl.* 60; see also *Spec.* 3.37–38; *Abr.* 135–136). Conversely, a woman usurping the penetrating role of men becomes a *gynandros*—the female counterpart of "androgyne" (Szesnat 1998, 1999).

Although Philo's use of gender is in line with his contemporaries', he disagrees with them on circumcision. In the Hellenistic and Roman world, the foreskin is associated with self-control and functions as an important attribute of masculinity. Circumcision, therefore, tends to be mocked; in addition, denigration of circumcised Jews contributes to stigmatizing barbarians as effeminate and lustful. Philo, however, turns circumcision into a symbol of the extraction of pleasures (*QG* 3.48) and defends the practice with the very arguments that Romans use against it (Neutel and Anderson 2014, 237). Explaining why only males are circumcised, Philo performs a curious inversion of male and female stereotypes: "The male creature feels venereal pleasures and desires matrimonial connections more than the female" (*QG* 3.47); he is perhaps implying that control of the passions is essentially a male business. More generally, Philo's sexual morality both absorbs and emulates Roman norms. Philo emphasizes diverse sexual prohibitions (pederasty, adultery, rape of children, prostitution, and sexual acts shameful for one's age) and claims that they incur the death penalty (*Hypoth.* 7.1; see also *Decal.* 121–131). These proscriptions, revolving around marital chastity and devotion to procreation, are very similar to Julian laws, if not more stringent (D'Angelo 2006).

Josephus relies on a comparable model of gender, although one more explicitly colored by politics (Mason 2007; Ehrenkrook 2011; Reeder 2015). His main purpose is to reassert the masculinity of the Jewish people despite their defeat by the Romans. Josephus draws upon Roman ideals of manliness—especially that of the courageous warrior—and applies them to the Jewish people. Models of manliness include the Hasmonean rulers, Antipater and his sons, as well as the Essene community (*B.J.* 2.119–161), which Josephus portrays as an embodiment of Spartan practices (Mason 2007). The Jewish troops also demonstrate manliness in their tenacious fight and willingness to die rather than surrender. As for Jewish women, Josephus casts them as extremely feminine and uninvolved in warfare: women's femininity is meant to increase, by way of contrast, men's masculinity (Reeder 2015). Defeat is blamed on rebellious factions, characterized by their gender deviance. Josephus, in particular, accuses his rival John of Gischala not only of tyranny but also of effeminacy (*B.J.* 4.560–563). John and his men, although they abuse women, also take pleasure in being sexually penetrated and in cross-dressing. The connection between tyranny and gender deviance is well attested in the early Flavian period. Sources convey "the capacity of effeminate emperors and other political figures to emasculate the state, as it were, to weaken, and ultimately endanger, Roman hegemony" (Ehrenkrook 2011, 159). Josephus assimilates this ideology: the rebels' transgressions prefigure the city's penetration and destruction by the Roman army; their effeminacy has spread, so to speak, to the people as a whole.

In general, early Jewish sources exhibit a fluid conception of gender. For example, the novel Joseph and Aseneth depicts several gender reversals, affecting both female and male characters. The heavenly man declares to Aseneth that she is a "pure virgin" and that her head is like that of a "young man" (15.1). Conversely, male characters refuse to "die like a woman" (24.7; 25.8). Gender roles, therefore, are at once encoded and blurred (Standhartinger 2017). Gender also affects the emotions both rejected and favored by the novel (Mermelstein 2017). Likewise, in the Testament of Job, the protagonist, consumed by suffering, compares himself to a woman: "I was exhausted, as a woman numbed in her pelvic region by the magnitude of birth pangs" (18.4). His body has lost its integrity: "My body was eaten by worms and discharges from my body were wetting the ground with moisture" (20.8). The body in pain, by its inability to retain its fluids, decreases in masculinity. Poverty, disease, and disability are thus integral to the marking of gender.

3.3. Gender as Structuring Category

Gender has been recognized by feminist theorists as a powerful tool for structuring other domains of human experience (see §1 of this essay). Scholarship on early Judaism has distinguished several ways in which gender and its categories organize varied (and overlapping) discourses, in particular those dealing with other aspects of human (and divine) beings, but also with textual authority, morality, and, more broadly, politics and empire.

Philo pervasively uses the category of gender to express notions that similarly assume a dynamic and hierarchical range (Mattila 1996; Conway 2003). Virtues (*Fug.* 51) are associated with masculinity; unformed and passive matter (*QG* 3.3), pleasure, and passions (*Leg.* 2.74; 3.68) are all associated with femininity. A gradient of masculinity is applied to the soul: "The rational part [of the soul] belongs to the male sex, being the inheritance of intellect and reason, but the irrational part belongs to the sex of woman, which is the lot also of the outward senses" (*Spec.* 1.201). The superiority of man over woman is comparable to the superiority of the mind over the senses, which it must always control (*Leg.* 3.222–224). The gender of Wisdom is more complex: it is female in relation to God, but male in relation to humanity. Conway (2003) argues that Philo's conception of divinity is likewise informed by gender; it displays a similar scale, composed of beings that are more or less divine or human. This hierarchy presents a fluidity comparable to that of gender: It was possible for a human to become closer to divine status, as the case of the emperor illustrates in the Roman world. Although Philo resists this deification of human beings (*Legat.* 118), he bestows on Moses a quasi-divine status: Moses "was called the god and king of the whole nation, and he is said to have entered into the darkness where God was…; he established himself as a most beautiful and godlike work" (*Mos.* 1.158). For Conway (2003), this proximity to divine standing is commended to Moses through his perfect masculinity (*Mos.* 1.1). Indeed, divinity is equated with the highest ideal of masculinity (*Fug.* 51). "The transcendent God may even be said to be more 'male' than 'male,' or 'ultramale'" (Mattila 1996, 126; against Baer 1970, 19).

Camp's (2013) study of the book of Sirach examines this instrumental use of gender. She argues that the consciousness of an emerging canon of authoritative texts is constructed as a gendered phenomenon, as both women and texts are appropriated as objects of a male desire for possession. Sirach displays considerable anxiety about women: their shame threatens male honor, and they must be kept in check, because of their uncontrollable desire and wild sexuality. Camp also discerns anxiety about the deity (and thus about texts that transmit the divine voice), especially in regard to moral accountability. The identification of Torah with the personified female figure of Wisdom addresses both sources of anxiety. By depicting the literary "body" as female, the author (Ben Sira) constructs the text as an object not only of heteroerotic desire (also Angel 2007), but also of possession and control. Since Ben Sira presents his own book as authoritative, he pictures himself as contributing to the production of this female body of divine texts, in an ultimate attempt to control and appropriate both women and divinity.

Morality is highly gendered in early Jewish literature. Virtues, as noted above in regard to Philo, are generally male. When a female character trait, such as patience, starts being hailed as a virtue, it tends to become male, as illustrated in 4 Maccabees (Shaw 1996). Sin is also colored by gender, especially as Eve is blamed for bringing sin into the world (Araujo 2017). Sirach states, "From a woman is the beginning of sin, and because of her we all die" (Sir 25:24); the text thus binds femininity, sin, and death together. In 4Q184 (4QWiles of the Wicked Women), a wicked woman, associated with the underworld, embodies sinful ways of life and leads men to their death (Goff 2008). In the Slavonic book of Enoch, the deity declares: "And I created for him a wife, so that death might come by his wife" (2 En. 30.10). Eve, by her very presence, elicits male free will; this role makes her responsible for sin and mortality. In the Sibylline Oracles, Eve is described as a betrayer (1.42), as she convinces an ignorant Adam to sin. The Greek Life of Adam and Eve intertwines two etiologies of sin, one based on Eve's culpability and another relying on the fallen angels' intercourse with women. This combination of discourses explains the identification of both Eve and the serpent with Satan; it also eases the association between sin and sexuality (Arbel 2012). Eve, by her sin, brings death not merely to Adam (Greek LAE 7.1) but to all humankind (14.2). At the same time, the Life of Adam and Eve exonerates Eve to a certain extent (17.1–2; chs. 31–42); her portrait thus includes both guilt and exemption (Levison 2000; Anderson 2004). However, the underlying discourse about gender remains unequivocal: sin is associated with the transgression of male authority (Arbel 2012).

The Testaments of the Twelve Patriarchs likewise associate femininity with sinfulness (Rosen-Zvi 2006). The Testament of Reuben expands the scriptural episode of Reuben's sexual intercourse with Bilhah (Gen 35:22); Bilhah, here naked and drunk (T. Reu. 3.11–15), is transformed into a temptress. The text emphasizes women's dangerousness: "Evil are women, my children" (5.1). In its interpretation of the Watchers myth (5.6–7), the Testament of Reuben likewise transforms the victims—the daughters of men—into the instigators of the transgression (Bachmann 2017). In both passages, women are "bringing upon themselves the male gaze," which is presented "as the women's own fault" (Rosen-Zvi 2006, 75). In this conception of gender, women elicit men's sexual desire; men, through an inner struggle, have to control this evil desire. This desire, *porneia*, is sent by Beliar and can be overcome only with divine help, in a kind of cosmic struggle raging inside the pious male. Sex therefore shifts "from an inter- to intra-personal issue" (Rosen-Zvi 2006, 92); sex becomes a matter of the (male) mind.

While gender stands at the core of Roman propaganda (see §1 of this essay), it also figures prominently in the Jewish response, which directly addresses the feminization of the conquered. Female characters, in early Jewish literature, often embody political weakness, while their unexpected rise to authority provides a symbolic sense of empowerment for the minority (esp. in Esther; Reinhartz 2017). Even more explicitly, oppressed female figures are masculinized through controlling their emotions. The martyred mother in 4 Maccabees and Mary in Josephus's *Bellum judaicum* (6.199–219) resist their maternal affection: The former encourages her seven sons to embrace martyrdom, while the latter roasts and eats her own baby in an act of defiance against both city guards and imperial power. Masculinity, in these two texts, is vicariously regained through self-control (Moore and Anderson 1998; Dijkhuizen 2008; Mirguet 2017). These texts present, to a minority that has been forcibly feminized, the possibility of a remasculinization—not in the political sphere, but through the control of the self. Interiority thus provides an alternative arena to restore a compromised masculinity. Gender, therefore, is intrinsic to the discourse and imagination of both the imperial power and the Jewish minority; its flexibility makes it not only a convenient tool for domination, but also—once internalized—a space for self-empowerment.

This last section illustrates the inseparability of gender vis-à-vis other notions, such as morality, power, and politics. The imperial context shapes early Jewish conceptions of gender considerably, not only through the pervasiveness of Roman ideology, but also because gender, as a hierarchical notion, necessarily intertwines with political discourses. Imperial hegemony deploys gender to assert itself and favor the internalization of its own rule; Jewish elites manipulate the same codes to defend their manliness. The development of interiority as a substitute—or even superior—area for cultivating agency grants gender new potentialities. Achieving, maintaining, and restoring masculinity, for late antique Jewish men, was not only a matter of bodily practices and military prowess, but also an internal undertaking, involving the pursuit of virtue and the control of emotions. Future research may further explore the intersection of gender with other aspects of human experience.

Bibliography

Anderson, Gary A. 2004. "The Culpability of Eve: From Genesis to Timothy." Pages 233–51 in *From Prophecy to Testament: The Function of the*

Old Testament in the New. Edited by Craig A. Evans. Peabody, MA: Hendrickson.

Angel, Andrew. 2007. "From Wild Men to Wise and Wicked Women: An Investigation into Male Heterosexuality in Second Temple Interpretations of the Ladies Wisdom and Folly." Pages 145–61 in *A Question of Sex? Gender and Difference in the Hebrew Bible and beyond*. Edited by Deborah W. Rooke. HBM 14. Sheffield: Sheffield Phoenix.

Araujo, Magdalena Díaz. 2017. "The Sins of the First Woman: Eve Traditions in Second Temple Literature with Special Regard to the Life of Adam and Eve." Pages 91–112 in *Early Jewish Writings*. Edited by Eileen Schuller and Marie-Theres Wacker. BW 3.1. Atlanta: SBL Press.

Arbel, Vita Daphna. 2012. *Forming Femininity in Antiquity: Eve, Gender, and Ideologies in the Greek Life of Adam and Eve*. Oxford: Oxford University Press.

Archer, Léonie J. 1990. *Her Price Is beyond Rubies: The Jewish Woman in Graeco-Roman Palestine*. JSOTSup 60. Sheffield: JSOT Press.

Atkinson, Kenneth. 2012. *Queen Salome: Jerusalem's Warrior Monarch of the First Century B.C.E.* Jefferson, NC: McFarland.

Bachmann, Veronika. 2017. "Illicit Male Desire or Illicit Female Seduction? A Comparison of the Ancient Retellings of the Account of the 'Sons of God' Mingling with the 'Daughters of Men' (Gen 6:14)." Pages 113–41 in *Early Jewish Writings*. Edited by Eileen Schuller and Marie-Theres Wacker. BW 3.1. Atlanta: SBL Press.

Baer, Richard A. 1970. *Philo's Use of the Categories Male and Female*. ALGHJ 3. Leiden: Brill.

Balla, Ibolya. 2011. *Ben Sira on Family, Gender, and Sexuality*. DCLS 8. Berlin: de Gruyter.

Beentjes, Pancratius C. 2013. "Daughters and Their Father(s) in the Book of Ben Sira." Pages 183–201 in *Family and Kinship in the Deuterocanonical and Cognate Literature*. Edited by Angelo Passaro. Berlin: de Gruyter.

Bernstein, Moshe J. 2013. "Women and Children in Legal and Liturgical Texts from Qumran." Pages 614–34 in *Reading and Re-reading Scripture at Qumran*. Edited by Moshe Bernstein. JSJSup 107. 2 vols. Leiden: Brill.

Berquist, Jon L. 1998. "Controlling Daughters' Bodies in Sirach." Pages 95–120 in *Parchments of Gender: Deciphering Bodies of Antiquity*. Edited by Maria Wyke. Oxford: Oxford University Press.

Biale, Rachel. 1984. *Women and Jewish Law: An Exploration of Women's Issues in Halakhic Sources.* New York: Schocken Books.

Bourdieu, Pierre. 1998. *La domination masculine.* Paris: Seuil.

———. 2001. *Masculine Domination.* Translated by R. Nice. Stanford: Stanford University Press.

Brooten, Bernadette J. 1982. *Women Leaders in the Ancient Synagogue: Inscriptional Evidence and Background Issues.* BJS 36. Chico, CA: Scholars Press.

———. 2000. "Female Leadership in the Ancient Synagogue." Pages 215–23 in *From Dura to Sepphoris: Studies in Jewish Art and Society in Late Antiquity.* Edited by Lee I. Levine and Zeev Weiss. JRASup 40. Portsmouth, RI: Journal of Roman Archeology.

Brown, Cheryl Anne. 1992. *No Longer Be Silent: First-Century Jewish Portraits of Biblical Women.* Gender and the Biblical Tradition. Louisville: Westminster John Knox.

Burrus, Virginia. 2006. "Mapping as Metamorphosis: Initial Reflections on Gender and Ancient Religious Discourses." Pages 1–10 in *Mapping Gender in Ancient Religious Discourses.* Edited by Todd Penner and Caroline Vander Stichele. BibInt 84. Leiden: Brill.

Butler, Judith. 1990. *Gender Trouble: Feminism and the Subversion of Identity.* New York: Routledge.

———. 1993. *Bodies That Matter: On the Discursive Limits of "Sex."* New York: Routledge.

Calduch-Benages, Núria, and Christl M. Maier, eds. 2014. *The Writings and Later Wisdom Books.* BW 1.3. Atlanta: SBL Press.

Camp, Claudia V. 2013. *Ben Sira and the Men Who Handle Books: Gender and the Rise of Canon-Consciousness.* HBM 50. Sheffield: Sheffield Phoenix.

Cawthorn, Katrina. 2008. *Becoming Female: The Male Body in Greek Tragedy.* London: Duckworth.

Conway, Colleen. 2003. "Gender and Divine Relativity in Philo of Alexandria." *JSJ* 34:471–91.

Crawford, Sidnie White. 2003. "Not according to Rule: Women, the Dead Sea Scrolls and Qumran." Pages 127–150 in *Emanuel: Studies in Hebrew Bible, Septuagint, and Dead Sea Scrolls in Honor of Emanuel Tov.* Edited by Shalom M. Paul, Robert A. Kraft, Lawrence H. Schiffman, and Weston W. Fields. VTSup 94. Leiden: Brill.

D'Angelo, Mary Rose. 2006. "Gender and Geopolitics in the Work of Philo of Alexandria: Jewish Piety and Imperial Family Values." Pages 63–88 in *Mapping Gender in Ancient Religious Discourses*. Edited by Todd Penner and Caroline Vander Stichele. BibInt 84. Leiden: Brill.

———. 2014. "Sexuality in Jewish Writings from 200 BCE to 200 CE." Pages 534–48 in *A Companion to Greek and Roman Sexualities*. Edited by Thomas K. Hubbard. BCAW. Chichester: Wiley Blackwell.

Dijkhuizen, Pieternella. 2008. "Pain, Endurance and Gender in 4 Maccabees." *JSem* 17:57–76.

Ehrenkrook, Jason von. 2011. "Effeminacy in the Shadow of Empire: The Politics of Transgressive Gender in Josephus's *Bellum Judaicum*." *JQR* 101:145–63.

Ellis, Teresa Ann. 2013. *Gender in the Book of Ben Sira: Divine Wisdom, Erotic Poetry, and the Garden of Eden*. BZAW 453. Berlin: de Gruyter.

Engberg-Pedersen, Troels. 1999. "Philo's *De Vita Contemplativa* as a Philosopher's Dream." *JSJ* 30:40–64.

Fausto-Sterling, Anne. 2000. *Sexing the Body: Gender Politics and the Construction of Sexuality*. New York: Basic Books.

Fiorenza, Elisabeth Schüssler. 1994. *In Memory of Her: A Feminist Theological Reconstruction of Christian Origins*. New York: Crossroad.

Frost, Samantha. 2011. "The Implications of New Materialisms for Feminist Epistemology." Pages 69–83 in *Feminist Epistemology and Philosophy of Science: Power in Knowledge*. Edited by Heidi E. Grasswick. Dordrecht: Springer.

Galor, Katharina. 2010. "Gender and Qumran." Pages 29–38 in *Holistic Qumran: Transdisciplinary Research of Qumran and the Dead Sea Scrolls*. Edited by Jan Gunneweg, Annemie Adriaens, and Joris Dik. STDJ 87. Leiden: Brill.

Goff, Matthew. 2008. "Hellish Females: The Strange Woman of Septuagint Proverbs and 4QWiles of the Wicked Woman (4Q184)." *JSJ* 39:20–45.

Goldberg, Shari. 2008. "The Two Choruses Become One: The Absence/Presence of Women in Philo's 'On the Contemplative Life.'" *JSJ* 39:459–70.

Grossman, Maxine L. 2004. "Reading for Gender in the Damascus Document." *DSD* 11/2:212–39.

———. 2010. "Women and Men in the Rule of the Congregation: A Feminist Critical Assessment." Pages 229–45 in *Rethinking the Dead Sea Scrolls: An Assessment of Old and New Methods and Approaches*. Edited by Maxine L. Grossman. Grand Rapids: Eerdmans.

———. 2015. "Gendered Sectarians: Envisioning Women (and Men) at Qumran." Pages 265–88 in *Celebrate Her for the Fruit of Her Hands:*

Essays in Honor of Carol L. Meyers. Edited by Susan Ackerman, Charles E. Carter, Beth Alpert Nakhai. Winona Lake, IN: Eisenbrauns.

Grosz, Elizabeth. 1994. *Volatile Bodies: Toward a Corporeal Feminism*. Theories of Representation and Difference. Bloomington: Indiana University Press.

Hallett, Judith P., and Marilyn B. Skinner, eds. 1997. *Roman Sexualities*. Princeton: Princeton University Press.

Halperin, David M., John J. Winkler, and Froma I. Zeitlin, eds. 1990. *Before Sexuality: The Construction of Erotic Experience in the Ancient Greek World*. Princeton: Princeton University Press.

Halpern-Amaru, Betsy. 1988. "Portraits of Biblical Women in Josephus' *Antiquities*." *JJS* 39:143–70.

———. 1999. *The Empowerment of Women in the Book of Jubilees*. JSJSup 60. Leiden: Brill.

Hancock, Rebecca S. 2013. *Esther and the Politics of Negotiation: Public and Private Spaces and the Figure of the Female Royal Counselor*. Emerging Scholars. Minneapolis: Fortress.

Heger, Paul. 2014. *Women in the Bible, Qumran, and Early Rabbinic Literature: Their Status and Roles*. STDJ 110. Leiden: Brill.

Henten, Jan Willem van. 2010. "Blaming the Women: Women at Herod's Court in Josephus's *Jewish Antiquities* 15.23–231." Pages 153–75 in *Women and Gender in Ancient Religions: Interdisciplinary Approaches*. Edited by Steven P. Ahearne-Kroll, Paul A. Holloway, and James A. Kelhoffer. WUNT 263. Tübingen: Mohr Siebeck.

Heschel, Susannah. 1990. "Anti-Judaism in Christian Feminist Theology." *Tikkun* 5:25–28, 95–97.

Hoek, Annewies van den. 2000. "Endowed with Reason or Glued to the Senses: Philo's Thoughts on Adam and Eve." Pages 63–75 in *The Creation of Man and Woman: Interpretations of the Biblical Narratives in Jewish and Christian Traditions*. Edited by Gerard P. Luttikhuizen. TBN 3. Leiden: Brill.

Holmes, Brooke. 2012. *Gender: Antiquity and Its Legacy*. Ancient and Modern Series. Oxford: Oxford University Press.

Ilan, Tal. 1995. *Jewish Women in Greco-Roman Palestine: An Inquiry into Image and Status*. TSAJ 44. Tübingen: Mohr Siebeck.

———. 1999. *Integrating Women into Second Temple History*. TSAJ 76. Tübingen: Mohr Siebeck.

———. 2010. "Women in Qumran and the Dead Sea Scrolls." Pages 123–47 in *The Oxford Handbook of the Dead Sea Scrolls*. Edited by Timothy H. Lim and John J. Collins. Oxford: Oxford University Press.

———. 2011. "Reading for Women in 1QSa (Serekh Ha-Edah)." Pages 61–76 in vol. 1 of *The Dead Sea Scrolls in Context: Integrating the Dead Sea Scrolls in the Study of Ancient Texts, Languages, and Cultures*. 2 vols. Edited by Armin Lange, Emanuel Tov, Matthias Weingold. VTSup 140. Leiden: Brill.

———. 2016. "Josephus on Women." Pages 210–21 in *A Companion to Josephus*. Edited by Honora Howell Chapman and Zuleika Rodgers. BCAW. Chichester: Wiley Blackwell.

———. 2017. "Flavius Josephus and Biblical Women." Pages 167–85 in *Early Jewish Writings*. Edited by Eileen Schuller and Marie-Theres Wacker. BW 3.1. Atlanta: SBL Press.

Konstan, David. 1994. *Sexual Symmetry: Love in the Ancient Novel and Related Genres*. Princeton: Princeton University Press.

Kraemer, Ross S. 1998. *When Aseneth Met Joseph: A Late Antique Tale of the Biblical Patriarch and His Egyptian Wife, Reconsidered*. New York: Oxford University Press.

———. 2011. *Unreliable Witnesses: Religion, Gender, and History in the Greco-Roman Mediterranean*. New York: Oxford University Press.

Laqueur, Thomas. 1990. *Making Sex: Body and Gender from the Greeks to Freud*. Cambridge: Harvard University Press.

Levine, Amy-Jill, ed. 1991. *"Women Like This": New Perspectives on Jewish Women in the Greco-Roman World*. EJL 1. Atlanta: Scholars Press.

Levison, John R. 2000. "The Exoneration and Denigration of Eve in the Greek Life of Adam and Eve." Pages 251–75 in *Literature on Adam and Eve: Collected Essays*. Edited by Gary A. Anderson, Michael E. Stone, and Johannes Tromp. SVTP 15. Leiden: Brill.

Lieber, Laura S. 2012. "Jewish Women: Texts and Contexts." Pages 329–42 in *A Companion to Women in the Ancient World*. Edited by Sharon L. James and Sheila Dillon. BCAW Malden, MA: Blackwell.

Liebowitz, Etka. 2015. "Josephus's Ambivalent Attitude towards Women and Power: The Case of Queen Alexandra." *JAJ* 6:182–205.

Lifshitz, Baruch. 1967. *Donateurs et fondateurs dans les synagogues juives: Répertoire des dédicaces grecques relatives à la construction et à la réfection des synagogues*. Paris: Gabalda.

Loader, William. 2009. *The Dead Sea Scrolls on Sexuality: Attitudes Towards Sexuality in Sectarian and Related Literature at Qumran*. Grand Rapids: Eerdmans.

Magness, Jodi. 2004. "Women at Qumran?" Pages 113–49 in *Debating Qumran: Collected Essays on Its Archaeology*. Edited by Jodi Magness. Interdisciplinary Studies in Ancient Culture and Religion 4. Leuven: Peeters.

Mason, Steve. 2007. "Essenes and Lurking Spartans in Josephus' *Judean War*: From Story to History." Pages 219–61 *Making History: Josephus and Historical Method*. Edited by Zuleika Rodgers. JSJSup 110. Leiden: Brill.

Mattila, Sharon L. 1996. "Wisdom, Sense Perception, Nature, and Philo's Gender Gradient." *HTR* 89:103–29.

McDonnell, Myles A. 2006. *Roman Manliness: Virtus and the Roman Republic*. Cambridge: Cambridge University Press.

Mermelstein, Ari. 2017. "Emotion, Gender, and Greco-Roman Virtue in Joseph and Aseneth." *JSJ* 48:331–62.

Meyers, Carol L. 2003. "Engendering Syro-Palestinian Archaeology: Reasons and Resources." *NEA* 66:185–97.

Mirguet, Françoise. 2017. *An Early History of Compassion: Emotion and Imagination in Hellenistic Judaism*. Cambridge: Cambridge University Press.

Moore, Stephen D., and Janice Capel Anderson. 1998. "Taking It Like a Man: Masculinity in 4 Maccabees." *JBL* 117:249–73.

Neutel, Karin B., and Matthew R. Anderson. 2014. "The First Cut Is the Deepest: Masculinity and Circumcision in the First Century." Pages 228–44 in *Biblical Masculinities Foregrounded*. Edited by Ovidiu Creangă and Peter-Ben Smit. HBM 62. Sheffield: Sheffield Phoenix.

Neusner, Jacob. 1980. *A History of the Mishnaic Law of Women*. SJLA 33. 5 vols. Leiden: Brill.

Niehoff, Maren. 2017. "Between Social Context and Individual Ideology: Philo's Changing Views of Women." Pages 187–203 in *Early Jewish Writings*. Edited by Eileen Schuller and Marie-Theres Wacker. BW 3.1. Atlanta: SBL Press.

Plaskow, Judith. 1980. "Blaming the Jews for Inventing Patriarchy." *Lilith* 7:11–12.

———. 1993. "Anti-Judaism in Feminist Christian Interpretation." Pages 117–30 in *A Feminist Introduction*. Vol. 1 of *Searching the Scriptures*. Edited by Elisabeth Schüssler Fiorenza and Shelly Matthews. New York: Crossroad.

Ramsby, Teresa R., and Beth Severy-Hoven. 2007. "Gender, Sex, and the Domestication of the Empire in Art of the Augustan Age." *Arethusa* 40:43–71.

Reeder, Caryn A. 2015. "Gender, War, and Josephus." *JSJ* 46:65–85.
Regev, Eyal. 2008. "Cherchez les femmes: Were the *yaḥad* Celibates?" *DSD* 15:253–84.
Reinhartz, Adele. 2017. "LXX Esther: A Hellenistic Jewish Revenge Fantasy." Pages 9–28 in *Early Jewish Writings*. Edited by Eileen Schuller and Marie-Theres Wacker. BW 3.1. Atlanta: SBL Press.
Roncace, Mark. 2000. "Josephus' (Real) Portraits of Deborah and Gideon: A Reading of *Antiquities* 5.198–232." *JSJ* 31:247–74.
Rosen-Zvi, Ishay. 2006. "Bilhah the Temptress: The Testament of Reuben and 'The Birth of Sexuality.'" *JQR* 96:65–94.
Schuller, Eileen M. 1999. "Women at Qumran." Pages 117–44 in vol. 2 of *The Dead Sea Scrolls after Fifty Years: A Comprehensive Assessment*. Edited by Peter W. Flint, James C. VanderKam. 2 vols. Leiden: Brill.
———. 2011. "Women in the Dead Sea Scrolls: Research in the Past Decade and Future Directions." Pages 571–88 in *The Dead Sea Scrolls and Contemporary Culture: Proceedings of the International Conference Held at the Israel Museum, Jerusalem (July 6–8, 2008)*. Edited by Adolfo D. Roitman, Lawrence H. Schiffman, and Shani Tzoref. STDJ 93. Leiden: Brill.
Schuller, Eileen, and Marie-Theres Wacker, eds. 2017. *Early Jewish Writings*. BW 3.1. Atlanta: SBL Press.
Scott, Joan Wallach. 1986. "Gender: A Useful Category of Historical Analysis." *American Historical Review* 91:1053–75.
Shaw, Brent D. 1996. "Body/Power/Identity: Passions of the Martyrs." *JECS* 4:269–312.
Sly, Dorothy. 1990. *Philo's Perceptions of Women*. BJS 209. Atlanta: Scholars Press.
Standhartinger, Angela. 2012. "Joseph and Aseneth: Perfect Bride or Heavenly Prophetess." Pages 578–85 in *Feminist Biblical Interpretation: A Compendium of Critical Commentary on the Books of the Bible and Related Literature*. Edited by Liuse Schottroff and Marie-Theres Wacker. Translated by Lisa E. Dahill et al. Grand Rapids: Eerdmans.
———. 2017. "Intersections of Gender, Status, Ethnos, and Religion in Joseph and Aseneth." Pages 69–87 in *Early Jewish Writings*. Edited by Eileen Schuller and Marie-Theres Wacker. BW 3.1. Atlanta: SBL Press.
Stocker, Margarita. 1998. *Judith: Sexual Warrior; Women and Power in Western Culture*. New Haven: Yale University Press.
Swancutt, Diana M. 2007. "*Still* before Sexuality: 'Greek' Androgyny, the Roman Imperial Politics of Masculinity and the Roman Invention of

the *Tribas*." Pages 11–61 in *Mapping Gender in Ancient Religious Discourses*. Edited by Todd Penner and Caroline Vander Stichele. BibInt 84. Leiden: Brill.

Szesnat, Holger. 1998. "'Pretty Boys' in Philo's *De Vita Contemplativa*." *SPhilo* 10:87–107.

———. 1999. "Philo and Female Homoeroticism: Philo's Use of γύνανδρος and Recent Work on 'Tribades.'" *JSJ* 30:140–47.

Taylor, Joan E. 2003. *Jewish Women Philosophers of First-Century Alexandria: Philo's 'Therapeutae' Reconsidered*. Oxford: Oxford University Press.

———. 2017. "Real Women and Literary Airbrushing: The Women 'Therapeutae' of Philo's *De vita contemplativa* and the Identity of the Group." Pages 205–23 in *Early Jewish Writings*. Edited by Eileen Schuller and Marie-Theres Wacker. BW 3.1. Atlanta: SBL Press.

Tervanotko, Hanna. 2016a. *Denying Her Voice: The Figure of Miriam in Ancient Jewish Literature*. JAJSup 23. Göttingen: Vandenhoeck & Ruprecht.

———. 2016b. "Unreliability and Gender: Untrusted Female Prophets in Ancient Greek and Jewish Texts." *JAJ* 6:358–81.

Trenchard, Warren C. 1982. *Ben Sira's View of Women: A Literary Analysis*. BJS 38. Chico, CA: Scholars Press.

Wassen, Cecilia. 2005. *Women in the Damascus Document*. AcBib 21. Atlanta: Society of Biblical Literature.

Wegner, Judith R. 1991. "Philo's Portrayal of Women—Hebraic or Hellenic?" Pages 41–66 in *"Women like This": New Perspectives on Jewish Women in the Greco-Roman World* Edited by Amy-Jill Levine. EJL 1. Atlanta: Scholars Press.

Winkler, John J. 1999. "Laying Down the Law: The Oversight of Men's Sexual Behavior in Classical Athens." Pages 171–209 in *Before Sexuality: The Construction of Erotic Experience in the Ancient World*. Edited by David M. Halperin, John J. Winkler, and Froma I. Zeitlin. Princeton: Princeton University Press.

Zlotnick, Helena. 2002. *Dinah's Daughters: Gender and Judaism from the Hebrew Bible to Late Antiquity*. Philadelphia: University of Pennsylvania Press.

Part 2
Methods, Manuscripts, and Materials

5
New Methodologies

RODNEY A. WERLINE

1. Introduction and the Early Days

Since the publication of the first edition of *Early Judaism and Its Modern Interpreters* (Kraft and Nickelsburg 1986), the use of new methodology has significantly increased. Many of the new methodological approaches focus on seemingly obvious starting places—analyses of genre, sectarianism, community formation, gender, and ritual. Others would not have been at all obvious in the 1980s. For example, in the mid-1980s, methodologies such as neuroscience, cognitive science, and analysis of emotions were not yet generally applied or anticipated within the discipline of Second Temple Judaism. This essay considers methodologies from these areas, as well as others. Because this volume contains essays on gender and sociological analyses, as well as reception criticism, these approaches are not generally, or thoroughly, addressed here. Further, as a supplement to the treatment of ritual in this essay, readers should consult Daniel K. Falk and Angela Kim Harkins's essay on prayer in this volume.

That first edition of *Early Judaism and Its Modern Interpreters* did not include a chapter on methodology. When that volume appeared in 1986, much of the basic groundwork for initial understandings of texts and the era still needed to be done. Not all of the Dead Sea Scrolls had been published. James Charlesworth's two volumes of *The Old Testament Pseudepigrapha* (1983, 1986; *OTP*) were published as *Early Judaism and Its Modern Interpreters*, first edition, was being planned, written, collected, and edited. The

---

I am very grateful to Matthias Henze and Judith H. Newman for reading this essay and for making many helpful suggestions.

assumed methodologies were those that had dominated biblical studies for about a century: textual, source, redaction, and form criticisms. That reliance on methodologies from biblical scholarship is not especially surprising, since many of the scholars who launched into the world of Second Temple Judaism had been trained in biblical studies (see Nickelsburg 1999, 89–91). However, in the 1980s, biblical scholars were experimenting with methods from such disciplines as anthropology, sociology (including Marxist theories), structuralism, and reader-response. This shift in biblical studies happened for several reasons. Pragmatically, one hundred years of the historical-critical approaches on a somewhat limited corpus—especially for canonically confined New Testament scholars—begged for some new entrée into the texts. Practically, biblical interpreters gained new colleagues in religious studies scholars, as programs in religious studies on university campuses were on the rise and postmodern methods with them. The time for challenging old assumptions and entertaining new questions had come—modernism was on the way out as postmodern methodologies took hold.

Because scholars of Second Temple Judaism remained occupied with some of the most basic problems of the discipline, the field lagged behind the new currents and advances in biblical studies. However, George Nickelsburg (1983) had already tested out a socio-ideological reading of Daniel and 1 Enoch in a critique of Hengel's notion that the Hasidim produced these apocalyptic traditions. Earlier, in his revised and published dissertation (1972), Nickelsburg showed a kind of intuitive "reinvention," as he would later say, of Vladimir Propp's Russian formalist analysis of folktales (see now Nickelsburg 2006, 7) in his tradition-history analysis of the "persecution and vindication of the righteous one." He would later return to Propp's formalism in order to explore the similarities between two quite different texts: Tobit and 1 Enoch (1996). More thorough applications of methods used on folklore were employed in the work of Susan Niditch and Robert Doran (1977), though structuralism was their tool of choice (cf. also Niditch 1987). Lawrence Wills (1990) noted that Niditch and Doran drew on the folklore schematic analysis of Antti Aarne and Stith Thompson (1928). As for his own early work, Wills (1990) compared the court tales in Daniel to tales in other ancient Near East texts through folktale analysis. Wills (1995) continued this new type of approach in his work on the Jewish novel.

Still, in 1999, Nickelsburg's assessment of fifty years of scholarship on the Dead Sea Scrolls included this observation: "Qumran scholarship continues to be dominated by the methods and approaches that typified biblical studies prior to the 1970s" (Nickelsburg 1999, 94; cf. also the assessment of Campbell 2005, 2). He sensed a potential methodological shift on the horizon, but he wondered if this would gain momentum. So, he exhorted his audience: "But there is much more to do if the minds and hands can be found to do it" (94). Indeed, Carol Newsom's mind and hands were already at work, and in a series of publications and conference papers on Qumran (e.g., 1992, 1993, 1997, 2001) she began to lay the groundwork for her epoch *The Self as Symbolic Space: Constructing Identity and Community at Qumran* (2004; see below). Nevertheless, as late as 2005, Jonathan G. Campbell lamented in his introduction to the collected essays in *New Directions in Qumran Studies* (Campbell, Lyons, Pietersen) that Qumran scholarship had made little use of new methodologies. The same could be said for most of the field.

2. New Literary Criticisms and Text Production and Transmission

Even as new editions of texts and translations of early Jewish texts were heading to print, postmodern methodologies began to expose anachronistic assumptions about the idea, production, transmission, and uses of texts in early Judaism. The full significance of these observations, by some measures, is only now being felt, though those who introduced the methods knew the implications of their findings. As is often the case, the Dead Sea Scrolls marked the starting place for this area of investigation. As confidence in the consensus theories of the origins of the community began to crack, so did trust in accepted theories about textual traditions and transmission. Indeed, the very idea of what constitutes a text would eventually need adjustments (see Tigchelaar 2010). Philip R. Davies (1987) brought awareness to these transmission problems in his assessment of CD and the pesharim, as he proposed that documents could be rewritten and redacted with completely new goals in mind. However, as Maxine Grossman (2002, ix, 17 n. 43) explains, Davies eschewed contemporary literary methods. While Davies spent little time on the implications of this observation, the idea of *the* author and original authorial intent became a problem.

Drawing on the work of John Barton on the Hebrew Bible, Campbell took on the inherent inconsistency in historical-critical analyses that identified the logical tensions within texts as indication of the introduction of different sources and reediting, while at the same time maintaining that texts generally exhibit an easily observable ideological coherency (1995, 34; see also Grossman 2002, 15–16). Campbell, though, actually relied little on new methodology in his analysis (34–35), and he chose not to fully engage the text in that mode (cf. assessment by Grossman 2002). Nevertheless, Grossmann identifies an important move in Campbell's study: from focus on authorial intent to audience reception and formation. This is where Grossman (2002, x) picks up in her work, and she more fully analyzes CD by using "New Historicism." She brings Terry Eagleton (1983), Roland Barthes, and Michel Foucault to bear on the text. Though she does not totally discard authorial intent, nor an interest in history, she takes seriously the reality that the text reflects more meanings than simply that of the author(s) (2002, 18–24). Siding with Barthes (1979), who emphasizes that texts must not be understood as what they *are* but what they *do* (i.e., their function), and with a nod to literary deconstruction theory, Grossman (2002) lays out her approach to "meaning" in CD: "Textual meaning, in this context, is always evocative and plural, rather than finite and potentially complete" (19; see also Grossman 2010b). As Grossman (2010b, 711–12) notes in a later essay, again using Barthes, "Textuality is never straightforward but instead always consists of texts in relationship to other texts" and that "the text is never capable of fully and straightforwardly saying … any one particular thing." With this she challenges the historical-critical notion of authorship.

Such approaches had an impact on textual criticism and reconstructed textual histories. As George Brooke (2005, 34) considered textual pluriformity in the Second Temple era of what became the biblical text, he proposed the following: "Faced with textual diversity in the earliest strata of the textual tell, the search for a pristine Ur-text has to be abandoned." Instead, he proposed that evidence from Qumran contributes to the conclusion that "textual-criticism needs to move beyond a quasi-ontological view of the text " and "move towards a more functional view of the text" that "concentrates far more on the transmission history of texts and asks … what they were copied for, whether it might have been for legal, political, didactic, liturgical, or some other communal or individual purpose" (42). Here one finds a tendency similar to that in Grossman, though both scholars were working on different problems. Brooke's view of parabiblical or so-called rewritten Bible is consistent with this pronouncement. In part, his view of the text arises from his interest in the production of these parabiblical texts, because it reveals scribal activity and aims. In his examination of intertextuality in the Dead Sea Scrolls, Brooke (2013b, 2013d) draws on both Julia Kristeva's and Gérard Genette's categories of hypertext and hypotext. Besides accounting for features of genre, including form and content, Brooke's (2013c, 123) approach considers the ability of a text "both to confer and to receive authority from the scriptural text that they seek to elucidate, re-present, or rewrite."

Brooke is not alone in these types of assessments. As Charlotte Hempel has summarized, work by Emanuel Tov and Shemaryahu Talmon additionally confirm a pattern of "insufficiently controlled copying" (Talmon's term quoted by Hempel 2010, 166) among scribes. These kinds of conclusions have wide-ranging effects on the understanding of textual transmissions in Second Temple Judaism. Hempel herself charted the developments in the Damascus Document over the many years that groups cherished it. The ongoing development and significance of this vein of scholarship becomes even more pronounced in Judith Newman's (2018) work. In part influenced by the kinds of conclusions one finds in Brooke, she starts from the position that texts are fluid in this era—not fixed. Further, she criticizes the underlying assumption of so much of scholarship that the text is inevitably moving toward a telos, its canonical form (4–6; and see below).

Scholars are beginning to test the usefulness of other linguistic theories in analyzing texts. Some examine the role of metaphor in carrying concepts and how humans rely on these to orient themselves to the world and act within it. Humans often scarcely notice how these metaphors shape their conceptual understandings. Important in such analysis is the work of George Lakoff and Mark Johnson (1980; see also Lakoff 1987). For example, Karina Hogan (2011) relies on the two theorists when she analyzes Mother Earth as a conceptual metaphor in 4 Ezra. As she notes, quoting Lakoff and Johnson, a conceptual metaphor refers to the process of "understanding and experiencing one kind of thing in terms of another" (75; see Lakoff and Johnson 1980, 5). These theories allow her to explain the "prevalence of both maternal and agricultural imagery" in 4 Ezra as a way for the author to imagine humans in their relationship to the earth and the earth's relationship to the apocalyptic world to come (Hogan 2011, 90). Trine Hasselbalch (2015) applies systemic functional linguistics developed by Michael A. K. Halliday (2004), along with other sociolinguistic theories, to selected texts in the Hodayot. With these theories, she can question the degree to which these texts actually offer information about the social structure of the community, as many scholars have assumed. Instead, she argues, the hymns reveal the community's self-understanding or identity.

3. Social-Scientific Approaches

With studies such as Wayne Meek's *The First Urban Christians* (1983) as a model for the value of hard social-scientific data, interpreters began to investigate such issues as literacy levels in Second Temple Judaism, which during this era were not high (see Harris 1989; Bar Ilan 1992; Hezser 2001). Catherine Hezser (2001) contributed the earliest, fullest treatment of this matter. These scholars recognized that knowledge about literacy might have broad implications for understanding social dynamics of the era, for example, the place of orality, production of texts, who used the texts, the role and standing of scribes (Carr 2005; Van der Toorn 2007), the formation of sects (Baumgarten 1997, 49–49), and the production of texts. The assessment of the role of scribes in Second Temple Judaism changed. No longer were they seen as simply copyists of authoritative texts (Brooke 2005, 38–40). Christine Schams (1998) determined that scribes could engage in diverse activities and occupied many different social locations. Application of newer methodology sought to elicit from texts and other artefacts a fuller understanding of the function of scribes (Portier-Young 2011, 2014; Horsley 1979a, 1979b, 2004, 2007).

In Qumran studies, Davies (e.g., 1987, 1995, 2000, 2005) pointed a way toward sociological analysis of the community in his work that distinguished the ideology of the Damascus Document from that in other scrolls. Further, Albert Baumgarten (1997) was able to show that deprivation theories do not explain all the reasons that people might join a sect. Baumgarten traced the flourishing of Jewish sects in the era to a general disappointment in leadership, especially in the encounter with Hellenism and foreign power. However, for many, especially the Jerusalem elites, disappointment developed with the Hasmonean dynasty's rule, which "provoked some" of them "to turn inwards, separating themselves off from a society which they felt had gone astray" (Baumgarten 1997, 113). Continuing to reject deprivation theory, like that represented in Kenelm Burridge's studies of millenarian groups (Baumgarten 1997, 164), Baumgarten argued that many factors, including victorious jubilations, can lead to eschatological and apocalyptic fervor (which he says is demonstrated in portions of 1 Enoch). Eyal Regev (2007), who acknowledges Baumgarten's influence on his work, brought a combined sociological and anthropological methodology to the analysis of the concept of Qumran sectarianism, including observations about seventeenth-century English Protestant sectarianism (16–17; cf. Baumgarten 1997, 201–8). Adopting the definition of sectarianism presented by Rodney Stark and William Sims Bainbridge, Regev (2007, 34) defines sect in this manner: "A religious group in *a state of tension* with the surrounding environment" (emphasis original; see also Stark and Bainbridge 1985, 23). Like these sociologists, Regev identifies "three markers of sub-cultural tension: antagonism, separation and difference" (34). He adds to this Bryan Wilson's lengthier list of ten features of "sectarian patterns of self-conception and social organization" (Regev 2007, 39–42, who cites, e.g., Wilson 1982, 91–93). Regev's analysis leads him through several Qumran and associated texts (e.g., Jubilees and 1 Enoch, as well as descriptions of the Essenes).

Michael Stone (2018) proposes that some of the groups from the era should be understood as secret societies that protected and passed on esoteric knowledge. This proposal shifts the sociological methods and models in current use to understand groups within the era. The theories of Georg Simmel (1906) and Lawrence Hazelrigg (1969) roughly underlie Stone's analysis. These groups, he asserts, "limited their membership and inducted new adherents into secret teachings and/or practices through a gradual initiation process" (1). Texts like 1 Enoch, 4 Ezra, and those from Qumran figure prominently in his examination. The apparent widespread availability of some apocalypses, like Daniel and 1 Enoch, suggests to Stone that these texts were actually pseudoesoteric and not secret. However, texts like these hint at additional secrets not available to the general public. These theories build on his early work "Lists of Revealed Things in Apocalyptic Literature" (1976) and his interest in religious experience (e.g., 2011, 90–121).

4. Spatial Theory

In the English-speaking world, spatial theory arose after the translation and publication of Henri Lefebvre, *The Production of Space* (1991). Edward W. Soja (1996) applied and promoted the theory in his *Thirdspace* and other publications (e.g., 1989). Firstspace consists of physical geography. Secondspace is space as culturally constructed and presented. Thirdspace holds the world as practiced and experienced (see, e.g., Berquist 2002; Harkins 2012; Schofield 2012). However, Claudia Camp (2002) found that distinguishing between these spaces may not always be as neat one hopes, as phenomena connected to a text may simultaneously occupy the same space or more than one space. This feature of the methodology becomes useful as she sorts through Ben Sira's relationships between priest, scribe, temple, and text. In the end, actually, Camp argues that "people also apparently read through people, not through books (or scroll)" (77).

Liv I. Lied (2005) relies on spatial theory in a quest for a new path through the long-standing problem of the meaning of "land of Damascus" in the Damascus Document. She focuses on Soja's idea of Thirdspace, which is characteristic in many of the uses of his theory. Thirdspace is more than a combination of Firstspace and Secondspace. Thirdspace emerges from the engagement of the first two spaces within lived experiences (121–25; see also Lied 2008). Read through this theory, Damascus becomes a multivalent term that can simultaneously evoke exile and blessing. Alison Schofield (2012, 470) found spatial theory helpful in handling "the ambiguous relationship between sect and land, Qumran and temple, priest and sanctuary (or lack thereof)." Her analysis leads to the following proposals: "1) In their texts, the *Yahad* members re-inscribed the desert as a new priestly space.... 2) As such, this sectarian space contested the alleged coherence and dominance of the Jerusalem temple, but *did not entirely supersede it*. 3) The creation of this new social spaces was a necessary part of cementing their sectarian movement, finalized through their practice, or regimentation of space" (470, emphasis original). An interesting parallel exists between Schofield's assessment of performance of Words of the Luminaries (4Q504–506) and Angela Harkins's (2015) analysis of the Hodayot (see below), as both emphasize the embodied experience of heterotopian space through liturgical enactment: "Whenever it [4Q504] was read, the performance of these communal prayers would have set apart a special liturgical space that suspended contemporary time and reflected upon the biblical wilderness age," which "would have produced in its speakers an embodied cognition of space at the intersection of story and reality, or text and experience, prayers through which the speakers could take on new virtual vestments of older priestly spaces" (Schofield 2012, 478–79). This experience may have mitigated separation from the Jerusalem temple.

Because apocalypses sometimes contain journeys through the cosmos and lengthy descriptions about its structures, spatial theory has enjoyed special application in analysis of the genre. Kelley Coblentz Bautch (2016) surveyed the possible functions of spatial theory for the analysis of the journeys in 1 Enoch. She especially noted the matter of construction of space by authors and communities, and the possible ways in which spatial construction might persuade an audience. Also relying on Kathryn M. Lopez (2008), she recognized all this as an act of resistance to power. Pieter

M. Ventor (2008) has argued that authors may combine space and time in the construction of group identity, which all then function together as a way to give structure to society and "control interrelationships" (643). Ventor (2003) has theorized that the construction of space in the journeys in 1 En. 12–36 assisted the editors in constructing their ideological critique. While not an apocalyptic text, Ventor (2006) has also explored Dan 1 for the way in which food restrictions and rites of passage construct liminal space and might provide paths of resistance. Lied (2008) proposed that 2 Baruch's construction of the land is fluid, and it is tied to the eschatological ideology of the book (cf. Nickelsburg 1991 on 1 Enoch). Further, 2 Baruch shapes its spatiality through a rhetoric of consolation. By highlighting the differences in the way that 1QS and 4Q286–290 (4QBer^{a-e}) imagine space, Andrew Krause (2018) questions the "liturgical homogeneity assumed" for those connected with the Qumran scrolls (218). Spatial theory also leads to notions about embodiment and bodies within spaces, an attribute of the theory that serves Harkins (2012) well in her examination of the Hodayot. She, however, draws on Foucault's ideas of utopia and heterotopia to attenuate the Marxist features of Soja's understanding of Thirdspace as a place of resistance (117–18).

5. The Construction of the Self

Perhaps the most important and influential volume that engages current methodology is Carol Newsom's *The Self as Symbolic Space: Constructing Identity and Community at Qumran* (2004). Affirming the centrality of language for the Qumran community, she structures her investigation as an analysis of discourse, the way in which it was regulated and engendered in the members. The methodological framework for her analysis is the sociolinguistic theories of Valentin Voloshinov and, especially, Mikhail Bakhtin, who claimed that language "is always socially stratified and socially stratifying" and that the impact of language is a "highly sensitive marker of social boundaries" (7). Language creates a space in which a community is formed and lives out its identity. In short, members of a particular group speak in a particular way and share knowledge that distinguishes them from others outside the group. This mode of speaking sits within a world of competing discourses, some of which originate much closer to the center of imperial power than the Qumran community's location. The Treatise of the Two Spirits (1QS III–IV) provides the community member with a map for understanding that world (79). However, speech also forms individuals (12), a claim that sets up the second emphasis in the book: "How to make a sectarian." Newsom (2004, 93) first relies on Dorothy Holland's (1998) theory of "figured worlds." These are practiced, embodied, socially constructed worlds in which humans assume roles and adopt the values and views of the group. Through practice, individuals embody these worlds and take on both identity and agency within them (94–95). At this moment, Newsom complements Holland with Michel Foucault's (1995, 1988) analysis of disciplinary institutions and his "technologies of the self."

Newsom (2004, 192; cf. 2001) then considers subjectivity, which she defines as "the culturally specific ways in which meaning of one's self is produced, experienced, and articulated." Because the Hodayot contain so many occurrences of "I," this becomes the testing ground for subjectivity in the Dead Sea Scrolls. Whoever the author or the voice in the text and whatever the setting for their performance, Newsom maintains that the members of the community would have viewed the "I" as "prototypical" for themselves and not as "unique to the reciter" (202). In the recitation of the Hodayot, a community member enacted a "drama" of "persecution" and "deliverance," and of "affinity" and "estrangement," a recognition of the implications of embodying the community's knowledge (274–75). The so-called Hymns of the Teacher "construct a figure who is a compelling object of loyalty," both in his relationships to God and community (345).

In a later essay, Newsom (2010) reviews the rhetorical strategies in the Damascus Document, Community Rule, and the Hodayot through the lens of Kenneth Burke. Her interest is in the "force of the language itself," and she emphasizes ongoing power of the texts to shape an audience in every new encounter or reencounter (2010, 201). Like Brooke and Grossman, Newsom assumes that the community updated texts to address changing times and new problems and demands, and explains this as follows: "Thus, the very model of *an* author addressing *an* audience in a *particular* setting is too simplistic" (201, emphasis original). Rodney A. Werline (2015), drawing on ritual theory and a form of reader-response theory, conducted a similar analysis of ritual in the Book of the Watchers in 1 Enoch in order to show the way in which rituals that appear within a text could continue to engage and form an audience. Newsom (2012) has also explored the potential of neuroscience for the construction of the self. She especially suggests the work of Patrick McNamara (2009), though she also employs ethnopsychology as presented in the theories of Paul Heelas and Andrew Lock (1981). With these theories in hand, she tackles the thorny matter of the self and moral agency in both the Hebrew Bible and Second Temple literature.

6. Emotions

Those researching emotion in early Judaism are now greatly assisted by Françoise Mirguet's (2019) highly detailed review of the scholarship on the subject, which, again, is only now beginning to pick up pace (Mirguet 2019; Gereboff 2009). As a caveat, David Lambert (2016) discouraged seeing much reflection about the inner life and emotions in the Hebrew Bible, and this included what most have thought of as remorse for sin as a constituent of repentance. However, Mirguet (2017) proposes that this might have shifted beginning in the Hellenistic period (see also Auerbach 1968; Ego 2015). In her book on compassion, Mirguet (2017) arrays the different attitudes toward emotions in the Hellenistic world and then focuses on how Judaism valued compassion as virtue. Emotion and visible related practices, she explains, structured identity among some groups (2017; see also 2019b).

Examining the role of emotions in Daniel, Ari Mermelstein (2015) proposes that the redactor seeks to transform the community's collective emotional state from fear to courage and hope through a correct appraisal of reality. Real power does not lie with the violent, threatening king—Antiochus IV—but with God and with God's people. Mermelstein also asserts that emotions are "conditioned by cultural values" (456), which he undergirds with Martha Nussbaum's (2001) philosophy and social constructivist theories.

In a conference proceedings volume edited by Stefan Reif and Renate Eggers-Wenzel (2015), Michael Duggan (2015) examines the laments in 1 Maccabees and determines that the author couples positive emotions and virtues in such a way as to distinguish Jews from gentiles. Simone Paganini (2015) considers Moses's opening intercessor prayer in Jubilees and the emotional effect that it has on God. In that same volume, Markus Witte (2015) is much more methodologically conscious about the cultural formation of emotions and applies that insight to an interpretation of emotions in the Wisdom of Solomon. Barbara Schmitz (2015) relies on Ben Zeʾev's (2010) phenomenology of emotions and reads Jdt 9 as an emotional response to change (cf. Egger-Wenzel 2012). Her results depict a Holefernes who has emotionally "lost his head," and a calm, resolute Judith, whose emotions only emerge in her prayer in chapter 9.

Harkins (2012), drawing on neuroscience, alerts her readers that scientists recognize that not every human experiences emotions in the same manner, and that emotions are culturally constructed (see, e.g., 2012, 43–45), complex cultural-cognitive processes (2016b, 468). Thus, she cautions against universalizing emotional experiences and expressions. Throughout her 2012 volume on the Hodayot, she emphasizes the place of emotions within texts that testify to ancient communities' interests in the reports of sensory, embodied experiences. Her approach to the Hodayot highlights the intensity and usefulness of recountings of heavenly journeys. Harkins' (2016b; cf. also 2016a, 2017, 2018) discussion of Ezra's penitential prayer in Ezra 9 gives her a chance to explore the role of ritual performance in constructing emotional responses. Jeremy Corley (2012) explores the emotional transformations on both the human and divine levels that take place in the apocryphal book of Baruch. The short text moves from penitence to the joyful return of the people to Jerusalem on the human level, and from anger to compassion on the divine.

7. Ritual Theory

In this area as well, biblical studies got out ahead of scholarship on Second Temple Judaism. For example, Ellen Juhl Christiansen (1995) examined ritual boundary markers in an exploration of distinguishing between early church communities and other Jewish groups. Bruce Malina's (1981) work provided a methodological model for her project.

Certainly, as with much of the scholarship of the era, the Dead Sea Scrolls provided a rich treasure for possible examination of ritual. The texts contain numerous prayers and liturgies, as well as discussions about other ritually related matters, like calendars, appropriate leadership, and so on. As the liturgical texts became available, interpreters such as Steven Weitzman (1997) soon saw the value of comparing these texts to other prayers from the era. He returned to the questions of the defunct myth and ritual school, eschewing its notion of its transcendent patterns, but insisting that new analyses of texts could bring new light to the interplay between ritual forms and story.

Robert Kugler (2002) was among the first to supply an inventory of rituals at Qumran. He organized his catalogue according to Catherine Bell's (1997, 91–169) six categories of rituals: rites of passage, feats and fasts, calendrical rites, rites of affliction, political rites, and rites of communion. He combined his lengthy list and brief explanations with Bell's notions of ritual intensity in order to argue that the thorough ritualization of life in the community transformed most of life—even from meals to the time of day—into a religious experience. Russell Arnold (2006) follows a somewhat similar agenda, but more thoroughly and in more detail. Like Kugler, he organizes his book according to Bell's six categories of rituals. Beginning with the theories of Mary Douglas about how ritual forms groups, he analyzes the way in which those connected to the scrolls established a strong sense of group and clear boundaries in part through liturgical performance, regulated speech, the calendar, and regulated community life (Arnold 2006, 29–51). Newsom's (2006, 52–71) work rightfully looms large in his analysis of entrance into the community. However, Arnold opts for a more functionalist approach, and his discoveries offer primarily sociological outcomes. Though he relies on Bell's categories, he does not employ Bell's theories of ritual as the enactment of power. Instead, the attention primarily settles on the way in which ritual establishes and maintains social boundaries.

An early treatment of purity at Qumran appeared in Hannah K. Harrington's scholarship (1993, 2004). While she examined Second Temple Jewish texts, she kept both eyes on the Hebrew Bible and rabbinic literature. Also notable is the collection of essays on purity by Susan Haber (2008), which was posthumously collected, edited, and published by Adele Reinhartz.

Jonathan Klawans in his *Impurity and Sin in Ancient Judaism* (2000), which especially focused on rabbinic texts, and in his *Purity, Sacrifice, and the Temple: Symbolism and Supersessionism in the Study of Ancient Judaism* (2006) displays a heavy theoretical interest and demonstrates its impact and payoff. The latter volume spans ritual texts in the Hebrew Bible, early Judaism, the New Testament, along with some treatment of rabbinic literature. Following a lengthy review, assessment, and critique of anthropological theories on these topics, Klawans contends that many theories on purity and sacrifice, including anthropological analyses, are flawed because they argue for a single explanation for the practice and purity. Further, he spots the general tendency among theorists to literalize a single metaphor for sacrifice and then prioritize it in order to explain all rituals and ritual systems in the Hebrew Bible. While Klawans (cf. 2008) appreciates Douglas's work in arguing against the Protestant bias against ritual in theorists like James Frazer and William Robertson Smith, he agrees with Ithamar Gruenwald that Douglas, like others who regard rituals as "ubiquitous symbolism," may be engaged in an "apologetic activity" of another kind. Klawans's (2006) aversion to any apologetic for interpreting early Jewish understanding of purity and ritual continues through the book, as he notes the tendency to spiritualize the temple and sacrifice in early Christian and rabbinic texts. In the end, Klawans's treatment is extensive and nuanced. However, one might summarize his position as an attempt to understand the way in which Jews of the Second Temple period were able to extend their understanding of the temple and its practices into their lives in order to remain connected to its practices and meaning.

8. Performance

Performance theory is an emerging discipline in the field. Its usefulness has been explained above in the discussion of Harkins's (see additionally 2017, 2018) work on the Hodayot and other texts. Newman advanced her previous work (1999) on the scripturalization of prayer by examining the nexus between liturgical practice, which includes prayer, and scripture by introducing "embodied cognition" into her research (2018). Her new methodology drew from the works the likes of Thomas Csordas (1994), Maurice Merleau-Ponty, Lakoff, and Johnson (1980; Johnson 2007) and integrated "anthropological and neurocognitive perspectives" (Newman 2018, 11), and her designation for the method signals a direct attack on the Cartesian dualism of mind and body, which many interpreters have started to criticize in the past few years. Informed by Pierre Bourdieu's theory of *habitus*, she expands the meaning of the term *liturgical* to include "the embodied practices around prayer and the learning of scriptures" (142). The site of all this activity—this phenomenon—is the "liturgical body," a term that she uses "to refer both to the individual biological body of the praying subject and to the communal, social body gathered together for the purposes of listening, praying and engagement" (13). From this vantage, she investigates the production and performance connected to an array of texts not normally considered together, such as Ben Sira; Dan 9; Bar 1:1–3:8; 2 Corinthians; and the Hodayot.

9. Cultural Memory Theory

Cultural memory theory traces its origins to Maurice Halbwachs (1941), who proposed that memory is not simply the internal recollections of an individual: "But individual memory is nevertheless a part or an aspect of group memory, since each impression and each fact, even if it apparently concerns a particular person exclusively, leave a lasting memory only to the extent that one has thought it over—to the extent that it is connected with the thoughts that come to us from the social milieu" (Halbwachs 1992, 53). Halbwachs's assertion bears the unmistakable influence of Emile Durkheim's collective consciousness (Halbwachs 1992; Werline forthcoming). Halbwachs (1941) applied his theory to an interpretation of the Jesus story and the geography of Palestine, while several years later the Egyptologist Jan Assmann (e.g., 2011) would develop the theory and test its usefulness for understanding the Hebrew Bible. Social memory theory maintains a group's memory of the past is always socially constructed—never how it actually was. The past has run through a social filter so that it serves the needs of the community and its coherence. Further, this past impinges on the present moment, as a community understands and acts in the present moment in a way that for them seems consistent with that memory. Communities keep the constructed past alive and in front of the community through myth, stories, festivals, sites, media, and various social institutions (e.g., Schwartz 2014). Likewise, the community structures its future vision based on this constructed history.

Given that Second Temple texts frequently interpret the present moment through remembering the past—or recall the past in light of the current moment—social memory theory holds much promise for unlocking new understandings of texts. The conference proceedings volume from a 2004 event in Durham displayed the value of the method (Barton, Stuckenbruck, Wold 2007). For example, Loren Stuckenbruck (2007; see also 2010) examines the process of remembering the Teacher of Righteousness at Qumran. He concluded that the texts say much more about the community itself in the act of remembering, its self-understanding, than they do about the historical Teacher of Righteousness, who remains mostly lost in the fog of the retelling. In the same volume, William Horbury (2007) explores memory in the Psalms of Solomon and suggests that memory in these psalms is the calling to mind of the deity and functioned as a defining aspect of the texts' image of piety. Werline (forthcoming) questions Horbury's emphasis on the memory as internal and contends that this neglects the social aspects of memory and the way in which memory in the Psalms of Solomon is connected to action.

Many other scholars recognized the value of social memory theory in interpreting texts from the era. Frances Flannery (2012) combined social memory theory and cognitive dissonance theory in an exploration of the construction of the character Ezra in 4 Ezra as a purveyor of esoteric mysteries. Brooke (2013d) applied memory theory to the reworked biblical traditions, especially in the Dead Sea Scrolls, and proposed four dimensions or processes: (1) embellishments that in some way relate to the group's institutionalization; (2) "distortion and obligation," which, as Assmann has argued, engenders a unique self-understanding and value system; (3) invention and organization; and (4) forgetting and omissions as a way to reconstruct memory (61–64).

10. Criticism of Imperial Ideology and Postcolonialism

Serious consideration of socioeconomic factors in imperial Rome and imperial ideology of domination migrated primarily from New Testament studies to Second Temple scholarship. This mostly resulted from the overlap with New Testament scholarship in the desire to reconstruct first-century Palestine, especially Galilee. Perhaps the most influential early book that fits this description—and somewhat shook the ground of biblical and Second Temple studies—was Richard Horsley and John S. Hanson's book, *Bandits, Prophets and Messiahs: Popular Movements at the Time of Jesus* (1985). The two authors dismantled the widely held notion that the Zealots were responsible for the Jewish revolt against Rome. Horsley had already been challenging these ideas in two articles (1979a, 1979b). This notion, they claimed, was "a modern scholarly construct" that "has little relation to actual Jewish history in the first century" (1985, xv). Instead, making use of the work of Eric Hobsbawm (e.g., 1981), the revolt was an uprising of the Jewish peasantry, especially in Galilee—a popular uprising. They gave serious consideration to imperial dominance, oppression, and the way some Jewish elites locally brokered and benefited from that power, and they were not content to explain the differences between Second Temple Jewish groups or sects as simply theological debates.

Horsley continued and expanded his socioeconomic and imperial critique of the Second Temple period in *Jesus and the Spiral of Violence: Popular Jewish Resistance in Roman Palestine* (1993). Soon, he began to apply the theories of James Scott (1990) on tactics of resistance among oppressed peoples (see Horsley 2004, 2007). Horsley eventually produced a monograph focused solely on Second Temple literature: *Scribes, Visionaries and the Politics of Second Temple Judea* (2007). Still aided by Scott's theories and an adjusted version of Gerhard Linski's (1966) assessment of agrarian societies, Horsley fit Judean society within a basic structure of patron-clients, retainers, and peasantry. Especially important in this work was his identification of scribes as the retainer class. In the shifting politics of the Greco-Roman era, groups of scribes could suddenly become disenfranchised and marginalized (cf. also Werline 2005).

Anathea Portier-Young (2011) engages many similar theorists as Horsley in her analysis *Apocalypse against Empire*. However, she breaks with Scott's idea of hidden transcript, which assumed a false dichotomy between mind and body, thought and action. As she asserts, "Scott does not allow for the ways in which practices shape consciousness" (36). For her, "what is remarkable about the apocalypses, however, is *not* their claim that there is an invisible, hidden world distinct from the visible world. It is their exposure of the hidden structures of false power and assertion of a more potent invisible power" (37, emphasis original). With these principles in mind she probes the way Alexander's successors and especially the Seleucids craft their hegemony and domination. Turning to Daniel and traditions in 1 Enoch, especially the Apocalypse of Weeks and the Book of Dreams, she elucidates the programs and the praxis of resistance presented in these texts—"all effective action that aims to limit, oppose, reject or transform hegemonic institutions and cosmologies as well as systems, strategies, and acts of domination" (379). The apocalypses invited the audience to see the world as the visionaries saw it and to act in the world with the courage and conviction that God is sovereign.

Meredith J. Stone (2018) combined postcolonial critique with feminist theory in her analysis of LXX Esther. Influenced by Scott, Horsley, and Warren Carter in her assessment of imperial power, she shows how a combination with feminist critique can elucidate various "arts of resistance" and negotiations of power. Portier-Young (2014) notes, the analyses of Jewish narratives, sometimes through folklore methodology, recognized the role of resistance within that genre. Further, monster theory shares the concerns of postcolonialism (Smith-Christopher 2014). Relying on Jeffery Jerome Cohen, Daniel Smith-Christopher argues that the monstrous body stands as a projection of culture. The cosmic disruptions and disorder arise to life in the hybridity of apocalyptic monsters (e.g., Dan 7), as they embody imperial domination and violence. Through these depictions, authors sought to subvert imperial or dominant powers and to reveal them as aberrations and violations of the true cosmic order. Their mixed character, however, also represent the fear of colonized people who worry that they, in fact, might adopt some of the cultural features of the subjugators (Smith-Christopher 2018; cf. Portier Young 2014).

11. Religious Experience

In 2005, the Society of Biblical Literature unit Religious Experience in Early Judaism and Early Christianity held its inaugural session. The founders, Flannery and Werline, sought to build and expand upon the observations and work of a small group of scholars of early Judaism who had brought attention to this matter: for example, Alan Segal (1990), Christopher Rowland (1982), Michael Stone (1974, 2003, cf. 2011), and Daniel Merkur (1989). The group hoped to take seriously the fact that in the end this discipline was not simply about genres, or histories of famous people, or philology, but of real people and the faith and practices of real people and their experience. At the moment, the group has published two volumes of collected essays (Flannery, Shantz, and Werline 2008; Shantz and Werline 2012). An easy criticism of the quest to describe experience is that one can never fully know the experience of a contemporaneous person, let alone a figure from the past. At best one only has access to the description of the experience but never the experience itself. Further, the representation of the experience will always be constructed according to social training and expectations. However, the group always recognized that access to the experience itself remains out of reach, but participants maintained that something can be observed in the recounting of the experiences. In addition, often overlooked aspects of texts received new attention (e.g., references to practices that lead to visionary experiences, see Merkur 1989). Those chasing understandings of experience have drawn on an assortment of methodologies—quite eclectic. There has been a tendency to determine what method might best serve the information that a text offers. The results of this group significantly differ from attempts at experience in the early 1900s. Current scholars scrupulously avoid speech about universal, and transcendent experiences of the divine. Instead, they focus on the embodied and cultural aspects of the phenomena.

12. Conclusions: Possibilities and Limitations

Grossman (2008, 293) summed up the two basic aims of the introduction of new methodologies into the study of early Judaism: "First, does the approach help the researcher to make observations or draw conclusions that would have been otherwise inaccessible? And, second, does the use of the approach spark readers to new insights and new lines of research of their own?" To speak broadly, the new methodological approaches of these texts and the era have produced new understandings of the material. They achieve this by asking questions of texts that more traditional historical-critical and literary methodologies are unable to propose. Kugler (2010) has warned about enshrining one particular discipline with a spirit of dogmatic commitment to the neglect of an eclectic, interdisciplinary enterprise that may pry new understanding from the texts. However, excitement about methodology can sometimes seduce scholars into going beyond the evidence that is available in a text. While much work is reconstructive in nature, including historical approaches, the text itself must be able to bear the weight of the interpretation.

Scholars can also state methodological approaches or theories as fact, apparently simply because they appear in lengthy and densely argued studies. Of course, methods and theories must not be reified, for every one of them is the construction of some theorist. Further, one must not forget that most anthropological and sociological theories arise from anthropologists' real observations of real people and reflections on the nature of their societies and cultures. Theories may be more particular and culturally delimited than imagined, and they may not transfer at all to our data. Scholars of Second Temple Judaism obviously cannot conduct such observations—participants from the culture cannot be interviewed. Thus, almost every application of any methodology from these disciplines, and from more literary disciplines, is always comparative. Along with comparative analyses come comparatively dangerous pitfalls. While new methodologies have undoubtedly produced new knowledge of and new perspectives on texts, each interpreter must approach the task with a degree of soberness and humility.

While not always the case, sometimes interpreters turn to new methodologies without recognizing that huge debates rage within these other disciplines. This opens up the possibility that an interpreter draws on two or more theorists who are completely at odds with one another. Thus, one cannot be naive and think that the application of a new theory solves the problems that one might find in a Second Temple text, nor that theory unambiguously opens a new explanation of a feature of a text. In fact, the application of a new theory exposes the text to a new assortment of issues. While this is not necessarily bad, matters are not completely solved.

Bibliography

Aarne, Antti, and Stith Thompson. 1928. *The Types of the Folk Tale: A Classification and Bibliography*. Folklore Fellows Communications 74. Helsinki: Suomalainen tiedeaktatemia.

Arnold, Russell C. D. 2006. *The Social Role of Liturgy in the Religion of the Qumran Community*. STDJ 60. Leiden: Brill.

Auerbach, Erich. 1968. *Mimesis: The Representation of Reality in Western Literature*. Translated by Willard R Trask. Princeton: Princeton University Press.

Assmann, Jan. 2011. *Cultural Memory and Early Civilization: Writing, Remembrance and Political Imagination*. Cambridge: University Press.

Bar Ilan, Meir. 1992. "Illiteracy in the Land of Israel in the First Centuries CE." Pages 46–61 in vol. 2 of *Essays in the Social Scientific Study of Judaism and Jewish Society*. Edited by Simcha Fishbane, Stuart Schoenfeld, and Alain Goldschloager. New York: KTAV.

Barthes, Roland. 1979. "From Work to Text." Pages 73–81 in *Textual Strategies: Perspectives in Post-Structuralist Criticism*. Edited by Josué Harari. Ithaca, NY: Cornell University Press.

Barton, Stephen C., Loren T. Stuckenbruck, and Benjamin G. Wold, eds. 2007. *Memory in the Bible and Antiquity: The Fifth Durham–Tübingen Research Symposium (Durham, September 2004)*. WUNT 212. Tübingen: Mohr Siebeck.

Baumgarten, Albert I. 1997. *The Flourishing of Jewish Sects in the Maccabean Era: An Interpretation*. JSJSup 55. Leiden: Brill.

Bell, Catherine. 1997. *Ritual: Perspectives and Dimensions*. Oxford: Oxford University Press.

Ben Ze'ev, A. 2010. "The Thing Called Emotion." Pages 41–62 in *The Oxford Handbook of Philosophy of Emotion*. Edited by Peter Goldie. Oxford: Oxford University Press.

Berquist, Jon L. 2002. "Critical Spatiality and the Construction of the Ancient World." Pages 14–29 in *"Imagining" Biblical Worlds: Studies in Spatial, Social, and Historical Constructs in Honor of James W. Flanagan*. Edited by David M. Gunn and Paula McNutt. JSOTSup 359. London: Sheffield Academic.

Brooke, George. 2005. "The Qumran Scrolls and the Demise of the Distinction between Higher and Lower Criticism." Pages 26–42 in *New Directions in Qumran Studies: Proceedings of the Bristol Colloquium on the Dead Sea Scrolls, 8–10 September 2003*. Edited by Jonathan G. Campbell, William John Lyons, and Lloyd K. Pietersen. LSTS 52. London: T&T Clark.

———. 2013a. *Reading the Dead Sea Scrolls: Essays in Method*. EJL 39. Atlanta: Society of Biblical Literature.

———. 2013b. "Controlling Intertexts and Hierarchies of Echo in Two Thematic Eschatological Commentaries from Qumran." Pages 85–97 in *Reading the Dead Sea Scrolls: Essays in Method*. Edited by George J. Brooke. EJL 39. Atlanta: Society of Biblical Literature.

———. 2013c. "Genre Theory, Rewritten Bible, and Pesher." Pages 115–36 in *Reading the Dead Sea Scrolls: Essays in Method*. Edited by George J. Brooke. EJL 39. Atlanta: Society of Biblical Literature.

———. 2013d. "Hypertextuality and the 'Parabiblical' Dead Sea Scrolls." Pages 67–84 in *Reading the Dead Sea Scrolls: Essays in Method*. Edited by George J. Brooke. EJL 39. Atlanta: Society of Biblical Literature.

Camp, Claudia V. 2002. "Storied Space, or, Ben Sira 'Tells' a Temple." Pages 64–80 in *"Imagining Biblical Worlds" Studies in Spatial, Social and Historical Constructs in Honor of James W. Flanagan*. Edited by David M. Gunn and Paula M. McNutt. JSOTSup 359. London: Sheffield Academic.

Campbell, Jonathan G. 1995. *The Use of Scripture in the Damascus Document 1–8, 19–20*. BZAW 228. New York: de Gruyter.

Campbell, Jonathan G., William John Lyons, and Lloyd K. Pietersen, eds. 2005. *New Directions in Qumran Studies: Proceedings of the Bristol Colloquium on the Dead Sea Scrolls, 8–10 September 2003*. LSTS 52. London: T&T Clark.

Carr, David M. 2005. *Writing on the Tablet of the Heart: Origins of Scripture and Literature*. Oxford: Oxford University Press.

Christiansen, Ellen Juhl. 1995. *The Covenant in Judaism and Paul: A Study of Ritual Boundaries as Identity Markers*. AGJU 27. Leiden: Brill.

Coblentz Bautch, Kelley. 2016. "Spatiality and Apocalyptic Literature." *HeBAI* 5:273–88.

Corley, Jeremy. 2012. "Emotional Transformation in the Book of Baruch." *DCLY* 2011:225–52.

Csordas, Thomas J., ed. 1994. *Embodiment and Experience: The Existential Ground of Culture and Self*. New York: Cambridge University Press.

Davies, Philip R. 1987. *Behind the Essenes: History and Ideology in the Dead Sea Scrolls*. BJS 94. Atlanta: Scholars Press.

———. 1995. "Was There Really a Qumran Community?" *CurBS* 3:9–35.

———. 2000. "The Judaism(s) of the Damascus Document." Pages 27–43 in *The Damascus Document: A Centennial of Discovery*. Edited by J. M. Baumgarten, Esther G. Chazon, and Avital Pinnick. STDJ 34. Leiden: Brill.

———. 2005. "Sects from Texts: On the Problems of Doing a Sociology of the Qumran Literature." Pages 69–82 in *New Directions in Qumran Studies: Proceedings of the Bristol Colloquium on the Dead Sea Scrolls, 8–10 September 2003*. Edited by Jonathan G. Campbell, William John Lyons, and Lloyd K. Pietersen. LSTS 52. London: T&T Clark.

Duggan, Michael W. 2015. "1 Maccabees: Emotions of Life and Death in Narrative and Lament." Pages 95–116 in *Ancient Jewish Prayers and Emotions: Emotions Associated with Jewish Prayer in and around the Second Temple Period*. Edited by Stefan C. Reif and Renate Egger Wenzel. DCLS 26. Berlin: de Gruyter.

Eagleton, Terry. 1983. *Literary Theory: An Introduction*. Minneapolis: University of Minnesota Press.

Egger-Wenzel, Renate. 2012. "Judith's Path from Grief to Joy—from Sackcloth to Festive Attire." *DCLY* 2011:189–223.

Ego, Beate. 2015. "Prayer and Emotion in the Septuagint of Esther." Pages 83–94 in *Ancient Jewish Prayers and Emotions: Emotions Associated with Jewish Prayer in and around the Second Temple Period*. Edited by Stefan C. Reif and Renate Egger Wenzel. DCLS 26. Berlin: de Gruyter.

Flannery, Frances. 2012. "Esoteric Mystical Practice in Fourth Ezra and the Reconfiguration of Social Memory." Pages 45–70 in *Linking Text and Experience*. Vol. 2 of *Experientia*. Edited by Colleen Shantz and Rodney A. Werline. EJL 35. Atlanta: Society of Biblical Literature.

Flannery, Frances, Colleen Shantz, and Rodney A. Werline, eds. 2008. *Inquiry into Religious Experience in Early Judaism and Early Christianity*. Vol. 1 of *Experientia*. SymS 40. Altanta: Society of Biblical Literature.

Foucault, Michel. 1986. "Of Other Spaces." *Diacritics* 16:22–27.

———. 1988. "Technologies of the Self." Pages 16–49 in *Technologies of the Self: A Seminar with Michel Foucault*. Edited by Lither H. Martin, Huck Gutman, and Patrick H. Hutton. London: Tavistock.

———. 1995. *Discipline and Punishment: The Birth of the Prison*. Translated by Alan Sheridan. New York: Vintage.

Gereboff, Joel. 2009. "Judaism." Pages 95–110 in *The Oxford Handbook of Religion and Emotion*. Edited by John Corrigan. Oxford: Oxford University Press.

Grossman, Maxine. 2002. "Priesthood as Authority: Interpretive Competition in First-Century Judaism and Christianity." Pages 117–31 in *The Dead Sea Scrolls as Background to Postbiblical Judaism and Early Chris-*

tianity: Papers from an International Conference at St. Andrews in 2001. Edited by James R. Davila. STDJ 46. Leiden: Brill.

———. 2008. Review of *New Directions in Qumran Studies: Proceedings of the Bristol Colloquium on the Dead Sea Scrolls, 8–10 September 2003*. Edited by Jonathan G. Campbell, William John Lyons, and Lloyd K. Pietersen. *DSD* 15:293–95.

———. 2010a. *Rediscovering the Dead Sea Scrolls: An Assessment of Old and New Approaches and Methods*. Grand Rapids: Eerdmans.

———. 2010b. "Roland Barthes and the Teacher of Righteousness: The Death of the Author of the Dead Sea Scrolls." Pages 709–22 in *The Oxford Handbook of the Dead Sea Scrolls*. Edited by Timothy H. Lim and John J. Collins. Oxford: Oxford University Press.

Haber, Susan. 2008. *"They Shall Purify Themselves": Essays on Purity in Early Judaism*. Edited by Adele Reinhartz. EJL 24. Atlanta: Society of Biblical Literature.

Halbwachs, Maurice. 1941. *La topographie légendaire des Évangiles en Terre Sainte: Étude de mémoire collective*. Bibliothèque de philosophie contemporaine. Paris: Presses universitaires de France.

———. 1992. *On Collective Memory*. Edited and translated by Lewis A. Coser. Heritage of Sociology. Chicago: University of Chicago Press.

Halliday, Michael A. K. 2004. *An Introduction to Functional Grammar*. 3rd ed. Revised by Christian M. I. M. Matthiesson. London: Hodder Education.

Harkins, Angela Kim. 2012. *Reading with an "I" to the Heavens: Looking at the Qumran Hodayot through the Lens of Visionary Tradition*. Ekstasis 3. Berlin: de Gruyter.

———. 2015. "A Phenomenological Study of Penitential Elements and Their Strategic Arousal of Emotion in the Qumran Hodayot (1QHa cols. 1[?]–8)." Pages 297–316 in *Ancient Jewish Prayers and Emotions: Emotions Associated with Jewish Prayer in and around the Second Temple Period*. Edited by Stefan C. Reif and Renate Egger Wenzel. DCLS 26. Berlin: de Gruyter.

———. 2016a. "Ritual Mourning in Daniel's Interpretation of Jeremiah's Prophecy." *Journal of Cognitive Historiography* 2:14–32.

———. 2016b. "The Pro-social Role of Grief in Ezra's Penitential Prayer." *BibInt* 24:466–91.

———. 2017. "The Function of Prayers of Ritual Mourning in the Second Temple Period." Pages 80–102 in *Functions of Psalms and Prayers in the Late Second Temple Period*. Edited by Mika S. Pajunen and Jeremy Penner. BZAW 486. Berlin: de Gruyter.

———. 2018. "Ritualizing Jesus' Grief at Gethsemane." *JSNT* 41:177–203.

Harrington, Hannah K. 1983. *The Impurity Systems of Qumran and the Rabbis: Biblical Foundations*. SBLDS 143. Atlanta: Scholars Press.

———. 2004. *The Purity Texts*. Companion to the Qumran Scrolls 5. London: T&T Clark.

Harris, William V. 1989. *Ancient Literacy*. Cambridge: Harvard University Press.

Hasselbalch, Trine Bjørnung. 2015. *Meaning and Context in the Thanksgiving Hymns: Linguistic and Rhetorical Perspectives on a Collection of Prayers from Qumran*. EJL 42. Atlanta: SBL Press.

Hazzelrigg, Lawrence E. 1969. "A Reexamination of Simmel's 'The Secret and the Secret Society': Nine Propositions." *Social Forces* 47:323–30.

Heelas, Paul, and Andrew Lock, eds. 1981. *Indigenous Psychologies: The Anthropology of the Self*. Language, Thought, and Culture. London: Academic Press.

Hempel, Charlotte. 2010. "Source and Redactions in the Dead Sea Scrolls: The Growth of Ancient Texts." Pages 162–81 in *Rediscovering the Dead Sea Scrolls: An Assessment of Old and New Approaches and Methods*. Edited by Maxine L. Grossman. Grand Rapids: Eerdmans.

Hezser, Catherine. 2001. *Jewish Literacy in Roman Palestine*. TSAJ 81. Tübingen: Mohr Siebeck.

Hobsbawm, Eric. 1981. *Bandits*. Rev. ed. New York: Pantheon.

Hogan, Karina Martin. 2011. "Mother Earth as a Conceptual Metaphor in 4 Ezra." *CBQ* 73:72–91.

Holland, Dorothy, William Lackicotte Jr., Debra Skinner, and Carole Cain. 1998. *Identity and Agency in Cultural Worlds*. Cambridge: Harvard University Press.

Horbury, William. 2007. "The Remembrance of God in *The Psalms of Solomon*." Pages 111–28 in *Memory in the Bible and Antiquity: The Fifth Durham-Tübingen Research Symposium (Durham, September 2004)*. Edited by Stephen C. Barton, Loren T. Stuckenbruck, and Benjamin G. Wold. WUNT 212. Tübingen: Mohr Siebeck.

Horsley, Richard A. 1979a. "Josephus and the Bandits." *JSJ* 10:37–63.

———. 1979b. "The Sicarii: Ancient Jewish Terrorists." *JR* 59:435–58.

———. 2004. *Hidden Transcript and the Arts of Resistance: Applying the Work of James C. Scott to Jesus and Paul*. SemeiaSt 48. Atlanta: Society of Biblical Literature.

———. 2007. *Scribes, Visionaries and the Politics of Second Temple Judaism*. Louisville: Westminster John Knox.

Horsley, Richard A., and John S. Hanson. 1985. *Bandits, Prophets, and Messiahs: Popular Movements at the Time of Jesus*. Minneapolis: Winston.

Klawans, Jonathan. 2000. *Impurity and Sin in Ancient Judaism*. Oxford: Oxford University Press.

———. 2006. *Purity, Sacrifice, and the Temple: Symbolism and Supersessionism in the Study of Ancient Judaism*. Oxford: Oxford University Press.

———. 2008. "Methodology and Ideology in the Study of Priestly Ritual." Pages 84–95 in *Perspectives on Purity and Purification in the Bible*. Edited by Naphtali S. Meshel, Jeffrey Stackert, David P. Wright, and Baruch J. Schwartz. LHBOTS 474. London: T&T Clark.

Kraft, Robert A., and George W. E. Nickelsburg, eds. 1986. *Early Judaism and Its Modern Interpreters*. BMI 2. Philadelphia: Fortress; Atlanta: Scholars Press.

Krause, Andrew. 2018. "Community, Alterity, and Space in the Qumran Covenant Curses." *DSD* 25:217–37.

Kugler, Robert. A. 2002. "Making All Experience Religious: The Hegemony of Ritual at Qumran." *JSJ* 33:131–52.

———. 2010. "Of Calendars, Community Rules, and Common Knowledge: Understanding 4QS^e–4QOtot, with Help from Ritual Studies." Pages 215–28 in *Rediscovering the Dead Sea Scrolls: An Assessment of Old and New Approaches and Methods*. Edited by Maxine Grossman. Grand Rapids: Eerdmans.

Lakoff, George. 1987. *Women, Fire, and Dangerous Things: What Categories Reveal about the Mind*. Chicago: University of Chicago Press.

Lakoff, George, and Mark Johnson. 1980. *The Metaphors We Live By*. Phoenix Books. Chicago: University of Chicago Press.

Lambert, David A. 2016. *How Repentance Became Biblical: Judaism, Christianity, and the Interpretation of Scripture*. Oxford: Oxford University Press.

Lefebvre, Henri. 1991. *The Production of Space*. Translated by Donald Nicholson Smith. Oxford: Blackwell.

Lied, Liv Ingeborg. 2005. "Another Look at the Land of Damascus: The Spaces of the Damascus Document in Light of Edward W. Soja's Thirdspace Approach." Pages 101–25 in *New Directions in Qumran Studies: Proceedings of the Bristol Colloquium on the Dead Sea Scrolls, 8–10 Sep-*

tember 2003. Edited by Jonathan G. Campbell, Willian John Lyons, and Lloyd K. Pietersen. LSTS 52. London: T&T Clark.

———. 2008. *The Other Lands of Israel: Imagination of the Land in 2 Baruch*. JSJSup 129. Leiden: Brill.

Linski, Gerhard E. 1966. *Power and Privilege: A Theory of Social Stratification*. Chapel Hill: University of North Carolina Press.

Lopez, Kathryn M. 2008. "Standing before the Throne of God: Critical Spatiality in Apocalyptic Scenes of Judgment." Pages 139–55 in *Constructions of Space II: The Biblical City and Other Imagined Spaces*. Edited by Jon L. Berquist and Claudia V. Camp. LHBOTS 490. New York: T&T Clark.

Malina, Bruce. 1981. *The New Testament World: Insights from Cultural Anthropology*. Atlanta: John Knox.

McNamara, Patrick. 2009. *The Neuroscience of Religious Experience*. Cambridge: Cambridge University Press.

Meeks, Wayne. 1983. *The First Urban Christians: The Social World of the Apostle Paul*. New Haven: Yale University Press.

Merkur, Daniel. 1989. "The Visionary Practices of Jewish Apocalypticists." *The Psychoanalytic Study of Society* 14:119–48.

Mermelstein, Ari. 2015. "Constructing Fear and Pride in the Book of Daniel: The Profile of a Second Temple Emotional Community." *JSJ* 46:449–83.

Mirguet, Françoise. 2017. *An Early History of Compassion: Emotion and Imagination in Hellenistic Judaism*. Cambridge: Cambridge University Press.

———. 2019. "The Study of Emotions in Early Jewish Texts: Review and Perspective." *JSJ* 50:557–603.

Newsom, Carol A. 1992. "The Case of Blinking I: Discourse of the Self at Qumran." *Semeia* 57:13–23.

———. 1993. "Knowing as Doing: The Social Symbolics of Knowledge at Qumran." *Semeia* 59:139–53.

———. 1997. "Disciplinary Power in the *Serek ha-Yahad*: Rewards and Punishments from a Foucauldian Perspective." Paper presented at the Annual Meeting of the Society of Biblical Literature. San Francisco, 23 November.

———. 2001. "Apocalyptic Subjects: Social Construction of the Self in the Qumran Hodayot." *JSP* 12:3–35.

———. 2004. *The Self as Symbolic Space: Constructing Identity and Community at Qumran*. STDJ 52. Leiden: Brill.

―――. 2010. "Rhetorical Criticism and the Dead Sea Scrolls." Pages 198–214 in *Rediscovering the Dead Sea Scrolls: An Assessment of Old and New Approaches and Methods*. Edited by Maxine Grossman. Grand Rapids: Eerdmans.

―――. 2012. "Models of the Moral Self: Hebrew Bible and Second Temple Judaism." *JBL* 131:5–25.

Newman, Judith H. 1999. *Praying by the Book: The Scripturalization of Prayer in Second Temple Judaism*. EJL 14. Atlanta: Scholars Press.

―――. 2018. *Before the Bible: The Liturgical Body and the Formation on Scriptures in Early Judaism*. New York: Oxford University Press.

Nickelsburg, George W. E. 1972. *Resurrection, Immortality, and Eternal Life in Intertestamental Judaism*. HTS 26. Cambridge: Harvard University Press.

―――. 1983. "Social Aspects of Palestinian Jewish Apocalypticism." Pages 641–54 in *Apocalypticism in the Mediterranean World and the Near East: Proceedings of the International Colloquium on Apocalypticism, Uppsala, August 12–17, 1979*. Edited by David Hellholm. Tübingen: Mohr Siebeck.

―――. 1991. "The Apocalyptic Construction of Reality in *1 Enoch*." Pages 51–64 in *Mysteries and Revelations: Apocalyptic Studies since the Uppsala Colloquium*. Edited by John. J. Collins and James H. Charlesworth. JSPSup 9. Sheffield: JSOT Press.

―――. 1996. "The Search for Tobit's Mixed Ancestry: A Historical and Hermeneutic Odyssey." *RevQ* 17:339–49.

―――. 1999. "Currents in Qumran Scholarship: The Interplay of Data, Agendas, and Methodology." Pages 79–99 in *The Dead Sea Scrolls At Fifty: Proceedings of the Society of Biblical Literature Qumran Section Meeting*. Edited by Robert A. Kugler and Eileen M. Schuller. EJL 15. Atlanta: Scholars Press.

―――. 2006. *Resurrection, Immortality, and Eternal Life in Intertestamental Judaism and Christianity*. Expanded ed. HTS 56. Cambridge: Harvard University Press.

Niditch, Susan. 1987. *Underdogs and Tricksters: A Prelude to Biblical Folklore*. San Francisco: Harper & Row.

Niditch, Susan, and Robert Doran. 1977. "The Success Story of the Wise Courtier: A Formal Approach." *JBL* 96:179–93.

Nussbaum, Martha C. 2001. *Upheavals of Thought: The Intelligence of Emotion*. Cambridge: Cambridge University Press.

Paganini, Simone M. 2015. "Adjusting the Narrative Emotions and the Prayer of Moses (Jub 1:19–21)." Pages 59–70 in *Ancient Jewish Prayers and Emotions: Emotions Associated with Jewish Prayer in and around the Second Temple Period*. Edited by Stefan C. Reif and Renate Egger Wenzel. DCLS 26. Berlin: de Gruyter.

Portier-Young, Anathea E. 2011. *Apocalypse against Empire: Theology of Resistance in Early Judaism*. Grand Rapids: Eerdmans.

———. 2014. "Jewish Apocalyptic Literature as Resistance Literature." Pages 145–62 in *The Oxford Handbook of Apocalyptic Literature*. Edited by John J. Collins. Oxford: Oxford University Press.

Regev, Eyal. 2007. *Sectarianism in Qumran: A Cross-Cultural Perspective*. RelSoc 45. Berlin: de Gruyter.

Reif, Stefan C., and Renate Egger Wenzel. 2015. *Ancient Jewish Prayers and Emotions: Emotions Associated with Jewish Prayer in and around the Second Temple Period*. DCLS 26. Berlin: de Gruyter.

Rowland, Christopher. 1982. *The Open Heaven: A Study of Apocalyptic in Judaism and Early Christianity*. London: SPCK.

Schams, Christine. 1998 *Jewish Scribes in the Second Temple Period*. JSOTSup 291. Sheffield: Sheffield Academic.

Shantz, Colleen, and Rodney A. Werline, eds. 2012. *Linking Text and Experience*. Vol. 2 of *Experientia*. EJL 35. Atlanta: Society of Biblical Literature.

Schmitz, Barbara. 2015. "Judith and Holofernes: An Analysis of the Emotions in the Killing Scene (Jdt 12:10–13:9)." Pages 177–92 in *Ancient Jewish Prayers and Emotions: Emotions Associated with Jewish Prayer in and around the Second Temple Period*. Edited by Stefan C. Reif and Renate Egger Wenzel. DCLS 26. Berlin: de Gruyter.

Schofield, Alison. 2012. "Re-placing Priestly Space: The Wilderness as Heterotopia in the Dead Sea Scrolls." Pages 469–90 in vol. 1 of *A Teacher for All Generations: Essays in Honor of James C. VanderKam*. Edited by Eric F. Mason. JSJSup 153. 2 vols. Leiden: Brill.

Schwartz, Barry. 2014. "Where There's Smoke, There's Fire: Memory and History." Pages 7–37 in *Memory and Identity in Ancient Judaism and Early Christianity: A Conversation with Barry Schwartz*. Edited by Tom Thatcher. SemeiaSt 78. Atlanta: SBL Press.

Scott, James C. 1990. *Domination and the Arts of Resistance: Hidden Transcripts*. New Haven: Yale University Press.

Segal, Alan F. 1990. *Paul the Convert: The Apostolate and Apostasy of Saul the Pharisee*. New Haven: Yale University Press.

Simmel, George. 1906. "The Sociology of Secrecy and Secret Societies." *American Journal of Sociology* 11:441–98.
Smith-Christopher, Daniel. 2014. "A Postcolonial Reading of Apocalyptic Literature: On Mixing Monsters." Pages 180–98 in *The Oxford Handbook of Apocalyptic Literature*. Edited by John J. Collins. New York: Oxford University Press.
Soja, Edward W. 1989. *Postmodern Geography: The Reassertion of Space in Critical Social Theory*. New York: Verso.
———. 1996. *Thirdspace: Journeys to Los Angeles and Other Real-and-Imagined Places*. Malden, MA: Blackwell.
Stark, Rodney, and William Sims Bainbridge. 1985. *The Future of Religion: Secularization, Revival and Cult Formation*. Berkley: University of California Press.
Stone, Meredith J. 2018. *Empire and Gender in LXX Esther*. EJL 48. Atlanta: SBL Press.
Stone, Michael E. 1974. "Apocalyptic: Vision or Hallucination?" *Milla wa-Milla* 14:47–56.
———. 1976. "Lists of Revealed Things in the Apocalyptic Literature." Pages 414–52 in *Magnalia Dei: The Mighty Acts of God: Essays on the Bible and Archaeology in Memory of G. Ernest Wright*. Edited by Frank Moore Cross, Werner E. Lemke, and Patrick D. Miller. Garden City, NY: Doubleday.
———. 2003. "A Reconsideration of Apocalyptic Visions." *HTR* 96:167–80.
———. 2011. *Ancient Judaism: New Visions and Views*. Grand Rapids: Eerdmans.
———. 2018. *Secret Groups in Ancient Judaism*. Oxford: Oxford University Press.
Stuckenbruck, Loren. 2007. "The Teacher of Righteousness Remembered: From Fragmentary Sources to Collective Memory in the Dead Sea Scrolls." Pages 75–94 in *Memory in the Bible and Antiquity: The Fifth Durham–Tübingen Research Symposium (Durham, September 2004)*. Edited by Stephen C. Barton, Loren T. Stuckenbruck, and Benjamin G. Wold. WUNT 212. Tübingen: Mohr Siebeck.
———. 2010. "The Legacy of the Teacher of Righteousness in the Dead Sea Scrolls." Pages 23–49 in *New Perspectives on Old Texts: Proceedings of the Tenth International Symposium of the Orion Center for the Study of the Dead Sea Scrolls and Associated Literature, 9–11 January, 2005*. Edited by Esther G. Chazon, Baruch Halpern-Amaru, and Ruth A. Clements. STDJ 88. Leiden: Brill.

Tigchelaar, Eibert. 2010. "Constructing, Deconstructing and Reconstructing Fragmentary Manuscripts: Illustrated by a Study of 4Q184 (4Q Wiles of the Wicked Woman)." Pages 26–47 in *Rediscovering the Dead Sea Scrolls: An Assessment of Old and New Approaches and Methods*. Edited by Maxine L. Grossman. Grand Rapids: Eerdmans.

Toorn, Karel van der. 2007. *Scribal Culture and the Making of the Hebrew Bible*. Cambridge: Harvard University Press.

Ventor, Pieter M. 2003. "Spatiality in Enoch's Journeys (1 Enoch 12–36)." Pages 211–30 in *Wisdom and Apocalypticism in the Dead Sea Scrolls and in the Biblical Tradition*. Edited by Florentino García Martínez. BETL 168. Leuven: Peeters; Leuven University Press.

———. 2006. "A Study of Space in Daniel 1." *OTE* 19:993–1004

———. 2008. "Space, Time and Group Identity in Jubilees 8–9." *HvTSt* 64:631–50.

Weitzman, Steven. 1997. "Revisiting Myth and Ritual in Early Judaism." *DSD* 4:21–54.

Werline, Rodney A. 2005. "The *Psalms of Solomon* and the Ideology of Rule." Pages 69–87 in *Conflicted Boundaries in Wisdom and Apocalypticism*. Edited by Lawrence M. Wills and Benjamin G. Wright III. SymS 35. Atlanta: Scholars Press.

———. 2015. "Ritual, Order and the Construction of an Audience in 1 Enoch 1–36." *DSD* 22:325–41.

———. Forthcoming. "Social Memory Features in the *Psalms of Solomon*." In *Psalms of Solomon: Texts, Contexts, and Intertexts; Proceedings of the Second International Meeting on the Psalms of Solomon*. Edited by Kenneth Atkinson, Anthony Keddie, and Patrick Pouchelle. EJL. Atlanta: SBL Press.

Wills, Lawrence. 1990. *The Jew in the Court of the Foreign King: Ancient Jewish Court Legends*. HDR 26. Minneapolis: Fortress.

———. 1995. *The Jewish Novel in the Ancient World*. Ithaca, NY: Cornell University Press.

Wilson, Bryan. 1982. *Religion in Sociological Perspective*. Oxford: Oxford University Press.

Witte, Markus. 2015. "Emotions in the Prayers of the Wisdom of Solomon." Pages 161–76 in *Ancient Jewish Prayers and Emotions: Emotions Associated with Jewish Prayer in and around the Second Temple Period*. Edited by Stefan C. Reif and Renate Egger Wenzel. DCLS 26. Berlin: de Gruyter.

6

THE DEAD SEA SCROLLS

ALISON SCHOFIELD

In March 1948, Professor William F. Albright examined a manuscript copy of the book of Isaiah only a few months after it had been discovered in a cave near the Dead Sea. He quickly recognized that this new find was part of what he determined to be the greatest manuscript discovery of the modern era, even though only seven scrolls had been uncovered. Neither Albright, nor other scholars of his day, could have imagined the extent of the manuscript evidence to emerge from the Judean Desert in the following years.

The Dead Sea Scrolls have significantly impacted the study of early Judaism, even though scrolls scholarship itself is a relatively new field of the past seventy years or so. Nevertheless, it has grown and changed rapidly. New manuscripts quickly came to light in the late 1940s to early 1950s, after bedouin and archaeologists uncovered an entire collection of scrolls from eleven caves near the site of Qumran. There was another influx of material during the 1990s and 2000s, when a majority of these texts were translated and finally published and made available. Editor-in-chief, Emanuel Tov greatly expanded the team working on the scrolls and led the publication of the bulk of the library between 1990 and 2009, when the last volume of the official publication series Discoveries in the Judaean Desert was completed. In the last thirty-five years since the first edition of *Early Judaism and Its Modern Interpreters* (Kraft and Nickelsburg 1986), exponential gains have been made not only in the amount of material available for study but also in what scholars have been able to understand about the entire collection of texts and their authors. This chapter will highlight some of these recent findings and other critical issues surrounding the Dead Sea Scrolls.

1. The Importance of the Scrolls for Early Judaism

The scrolls are significant because of the relative quantity of texts preserved and because this written material even exists at all. Before the discovery of the scrolls, scholars had very few examples of writing on perishable material from the Second Temple period. Most assumed that there were other libraries or manuscript collections from this time, in Jerusalem and elsewhere, but few expected notable amounts of animal skin or papyrus to survive for over two thousand years. Yet the Dead Sea Scrolls survived under an unusual set of conditions. At the lowest point on earth, the Judean Desert provided a hot and dry environment, and the scroll caves were relatively stable in temperature and humidity levels. Further, these hiding places were also relatively inaccessible and undisturbed by later human settlement until the caves were systematically explored and searched by bedouin and archaeologists during the mid-twentieth century.

Second, the Dead Sea Scrolls are perhaps most notable for how they illuminate the history and development of the Bible. Approximately 40 percent of the nearly one thousand different scrolls discovered are copies of portions of the Hebrew Bible. These biblical scrolls constitute many of the earliest-known copies of what would later become books of the Jewish Bible (or Christian Old Testament). Yet the evidence from the caves highlights the fact that the term *Bible* is in many ways an anachronistic term for the late Second Temple period. Various copies of the same biblical book among the scrolls were not uniform in content, nor did they always represent the same text-type, such as that of the Masoretic Text (MT), underlying most translations today. Rather, they preserved various snapshots of what appeared to be a much more diverse and fluid development of the Bible, before the text was fixed and the canon of scriptural books set during later stages of Judaism and Christianity. Third, the scrolls contain valuable information about how biblical interpretation began, and they include the earliest known biblical commentaries. Among the various examples found are modes and genres of biblical interpretation not otherwise known from later rabbinic and Christian sources.

Fourth, the Dead Sea Scrolls contain some of the earliest evidence of later Jewish beliefs and practices. The authors of a few scrolls record very early, developed understandings of Jewish messianic expectations and eschatology. Of the latter, some write in expectation of a new, heavenly temple and a new Jerusalem to come (e.g., New Jerusalem, Temple Scroll).

Not only did members of the scrolls communities copy and preserve some of our earliest translations of the Jewish scriptures, they also included what some would call the first mystical or semimystical Jewish texts, liturgies, and prayers, frequently derived from scriptural texts, and the first, otherwise unknown, exorcistic prayers (11Q5; 4Q510–511). The material and textual remains from Qumran also shed much light on later Jewish practices. Their authors copied very small texts housed within tefillin, or Jewish phylacteries, which they wore for prayers, and they left behind the first confirmed example of a mezuzah (8Q4). Further, in their writings, the members of these communities preserved what are now some of the oldest preserved legal traditions, or halakah, outside of the Bible. This includes the first evidence of the Jewish quorum of ten, or minyan, first mentioned in some of the communities' own texts (see 1QS; 1QSa; CD), as well as descriptions of ritual bath (mikvaot) and Sabbath practices. The authors of the scrolls engaged in debates over proper Jewish praxis (see 4QMMT), as an early example of what the later rabbis describe as halakic debates between Pharisees and Sadducees and others.

And fifth, the scrolls are important because they illuminate the diversity of Judaisms during the late Second Temple period, before any normative Judaism or Christianity emerged. The Jewish authors of the scroll texts, who self-identified as the Yahad, composed their own sectarian texts which reflect distinct, but yet consistent, perspectives on praxis and theology among the various writings. For example, they recorded written law codes (penal codes), reflecting their specific community rules for living, which are otherwise unattested in later Jewish sources. If these are written records of their own oral laws or traditions, this group of priests went against the later rabbinic prohibition of writing down the oral torah (b. Git. 60b). Finally, the scrolls have also increased our understanding of scribal practices and scribal training in the early Jewish context (Carr 2005, 2011; Delamarter 2010; Tigchelaar 2019; Tov 2004), shedding light on how Jewish religious culture shifted from a priest and cultic center toward that based on the study of sacred texts.

2. Overview of the Collection

The Dead Sea Scrolls can be taken to mean manuscript collections from eighteen total sites in the Judean Desert from the seventh century BCE to the eighth to eleventh centuries CE, including those from Qumran, as well as near-by sites such as Naḥal Ḥever, Wadi Murabbaʿat, Khirbet Mird, and Masada (Eshel 2010; Tov 2010). However, this brief overview will be limited to the more common definition of the Dead Sea Scrolls as only those manuscripts discovered in 1947–1956 in the caves near the site of Qumran.

Penned between 250 BCE and 68 CE, the scrolls include between nine hundred and one thousand discrete texts. However, very few manuscripts were found completely intact; most were recovered only in fragmentary pieces. And these fragments were spread among eleven caves of varying distance from the settlement at Qumran. Caves 4–10 are clustered within about 150 m of the site. Caves 1, 2, 3, and 11 are within 1–2 km north of the site, while Cave 3 is the farthest from Qumran. Cave 4 contained the greatest number of manuscripts (seven hundred), followed by Cave 1 (eighty) and Cave 11 (thirty-one); other caves yielded a handful of fragments or, in the case of Cave 10, only one pottery sherd with two letters.

Only a small minority of scholars still question the link between the caves and the site (Cansdale 1997; Golb 1995; Hirschfeld 2004; Magen and Peleg 2007; Stacey and Doudna 2013). Most others point to what they consider to be very strong evidence that connects these scrolls with the neighboring settlement at Qumran: such as their close geographical proximity (esp. Caves 4–10), contemporaneous time frame, and the evidence of writing and multiple inkwells from Qumran. Further, archaeologists have highlighted how the pottery from the caves (e.g., Caves 4, 6, 7, 8) parallels pottery found in the neighboring settlement (Humbert 2016; Lemaire 2003; Magness 2002, 2016; Mizzi 2019; Zangenberg 2016).

The entire collection of scrolls reflects a wide array of literary and religious material. One can find the genre of prayers, hymns, liturgical texts, legal material, community rule-texts for the Yahad alongside calendrical texts, eschatological material, wisdom texts, biblical texts, and examples of biblical interpretation. Also preserved are some texts later classified as apocrypha and pseudepigrapha, as well as the earliest translations, or targumim, of the biblical text into Aramaic. Unlike the manuscript collections found elsewhere in the Judean desert, only a very small number of the Dead Sea Scrolls could be classified as documentary, or nonliterary, texts (letters, a record of debt, documents dealing with the sale of land, etc.). Yet there is some debate about whether these documents actually originated in Qumran or some other site nearby, and it is clear that, as a whole, the scrolls are overwhelmingly literary and religious in nature.

The physical characteristics of the Qumran manuscripts are varied. Most of the manuscripts (85–90 percent) were copied onto parchment, or treated animal skins, from domesticated goats and ibexes and possibly calfskin. The remaining scrolls (10–15 percent) were written on papyrus, and one was inscribed onto a thin, copper sheet (3Q15). A few other scattered inscriptions were found on jars and ostraca, as well as one limestone plaque. Some extant scrolls are as long as eight meters (11Q19), while others were copied onto tiny pieces of parchment, as in the case of the tefillin. Approximately 85 percent of the Qumran collection was written in Hebrew, often in an archaizing form closer to Biblical Hebrew than the vernacular of its day (but cf. 3Q15). Roughly 11–12 percent of the collection is in Aramaic, and a few fragments in Greek exist. Most of the Hebrew and Aramaic texts were penned in the common square script, or Aramaic script, of their day, but a small number of Hebrew manuscripts were written in paleo-Hebrew or an otherwise-unknown cryptic Hebrew script, which likely was invented by the authors of the scrolls and could have provided some secrecy for the Yahad and their sectarian texts.

2.1. Authorship and Ownership: Who Hid the Dead Sea Scrolls?

Who wrote the Dead Sea Scrolls? Since early on in scrolls scholarship, the standard view has been that the Essenes wrote the Dead Sea Scrolls, under the direction of the so-called Teacher of Righteousness, and in protest against other Jews and the Jerusalem priesthood. This group of priests disagreed with other Jews about the proper calendar, advocating for a 364-day solar calendar rather than the lunar-based calendar of the temple, and these priestly protestors withdrew from Jerusalem to settle in the desert near the Dead Sea.

Recently, some have challenged many of these ideas as oversimplified or have added nuance to what we can conclude about the Yahad in light of the entire body of evidence from Qumran. Most generally agree that the Yahad was related to the Essenes rather than the Pharisees, Sadducees, or another known Jewish group. Yet the exact relationship between the Yahad and the Essenes is still not entirely clear. Partly, this is due to a lack of primary sources contemporaneous to the Essenes and other Jewish sects of the late Second Temple period. The most closely related classical sources (such as Josephus, Philo, and Pliny the Elder) are ambiguous or biased and were likely composed not from primary observation but earlier sources (see also VanderKam 2010, 2019). The Essenes are not mentioned at all in the New Testament, which may have been because they were not useful foils to the characterization of Jesus and his early followers.

The authors of the scrolls themselves never identify themselves as Essenes, a term derived from Greek and Latin sources, although it is probably based on their Hebrew description of themselves as "doers ['ośê] of the torah" (e.g., 1QpHab VII, 10–12; see VanderKam 1999). Yet the most common term the authors of the scrolls use to identify themselves, Yahad, is never directly translated into the Greek or Latin classical sources often used to understand this group. It is clear that the authors of the scrolls understood themselves to be a righteous minority in marked contrast to their fellow Jewish contemporaries. They called themselves the "children of light," "people of righteousness," "children of truth," and the "elect of righteousness." They stood in opposition to the "children of darkness," "people of wickedness," "people of mockery," and so on, whom they perceived to be Jews who did not follow the appropriate Jewish praxis, calendar, and revelation from God. The authors of the Yahad's charter text, Community Rule, for example, believed themselves to be the true covenant-keeper of Israel and pious priests, who willingly observe the statutes of God (1QS I, 7; VIII, 10). Among other things, they were called to uphold the virtues of truth, righteousness, humility, justice, introspection, and covenantal love (1QS I, 5–6; V, 3–4; VIII, 2).

2.2. Did the Dead Sea Scrolls Constitute a Library?

Questions remain about the character and origin of the Qumran texts and whether we can call the scrolls a library (see Crawford and Wassen 2016; Martone 2016; Lange 2006; Werrett 2016). The scrolls can be dated paleographically to roughly the same time frame in the late Second Temple period, and the scroll caves are clearly interlinked, as many of the same texts were found in more than one copy among the various caves. Cave 4 itself contained copies of almost all of the other works (Dimant 1995). Further, scrolls from multiple caves share similar handwriting and other paleographic features. For example, one scribe penned both the Cave 1 copy of the Community Rule (1QS) and a few texts from Cave 4 (4Q175 [Testimonia]; and a copy of Samuel, 4Q53 [4QSam^c]) (Ulrich 1979).

Those who collected the scrolls shared a similar religious self-understanding, as the scrolls record the same unique terminology, shared legal traditions, and common approaches to scriptural interpretation (see also Tigchelaar 2012). In light of these characteristics and the close proximity in which they were found, many scholars label Qumran as a library or at least an intentional collection of texts (Dimant 1995, 2015 with bibliography). At least it is clear that the scrolls do not reflect the entirety of contemporaneous Jewish literature, nor do they represent a disparate collection of random Jewish texts.

But were all of the Dead Sea manuscripts part of a single, working library? Most scholars would disagree with this characterization of the scrolls as a library, at least in the modern sense of the term (Stökl ben Ezra 2007, 2011). The texts from all Qumran caves appear to be a related and possibly even a communal or school-like collection (Taylor 2012). Yet it is not clear that all of these scrolls were accessed to the same degree nor even simultaneously. Some argue that some or most of these scrolls could have been part of an ancient genizah, or ritual storage area for discarded texts (Brooke 2005; Taylor 2012). Others conclude that these scrolls were in use but hidden together only as a one-time or even urgent move (García Martínez 2010; White Crawford 2012).

Further, many scholars are increasingly convinced that at least some of the scrolls could not have been penned at Qumran, especially since some of the scrolls predate the settlement at Qumran by up to 120 years and because an unusually high number of scribal hands are represented for a small desert community of no more than 100–150 inhabitants (Alexander 2003). At least some scrolls likely originated in different localities (see §2.2.1), only eventually to end up in caves near Qumran, possibly brought over time by Yahad members from inside and outside of the area (see CD description of rules for members traveling between communities), and/or some may have also been hidden simultaneously in the remote Judean desert in the face of the Roman threat (Schofield 2009). The latter scenario would be similar to how other manuscripts were deposited in the Judean Desert alongside those seeking refuge (for descriptions of scrolls being scattered in times of war, see 2 Macc 2:14–15). Recent Instrumental Neutron Activation Analysis (INAA) of pottery found among the scrolls has confirmed that at least some of the unique scroll-shaped jars found at Qumran originated from clay sources far from the site (Yellin, Broshi, and Eshel 2001; Gunneweg and Balla 2006). These data could indicate that these scroll jars also traveled to Qumran with scrolls inside, but that remains unconfirmed.

2.3. Forms of Community

The group's self-identification as Yahad arises from a Hebrew root word indicating togetherness or unity. This term reflects their common activities and daily life among members, who share property, eat together, give counsel to one another, pronounce blessings and curses together, and meet each evening to study and worship (see the Community Rule, etc.).

The social context of the Yahad was highly structured, with a hierarchical leadership concentrated around increasingly authoritative priestly groups (Levites, Aaronites, and Zadokites; e.g., 1QS I, 18–23; II, 19–23; V, 2–3). They describe their meetings, meals, and festivals as those in which members physically organize themselves along the lines of their authority, with incoming, proselyte members having the most peripheral roles in the rituals. The sectarian texts mention leaders, not by personal name but by titles, such as the Teacher of Righteousness, who is associated with the foundational years of the movement (CD I, 1–11) and who is elsewhere called a priest and equated with "The Interpreter of the Law." This title may have referred to a position passed down to others in subsequent years. While their authors never clarify the roles of specific leaders, some texts mention a prominent figure, the Instructor (Maskil), in addition to the Overseer (Mebaqqer), the latter of which is associated with an important governing body within the Yahad, the Many (Rabbim). The Many constitutes a majority, judicial body of fully fellowshipped members that is charged with assembling, examining prospective members, and undertaking other decisions by vote (CD XIII, 7; XIV, 7; 1QS V, 2–3; VI, 1–25; VII, 3).

Soon after the scrolls were discovered, many equated the two prominent sectarian rule texts, the Damascus Document (CD) and the Community Rule (1QS), with two distinct groups of sectarians mentioned in Josephus: an order of Essenes who marry (*B.J.* 1.160) and a pious group who are celibate, respectively. In 1QS, there is no explicit mention of women, and although it never proscribes celibacy, one could be celibate and follow its rules. Yet, in recent years, many have questioned this simplistic understanding of two monolithic CD and 1QS communities. As Maxine Grossman (2010a, 241) reminds us, in androcentric texts "the absence of women in the wording should not lead us to assume their absence from the world imagined in the text." Eventually other rule texts were published, especially in the 1990s, and they depict a more complex and diverse set of sectarian audiences and concerns. For example, one rule text mentions both the Yahad and the Many, alongside legislation for childbirth and family life (4Q265), and another parallels segments of 1QS (1QS IV, 4–6) and also descriptions of women, wives, and procreation (4Q502 [Ritual of Marriage]).

In general, more scholars have come to see the Yahad itself encompassing more than Qumran (Collins 2010; Elgvin 2005; Schofield 2008, 2009). Multiple communities are mentioned in the Community Rule ("In this way they shall behave in all of their places of residences," 1QS VI, 1), and these settlements are similar in description to the various "camps" mentioned in CD and elsewhere (1QM, 4QMMT, etc.), although different terminology is used to describe each. Nevertheless, the hypothesis that the scrolls, and the Community Rule, were the product of one celibate community living at Qumran by the Dead Sea is no longer tenable (more below).

2.4. Categories and Genre

Since 2009, upon completion of the final volume of Discoveries in the Judean Desert, scrolls scholars have shifted their work from primarily assembling and translating fragments to assessing the meaning and overall picture of the Qumran collection. In light of the entire body of evidence, many have rightly questioned or deconstructed previous labels, categories, and genres first applied to the scrolls. Initially, scholars divided the scrolls into three categories: (1) biblical texts, (2) apocrypha and pseudepigrapha, and (3) sectarian (Essene) scrolls. Yet these categories have not sufficiently accounted for all the textual evidence (for recent classifications, see Lange and Mittmann-Richert 2002). The categories of biblical and nonbiblical assume a relatively normative or canonized understanding of the Bible, which did not yet exist in the latter days of the Second Temple (Tigchelaar 2012). Additionally, identifying sectarian versus nonsectarian texts has proven to be problematic; it is not always clear from the language alone which content was authored by Yahad members. Further, we lack much knowledge about the relationship between various Jewish groups (or sects) in this time, and there is no comparable first-hand textual evidence from other groups to which we may compare the collection of scrolls.

The idea of genre itself is a scholarly construct, and one that can limit our understanding and analysis of the scrolls (e.g., Bernstein 2013; Brooke 2013; Collins 2016; Metso 2012; Najman 2012; Wright 2010; and esp. *DSD* 17). At least when applying modern, constructed categories, many recognize that the evidence from Qumran does not easily fit. Many scrolls contain a variety of previously unknown and genre-bending categories of texts, such as the Community Rule, which interlaces liturgical-type material, wisdom literature, legal code, and hymn/poetic texts (and, in one example, a calendar of priestly rotations, 4Q259 [4QS^e]). Other examples include mysteries (1Q27; 4Q299–300), which mix prophetic, priestly, and sapiential elements, with clear verbal similarities to the wisdom text, 4Q418 (Instruction; Thomas 2019), or 4Q176 (Consolations), inextricably mixing both liturgical and wisdom elements. The latter example seamlessly moves between scriptural and nonscriptural elements, posing a literary challenge to the current notion of Bible itself.

3. Bible and Authoritative Scriptures

Some 220 scrolls have been labeled as biblical or works that eventually became recognized as part of the Hebrew Bible. Copies of every book of the Jewish/Protestant Hebrew Bible have been found among the scrolls, with the exception of Esther. In some cases, the Qumran fragments are 1,200 years earlier than the Leningrad Codex of the MT (ca. 1008 CE) and up to 600 years prior to the earliest, relatively complete copies of the Old Greek translation (the Septuagint, or LXX). However, which scrolls the Yahad considered to be scripture is not always clear, and they likely included more authoritative texts than what later became part of the Jewish biblical canon.

3.1. Scripture and Authority at Qumran

In general, *canon* itself is a notion more suited to the postbiblical period (Lange 2002; Ulrich 2015; VanderKam 2002; VanderKam and Flint 2002). Yet, some scrolls from Qumran were clearly more authoritative than others. James VanderKam proposes a few criteria for authoritative or scriptural texts from Qumran: (1) includes language indicating scriptural status (e.g., "As it is written," "thus it is written," "as God promised") or (2) associates a particular book or writing with prophecy or divine authority. For example, the Great Psalms Scroll from Qumran (11Q5 [11QPs^a]) refers to David composing these psalms through prophecy, Jubilees refers to itself as divine revelation, and the Temple Scroll records a version of Deuteronomy and places it in the mouth of God, spoken in the first person. Authoritative texts (3) are preserved in a relatively large number of copies, (4) may have their own commentaries, or (5) may be found alongside translations of their text. Or, finally, (6) they may be quoted or alluded to in another manuscript, such as in the New Testament book of Jude, which quotes from 1 En. 1.9 and references it as prophecy (VanderKam and Flint 2002, 172–80; see also Tigchelaar 2012; Ulrich 2010b).

The most popular texts from Qumran were the Psalms (thirty-six copies), Deuteronomy (thirty), Isaiah (twenty-one), Genesis (twenty), Exodus (fifteen to seventeen), Jubilees (fifteen), Leviticus (twelve to thirteen), 1 Enoch (twelve), and Daniel (eight) (see also Berthelot 2019; Popović 2010). Jubilees and 1 Enoch were very likely considered to be scriptural for the authors of the scrolls, given their content, how they are referenced in other works, and how many copies were found (Lange 2002; Ulrich 2015; VanderKam 2002). Fragments of the Apocrypha, such as Tobit, Ben Sira, and the Letter of Jeremiah were also discovered at Qumran, but it is not entirely clear that any had reached scriptural status. Also, it is likely that "authoritative scripture" may not have been a formal category, for which they viewed texts as either scripture or not, but one that was graduated and variable in its degree of authority (see also Bautch and Weinbender 2019). In this way, one is reminded that as modern readers, we should not privilege the category of Bible, especially the MT, when reading these early Jewish texts in order to understand the dynamic nature of sacred writings and the true diversity of early Jewish literature (Mroczek 2016).

3.2. Variants and Versions

On the closest, textual level, copies of biblical and related material from Qumran diverge in orthography, language, and expression. That multiple manuscripts of the same biblical book vary in spelling and wording is not surprising, given that many of these texts had not been standardized yet and were copied by hand in various locations. From the beginning, most scholars classified the biblical fragments according to their relative similarity with the Masoretic text-type (proto-MT), or the text was equated to the Hebrew underlying the Greek translation (LXX) or the language of the Samaritan Pentateuch. Yet many copies of biblical books did not easily align with the previously known text-types, often preserving previously unknown variants in the biblical text (Tov 2012). The most prominent example includes a missing paragraph of text between 1 Sam 10–11, preserved in one copy of Samuel (4Q51 [4QSam[a]]), which had clearly fallen out relatively early due to scribal error and was not preserved in later Hebrew versions of this text (although Josephus knew of this content in A.J. 6.68–69) (for more examples, see VanderKam and Flint 2002). That such a diversity in biblical text was found side by side in the Qumran caves should lead us to problematize any simplistic efforts to categorize the content of these biblical scrolls along the lines of later, known biblical types.

On a larger scale, the overall content of these books was sometimes quite fluid, even as they approached scriptural status. The lack of any normative version did not appear to cause much interpretive alarm for the Yahad members. At least, they kept or stored different versions of the same work side-by-side, such as the longer version of Jeremiah found in most Bibles today (which aligns with the MT; 4Q70 [4QJer^a]; 4Q72 [4QJer^c]), which was stored alongside the notably shorter edition (cf. the LXX; 4Q71 [4QJer^b]; 4Q72a [4QJer^d]). Nor did the authors of the scrolls record any explicit concerns about having multiple versions of the same biblical material, but rather they seem to assume that any authority lay in the work itself, rather than in its specific text type or edition (see also Berthelot 2019). The Yahad did not privilege the MT version of the Bible, as did later Jewish and Christian communities. Therefore, we should not assume that the MT (or proto-MT) is necessarily an earlier or more reliable witness to the biblical text.

4. Interpreting Scripture

One effect of the gradual closing of the biblical canon was that Jewish readers increasingly needed to interpret the biblical text as they began to turn to previous scripture for guidance rather than generate new authoritative texts. There was already a need to interpret words and phrases that had fallen out of use by the late Second Temple period and also a need to explain gaps, ambiguities, and apparent inconsistencies in the text (see Kugel 1998). But perhaps most importantly, the Yahad looked to earlier authoritative texts to help them understand the politically and socially turbulent age in which they found themselves (see Henze 2005).

As with their Jewish contemporaries, the Yahad encountered divine revelation in various sources and formats (Najman 2003). Ongoing revelation for the Yahad may have resulted from an embodied or even ecstatic experience (e.g., Harkins 2012; Newman 2018). But more likely, some or most of this inspiration was text-generated, where community members drew new meanings from earlier biblical texts. They record various expressions of divine revelation in the scrolls, including new interpretations of biblical texts, often voiced through the mouths of angels or biblical figures of the past or through direct commentaries on the Bible. In this way, certain scribes of the scrolls authorized and reworked earlier biblical traditions in a variety of ways, as they understood themselves to be the recipients of specialized or even secret knowledge. In their self-descriptions, they even describe themselves as the Israelites who were at the foot of Sinai, special inhabitants of the desert, where one could have direct access to divine revelation (Schofield 2008, 2011).

4.1. Rewritten Bible or the Parabiblical Texts

A subgroup of texts from the Qumran collection were first called "rewritten Bible" because they were interpretive retellings or paraphrasings of one or more sections of the Bible (see Falk 2007; Mroczek 2016; Najman 2003; Zahn 2019). Often these rewritings would presumably derive from the author's own interpretation or would contain material from wider traditions or sources. These works are not unlike some examples of rewritten Bible in the Bible itself (such as with Deuteronomy or Chronicles). In at least one case in these scrolls, the author claims that God told the community leader, the Teacher of Righteousness, the true understanding of biblical prophecy, as first recorded in Habakkuk (1QpHab VII, 3–5). So, revelation, at least in some form, was believed to continue beyond the lives of the original biblical authors and was relevant to the current context of the Yahad.

Scholars of biblical interpretation have shown notable interest in the rewritten Bible texts, given how their authors took liberties in reworking an earlier authoritative text; however, many have recently added nuance to the conversation about these scrolls and their classification (see Bernstein 2005; Brooke 2010; Campbell 2014; Najman and Tigchelaar 2014; Segal 2005; Crawford 2008). Since the 1990s, many have preferred the alternate *parabiblical* (or even *parascriptural*; Kraft 2007) as a label for these texts, since the base text and the rewritten version are not always fixed or clear to us today (Segal 2012; Crawford 2012). The rewritten texts were not necessarily of secondary status to those versions later included in the Hebrew Bible, despite the fact that many early scholars assumed that they were of a derivative (and secondary) nature (see Zahn 2019). Nor can one assume that each parabiblical book from Qumran was derivative of the biblical text as we now have it (MT), given how fluidly traditions developed in the Second Temple period (Mroczek 2016; Ulrich 2015). Some of these parabiblical texts may have developed relatively early (4Q47? [4QJosh^a]), simultaneously with other biblical traditions, and possibly even influenced the ongoing development of these biblical books to which they were related (Popović 2010).

Two prominent examples of these parabiblical texts from Qumran themselves claim to be authoritative, or even scriptural. The Temple Scroll lays claim to divine inspiration by re-presenting material from the Pentateuch with God speaking in the first rather than the third person ("and I said"). The most complete copy of the Temple Scroll (11Q19) is the longest of the Dead Sea Scrolls (more than eight meters) and contains a reworking of various laws and biblical texts generally drawn from Deuteronomy but shaped to reflect the 364-day solar calendar and similar legal material found in the Dead Sea Scrolls (Schiffman forthcoming). Also, the author of Jubilees presents this work as a revelation from God, through an angel, who in turn tells it to Moses to write down. The work includes a reworking of Gen 1 through Exod 19:24, concluding with Moses's ascension of Mount Sinai. The author(s) modifies the biblical stories in order to authorize their unique view on theological and legal matters, including the use of the 364-day solar calendar known from Qumran scrolls. Given this self-authorization, in addition to the number of copies found and that it is cited as an authority in other sectarian texts, makes it likely that Jubilees was considered to be scripture at Qumran. This status is further confirmed by the presence of rewritten(?) versions of this text among the Qumran scrolls (Pseudo-Jubilees [4Q225–227; etc.]).

Other parabiblical texts rework a biblical tradition in order to address inconsistencies or other exegetical issues in the earlier text (e.g., 1QapGen; 4Q22 [4QpaleoExod^m]; 11Q10) or to adapt a previous biblical work into a liturgical setting (e.g., 4Q41). Sometimes the authors rework an entire tradition, such as that around Moses (Apocryphon of Moses [2Q20; 4Q375–377]; Pseudo-Moses [4Q385–390]) or around the prophets Jeremiah (Apocryphon of Jeremiah [4Q383–385; 4Q387; 4Q389]) or Ezekiel (Pseudo-Ezekiel [4Q385–388; 4Q391]). Other parabiblical scrolls, such as Wiles of the Wicked Woman (4Q184) and Beatitudes (4Q525), engage biblical books passages intertextually, such as Prov 1–9 (Tigchelaar 2012) or contain a pastiche of biblical quotations and allusions (Words of the Luminaries [4Q504–506]). It is unclear whether the authors of these works meant them to complement, supplement, or even replace the earlier biblical version (Tigchelaar 2012).

4.2. Biblical Commentaries

The authors of the scrolls interpreted scripture in other, more explicit ways, clearly distinguishing between Bible and commentary. Seventeen or eighteen texts have been labeled continuous commentaries, or pesharim, featuring a quotation of a biblical work followed by its interpretation. Only texts that were considered to be prophetic literature included these types of commentaries: Isaiah (six), Psalms (three), Hosea (two), Micah (two), and Zephaniah (two), as well as one each on Habakkuk and Nahum (the Psalms themselves were considered to be prophetic during this time). Scholars have mined these commentaries on scripture for historical details about their authors, who find guidance in these earlier prophetic texts for their specific historical circumstances. For example, the Habakkuk Pesher speaks of the "Kittim" (likely the Romans) and describes "the Wicked Priest who pursued the Teacher of Righteousness to the house of his exile" (1QpHab XI, 2–4), which have spawned much debate on how these figures related to known historical figures.

Other commentaries, known as thematic pesharim, do not interpret a sequence of verses from a biblical book but rather compile verses from various biblical sources that all relate to a particular theme. Their authors create meaning through what passages they select and how they arrange them. Florilegium (4Q174) also incorporates the term midrash, which may explain the type of thematic interpretation present here, as well as in other works such as Testimonia (4Q175), Melchizedek (11Q13), and possibly Ages of Creation (4Q180) and Commentary on Genesis A (4Q252).

5. Legal Material

Relatively few texts from Qumran are comprehensive, organized collections of legal statutes, yet the legal material that is represented reflects a diversity in styles, terminology, and ways in which their authors authorize their legal content. These texts are primarily concerned with issues surrounding observing the Sabbath, purity, and cultic regulations, and concerns about the structure and function of the Jerusalem temple (the Temple Scroll). Alongside regulations about ritual purity are moral concerns as well (H. Harrington 2004; Klawans 2006; Werrett 2007; Wassen 2019). Only since the late 1970s and early 1980s has the extent of the legal material been recognized and systematically analyzed in relation to later Jewish rabbinic law (Amihai 2017; Jassen 2012, 2014; Nitzan 2010; Schiffman 2010, 2019; Shemesh 2009, 2012; Shemesh and Werman 2003). The most important legal texts discovered include the Temple Scroll, Miqṣat Maʿaśê ha-Torah (4QMMT), Ordinances (4Q159; 4Q513–514), Miscellaneous Rules (4Q265); Halakhah A and B (4Q251; 4Q264), Tohorot (4Q274), and the legal sections within the Damascus Document.

Miqṣat Maʿaśê ha-Torah (4QMMT) is unique among the scrolls because it is written in the form of an epistolary treatise, where the authors take issue with a number of practices or interpretations about some purity regulations, sacrifices, and other temple regulations, priestly gifts, and illegal marriages. When it was first discovered, most scholars assumed that this was a letter written by the Teacher of Righteousness to the Wicked Priest, a high priest in Jerusalem and one of the teacher's main opponents (see also 4Q171 [4QpPsalms^a]). In recent years, most have abandoned this view or question whether it was even meant to be a letter at all (Doering 2012; Hempel 2010; von Weissenberg 2009). Whatever its function, the Halakic Document deals with matters of priestly concern, and the positions taken by the author(s) are generally stricter than those of the addressees and they support their arguments by citing or alluding to scriptural source texts (Kratz 2006; von Weissenberg 2009). The concerns with temple matters could reflect their hope that the temple cult would be purified (Hempel 2010; von Weissenberg 2010), or it may have been used to instruct and strengthen the identity of new Yahad members (Fraade 2000; Grossman 2001).

6. The Rule Texts

From the Qumran collection emerged an otherwise unknown and distinctive type of literature regarding the Yahad, known as the rule texts. Generally, these compositions include information about community identity and leadership, as well as theological and liturgical material, instruction, organizational procedures, rule codes for proper conduct within the community, and hymns (for more about this category of texts, see Collins 2010; Hempel 2019; Metso 2007; Newsom 2004).

The rule texts offer us an unprecedented look into the beliefs, practices, and self-understanding of the authors of the Dead Sea Scrolls, and the two most important examples of these, the Community Rule and the Damascus Document, have been the subject of ongoing debates and analysis. Both of these texts appear in multiple copies and different versions, which attest to a long and dynamic history of development for both sets of traditions. Both contain overlapping material, such as how one enters a specific group, and the punishments involved when one does not follow the regulations of the community. Yet these two texts diverge somewhat in content as well as in rhetorical design. These and other related texts are different enough that some have recently challenged whether we should even categorize the rule texts as a genre or simply texts with a shared family resemblance (Newsom 2010; Hempel 2013, 2019).

6.1. The Community Rule

One of the first few scrolls to be discovered was the Cave 1 copy of the Community Rule (1QS). The Community Rule describes the ideology of the community and an annual covenant renewal ceremony, alongside a theological Treatise on the Two Spirits, a collection of rules, guidance on oaths, information about the purpose of the community, and a thanksgiving hymn. Given its well-preserved state and relatively early appearance, 1QS became the standard text to which all others of the rule category were compared. Early scholars quickly correlated its rich descriptions of covenant renewal ceremonies, organizational meals and meetings, community entry procedures, and depictions of daily life to similar descriptions of the Essenes in the writings of Josephus and Philo of Alexandria. Most assumed that the authors and audience of the Community Rule were synonymous with the Qumran community.

Yet later discoveries and recent studies have challenged this equation as overly essentializing. Ten additional copies of the Community Rule were discovered in Cave 4, along with related material. Major differences between the Cave 4 and Cave 1 copies were revealed, not only when describing different authorities within the community ("the Many" in 4Q256; 4Q258 [4QS^{b,d}] versus "the Sons of Zadok" in 1QS), but also in content. For example, some Cave 4 copies are missing columns 1–4 of 1QS, and 4Q259 [4QS^e] includes an otherwise-unknown calendrical text at the end. Scholars have argued that there is no obvious, single line of textual development of the materials (Alexander and Vermès 1998; Hempel 2006; Metso 1997; Schofield 2009). Further, some have questioned whether the Community Rule was composed in, and should apply only to the Qumran community, given its complex textual history and contradictory regulatory material (Schofield 2009).

6.2. The Damascus Document

The Damascus Document recounts the origins and early history of its authors alongside important information about their organization. It contains regulations for community structure, guidance on marriage, family life, and how to engage non-Essenes, among other things. Ten copies were discovered in the Qumran caves (4Q266–273; 5Q12; 6Q15). While the Damascus Document exhibits less variation among the copies than those of the Community Rule, its history and development is no less complicated. Two copies were also discovered in Cairo in a Karaite synagogue (CD A and CD B), dating to the tenth and twelfth centuries, and it is unclear how (or why) this otherwise unknown text would be preserved in a later, distant context. Surprisingly, there is close textual correspondence between the medieval copies of the Damascus Document from Cairo and those copied over one thousand years earlier and hidden away in Cave 4.

Even more complicated is the relationship between the Damascus Document and the Community Rule. They share organizational terminology and both contain a penal code of regulations for members (but only in the Cave 4 versions of the Damascus Document, not in the Cairo Genizah copies). Both rule texts refer to a subgroup of those who have obtained a higher degree of holiness and both contain legal material related to the Sabbath, oaths and vows, trials, purity and impurity, as well as engagement with gentiles, but otherwise they also record different content and legal material. Do they describe separate communities? Some scholars have found that the Damascus Document and the Community Rule represent separate, even polemical groups, but given that so many manuscripts of the Damascus Document were copied and preserved at Qumran, that scenario seems less likely. Some have found the Damascus Document to represent earlier sectarian content and terminology (Hultgren 2007) and even some evidence of a Qumran redaction of the Damascus Document, bringing it closer in line to the later realities of the Yahad and the Community Rule traditions (Hempel 2000).

7. Poetic and Liturgical Texts

The authors of the Dead Sea Scrolls composed and/or preserved poetic religious texts, including liturgies, prayers, blessings, and hymns, presumably for both private and public rituals. Some of these might best be described as prayers and hymns. Others were marked as liturgical texts, for daily blessings, for the Sabbath sacrifice, festival prayers, and other daily prayers, preceding the rabbinic forms of institutionalized prayer by up to a few hundred years. Yet there is disagreement about categorizing these texts. It is not always clear that a specific text is simply poetry or a hymn, especially given that we have limited access to the actual performances, if any, of these texts. In general, poetry among the scroll texts can be classified as a literary mode of expression and therefore overlap many other genres of texts. Poetic texts may be divided into (1) blessings and curses, (2) eschatological or prophetic poetry, (3) magical poetry, (4) mystical poetry, and (5) songs of praise, (6) laments, and (7) sapiential poetry (Nitzan 1994).

Categorizing something as a liturgical text, however, requires us to presume a context or performance, but this can be unclear unless it is explicitly identified or assigned to a time of the calendar, such as we have for Words of the Luminaries (4Q504; 4Q505?; 4Q506) and Songs of the Sabbath Sacrifice (4Q400–407; 11Q17). These liturgical texts may have been communally performed and may have been used to transform the participants through the repetition of the terse language and (semi-)mystical images (Angel 2010; Newman 2008). Other poetic works may also have been performed and used to generate religious experience, such as the Hodayot, a collection of poetic hymns likely used in communal gatherings (4Q427–432 [1QH^{a-e}]; and related texts 4Q433; 4Q433a; and 4Q440). When read and reenacted, these prayer texts could engender a particular emotional or transformational experience in the participant (Harkins 2012), or they could be of the tradition of lament and thanksgiving psalms in the Bible, read as part of and authorizing the Yahad's system of bringing in members to their community (Newsom 2004).

8. Sapiential Texts

From the many scrolls discovered, scholars identified a number of new examples of wisdom literature or those containing sapiential material. These are pedagogical texts that contain at least some of the following: instruction or exhortation, proverbial or didactic material encouraging one to seek the acquisition of knowledge, concern with the order of cosmos, the meaning of life and death, and other wisdom-related content (see Goff 2006; Harrington 1996; Hempel, Lange and Lichtenberger 2012; Kampen 2011; Tigchelaar 2012). Yet some point out that there is no evidence that the authors of the scrolls recognized any specific literary, wisdom genre, and such categorizations are more appropriate constructs for the modern-day reader (Goff 2010; Newsom 2004; and above).

For example, Instruction (*Musar le-Mevin*; 4Q415–418a; 4Q423; 1Q26) contains teachings about practical matters, such as wealth, money, and agriculture, but it also reflects a wider metaphorical or even apocalyptic worldview. The addressee is exhorted to gain wisdom and to behave appropriately, not only for rewards in this life but because of impending judgment in the afterlife as well. In this, the connection between wisdom and apocalyptic elements is made explicit (see also Rey 2009; Wold 2018). Other examples, such as The (Book of) Mysteries and Beatitudes, also contain some eschatological assumptions about a future judgment, and in Wiles of the Wicked Woman, eschatological connection is made explicit by rewriting Prov 1–9 through the lens of the eschaton (Uusimäki 2016).

9. Apocalyptic and Eschatological Texts

The authors of the scrolls appropriated and greatly expanded upon eschatological themes already present in the Hebrew Bible. They interpreted history and understood it to be divided into eras in which good or evil would prevail. This periodization of history, already present in books such as Daniel and 1 Enoch, set the stage for their belief that they were living in a critical epoch of history, one that would end with a cosmic battle of good against evil. Utilizing the expression "end of days" (*aḥarit ha-yamim*) more than thirty times, these authors understood themselves to be standing at the cusp of the final days of judgment (e.g., "this is the end of days," 4Q394–399 [MMT]; also 4Q174 I, 14–15 [Florilegium]; Steudel, 1993). During this time, they imagined that they were part of the forces of good, or the "children of light," who would battle and eventually triumph over the "children of darkness," including both non-Jewish and apostate Jewish antagonists (1QM [War Scroll]). They even included a "rule for the congregation of Israel in the End of Days" (1Q28a), which appears to be some sort of sectarian rule text for the postmessianic era.

Their end-time expectations included the notion that all would be subject to divine judgment after death, resulting in either everlasting damnation or salvation. This underlies the authors' calls to follow the law and endure testing and purification (e.g., 4Q177 2, 9–10 [4QCatena[a]]) and to expect eternal rewards or punishments after death (1QS IV, 6–8; IV, 11–14). Elsewhere, the cosmological forces of good are led by Melchizedek, a divine or semidivine figure, who would act as a final judge (11Q13 [11QMelchizedek]). Yet the full realization of this end time had not yet occurred, and they even claim that the last days will be delayed for them ("the final end time is drawn out for them, for all of God's end times will come according to their fixed order," 1QpHab VII, 6–13). According to some scholars, the Yahad members also expected bodily resurrection as part of this divine restitution of good (Puech 1993, 2006; but contrast Nickelsburg 2006).

The authors of the scrolls refer to one (or two) messianic figures in relation to the end times. This messiah is likely the "Branch of David," mentioned in 1Q174 (cf. also 4Q252; 4Q161 [4QpIsa^a]). The coming of the "messiah of Aaron and Israel" is mentioned in the Damascus Document (CD XII, 23–XIII, 1; XIV, 19; XIX, 10–11), which a few scholars first took to refer to one individual; yet in light of other scrolls, most regard this and other references to mean that the Yahad expected two messiahs, mentioned elsewhere in the plural (1QS IX, 10–11; Pomykala 2019). Yet the messiah(s) do not necessarily take a central role in the eschatological texts, despite the fact that they are to be present at the eschatological banquet (1Q28a 2 [1QSa]) and will encourage the children of light at the final battle (1QM). Overall, however, the scrolls do not represent one unified or monolithic understanding of the "end times," nor of the divine players they imagined would come to their aid at the end (Collins 2000).

10. Other Issues and Developments in the Dead Sea Scrolls Scholarship

In light of all of the evidence, many old assumptions about the scrolls are being challenged. First, our current concepts of a manuscript or version are themselves scholarly constructs (Tigchelaar 2010), and not all agree with the labels or assignments the early scroll editors first gave to various assortments of fragments. Also, as noted above, multiple copies of the same textual tradition exhibit traces of editing and reworking (e.g., the Damascus Document and the Community Rule), and this was often not done in linear, easily explainable ways. As such, more now emphasize the fact that many of the Yahad's texts were in many ways malleable, collective compositions, developed by various hands over time and in multiple places (Alexander 2003; Schofield 2009). At least, it seems less tenable to assume that the fragments from Qumran were original compositions, or were even authored in the single-handed, one-time, authorship experience we generally experience today.

10.1. The Study of Sectarianism and Social-Scientific Models

Many studies have explored what the terms *sect* and *sectarian* could mean in the context of the Second Temple. Increasingly, scholars of the social sciences have cautioned against the uncritical application of sect and its categories to the Yahad without carefully considering the historical context of the movement vis-à-vis modern sectarian movements (Jokiranta 2010a, 2010b). This label can be somewhat anachronistic or even problematic, as it draws on a Christian paradigm of a normative church versus outlying sect, a situation that was not applicable to Judaism at that time (Regev 2007).

Other scholars have shifted the discussion from identifying a historical Yahad sect or other Jewish sectarian groups, to the sociological study of identity formation. Drawing from social psychology, some apply social identity theory to understand the formation of a Yahad-consciousness. Social identity theory demonstrates that in some texts, the authors reinforced a sense of intragroup identity (similarities) at the same time distancing itself from the Jewish Other in order to create an ideal prototype of group membership over against the out-groups of wider contemporaneous society (Jokiranta 2005; Lawrence 2005).

Others emphasize that members of the Yahad constructed individual and group identities first on a linguistic level by using the Hebrew language to mark out certain social boundaries between those who agree with certain ideological perspectives and those who do not. Second, on a textual or rhetorical level, the Yahad constituted and maintained their group identity through speech acts, or shared community discourse, in texts composed and copied by Yahad members. This written (and also recited) material would have reinforced and reproduced the very idea that the readers and authors of these texts belonged to a community and were participating in a unique social discourse (Newsom 2004).

10.2. Theology and Beliefs

The Yahad's theology is revealed both explicitly, in the rule texts, for example, but also indirectly through a large number of poetic-liturgical texts. First, the scrolls present a strong dualistic worldview, as reflected in the common word pairs of light/darkness, truth/falsehood, or iniquity/righteousness. Such beliefs are present in Jewish prayer texts, such as Barkhi Nafshi (4Q434–438). These hymns of praise to God reflect a dualistic understanding of the world between the authors and outsiders as well as with the internal struggle against the evil inclination. There is a deterministic undercurrent to these communal hymns, emphasizing that God has removed the condition of sinfulness in the elect and that this spiritual superiority is inscribed in the physical bodies of the elect (Brand 2013; Brooke 2000; Falk 1998). This idea underlies the Yahad's practice of physiognomy for spiritual discernment and initiation into the community mentioned in other texts.

Second, the sectarian scrolls reflect a sometimes contradictory understanding of free will and determinism, where members are divinely chosen and born with a lot of good versus evil, yet elsewhere followers are called to rise up in the ranks of righteous ones. Instruction embodies this tension in that it affirms the righteous has an allotment in the hereafter yet simultaneously exhorts the addressee to live a life in accordance with wisdom, lest punishment ensue (Wold 2018).

Further, the scrolls reflect other beliefs about the relationship between the elect and the heavenly realm. First, it is seen in a belief that humans and angels are united (connected?) in worship (e.g., Blessings [Berakhot], Chazon 2003; Songs of the Sabbath Sacrifice [4Q400–407; 11Q17]), even if they imagined that communion to take place only for Yahad members. A version of this same worldview is laid out in the Community Rule, where the community members are described as if they were the actual embodiment of the temple and its sacrifices, a "house of holiness," "foundation of the holy of holies for Aaron," and "precious cornerstone" there to atone for the land (1QS VIII, 5–7).

10.3. Other Approaches and Postmodern Methods

More scholars have applied postmodern approaches to the study of the scrolls in recent years (Grossman 2010a). Some have attempted to reclaim women and their voices from these ancient texts, especially in light of how most early scholars assumed that the Yahad was only a celibate community of men living a remote desert life. Yet new studies further illuminate the role of women and families underlying sectarian rule texts (Crawford 2003; Ilan 2010, 2011; Schuller 1999; Wassen 2005), and fresh questions have been raised about how the authors of these texts construct gender and identity (Grossman 2010a, 2010b). Only a few have studied the intersectionality of gender and other identities, although some approach the topic of disability studies and the Dead Sea Scrolls (e.g., Shemesh 1997). Others have begun to read the scrolls through the lens of critical spatial theory (Schofield 2011; Harkins 2012), yet much remains ripe for study from this perspective.

11. Conclusions

Since many of the scrolls were published since the 1990s, scholars have only recently had the entire Qumran library at their disposal. In the past few decades, many have rightly revisited and nuanced many early theories about the Dead Sea Scrolls. By applying increasingly diverse methods of studying the scrolls, they have posed new questions of these texts that were not possible in the first few decades of scrolls research. The Dead Sea Scrolls have contributed greatly to many areas in the study of early Judaism, and yet, they continue to raise more questions and inspire new debates. They provide valuable evidence for a period with few extant primary sources and have rightly complicated previous views about Judaism in the prerabbinic period. The scrolls themselves witness to a greater diversity of early Jewish communities, beliefs, and practices than ever imagined prior to their discovery.

Bibliography

Translations

Abegg, Martin, Peter W. Flint, and Eugene Ulrich. 2002. *The Dead Sea Scrolls Bible*. New York: HarperCollins.

García Martínez, Florentino, and Eibert J. C. Tigchelaar. 1997–1998. *The Dead Sea Scrolls Study Edition*. 2 vols. Grand Rapids: Eerdmans; Leiden: Brill.

Vermès, Géza. 2003. *The Complete Dead Sea Scrolls in English*. Rev. ed. New York: Penguin Books.

Wise, Michael O., Martin G. Abegg, and Edward M. Cook. 2005. *The Dead Sea Scrolls: A New Translation*. San Francisco: HarperSanFrancisco.

Secondary Literature

Alexander, Philip S. 2003. "Literacy among Jews in Second Temple Palestine: Reflections on the Evidence from Qumran." Pages 3–24 in *Hamlet on a Hill: Semitic and Greek Studies Presented to Professor T. Muraoka on the Occasion of His Sixty-Fifth Birthday*. Edited by Martin F. J. Baasten and Willem Th. van Peursen. OLA 118. Leuven: Peeters.

Alexander, Philip S., and Géza Vermès. 1998. *Qumran Cave 4.XIX: 4QSerekh Ha-Yaḥad and Two Related Texts*. DJD 26. Oxford: Clarendon.

Amihai, Aryeh. 2017. *Theory and Practice in Essene Law*. New York: Oxford University Press.

Angel, Joseph L. 2010. *Otherworldly and Eschatological Priesthood in the Dead Sea Scrolls*. STDJ 83. Leiden: Brill.

Bautch, Kelley Coblentz, and Jack Weinbender. 2018. "Authoritative Scriptures (Other Texts)." Pages 278–83 in *T&T Clark Companion to the Dead Sea Scrolls*. Edited by George J. Brooke and Charlotte Hempel. T&T Clark Companions. London: T&T Clark.

Bernstein, Moshe J. 2005. "'Rewritten Bible': A Generic Category Which has Outlived Its Usefulness?" *Text* 22:169–96.

———. 2013. "Pseudepigraphy in the Qumran Scrolls: Categories and Functions." Pages 421–47 in vol. 2 of *Reading and Re-reading Scripture at Qumran*. Edited by Moshe J. Bernstein. STDJ 107. Leiden: Brill.

Berthelot, Katell. 2019. "Authoritative Scriptures: Torah and Related Texts." Pages 264–68 in *T&T Clark Companion to the Dead Sea Scrolls*. Edited by George J. Brooke and Charlotte Hempel. T&T Clark Companions. London: T&T Clark.

Brand, Miryam T. 2013. *Evil within and without: The Source of Sin and Its Nature as Portrayed in Second Temple Literature*. JAJSupp 9. Göttingen: Vandenhoeck & Ruprecht.

Brooke, George J. 2000. "Rewritten Bible." Pages 777–80 in *Encyclopedia of the Dead Sea Scrolls*. Edited by Lawrence H. Schiffman and James C. VanderKam. Oxford: Oxford University Press.

———. 2005. *Qumran and the Jewish Jesus: Reading the New Testament in the Light of the Scrolls*. Groove Biblical Series 35. Cambridge: Groove Books.

———. 2010. "Hypertextuality and the 'Parabiblical' Dead Sea Scrolls." Pages 43–64 in *In the Second Degree: Paratextual Literature in Ancient Near Eastern and Ancient Mediterranean Culture and Its Reflections in Medieval Literature*. Edited by Philip Alexander, Armin Lange, Renate J. Pillinger. Leiden: Brill.

———. 2013. *Reading the Dead Sea Scrolls: Essays in Method*. EJL 39. Atlanta: Society of Biblical Literature.

Campbell, Jonathan G. 2014. "Rewritten Bible: A Terminological Reassessment." Pages 49–81 in *Rewritten Bible after Fifty Years: Texts, Terms or Techniques? A Last Dialogue with Géza Vermès*. Edited by József Zsengellér. JSJSup 166. Leiden: Brill.

Cansdale, Lena. 1997. *Qumran and the Essenes: A Re-evaluation of the Evidence*. TSAJ 60. Tübingen: Mohr.

Carr, David. 2005. "Response to W. M. Schniedewind, How the Bible Became a Book: The Textualization of Ancient Israel." *JHebS* 5. https://tinyurl.com/SBL9027f.

———. 2011. *The Formation of the Hebrew Bible: A New Reconstruction*. New York: Oxford University Press, 2011.

Chazon, Esther G. 2003. "Human and Angelic Prayer in Light of the Dead Sea Scrolls." Pages 35–47 in *Liturgical Perspectives: Prayer and Poetry in Light of the Dead Sea Scrolls*. Edited by Esther G. Chazon, Ruth Clements, and Avital Pinnick. STDJ 48. Leiden: Brill.

Collins, John J. 2000. "The Nature of Messianism in the Light of the Dead Sea Scrolls." Pages 199–217 in *The Dead Sea Scrolls in Their Historical Context*. Edited by Timothy H. Lim, Larry W. Hurtado, A. Graeme Auld, and Alison M. Jack. Edinburgh: T&T Clark.

———. 2010. *Beyond the Qumran Community: The Sectarian Movement of the Dead Sea Scrolls*. Grand Rapids: Eerdmans.

———. 2016. "The Genre Apocalypse Reconsidered." *ZAC* 20:21–40.

Crawford, Sidnie White. 2003. "Not According to Rule: Women, the Dead Sea Scrolls and Qumran." Pages 127–50 in *Emanuel: Studies in Hebrew Bible, Septuagint and Dead Sea Scrolls in Honor of Emauel Tov*. Edited by Shalom M. Paul, Robert A. Kraft, Lawrence H. Schiffman, and Weston W. Fields. VTSup 94. Leiden: Brill.

———. 2008. *Rewriting Scripture in Second Temple Times*. Grand Rapids: Eerdmans.

———. 2012. "'Biblical' Text—Yes or No?" Pages 113–19 in *What Is Bible?* Edited by Armin Lange and Karin Finsterbusch. CBET 67. Leuven: Peeters.

Crawford, Sidnie White, and Cecilia Wassen. 2016. *Introduction to The Dead Sea Scrolls at Qumran and the Concept of a Library*. STDJ 116. Leiden: Brill.

Delamarter, Steve. 2010. "Sociological Models for Understanding the Scribal Practices in the Biblical Dead Sea Scrolls." Pages 182–97 in *Rediscovering the Dead Sea Scrolls: An Assessment of Old and New Approaches and Methods*. Edited by Maxine L. Grossman. Grand Rapids: Eerdmans.

Dimant, Devorah. 1995. "The Qumran Manuscripts: Contents and Significance." Pages 23–58 in *Time to Prepare the Way in the Wilderness: Papers on the Qumran Scrolls by Fellows of the Institute for Advanced Studies of the Hebrew University, Jerusalem, 1989–1990*. Edited by Devorah Dimant and Lawrence H. Schiffman. STDJ 16. Leiden: Brill.

———. 2015. "The Library of Qumran in Recent Scholarship." Pages 5–14 in *The Dead Sea Scrolls at Qumran and the Concept of a Library*. Edited by Sidnie White Crawford and Cecilia Wassen. STDJ 116. Leiden: Brill.

Doering, Lutz. 2012. *Ancient Jewish Letters and the Beginnings of Christian Epistolography*. WUNT 298. Tübingen: Mohr Siebeck.

Elgvin, Torleif. 2005. "The Yaḥad Is More Than Qumran." Pages 273–79 in *Enoch and Qumran Origins: New Light on a Forgotten Connection*. Edited by Gabriele Boccaccini. Grand Rapids: Eerdmans.

Eshel, Hanan. 2010. "Gleaning of Scrolls from the Judaean Desert." Pages 49–87 in *The Dead Sea Scrolls: Texts and Context*. Edited by Charlotte Hempel. STDJ 90. Leiden: Brill.

Falk, Daniel K. 1998. *Daily, Sabbath, and Festival Prayers in the Dead Sea Scrolls*. STDJ 27. Leiden: Brill.

———. 2007. *The Parabiblical Texts: Strategies for Extending the Scriptures among the Dead Sea Scrolls*. LSTS 63. London: T&T Clark.

Fraade, Steven D. 2000. "To Whom It May Concern: 4QMMT and Its Addressee(s)." *RevQ* 19 (76):507–26.

García Martínez, Florentino. 2010. "Reconsidering the Cave 1 Texts Sixty Years after Their Discovery: An Overview." Pages 1–13 in *Qumran Cave 1 Revisited: Texts from Cave 1 Sixty Years after Their Discovery: Proceedings of the Sixth Meeting of the IOQS in Ljubljana*. Edited by Daniel K. Falk, Sarianna Metso, Donald W. Parry, and Eibert J. C. Tigchelaar. STDJ 91. Leiden: Brill.

Goff, Matthew J. 2006. *Discerning Wisdom: The Sapiential Literature of the Dead Sea Scrolls*. VTSup 116. Leiden: Brill.

———. 2010. "Qumran Wisdom Literature and the Problem of Genre." *DSD* 17:286–306.

Golb, Norman. 1995. *Who Wrote the Dead Sea Scrolls? The Search for the Secret of Qumran*. New York: Scribner.

Grossman, Maxine L. 2001. "Reading 4QMMT: Genre and History." *RevQ* 20:3–22.

———. 2010a. "Women and Men in the Rule of the Congregation: A Feminist Critical Assessment." Pages 229–45 in *Rediscovering the Dead Sea Scrolls: An Assessment of Old and New Approaches and Methods*. Edited by Maxine L. Grossman. Grand Rapids: Eerdmans.

———. 2010b. "Rethinking Gender in the *Community Rule*: An Experiment in Sociology." Pages 495–512 in *The Dead Sea Scrolls in Contemporary Culture: Proceedings of the International Conference Held at the Israel Museum, Jerusalem (July 6–8, 2008)*. Edited by Adolfo D.

Roitman, Lawrence H. Schiffman, and Shani Tzoref. STDJ 93. Leiden: Brill.

Gunneweg, Jan, and Marta Balla. 2006. "The Provenance of Qumran Pottery by Instrumental Neutron Activation Analysis." Pages 99–108 in *Bio- and Material Cultures at Qumran: Papers from a COST Action G8 Working Group Meeting Held in Jerusalem, Israel on 22–23 May 2005*. Edited by Jan Gunneweg, Charles Greenblatt, Annemie Adriaens. Stuttgart: Fraunhofer IRB.

Harkins, Angela Kim. 2012. *Reading with an "I" to the Heavens: Looking at the Qumran Hodayot through the Lens of Visionary Traditions*. Ekstasis 3. Berlin: de Gruyter.

Harrington, Daniel J. 1996. *Wisdom Texts from Qumran*. Literature of the Dead Sea Scrolls. London: Routledge.

Harrington, Hannah. 2004. *The Purity Texts*. CQS 5. London: T&T Clark.

Hempel, Charlotte. 2000. *The Damascus Texts*. CQS 1. Sheffield: Sheffield Academic.

———. 2006. "The Literary Development of the S Tradition—A New Paradigm." *RevQ* 22:389–401.

———. 2010. "Sources and Redaction in the Dead Sea Scrolls: The Growth of Ancient Texts." Pages 162–81 in *Rediscovering the Dead Sea Scrolls: An Assessment of Old and New Approaches and Methods*. Edited by Maxine L. Grossman. Grand Rapids: Eerdmans.

———. 2013. *The Qumran Rule Texts in Context: Collected Studies*. TSAJ 154. Tübingen: Mohr Siebeck.

———. 2019. "Bildung und Wissenswirtschaft im Judentum zur Zeit des Zweiten Tempels." Pages 229–44 in *Was ist Bildung in der Vormoderne?* Edited by Peter Gemeinhardt. Studies in Education and Religion in Ancient and Pre-Modern History in the Mediterranean and Its Environs 4. Tübingen: Mohr Siebeck.

Hempel, Charlotte, Armin Lange, and Hermann Lichtenberger, eds. 2002. *The Wisdom Texts from Qumran and the Development of Sapiential Thought*. BETL 159. Leuven: Peeters.

Henze, Matthias, ed. 2005. *Biblical Interpretation at Qumran*. SDSS. Grand Rapids: Eerdmans.

Hirschfeld, Yizhar. 2004. *Qumran in Context: Reassessing the Archaeological Evidence*. Peabody, MA: Hendrickson.

Hultgren, Stephen. 2007. *From the Damascus Covenant to the Covenant of the Community: Literary, Historical, and Theological Studies in the Dead Sea Scrolls*. STDJ 66. Leiden: Brill.

Humbert, Jean-Baptiste. 2016. "Cacher et se cacher à Qumrân: Grottes et refuges; Morphologie, fonctions, anthropologie." Pages 34–63 in *The Caves of Qumran: Proceedings of the International Conference, Lugano 2014*. Edited by Marcello Fidanzio. STDJ 118. Leiden: Brill.

Ilan, Tal. 2010. "Women in Qumran and the Dead Sea Scrolls." Pages 123–47 in *The Oxford Handbook of the Dead Sea Scrolls*. Edited by Timothy H. Lim and John J. Collins. Oxford: Oxford University Press.

———. 2011. "Reading for Women in 1QSa (Serekh Ha-Edah)." Pages 61–76 in vol. 1 of *The Dead Sea Scrolls in Context: Integrating the Dead Sea Scrolls in the Study of Ancient Texts, Languages, and Cultures*. Edited by Armin Lange, Emanuel Tov, and Matthias Weingold. VTSup 140. Leiden: Brill.

Jassen, Alex. 2012. "American Scholarship on Jewish Law in the Dead Sea Scrolls." Pages 101–54 in *The Dead Sea Scrolls in Scholarly Perspective: A History of Research*. STDJ 99. Edited by Devorah Dimant. STDJ 99. Leiden: Brill.

———. 2014. *Scripture and Law in the Dead Sea Scrolls*. New York: Cambridge University Press.

Jokiranta, Jutta. 2005. "Identity on a Continuum: Constructing and Expressing Sectarian Social Identity in Qumran Serakhim and Pesharim." PhD diss., University of Helsinki.

———. 2010a. "Social-Scientific Approaches to the Dead Sea Scrolls." Pages 246–63 in *Rediscovering the Dead Sea Scrolls: An Assessment of Old and New Approaches and Methods*. Edited by Maxine L. Grossman. Grand Rapids: Eerdmans.

———. 2010b. "Sociological Approaches to Qumran Sectarianism." Pages 200–31 in *The Oxford Handbook of the Dead Sea Scrolls*. Edited by Timothy H. Lim and John J. Collins. Oxford: Oxford University Press.

———. 2013. *Social Identity and Sectarianism in the Qumran Movement*. STDJ 105. Leiden: Brill.

Kampen, John. 2011. *Wisdom Literature*. ECDSS 14. Grand Rapids: Eerdmans.

Klawans, Jonathan. 2006. *Purity, Sacrifice, and the Temple: Symbolism and Supersessionism in the Study of Ancient Judaism*. New York: Oxford University Press.

Kraft, Robert. 2007. "Para-mania: Beside, before and beyond Bible Studies." *JBL* 126:5–27.

Kraft, Robert A., and George W. E. Nickelsburg, eds. 1986. *Early Judaism and Its Modern Interpreters.* BMI 2. Philadelphia: Fortress; Atlanta: Scholars Press.

Kratz, Reinhard G. 2006. "Mose und die Propheten: Zur Interpretation von 4QMMT C." Pages 151–76 in *From 4QMMT to Resurrection: Mélanges qumraniens en hommage à Émile Puech.* Edited by Florentino García Martínez, Annette Steudel, and Eibert J. C. Tigchelaar. STDJ 61. Leiden: Brill.

Kugel, James L. 1998. *Traditions of the Bible: A Guide to the Bible as It Was at the Start of the Common Era.* Cambridge: Harvard University Press.

Lange, Armin. 2002. "The Status of Biblical Texts in the Qumran Corpus and the Canonical Process." Pages 21–30 in *The Bible as Book: The Hebrew Bible and the Judean Desert Discoveries.* Edited by Edward D. Herbert and Emanuel Tov. London: British Library.

———. 2006. "The Qumran Dead Sea Scrolls: Library or Manuscript Corpus." Pages 177–93 in *From 4QMMT to Resurrection: Mélanges qumraniens en hommage à Émile Puech.* Edited by Florentino García Martínez, Annette Steudel, and Eibert J. C. Tigchelaar. STDJ 61. Leiden: Brill.

Lange, Armin, and Ulrike Mittmann-Richert. 2002. "Annotated List of the Texts from the Judaean Desert Classified by Content and Genre." Pages 115–64 in *The Texts from the Judaean Desert: Indices and an Introduction to the Discoveries in the Judaean Desert Series.* Edited by Emanuel Tov. DJD 39. Oxford: Clarendon.

Lawrence, Louise J. 2005. "'Men of Perfect Holiness' (1QS 7.20): Social-Scientific Thoughts on Group Identity, Asceticism and Ethical Development in the Rule of the Community." Pages 83–100 in *New Directions in Qumran Studies: Proceedings of the Bristol Colloquium on the Dead Sea Scrolls, 8–10 September 2003.* Edited by Jonathan G. Campbell, William John Lyons, and Lloyd K. Pietersen. LSTS 52. London: T&T Clark.

Lemaire, André. 2003. "Inscriptions du khirbeh, des grottes et de 'Aïn Feshkha." Pages 341–88 in *Khirbet Qumrân et 'Aïn Feshkha II: Études d'anthropologie, de physique et de chimie.* NTOA.SA 3. Göttingen: Vandenhoeck & Ruprecht; Fribourg: Academic Press.

Magen, Yitzhak, and Yuval Peleg. 2007. *The Qumran Excavations 1993–2004: Preliminary Report.* Judea and Samaria Publications 6. Jerusalem: Israel Antiquities Authority.

Magness, Jodi. 2002. "Women at Qumran." Pages 89–123 in *What Athens Has to Do with Jerusalem: Essays on Classical, Jewish and Early Chris-*

tian Art and Archaeology in Honor of Gideon Foerster. Edited by Leonard V. Rutgers. Leuven: Peeters.

———. 2016. "The Connection between the Site of Qumran and the Scroll Caves in Light of the Ceramic Evidence." Pages 184–94 in *The Caves of Qumran: Proceedings of the International Conference, Lugano 2014*. Edited by Marcello Fidanzio. STDJ 118. Leiden: Brill.

Martone, Corrado. 2016. "The Qumran Library and Other Ancient Libraries: Elements for a Comparison." Pages 55–77 in *The Scrolls from Qumran and the Concept of a Library*. Edited by Sidnie White Crawford and Cecilia Wassen. STDJ 116. Leiden: Brill.

Metso, Sarianna. 1997. *The Textual Development of the Qumran Community Rule*. STDJ 21. Leiden: Brill.

———. 2007. *The Serekh Texts*. LSTS 62. London: T&T Clark.

———. 2012. "Leviticus outside the Legal Genre." Pages 379–88 in *A Teacher for All Generations: Essays in Honor of James C. VanderKam*. Edited by Eric F. Mason, Samuel I. Thomas, Alison Schofield, and Eugene Ulrich. JSJSup 153.1. Leiden: Brill.

Mizzi, Dennis. 2016. "Miscellaneous Artefacts from the Qumran Caves: An Exploration of their Significance." Pages 137–60 in *The Caves of Qumran: Proceedings of the International Conference, Lugano 2014*. Edited by Marcello Fidanzio. STDJ 118. Leiden: Brill.

Mroczek, Eva. 2016. *The Literary Imagination in Jewish Antiquity*. New York: Oxford University Press.

Najman, Hindy. 2003. *Seconding Sinai: The Development of Mosaic Discourse in Second Temple Judaism*. JSJSup 77. Leiden: Brill.

———. 2012. "The Idea of Biblical Genre: From Discourse to Constellation." Pages 307–21 in *Prayer and Poetry in the Dead Sea Scrolls and Related Literature: Essays in Honor of Eileen Schuller on the Occasion of Her Sixty-Fifth Birthday*. Edited by Jeremy Penner, Ken M. Penner, and Cecilia Wassen. STDJ 98. Leiden: Brill.

Najman, Hindy, and Eibert J. C. Tigchelaar. 2014. "A Preparatory Study of Nomenclature and Text Designation in the Dead Sea Scrolls." *RevQ* 26:305–25.

Newman, Judith H. 2008. "Priestly Prophets at Qumran: Summoning Sinai through the *Songs of the Sabbath Sacrifice*." Pages 29–72 in *The Significance of Sinai: Traditions about Sinai and Divine Revelation in Judaism and Christianity*. Edited by George J. Brooke, Hindy Najman, and Loren Stuckenbruck. TBN 12. Leiden: Brill.

———. 2018. *Before the Bible: The Liturgical Body and the Formation of Scriptures in Early Judaism*. Oxford: Oxford University Press.

Newsom, Carol. 2004. *The Self as Symbolic Space: Constructing Identity and Community at Qumran*. STDJ 52. Leiden: Brill.

———. 2010. "Rhetorical Criticism and the Dead Sea Scrolls." Pages 198–214 in *Rediscovering the Dead Sea Scrolls: An Assessment of Old and New Approaches and Methods*. Edited by Maxine Grossman. Grand Rapids: Eerdmans.

Nickelsburg, George W. E. 2006. *Resurrection, Immortality, and Eternal Life in Intertestamental Judaism and Christianity*. Expanded ed. HTS 56. Cambridge: Harvard University Press.

Nitzan, Bilhah. 1994. *Qumran Prayer and Religious Poetry*. STDJ 12. Leiden: Brill.

———. 2010. "The Continuity of Biblical Interpretation in the Qumran Scrolls and Rabbinic Literature." Pages 337–50 in *The Oxford Handbook of the Dead Sea Scrolls*. Edited by Timothy H. Lim and John J. Collins. Oxford: Oxford University Press.

Pomykala, Kenneth E. 2019. "Eschatologies and Messianisms." Pages 496–504 in *T&T Clark Companion to the Dead Sea Scrolls*. Edited by George J. Brooke and Charlotte Hempel. T&T Clark Companions. London: T&T Clark.

Popović, Mladen. 2010. *Authoritative Scriptures in Ancient Judaism*. JSJSup 141. Leiden: Brill.

Puech, Emile. 1993. "Messianism, Resurrection, and Eschatology at Qumran and in the New Testament." Pages 235–56 in *The Community of the Renewed Covenant: The Notre Dame Symposium on the Dead Sea Scrolls*. Edited by Eugene Ulrich and James C. VanderKam. CJAn 10. Notre Dame: University of Notre Dame Press.

———. 2006. "Resurrection: The Bible and Qumran." Pages 247–81 in *The Bible and the Dead Sea Scrolls, 2: The Dead Sea Scrolls and the Qumran Community; the Second Princeton Symposium on Judaism and Christian Origins*. Edited by James H. Charlesworth. Waco, TX: Baylor University Press.

Regev, Eyal. 2007. *Sectarianism in Qumran: A Cross-Cultural Perspective*. RelSoc 45. Berlin: de Gruyter.

Rey, Jean-Sébastien. 2009. *4QInstruction: Sagesse et eschatology*. STDJ 81. Leiden: Brill.

Schiffman, Lawrence H. 2010. *Qumran and Jerusalem: Studies in the Dead Sea Scrolls and the History of Judaism*. SDSS. Grand Rapids: Eerdmans.

———. 2019. "Second Temple Jewish Law in Light of the Dead Sea Scrolls: Widening the Paradigm." Pages 1–26 in *Law, Literature, and Society in Legal Texts from Qumran: Papers from the Ninth Meeting of the International Organisation for Qumran Studies, Leuven 2016*. Edited by Jutta Jokiranta and Molly Zahn. STDJ. 128. Leiden: Brill.

———. forthcoming. *The Temple Scroll*. Edited by Martin Abegg, Daniel K. Falk, and Alison Schofield. Dead Sea Scroll Editions. Leiden: Brill.

Schofield, Alison. 2008. "The Wilderness Motif in the Dead Sea Scrolls." Pages 37–52 in *Israel in the Wilderness: Interpretations of the Biblical Narratives in Jewish and Christian Traditions*. Edited by Kenneth Pomykala. TBN 10. Leiden: Brill.

———. 2009. *From Qumran to the Yaḥad: A New Paradigm of Textual Development for The Community Rule*. STDJ 77. Leiden: Brill.

———. 2011. "Re-placing Priestly Space: The Wilderness as Heterotopia in the Dead Sea Scrolls." Pages 469–90 in vol. 1 of *A Teacher for All Generations: Essays in Honor of James C. VanderKam*. Edited by Eric Mason. JSJSup 153. Leiden: Brill.

Schuller, Eileen M. 1999. "Women in the Dead Sea Scrolls." Pages 117–44 in vol. 2 of *The Dead Sea Scrolls after Fifty Years: A Comprehensive Assessment*. Edited by Peter Flint and James C. VanderKam. Leiden: Brill.

Segal, Michael. 2005. "Between Bible and Rewritten Bible." Pages 10–28 in *Biblical Interpretation at Qumran*. Edited by Matthias Henze. SDSS. Grand Rapids: Eerdmans.

———. 2012. "Biblical Interpretation—Yes and No." Pages 63–80 in *What Is Bible?* Edited by Armin Lange and Karin Finsterbusch. CBET 67. Leuven: Peeters.

Shemesh, Aharon. 1997. "The Holy Angels Are in Their Council: The Exclusion of Deformed Persons from Places in Qumranic and Rabbinic Literature." *DSD* 4:179–206.

———. 2009. *Halakhah in the Making: The Development of Jewish Law from Qumran to the Rabbis*. Taubman Lectures in Jewish Studies. Berkeley: University of California Press.

———. 2012. "Biblical Exegesis and Interpretation from Qumran to the Rabbis." Pages 467–89 in *A Companion to Biblical Interpretation in Early Judaism*. Edited by Matthias Henze. Grand Rapids: Eerdmans.

Shemesh, Aharon, and Cana Werman. 2003. "Halakhah at Qumran: Genre and Authority." *DSD* 10:104–29.

Stacey, David, and Gregory Doudna. 2013. *Qumran Revisited: A Reassess-*

ment of the Archaeology of the Site and Its Texts. BARIS 2520. Oxford: Archaeopress.

Steudel, Annette. 1993. "'אחרית הימים [End of Days]' in the Texts from Qumran." *RevQ* 16:225–46.

Stökl Ben Ezra, Daniel. 2007. "Old Caves and Young Caves: A Statistical Reevaluation of a Qumran Consensus." *DSD* 14:313–33.

———. 2011. "Wie viele Bibliotheken gab es in Qumran?" Pages 327–46 in *Qumran und die Archäologie: Texte und Kontexte*. Edited by Jörg Frey, Carsten Claussen, and Nadine Kessler. WUNT 278. Tübingen: Mohr Siebeck.

Taylor, Joan E. 2012. *The Essenes, the Scrolls, and the Dead Sea*. Oxford: Oxford University Press.

Thomas, Samuel I. 2019. "Mysteries." Pages 329–31 in *T&T Clark Companion to the Dead Sea Scrolls*. Edited by George J. Brooke and Charlotte Hempel. T&T Clark Companions. London: T&T Clark.

Tigchelaar, Eibert J. C. 2010. "Constructing, Deconstructing, and Reconstructing Fragmentary Manuscripts: Illustrated by a Study of 4Q184 (4QWiles of the Wicked Woman)." Pages 26–47 in *Rediscovering the Dead Sea Scrolls: An Assessment of Old and New Approaches and Methods*. Edited by Maxine L. Grossman. Grand Rapids: Eerdmans.

———. 2012. "The Dead Sea Scrolls." Pages 204–27 in *Early Judaism: A Comprehensive Overview*. Edited by Daniel C. Harlow and John J. Collins. Grand Rapids: Eerdmans.

———. 2019. "The Scribes of the Scrolls." Pages 524–32 in *T&T Clark Companion to the Dead Sea Scrolls*. Edited by George J. Brooke and Charlotte Hempel. T&T Clark Companions. London: T&T Clark.

Tov, Emanuel. 2004. *Scribal Practices and Approaches Reflected in the Texts Found in the Judean Desert*. STDJ 54. Leiden: Brill.

———. 2010. *Revised Lists of the Texts from the Judaean Desert*. Leiden: Brill.

———. 2012. *Textual Criticism of the Hebrew Bible*. 3rd ed. Minneapolis: Augsburg Fortress.

Ulrich, Eugene C. 1979. "4QSam^c: A Fragmentary Manuscript of 2 Samuel 14–15 from the Scribe of the *Serek Hay-yaḥad* (1QS)." *BASOR* 235:1–25.

———. 2010a. *The Biblical Qumran Scrolls: Transcriptions and Textual Variants*. VTSup 13. Leiden: Brill.

———. 2010b. "Methodological Reflections on Determining Scriptural Status in First Century Judaism." Pages 145–61 in *Rediscovering the*

Dead Sea Scrolls: An Assessment of Old and New Approaches and Methods. Edited by Maxine L. Grossman. Grand Rapids: Eerdmans.

———. 2015. *The Dead Sea Scrolls and the Developmental Composition of the Bible*. VTSup 169. Leiden: Brill.

Uusimäki, Elisa. 2016. *Turning Proverbs towards Torah: An Analysis of 4Q525*. STDJ 117. Leiden: Brill.

VanderKam, James C. 1999. "The Judean Desert and the Community of the Dead Sea Scrolls." Pages 159–71 in *Antikes Judentum und frühes Christentum: Festschrift für Hartmut Stegemann zum 65. Geburtstag*. Edited by Bernd Kollmann, Wolfgang Reinbold, and Annette Steudel. BZNW 97. Berlin: de Gruyter

———. 2002. "Questions of Canon in Light of the Dead Sea Scrolls." Pages 91–109 in *The Canon Debate*. Edited by Lee Martin McDonald and James A. Sanders. Peabody, MA: Hendrickson.

———. 2010. *The Dead Sea Scrolls Today*. 2nd ed. Grand Rapids: Eerdmans.

———. 2019. "Uses of Earlier Literature in Some Second Temple Texts." Pages 135–52 in *Scribal Practice, Text and Canon in the Dead Sea Scrolls: Essays in Memory of Peter W. Flint*. Edited by John J. Collins and Ananda Geyser-Fouché. STDJ 130. Leiden: Brill.

VanderKam, James C., and Peter Flint. 2002. *The Meaning of the Dead Sea Scrolls: Their Significance for Understanding the Bible, Judaism, Jesus, and Christianity*. New York: HarperCollins.

Wassen, Cecilia. 2005. *Women in the Damascus Document*. AcBib 21. Atlanta: Society of Biblical Literature.

———. 2019. "Purity and Holiness." Pages 513–23 in *T&T Clark Companion to the Dead Sea Scrolls*. Edited by George J. Brooke and Charlotte Hempel. T&T Clark Companions. London: T&T Clark.

Weissenberg, Hanne von. 2009. *4QMMT: Reevaluating the Text, the Function, and the Meaning of the Epilogue*. STDJ 82. Leiden: Brill.

———. 2010. "The Centrality of the Temple in 4QMMT." Pages 293–305 in *The Dead Sea Scrolls: Texts and Context*. STDJ 90. Edited by Charlotte Hempel. Leiden: Brill.

Werrett, Ian C. 2007. *Ritual Purity and the Dead Sea Scrolls*. STDJ 72. Leiden: Brill.

———. 2016. "Is Qumran a Library?" Pages 78–105 in *The Dead Sea Scrolls at Qumran and the Concept of a Library*. Edited by Sidnie White Crawford and Cecilia Wassen. STDJ 116. Leiden: Brill.

White, Sidnie Crawford, and Cecilia Wassen. 2016. *Introduction to The*

Dead Sea Scrolls at Qumran and the Concept of a Library. STDJ 116. Leiden: Brill.

Wold, Benjamin G. 2018. *4QInstruction: Divisions and Hierarchies*. STDJ 123. Leiden: Brill.

Wright, Benjamin G., III. 2010. "Joining the Club: A Suggestion about Genre in Early Jewish Texts." *DSD* 17:289–314.

Yellin, Joseph, Magan Broshi, and Hanan Eshel. 2001. "Pottery of Qumran and Ein Ghuweir: The First Chemical Exploration of Provenience." *BASOR* 321:65–78.

Zahn, Molly. 2019. "The Levites, the Royal Council, and the Relationship between Chronicles and the Temple Scroll." Pages 253–69 in *Law, Literature, and Society in Legal Texts from Qumran: Papers from the Ninth Meeting of the International Organisation for Qumran Studies, Leuven 2016*. Edited by Jutta Jokiranta and Molly Zahn. STDJ 128. Leiden: Brill.

Zangenberg, Jürgen K. 2016. "The Functions of the Caves and the Settlement of Qumran: Reflections on a New Chapter of Qumran Research." Pages 195–209 in *The Caves of Qumran: Proceedings of the International Conference, Lugano 2014*. Edited by Marcello Fidanzio. STDJ 118. Leiden: Brill.

For the most complete, up-to-date bibliography on the Dead Sea Scrolls, see the Orion Center's Dead Sea Scrolls Bibliography at http://orion.mscc.huji.ac.il.

7
Early Jewish Epigraphy

PIETER W. VAN DER HORST

1. Introduction

Students of ancient Judaism tend to pay attention primarily to Jewish literature of the Hellenistic, Roman, and early Byzantine periods. That is logical, for this literature is our most important source of information and, moreover, it is rich: we have tens of thousands of pages of the Dead Sea Scrolls, the Pseudepigrapha, Philo, Josephus, rabbinic literature, the *hekhalot* texts, and more. Yet there is another important source for our knowledge of early Jewish life and thought that usually receives much less attention, although it, too, provides us with fascinating information that one often cannot find elsewhere, namely, Jewish epigraphy, that is, inscriptions on stones, ostraca, graffiti walls, metal objects, and other surfaces. These inscriptions consist mainly of epitaphs (tomb inscriptions) and of decrees in honor of benefactors. It is telling that in the first edition of *Early Judaism and Its Modern Interpretations* (Kraft and Nickelsburg 1986), there is no chapter on epigraphy, only some very short paragraphs that amount to no more than three pages (66–67, 197–99). In the past three decades, however, the field of early Jewish epigraphy has developed rapidly so as to become a specialization of its own.

Through ancient Jewish literature we come into contact with the literate circles of Jewish society and so we come to know the ideas of the elite. The voices of the less educated (or illiterate) common people are not heard in those pages. It is precisely in introducing us to ordinary Jewish people, their thoughts and actions, their hopes, griefs, and joys, that inscriptions make a most valuable contribution to our knowledge of the world of ancient Judaism. Even though many Jewish inscriptions are products of the elite, it is an undeniable fact that—unlike the literary sources—in many others we hear the voices of the lower classes. Inscriptions derive "from the nearly illiterate poor … to the wealthy patrons of funerary poetry" (Kant 1987, 674). Importantly, inscriptions sometimes express beliefs that have not been censored out by a later normative Jewish tradition.

2. The History of Scholarship

Up until the early 1990s , scholars had to make do with several partial collections of Jewish inscriptions and one collection that had aimed at comprehensiveness but failed to achieve what it promised. Aside from the late nineteenth and early twentieth century collections of Jewish inscriptions that covered only one country or city or site, it was in 1936 that the Jesuit Father Jean-Baptiste Frey published the first volume of what was meant to be a comprehensive collection of all Jewish epigraphic material from antiquity, the *Corpus Inscriptionum Judaicarum*. The second volume was published posthumously in 1952 (*CIJ*). The manuscript of both volumes had been completed by 1935. So the work reflects the state of knowledge of more than eighty years ago, or rather, Frey's state of knowledge, for Frey was severely criticized by some leading epigraphers not only for being sloppy in the presentation of the evidence but also for having overlooked quite a number of inscriptions and for having included several that did not belong there (Robert 1937; 1954; Ferrua 1941). Many of these defects were remedied for the first volume (which covers Europe) by Baruch Lifshitz, who wrote an extensive prolegomenon to the 1975 reprint of volume one (Lifshitz 1975), in which he proposed a considerable number of corrections and additions. But, unfortunately, Lifshitz died before he could start to work on volume 2 (covering Asia [including Palestine] and Egypt), which is still more deficient than volume 1.

This unsatisfactory situation lasted for several decades. I here mention briefly only the most important partial collections from the four decades between Frey's second volume of 1952 and the new harvest that began in 1992. The group of epitaphs from Dominus Flevit (on the Mount of Olives) was edited by Bellarmino Bagatti and Józef Tadeusz Milik (1958). David M. Lewis (1964) published the inscriptions from Egypt; Yann le Bohec (1981) those of the rest of North Africa; Gert Lüderitz (1983) those of the Cyrenaica; Alexander Scheiber (1983) those of Hungary; Harry J. Leon (1960, 263–346) those of Rome; Benjamin Mazar, Moshe Schwabe, Baruch Lifshitz, and Nahman Avigad those from the catacombs of Beth She'arim (*BS*).

Lifshitz (1967) published synagogal donor inscriptions in general; Joseph Naveh (1978 [Hebrew]) the Hebrew and Aramaic synagogal inscriptions from Israel and elsewhere; Lea Roth-Gerson (1987 [Hebrew]) the Greek ones from the synagogues in Israel; Frowald G. Hüttenmeister and Gottfried Reeg (1977) all synagogue inscriptions from Israel; Rachel Hachlili (1979) the epitaphs of the Goliath family in Jericho; and L. Y. Rahmani (1994) those on ossuaries (small bone boxes) from Israel.

By the beginning of the 1990s, some two thousand Jewish inscriptions were available to the scholarly world. At the time of the publication of this essay, however, we know at least some four thousand Jewish inscriptions from the period between circa 300 BCE and circa 700 CE—nota bene, two-and-a-half times as many as in Frey's *Corpus Inscriptionum Judaicarum*, which contained some sixteen hundred (for comparison's sake: we have hundreds of thousands of pagan and Christian inscriptions in Greek and Latin, so four thousand is still a tiny number). This dramatic increase in numbers is primarily due to the fact that especially in the last twenty-five to thirty years the pace of the study of ancient Jewish inscriptions has greatly accelerated. A flurry of epigraphic activity took place, especially thanks to two projects at the universities of Cambridge (UK) and Tübingen, respectively. The British scholar David Noy was the main organizer of and contributor to these enterprises. In 1992, together with William Horbury, Noy published *Jewish Inscriptions of Graeco-Roman Egypt* (*JIGRE*); in 1993 Noy as sole editor published the first volume of his *Jewish Inscriptions of Western Europe I: Italy (excluding the City of Rome), Spain and Gaul* (*JIWE* 1), and in 1995 the second volume appeared as *Jewish Inscriptions of Western Europe II: The City of Rome* (*JIWE* 2). A new peak of epigraphic activity was reached in 2004 when the three volumes of the *Inscriptiones Judaicae Orientis* (*IJO*) were published simultaneously. Two of the three volumes were edited, again, by Noy, in collaboration with Hans-Wulf Bloedhorn and Alexander Panayotov (Greece, the Greek islands, the rest of Eastern Europe [*IJO* 1]; Syria, Cyprus [*IJO* 3]); the volume on Asia Minor was the work of Walter Ameling alone [*IJO* 2]).

Apart from these six major volumes, in 1999 E. Leigh Gibson published the Jewish manumission inscriptions of the Bosporan kingdom. Also in 1999, Elena Miranda published the inscriptions of the Jewish community of Phrygian Hierapolis. And in 2001 John Kroll finally published the Greek inscriptions of the famous Sardis synagogue (they had been found some forty years before!). But all of this material (from the Bosporus, Hierapolis, and Sardis) has now also been included in the volumes of *IJO*. Further there was, of course, the usual host of minor publications in various journals (see Williams 2003–2004; cf. Williams 1999).

The only area that is still partly lacking in these recent publications, apart from Northern Africa, is the land of Israel itself. For that gap we have to await the completion of the new large-scale Israeli project *Corpus Inscriptionum Iudaeae/Palestinae* (*CIIP*), of which Hannah Cotton and Jonathan Price are the main organizers and editors. That enterprise has started to yield its first results. The *Corpus Inscriptionum Iudaeae/Palestinae* is to be a new corpus of all inscriptions (not only Jewish but also pagan and Christian), in all languages, arranged topographically, found in Israel and dating from the fourth century BCE to the seventh century CE. A provisional estimate is that there will be more than twelve thousand texts in the corpus, some three thousand of them (but probably more) of Jewish provenance. Since 2010, the first four volumes (in six parts) of the project were published, covering the material from Jerusalem (*CIIP* 1), Caesarea Maritima and the middle coast (*CIIP* 2), the southern coast (*CIIP* 3), and the rest of Judea and Idumaea (*CIIP* 4). Six more volumes are to follow. Only after the completion of this project will Frey's *Corpus Inscriptionum Judaicarum* definitively belong to the past.

3. Criteria for Identifying Jewish Inscriptions

A crucial question is: What are the minimal requirements for an inscription to be regarded as certainly (or almost certainly) Jewish? This difficult question is a matter of much scholarly debate (Van der Horst 1991, 16–18; Kraemer 1991; Bij de Vaate and Van Henten 1995; *IJO* 2.8–21; Williams 2013, 231–36). In order not to distort the picture to be drawn of early Judaism, it is of paramount importance to define which criteria are valid and which are not in making a distinction between Jewish and non-Jewish material. It is clear that an epitaph found in a Jewish catacomb or cemetery, containing biblical names with the term *Ioudaios* added, referring to biblical passages, mentioning the function of head of the synagogue, and adorned with symbols such as the menorah, *ethrog*, *lulav*, or shofar—that such an inscription should be regarded as Jewish without any doubt. It is also clear that a tomb inscription found in a pagan necropolis, invoking pagan deities, and without any Jewish symbols or biblical names is almost certainly not Jewish. The problem is, however, that there are so many instances that are far less clear-cut than those just mentioned. What are we to make, for example, of an epitaph found in a Jewish catacomb, beginning with *DM*

(= D[is] M[anibus], "to the gods of the netherworld"), mentioning pagan theophoric proper names, showing no Jewish symbols, and having no reference to the Bible or the synagogue? Or an epitaph found *not* in a Jewish burial place and showing no Jewish symbols but mentioning names such as Isaac and Sabbatis and quoting the Septuagint? Or an epitaph with Jewish names and a menorah but also a cross?

In the introduction to the *Corpus Papyrorum Judaicarum*, Victor Tcherikover uses the following criteria for regarding a papyrus as Jewish (*CPJ* 1:xvii–xx): a papyrus is identified as Jewish (1) if the word *Ioudaios* or *Hebraios* occurs in it; (2) if technical terms such as synagogue or sabbath appear in it; (3) if it originates from what are known to have been places of exclusively Jewish settlement; (4) if it contains Jewish names. When *taken together*, these four criteria surely establish a solid case for regarding a papyrus, or an inscription, for that matter, as Jewish. Tcherikover, however, considers them to be valid indicators of Jewishness *also when they occur in isolation*. But that position is problematic for the following reasons. (1) The words *Ioudaios* or *Hebraios* (or their Latin equivalents) make an epitaph Jewish *only* if said of the deceased or honored person(s) or the dedicator(s) but *not*, for example, when a fifth- or sixth-century inscription found in a church on the island Icaria says that "it is impossible that one will ever hear the truth from Jews of Icaria" (*IJO* 2.5a) or when an inscription states that the man or woman who set up the stone forbids pagans, Jews, and Christians to efface its inscription (see, e.g., *IJO* 1.Dal3). (2) Technical terms are indications of Jewishness *only* if they are exclusively Jewish. But that is not the case, for example, with the term *synagōgē* (which could mean any meeting or assembly of non-Jews as well) and with several other "Jewish" termini technici (e.g., *archisynagōgos*, "head of the synagogue," or *presbyteros*, "elder"). This criterion applies with greater force only *in combination with other criteria*. (3) Exclusively Jewish places are very rare, especially in the diaspora, except perhaps for the Jewish catacombs in Rome. But even there it is not impossible that, after these burial places ceased to be used by Jews, pagans or Christians deposited the bodies of their deceased in these catacombs. (4) Finally the criterion of Jewish names. Are there exclusively Jewish names? Actually, there are very few names (if any) that have demonstrably been used *only* by Jews and never by Christians or pagans (Kraemer 1986). Highly instructive in this respect is the name Sabbation (and its variants) of which Menahem Stern (*CPJ* 3:43–56) demonstrated that, whereas in the Hellenistic period it was by and large a typically Jewish name (as a hellenized form of the Hebrew Shabbetai), in the Roman and

Byzantine periods a great many non-Jews adopted it, probably without being aware of its original connotations. It should be added, even Jewish symbols are not an absolute guarantee for Jewishness either because these could be—and were—used also by Jewish Christians and even by some gentile Christians.

In his edition of the Jewish inscriptions of Asia Minor (*IJO* 2), Ameling lists five criteria that identify an inscription certainly as Jewish: (1) The identification of a person as *Ioudaios*; Ameling rightly rejects the geographical interpretation (person from Judea). (2) Mention of Jewish realia, such as Jewish feasts, their holy scriptures, synagogues, and so on. Here, however, one should not rule out the possibility that Judeo-Christian groups could refer to the same realia. (3) Provenance from unquestionably Jewish buildings such as synagogues or exclusively Jewish catacombs (such as Beth She'arim). (4) Occurrence of Jewish symbols such as menorah, *lulav*, *ethrog*, shofar, and so on. Ameling does concede, however, that sometimes Christians used some of these symbols as well. (5) The use of Hebrew, which was the sacred language of none but the Jews. Ameling (2007, 266) is also aware, however, of the fact that, whatever criteria we use, it is inevitable that we overlook Jewish inscriptions that cannot be identified as such for the simple reason that they are not distinguishable in any way from non-Jewish inscriptions.

It is clear that the matter is far from being simple (see also Price and Misgav 2006, 461). A rigorous application of criteria would require us to regard an inscription as Jewish only when a number of criteria corroborate one another, for example, a Jewish burial place plus typically Jewish symbols and epithets (e.g., *philentolos*, "lover of the commandments"), or biblical names plus Jewish technical terms and functions (e.g., *archisynagōgos*, "head of the community"). The only case in which no more than one criterion suffices to establish Jewishness is the use of Hebrew, since only Jews used that language in antiquity (Samaritan Hebrew had a different script). In all other cases more than one criterion is required. With such methodological strictness one does run the risk of excluding material the Jewishness of which is not manifest enough. On the other hand, methodological slackness runs the risk of including non-Jewish material. It is better, for the sake of clarity, to keep on the strict side, without being overly rigorous. That is to say, application of two or three criteria together is to be much preferred to applying only one, the more so since in late antiquity Judaism, Christianity, and paganism were not always mutually exclusive categories.

4. Geographical and Chronological Distribution

From Rome we have some 600 inscriptions (see *JIWE* 2), but it should be emphasized that this number is exceptional. From no other city do we have so many Jewish inscriptions, except Jerusalem, which has some 700. One of the problems of the study of early Jewish epigraphy is the very uneven distribution of the evidence. For the whole of Asia Minor, for instance, including all major cities there, we have no more than some 250 inscriptions (*IJO* 2); for Syria, including Phoenicia, some 130 (*IJO* 3); for Egypt some 135 (*JIGRE*). And even more telling is a comparison of Rome with another major metropolis of the ancient world, Alexandria. We know from several sources that Alexandria had for more than four centuries (ca. 300 BCE–115 CE) the largest Jewish urban population of the Hellenistic and Roman diaspora, definitely much larger than that of Rome. From Rome we have some 600 inscriptions, but from Alexandria we have no more than 20. This disproportionate situation is typical for the field of research as a whole. This situation is due to the vicissitudes of history and to the arbitrariness of archaeological discoveries. A couple of new finds could change the whole picture. Imagine the discovery of a huge Jewish necropolis in ancient Alexandria with thousands of epitaphs! That could well force us to revise our image of diaspora Judaism considerably. Furthermore it is notable that the evidence tends to have mainly an urban provenance; the countryside yields much less material.

There is also an unevenness in chronological distribution of the epigraphic material. The evidence ranges in time from ca. 300 BCE to 700 CE, thus covering the Hellenistic, Roman, and early Byzantine period in which Greek epigraphic habits influenced many Jews. However, the earlier centuries in this time span do not yield nearly as much evidence as the later centuries. To be more precise, there is a conspicuous concentration of material from the third to fifth centuries CE, which is exactly the period in which the epigraphic habit of the Roman Empire was in decline. This is a striking and still somewhat enigmatic situation.

5. Genres

The majority of our evidence consists of epitaphs (some 75–80 percent). These range from very simple scratches on a grave wall or ossuary, consisting of only a name, on the one hand, to elaborate poetic laments in Greek hexameters beautifully executed on marble sarcophagi on the other (on the latter, see Van der Horst 1994). There are, however, also other epigraphic genres (Kant 1987, 675–81). First, there are honorific inscriptions, that is, decrees passed by an official body (usually a synagogal community) in honor of persons who aided financially or treated a Jewish community kindly in other ways (Lifshitz 1967). The competition in striving after epigraphic honor that is so characteristic of Greco-Roman honorific epigraphy here clearly influenced the Jews (Ameling 2007, 272; Rajak 2001, 374, 380). Further, there are legal texts, mainly in the form of Jewish manumission inscriptions that legally formalize the freedom of slaves—we have quite a few instances from both Delphi and the Bosporan kingdom (Gibson 1999; *IJO* 1.Ach42–45). Moreover, we have lists of persons, both Jewish and non-Jewish, who have contributed to the realization of a Jewish building or other project (e.g., a cemetery), such as the famous donor inscription from Aphrodisias in Caria (Reynolds and Tannenbaum 1987; *IJO* 2.14). It should be stressed that these epigraphic genres owe their origin to the heavy influence of Greek models.

6. Languages

One of the most striking features of the epigraphic material is the heavy preponderance of Greek, not only in evidence from the diaspora but also in that from the Jewish homeland, Palestine (Van der Horst 2001; for the peculiarities of this Greek see Van der Horst 2015, 88–95). In the diaspora some 85 percent of the evidence is in Greek, and in Palestine the percentage is some 60–65 percent (a provisional estimate). Only a quarter—or, for Israel, one-third—is in Hebrew, Aramaic, Latin, and other languages. But there are significant local variations. For instance, we find that of the approximately six hundred inscriptions from the Jewish catacombs in Rome, 78 percent are in Greek, whereas only 21 percent are in Latin and 1 percent in Hebrew or Aramaic. There are also considerable differences in the use of the three languages in the three greatest catacombs (out of seven) in Rome: the Via Appia catacomb (the most Romanized of all) has approximately 65 percent Greek inscriptions, 23 percent in Latin, 12 percent bilinguals; the Via Nomentana catacomb has 99 percent in Greek, none in Latin, and 1 percent bilinguals; and the Monteverde catacomb has approximately 79 percent in Greek, 13 percent in Latin, 1.5 percent in Hebrew or Aramaic, and 6.5 percent bilinguals (Greek/Latin; Greek/Hebrew; Greek/Aramaic) (Leon 1960, 77; with corrections by Rutgers 1995, 176–78). What deserves our attention is the degree of linguistic hellenization of the Jews, even in a predominantly Latin-speaking city such as Rome. Greek had become the lingua franca of the Jews all over the Mediterranean world and the inscriptions testify most eloquently to that high degree of linguistic hellenization. In Asia Minor, for instance, the total of Jewish inscriptions in Greek is above 95 percent. Of Hebrew and Aramaic we find only some superficial traces such as the word *shalom*. One should not assume that they used Greek only on their tombstones as a kind of sacred language, for their sacred language remained Hebrew, as is witnessed by the many Greek and Latin inscriptions ending in the single Hebrew word *shalom*, or expressions such as *shalom ʿal mishkevo* ("peace be upon his resting place") and *shalom ʿal Yisraʾel* ("peace be upon Israel"). Almost all epigraphic biblical quotations are from the Septuagint or Aquila (Van der Horst 2014).

This brings us to another, much debated matter, the role of Greek as a spoken language in Jewish Palestine in light of epigraphy (Lieberman 1942; Van der Horst 2001; Chancey 2005, 122–65; Wise 2015). When we try to establish the percentage of Greek inscriptions in the Jewish evidence from Israel, we find that of Frey's 530 inscriptions, 315 are in Greek (several of them in fact being bilingual), which is about 60 percent. Further, of the 43 inscriptions from the cemetery of Dominus Flevit in Jerusalem, 12 are in Greek, which is 29 percent. In the catacombs of Beth Sheʿarim, however, of the 246 epitaphs no less than 218 are in Greek, which is 88 percent. Of the 32 tomb inscriptions of the Goliath family in Jericho 17 are in Greek, which is 53 percent. And of the 240 inscribed ossuaries in the collection of Rahmani, 87 are in Greek (16 of which are bilingual), which is 37 percent. These percentages vary widely, from 29–88 percent, but the overall average of Greek inscriptions is slightly more than 53 percent.

It is hard to predict how this will compare to the average in the final database of the *CIIP*. The percentage of Greek inscriptions in this comprehensive collection cannot yet be established with any certainty, but a provisional estimate is that more than half of the Jewish inscriptions are in Greek (or have some Greek writing on them in the considerable number that are bilingual, containing both Greek and Hebrew or Aramaic). If for the sake of convenience we round this off to some 55 percent, we see something very significant. This is not only very close to the average of 53 percent that we have just arrived at, but it is also consonant with the 60 percent of Greek inscriptions in the old collection of Frey. So even though in the past eighty years the evidence has more than doubled, the numerical ratio of Greek and non-Greek material has not changed at all. In this connection it is telling that of the 609 papyri from the Roman Near East in general found outside Egypt—the *vast majority* of which are from Roman and Byzantine Palestine—some 325 are in Greek: that is almost 55 percent! (Cotton, Cockle, Millar 1995).

If at least half of the Palestinian Jewish epigraphic material from the period between Alexander and Muhammad is in Greek, can we then draw the conclusion that for at least half of the Jewish people in their homeland the native language was Greek, not Aramaic (cf. the discussion of the choice of language for Jewish epitaphs in Italy by Noy 1997)? That would be an overhasty conclusion, for we first have to address the question of the representativeness of this material. This is a very difficult matter, the more so if we take into account Josephus's somewhat enigmatic remark, "Our people do not favor those who have mastered the languages of many nations'" (*A.J.* 20.264).

The burden of proof would seem to be on the shoulders of those who maintain that Greek was *not* the lingua franca of many Palestinian Jews in the Hellenistic-Roman-Byzantine period in view of the fact that more than 50 percent of the inscriptions are in "the language of Japheth" (a rabbinic expression for Greek). The minimalist interpretations that have been put forward by several scholars are unconvincing. It is on the basis of the epigraphic evidence that as early as 1965 the great Jewish epigrapher Lifshitz was able to conclude: "The Greek language and Greek culture had penetrated all the Jewish communities of the Greek East" (Lifshitz 1965, 538; cf. Lifshitz 1970; similarly Lieberman 1942, 39). Lifshitz was probably by and large right, but his statement should be qualified by adding that this does not imply that a majority, or even a large minority, of Jews were monolingual Greek-speakers. For most, or at least many, of the Jews in Palestine, Greek most probably remained a second language, certainly outside the urban areas. We may tentatively conclude that Roman Palestine was a largely bilingual, or even trilingual, society (Wise 2015; cf. Spolsky 1985)—alongside the vernacular Aramaic (and, to a much lesser extent, Hebrew), Greek was widely used and understood—but the degree of use and understanding of Greek probably varied strongly according to locality and period, social status and educational background, occasion, and mobility.

7. Nonrabbinic Judaism

The inscriptions demonstrate that diaspora communities remained outside the sphere of influence of the rabbis until the end of antiquity. To be sure, there are sixty-seven inscriptions that do mention rabbis, but the vast majority (sixty) are from Palestine (Lapin 2011; the largest number is from the Beth She'arim catacombs), and, moreover, it is highly doubtful whether the persons designated rabbi were rabbis in the technical sense of ordained community leaders (Cohen 1981; Lapin 2011; Stemberger 2017, 601–3). Hardly any epigraphical rabbi can be securely identified with a known member of the rabbinic movement (*pace* Rosenfeld 2010). First, in antiquity the term *rabbi* was often used to designate anyone of high standing in a community and hence very often had the meaning of "prominent person" (Levine 1989, 15). Second, it is the inscriptions themselves that make clear that the real community leaders were the *archontes* (leaders), the *archisynagōgoi* (heads of the synagogue), the *gerousiarchai* (heads of the council of elders), and so on. Rabbis mentioned in inscriptions appear almost always as donors or benefactors, not as leaders of the community, and it makes no sense to assume that all epigraphical rabbis in antiquity were talmudic scholars (Cohen 1981, 14; cf. Williams 1999, 80; Lapin 2011). Some of the very few rabbis mentioned in diaspora inscriptions might perhaps have been rabbis in a technical sense (e.g., *JIWE* 1.22, 36, 86; these are from fifth through sixth century Italy and possibly indicate a beginning rabbinization of this area). But the term *rabbinic Judaism* would be a glaring misnomer for the Jewish communities in the Western diaspora as a whole. These communities often flourished for centuries without rabbis being around, let alone as community leaders. That also explains why outside Byzantine Palestine (where we have the sixth-century halakic inscription from Rehov [Naveh 1978, no. 49]), there are no inscriptions that reflect any specifically rabbinic ideas or practices. The vast majority of the Jews in the Roman Empire never saw a rabbi and never heard of the Mishnah or the Talmud (Stemberger 2017, 603–6).

Even so, attachment to the synagogue and the Jewish community with its value system, which was based upon the torah, is apparent from, for example, telling epithets that several of the deceased are adorned with in epitaphs. Apart from the most frequently occurring epithet *hosios* (pious), we find designations which are very unusual or even nonexistent in the non-Jewish world, such as *philosynagōgos* (loving the synagogue/community, *JIWE* 2.271), *philonomos* (loving the torah, *JIWE* 2.212, 502), *philentol(i)os* (loving the commandments, *JIWE* 1.163; *JIWE* 2.240, 281, 564, 576), *philopenēs* (loving the poor, *JIWE* 2.240), *philogeitōn* (loving one's neighbors, *JIGRE* 84); plus more. It is also noteworthy that the daughter of a Roman "father of the synagogue" is said "to have lived a good life in Judaism" or "to have lived a good Jewish life" (*kalōs biōsasa en tōi Ioudaïsmōi, JIWE* 2.584). In *IJO* 1.Mac1 (Macedonia), a "father of the synagogue" at Stobi proudly states that he "lived all [his] life according to [the prescriptions of] Judaism" (*politeusamenos pasan tēn politeian kata ton Ioudaïsmon*). These epithets and statements reveal a strong sense of Jewish identity and of attachment to the Jewish tradition on the part of these diaspora Jews. It is also clear from this (and other) evidence that the torah had taken center stage in their lives. The centrality of the torah "is something about which the epigraphic record leaves us in no doubt" (Williams 1999, 83). It is not only epithets such as *philonomos* and *philentolos* that highlight this but also the proud mention of synagogal functions such as *nomodidaskalos* (teacher of the torah), *didaskalos nomomathēs* (teacher and scholar of the torah), and the frequent depiction of Torah shrines on tombstones that make this abundantly clear (references in Williams 1999, 83). In Palestinian inscriptions one is struck by the frequent mention of a person's having been a priest, or of priestly descent, even long after 70 CE. Apparently one took great pride in that.

Functions in the religious community, in the synagogue, are mentioned significantly more frequently in the inscriptions than secular professions, which is indicative of their importance to the holders of these offices (see the lists of secular occupations in Williams 1998, 231; Van der Horst 2015, 52). "Inscriptions reveal more clearly than any other type of source material the early emergence of the synagogue as the most characteristic feature of the established diasporan community and its development from simple prayer-hall into multi-purpose community centre" (Williams 1999, 77). It is telling that in many inscriptions the synagogue is called "the (most) holy synagogue" or "the holy place" (or "sacred precinct") (Goodman 2007, 219–31), a clear indication of the great importance of the synagogue as a religious institution. It is two inscriptions from the second half of the third century BCE in Egypt that are the earliest secure attestations of the existence of synagogues as Jewish religious buildings (*JIGRE* 22 and 117). It is an inscription from mid-first-century CE Jerusalem that explicitly states what the synagogue had been built: "for reading of the Law and instruction in [or: teaching of] the commandments" (*CIIP* 1.9). Synagogal functionaries (other than rabbis) are mentioned frequently in the inscriptions, especially throughout the later Roman period. It is apparently with pride that commemorative and honorary inscriptions mention that the persons concerned are (or were) *archōn* (ruler, leader of the community), *archisynagōgos* (head of the community), *gerousiarchēs* (president of the council of elders, also called *epistatēs tōn palaiōn*), *grammateus* (secretary or scribe of the community), *hypēretēs* (servant or attendant), *mellarchōn* (archon-elect), *patēr synagōgēs* (father of the synagogue), *phrontistēs* (manager, possibly the overseer of the finances), *presbyteros* (elder = member of the council of elders), *prostatēs* (president or patron, a rather unclear function), *psalmōidos* (singer of psalms), and so on (references in Burtchaell 1992, 228–71; esp. Williams 1998, 37–50; Levine 2000, 387–428; Claußen 2002, 256–93). Regrettably enough, more often than not these inscriptions deny us any information about the precise duties and responsibilities of these offices. Neither do they tell us which offices were honorary and which were not, although we can be sure that the cases of infant office holders (such as an *archisynagōgos* of three years, *JIWE* 1.53; more instances in Williams 1998, 149) were bestowed their titles because the community wanted to honor the family of the child. That the child was not an office holder was taken for granted.

It is a matter of debate whether the inscriptions mentioning women as leaders of the community have to be taken literally or as honorific designations, for example, to indicate that the woman concerned had a husband who was the leader of the synagogue (Brooten 1982; Horbury 1999). We find women as *archisynagōgos* or *archisynagōgissa* (leader of the synagogue; *IJO* 1.Cre3; *IJO* 2.25; *IJO* 2.43); as *presbytera* or *presbyterissa* ([female] elder; *JIWE* 1.59; *JIWE* 1.62; *JIWE* 1.72; *JIWE* 1.163; *IJO* 1.Thr3; *IJO* 1.Cre3; plus more); as *matēr synagōgēs* (mother of the synagogue; *JIWE* 2.251, 542, 577). It would seem that, although the practice of conferring honorific titles upon women did exist in some circles, this does definitely not exclude the possibility that, in nonrabbinic synagogues of the Western diaspora, women had more opportunities to climb the social ladder in their communities than was possible elsewhere, especially in Palestine.

All this evidence shows us different kinds of synagogue organization—apparently there was great freedom in the diaspora to structure the community according to local needs. Again, it also highlights the centrality and great importance of the synagogue in the lives of individual Jews.

The fact that numerous inscriptions from the land of Israel, especially from Beth She'arim and Jaffa, show that many diaspora Jews came to live there may indicate that they regarded Israel as the Holy Land where they wanted to be buried, but others may also have moved there for reasons of trade (e.g., *BS* 2.141 [from Antioch], 147 [from Tyre], 148 [from Beirut],

172 [from Sidon]; Jaffa: *CIIP* 2176 [from Emesa], 2180, 2191, 2196 [all from Alexandria]).

8. Manumission of Slaves and Other Examples of Greek Influence

It is only through epigraphic evidence that we learn about release rituals (manumissions) of Jewish slaves. This evidence comes mainly from Delphi and the Bosporan kingdom (*IJO* 1.Ach42–45; *IJO* 1.BS5–9, 17–25). For instance, a second-century BCE inscription from Delphi tells us that the slave, "*Ioudaios* by name, *Ioudaios* by nation" (for *Ioudaios* as both a name and an ethnic label see Williams 2013, 267–88) was sold to the god Apollo (!, *IJO* 1.Ach42), a not uncommon manumission procedure at the time among Greeks (see also 1.Ach43 and 44). Even though the involvement of Apollo was probably at the initiative of the manumittor, it is revealing to read in another inscription that the liberated slave, Moschus, who is explicitly identified as a Jew, set up a stela on which he states that he had a dream in which the Greek gods Amphiaraus and Hygieia ordered him to record his manumission on the stone and set it up by their altar (*IJO* I.Ach45, third century BCE). This sheds a striking light on the degree of assimilation that was possible among Jewish slaves of pagan owners. In the Bosporan inscriptions (most of them from the first century CE), we find that Jewish slaves were set free in the prayer-house (*proseuchē* = synagogue) and that the community of the Jews (*synagōgē tōn Ioudaiōn*) provided guardianship (e.g., *IJO* 1.BS5–7). This final remark probably means that "the synagogue is bound to uphold the contract between owner and now freed slave" (Gibson 1999, 150). Some other Bosporan manumissions, however, state that the Jewish slaves were set free "under [the gods] Zeus, Gê, and Helios" (*IJO* 1.BS20, 22), a common pagan Greek juridical formula, even though the transaction took place in the synagogue (Gibson 1999, 119–21).

Whether the Jewish participants attached much significance to such formulas may be doubted, as it may in the case of the many instances of the Latin formula *Dis Manibus* (*DM*), "to the gods of the netherworld," on many tombstones in the Jewish catacombs of Rome. Yet there are many other epigraphic instances of influence of pagan ideas and practices on Jews (Williamson 1999, 82–83, 87–88). Also pagan theophoric names became fashionable among Jews under Greek influence (e.g., Isidorus, "gift of Isis"; many other instances in Ilan 2002–2011).

9. Pagan Donors

Again another area that Jewish literary sources are silent about is that of pagan donors of synagogues. The best-known example is mentioned in the New Testament, where the Gospel of Luke tells about a Roman centurion in Capernaum who had the synagogue built for the local Jews (Luke 7:4–5). We have impressive epigraphical corroboration of this phenomenon. It is an inscription from Acmonia in Phrygia in which it is said that the house built by Julia Severa was restored by some prominent members of the local Jewish community who were honored for this by the synagogue (*IJO* 2.168). Julia Severa is well known to us. In the middle of the first century CE, she was priestess of the local emperor cult. So she was not Jewish but played a prominent role in a pagan cult of the city. Even so, this inscription testifies to her interest in and sympathy for the Jewish community: she had its synagogue built at her own cost. Julia Severa was a woman from an aristocratic family (her son later became a senator in Rome), a lady who had close ties to members of the distinguished Roman family of the Turronii: one of them, Turronius Rapo, was a priest of the emperor cult as well, but another member of that family, Turronius Cladus, is mentioned in our inscription as the "leader of the community" (*archisynagōgos*) who saw to it that the restoration was carried out properly. So he must have been a proselyte. The fact that here a socially very prominent woman from a distinguished family with an explicitly pagan role in the city makes a very generous gesture toward the Jewish community bespeaks a very successful integration of the Acmonian Jews and of the sympathy they had won with the non-Jewish inhabitants of that city (other instances in Feldman 1993, 310). Here a single inscription provides us with a unique insight into gentile-Jewish relations in first-century CE Asia Minor. So does—for a later period—the great donor inscription from Aphrodisias (*IJO* 2.14), which shows that more than fifty often prominent non-Jews (called *theosebeis*, Godfearers) contributed substantially to the financing of a Jewish institution.

10. Afterlife

A sign of influence of Greek (and Roman) epigraphy is the mention of the age at death of the deceased in epitaphs. Whereas early Jewish literary sources hardly ever mention someone's age at death, we have several hundred tombstones that do so. The average age at death for Jews in the period under review turns out to be about twenty-eight years—some twenty-nine years for men and twenty-seven for women (Van der Horst 1991, 73–84). These low numbers hardly deviate from averages for other groups in the Hellenistic and Roman world. It should be borne in mind that less than half of those born reached the age of five (Burn 1953). That may have fostered a longing for an afterlife.

The vast majority of tomb inscriptions, however, are disappointingly silent about belief in the afterlife (Van der Horst 1991, 114–26; Park 2000). For instance, 97 percent of the hundreds of funerary inscriptions from the Jewish catacombs in Rome show no signs of belief in the afterlife (Williams 1999, 90). Those that do yield information about some forms of belief in life after death, however, show us a great variety of ideas. Jewish literary sources from the Hellenistic and Roman period tend to suggest that most Jews believed in either the resurrection of the body or the immortality of the soul (or related concepts such as astral immortality, e.g., *IJO* 2.236), but the inscriptions clearly demonstrate that in that period many Jews still preserved the image that the Hebrew Bible pictures of humans' fate after death, that of a somber life in a gloomy netherworld (Sheol). Sometimes one finds there a downright denial of afterlife reminiscent of what we know about the Sadducees. It would seem that "a significant number of people who considered themselves to be Jews either denied, or held to a minimal conception of, afterlife" (Park 2000, 202). On the other hand, the large number of epitaphs from Beth She'arim containing the formula *eumoirei* ("may your lot be good") are probably best interpreted as indicating a belief in life after death. Also the many inscriptions (especially from Rome) in which the deceased's relatives wish that "his/her sleep may be in peace" are open to an eschatological interpretation, although that is a much debated issue. But there is less than a handful of inscriptions that do explicitly state that resurrection of the body was what one hoped for or believed in (*JIWE* 2.103; *BS* 2.162, 194). It is paradoxical that this most typical of Jewish beliefs finds its clearest expression in one of the most atypical Jewish epitaphs from antiquity, namely, in a Latin poem of thirteen hexameters from third- or fourth-century CE Rome (*JIWE* 2.103):

> Here is buried Regina, covered by such a tomb,
> which her husband set up in accordance to his love for her.
> After twice ten (years), she spent with him a year
> and a fourth month with eight days more.
> She will live again, return to the light again.
> For she can hope that she may rise into the life

promised for both the worthy and the pious, a true pledge,
she who deserved to have an abode in the venerable land.
Your piety has achieved this for you, your chaste life,
your love for your people, your observance of the law,
the merit of your marriage, whose honor was your concern.
From these deeds there is future hope for you,
and therein your grieving spouse seeks his consolation.

Even though it will always remain impossible to say how representative the beliefs expressed in these inscriptions are for the Jewish people as a whole, there can be little doubt that here, too, we see at least that a wide variety of ideas about and attitudes toward life after death continued to be a feature of Judaism till the very end of antiquity (and even thereafter).

11. Judeo-Greek Culture after 70 CE

The most important contribution of Jewish epigraphy is that the inscriptions reveal to us a world of Judeo-Greek culture that we would hardly know of otherwise. Many scholars tend to think that the various forms of Judeo-Greek culture that came into being and flourished in the centuries between 300 BCE and 100 CE, disappeared completely after the first century. It is for that reason, so it is assumed, that we do not know any Jewish literature in Greek after Josephus: Jews simply stopped writing in Greek by the end of the first century CE and apparently chose to express their Judaism in the Hebrew and Aramaic of the rabbinic literature. But this assumption "is contradicted by the thousands of Greek inscriptions set up by Mediterranean Jews between the second and sixth centuries CE" (Goodman 2010, 67). Why Judeo-Greek literature from these later centuries was not preserved by the Jews is a much debated matter on which there exists no consensus. Be that as it may, since we do not have Judeo-Greek literature that was written after the first century CE, and since the Jewish literature we do have from that period (i.e., rabbinic writings) does not inform us about the Western diaspora, it is again only epigraphy (and, of course, archaeology) that allows us glimpses into the rich nonrabbinic Jewish culture of this diaspora.

Bibliography

Ameling, Walter. 2007. "Die jüdische Diaspora Kleinasiens und der 'epigraphic habit.'" Pages 253–82 in *Jewish Identity in the Greco-Roman*

World. Edited by Jörg Frey, Daniel R. Schwartz, and Stephanie Gripentrog. AJEC 71. Leiden: Brill.

Bagatti, Bellarmino, and Józef Tadeusz Milik. 1958. *Gli scavi del "Dominus Flevit" (Monte Oliveto—Gerusalemme), Parte I: La necropoli del periodo romano*. PSBF 13.1. Jerusalem: Franciscan.

Bij de Vaate, Alice J., and Jan Willem van Henten. 1995. "Jewish or Non-Jewish? Some Remarks on the Identification of Jewish Inscriptions from Asia Minor." *BO* 53:16–28.

Bohec, Yann le. 1981. "Inscriptions juives et judaïsantes de l'Afrique Romaine." *Antiquités Africaines* 17:165–207.

Brooten, Bernadette J. 1982. *Women Leaders in the Ancient Synagogue: Inscriptional Evidence and Background Issues*. BJS 36. Chico, CA: Scholars Press.

Burn, A. R. 1953. "*Hic breve vivitur:* A Study of the Expectation of Life in the Roman Empire." *Past & Present* 4:1–31.

Burtchaell, James Turstead. 1992. *From Synagogue to Church: Public Services and Offices in the Earliest Christian Communities*. Cambridge: Cambridge University Press.

Chancey, Mark A. 2005. *Greco-Roman Culture and the Galilee of Jesus*. SNTSMS 134. Cambridge: Cambridge University Press.

Claußen, Carsten. 2002. *Versammlung, Gemeinde, Synagoge: Das hellenistisch-jüdische Umfeld der frühchristlichen Gemeinden*. SUNT 27. Göttingen: Vandenhoeck & Ruprecht.

Cohen, Shaye J. D. 1981. "Epigraphical Rabbis." *JQR* 72:1–17.

Cotton, Hannah M., W. E. H. Cockle, and F. G. B. Millar. 1995. "The Papyrology of the Roman Near East: A Survey." *JRS* 85:214–35.

Feldman, Louis H. 1993. *Jew and Gentile in the Ancient World*. Princeton: Princeton University Press.

Ferrua, A. 1941. "Addenda et corrigenda al CIJ." *Epigraphica* 3:30–46.

Gibson, E. Leigh. 1999. *The Jewish Manumission Inscriptions of the Bosporus Kingdom*. TSAJ 75. Tübingen: Mohr Siebeck.

Goodman, Martin. 2007. "Sacred Space in Diaspora Judaism." Pages 219–31 in *Judaism in the Roman World*. AJEC 66. Leiden: Brill.

———. 2010. "Under the Influence: Hellenism in Ancient Jewish Life." *BAR* 36.1:60–67.

Hachlili, Rachel. 1979. "The Goliath Family in Jericho: Funerary Inscriptions from a First-Century A.D. Jewish Monumental Tomb." *BASOR* 235:31–66.

Horbury, William. 1999. "Women in the Synagogue." Pages 358–401 in *The Early Roman Period*. Edited by William Horbury, W. D. Davies, and John Sturdy. CHJ 3. Cambridge: Cambridge University Press.
Horst, Pieter W. van der. 1991. *Ancient Jewish Epitaphs: An Introductory Survey of a Millennium of Jewish Funerary Epigraphy (300 BCE–700 CE)*. CBET 2. Kampen: Kok Pharos.
———. 1994. "Jewish Poetical Tomb Inscriptions." Pages 129–47 in *Studies in Early Jewish Epigraph*. Edited by Jan Willem van Henten and Pieter W. van der Horst. AGAJU 21. Leiden: Brill.
———. 2001. "Greek in Jewish Palestine in the Light of Epigraphy." Pages 154–74 in *Hellenism in the Land of Israel*. Edited by John J. Collins and Gregory E. Sterling. CJAn 13. Notre Dame: University of Notre Dame Press.
———. 2014. "Biblical Quotations in Judaeo-Greek Inscriptions." Pages 66–79 *Studies in Ancient Judaism and Early Christianity*. AJEC 87. Leiden: Brill.
———. 2015. *Saxa Judaica Loquuntur: Lessons from Early Jewish Inscriptions*. BibInt 134. Leiden: Brill.
Hüttenmeister, Frowald G., and Gottfried Reeg. 1977. *Die antiken Synagogen in Israel*. BTAVO 12. 2 vols. Wiesbaden: Reichert.
Ilan, Tal. 2002–2011. *Lexicon of Jewish Names in Late Antiquity*. TSAJ 91, 126, 141, and 148. 4 vols. Tübingen: Mohr Siebeck.
Kant, Laurence H. 1987. "Jewish Inscriptions in Greek and Latin." ANRW 20.2:671–713.
Kraemer, Ross S. 1986. "Hellenistic Jewish Women: The Epigraphical Evidence." Pages 183–200 in *Society of Biblical Literature 1986 Seminar Papers*. SBLSP 25. Missoula, MT: Scholars Press.
———. 1991. "Jewish Tuna and Christian Fish: Identifying Religious Affiliation in Epigraphic Sources." HTR 84:141–62.
Kraft, Robert A., and George W. E. Nickelsburg, eds. 1986. *Early Judaism and Its Modern Interpreters*. BMI 2. Philadelphia: Fortress; Atlanta: Scholars Press.
Kroll, John H. 2001. "The Greek Inscriptions of the Sardis Synagogue." HTR 94:5–55.
Lapin, Hayim. 2011. "Epigraphical Rabbis: A Reconsideration." JQR 101:311–46.
Leon, Harry J. 1960. *The Jews of Ancient Rome*. Philadelphia: Jewish Publication Society.

Levine, Lee I. 1989. *The Rabbinic Class of Roman Palestine in Late Antiquity*. Jerusalem: Yad ben-Zvi; New York: Jewish Theological Seminary.

———. 2000. *The Ancient Synagogue: The First Thousand Years*. New Haven: Yale University Press.

Lewis, David M. 1964. "Appendix I: The Jewish Inscriptions of Egypt." Pages 138–66 in vol. 3 of *Corpus Papyrorum Judaicarum*. Edited by Victor Tcherikover, Alexander Fuks, and Menahem Stern. 3 vols. Cambridge: Harvard University Press; Jerusalem: Magnes.

Lieberman, Saul. 1942. *Greek in Jewish Palestine*. New York: Jewish Theological Seminary.

Lifshitz, Baruch. 1965. "L'hellénisation des Juifs en Palestine á propos des inscriptions de Besara (Beth-Shearim)." *RB* 72:520–38.

———. 1967. *Donateurs et fondateurs dans les synagogues juives*. CahRB 7. Paris: Gabalda.

———. 1970. "Du nouveau sur l'hellénisation des Juifs de Palestine." *Euphrosyne* NS 3:113–33.

———. 1975. "Prolegomenon." *CIJ* 1:21–104.

Lüderitz, Gert. 1983. *Corpus jüdischer Zeugnisse aus der Cyrenaica*. BTAVO 53. Wiesbaden: Reichert.

Miranda, Elena. 1999. "La comunità giudaica di Hierapolis di Frigia." *Epigraphica Anatolica* 31:109–56.

Naveh, Joseph. 1978. *On Stone and Mosaic: The Aramaic and Hebrew Inscriptions from Ancient Synagogues* [Hebrew]. Jerusalem: Israel Exploration Society.

Noy, David. 1997. "Writing in Tongues: The Use of Greek, Latin and Hebrew in Jewish Inscriptions from Roman Italy." *JJS* 48:300–11.

Park, Joseph S. 2000. *Conceptions of Afterlife in Jewish Inscriptions*. WUNT 2/121. Tübingen: Mohr Siebeck.

Price, Jonathan J., and Haggai Misgav. 2006. "Jewish Inscriptions and Their Use." Pages 461–83 in *The Literature of the Sages: Part 2*. Edited by Shmuel Safrai, Zeev Safrai, Joshua Schwartz, and Peter J. Tomson. CRINT 2.3b. Assen: Van Gorcum; Minneapolis: Fortress.

Rahmani, L. Y. 1994. *A Catalogue of Jewish Ossuaries in the Collections of the State of Israel*. Jerusalem: Israel Academy of Sciences and Humanities.

Rajak, Tessa. 2001. *The Jewish Dialogue with Greece and Rome: Studies in Cultural and Social Interaction*. AGAJU 48. Leiden: Brill.

Reynolds, Joyce Marie, and Robert F. Tannenbaum. 1987. *Jews and God-Fearers at Aphrodisias: Greek Inscriptions with Commentary*. Cambridge: Cambridge Philological Society.

Robert, Louis. 1937. "Un corpus des inscription juives." *REJ* 101:73–86.

———. 1954. Review of *Corpus Inscriptionum Judaicarum: Recueil des inscriptions juives qui vont du IIIe siècle avant Jésus-Christ au VIIe siècle de notre ère*, vol. 2, by Jean-Baptiste Frey. *Bulletin Épigraphique* 67:101–4.

Rosenfeld, Ben-Zion. 2010. "The Title 'Rabbi' in Third- to Seventh-Century Inscriptions in Palestine." *JJS* 61:234–56.

Roth-Gerson, Lea. 1987. *The Greek Inscriptions from the Synagogues in Israel* [Hebrew]. Jerusalem: Yad Ben-Zvi.

Rutgers, L. V. 1995. *The Jews of Late Ancient Rome: Evidence of Cultural Interaction in the Roman Diaspora*. RGRW 126. Leiden: Brill.

Scheiber, Alexander. 1983. *Jewish Inscriptions in Hungary from the Third Century to 1686*. Budapest: Akadémiai Kiadó; Leiden: Brill.

Spolsky, Bernard. 1985. "Jewish Multilingualism in the First Century: An Essay in Historical Sociolinguistics." Pages 35–50 in *Readings in the Sociology of Jewish Languages*. Edited by Joshua A. Fishman. Leiden: Brill.

Stemberger, Günter. 2017. "Rabbi." *RAC* 28:593–613.

Williams, Margert H. 1998. *The Jews among the Greeks and Romans: A Diaspora Sourcebook*. Baltimore: Johns Hopkins University Press.

———. 1999. "The Contribution of Jewish Inscriptions to the Study of Judaism." Pages 75–93 in *The Early Roman Period*. Edited by William Horbury, W. D. Davies, and John Sturdy. CHJ 3. Cambridge: Cambridge University Press.

———. 2003–2004. "Jewish Inscriptions of the Graeco-Roman Period—An Update." *Bulletin of Judaeo-Greek Studies* 33:40–46.

———. 2013. *Jews in a Graeco-Roman Environment*. WUNT 312. Tübingen: Mohr Siebeck.

Wise, Michael O. 2015. *Language and Literacy in Roman Judaea: A Study of the Bar Kochba Documents*. ABRL. New Haven: Yale University Press.

8
Documentary Papyri

ROBERT KUGLER

Apart from an exceptionally cursory listing of some of the evidence in an essay on "Other Manuscript Discoveries" (Brock 1986, 164–67), one searches in vain to find a sustained discussion of documentary papyri within any of the chapters collected in *Early Judaism and Its Interpreters* (Kraft and Nickelsburg 1986), let alone a standalone treatment of the topic such as the present essay. The absence of any sustained discussion of documentary evidence in *Early Judaism and Its Interpreters* is explained in part by the fact that the burgeoning research of the 1980s on Jewish origins in Greco-Roman world was understandably driven largely by the array of *literature* that had been discovered and rediscovered in the decades preceding, most especially the Dead Sea Scrolls and related (and unrelated) pseudepigrapha. Even if there was a wealth of data available in Victor Tcherikover and Alexander Fuks (*CPJ* 1–3) well before the creation of *Early Judaism and Its Interpreters*, without significant archives like the Herakleopolis archive, first published in 2001, and the Babatha and Salome Komaise archives from the Judean desert, largely unpublished until the late 1990s, the documentary record held little of interest to researchers. The availability of all three archives has stirred greater interest in the documentary record, as has the emerging recognition in the wider field that nonliterary evidence can reveal aspects of Jewish life apart from the literate elite and tell us something of the audiences targeted by the literature that has so fascinated recent generations of scholars. This brief treatment orients readers to the most important documentary evidence available.

1. A Survey of the Evidence

1.1. Egypt

The number of documentary papyri recovered from the sands of Egypt—from refuse dumps, as in Oxyrhynchus and from cartonnage as in the Herakleopolite and other locales in the Nile Valley—number in the thousands (for an introduction to documentary papyri, see Pestman 1984). Among these are several hundred that have been definitively identified as relating to Jews—either they were authored by Jews or they involve Jews in some way. These Jewish documentary papyri constitute a significant body of evidence for the daily life of nonelite Jews in Greco-Roman and Byzantine Egypt.

Although they predate the period covered by the *Early Judaism and Its Interpreters* volumes, the Aramaic papyri from fifth century BCE Elephantine require attention in this context—they give important insight into the life of Jews in Egypt leading up to the Greco-Roman era and provide strong evidence for viewing specific moments of Jewish experience in Egypt within a continuum from the Persian to the Byzantine periods (Porten 1968). Found mostly on the Nile island of their namesake in Upper Egypt, the papyri were associated with the Jewish soldiers and their families assigned to a military outpost that served the Persians who ruled Egypt at the time. The most relevant papyri include private and official letters and contracts. (The archive also contains small numbers of literary and historical texts, as well as accounts and lists.) Private letters are concerned with, among other things, the sending of needed items, concerns about salary payments, and the wellbeing of the addressees and the senders, with one even expressing frustration with the addressee's lack of interest in the welfare of the sender (Porten 2011, 103). We learn much about daily life from the private correspondence. Among the official letters, two stand out: a letter to a community leader, Jedaniah, dating to 419/418 from a certain Hananiah invoking the Persian king's authority and addressing aspects of Passover observance among the Elephantine Jews (Porten 2011, 126–27) and a letter dating to 410 BCE from Jedaniah and the Jews of Elephantine to the governor of Judah asking for the reconstruction of their temple, which had been destroyed by Egyptian priests of Khnum (Porten 2011, 141–46). Among the contracts, the multigenerational archives of Mibtahiah and Anani reveal a great deal about the conveyance of property between generations, as well as the ways marriages were formed and the terms that governed husbands and wives.

The major source for documentary papyri relating to Jews of Greco-Roman Egypt, *CPJ* 1–3, is quite dated, having been completed in 1960. However, an update to *CPJ* 1–3, referred to here as *CPJ* 4 is underway and will provide a comprehensive update of *CPJ* 1–3, gathering in one place the documentary texts relating to the Jews of the Greco-Roman and Byzantine periods published since the completion of *CPJ* 1–3 (as well as publishing some non-Greek texts known when *CPJ* 1–3 was edited, but not included in those volumes; see *CPJ* 4). While there can be no substitute for browsing the texts themselves to get a sense of the wealth of insight they offer—both those presently available in *CPJ* 1–3 and those to appear in *CPJ* 4—a summary of the criteria for including texts in the volumes, a general survey of the contents of the *CPJ*, and brief descriptions of significant clusters of texts and archives assembled in the volumes can orient users of the volumes and to the data they contain.

The editors of *CPJ* 1–3 used four criteria to determine if a text from among the thousands of documentary papyri recovered chiefly from Egypt could be included in the collection, three of which are used by the editors of *CPJ* 4: (1) the appearance of the terms *Ioudaios* or *Hebraios* in Greek texts (*CPJ* 1–3 and 4) and related terms in Hebrew, Aramaic, and Demotic texts (*CPJ* 4; the editors of *CPJ* 4 depart from the Greek-only standard held to by the editors of *CPJ* 1–3); (2) the use of technical terms or references to events that point to Jews (e.g., the term *proseuche*, or a reference to the Jewish revolt of 115–17 CE); and (3) the appearance of indubitably Jewish names (i.e., biblical names; the editors of *CPJ* 4 take a more conservative view on two contested names, Dositheos and Shabbtai in view of the more recent understanding that these were often used by non-Jews, as well). The fourth criterion used by the editors of *CPJ* 1–3, a document's origin from a place (thought to be) exclusively a Jewish settlement, has been set aside by the editors of *CPJ* 4, in recognition of the fact that such places did not in fact exist in Greco-Roman Egypt. By these criteria, once *CPJ* 4 is published, scholars will have in hand around 210 documentary papyri from Ptolemaic Egypt and just short of 380 from the Roman period.

Even leaving aside the literary and magical papyri included in *CPJ* 4, the range of genres among the documentary texts gathered in *CPJ* 1–3 and *CPJ* 4 is impressive. There are petitions individuals addressed to courts and officials seeking remedies for wrongs done to them by other private individuals (e.g., *CPJ* 1.128), public officials (*CPJ* 1.43), or institutionalized powers such as systems for tax collection (e.g., *CPJ* 1.130); police reports (e.g., *CPJ* 1.131); personal and official letters (*CPJ* 2.424 and *CPJ* 1.132 respectively); contracts for sale, loans, leases, and other business relationships (e.g., *CPJ* 1.25–26; 2.414); receipts for payment of purchase prices, taxes, and other transactions involving exchanges of goods, services, and monies (e.g., *CPJ* 1.48–111; 2.409, 422); business accounts, lists of persons and property, (e.g., *CPJ* 1.28–30, 39; 2.415); testaments and wills (e.g., *CPJ* 1.126); documents related to marriage and divorce (e.g., *CPJ* 2.144; P.Polit. Iud. 4, 5); and much more.

The Ptolemaic-era documentary texts contained in *CPJ* 1–4 can be sorted into six groupings: (1) assorted individual texts associated with persons who are demonstrably Jewish (chiefly receipts, accounts, and other minor business and commercial records, but also petitions, personal communications, and other documents related to daily life apart from business transactions); these are drawn from a wide variety of different archives and collections of related documentary texts from Hellenistic Egypt and are provenanced to places throughout Egypt; (2) texts drawn from the Zenon papyri that relate to Jews in Egypt and in Palestine (see further below); (3) a group of tax registers from the Fayum, and especially Trikomia, a village identified as being home to a significant number of Jews (see P.Count 23, 26, 27, 29, 34, and 36 in Clarysse and Thompson 2006; Clarysse 1994); (4) a small collection of entries in a contracts register from Theogenis involving Jews in Samareia (see further below); (5) texts related to Dositheos son of Drimylos; and (6) the Herakleopolis *politeuma* papyri (see further below).

The Roman-era texts contained in *CPJ* 1–4 likewise can sorted into a number of more or less well-defined groupings: (1) assorted individual texts associated with persons who are demonstrably Jewish (again, chiefly receipts, accounts, and other minor business and commercial records); (2) texts that give evidence for the Jews of Alexandria in the early Roman period (including, among other things, a deed of divorce, a wet nurse contract, a receipt for the payment of a debt); (3) texts related to the disruptions Jews experienced in 38–41 BCE; (4) in *CPJ* 2 a collection of tax record ostraca from Edfu, a place that the lead editor of *CPJ* 1–3, Tcherikover, in particular regarded as a Jewish settlement (see the comments of his colleagues after his passing indicating their decision to include the full collection of ostraca proposed by Tcherikover in spite of their misgivings that Edfu was not nearly so completely Jewish as once thought, ensuring that many of the ostraca were not in any way Jewish); and (5) texts related to the revolt of 115–117 CE.

A number of these texts groups deserve special comment. The Zenon archive, dated to the middle of the third century BCE, is a large number of documents that were collected by the archive's namesake, a secretary to Apollonios, a high-ranking administrative official who served Ptolemy II. At one point in his service to Apollonios, Zenon traveled to Palestine on his behalf and sent and received (and saved) correspondence related to that journey, giving a record of, among other things, dealing with Toubias, a Jewish figure in the Transjordan we know of from Josephus (*CPJ* 1.1–5; Tcherikover 1989). Zenon also included in his collection documents that mention dealing with Jews in Egypt. Thus, the archive's texts that meet criteria for inclusion in the *CPJ* volumes provide invaluable insight on the affairs of everyday Jews in the third century both in Egypt and Palestine and indicate something of how non-Jewish Ptolemaic officials interacted with Jews in Egypt—pretty much as they did with any other Hellenes in the kingdom.

The small collection of entries in a contracts register from a records office in Theogenis involving Jews from the village of Samareia also deserves special mention (*CPR* 18.7–9, 11 in Kramer 1991). Even if the texts are from a contracts register, and as such are little more than abstracts of more complete documentary texts that do not survive, they provide a wealth of data. The collection includes a lease agreement for a vineyard, a dowry receipt, a receipt for the restitution of a dowry, and a contract of lease and cultivation of a vineyard executed between the man who restored the dowry and the former mother-in-law to whom he returned it. The cluster of abstracts is especially significant for its testimony to the business dealings of a group of related Jews.

The texts assembled in *CPJ* 1–3 that give evidence of Jews in Alexandria, though few in number because physical conditions in the delta and the city itself far reduce the chances that organic material like papyrus might survive, are a precious resource for a relatively overlooked reason: they largely demonstrate that the concerns and interests of Jews in the main city and those shared by Jews inhabiting the villages, town, and countryside in the *chora* were, in fact, not that different. To be sure, *CPJ* 1.151, the well-known Helenos son of Tryphon text is a reminder of the special status that Alexandrian residency (and citizenship) could (or could not) grant. But otherwise, the issues addressed in texts associated with Alexandria are typical of Jews elsewhere in Egypt—they address disputes and agreements about land, debts, and loans (*CPJ* 1.142, 145, 148, 149), arrangements regarding legacies (*CPJ* 1.143), divorce agreements (*CPJ* 1.144), and wet nurse contracts (*CPJ* 1.146, 147). The tendency in much secondary literature to draw a sharp distinction between Jewish life in the *chora* and in Alexandria (and the other Greek cities of Egypt) is perhaps mistaken.

The most spectacular collection of texts in *CPJ* 1–4 deserving special attention are the twenty-one texts in the archive from the Jewish *politeuma* in Herakleopolis (P.Polit.Iud. 1–20 in Cowey and Maresch 2001; *CPJ* 4.557). Dating between 144/143 and 133/132 BCE, they include seventeen petitions (four of which are too small and broken to be of much interest) and four communiqués between leaders of the *politeuma* and Herakleopolis and Jews in villages in the region (nome). The petitions provide abundant insight on the daily lives and concerns of Jews in the Herakleopolite, as well as something of their connection to their ancestral legal traditions. They address violations of a person's integrity (e.g., improper incarceration, a verbal assault in public), disputes related to marriage agreements and other family matters (e.g., an aborted betrothal, failure to meet obligations related to a dowry promise), and arguments over property and contractual obligations (e.g., an unpaid loan secured by a mortgaged vineyard, an unfulfilled contract for spinning wool). Particularly the last group of petitions demonstrates the degree to which at least these Jews adhered to the Greek normative system that had come to dominate daily practice in Egypt under the Ptolemies. At the same time, though, close examination of the petitions that address violations of the integrity of the person and marriage and family matters reveals significant dependence on normative principles traceable to the Greek Torah, as well as on some Egyptian norms—the legal reasoning of the Jewish petitioners in the Herakleopolite was decidedly pluralistic (Kugler 2013, 2016). The texts also give us some insight on ethnic identity among these Jews (see, among others, Honigman 2003). As to the communiqués, they reveal a high degree of cooperation between officials of the *politeuma* in Herakleopolis and leaders of Jewish communities in outlying villages of the Herakleopolite and adjacent nomes, indicating something of the reach of this *politeuma*'s jurisdiction. Of course, the archive as a whole proves that at least the Jews of Herakleopolite in the second century BCE had the privilege of the *politeuma*, settling a longstanding debate as to whether the Ptolemies permitted the Jews the privilege at all (see, e.g., Kasher 20008; Lüdertz 1994). And because the archive yields an unprecedented amount of information regarding the nature and operation of a *politeuma* in Hellenistic Egypt, much has been made of it on that account as well (e.g., Kruse 2015; Sänger 2019).

1.2. Judea

Because physical conditions in Palestine, unlike those in Egypt, do not favor the survival of organic material over long periods of time, we have far fewer documentary papyri from Greco-Roman Judea (and other sites outside of Egypt; for a summary of the evidence from the Roman East, see Cotton, Cockle, and Millar 1989). Nonetheless, some finds of varying significance have been recovered from the region. Those with modest significance are the most numerous. A small number of papyri were recovered at Masada and provide (ambiguous) evidence for circumstances at the fortress near the end of the first revolt: there are some papyri inscribed in Latin that were likely left behind by the victorious Roman army (one of which is a pay record of some interest [Cotton and Geiger 1989, no. 722], and another a letter to a Roman that has been argued to have a bearing on setting the date of the fall of Masada [Cotton and Geiger 1989, no. 724]), and there is a bilingual text in Latin and Greek (Cotton and Geiger 1989, no. 748) that may list names of Jews pressed into service for the Romans in some capacity. In fact, the more significant documentary finds from Masada are the 275 ostraca likely used as food rationing coupons during the Roman siege of the desert fortress (Yadin and Naveh 1989). The Wadi Daliyeh Samaria papyri are extremely fragmentary legal documents—most of them deeds of sale, pledge, and consignment—that date to the fourth century BCE (DJD 28.1–27 [Gropp 2001]). Texts from near Jericho, also quite fragmentary, date to the second revolt and provide some insight on property transactions and loans in the relevant period (DJD 38.1–19 [Charlesworth et al. 2000]); the most notable text among them is an Aramaic list of loans that may date as early as the fourth century BCE (DJD 38.1 [Charlesworth et al. 2000, 21–30]). The most significant material from Qumran proper is a handful of texts published in DJD 27 (Cotton and Yardeni 1997; 4Q342–359), fragments of letters, deeds, accounts, and acknowledgements; however, at least one of these Ada Yardeni (1997, 284) has shown to be from Wadi Seiyal, so it is uncertain as whether it is really Qumran material. Gathered in DJD 38 we have a promissory note from Wadi Sdeir, a list of names and an account from Nahal Mishmar, and a deed and a census list from Nahal Seʾelim. Also, a single text from Seʾelim (DJD 27.13), is thought to be a separation notice sent by a wife to her husband during the second revolt, signaling a woman's right to divorce her husband, but it can also be read quite contrarily as a woman's declaration that she has no claims against a husband who divorced her (see Ilan 1996;

Schremer 1998). From Murabbaʿat we have most significantly a loan agreement dating to 55–56 CE that seems to include a clause whereby the debtor would forego the cancellation of debt in a sabbatical year (the so-called *prosbul*; DJD 2.18 [Benoit, Milik, and de Vaux 1961]).

The most significant documentary papyri from the Judean desert are the archives of two women who likely perished in the Second Revolt. The Babatha archive, discovered in 1961 in a cave in Wadi Hever near the Dead Sea, amounts to thirty-five legal documents pertaining to the affairs of the archive's namesake—a Jewish woman who took refuge in the Judean desert in the Second Revolt—as well as of others related to her (Lewis 1989; Yadin et al. 2002). The documents are in Greek, Aramaic, and Nabatean. Babatha seems to have brought the documents in a single pouch with her when she took refuge (unsuccessfully) from the Roman army in the Judean desert. Dating between the mid 90s CE and 132 CE, the papyri include property purchase and wedding contracts, loan documents, land registrations, and documents relating to Babatha's legal entanglements (especially over guardianship of her son, Jesus, and the disposition of property from the estate of her deceased husband, Judah). The Salome Komaise archive, also named for the woman who features most prominently in its texts, is smaller, amounting to only eight documents, ranging in date roughly from around 100 to 130 CE (Cotton 1995; Cotton and Yardeni 1997; Eshel 2002; Starcky 1954). Among them are a sales contract, a receipt for taxes, census documents, a marriage contract, a renunciation of claims to property, and a deed of gift. The information contained in the two archives covering four decades provides important insight on marriage, guardianship, commercial, and real estate practices among Jews in the Roman East, as well as some insight on their tax status. While they also testify to the staying power of the legal practices and norms developed among the Greeks going back to the classical period, we see in these texts the same legal pluralism evident in the Herakleopolis archive from Egypt—in this case a mix of Nabataean, Jewish, Greek, and Roman norms (see now Czajkowski 2017).

2. Conclusion

The foregoing provides only a basic—and incomplete—survey of the Greco-Roman era documentary papyri created by and relating to Jews. I hope that it is sufficient, though, to indicate the wealth of information available from these texts and point the way toward greater interest in learning what we can from them in expanding our understanding of Jewish origins.

Bibliography

Benoit, Pierre, Józef T. Milik, and Roland de Vaux. 1961. *Les Grottes de Murabba'ât*. DJD 2. Oxford: Clarendon.
Brock, Sebastian. 1986. "Other Manuscript Discoveries." Pages 157–73 in *Early Judaism and Its Modern Interpreters*. Edited by Robert A. Kraft and George W. E. Nickelsburg. BMI 2. Philadelphia: Fortress; Atlanta: Scholars Press.
Charlesworth, James, et al. 2000. *Miscellaneous Texts from the Judaean Desert*. DJD 38. Oxford: Clarendon.
Clarysse, Willy. 1994. "Jews in Trikomia." Pages 193–203 in *Proceedings of the Twentieth International Congress of Papyrologists: Copenhagen, 23–29 August, 1992*. Edited by Adam Bülow-Jacobsen. Copenhagen: Museum Tusculanum Press.
Clarysse, Willy, and Dorothy Thompson. 2006. *Counting the People in Hellenistic Egypt*. CCS. 2 vols. Cambridge: Cambridge University Press.
Cotton, Hannah M. 1995. "The Archive of Salome Komaise Daughter of Levi: Another Archive from the 'Cave of Letters.'" *ZPE* 105:171–208.
Cotton, Hannah, W. E. H. Cockle, and Fergus Millar. 1995. "The Papyrology of the Roman Near East: A Survey." *JRS* 85:214–35.
Cotton, Hannah, and Joseph Geiger. 1989. *Masada II, the Yigael Yadin Excavations 1963–1965: Final Reports; Latin and Greek Documents*. Jerusalem: Israel Exploration Society.
Cotton, Hannah M., and Ada Yardeni. 1997. *Aramaic, Hebrew, and Greek Documentary Texts from Nahal Hever and Other Sites*. Seiyal Collection 2. DJD 27. Oxford: Oxford University Press.
Cowey, James M. S., and Klaus Maresch. 2001. *Urkunden des Politeuma der Juden von Herakleopolis (144/3–133/2 v.Chr.): (P. Polit. Iud.)*. Papyrologica Coloniensia 29. Wiesbaden: Westdeutscher.
Czajkowski, Kimberley. 2017. *Localized Law: The Babatha and Salome Komaise Archives*. Oxford Studies in Roman Society and Law. Oxford: Oxford University Press.
Eshel, Hanan. 2002. "Another Document from the Archive of Salome Komaise Daughter of Levi." *SCI* 21:169–71.
Gropp, Douglas. 2001. *Wadi Daliyeh II: The Samaria Papyri from Wadi Daliyeh*. DJD 28. Oxford: Clarendon.

Honigman, Sylvie. 2003. "*Politeumata* and Ethnicity in Ptolemaic and Roman Egypt." *Ancient Society* 33:61–102.

Ilan, Tal. 1996. "On a Newly Published Divorce Bill from the Judaean Desert." *HTR* 89:195–202.

Kasher, Aryeh. 2008. "The Jewish *politeuma* in Alexandria: A Pattern of Jewish Communal Life in the Greco-Roman Diaspora." Pages 109–25 in *Homelands and Diasporas: Greeks, Jews and Their Migrations*. Edited by Minna Rozen. London: Taurus.

Kraft, Robert A., and George W. E. Nickelsburg, eds. 1986. *Early Judaism and Its Modern Interpreters*. BMI 2. Philadelphia: Fortress; Atlanta: Scholars Press.

Kramer, Bärbel. 1991. *Das Vertragsregister von Theogenis (P. Vindob. G 40618)*. Corpus Papyrorum Raineri 18. Griechische Texte 13. Vienna: Hollinek.

Kruse, Thomas. 2015. "Ethnic *Koina* and *Politeumata* in Ptolemaic Egypt." Pages 270–300 in *Private Associations and the Public Sphere: Proceedings of a Symposium Held at the Royal Danish Academy of Sciences and Letters, 9–11 September 2010*. Edited by Vincent Gabrielsen and Christian A. Thomsen. Copenhagen.

Kugler, Robert. 2013. "Uncovering Echoes of LXX Legal Norms in Hellenistic Egyptian Documentary Papyri: The Case of the Second-Century Herakleopolite Nome." Pages 143–54 in *XIV Congress of the International Organization for Septuagint and Cognate Studies*. Edited by Melvin Peters. SCS 59. Atlanta: Society of Biblical Literature.

———. 2016. "Judean Marriage Custom and Law in Second-Century BCE Egypt: A Case of Migrating Ideas and a Fixed Ethnic Minority." Pages 123–39 in *Minderheiten und Migration in der griechisch-römischen Welt*. Edited by Patrick Sänger. Paderborn: Schöningh.

Lewis, Naphtali. 1989. *The Documents from the Bar Kochba Period in the Cave Letters: Greek Papyri*. JDS 2. Jerusalem: Israel Exploration Society.

Lüdertz, Gerd. 1994. "What Is the Politeuma?" Pages 183–225 in *Studies in Early Jewish Epigraphy*. Edited by Jan Willem van Henten and Pieter van der Horst. AGJU 21. Leiden: Brill.

Pestman, Pieter W. 1994. *The New Papyrological Primer*. Leiden: Brill.

Porten, Bezalel. 1968. *Archives from Elephantine: The Life of an Ancient Jewish Military Colony*. Berkeley: University of California Press.

———. 2011. *The Elephantine Papyri in English: Three Millennia of Cross-Cultural Continuity and Change*. DMOA 22. 2nd ed. Leiden: Brill.

Sänger, Patrick. 2019. *Die ptolemäische Organisationsform politeuma: Ein Herrschaftsinstrument zugunsten jüdischer und anderer hellenischer Gemeinschaften*. TSAJ 178. Tübingen: Mohr Siebeck.
Schremer, Adiel. 1998. "Divorce in Papyrus Şe'elim 13 Once Again: A Reply to Tal Ilan." *HTR* 91:193–202.
Starcky, Jean. 1954. "Un contrat Nabatéen sur papyrus." *RB* 61:161–81.
Tcherikover, Victor. 1989. "The Tobiads in Light of the Zenon Papyri." Pages 77–99 in *Emerging Judaism: Studies on the Fourth and Third Centuries B.C.E.* Edited by Michael Stone and David Satran. Minneapolis: Fortress.
Yadin, Yigael, Jonas Greenfield, Ada Yardeni, and Baruch Levine. 2002. *The Documents from the Bar Kochba Period in the Cave of Letters: Hebrew, Aramaic and Nabataean-Aramaic Papyri*. JDS 2. Jerusalem: Israel Exploration Society.
Yadin, Yigael, and Joseph Naveh. 1989. *Masada I, the Yigael Yadin Excavations 1963–1965: Final Reports; the Aramaic and Hebrew Ostraca and Jar Inscriptions*. Jerusalem: Israel Exploration Society.
Yardeni, Ada. 1997. "Appendix: Documentary Texts Alleged to Be from Qumran Cave 4." Pages 283–318 in *Aramaic, Hebrew and Greek Documentary Texts from Nahal Hever and Other Sites*. Edited by Hannah Cotton and Ada Yardeni. Seiyal Collection 2. DJD 24. Oxford: Clarendon.

9
THE ARCHAEOLOGY OF EARLY JUDAISM

ERIC M. MEYERS

The scope and direction of this article when compared to the original version, which appeared in 1986, is pretty much a consequence of the fact that after three decades there has been a major buildup of new data as a result of recent work relating to the material world of early Judaism. Most of this has come from archaeological fieldwork in Israel and in the West Bank. Some scholars refer to the beginning of the Second Temple period as the postexilic era, and I will use that to refer to the period of Achaemenid oversight of Judea and Samaria, from around 538 BCE, the Edict of Cyrus allowing the Jews to return to their homeland, to the Hellenistic period, which begins with Alexander the Great around 332 BCE. The Hellenistic period ends with the beginning of the Roman period in 63 BCE when Palestine falls under direct Roman control, which lasts until the era of Emperor Constantine in the fourth century CE. Since so much of this new work and data comes from the Holy Land this essay skews in favor of the land of Israel rather than the diaspora. Unfortunately, there has not been a similar explosion of work in the diaspora when it comes to the material world of early Judaism. Recent surveys have rather focused on the land of Israel (E. Meyers and Chancey 2012; Magness 2012). A few studies, however, have shed new light on the Jewish remains from Rome (Burrus 2017; E. Meyers and Burrus, forthcoming) while other studies have focused on such special topics as the polychrome nature of the Arch of Titus (Fine 2012) and other new and old discoveries from diasporic lands (Fine 1996; Hachlili 1998, 2013).

This article is dedicated to the memory of A. Thomas Kraabel, who coauthored the first version of this article.

A few words must be said regarding the phrase *the archaeology of early Judaism*. To the best of my knowledge the phrase was coined by the late G. Ernest Wright in the mid-1960s when as president of the American Schools of Oriental Research (ASOR) and based at Harvard University where he was Parkman Professor of Divinity, he selected me to head a new excavation in Israel that would shed new light on early Judaism. Tom Kraabel, then a ThD candidate in New Testament in the Divinity School, was already working in this area while on the staff of the excavations at Sardis. The result of Wright's efforts to push ahead in this new direction, at least for ASOR, was that Kraabel came on as Assistant Director of the new excavations at Khirbet Shemaʿ in Upper Galilee (E. Meyers and Kraabel 1986, 175; E. Meyers 2015, 414–23). The first phase of that project lasted from 1969 to 1981 and is best known as the Meiron Excavation Project, which uncovered four synagogues and four villages there. The two final reports of that project appeared after the 1986 article and faithfully record the data from Gush Halav (E. Meyers, C. Meyers, and Strange 1990) and Nabratein (E. Meyers and C. Meyers 2009) as well as point to regional factors that are reflected in the material remains presented.

1. New Developments in the Persian Period

With the publication of Ephraim Stern's (1982, 2001) important volume on biblical archaeology that culminated with the material of the Persian period following his programmatic monograph on the material culture of the Persian period, a genuine reengagement with the early postexilic period began. While biblical scholars such as Peter Ackroyd and others (E. Meyers 2009, 2020) had written extensively to show how the last of the prophets Haggai, Zechariah, and Malachi as well as other postexilic writings assigned to this period were to be positively evaluated, Stern's works and the continuing excavation of Jerusalem led to a surprising reassessment of the demographic picture of postexilic Yehud or Judaea. Put succinctly, a group of scholars basing their numbers on the most recent archaeological work concluded that the population of the province of Yehud and Jerusalem was much smaller than previously believed, the holy city with as few as four hundred or so in the time of Nehemiah (Finkelstein 2016), and Yehud with as few as twelve thousand (Lipschits 2005, 2009; Geva 2014, 141–43). Other scholars have higher numbers but all are far below what previous generations had thought. All of this has led to a debate on what really was happening in Jerusalem and the temple and what the precise role of the elites in the priesthood and scribal class was in the early editing of the Hebrew Bible.

Similar to Jerusalem and its temple complex was Mount Gerizim in the highlands of Samaria, a Yahwistic cult center near modern day Nablus. On that hillside site excavations have revealed the Samaritan temple and a small residential area that was inhabited by the priestly class of that schismatic group (Magen 2008). There the remnants of the city of Samaria who fled after the 722 BCE destruction ultimately located and tended to their own histories and traditions that were limited to their own version of the Pentateuch. In the national park at the site the remains from the Persian and Hellenistic period are fairly extensive and well preserved.

In commenting on Haggai and Zechariah, Carol Meyers and I have noted that Persian rule through an imperial governor and an appointed high priest allowed the Persians to stay at a relative distance and allow a measure of independence in running local affairs in Yehud and within the sacred precincts of the temple (C. Meyers and E. Meyers 1987, xxix–xliv; E. Meyers 2018). The policy while appearing to be progressive was rooted in the idea that conquered peoples would remain more loyal if given certain prerogatives such as freedom to maintain their own traditions and to rebuild their historic sanctuary. The recently concluded excavations at Ramat Raḥel just four kilometers south of Jerusalem illustrate this principle by virtue of its identification as a tax collection center for the province of Yehud (Lipschits, Gadot, and Langgut 2012). The large number of Yehud jar stamps uncovered there (Lipschits and Vanderhooft 2011, 31–41) and elaborate gardens (Gordon forthcoming) also support the idea of the importance of the site in the middle of the fifth century BCE. Given what we have indicated about the size and population of Yehud we would not want to overemphasize what those numbers meant for the province as a whole.

The low demographic profile of the Persian era in Yehud changed radically after the Maccabean period in the late Hellenistic period and biblical scholarship is now facing the challenge of dealing with the issue of how so few could have accomplished so much in the way of literary achievement. From the editing of the Deuteronomic history to the last of the prophets, to Ezra-Nehemiah and Chronicles and other hagiographical writings, the Persian period is today viewed as one of enormous creativity and prodigious literary output. How this came to be and its implications for the remainder of the Second Temple period is an issue that requires continued engagement (Carter 2016).

Another topic that has emerged in recent years that pertains to the Persian period is the origin of the synagogue. For centuries scholars have related the idea of prayer outside the temple to the period after destruction of the first temple in 586 BCE when Judeans learned to pray in small groups referred to by Ezekiel as "the little temple" or *miqdash me'at* (11:16) and in later rabbinic literature as the beginning of the synagogue (b. Meg. 29a). Lee Levine (2000, 30) was the first to propose that it was the city gate that was the model for the synagogue. After all, that was where justice was meted out and business conducted and where the torah was read by Ezra (Neh 8) on the first day of the seventh month—at the Water Gate in Jerusalem from early morning to midday. The idea, which can be traced back to the preexilic period as well, goes along well with new theories regarding literacy in the biblical period (Rollston 2016). Once again it would seem that integral to these literary and editorial developments in association with the temple were the priests and the scribal class.

There is one final area for early postexilic studies that is now in its infancy that has rich potential for influencing how we think about the Persian period and the ways in which the diaspora communities may have identified with their past. It has to do with the Babylonian Jewish community that is attested in two large cuneiform archives, the Murashu archives (Coogan 1976) and the al-Yahudu corpus (Pierce 2006). At the very least they indicate that the exiles did quite well after their expulsion from the homeland and after some time managed in numerous ways to maintain their identity as Yahwists and as a distinct ethnicity. No doubt this was the kernel of the community that a millennium later was responsible for the Babylonian Talmud. Biblical scholars who would locate the major editorial activity of the early, precanonical Hebrew Bible in Mesopotamia, would go so far as to credit the golah-community with articulating monotheism, originating the synagogue and private prayer, and inspiring a spate of unusual literary creativity (Carter 2016, 231–35). In my 2020 publication, I have maintained that this creative literary surge was produced in the homeland despite the low demographic profile. With our increasing focus on developments within the homeland of the land of Israel let us also remain mindful of the diasporic communities and their achievements even though they are more elusive in terms of material culture.

2. The Advent of Hellenism

Much has changed over the past decades in respect to viewing how the land of Israel was affected by the so-called conquest of Alexander the Great and his idea of how the civilized world should be organized according to language, culture, architecture, and educational norms (E. Meyers and Chancey 2012, 11–21). While former scholarship had proposed that with the arrival of the Greek colonists and the establishment of *poleis* the Greek ideal envisioned by Alexander took root rather rapidly (Hengel 1974, 310–14), more recent treatments are much more cautious in their assessment of how Hellenism was more gradually accepted and integrated into various aspects of life and culture (E. Meyers 2002, 140–43). Today I would argue that the consensus points to the adoption of Hellenistic ways in only certain elite circles alongside the persistence of a more traditional lifestyle that harkens back to the early postexilic and even preexilic eras (Tal 2006). Even after the beginning of the Roman period indigenous ways especially in the Galilee continued to prosper, ultimately alongside the newer and more fashionable Greco-Roman style. Resistance to Alexander's armies in 332 BCE was rather limited and most notably is attested at the site of Samaria (Sebaste) where rebels offered strong opposition and were pursued to the caves of Wadi Daliyeh to the east (E. Meyers and Chancey 2012, 9). Well-preserved Hellenistic round towers were constructed there after the event. The Samaritan temple on Mount Gerizim was built around this time as well, and while modeled roughly on the Jerusalem temple, it became a symbol of their national identity and has remained so until this day. As noted above, the repopulation of Judaea occurred only after the Hasmonean expansion in the middle of the second century. Hence there is little in the way of material culture to illuminate the late Hellenistic period in Jewish areas, though the ongoing work in Jerusalem has and will continue to produce new discoveries.

Still, the transformation of the land began in earnest as many sites and cities were repopulated, sometimes with outsiders as with Macedonians in Samaria. Beth Shean was resettled at the base of the tel and renamed Scythopolis. A municipal council would have been set up and was called the *boule*. Greek deities and myths and stories of them were now associated with the new cities often symbolized on coins. Many cities now included a stadium for races, a theater for performances and entertainment of other kinds, and educational institutions. This initial wave of urbanism was the mechanism for realizing the cultural and ecumenical ideas of Alexander and implanting the material symbols of them on the ground (Freyne 1980, 99–138). The Romans would do this later as well especially after the two revolts in 70 and 135 CE. Other new cities were Banias (Paneas), later Caesarea Phillippi, Antiochia, Seuluecia, Akko, later renamed Ptolemais, Dor, Strato's Tower, later renamed Caesarea Maritima, Maresha/Marissa, later Eleutheropolis, Tyre, and Sidon.

After Alexander's death in 323 in Babylon, his generals who vied to succeed him in what is called the period of the Diadochi or successors were Antigonus, Ptolemy, and Seleucus. While Antigonus was the most powerful of the three, he was defeated at the battle of Ipsus in 301 by Ptolemy, who won control over Coele-Syria (E. Meyers and Chancey 2012, 14–15). Ptolemy was subsequently challenged by Seleucus and the next century was marred by continual warring between the Ptolemies and the Seleucids. The end result of these five Syrian Wars was that the Ptolemies would take control of Palestine and south-central Phoenicia. In order to maintain control they sent out soldiers, merchants, and tax collectors, Joseph the Tobiad being the most famous of them, who as envoy of the Jews won the office of tax collector from Ptolemy Epiphanes (Josephus, *A.J.* 12.164–176). His family's wealth and influence is represented in the fabulous Qasr el-Abd built around 169 BCE as a "mighty manor" (Josephus, *A.J.* 12.230–233) with its twenty-one fluted Corinthian columns on the east and west side and northern facade featuring a monumental entrance *distylos in antis*, with high-relief lions in the four corners (E. Meyers and Chancey 2012, 19). Located at the site of Iraq el-Emir in Ammon in Jordan, it is by far the best preserved of any Hellenistic ruin of this period.

Along with Ptolemaic rule and a more rigid tax system, growing signs of Hellenistic influence appeared in the coinage of the land, on the forms of dress, and in the adoption of the orthogonal town plan in many places. With the disappearance of the secular authority of governor that had dominated in the Persian period, the stage is set for a more theocratic government in the remainder of the Second Temple period. This meant the emergence of a more powerful temple establishment in the affairs of state, in part reflected in the secondary Jewish inscription on coins. In Jerusalem and in the heartland of Judea, however, the Jewish towns and villages remained largely unaffected by Hellenism, though they were surrounded by Hellenistic settlements to the north in Samaria and Idumea in the south. In fact, the discovery of a late form of the YHD stamp with only *y* and *h* suggests an administrative continuity between the Persian and Hellenistic periods (Carter 2016, 227–28). However, Ptolemaic rule allowed the emergence of a new Jewish middle class that was to play a significant role in the Hasmonean era. Burial practices slowly began to change as well with the introduction of the individual coffin or burial receptacle. In the Hellenistic and Roman periods these containers or receptacles for the bones of the dead or ossuaries were often inscribed with the names of the dead (E. Meyers 2002, 142).

Far and away the most significant product of the third century BCE, in the time of Ptolemy II Philadelphus, is the translation of the Torah known as the Septuagint. Can there be any more dramatic sign of the changing nature of the times than this? The story of the seventy-two sages who were brought from Jerusalem to Alexandria is preserved in the Letter to Aristeas (Grabbe 2000, 49–50). We cannot underestimate the importance of this translation work: nothing more than the Septuagint better symbolizes the spread of Greek language and culture at this early date. It also meant that the holy scriptures of the Jewish community in the land of Israel could be read in the diaspora where Greek was becoming the new lingua franca; and it was the Septuagint in the time of the spread of early Christianity that was the version of the Bible most used.

3. Jerusalem and the Early Synagogue

Among the most important developments through the years has been the amount of new excavation in Jerusalem and the number or pre-70 synagogues now identified. We have noted that, with the Hasmonean expansion of the kingdom in the second century BCE, the population also began to increase, especially in the first century BCE after the northern campaigns of Aristobolus I. The material remains of the city reflect those changes whether in the tomb monuments of the Kidron Valley or the monumental tomb of Jason or others such as the Sanhedria tomb complex (Kloner and Zissu 2007, 621–25, 516–7; E. Meyers and Chancey 2012, 39–44). Besides the tombs, however, the late Hellenistic remains in Jerusalem have remained somewhat elusive, though with so much ongoing work this may well change in the years to come. The site of Modi'in, Umm el-'Umdan, identified with the Maccabees, provides an exception to this picture (Onn and Weksler-Bdolah 2008, 2061–63). There a pillared building has been revealed and identified as an early second-century BCE synagogue, which would make it the oldest thus far excavated in the land of Israel. The monumental Hasmonean tomb attributed to Simon Maccabee (143–134 BCE) at the site (1 Macc 13:27–29) allows us to observe the degree to which the leadership of the Jewish community in the second century dealt with the problematics of Jewish art and Hellenistic influence (Fine 2005, 61). The absence of any images is noteworthy, especially the menorah, which becomes so dominant in later times. Adi Erlich (2010, 110–12, 119–20) has observed that there is no single example of three-dimensional art in the entire Hellenistic corpus and that art would be embraced only in the Herodian era. The design of the tomb resembles most closely the Tomb of Absalom in the Kidron Valley but also shares stylistic elements, the conical pyramid, with Jason's Tomb and other monument in the Kidron, as well as motifs that we find on ossuaries (Fine 2005, 62–65). The site and the tomb in particular demonstrate the ambitions of the Hasmonean dynasty at an early point in their history, which is abundantly reflected also in their coinage and the symbols on them (Regev 2013, 175–223). Their ambitious agenda in the area of building and construction is also reflected in their palatial residences in Jericho (Netzer 2001).

Despite a dearth of representational art in the late-Hellenistic or Hasmonean era we can say without equivocation that the adoption of many aspects of Greek culture was fully underway and is reflected mostly in the elite circles of the population, as we have noted, which is also true for the Hasmoneans. The thoroughgoing transformation of Jerusalem and many places throughout the land was to come at the hands of the greatest of all the royals, Herod the Great, who quite literally embarked on one of the greatest building campaigns in history. The Hasmonean era is marked by a discernable shift to more conservative religious practice reflected in the observance of purity laws and the adoption of ritual baths in numerous places. The early Roman period (until ca. 135 CE), however, would witness a more systematic change in this regard both in Judea and in Galilee.

For a consideration of the archaeology and place of the community of Qumran and the Dead Sea Scrolls at the end of the Second Temple period see the article of Alison Schofield in this volume.

4. The Early Synagogue, Pre-70 CE

As already noted, we have not gained much new archaeological knowledge about the diaspora these past years, since the large spurt in new excavations has been more or less confined to the land of Israel. Hence, I can honestly say that the earlier version of this article (E. Meyers and Kraabel 1986) in respect to the situation in the diaspora may still be reliably used, though with some refinements. Ongoing excavations at Ostia in Italy by the University of Texas under the direction of Michael White have not yet been published, and the state of the so-called early synagogue there is not known, though numerous scholars still support a pre-70 phase (E. Meyers and Chancey 2012, 207). Important new work on the synagogue of Delos in the Cyclades, however, has been conducted and a consensus has been arrived at that it is indeed a synagogue (Levine 2000, 11–15; E. Meyers and Chancey, 2012, 2005–7; Trümper 2004). Possibly built in the second century BCE or a bit later, the building is situated on the eastern shore of the Aegean island near a residential area and gymnasium. The building might well have been a residence in its initial phase and later converted into a synagogue. A possible seat of Moses in marble has been identified along with a possible ritual bath, and there is one inscription with the mention of the term *proseuche* (Kraabel 1979, 491) meaning house of worship. There are also indications that the site might have been settled by Samaritans.

Notwithstanding these new developments, we should reiterate that there is abundant literary and epigraphical data on the diaspora synagogue in Egypt where there are twelve inscriptions and papyri, though no physical remains, and, of course, the evidence from Philo, the most famous reference being to the great synagogue of Alexandria (*Legat*. 143).

I have already noted the identification of the synagogue at Modi'in (Umm el-'Umdan) and the probability of it being from the second century BCE. The only other synagogue that might be dated as early is Jericho, a hypothesis that has not won much scholarly support (Netzer, Laureys-Chachy, and Kalman 2004, 159–94). Nonetheless, Ehud Netzer's identification and dating to the Hasmonean period must be taken seriously. Other synagogues from the late Second Temple period are Gamla in the Golan, Herodium and Masada in the Judean desert, and Qiryat Sefer near Modi'in (Magen and Tzionit 2008, 2000–2003). Rachel Hachlili (2013, 23–54) lists fifteen synagogues from this period. The most notable newcomer in this grouping comes from Magadala or Taricheae, on the western shore of the Sea of Galilee. There along the lake only one meter below modern surface a first-century synagogue has been uncovered in a well-preserved town with several small villas uncovered with extremely well-constructed ritual baths with the walls. In the center of the synagogue a uniquely decorated stone, with an amphora, menorah, and other temple symbols on it, was discovered and it has been the focus of much scholarly interest in recent years. Some have suggested it is the base of a Torah reader's platform (Aviam 2013), some that it was originally a seat of honor for an elder, a base for a lampstand, or possibly a table for a food offering of some kind (Binder 2014, 41–44). As of today there is no consensus among scholars as to its practical function. The building is today associated with Mary Magdalene and surely dates to the time of Jesus and possibly was constructed a bit earlier (E. Meyers and Chancey 2012, 211–12). The site is being reconstructed and excavated by the Roman Catholic Church and supported by the Legionnaires of Christ who have established a retreat center for women on top of and alongside the ruin.

The main nonliterary, epigraphical evidence for the pre-70 synagogue is the Theodotus inscription from Jerusalem, which is dated to the first century CE. Foremost, it points to the synagogue as a social grouping and building with special features. The name Vettenos, priest and *archisynagogus*, associates the synagogue with Jews who came from Rome: Theodotus who built it, and his ancestors who came three generations earlier, which would put its founding in the first century BCE. Though the building is not preserved, the inscription provides vivid and inalterable testimony to the nature of the synagogue in Jerusalem. It goes on to detail these main functions: reading of scripture, studying the commandments, and providing hospitality to visitors (E. Meyers and Chancey 2012, 208–10). Each of these functions would seem to survive the Second Temple era and continue as main features of the post-70 synagogue, supplemented mainly by the development of a rich liturgy that is usually dated to the late second century CE (Levine 2000, 69–70).

5. The Roman Period (63 BCE –313 CE)

We refer to this long period as *Roman* since it demarcates the time when Roman control was realized in the holy land; it ends a year after Constantine's conversion to Christianity at Milan when the Edict of Toleration adopted there in 313 CE. That edict reversed Diocletian's policy of persecuting Christians and declared Christianity a legal religion of the empire. While in Judea the hellenization process accelerated and expanded in the late Second Temple period, especially under Herod the Great, Galilee only began to catch up in the latter part of the first century CE and especially later. In Jerusalem, though ample remains underscore that purity laws and others aspects of Jewish practice were followed, there is no doubt that the city was the most hellenized in all the land in terms of "its population, languages, institutions, and general cultural ambience" (Levine 2002, 281). The major test case for this in the north has been the excavations at Sepphoris, which have shown that Herod's son, Antipas, accomplished less than had been thought and that only with the influx of Jews after the two wars with Rome did the site and Galilee as a whole begin to be transformed (E. Meyers, C. Meyers, and Gordon 2015, 2018). Benjamin Gordon in a recent article vividly depicts the extent of influence of Herod the Great on the archaeology of the land of Israel toward the end of the Second Temple period:

> The excavated remains at Masada, Caesarea-Maritima, Herodium, and elsewhere reveal the king to have been an avid patron of the arts, a skilled host and entertainer, an aficionado of Roman cuisine, and an oenophile. As Netzer's archeological investigations made abundantly clear, Herod was a prolific builder, benefactor, and client to architects utilizing innovative and bold designs. Among Herod's Italian architectural imports to Judea are the theater and amphitheater, the prostyle imperial cult temple, the bathhouse caldarium with Campanian-style hypocaust, and the artificial concrete harbor. The Roman cultural institutions he introduced to the region catered to a more cosmopolitan population than was tolerated by his Hasmonean predecessors. This is a picture of Herod the multiculturalist. (Gordon forthcoming)

This summary of Herod's career points out that Herod's stamp on the physical space that is the land of Israel and even beyond was so great that we can today identify Herodian archaeology as a specialty within the larger field of biblical archaeology. With Netzer its chief architect and proponent (Netzer 2006; E. Meyers and Chancey 2012, 5–82; Richardson 2004, 225–308) along with excessive excavation in Jerusalem the past two decades, it is simply impossible to avoid the larger than life figure of Herod the Great, builder and statesman or his single greatest achievement, the Jerusalem temple, one of the wonders of the ancient world (Bahat 2011, 34–63). Herod's many accomplishments are recounted and lavishly illustrated and published in the magnificent catalogue that accompanied the Herod the Great exhibit at the Israel Museum in 2013, the most ambitious and expensive exhibit every carried out in Israel (Rozenberg and Mevorah 2013). The exhibit and focus on Herod was prompted in the main by the discovery of his tomb at Herodium by Netzer, though not everyone agrees on this identification today.

We should mention that among the less dramatic finds of recent years the study of miqvaot (or ritual baths) and stone vessels has advanced the idea that the population of all regions, north and south, were more dedicated to purity practices normally associated with priests regardless of the extent of their acculturation and identification with Greco-Roman culture. Ronny Reich's (2013) study recently updated and published and the important supplementary studies by Adler (2014a, 2014b) have noted that around nine hundred ritual baths have been excavated and/or identified in private and public spaces as well as industrial contexts. All of these may be dated to the late Second Temple period—from the late Hellenistic period onward. They seem to diminish in number as specially built structures by the middle of the Roman period or in the second century CE, but according to Miller (2014, 45–55, 324–31; E. Meyers, C. Meyers, and Gordon 2018) the practice of ritual immersion hardly disappeared but rather was practiced in different ways and physical settings. The material from Sepphoris on the western summit has been very helpful in nuancing this development. Together with chalkstone vessels found during the same period and frequently in association with ritual baths, with quarries and industries in the north and south to produce them, they have become synonymous with purity practices, since vessels made from soft chalkstone could not conduct or transfer impurity (Magen 2008; Miller 2014, 153–83). At Sepphoris, this evidence is supplemented by analysis of faunal remains that shows that in Jewish contexts virtually no pork was consumed (Grantham 2018). This sort of information and an increasing sophistication in the analysis of Roman-period ceramics, including lamps has made it possible to add provenience as a control when examining archaeological materials (Lapp 2016, 177–80; Adan-Bayewitz 1993; Adan-Bayewitz et al 2008). As a result we are much better able today to speak of regional trade and production centers than ever before.

6. The Synagogue after 70 CE

Just as before 70 CE we have witnessed an enormous amount of new material, so too for the period after 70 CE can we note a huge increase in the amount of new data and observe a significant number of new synagogues discovered and excavated. As in the other sections of this essay we can only highlight the trends and new insights that are provided by this new corpus of evidence. For much of the past several decades a serious debate has emerged over the dating of synagogues after 70 and the significance of a late dating. Let me simplify a bit by stating that one of the assumptions of Levine's groundbreaking study of the ancient synagogue in 2000 was his musing about the apparent absence or small number of synagogues before the beginning of the Byzantine period in the fourth century CE. In a Festschrift in his honor, I questioned this assumption and suggested that this might well not be more than accidental since several buildings from the second century had already been uncovered, for example, Nabratein, Kh. Ethri, and Magdala (?) (E. Meyers 2010, 435–48), and there are others today such as Tel Rechesh near Mount Tabor discovered in 2016 built in the pre-70 era but surviving until the early second century CE (Aviam 2016). Another aspect of the dating discussion was the issue of how to assign a date and use ceramics to date different layers in association with a synagogue, an issue I have addressed in several articles but most recently in an encyclopedia entry (E. Meyers 2013, 253–55). It has been my contention that even if a type of vessel has a use-phase of hundreds of years, the presence of such a vessel should not be used to date on its extreme points, high or low, but rather should be used and dated on the basis of the abundance of sherds that accompany such a type. Simply taking the latest possible date of such a vessel and ignoring the homogeneous pottery reading of a given locus is simply not proper methodology.

One of the most controversial inferences to be drawn from the possibility of a lack of securely dated synagogues from the period after 70 is Seth Schwartz's (2001) idea that Judaism after 70 did not really fully develop until Christianity became more established in the land, a view strongly rejected by this author and others (Miller 2017, 437–40, 447–50). In his view, the presence of pagan institutions in Jewish centers such as Sepphoris and Tiberias, as well as the presence of pagan images on coins, supports the idea that Jewish society and religiosity were shattered and shallow after the two wars with Rome. Schwartz goes on to accuse rabbinic scholars of being maximalists because they see a smooth transition from Second Temple Judaism to synagogue/community. I do not think that the existence of a small number of synagogues from the second or third centuries CE proves that there was such a smooth transition or points to the degree to which the Jewish community was following rabbinic law or not at that time. However, it certainly says something about the nature of common Judaism. If anything, the material evidence suggests a serious divergence from rabbinic law, as in the case of Khirbet Shema', where the third century CE synagogue is built next to a tomb mausoleum and underground tomb complex (E. Meyers 2014, 312–14). I would even say that the material evidence in general apart from synagogues suggests serious divergence from the rabbinic law, though at the same time it points to continuity with a form of common Judaism (E. Meyers 2014, 314–19). We may also explain the late dating of so many synagogues by noting that they are preserved in their last or most recent use-phase. In no way does it prove that the synagogue arose in response to the development of the church. In my opinion, the *consensus communis* is that the Jewish response to the loss of the temple was immediate and definitive as evidenced by the publication of the Mishnah and tannaitic literature and the emergence of the synagogue. The rise of imperial Christianity surely gave a new impetus to local communities to secure their ties to the traditions of the past in the face of a new expression of religion that in large part was based on the Hebrew Bible. The synagogue remained the centerpiece of that tradition.

Another aspect of recent scholarship concerns the meaning and significance of a robust visual culture that is best represented in the mosaics of ancient synagogues. While the old consensus was that this visual culture began after Constantine, especially in the fifth century CE, with the excavation of the Wadi Hamam synagogue in eastern Galilee with mosaics depicting artisan and workers and possibly biblical themes, along with the third-century CE mosaics in the Dionysos mansion at Sepphoris in a Jewish context, there is every reason to believe that it began at the end of the Roman period, in the third or early fourth century (E. Meyers and Chancey 2012, 231–33). One of the biases of past generations of Jewish scholarship that dealt with the material world, was the belief in the "artless Jew" or that Jews were devoid of art because of a literal view of the Second Commandment. Steven Fine (2005), Levine (2012), and others have chronicled the latest trends in this field of Jewish visual studies while Kalman Bland (2000) has written about the modern philosophical roots of it. The discovery of the rich mosaics in the ancient, Byzantine-period (fifth-century CE) synagogue of Huqoq by Jodi Magness (2019) has put the subject of Jews and art at the center of the discussion of late antique Judaism in the land of Israel. We anticipate an emerging debate over their meaning and whether some scenes are inspired by biblical themes and others by noncanonical literature and events as the excavator has maintained in public discussion. In addition, the relationship between Jewish art and Christian art in this period is surely to stay high on any agenda (Hachlili 1988, 366–75). We also anticipate that this renewed interest in art and the visual in the holy land will influence discussion of Jewish art in the diaspora as well (Hachlili 1998).

7. New Issues and New Directions

In addition to these important new areas for discussion concerning the ancient synagogue, there is an emerging new consensus in light of these new finds. Today no one could doubt that there is simply no substitute for solid data from controlled excavation in the argument over dating and there is no dearth of new material coming from such excavations in Israel (Hachlili 2013, 600–605). Dating based on arguments over architectural style and floor layout has also been discredited (Hachlili 2013, 605–7). Similarly, statements about the old typology of basilical, broad house, or apsidal are to be ignored, though we have yet to find an apsidal building in an early context. The decorations on the stone fragment with a menorah found at Magdala has demonstrated that even at the end of the Second Temple period in a first-century synagogue, attachment to the temple was strong. And if we can believe the early publications and press releases, a good many scholars believe that the Magdala synagogue shows the importance of the idea of sacred orientation as well. In none of the pre-70 CE synagogues do we find a bema for the elevated reading of scripture or storage of the scrolls. The earliest example of this is the broadhouse Synagogue 1 at Nabratein (E. Meyers 2013, 252; E. Meyers and Chancey 2012, fig. 8.9). The pre-70 CE synagogues were mostly used for Torah reading and study with the focus on the center of the structure and community meeting. The fixed Torah shrine (a nearly complete pediment was found at Nabratein in Synagogue 2) in later synagogues is typically found on the southern, Jerusalem-facing wall. In most early pre-70 CE remains, decoration is very simple and benches all around are common (Magdala has a very plain but elegant mosaic). In general, the later the synagogue the more elaborate its decoration both inside and outside, and the benches would face the Torah shrine. Regional differences played a significant role in how one building differed from another, as did local topographic features and geological resources. The Golan synagogues, for example, are consistently made from basalt and usually have a single entrance on the Jerusalem-oriented wall. The Galilean synagogues often have a triple facing toward the south, though many do not.

The issue of localism thus should be emphasized overall, and attention to regional trends and patterns is advised as well. The inscriptions found in synagogues and tombs offer a huge repository of material for further insight into the nature of each community and region, and individual field reports should be consulted to determine the precise context of building and text. Therefore, also of importance in such discussions is the nature of the town or settlement in which the building is found. Greater attention to items of everyday life is very relevant to evaluating the nature of a particular community with a synagogue structure. I sincerely hope that the appearance of the final report on Sepphoris (E. Meyers, C. Meyers, and Gordon 2018) makes this abundantly clear, while also demonstrating that there is as much to learn from the contents of a private domicile as from a house of worship. In this regard, the future looks very bright, since so many digs from the past several decades are in the final stages of publication and they will surely raise many news issues.

Bibliography

Adan-Bayewitz, David. 1993. *Common Pottery in Roman Galilee: A Study in Local Trade*. BISNEL. Ramat-Gan: Bar Ilan University Press.

Adan-Bayewitz, David, Frank Asaro, Moshe Wieder, and Robert D. Giauque. 2008. "Preferential Distribution of Lamps from the Jerusalem Area in the Late Second Temple Period (Late First Century B.C.E.–70 C.E.)." *BASOR* 350:37–85.

Adler, Yonatan. 2014a. "Tosefta Shabbat 1:14—'Come See the Extent to Which Purity Had Spread': Archaeological Perspective on the Historical Background to a Late Tannaitic Passage." Pages 63–82 in *Talmuda de-Eretz Israel: Archaeology and the Rabbis in Late Antique Palestine*. Edited by Steven Fine and Aaron Koller. SJ 73. Berlin: de Gruyter.

———. 2014b. "The Myth of the 'Oṣar' in Second Temple Period Ritual Baths: An Anachronistic Interpretation of a Modern-Era Innovation." *JJS* 64:263–83.

Aviam, Mordechai. 2013. "The Decorated Stone from the Synagogue at Migdal: A Holistic Interpretation and a Glimpse into the Life of Galilean Jews at the Time of Jesus." *NovT* 55:205–20.

———. 2016. "Tel Rechesh." https://tinyurl.com/SBL9027c.

Bahat, Dan. 2011. *The Carta Jerusalem Atlas*. 3rd ed. Jerusalem: Carta.

Binder, Donald D. 2014. "The Mystery of the Magdala Stone." Pages 17–48 in *A City Set on A Hill: Essays in Honor of James F. Strange*. Edited by Daniel A. Warner and Donald D. Binder. Mountainhome, AR: Borderstone.

Bland, Kalman P. 2000. *The Artless Jew*. Princeton: Princeton University Press.

Burrus, Sean P. 2017. "Remembering the Righteous: Sarcophagus Sculpture and Jewish Patrons in the Roman World." PhD diss., Duke University.

Carter, Charles E. 2016. "(Re) Defining 'Israel': The Legacy of the Neo-Babylonian and Persian Periods." Pages 215–40 in *The Wiley Blackwell*

Companion to Ancient Israel. Edited by Susan Niditch. Malden, MA: Wiley Blackwell.
Coogan, Michael. 1976. *West Semitic Names in the Murašu Documents*. HSM 7. Missoula, MT: Scholars Press.
Erlich, Adi. 2012. *The Art of Hellenistic Palestine*. BARIS 2010. Oxford: Archaeopress.
Fine, Steven. 1996. S*acred Realm: The Emergence of the Synagogue in the Ancient World*. New York: Oxford University Press.
———. 2005. *Art and Judaism in the Greco-Roman World: Toward a New Jewish Archaeology*. Cambridge: Cambridge University Press.
———. 2012. "Menorahs in Color: Polychromy in Jewish Visual Culture of Roman Antiquity." *Images* 6:3–25.
Finkelstein, Israel. 2016. "Jerusalem and Judah 600–200 BCE: Implications for Understanding Pentateuchal Texts." Pages 6–18 in *The Fall of Jerusalem and the Rise of Torah*. Edited by Peter Dubovsky, Dominik Markl, and Jean-Pierre Sonnet. FAT 107. Tübingen: Mohr Siebeck.
Freyne, Sean. 1980. *Galilee: From Alexander the Great to Hadrian; A Study of Second Temple Judaism*. Wilmington, DE: Glazier; Notre Dame: University of Notre Dame.
Geva, Hillel. 2007. "Estimating Jerusalem's Population in Antiquity: A Minimalist's View" [Hebrew]. *ErIsr* 28:50–65.
Gordon, Benjamin D. 2018. "Archaeology of the Postexilic Period and Writings." Pages 49–63 in *The Oxford Handbook of the Writings of the Hebrew Bible*. Edited by Donn F. Morgan. Oxford: Oxford University Press.
———. Forthcoming. "The Archaeology of the Second Temple Period in Judea: New Discoveries and Research." In *The State of Jewish Studies: Perspectives on the Premodern Periods*. Edited by Carl Ehrlich and Sara Horowitz. Berlin: de Gruyter.
Grabbe, Lester L. 2000. *Judaic Religion in the Second Temple Period: Belief and Practice from the Exile to Yavneh*. London: Routledge.
Grantham, Billy J. 2018. "The Faunal Remains." Pages 871–88 in Eric M. Meyers, Carol L. Meyers, and Benjamin D. Gordon. *The Architecture, Stratigraphy, and Artifacts of the Western Summit of Sepphoris*. Sepphoris 3. University Park, PA: Eisenbrauns.
Hachlili, Rachel. 1988. *Ancient Jewish Art and Archaeology in the Land of Israel*. HdO 7. Leiden: Brill.
———. 1998. *Ancient Jewish Art and Archaeology in the Diaspora*. HdO 35. Leiden: Brill.

———. 2013. *Ancient Synagogues—Archaeology and Art: New Discoveries and Current Research*. HdO 104. Boston: Brill.

Hengel, Martin. 1974. *Judaism and Hellenism: Studies in Their Encounter in Palestine during the Early Hellenistic Period*. Translated by John Bowden. Philadelphia: Fortress.

Kloner, Amos, and Boaz Zissu. 2007. *The Necropolis of Jerusalem in the Second Temple Period*. Leuven: Peeters.

Kraabel. A. Thomas. 1979. "The Diaspora Synagogue: Archeological and Epigraphic Evidence Since Sukenik." *ANRW* 19.1:477–510.

Lapp, Eric C. 2016. *The Clay Lamps from Ancient Sepphoris: Light Use and Regional Interactions*. Sepphoris 2. Winona Lake, IN: Eisenbrauns.

Levine, Lee I. 2000. *The Ancient Synagogue: The First Thousand Years*. New Haven: Yale University Press.

———. 2002. *Jerusalem: Portrait of the City in the Second Temple Period (538 BCE–70 CE)*. Philadelphia: Jewish Publication Society.

———. 2012. *Visual Judaism in Late Antiquity: Historical Contexts of Jewish Art*. New Haven: Yale University Press.

Lipschits, Oded. 2005. *The Fall and Rise of Jerusalem: Judah under Babylonian Rule*. Winona Lake, IN: Eisenbrauns.

———. 2009. "Persian Period Finds from Jerusalem: Facts and Interpretation." *JHebS* 9. https://tinyurl.com/SBL9027d.

Lipschits, Oded, and David S. Vanderhooft. 2011. *The Yehud Stamp Impressions: A Corpus of Inscribed Impressions from the Persian and Hellenistic Periods*. Winona lake, IN: Eisenbrauns.

Lipschits, Oded, Yuval Gadot, and Dafna Langgut. 2012. "The Riddle of Ramat Rahel: The Archaeology of a Royal Persian Period Edifice." *Transeu* 21:57–79.

Magen, Yitzhak. 2008. *A Temple City*. Vol. 2 of *Mount Gerizim Excavations*. JSP 8. Jerusalem: Staff Officer for Archaeology, Civil Administration of Judea and Samaria.

Magen, Yitzhak, and Yoav Tzionit. 2008. "Qiryat Sefer (Khirbet Badd 'Isa)." *NEAEHL* 5:2000–20003.

Magness, Jodi. 2012. *The Archaeology of the Holy Land: From the Destruction of Solomon's Temple to the Muslim Conquest*. Cambridge: Cambridge University Press.

Magness, Jodi, et al. "The Huqoq Excavation Project 2004–2017: Interim Report." *BASOR* 380:61–131.

Meyers, Carol L., and Eric M. Meyers. 1987. *The Books of Haggai, Zechariah*

1–8: A New Translation with Introduction and Commentary. AB25B. Garden City, NY: Doubleday.

Meyers, Eric M. 2002. "Jewish Culture in Greco-Roman Palestine." Pages 135–79 in *Cultures of the Jews: A New History*. Edited by David Biale. New York: Schocken Books.

———. 2009. "Exile and Restoration in Light of Recent Archaeological Work." Pages 166–73 in *Exile and Restoration Revisited: Essays on the Babylonian and Persian Periods in Memory of Peter R. Ackroyd*. Edited by Gary N. Knoppers and Lester Grabbe. Edinburgh: T&T Clark.

———. 2010. "The Problem of the Scarcity of Synagogues from 70 to ca. 250 CE. The Case of Synagogue 1 at Nabratein (Second–Third Century CE)." Pages 435–48 in *"Follow the Wise": Studies in Honor of Lee I. Levine*. Edited by Zeev Weiss, Oded Irshai, Jodi Magness, and Seth Schwartz. Winona Lake, IN: Eisenbrauns.

———. 2013. "Palestine, Synagogues." Pages 249–58 in *The Oxford Encyclopedia of the Bible and Archaeology*. Edited by Daniel M. Masters. Oxford: Oxford University Press.

———. 2014. "The Use of Archaeology in Understanding Rabbinic Materials: An Archaeological Perspective." Pages 303–19 in *Talmuda de-Eretz Israel: Archaeology and the Rabbis in Late Antique Palestine*. Edited by Steven Fine and Aaron Koller. SJ 73. Berlin: de Gruyter.

———. 2015. "The Ancient Synagogue and Village of Khirbet Shema." Pages 414–23 in *The Archaeological Record from Towns and Villages*. Volume 2 of *Galilee in the Late Second Temple and Mishnaic Periods*. Edited by David A. Fiensy and James Riley Strange. Minneapolis: Fortress.

———. 2018. "Haggai and Zechariah: A Maximalist View of the Return in a Minimalist Social Context." Pages 433–48 in *Enemies and Friends of the State: Ancient Prophecy in Context*. Edited by Christopher Rollston. University Park, PA: Eisenbrauns.

———. 2020. "The Rise of Scripture in a Minimalist Demographic Context." Pages 379–94 in *Stones, Tablets and Scrolls: Periods of the Formation of the Bible*. Edited by Peter Dubovsky and Federico Giuntoli. Archaeology and Bible 3. Tübingen: Mohr Siebeck.

Meyers, Eric M., and Mark A. Chancey. 2012. *Archaeology of the Land of the Bible*. Vol. 3 of *Alexander to Constantine*. ABRL. New Haven; Yale University Press.

Meyers, Eric M., and A. Thomas Kraabel. 1986. "Archaeology, Iconography, and Nonliterary Remains." Pages 175–210 in *Early Judaism and*

Its Modern Interpreters. Edited by Robert A. Kraft and George W. E. Nickelsburg. BMI 2. Atlanta: Scholars Press; Philadelphia: Fortress.

Meyers, Eric. M., and Carol L. Meyers. 2009. *Excavations at Ancient Nabratein: Synagogue and Environs*. MEP 6. Winona Lake, IN: Eisenbrauns.

Meyers, Eric M, Carol L. Meyers, and Benjamin D. Gordon. 2015. "Residential Area of the Western Summit." Pages 39–52 in *The Archaeological Record from Cities, Towns, and Villages*. Vol. 2 of *Galilee in the Late Second Temple and Mishnaic Periods*. Edited by David A. Fiensy and James Riley Strange. Minneapolis: Fortress.

———. 2018. *The Architecture, Stratigraphy, and Artifacts of the Western Summit of Sepphoris*. Sepphoris 3. University Park, PA: Eisenbrauns.

Meyers, Eric M., and Carol L. Meyers, with James F. Strange. 1990. *Excavations at the Ancient Synagogue of Gush Halav*. MEP 5. Winona Lake, IN: Eisenbrauns.

Miller, Stuart S. 2014. *At the Intersection of Texts and Material Finds: Stepped Pools, Stone Vessels, and Ritual Purity among the Jews of Roman Galilee*. JAJSup 16. Göttingen: Vandenhoeck & Ruprecht.

———. 2017. "The Study of Talmudic Israel and/or Roman Palestine: Where Matters Stand." Pages 433–54 in *The Faces of Torah: Studies in the Texts and Contexts of Ancient Judaism in Honor of Steven Fraade*. Edited by Michal Bar-Asher Siegel, Tzvi Novick, and Christine Hays. JAJSup 22. Göttingen: Vandenhoeck & Ruprecht.

Netzer, Ehud. 2001. *The Palaces of the Hasmoneans and Herod the Great*. Jerusalem: Yad Ben-Zvi; Israel Exploration Society.

———. 2006. *The Architecture of Herod, the Great Builder*. TSAJ 117. Tübingen: Mohr Siebeck.

Netzer, Ehud, Rachel Laureys-Chachy, and Ya'akov Kalman. 2004. "The Synagogue Complex." Pages 159–92 in *Stratigraphy and Architecture*. Vol. 2 of *Hasmonean and Herodian Palaces at Jericho*. Edited by Ehud Netzer. Jerusalem: Israel Exploration Society.

Onn, Alexander, and Shlomit Weksler-Bdolah. 2008. "Umm el-'Umdan, Khirbet (Modi'in)." *NEAEHL* 5:2016–63.

Pierce, Laurie E. 2006. "New Evidence for Judeans in Babylonia." Pages 399–411 in *Judah and the Judeans in the Persian Period*. Edited by Oded Lipschits and Manfred Oeming. Winona Lake, IN: Eisenbrauns.

Regev, Eyal. 2013. *The Hasmoneans; Ideology, Archaeology, Identity*. JAJSsup 10. Göttingen: Vandenhoeck & Ruprecht.

Reich, Ronnie. 2013. *Miqwa'ot (Jewish Ritual Baths) in the Second Temple, Mishnaic and Talmudic Periods* [Hebrew]. Jerusalem: Yad Ben-Tzvi.

Richardson, Peter. 2004. *Building Jewish in the Roman East.* JSJSup 92. Leiden: Brill; Waco, TX: Baylor University Press.

Rollston, Christopher. 2016. "Inscriptional Evidence for the Writing of the Earliest Texts of the Bible: Intellectual Infrastructure in the Tenth- and Ninth-Century Israel, Judah, and the Southern Levant." Pages 15–45 in *The Formation of the Pentateuch: Bridging the Academic Cultures of Europe, Israel, and North America.* Edited by Thomas C. Römer, Jan C. Gertz, Bernard Levinson, Dalit Rom-Shilomi, and Konrad Schmidt. FAT 111. Tübingen: Mohr Siebeck.

Rozenberg, Silvia, and David Mevorah, eds. 2013. *Herod the Great: The King's Final Journey.* Jerusalem: Israel Museum.

Schwartz, Seth. 2001. *Imperialism and Jewish Society 200 B.C.E. to 640 C.E.* Princeton: Princeton University Press.

Stern, Ephraim. 1982. *Material Culture of the Land of the Bible in the Persian Period (538–332 B.C.).* Warminster: Aris & Phillips.

———. 2001. *The Assyrian, Babylonian, and Persian Periods (732–332 BCE).* Vol. 2 of *Archaeology of the Land of the Bible.* ABRL. Garden City, NY: Doubleday.

Tal, Oren. 2006. *The Archaeology of Hellenistic Palestine: Between Tradition and Renewal* [Hebrew]. Jerusalem: Bialik.

Trümper, Monica. 2004. "The Oldest Original Synagogue Building in the Diaspora: The Delos Synagogue Reconsidered." *Hesperia* 73:513–98.

10
Early Judaism and Modern Technology

TODD R. HANNEKEN

The most dramatic development in the work of early Judaism research over recent decades has been the expansion of digital technology. Computer-aided discovery went from a small niche, using punch cards in the 1960s, to nearly universal. Tasks that were possible with paper, pen, and typewriter became increasingly quick and easy. Tasks that required processing of large data sets beyond human comprehension became possible. By digital we mean information is stored, transmitted, and processed as a series of numbers, ultimately ones and zeros in binary code. Some of the advantages of digital technology mirror the changes in scholarship with the advent of the printing press and affordable paper. Like the printing press (and more so), digital technology can create exact duplicates of information. Unlike analog duplicates, each digital copy is identical to the original, no matter how many copies are made. Like paper, digital information can be stored and transmitted at relatively low cost. Optical media, such as CD-ROM and DVD-ROM, rose above magnetic media for their low cost and were in turn replaced by magnetic and electronic media with higher capacity. More importantly, the transmission of digital information became quick, easy, and relatively affordable with the spread of standards known collectively as the internet.

Rudimentary uses of digital technology in early Judaism research can be thought of as quicker, easier, and cheaper versions of predigital technologies, such as paper. One trend in recent decades has been increased utilization of the nature of digital information not only for storage and transmission, but processing. Once information is machine-readable, it becomes more than a conduit of human-readable information. The machine can find and transform information in ways that would be impossible or extremely time consuming otherwise. Digitization, or making information machine readable, occurs at many levels of abstraction. A page of a book can be digitized at the basic level of an image of the page, with black and white dots representing ink and paper. That information can be stored, transmitted, and presented to another human that may understand it, but the machines themselves have no greater understanding of the content than did the paper. The next level of abstraction is to digitize the text on the page, not just as black and white dots, but encoded as characters in an alphabet. This encoding can be done by human data entry or through a form of machine learning called Optical Character Recognition (OCR). (The encoding of non-Latin alphabetic characters is another development discussed below.) At this level of machine understanding the text can be searched for text strings, although inexact matches or matches that span lines of text require an additional level of machine understanding. Higher levels of abstraction, easy for an informed human reader, require additional human encoding or machine learning. Humans easily distinguish whether italics indicate a title of a book or journal, a word in a foreign language, or emphasis. We distinguish a series of capital letters as an acronym or a roman numeral and easily equate different standards for citation. Other levels of data about the data on the page (metadata) might include language and catalog information of the work in which the page is found. Recent decades have seen significant advances in digital technology moving from a dumb to smart medium through metadata standards, human encoding, and machine learning. Nevertheless, awareness of the challenges and levels of abstraction of machine learning can help the researcher troubleshoot problems. For example, a search for "Is 40:5" may not find a reference to "Isa XL.5." A search for a word with an "m" may fail if the optical character recognition read "rn" (and failed to detect the language from context and that the word with "m" is a dictionary word in that language). Machine understanding of information in context is a trend in artificial intelligence applied to early Judaism research but cannot yet be taken for granted.

Another general trend in digital technology in early Judaism research has been progress from proprietary and closed tools to open and interoperable standards. The term *silo* is applied to a software application or website that may be very powerful within itself but unable to share or receive information from outside sources. In decades past even the simple ability to copy and paste text from a Bible program to a word processor could not be taken for granted. In general this kind of problem occurs when there is no standard for encoding and transmitting information, or the standard is not followed. Many application developers find it easier to reach short-term goals by inventing their own system, rather than adopting a system understood by other applications. The advantages of interoperable standards apply to many levels, including image repositories, textual analysis, and bibliographic data. A simple example can be seen in the development of encoding Hebrew, ultimately leading to Unicode. Hebrew posed challenges mainly in that the alphabet is non-Latin and the direction is right-to-left, with more problems arising with masoretic pointing. Early systems relied on some degree of transliteration but were neither standardized nor machine-readable. The system most designed for machine processing was Beta Code, which would render אחר as ")XR". Systems designed to look like Aramaic script in word processing programs were not standardized and relied on tricks with fonts. A font could be designed such that a character ")" or "a" could look like א, but the computer system had no understanding that the language and script were other than English. The user had to type backward, manually manage line breaks, and tell the spell checker to ignore rHa for אחר. A better solution, though rarely used for Hebrew outside of Israel, was to use an alternative character set. An 8-bit character set can encode 256 distinct characters. Some of those could be assigned to Hebrew letters, but support for additional character sets was limited. The ultimate solution was the development of the Unicode standard, which uses up to 16-bits per character and has the ability to encode 65,536 characters without tricking an "a" to look like an aleph or alpha. Researchers today are unlikely to encounter problems with character sets unless working with digital materials from before the turn of the century (in which case further reading about ASCII, ANSI, Unicode, UTF-8, ISO-8859, and Windows-1252 might be helpful). Unicode also allows signals for text direction, that is, switching between right-to-left (RTL) and left-to-right (LTR). In this case the existence of a standard and general compliance does not guarantee that there will not be problems across different implementations. Problems with multiline right-to-left text in otherwise left-to-right paragraphs in Microsoft Word for Macintosh persisted long after standards existed to solve that problem. Other standards deal with much more complicated problems. When successful, standards for interoperability make it possible to aggregate, search, process, and visualize data from many sources. Again, progress over recent decades is remarkable, but when troubleshooting or identifying limitations in research methods it is often helpful to understand the underlying standards for interoperability.

Specific tools for early Judaism research are discussed below in the categories of (1) primary sources search and access, (2) secondary sources search and access, (3) images of manuscripts and artifacts, (4) data visualization, and (5) publication and dissemination.

1. Primary Sources Search and Access

Digital collections of primary sources are widely available and typically divided by language and corpora. Resources are further divisible into those that are freely available and those that require purchase or subscription. With some notable exceptions of projects funded by universities and grants, resources freely available on the internet often use editions and translations that are in the public domain and out of date. Software packages and subscription services can be expensive for individuals, especially those working in multiple corpora. Research universities typically provide access to visitors physically on campus.

Digital resources are most bountiful for the biblical canon, particularly the Protestant canon. These platforms have been expanded to include additional corpora, including pseudepigrapha, Philo, Josephus, and the ability to create custom versions. Web-based resources such as BibleGateway.com (free, ad supported; https://www.biblegateway.com/) offer many translations and simple searching. Locally installed software such as Logos (https://www.logos.com/) and Accordance (https://www.accordancebible.com/) (and BibleWorks, until it closed in 2018) offers substantially more power, including search by morphology and instant access to parsing and lexicons. Additional resources are often included or available as upgrade packages (e.g., maps, commentaries, and dictionaries).

For Greco-Roman materials, the Perseus Digital Library (http://www.perseus.tufts.edu/hopper/) at Tufts University is an early star of digital humanities projects, having originated in 1985. Texts in Greek and Latin are linked to morphological information, and forms can be entered to show possible and likely parsings and lexicon entries. A related project, Perseids (http://www.perseids.org/), uses open standards to build editions of ancient documents. Alpheios (https://alpheios.net/) provides tools for philological analysis. Pelagios (http://pelagios.org/) extends the principles of linked open data with a focus on geography in the ancient world. These projects originated with a focus on Greek and Latin and expanded to the classical Mediterranean world. Because they utilize open standards, inclusion of Hebrew and Aramaic materials is easily imaginable.

Another free, web-based resource is the Online Critical Pseudepigrapha (http://ocp.tyndale.ca/). Among resources that require a subscription for full access, the Thesaurus Linguae Graecae (TLG; http://stephanus.tlg.uci.edu/) at the University of California Irvine is the oldest (1972) and most comprehensive. An abridged collection and lexica are available with free registration. The Loeb Classical Library (https://www.loebclassics.com/) at Harvard University is also available with subscription in a searchable digital format. Other databases specialize in specific media, such as papyri and inscriptions from the ancient world, not necessarily related to early Judaism. Papyri.info (http://papyri.info/) at Duke University exemplifies use of open standards in aggregating information from and about papyri. The Packard Humanities Institute's (https://inscriptions.packhum.org/) database of ancient Greek inscriptions covers direct written evidence, as opposed to literary texts copied in manuscripts.

Electronic resources for the Dead Sea Scrolls are available as optional additions to some Bible software packages described above. The most powerful dedicated tool is the Dead Sea Scrolls Electronic Library (https://brill.com/view/package/dsso) published by Brill and Brigham Young University. The transcription and English translations are fully searchable and linked to Palestine Antiquities Museum (PAM) images, though not necessarily the best available images (for which see Images of Manuscripts below). The Dead Sea Scrolls Electronic Library was published as a specialized application on CD-ROM in 1999 (biblical) and 2006 (nonbiblical), and converted to BrillOnline Reference Works in 2015 and 2016, respectively. This resource is available only with subscription and is not interoperable with open standards.

The oldest and most comprehensive digital collection of rabbinic literature is the Responsa Project at Bar-Ilan University (https://www.responsa.co.il/home.en-US.aspx). The project traces its origins to the 1960s and released its first version in 1992. After versions on CD-ROM and USB drive, the project is now available by subscription in a web browser. The project supports browse and search across corpora but lacks interoperability and other advanced features. Another significant subscription-based resource for rabbinic primary sources is the Lieberman Institute (https://www.lieberman-institute.com). Their Cooperative Development Initiative includes all major manuscript witnesses for the Babylonian Talmud, as well as the secondary literature index discussed below. The most widely accepted English translation of the Babylonian Talmud is the Soncino edition, which is in the public domain. It is freely available online from halakhah.com (http://halakhah.com). In recent years Sefaria (https://www.sefaria.org/texts) has made significant progress in adding new resources while maintaining open access. It does so by use of crowdsourcing (outsourcing to the crowd), which originated as a term, if not a concept, in the context of digital technologies and the internet. The advantages and disadvantages of crowdsourcing can be seen in its most famous exemplar, Wikipedia (wikipedia.org). The reliability and intentions of information provided by mostly unvetted, unpaid sources must be met with skepticism. The advantages of crowdsourced information are that the information is typically free and more easily updated. When a resource exists from a major publisher, one can expect it to be more reliable than its crowdsourced counterpart. Often, however, there is no competition from major publishers for information that is obscure or requires frequent updating. Crowdsourced resources may be the only available or only freely available even when not the best available. Sefaria is also noteworthy in providing applications (apps) for mobile devices, open-source code, and application programming interfaces (APIs) to allow other resources to interoperate with its database.

The Comprehensive Aramaic Lexicon (http://cal.huc.edu/) at the Hebrew Union College Jewish Institute of Religion includes three million words from the history of the Aramaic language, with morphological parsing and lexical entries. In addition to search and browse, the interface supports key word in context, which shows a word with a few words before and after from every instance in the database. The Digital Syriac Corpus (https://syriaccorpus.org/) provides a massive repository of literature compliant with interoperable standards for accessible linked data. The corpus, along with Syriaca.org (http://syriaca.org/) at Vanderbilt University and compatible tools such as Pelagios (http://pelagios.org/) and Pleiades (e.g., http://syriaca.org/place/78.html together with http://pleiades.stoa.org/places/658457), place Syriac studies ahead of the pack of fields supported by digital humanities resources. Similarly, Papyri.info and Coptic Scriptorium (http://copticscriptorium.org/) deserve mention as exemplars of the potential of open standards and digital tools.

2. Secondary Sources Search and Access

Secondary literature has several characteristics that make it easier to aggregate and discover than ancient sources. Publications in recent decades are typically born digital, meaning they were created on computers in the first place so do not require digitization such as scanning and character recognition. (Errors still occur when a digital source is printed to paper and redigitized.) Modern publications have objective characteristics such as author and date, unlike ancient sources that may require several paragraphs to describe the likely range of possibilities. Data about data, or metadata, can be entered, aggregated, indexed, and searched far more easily when the metadata is simple and machine readable. Standards for recording bibliographic data certainly exist, yet different interpretations can still cause a search to fail or the same work to appear twice in a search. This is especially the case for translations, multivolume works, and works in a series within a series. For example, the series Discoveries in the Judaean Desert follows a sequence for all volumes in the series, but additional internal numbering adds confusion. The volume scholars call "DJD 13" also includes a cave number (4), the volume number for that cave (8), and a part number (1), in addition to the overall series volume (13), with roman numerals to add to the fun (Attridge et al. 1994). The combination is confusing enough for beginning scholars in Dead Sea Scrolls research. Machine learning and librarians attempting to fit the reference to an interoperable standard are likely to arrive at different interpretations of the standard or simply make mistakes. To the extent to which modern scholarship falls neatly into the categories anticipated by metadata standards, which is a large extent overall, it is easy for aggregators to collect bibliographic information and make it easily searchable. The largest aggregator of catalog metadata is World-Cat (http://www.worldcat.org/), which ingests catalog information from libraries all over the world. Errors made by any one of those libraries will be perpetuated in WorldCat, but it remains an excellent resource for discovery. A work is more likely to be duplicated than missing in WorldCat.

Searching for secondary literature becomes more complicated when searching for information not included in the standard library catalog metadata. Unlike catalog data, the contents of a work are typically restricted by copyright. Google Books (https://books.google.com/) addresses this problem by indexing all of the content of a book even if it cannot show that content. Thus searching Google Books might indicate if the content of a work matches search terms. Large scale, free resources rely on simple machine learning, which may work well for specific terms but fail to distinguish a search about the book of Job from a search for a job (employment). Many researchers prefer more focused and/or subscription-based databases that rely more on informed human interpretation. Among free bibliographic search tools related to early Judaism, the most complete is Rambi, The Index of Articles on Jewish Studies from the National Library of Israel (http://web.nli.org.il/sites/NLI/English/infochannels/Catalogs/bibliographic-databases/rambi/Pages/rambi.aspx). More focused (but not too narrowly) on Dead Sea Scrolls research is the bibliography maintained by The Orion Center for the Study of the Dead Sea Scrolls and Associated Literature (http://orion-bibliography.huji.ac.il/). For the proper amount of money, more often paid by libraries than individuals, subscription services maintain a more curated index, and sometimes the complete work as PDF or e-book. EBSCO Research Databases categorize scholarship into many categories, including the EBSCO Jewish Studies Source (https://www.ebsco.com/products/research-databases/jewish-studies-source). Atla also maintains a religion database (https://www.atla.com/products/prodinfo/Pages/ATLA-RDB.aspx). Many libraries subscribe to several databases and make efforts to unify search and results, such that users may not need to know the databases involved behind the user interface. One can expect to see further progress in aggregation of search and access, especially for works in the public domain or openly licensed. An example of the concept of an aggregator discovery tool, though more relevant to American history than early Judaism, is the Digital Public Library of America (https://dp.la/).

Many researchers would like to search for secondary scholarship that deals with a particular primary source. This is sometimes easy if the citation appears in the title, keywords, or abstract in an expected form. An index of ancient works cited in a monograph may be searchable in Google Books, but only if the search string matches exactly with no dependence on contextual common sense. This situation will improve with better artificial intelligence and better tagging of metadata into machine-readable formats. If the primary source is specifically Talmudic, the Lieberman Index (http://lieberman-index.org; subscription required) claims to index ancient and modern treatments of any given passage. Researchers may also wish to search for more recent discussion of a subject treated by an older secondary source. It is easy to find bibliography going back in time but harder going forward. The best resource for searching newer works that cite an older source is Google Scholar (https://scholar.google.com/). Links labeled "cited by" and "related articles" may aid discovery, though one may not assume that there are no more citations.

Researchers may also wish to know about works that have not yet, or just recently, appeared in print. Often years go by between the first presentable version of research and the final publication. As discussed below, authors have many options for making their work public other than established print publishers. Google and Google Scholar index major repositories such as Humanities Commons (https://hcommons.org/) and Academia.edu (https://www.academia.edu/). Researchers can also search these repositories directly or join them for notifications. Researchers may find relevant news by following the right accounts on Twitter (such as Annette Y. Reed [https://twitter.com/annetteyreed]) or blogs (such as Jim Davila's PaleoJudaica [https://paleojudaica.blogspot.com/]). Researchers may find that resources published on the internet may disappear (dead links) for a variety of reasons. Google sometimes displays a recently cached version of a webpage that is currently unavailable. For older dead links, one's best hope is the Internet Archive's Wayback Machine (https://archive.org/web/). This tool allows users to go to a web address or browse the web as it appeared in the past.

3. Images of Manuscripts and Artifacts

For many researchers the most primary of primary sources is not a modern print edition but a digital facsimile of a manuscript or other artifact. Digital technology has already brought tremendous improvements over microfilm and photographic plates in printed editions. The cost of production and transmission is lower, and quality is typically higher. As high-quality digital scanning expanded in the 1990s, and digital photography surpassed film photography in the 2000s, digital access to artifacts expanded and is continuing to expand. For some researchers, the only question is whether the object has yet been digitized and made accessible. For others, various questions determine whether the benefits of digital technology for research into ancient artifacts have already reached maturity or are just beginning to blossom.

One question is whether the information sought is easily digitized. It is easy to create a simple digital equivalent of a photograph or microfilm. Information is not so easily digitized if the markings are damaged or otherwise illegible. In the case of palimpsests (erased and overwritten manuscripts), a simple photograph may not suffice to make the erased text legible. Spectral imaging may be necessary to enhance images. For research in early Judaism as mediated by early Christianity, the largest project to make palimpsests legible and available online has been the Sinai Palimpsests Project (http://sinaipalimpsests.org/; free registration required). Artifacts can also be difficult to photograph and digitize if texture is the primary or essential conveyor of meaning. Bad (diffuse) lighting may make cuneiform tablets, stone inscriptions, coins, amulets, and so forth illegible. West Semitic Research (https://dornsife.usc.edu/wsrp/) pioneered applying technology for dynamic relighting (Reflectance Transformation Imaging) to artifacts related to early Judaism. Their InscriptiFact Digital Image Library (http://www.inscriptifact.com/; free registration required) has thousands of relightable images, with thorough catalog information for search and browse. The Jubilees Palimpsest Project (http://jubilees.stmarytx.edu/) combines spectral imaging with dynamic relighting for all of Latin Moses (Latin Jubilees and the Testament of Moses) and a few other artifacts.

Another question is whether the researcher already knows the catalog information of the object sought. It is easy to find (or confirm the unavailability) of an artifact if one already knows the owner and designator (call number or shelf mark). High quality, sometimes spectrally enhanced, images of the Dead Sea Scrolls are available from the Leon Levy Dead Sea Scrolls Digital Library (https://www.deadseascrolls.org.il). Other images are available from the Israel Museum Digital Dead Sea Scrolls (http://dss.collections.imj.org.il). The Aleppo Codex is available as its own site (http://www.aleppocodex.org/; Adobe Flash required). The Leningrad Codex is available from the Internet Archive (https://archive.org/details/Leningrad_Codex/page/n0). Similarly, Codex Sinaiticus (http://www.codexsinaiticus.org/en/) and Codex Vaticanus (https://digi.vatlib.it/view/MSS_Vat.gr.1209) can be viewed online. For lower profile artifacts, the researcher is at the mercy of the holding institution. Some institutions, such as the Bibliothèque nationale de France (http://www.bnf.fr/), have systematic programs for digitization and follow open standards for accessibility. In all these cases, however, images of the artifacts are only discoverable if the researcher already has the catalog information. This could be gained from critical editions, secondary scholarship, or perhaps aggregators such as Trismegistos (https://www.trismegistos.org/). As artifacts are increasingly annotated with machine-readable linked data, it will become increasingly effective to search for artifacts not just by owner and shelf mark but by scribal features (support, columns, lines, hand, provenance) and contents of the text.

Another question that will determine one's experience of the progress already made in digital access to artifacts is what one wishes to do with the images. If one wishes only to read a text on screen, one can expect decent options for pan and zoom. If one wishes to recontextualize the image in any way, it will make a difference whether the image source complies with standards for interoperability. Many of the aforementioned sites are closed silos and seem to wish to prevent the user from saving the image (although it is difficult to prevent a simple screen capture). Other sites favor open standards for interoperability. Exemplary in this regard is vHMML (https://www.vhmml.org/), the virtual library of the Hill Museum and Manuscript Library at Saint John's Abbey and University (http://hmml.org/). The collection focuses on digital preservation of threatened collections, mostly Christian and Islamic. To the extent possible in light of intellectual property restrictions, the project favors open access, open standards, and open-source software. One notable set of open standards is the International Image Interoperability Framework (IIIF; https://iiif.io/). With IIIF compliance, images and collections can be reused outside their silos without divorcing them from the metadata and information provided by the original repository. Alternative viewers and collections can be easily implemented, along with sophisticated systems for annotation and collaboration. Once information and its relationship to other information becomes machine readable through defined standards, the possibilities for computer-assisted recontextualizing of information become limitless.

4. Data Visualization

Sometimes discovery and learning benefit from rendering data in ways other than linear strings of text. Data visualization can communicate in a glance what otherwise would have required extensive work and abstract thinking. One of the core advantages of digital technology is the ability to store and process massive quantities of data. The great predigital scholars were able to comprehend, retain, and notice patterns in huge amounts of literary data, but even they had their limits. Visualization tools that developed in the past decades have the ability to summarize information that would have been extremely time consuming or impossible in earlier generations.

For example, word clouds quickly visualize the words that appear most frequently in a set of text by rendering the more frequently used terms in larger letters. This can quickly convey themes and emphases in a work. One could quickly visualize the frequency of personal names that appear in a work, such as the Hebrew Bible, and compare it to the relative frequency of those names in the New Testament or Talmud. If properly coded, names could be expressed in colors for gender, ethnicity, and any other object of study. Color can be used to express any dimension in a data set using heat maps. Charts can express the relative frequency of a lexical variant or synonym in one corpus or period relative to others. Dendrograms can be automatically generated to visualize trees of manuscript families based on degree of textual similarity. The key word in context became more popular and easier to generate with digital texts and shows more of the context than a lexicon or concordance normally would. One can also easily create geographic maps with pins or colors representing mentions or more detailed information about place names in a work. In the past scholars have argued that geographic information mentioned in a work (if accurate) might indicate provenance of composition. Simple mapping software makes it easy to apply that line of inquiry to any text, compare it to other texts, and present arguments visually to reach a wider audience more quickly. In general, research questions that might have been intuited or manually tabulated with relatively small and well-referenced corpora such as the biblical canon can be asked of much larger corpora as long as they are adequately machine readable. For a collection of data visualizations pertaining to rabbinic literature see the index of visualizations at Sefaria.org (sefaria.org/visualizations).

5. Publication and Dissemination

Digital technology has not replaced the conference paper and printed volume, but it has added substantial new options. Email might be thought of as a quicker and easier version of preexisting media, such as mail. Other electronic media facilitate communication globally that before could only have been imagined in physical proximity. Web logs (blogs) and then Twitter offered an easy way to share announcements and ideas, especially in their nascent stages. Academia.edu gained popularity as a resource for authors to share their ideas and reach readers (and also gained controversy in its for-profit use of personal information). Nonprofit alternatives such as Humanities Commons and institutional repositories were built to have the same or improved capabilities for search, notification, and discussion without selling personal information. In addition to published material, such online forums can be used for conference papers, slideshows, syllabi, data sets, videos, and so on. Audio-visual materials are more common for reaching popular audiences (e.g., the Society of Biblical Literature's Bible Odyssey project [https://www.bibleodyssey.org/] or James McGrath's *Religion Prof Podcast* [https://anchor.fm/religionprof]), but that could easily change.

Even with some help from the Internet Archive's Wayback Machine, it is reasonable to wonder if digitally disseminated information and ideas will have the endurance of printed paper volumes or the parchment and papyri we study. The vast majority of the information we have from antiquity, we have not because it was durable but because it was copied. It was copied because it was deemed worthy of copying. To the extent that information on the internet is deemed worthy of copying and archiving it will be preserved more easily than its predigital analogs. The copying of digital information is the easy part. Archiving also requires attention to formats. Portable Document Format (PDF) is popular as a substitute for paper and thus is very human readable but less machine-readable. For important works and editions, the Text Encoding Initiative (http://www.tei-c.org/) provides an archival standard for texts to be readable to machines as well as humans.

The ease of copying digital information raised in a new way questions of intellectual property and copyright protection. From one perspective, copyright restrictions create a barrier to access, copying, and in that way preservation. From another perspective, copyright restrictions protect the rights of authors and publishers. Digital media have not displaced the traditional benefits of print publication for making information accessible in standard form. Besides the massive copying and dissemination implicit in the production and sale of physical books, publishers have performed functions such as vetting the quality of work. This vetting is often the best available metric in the career of a researcher, specifically for promotion and tenure. At one point there was a perceived divide separating digital access from print publication, associated with peer review and reliability. The lines have blurred substantially as publishers have found markets for online subscription- or open-access alongside or complementary to print publications. Meanwhile, open-access online-only journals not affiliated with a traditional print publisher have built strong reputations based on quality of editorial board, peer review, permanence, and preservation. The category of open access can be nuanced with standard licenses, such as Creative Commons (https://creativecommons.org/) licenses, which specify exactly what can and cannot be done with work published online. As with other widely adopted standards, the Creative Commons licenses facilitate the spread of information through machine aggregators. The best online journals have plans for permanence and preservation, often by agreements with archival repositories at major universities. Online resources require maintenance and could easily disappear, especially if the provider is a for-profit service that ceases to be profitable. Print publications are implicitly archived by libraries that hold them even if the publisher goes out of business. Today a library may provide access to an external digital subscription without maintaining its own copy. An institutional repository, however, implies commitment to preservation including replacement of storage hardware, following archival formats, and converting formats before they become inaccessible through obsolescence. A researcher has more options than ever for making information and ideas accessible to a large number of people in the present, preserved for the future, and vetted for quality.

6. Conclusion

Research in early Judaism has changed dramatically since the 1986 publication of the first edition of *Early Judaism and Its Modern Interpreters* (Kraft and Nickelsburg 1986). Research that had been possible with difficulty became easy. Research that had been impossible became possible. Information that had been accessible to very few became accessible to many. Along with social trends not directly linked to digital technology, there were changes in the questions being asked. Digital technology also impacted related aspects of the life of a researcher. Not least among these is teaching, both in general and specific to early Judaism. Digital media, course management systems, video conferencing technology, and so forth changed the list of things that could only happen in a classroom, such as showing a video, giving a lecture, or having a discussion. The role of memorization came into question for information that could be quickly accessed using digital tools. The importance of teaching students how to use digital tools left in question the necessity of teaching predigital tools. Especially at introductory levels, digital tools that give lexical and parsing information opened the possibility of teaching just enough of a language to use these tools. In addition to teaching, related interests such as publishing and museum and library science were impacted by the developments discussed above from the perspective of the researcher. As with previous generations in which new tools became available, the distinction between the possible and the beneficial, what one can do and what one should do, became vital.

Computer-assisted research developed from a set of tools into a self-reflective discipline in its own right. Digital humanities, a vague and problematic term among many in the history of research, became a buzzword that encompasses a range from doing the same kind of research with a computer, to self-reflection on the nature and role of the discipline itself. As digitally enabled tools impacted not only research but all aspects of the life of the researcher in society, the system of intertwined benefits and hazards of digital technology became important objects of study. All researchers in early Judaism have been impacted by at least some tools from digital technology. For some researchers, the relationship between early Judaism and digital humanities became a fruitful avenue of interdisciplinary inquiry, taking its place along with other interdisciplinary approaches in the history of the discipline.

Bibliography

Attridge, Harold W., et al. 1994. *Qumran Cave 4.VIII: Parabiblical Texts, Part 1*. DJD XIII. Oxford: Clarendon.
Kraft, Robert A., and George W. E. Nickelsburg, eds. 1986. *Early Judaism and Its Modern Interpreters*. BMI 2. Philadelphia: Fortress; Atlanta: Scholars Press.

Part 3
Early Jewish Literatures

11
THE LITERATURE OF EARLY JUDAISM

TIMOTHY H. LIM

At the head of a discussion of Jewish writings in the Hellenistic and early Roman periods are conceptual, terminological, historical, and methodological disagreements over how one describes this literature. Should one evoke the terms *Bible*, *Apocrypha*, and *Pseudepigrapha*? Is it more justifiable to employ the term *scripture*, connoting a valued and authoritative writing? Would this effectively avoid the implications of the designation *canon*, a term that might, depending on the context, produce obvious anachronisms, as well as signal theological assumptions? A determination of how and when the canon of the Hebrew Bible emerges is a complicated matter—who was responsible for its construction and what process and criteria determined which books to include? Further, assessments of the Dead Sea Scrolls and other finds from the Judean desert bear on these issues.

1. Terminology of Apocrypha and Pseudepigrapha

The English term *apocrypha* is most commonly associated with the Protestant (Lutheran and Reformed) definition of those books that were not included in the canon of the Hebrew Bible but appear in the LXX (Fricke 1991; Neuser 1991). The term is a transliteration of the Latin *apocrifa*, which in turn is a romanized and collective reference to the Greek apocryphal books (*biblioi apocryphoi*). Within the codices of the Greek Bible and the writings of the church fathers, the number of books to be listed in the Apocrypha varies (Stuckenbruck 2012, 96–97). In modern textbooks, the number is generally sixteen: Tobit, Judith, Additions to Esther, Wisdom of Solomon, Sirach, Baruch, Letter of Jeremiah, Additions to Daniel, 1

Maccabees, 2 Maccabees, 1 Esdras, the Prayer of Manasseh, Psalm 151, 3 Maccabees, 2 Esdras, and 4 Maccabees (Harrington 1999; Goodman 2001), while Raymond Brown, Pheme Perkins, and Anthony Saldarini (1990, 1056) count fifteen.

However, these two lists differ from the Reformers. In the complete German Bible of 1534, Martin Luther enumerated eight books of the Apocrypha in the following order: Judith, Wisdom, Tobias, Sirach, Baruch, Maccabees, parts of Esther, and parts of Daniel. He defined this category as those books that are not equal to holy scripture yet "are useful and good to read." This definition, then, does not extend to the sixteen books listed above that were excluded from the Hebrew Bible but involves only those that had already been deemed by church tradition to belong to the Apocrypha. This tradition follows Jerome who, in the last decade of the fourth century, distinguished between the books on his canonical list, the books of the Hebrew Bible, and those that had been set apart. His distinctions appear in his "Preface to the Scriptures," which he placed at the beginning of his Latin translation of "Reigns" (i.e., the books of Samuel and Kings). He explained that the books not included on his canonical list (*non sunt in canone*) should be "set to one side" among the apocrypha (*inter apocrifa seponendum*; *Prologus Galeatus*, 52–57; Latin text in Weber 1984, 365). He then listed seven books of the Apocrypha: Wisdom of Solomon, Wisdom of Jesus ben Sira, Judith, Tobit, the Shepherd of Hermas, and 1 and 2 Maccabees. The inclusion of the early Christian work of the Shephard of Hermas on this list is surprising but explicable by the early church's practice of treating disputed books of the Old and New Testaments together (Horbury 1994, 152). Jerome did not use the term *apocrifa* consistently, sometimes referring to the same book (e.g., Wisdom of Solomon) as "apocryphal" or "pseudepigraphical" (Stuckenbruck 2012, 184). However, his view that the Old Testament canon was the canon of the Hebrew Bible, and not that of the larger Septuagint, persisted (Brown 1992, 62–67; Gallagher 2012a).

Apocrypha has also been applied to works discovered among the manuscripts of the Judean Desert (e.g., Genesis Apocryphon [1Q20], Apocryphon of David [2Q22]). This use of the term is generic and depends on the etymological derivation of *apocryphos* to mean "hidden" and carries the sense of not having been preserved by tradition (Stuckenbruck 2012, 186). That the Greek term may derive from the Hebrew *genuz*, "hidden, sealed, covered up," to indicate certain words, for example, Dan 8:26; 12:4, 9–10, and books, for example, 4 Ezra 12.37; 14.5, 45–48; 2 Bar.

20.3–4; 87.1, are reserved for the wise (see Brown, Perkins, Saldarini 1990, 1056). Only later, in the patristic church's dispute with gnosticism, did the term apocrypha assume a pejorative connotation of works not to be read in public worship (cf. Origen, *Comm. Matt.* 10.18).

There are, then, two main uses of the term, the traditional and the contemporary. The traditional designates Apocrypha as the list of books (of varying number) not included in the Hebrew Bible but found in the Greek and Latin Bibles. This traditional meaning of Apocrypha assumes that there was already a canon of the Hebrew Bible. The contemporary use of the cognate terms, apocryphon or apocryphal is generic and does not imply a canon.

The other frequently used term to describe the literature of early Judaism, *the Pseudepigrapha*, has a similarly complex history of usage. It is often used loosely and interchangeably with apocrypha (Sparks 1987, xvii; Adler 2002, 212–15). The etymological meaning of *pseudepigrapha*, as "false writings," in its earliest, patristic usage applied to a gospel that falsely, so it was thought, bore the name of Peter (Eusebius, *Hist. eccl.* 6.12.1–4). Serapion rejected this gospel as heretical, since it was not handed down in the orthodox tradition. However, his criterion for pseudonymity, which displays an obvious Christian context in its guarding against heresy, is problematic if applied to pseudepigraphical works of early Judaism. Moreover, for modern scholars of the Hebrew Bible and New Testament, who consider many of these ancient texts to have been written by someone other than the person named in the writing, the definition is problematic. Finally, not until the modern era does the term define a collection of works.

Despite these observations, the current use of pseudepigrapha serves as a convenient label of a loose collection of all those works that are not included in the Hebrew Bible or Apocrypha. As R. H. Charles (1913 2:iv) famously stated, "pseudepigrapha" refers to "all the remaining extant non-Canonical Jewish books written between 200 B.C. and A.D. 100 with possibly one or two exceptions." His definition is problematic, because it assumes that Hebrew Bible canon was closed by 200 BCE. Further, the definition assumes that the Apocrypha was already defined as a distinct collection. Finally, not all of the noncanonical books to which he refers were Jewish. Rather, some (e.g., 2 Esdras) are composites and combine Christian and Jewish works together (see Davila 2005 for methodological problems in determining Jewish or Christian provenance of a work). Subsequent scholarship expands Charles's definition, so that the pseudepigrapha are no longer considered "*prima facie* as a group of writings representative of Early Judaism" (*OTP* 1:xv; also Bauckham, Davila, and Panayotov 2013, xxvi–xxx).

The three-volume work of noncanonical, early Jewish literature called *Outside the Bible: Ancient Jewish Writings Related to the Scripture*, edited by Louis Feldman, James Kugel and Lawrence Schiffman (2013), offers an alternative way of categorizing early Jewish literature by dividing it into "Scripture" and "outside books." The editors' surprisingly brief justification argues that outside books avoid perpetuating "the fragmented perception of these writings as the singular products of isolated Second Temple Jewish writers" (xvi–xvii). The central feature of most of the documents included in this multivolume work is their relationship to the Hebrew Bible. The editors arrange the material according to translations of biblical texts, biblical commentaries, rewritten biblical narratives, laws, and liturgies. The editors also realize that not all early Jewish literature is immediately related to the Hebrew Bible. This commendable categorization avoids anachronism and is bolstered by the fact that the historical categories are more historically appropriate (see below).

2. The Category of Bible

Scholars also disagree on the use of the adjective *biblical* to describe the books of the Hebrew Bible in this period. The disagreements generally center on the understanding of whether the canon was open or closed in the Second Temple period. If one views the canon as closed, then the use of biblical is defensible to that scholar. On the other hand, for someone who holds that the canon remained open well after the Second Temple period, the adjective is quite problematic. The closing of the canon of the Hebrew Bible has been variously dated by scholars to the end of the fifth century BCE (Freedman 1991; Steinman 1999), the second century BCE (Leiman 1976; Beckwith 1985), and the third century CE (Barton 1986, 1997, following Sundberg 1964; but first century CE in Barton 2017, 82–83, following Lim 2013a). It is widely agreed that by the first century CE there was a canon of the Hebrew Bible. How far back this canonization process is to be traced remains disputed.

Some argue against laying out a trajectory of development based on a teleological reading of the evidence, that is, with the end result of the canon in mind, which would constitute a kind of teleological fallacy. Robert Kraft (2007) has programmatically called for a broader perspective of a "paratextual" and "parahistorical" approach, in which canonical texts do not exert an unwarranted influence on the understanding of the traditions of the past. While this caution is a useful reminder in general terms,

Kraft seems to define canon in codicological terms (when the books are bound in a single codex) and minimizes the significance of ancient canonical lists. Moreover, he operates with a definition of the Bible based on the Greek tradition, which includes both the Old and New Testaments (Kraft 2007, 10). Jewish tradition, however, did not adopt the codex until the postrabbinic period and prior to this era focused on the *sepher* or scroll (see Lim 2017c). Following Kraft's approach, Eva Mroczek (2016, 23–25) applies these assumptions to an investigation of the Great Psalms Scrolls (11Q5 [11QPs^a]) as a collection of psalms.

Philip Davies (2006, 57) in his warning about the teleological fallacy argues against constructing "a single line of evolution" that results in a single canon by reading the final shape of the Hebrew Bible back into prerabbinic Judaism. His warning is worth heeding, but it has to be recognized that earlier collections of authoritative scriptures do overlap to a large extent with books found on the canonical notices (Josephus, *C. Ap.* 1.38–41; 4 Ezra 14.45–48; m. Yad. 3:5) and lists (Bryennios list [ca. 150 CE; folio 76a of MS 54 of the Greek Patriarchate Library of Jerusalem]; Melito of Sardis [ca. 190; Eusebius, *Hist. eccl.* 4.26]; B. Bat. 14–15, Origen [ca. before 232], *Commentary on the Psalms*; Eusebius, *Hist. eccl.* 6.25; Jerome [ca. 390s], *Prologus Galeatus*). These canonical notices date to the first four centuries of the Common Era and did not materialize ex nihilo. Their existence suggests that the Hebrew Bible canon was in the process of being formed prior to the turning of the era.

Moreover, the rabbinic canon, which is identical to the traditional canon of the Hebrew Bible, is the canon of only one group in prerabbinic Judaism, the Pharisees, since there were several other groups who held different collections of authoritative writings (e.g., Samaritans and Alexandrians considered only the Pentateuch authoritative; see Lim 2013a, 2017b). One need not assume that the Pharisees represented normative or common Judaism before 70 CE, a concept that is itself debated (cf. Neusner 1981; Sanders 1992; see the collection of essays edited by McCready and Reinhartz 2008). Before the refounding of Judaism in the aftermath of the Roman destruction of Jerusalem, there were different collections of authoritative scriptures used by Jewish groups. The Pharisaic canon of twenty-two holy scriptures (according to Josephus, *C. Ap.* 1.38–41) or twenty-four public books (according to 4 Ezra 14.45–48) became the canon of rabbinic Judaism because the majority of those who refounded Judaism after the destruction of Jerusalem were Pharisees (Cohen 1984; Collins 1995; Lim 2013b).

The legitimacy of the binary classification of literature of early Judaism as either biblical or nonbiblical depends on the canonical and chronological parameters of an investigation. More clarity can be gained if we date early Judaism to the period between 323 BCE and 200 CE. In this period there was already a concept of Bible, as evidenced by the prologue of the Wisdom of Ben Sira (Sir 39:1–3), the Hebrew rolls that were translated into Greek (Letter of Aristeas), and the references to the twenty-two or twenty-four books of sacred scriptures dating to the first century CE (Josephus, *C. Ap.* 1.38–41; 4 Ezra 14.45–48). The canonical lists of Bryennios (folio 76a of MS 54 of the Greek Patriarchate Library of Jerusalem) and Melito (Eusebius, *Hist. eccl.* 4.26), and the implied list of m. Yad. 3:5 ("all holy scriptures defile the hands"), dating to the second century CE, corroborate this fixed sense of the Bible (Lim 2013a, 35–53). Moreover, the Mishnah records a saying attributed to Rabbi Akiba that the one who reads "the heretical books" (lit. "the outside books," *sepharim ha-hitzonim*, Sanh. 10:1) does not have a place in the world to come. If the rabbis knew what were "outside books," then they must have known what were "inside books." But they did not call them "inside books"; they called them "holy scriptures" (*kitvey ha-qodesh*; e.g., m. Yad. 3:5).

3. The Gathering at Yavneh

In the Hellenistic and early Roman period, then, the literature of early Judaism was divided between the scriptural and nonscriptural books. What was the process that led to this division? Was there an institution that decided on the books of the canon?

In the past, it was thought that the canonization of the Hebrew scriptures took place at the gathering of rabbis at Yavneh in 90 CE, a position now contested, which was labeled a *synode* by Heinrich Graetz (1871, 149). In using this terminology, it is possible that he was influenced by Baruch Spinoza's earlier description of a "*concilium pharisaeorum*" (so Aune 1991; doubted by Lewis 2002, 159). Graetz proposed that the third division of the Writings was assembled in two stages, first by the Pharisees and Sadducees in 65 CE and then at the *synode* of Yavneh. For Graetz, the final closing of the canon took place only with the redaction of the Mishnah, which he dated to 189 CE (1871, 149).

This model of the gathering at Yavneh was patterned after the ecclesiastical councils. Jack Lewis (1964, 128) objected to the use of the label *council* because the Christianizing description carried with it an authority that was not evident in the decisions taken at the court or assembly at Yavneh. Many scholars follow Lewis in eschewing the label council, but nonetheless think that the assembly at Yavneh was an important moment in the canonization of the Hebrew Bible. Lewis's assumptions, however, are open to question. It is to be doubted that the ecclesiastical councils, including the regional council of Laodicea (363–364 CE), where the Old Testament canon was first discussed, had the authority and decision-making power that Lewis attributed to them (see Tanner 1990, 2001). Moreover, the link between Yavneh and canonization is based on m. Yad. 3:5, which reports that R. Eleazar ben Azariah replaced Rabban Gamaliel as head of the academy, a tradition that is textually and historically unsound (Alexander 2007, 63–64). The significance of Yavneh is not in the canonization of the Hebrew Bible, but the establishment of "a grand coalition" of different groups and parties and the end of sectarianism (Cohen 1984, 50).

4. The Closing of the Canon

Another source of scholarly disagreement lies in the ambiguous concept of the closing of the canon. Scholarly consensus between the end of the nineteenth century and first half of the twentieth century posited a three-stage theory of the canonization process. Notably following the tripartite subdivision of the traditional Hebrew Bible, this consensus held that the Torah or Pentateuch closed around 500 BCE, followed by the books of the prophets (*Nevi'im*) in the third or fourth century, and finally the Writings (*Ketuvim*) in the so-called council of Jamnia in 90 CE (Buhl 1891; Wildeboer 1891; Ryle 1892); H. E. Ryle (1892) even described the closing of each subsection as the closing of the first, second, and third canon.

In the past generation, this three-stage theory has been challenged. Roger Beckwith (1985, 165) argued that the canon of the Old Testament was closed in two, not three, stages: the Torah first, followed by the subdivision of the non-Mosaic material into the Prophets and Writings in the second century BCE. Beckwith believed that all the books of the Old Testament were canonized very early on. In the same vein, Andrew Steinmann (1999) believed that the whole canon was closed by the end of the fifth century BCE, before splitting into two strands that subdivided the books either into "the Law and the Prophets" or "the Law, the Prophets, and the Writings/Psalms."

John Barton (1986, 44, 55–82) also found difficulties with the three-stage theory and proposed that throughout the postexilic period to the time of the New Testament and beyond, "scripture was bipartite rather than tripartite," consisting of the Torah and an open category of the prophets. Barton (1986, 68–71; 1997, 108–21; 2005, 1–7) means by openness the inclusion of books *in addition* to those that were eventually canonized and not that the bipartite canon lacked any of the biblical books.

Timothy Lim (2013a, 18–21) questioned the three-stage theory's reconstruction of the closing of the canon, both in the way that it described the so-called council of Yavneh (see above) and also in the reconstruction of the so-called Samaritan schism. Ryle (1892, 93) had argued that when the Samaritans separated from the Jews in 432 BCE, they took with them the Pentateuch, which they had already considered canonical. He inferred that the Pentateuch must have been closed earlier in the fifth century. But there was no schism in the way that implied that the Samaritans split off from the Jews. The Samaritans were remnants of the northern Israelites who remained in the land after the Assyrians exiled part of the population. These northern Israelites built a sacred precinct on Mount Gerizim in the Persian period that lasted to Hellenistic times, and the Gerizim temple was destroyed along with Schehem and Mareshah in 110 BCE (Magen 2007; Kartveit 2009; Knoppers 2013; Lim 2017b).

The very meaning of closing also encountered problems. Does it refer to the closing of the section of the Torah, the Prophets, or the Writings? Is it justifiable to reconstruct a sequential closing of each subsection of the Hebrew Bible? Does a list of authoritative writings, a codex of books constitute closing, or simply the absence of dispute over the canonical status of an agreed set of books?

Beckwith (1988, 59) is surely correct when he questioned the absolute sense that one might attach to the closing of the canon. The canon has never been closed, if by this is meant an absence of any doubt whatsoever by anyone about the canonical status of the books of the Hebrew Bible. Lim (2013a, 180–81) likens the closing of the rabbinic canon to the reaching of a scholarly consensus. It does not imply the absence of dissenting voices. Rather, it means that most accepted the twenty-two or twenty-four books of the canon.

5. The Temple of Jerusalem

Another institution thought to have been important for the canonical process is the temple of Jerusalem. Accordingly, several scholars believe that the temple not only served as the cultic center of early Judaism but that it also promulgated the official or public canon of the Hebrew Bible (Leiman 1976, 24, 131; Beckwith 1985, 153, 165; Van der Kooij 1998, 32–33; 2003, 31–33). As mentioned above, Beckwith theorized that the tripartite canon was closed in two stages: the Torah followed by the subdivision of the non-Mosaic collection into the Prophets and the Writings. He argued that Judas Maccabeus (164 BCE) founded a library and compiled a canonical list, and that list may be the same as the one found in B. Bat. 14a. Beckwith's interpretation of 2 Macc 2:13–15, however, is questionable (Barton 1986, 57, Van der Kooij 1998, 25). The passage does not mention Judas establishing a library; rather, it refers to Judas collecting all the books, damaged during the persecution of Antiochus Epiphanes (1 Macc 1:56), which he gave back to the people. The Greek of 2 Macc 2:14 is correctly translated as all the books "fallen to pieces" (*ta diapeptōkota*), and not "lost," on account of the war (Lim 2013a, 116).

There were no temple scriptures that served as the public, common, or official canon of all Jews (Klijn 1977, 265–72), but scriptural scrolls were kept at the cultic center for various purposes and at times they carried with them an authoritative function. The discovery of "the book of the torah" in the seventh century BCE is questionable as early evidence of the temple functionaries' role in the canonization of the Hebrew Bible. In the reign of Josiah (622 BCE), the high priest Hilkiah discovered a *sepher ha-torah*, which is widely understood to be an earlier version of the book of Deuteronomy or *Urdeuteronomium* (2 Kgs 22). This event was not the canonization of a collection of books, but the discovery of one book that served as the basis of a short-lived cultic reform (Lim 2013a, 31–32).

There is no doubt that the temple served as the depository of some of the scriptures, especially the Torah and the Psalms (see Josephus, *B.J.* 7.148, 150, 162; *A.J.* 12.323). These books would have been used in rituals and worship. But depositing scrolls at the temple is not the same as canonizing texts as scripture. Other noncanonical writings, such as priestly genealogies, were also deposited at the temple, available for consultation in the event that doubt was cast over a sacerdotal claim (Josephus, *C. Ap.* 1.34–36; cf. *B.J.* 2.247; 6.354; *Vita* 1.6). Conversely, scriptural scrolls were also deposited in synagogues and not just at the temple (Josephus, *A.J.* 16.164; see Lim 2013a, 30).

Several rabbinic passages refer to the discovery of three scrolls of the Torah in the temple court, and they have been understood by some as evidence of the canonizing function of the temple (Beckwith 1985, 80–86). The most important of these texts are y. Taʿan. 4:2; 68a, which Shemaryahu

Talmon (1962, 57) understands to be the defense of the Textus Receptus; for him, these rabbinic notices attest to the confirmation and authorization of the proto-Masoretic Text. Thus, they are not about canonization. Elsewhere, Talmon (2002, 12) argued that there is no evidence whatsoever that "an official agency ever legislated the inclusion of a book in a canon of Scripture." There were scribes who worked at the temple, and in copying various scrolls they would have compared variant readings of the same text. Faced with this situation, they conducted what amounts to be a rudimentary form of textual criticism where the textual variant of the majority of two of the three scrolls was accepted (Lim 2013a, 33–34).

Neither the gathering at Yavneh nor the temple of Jerusalem, then, functioned as an authoritative body that decided the books that were to be included in the canon. If no institution was responsible for the canonization of the Hebrew Bible, then how was the canon formed? How did the literature of early Judaism come to be distinguished into scripture and nonscripture?

6. The Selection of the Books of the Canon

The process that led to the canonization of the books of the Hebrew Bible was protracted and complex and cannot be explained by a single factor (Lim 2013a, 181). There was no central authority that determined which books were to be included in the canon. Each community (Judeans, Samaritans, Alexandrians, Essenes, Therapeutae, Pharisees, etc.) constructed its own understanding of authoritative writings. These collections were not mutually exclusive; rather, they overlapped to a large extent and included a core of writings that were eventually included in the canon.

Different historical factors impacted on the formation and emergence of these authoritative collections. Several of these factors were external. First, the Persian intervention into the religious affairs of the Judeans contributed to the rise of the Torah in the fifth century BCE (Frei 1984; 2001; Lee 2011). Second, the standardization of the Homeric epics spurred the Alexandrian Jews to initiate a project of translating the Hebrew laws into Greek in the second century BCE (Honigman 2003; Lim 2013a, 74–93). Third, the controversies between Jews and their Greek detractors over the historical veracity of Jewish writings led to the first, explicit articulation of the canon by Josephus in the first century CE (*C. Ap.* 1.37–38; see also Alexander 2007; Lim 2013a). Finally, the high value attributed to the Homeric epics and the emergence of the Christian gospels in the tannaitic period caused the rabbis to rule that these writings do not "defile the hands," a cryptic and enigmatic shorthand to mean that they are not to be considered holy scriptures (Leiman 1976, 115-17; Barton 1986, 68-71; Goodman 1990; Lim 2010b, 2013a). Internally, the study, interpretation, and scribal transmission of Jewish writings contributed to the recognition that certain books had an authority in governing the pattern of daily life, rites of passage, and the construction of beliefs (Lim 2017a, 19-21).

These factors, however, do not explain why some books were included in the canon, while others were not. As Shaye Cohen (2014, 188-189) rightly asked: "Why these, and not those [books]?" What inherent distinctiveness can one identify between the books, quite apart from the fact that some were included in the canon and others were not?

Josephus provides one explanation when he defends the Jewish people against Greek detractors (*C. Ap.* 1.1-4). According to him, the books of sacred scriptures differ from other Jewish writings in their trustworthiness (*C. Ap.* 1.38-41). He counted a total of twenty-two biblical books: five books of Moses, thirteen books of the prophets, and four books of hymns to God and instructions for life. There is wide agreement that the five books of Moses refer to the Pentateuch. There is some disagreement over the third category of books, but they are thought to include the Psalms, Proverbs, Ecclesiastes, and the Song of Songs.

It is the second category of prophetic books that has engendered scholarly debate and speculation. There are indeed thirteen prophetic books, as also attested by Josephus elsewhere (*A.J.* 10.35), but what are they and how should they be ordered? Beckwith (1985, 119) suggested that they are Job, Joshua, Judges (+ possible Ruth), Samuel, Kings, Isaiah, Jeremiah (+ possible Lamentations), Ezekiel, Twelve Minor Prophets, Daniel, Chronicles, Ezra-Nehemiah, and Esther. For Beckwith, the uncertainty is whether Ruth and Lamentations should appear with the books of the prophets or in the third division of the hymns, combined with Psalms and Song of Songs respectively.

Steinmann (1999, 116), on the other hand, offers an alternative enumeration, based on Josephus's use of the biblical books: Joshua, Judges-Ruth, Samuel, Kings, Chronicles, Ezra-Nehemiah, Esther, Job, Isaiah, Jeremiah-Lamentations, Ezekiel, Daniel, and the Twelve Prophets. But Job and Chronicles were not used by Josephus, and Steinmann added them to his reconstructed list because they were attested in the Wisdom of Ben Sira in the second century BCE.

There really is no way of knowing precisely which books, let alone their order, Josephus had in mind in his second category of prophetic books. Steve Mason (2002, 114) has argued that Josephus's classification of the writings was according to genre and not according to the tripartite division of the canon. The uncertainty, however, does not nullify the fact that he considered the twenty-two books as scriptures (*C. Ap.* 1.42; Lim 2013a, 45). According to Josephus, the nonscriptural books were "not worthy of the same trust" as the scriptural books on the absence of an exact line of prophetic succession. In what sense they are less trustworthy is not explained, although, given the context, one suspects that Josephus had in mind historical trustworthiness. His implied classification of scriptures and nonscriptures is nonetheless based on this criterion of trustworthiness. In practice, however, he does not follow the principle. In drafting his *Antiquitates judaicae*, Josephus not only paraphrased the scriptural texts, but also the nonscriptural writings of the Letter of Aristeas, Esdras, 1 Maccabees, new sources, as well as his own earlier work, the *Bellum judaicum* (Cohen 2002, 24–48). Josephus used criterial logic to account for the formal distinction between scriptural and nonscriptural books, but he could not account for their qualitative difference (Lim 2017a, 15–18).

Scholars, both ancient and modern, have attempted to account for the criteria used in the selection of the books of the canon. Origen and Africanus argued that the use of certain books in synagogues and churches should serve as canonical criteria (*Letter to Africanus*; see the edition and commentary of Harl and de Lange 1983). They also sought the criterion of the original Hebrew language of a composition. But these are clearly *ex post facto* rationalizations. Edmond Gallagher (2012b), basing his discussion on this dispute between Origen and Africanus over the status of the book of Susanna, suggests that the Hebrew criterion was already evident in prerabbinic Judaism and was operative in the canonical process. But this criterion does not explain why books composed in Hebrew (e.g., Ben Sira, Jubilees, the Temple Scroll) were left out of the rabbinic canon, while other books (e.g., Ezekiel, Qoheleth, the Song of Songs) were disputed by rabbis, despite being written in Hebrew (Lim 2017a, 1–3).

Jewish tradition points to another criterion: the divine inspiration of holy scriptures. Accordingly, books that were composed by divine inspiration, through the agency of the holy spirit and prophetic oracles, were thought to be holy scriptures. According to rabbinic tradition the holy spirit ceased with the death of the last prophets, Haggai, Zechariah and Malachi (t. Sotah 13:2), and so the canon was thought to have closed by

450 BCE (Leiman 1981, 61). But other Jewish writings after this period continued to claim divine inspiration (e.g., 1 En. 1.1–2; Prologue of the book of Jubilees; 1QpHab VII, 1–5). Moreover, the rabbinic concept of the *bat qol*, or "heavenly voice," implies that divine revelation continued and did not cease, at least in one strand of rabbinic Judaism (e.g., t. Sotah 13:3; see also Cook 2011).

7. The Nature of Scriptural Authority in Dead Sea Scrolls

Probably the most significant contribution to our understanding of the literature of early Judaism in the past generation is the discovery of manuscripts of the Judean Desert, especially those recovered from the caves by Khirbet Qumran. These scrolls not only add to the collection of Jewish literature in the Hellenistic and Roman period, they also challenge the distinction drawn between scripture and nonscripture.

The Dead Sea Scrolls comprise between nine hundred and a thousand original scrolls, dating between 300 BCE and 100 CE, and by convention they have been classified into three broad categories. About a quarter of these scrolls are biblical, attesting to all the books of the Hebrew Bible except Esther. An unprovenanced copy of Nehemiah (MS 5426) from the Schøyen collection has recently been published, but its authenticity is disputed (Davis et al. 2017, 221–25). Nonetheless, Nehemiah could still be counted among the biblical books on the strength of a scroll of Ezra (4Q117), with which it is combined in the traditional canonical arrangement. Other scrolls found include those that were preserved by Jewish and Christian traditions, designated variously as apocryphal, pseudepigraphical and/or deuterocanonical (e.g., 1 Enoch, Jubilees). There are also scrolls of previously unknown writings (e.g., 1Q20; 1Q22; 1Q29; 2Q21; 4Q375; 4Q376; 4Q408), and they are generically designated as apocryphon (e.g., of Genesis or Moses; see above). The third category of compositions are those designated as sectarian (e.g., Rule of the Community, Damascus Document), writings that represent the ideology and teachings of a sect or school of thought most commonly identified with the Essenes.

This conventional way of describing the Dead Sea Scrolls has, in recent years, been questioned by scholars who investigate the expanded literature of early Judaism. Should the Dead Sea Scrolls be described as the "library of the Essenes" (see Cross 1958, 3rd ed. 1995; Pedley 1959; Stegemann 1993)? The implication of this description is that all the scrolls found in the collection were carefully collected and curated, reflecting the ideology of the Qumran-Essene community. It was often said that such-and-such a scroll is authoritative because it was found among the Qumran library. But if the corpus of Dead Sea Scrolls is a heterogeneous collection of scrolls deposited in the caves at different times and by different groups, then not every scroll can be understood to reflect the sectarian point of view (Lim and Collins 2010, 2–3). For instance, the scrolls that attest to copies of books that were eventually included in the canon (the so-called biblical scrolls) are not Essene compositions, since they do not show any sectarian features (Ulrich 2002, 180–83). These biblical scrolls belong to Judaism of the Second Temple period.

One way of investigating the authoritativeness of certain writings is to study the citations and references in the sectarian scrolls. Which texts did the Essene communities cite in their own writings? Ian Eybers (1962; 1965), James VanderKam (1998, 389–96) and Lim (2001, 27–35) have argued that the communities reflected in the Dead Sea Scrolls considered the Pentateuch authoritative. The sectarians cited verbatim, with or without introductory formulas, from all five books attributed to Moses (e.g., Gen 1:27 in CD IV, 20–21; Exod 23:7 in 1QS V, 15; Lev 18:13 in CD V, 8–9; Num 24:17 in CD XVII, 19–21; Deut 23:24 in CD XVI, 6).

VanderKam (1998; 2000, 23–30; 2002, 108), however, has argued that the Essene Torah may have additionally included the book of Jubilees, 1 Enoch, the Temple Scroll (11Q19; 11Q20; 4Q524) and the Reworked Pentateuch (4Q158; 4Q364; 4Q365; 4Q366; and 4Q367). The book of Jubilees and 1 Enoch have the strongest claim to authoritative status, followed by the Temple Scroll (Lim 2010a, 314–18). The Reworked Pentateuch, now considered a pentateuchal text, was never cited by the sectarians in their own writings (Lim 2010a, 317). There is moreover no evidence that the sectarians had an open canon, nor did they call the book of Jubilees torah. To be sure, the book of the Divisions of the Times by Jubilees and Weeks was considered authoritative. In CD XVI, 1–3, it is called a *perush* or explanation, and its authority on chronological matters is specified for sectarian religious practice.

Eybers (1965, 206–7) has argued that the sectarians had a closed collection of the books of the prophets from Joshua to Malachi. But there is no evidence to suggest that the sectarians had a fixed list of prophetic books (Lim 2010a, 308–10). There are indeed citations of various books of the prophets (e.g., Josh 6:26 in 4Q175 21–23; 1 Sam 25:26, 31, 33 in CD IX, 9–10), and some of these references imply a collection (e.g., from reigns of Jeroboam to Zedekiah in Samuel-Kings [4Q397 14–21, 15]; a collection of minor prophets). But the book of Daniel was also considered prophetic ("as it is written in the book of Daniel the prophet," 4Q174 1-3, II, 3, citing a conflated quotation of Dan 12:10 + 11:32; cf. Dan 9:25-26 in 11Q13 [11QMelch] 1; 2i; 3i; 4 II, 18). Eybers (1965, 141, 145, and 158; cf. Lim 2010a, 309) takes a maximalist approach to the evidence, combining sectarian citations with a reading of the biblical scrolls that is tendentious.

There is no evidence for the third division of the Writings. Some books that were eventually classified among the Ketuvim were cited as authoritative (e.g., Prov 15:8 in CD IX, 20-21), but there is no evidence of a collection, apart from the Psalms (Lim 2010a, 310). The Psalms were considered authoritative, the sectarians having devoted three continuous pesharim to their interpretation (1Q16 [1QpPs]; 4Q171 [4QpPs^a]; and 4Q173 [4QpPs^b]); 11Q13, a thematic pesher introduces its citation of Ps 82:1 by the formula "as it is written concerning him [i.e., Melchizedek] in the psalms of David" (11Q13 I, 10). It is possible that the reference to *sepher ha-tehilim* in a version of the War Scroll (4Q491 17, 4) may be a reference to the book of psalms (Lim 2013a, 127).

As for the Great Psalms Scroll (11Q5), its authoritative status among the sectarians is unclear. James Sanders (1974, 1993) had originally argued that the Essenes, when they separated from the temple, took with them one version of the psalter and added to them their own Hasidic and proto-Essene poems. This would in effect mean that 11Q5 was a sectarian psalter, a secondary collection (Lim 2013a, 123-24). But Sanders either changed his mind or clarified his view and later argued that 11Q5 was a true psalter. Peter Flint (1997, 202-27) dubbed Sanders's theory "the Qumran Psalms Hypothesis" and supported Sanders claim that 11Q5 evidences the gradual stabilization of the Psalter and argues for variant literary editions of the psalter. But 11Q5 is not cited by any of the sectarian scrolls, and as such it is unknown how the Essenes understood its authoritative status (Lim 2013a, 126; Mroczek 2016).

The concept of canon among the sectarians of the Dead Sea Scrolls is not well developed. At most, one can say is that they had a broadly bipartite canon, corresponding to the Pentateuch and an undefined collection of prophetic books, but the sectarians did not limit their authoritative scriptures to the biblical scrolls (Lim 2013a, 119-47). Thus, the bifurcation of the literature of early Judaism into scripture and nonscripture does not adequately capture the sectarians' understanding of textual authority. Other books (e.g., Jubilees, 1 Enoch) likewise had an authority that complemented the Scriptures. Lim has suggested that between the poles of scripture and nonscripture, the sectarians had a dual (in the case of the Torah and its authoritative explanation) and graded authority (in the way that the sectarian writings themselves, like the pesharim, rules, hodayot, and 4Q418 [4QInstruction], functioned authoritatively).

8. Conclusions

By the first century CE, the literature of early Judaism had been divided into the categories of scripture and nonscripture (or "outside books"). This was the tradition of one strand of ancient Judaism, the Pharisaic and rabbinic. Josephus, the anonymous author of 4 Ezra, and the rabbis all recognized a collection of twenty-two or twenty-four books of the Hebrew Bible, which the Mishnah called holy scriptures. They did not specify what were noncanonical or outside books. Christian tradition and modern scholarship designate these nonscriptural books as apocrypha and pseudepigrapha, but these terms are problematic. They continue to be used in contemporary scholarship for convenience.

The Pharisaic-rabbinic definition of early Jewish literature, however, is not without its problems. Other non-Pharisaic Jews, before and after the first century CE, conceived their authoritative scriptures differently. The Jews of Alexandria in Ptolemaic Egypt translated the Hebrew rolls of the Pentateuch into Greek and hailed them as a new Torah. The Samaritans likewise held and continue to hold the canonical status of only the first five books of the Hebrew Bible. The Essenes had a broadly bipartite canon of the Torah and prophets, but they also held as authoritative books that were not included in the Hebrew Bible, including their own sectarian writings.

The Pharisaic-rabbinic distinction between scripture and outside books is, moreover, dependent upon the formation and closing of the canon in the first century CE. The rabbis who assembled at Javneh did not form a council by another name that pronounced on the sacred status of the two remaining disputed books of the Song of Songs and Qoheleth. The description of this gathering of rabbis as a council is unsuitable. Before the first century, the priests of the temple of Jerusalem kept books within the sacred precinct, but they did not serve as a council to prescribe the books of the canon. The formation of the canon of the Hebrew Bible is complex and cannot be easily generalized. Many historical factors contributed to the elevation of the traditional writings of Jews to the status of authoritative scriptures.

Finally, the Pharisaic-rabbinic definition of the literature of early Judaism has been called into question by the discovery and study of the scrolls from the Judean Desert. The categories of scripture and nonscripture do not adequately describe how Jews understood the authoritative nature of their writings. To be sure, the biblical texts in various collections were authoritative, but authority also rested in other books that were not eventually included in the canon, as well as the sectarians' own writings.

Bibliography

Adler, William. 2002. "The Pseudepigrapha in the Early Church." Pages 211–28 in *The Canon Debate*. Edited by Lee Martin McDonald and James A. Sanders. Peabody, MA: Hendrickson.

Alexander, P. S. 2007. "The Formation of the Biblical Canon in Rabbinic Judaism." Pages 57–80 in *The Canon of Scripture in Jewish and Christian Tradition / Le canon des Ecritures dans les traditions juive et chrétienne*. Edited by Philip S. Alexander and Jean-Danul Kaestli. Lausanne: Zèbre.

Aune, David E. 1991. "On the Origins of the 'Council of Javneh' Myth." *JBL* 110:491–93.

Barton, John. 1986. *Oracles of God: Perceptions of Ancient Prophecy in Israel after the Exile*. London: Darton, Longman & Todd.

———. 1997. *The Spirit and the Letter: Studies in the Biblical Canon*. London: SPCK.

———. 2005. "The Canonicity of the Song of Songs." Pages 1–7 in *Perspectives on the Song of Songs/Perspektiven der Hoheliedauslegung*. Edited by Anselm Hagedorn. Berlin: de Gruyter, 2005.

———. 2017. "Canon and Content." Pages 82–94 in *When Texts Are Canonized*. Edited by Timothy H. Lim. BJS 359. Providence, RI: Brown Judaic Studies.

Bauckham, Richard, James R. Davila, and Alexander Panayotov, eds. 2013. *Old Testament Pseudepigrapha: More Nonocanonical Scriptures*. Vol. 1. Grand Rapids: Eerdmans.

Beckwith, Roger. 1985. *The Old Testament Canon of the New Testament Church and Its Background in Early Judaism*. London: SPCK.

———. 1988. "Formation of the Hebrew Bible." Pages 39–86 in *Mikra: Text, Translation, Reading and Interpretation of the Hebrew Bible in Ancient Judaism and Early Christianity*. Edited by M. J. Mulder. CRINT 2.2. Assen: Van Gorcum; Minneapolis: Fortress.

Brown, Dennis. 1992. *Vir Trilinguis: A Study in the Biblical Exegesis of Saint Jerome*. Kampen: Kok Pharos.

Brown, Raymond E., Pheme Perkins, and Anthony J. Saldarini. 1990. "Apocrypha; Dead Sea Scrolls; Other Jewish Literature." Pages 1055–82 in *The New Jerome Biblical Commentary*. Edited by Raymond E. Brown, Joseph A. Fitzmyer, and Roland E. Murphy. 2nd ed. London: Chapman.

Buhl, Frants. 1891. *Kanon und Text des Alten Testaments*. Leipzig: Faber.

Charles, R. H. 1913. *The Apocrypha and Pseudepigraph of the Old Testament in English*. 2 vols. Oxford: Clarendon.

Cohen, Shaye J. D. 1984. "The Significance of Yavneh: Pharisees, Rabbis, and the End of Jewish Sectarianism." *HUCA* 55:27–53.

———. 2002. *Josephus in Galilee and Rome: His Vita and Development as a Historian*. Columbia Studies in the Classical Tradition 8. Leiden: Brill.

———. 2014. *From the Maccabees to the Mishnah*. 3rd ed. Louisville: Westminster John Knox.

Collins, John J. 1995. "Before the Canon: Scriptures in Second Temple Judaism." Pages 225–241 in *Old Testament: Past, Present, and Future; Essays in Honor of Gene M. Tucker*. Edited by James L. Mays, David L. Petersen, and Kent H. Richards. Nashville: Abingdon.

Cook, Stephen L. 2011. *On the Question of the "Cessation of Prophecy" in Ancient Judaism*. TSAJ 145. Tübingen: Mohr Siebeck.

Cross, Frank Moore. 1958. *The Ancient Library of Qumrân and Modern Biblical Studies*. Garden City, NY: Doubleday.

———. 1995. *The Ancient Library of Qumrân and Modern Biblical Studies*. 3rd ed. Minneapolis: Fortress.

Davies, Philip R. 2006. "Loose Canons: Reflections on the Formation of the Hebrew Bible." *JHebS* 5. https://tinyurl.com/sbl9027e.

Davila, James R. 2005. *The Provenance of the Pseudepigrapha. Jewish, Christian or Other?* JSJSup 105. Leiden: Brill.

Davis, Kipp, Ira Rabin, Ines Feldman, Myriam Krutzsch, Hasia Rimon, Årstein Justnes, Torleif Elgvin, and Michael Langlois. 2017. "Nine Dubious 'Dead Sea Scrolls' Fragments from the Twenty-First Century." *DSD* 24:189–228.

Eybers, I. H. 1962. "Some Light on the Canon of the Qumran Sect." *OTWSA* 5:1–14.

———. 1965. "Historical Evidence on the Canon of the Old Testament with Special Reference to the Qumran Sect." 2 vols. PhD diss., Duke University.

Feldman, Louis H., James L. Kugel, and Lawrence H. Schiffman, eds. 2013. *Outside the Bible: Ancient Jewish Writings Related to the Scripture.* 3 vols. Lincoln: University of Nebraska Press; Philadelphia: Jewish Publication Society.

Flint, Peter W. 1997. *The Dead Sea Psalms Scrolls and the Book of Psalms.* STDJ 17. Leiden: Brill.

Freedman, David Noel. 1991. *The Unity of the Hebrew Bible.* Ann Arbor: University of Michigan Press.

Frei, Peter. 1984. "Zentralgewalt und Lokalautonomie im Achamenidenreich." Pages 8–43 in *Reichsidee und Reichsorganisation im Perserreich.* Edited by Peter Frei and Klaus Koch. OBO 55. Fribourg: Universitätsverlag; Göttingen: Vandenhoeck & Ruprecht.

———. 2001. "Persian Imperial Authorization: A Summary." Pages 5–40 in *Persia and Torah: The Theory of Imperial Authorization of the Pentateuch.* Edited by James W. Watts. SymS 17. Atlanta: Society of Biblical Literature.

Fricke, Klaus Dietrich. 1991. "The Apocrypha in the Luther Bible." Pages 46–87 in *The Apocrypha in Ecumenical Perspective: The Place of the Late Writings of the Old Testament among the Biblical Writings and Their Significance in the Eastern and Western Church Traditions.* Edited by Siegfried Meurer and Paul Ellingworth. UBS.MS 6. New York: United Bible Societies.

Gallagher, Edmond. 2012a. "The Old Testament 'Apocrypha' in Jerome's Canonical Theory." *JECS* 20:213–33.

———. 2012b. *Hebrew Scripture in Patristic Biblical Theory: Canon, Language, Text.* VCSup 114. Leiden: Brill.

Goodman, Martin. 1990. "Sacred Scripture and 'Defiling the Hands.'" *JTS* 41:99–107.

———, ed. 2001. *The Apocrypha.* Oxford Bible Commentary. Oxford: Oxford University Press.

Graetz, Heinrich. 1871. "Der alttestamentliche Kanon und sein Abschluss." Pages 147–73 in *Kohelet oder der Salomonische Prediger übersetz und kritisch erläutert.* Edited by Heinrich Graetz. Leipzig: Winter.

Harl, Marguerite, and Nicholas de Lange, eds. 1983. *Origène: Philocalie, 1–20; Sur les Écritures et la Lettre à Africanus sur l'Histoire de Suzanne.* SC 302. Paris: Cerf.

Harrington, Daniel J. 1999. *Invitation to the Apocrypha.* Grand Rapids: Eerdmans.

Honigman, Sylvie. 2003. *The Septuagint and Homeric Scholarship in Alexandria: A Study in the Narrative of the Letter of Aristeas.* London: Routledge.

Horbury, William. 1994. "The Wisdom of Solomon in the Muratorian Fragment." *JTS* 45:149–59.

Kartveit, Magnar. 2009. *The Origin of the Samaritans.* VTSup 128. Leiden: Brill.

Klijn, A. F. J. 1977. "A Library of Scriptures in Jerusalem?" Pages 265–72 in *Studia Codicologica.* Edited by Kurt Treu. TUGAL 124. Berlin: Akademie.

Knoppers, Gary N. 2013. *Jews and Samaritans: The Origins and History of Their Early Relations.* Oxford: Oxford University Press.

Kooij, Arie van der. 1998. "The Canonization of Ancient Books Kept in the Temple of Jerusalem." Pages 17–40 in *Canonization and Decanonization: Papers Presented to the International Conference of the Leiden Institute for the Study of Religions (LISOR) Held at Leiden 9–10 January 1997.* Edited by Arie van der Kooij and Karel van der Toorn. Numen 82. Leiden: Brill.

———. 2003. "Canonization of Ancient Hebrew Books and Hasmonean Politics." Pages 27–33 in *The Biblical Canons.* Edited by J.-M. Auwers and H. J. de Jonge, Leuven: Leuven University Press.

Kraft, Robert. 2007. "Para-mania: Beside, before and beyond Bible Studies." *JBL* 126:5–27.

Lee, Kyong-Jin. 2011. *The Authority and Authorization of Torah in the Persian Period.* CBET 64. Leuven: Peeters.

Leiman, Sid. 1976. *The Canonization of Hebrew Scripture: The Talmudic and Midrashic Evidence.* Hamden: Archon.

———. 1981. "Inspiration and Canonicity: Reflections on the Formation of the Biblical Canon." Pages 56–63 in *Jewish and Christian Self-Definition.* Vol. 2 of *Aspects of Judaism in the Graeco-Roman Period.* Edited by E. P. Sanders, Albert I. Baumgarten, and Alan Mendelson. London: SCM.

Lewis, Jack P. 1964. "What Do We Mean by Jabneh?" *JBR* 32:125–32.

———. 2002. "Jamnia Revisited." Pages 146–62 in *The Canon Debate.* Edited by Lee Martin McDonald and James A. Sanders. Peabody, MA: Hendrickson.

Lim, Timothy H. 2001. "An Alleged Reference to the Tripartite Division of the Hebrew Bible." *RevQ* 77:23–37.

———. 2010a. "Authoritative Scriptures and the Dead Sea Scrolls." Pages 303–22 in *The Oxford Handbook of the Dead Sea Scrolls*. Edited by Timothy H. Lim and John J. Collins. Oxford: Oxford University Press.

———. 2010b. "Defilement of the Hands as a Principle Determining the Holiness of Scriptures." *JTS* 61:501–15.

———. 2013a. *The Formation of the Jewish Canon*. ABRL. New Haven: Yale University Press.

———. 2013b. "A Theory of the Majority Canon." *ExpTim* 124:365–73.

———. 2017a. "An Indicative Definition of the Canon." Pages 1–24 in *When Texts Are Canonized*. Edited by Timothy H. Lim. BJS 359. Providence, RI: Brown Judaic Studies.

———. 2017b. "The Emergence of the Samaritan Pentateuch." Pages 89–104 in *Reading the Bible in Ancient Traditions and Modern Editions: Studies in Memory of Peter W. Flint*. Edited by Andrew Perrin, Kyung Baek, and Daniel Falk. EJL 47. Atlanta: SBL Press.

———. 2017c. "Rabbinic Concept of Holy Scriptures as Sacred Objects." Pages 127–42 in *Scribal Practices and the Social Construction of Knowledge in Antiquity, Late Antiquity and Medieval Islam*. Edited by Myriam Wissa. OLA 226. Leuven: Peeters.

Lim, Timothy H., and John J. Collins. 2010. "Current Issues in Dead Sea Scrolls Research." Pages 1–18 in *The Oxford Handbook of the Dead Sea Scrolls*. Edited by Timothy H. Lim and John J. Collins. Oxford: Oxford University Press.

Magen, Yitzhak. 2007. "The Dating of the First Phase of the Samaritan Temple on Mount Gerizim in Light of the Archaeological Evidence." Pages 157–211 in *Judah and the Judeans in the Fourth Century B.C.E.* Edited by Oded Lipschits, Gary N. Knoppers, and Rainer Albertz. Winona Lake, IN: Eisenbrauns.

Mason, Steve. 2002. "Josephus and His Twenty-Two Book Canon." Pages 110–27 in *The Canon Debate*. Edited by Lee Martin McDonald and James A. Sanders. Peabody, MA: Hendrickson.

McCready, Wayne O., and Adele Reinhartz, eds. 2008. *Common Judaism: Explorations in Second-Temple Judaism*. Minneapolis: Fortress.

Mroczek, Eva. 2016. *The Literary Imagination in Jewish Antiquity*. Oxford: Oxford University Press.

Neuser, Wilhelm H. 1991. "The Reformed Churches and the Old Testament Apocrypha." Pages 88–115 in *The Apocrypha in Ecumenical Perspective: The Place of the Late Writings of the Old Testament among the Biblical Writings and Their Significance in the Eastern and Western*

Church Traditions. Edited by Siegfried Meurer and Paul Ellingworth. UBS.MS 6. New York: United Bible Societies.

Neusner, Jacob. 1981. *Judaism: The Evidence of the Mishnah*. Chicago: University of Chicago Press.

Pedley, Katharine Greenleaf. 1959. "The Library at Qumran." *RevQ* 5:21–41.

Ryle, H. E. 1892. *The Canon of the Old Testament: An Essay on the Gradual Growth and Formation of the Hebrew Canon of Scripture*. London: MacMillan.

Sanders, E. P. 1992. *Judaism: Practice and Belief 63 BCE–66 CE*. London: SCM.

Sanders, James. 1974. "Cave 11 Surprises and the Question of Canon." Pages 37–51 in *The Canon and Masorah of the Hebrew Bible: An Introductory Reader*. Edited by Sid Z. Leiman. New York: Ktav.

———. 1993. "Psalm 154 Revisited." Pages 296–306 in *Biblische Theologie und gesellschaftlicher Wandel: Für Norbert Lohfink*. Edited by Georg Braulik, Walter Gross, and Sean McEvenue. Freiburg im Breisgau: Herder.

Sparks, H. F. D., ed. 1987. *The Apocryphal Old Testament*. Oxford: Clarendon.

Stegemann, Hartmut. 1993. *Die Essener, Qumran, Johannes der Täufer und Jesus: Ein Sachbuch*. Freiburg im Breisgau: Herder.

Steinmann, Andrew E. 1999. *The Oracles of God: The Old Testament Canon*. Saint Louis: Concordia.

Stuckenbruck, Loren. 2012. "Apocrypha and Pseudepigrapha." Pages 179–203 in *Early Judaism: A Comprehensive Overview*. Edited by John J. Collins and Daniel C. Harlow. Grand Rapids: Eerdmans.

Sundberg, Albert. 1964. *The Old Testament of the Early Church*. HTS 20. Cambridge: Harvard University Press.

Talmon, Shemaryahu. 1962. "The Three Scrolls of the Law That Were Found in the Temple Court." *Text* 2:14–27.

———. 2002. "The Crystallization of the 'Canon of Hebrew Scriptures' in the Light of Biblical Scrolls from Qumran." Pages 5–20 in *The Bible as Book: The Hebrew Bible and the Judaean Desert Discoveries*. Edited by Edward D. Herbert and Emanuel Tov. London: British Library.

Tanner, Norman P., ed. 1990. *The Decrees of the Ecumenical Council*. 2 vols. London: Sheed & Ward.

———. 2001. *The Council of the Church: A Short History*. New York: Crossroad.

Ulrich, Eugene C. 2002. "The Absence of 'Sectarian Variants' in the Jewish Scriptural Scrolls Found at Qumran." Pages 179–95 in *The Bible as Book: The Hebrew Bible and the Judaean Desert Discoveries*. Edited by Edward D. Herbert and Emanuel Tov. London: The British Library.

VanderKam, James C. 1998. "Authoritative Literature in the Dead Sea Scrolls." *DSD* 5:382–402.

———. 2000. "Revealed Literature in the Second Temple Period." Pages 1–30 in *From Revelation to Canon: Studies in the Hebrew Bible and Second Temple Literature*. Edited by James C. VanderKam. JSJSup 62. Brill: Leiden.

———. 2002. "Questions of Canon Viewed through the Dead Sea Scrolls." Pages 91–109 in *The Canon Debate*. Edited by Lee Martin McDonald and James A. Sanders. Peabody, MA: Hendrickson.

Weber, Robert, ed. 1984. *Biblia Sacra: Iuxta Vulgatam Versionem; Editio Minor*. 3rd ed. Stuttgart: Deutsche Bibelgesellschaft.

Wildeboer, G. 1891. *Die Entstehung des alttestamentlichen Kanons: Historisch-kritische Untersuchung*. Gotha: Perthes.

12

Alexandrian Judaism

MAREN R. NIEHOFF

In 1986 Alexandria was not yet on the map of scholarship as a significant category for the study of early Judaism and therefore did not receive independent treatment in the first edition of *Early Judaism and Its Modern Interpreters* (Kraft and Nickelsburg 1986). Since then the situation has radically changed as a result of two factors: key-texts became available in English and diaspora Judaism has been appreciated as a vibrant form of Judaism, which had more influence on the homeland and thus on the shaping of normative Judaism than had hitherto been recognized. In 1987 F. H. Colson (Colson, Whitaker, and Marcus 1929–1987) completed his twelve-volume Greek-English edition of the works of Philo of Alexandria, the most prolific and best-preserved author among the Alexandrian Jews. In 1996 Carl Holladay reprinted his Greek-English edition of the fragments of Alexandrian-Jewish literature prior to Philo. Moreover, scholars began to recognize that the sensational discovery of the Dead Sea Scrolls in 1946–1947 cannot fully explain the emergence of rabbinic Judaism in the land of Israel. While the documents from Qumran are written in the same language as rabbinic literature, namely, Hebrew and Aramaic, they are too sectarian and too apocalyptic to account for the rabbinic movement, which developed as a distinctly urban phenomenon in the Greco-Roman cities of late antique *Palaestina* (Lapin 1999, 2000, 2012; Dohrmann 2003; for different views, Rosen-Zvi in this volume). Rabbinic sources are replete with Greek loanwords and point to a wider Hellenistic context. Catherine Hezser (2016) speaks about the "diasporization" of Judaism in the rabbinic period. Steven Fine (1996) has drawn attention to the Great Synagogue in

---

Thanks to Steve Mason for helpful comments on a draft of this essay.

Alexandria as a model for rabbinic notions of the prayer house. Yakir Paz (2012) pointed to the use of Alexandrian exegetical methods among the rabbis. Following such insights as well as the availability of Alexandrian-Jewish texts in accessible, bilingual editions, Alexandrian Judaism has emerged as an important form of Judaism, which deserves our full attention not only in its own right, but also as a significant factor for a broader understanding of classical Judaism.

Initially, we need to define the boundaries of Alexandrian Judaism. Which texts and sources belong in this category? Undoubtedly, the oeuvre of Philo of Alexandria provides the most important insight into Alexandrian Judaism. Active in the first half of the first century CE, he speaks about Alexandria as "our" city (*Legat.* 150) and describes its history during the pogrom in 38 CE. Philo is the first systematic Jewish Bible interpreter, who has left behind many volumes of detailed commentary on the books of Genesis and Exodus. He is also the first extant Jewish philosopher, who offered a synthesis of Platonic and Stoic thought with the biblical heritage, while at the same time giving new impulses to middle Platonic discourses. Throughout his work Philo refers to other Jewish voices, yet without identifying their names or directly quoting their works. Who were these other Jews and in what kind of Jewish environment did Philo develop his ideas? Fortunately, the Jewish community of Alexandria is the best-documented and probably also the most flourishing Jewish community of the Second Temple period. The Septuagint, that is, the Greek translation of the Bible, which later became canonical for Christian authors, was produced in this city and represents the first monument of Jewish-Alexandrian culture. We moreover possess the Letter of Aristeas telling the story of the Greek translation and opening a window into the cultural life of the Jewish community in Alexandria. Other fragmentary writers have been preserved in the quotations of Christian authors, especially Clement of Alexandria and Eusebius, bishop of Caesarea. We thus know of a Jewish tragedian called Ezekiel, whose play on the exodus is partly extant. We also know of Demetrius, famous for his studies of the consistency of the biblical text, often based on a calculation of the dates provided in the different stories. We furthermore get a glimpse into Aristobulus's philosophical inquiries into the Bible. These authors most likely worked in Alexandria, since they assume a distinctly urban context. A different matter is Artapanus, a historian known for his exceptionally positive appreciation of the Egyptian animal cult, who was on that account placed by scholars in the countryside. The papyri moreover testify to numerous Jewish communities outside Alexandria, who organized themselves in the form of an autonomous *politeuma* but left no texts providing insights into their cultural life (Sänger 2019). Finally, the romance Joseph and Aseneth may have emerged from Alexandria, as has been assumed for a long time. This assumption, however, was challenged by Ross Kraemer (1998), who opted for Asia Minor as its place of composition and a Christian monk as its author. While these alternatives, especially the Christian authorship of this work, are unlikely, an Alexandrian provenance is no longer certain.

Today it is relatively easy to access Alexandrian Judaism through the available reference books and commentaries on the Letter of Aristeas, the fragmentary authors and Philo (for research on the Septuagint, see separate chapter in this volume). Benjamin G. Wright published in 2015 a comprehensive commentary on the Letter of Aristeas, which provides excellent translations, explanations, and discussions of scholarly debates. White and Keddie (2018) published the Greek text of the Letter of Aristeas and other epistolary works from Hellenistic Egypt together with excellent translations, annotations, and comparative epigraphic materials. Holladay (1983–1996) remains the standard work on the fragmentary authors, which includes detailed commentaries and discussions of scholarly debates. Lester Grabbe (2008) provides a more updated survey. Adam Kamesar (2009) offers a comprehensive handbook of Philonic studies with detailed discussions of the state of scholarship. The *Studia Philonica Annual* was launched in 1989 and offers articles on specific topics as well as detailed bibliographies of Philonic research. A commentary series on each of Philo's works has begun to appear, with David Runia (2001), Pieter van der Horst (2003), Walter Wilson (2010), and Albert Geljon and Runia (2013) as pioneering volumes. Gregory Sterling (2010), Mireille Hadas-Lebel (2012), Francesca Calabi (2013), and Torrey Seland (2014) are useful introductions and surveys. Maren Niehoff (2018a) offers the first intellectual biography of Philo, which gathers all snippets of information about his person and life, while at the same time establishing the chronology of his numerous works. Niehoff traces Philo's development from Platonic Bible exegete among Alexandrian Jews to apologist of Judaism in Rome. While previous scholars had pointed to special features of individual works or series of works (Runia 1981, 1987; Sterling 1990, 1991, 2012b; Birnbaum 1996), Niehoff analyzes all of Philo's series and systematically collects the internal and external evidence for their dating, giving special attention to the impact of Philo's embassy to the emperor Gaius Caligula in Rome (38–41 CE). Philo is appreciated here as an important Jewish intellectual in the broader context of his time, who plays a significant role in the negotiation of the Greek East with Roman discourses, especially Roman philosophy. Philo is moreover shown to engage with different forms of Judaism and to anticipate rabbinic Judaism in significant ways.

My assessment of scholarship on Alexandrian Judaism will revolve around the following key-issues: (1) the diaspora as an independent form of Judaism; (2) Bible interpretation in Alexandria; (3) Jewish-Alexandrian philosophy; (4) Philo as a historian; (5) Philo on women; (6) and Alexandrian Judaism in context.

1. Greek or Hebrew? The Diaspora as an Independent Form of Judaism

From the inception of modern scholarship, when Alexandrian Judaism first drew attention, scholars debated how to conceptualize it and how to understand it in relation to the form of Judaism that would become normative, namely, Judaism in the land of Israel. Already in the nineteenth century the main approaches to this question were outlined: Alexandrian Judaism was either seen as an extension of Palestinian Judaism, as a kind of ambassador abroad, or as a very different sort of Judaism, which was either dismissed as a degradation and preparation of Christianity or praised as a more liberal type of Reform Judaism anticipating Jewish experiences in medieval Spain and modern Germany (Niehoff 1999). Crucial in this context is the question of Hebrew: did the Alexandrian Jews cultivate enough Hebrew to engage contemporary Palestinian Judaism, or did they acculturate so quickly and thoroughly that they produced the Septuagint for their own purposes, including the liturgy, and used it ever after—while forgetting Hebrew? This question is hotly debated even today and resurfaces in different contexts, especially regarding the Letter of Aristeas and Philo.

The Letter of Aristeas suggests that the initiative for the Greek translation of the Bible came from outside, namely, from the director of the famous Alexandrian library who sought to build up a comprehensive collection of scrolls and requested the Torah of the Jews in the lingua franca of the day, namely, Greek. The project quickly gained the Ptolemaic king's support and was executed under royal patronage. While the historicity of this account has been questioned by Sara Raup Johnson (2004), it has been affirmed by Sylvie Honigman (2003) and, with some qualifications, by Tessa Rajak (2009) and Wright (2015). Radical conclusions have been drawn by Nina Collins (2000), who argued that Alexandrian Jews were opposed to the Greek translation of the Bible and instead wished to cherish Hebrew culture among themselves. This conclusion, however, cannot be maintained in the face of overwhelming evidence for the use of the Septuagint by all Alexandrian Jews, beginning, as Holladay (1983–1996) has amply documented, with our earliest witnesses. In fact, even the letter itself shows no traces of access to the Hebrew layer of the Bible.

Similar questions have been raised concerning Philo of Alexandria, who devoted most of his works to the interpretation of the books of Genesis and Exodus. Is it possible, many will ask, that this leading intellectual never consulted the original text, as any serious graduate student would do nowadays? Peter Katz (1950) in a pioneering study demonstrated that Philo only quotes the Septuagint and does not take recourse to the Hebrew original. This conclusion has been confirmed by Yehoshua Amir (1988) and Gregory Sterling (2010, 2012a). Philo's commitment to Greek is understandable in the context of his hometown Alexandria, which created a monolingual Greek culture in contrast, for example, to Rome, where intellectuals were fluent not only in their mother tongue Latin, but also in Greek. Rajak (2009), however, reopened the question of Philo's exposure to Hebrew and pointed to his use of Hebrew etymologies in his Bible interpretation, which suggest to her that he must have known Hebrew. However, Amir (1988) already addressed the issue of the etymologies and suggested that they may well have been drawn from special lists in Greek, as attested elsewhere. Niehoff (2011, 133–51) has moreover shown that Philo never solves a textual problem raised by critical colleagues by recourse to the Hebrew, which would in many cases have solved the problem. Disputes over the meaning of the Jewish Bible were thus handled in Alexandria in the exclusively Greek context of the Septuagint. The Hebrew language seems to have been forgotten rather quickly after the Greek translation became available. Alexandrian Jews were proud citizens of one of the most thriving cultural centers of the Greco-Roman world and hardly looked to Jerusalem for inspiration. For details on Alexandria as a thriving cultural center, see Fraser 1972.

2. Bible Interpretation in Alexandria

Throughout the centuries during which we have evidence of the Jewish community of Alexandria the Bible constituted a backbone for negotiating and constructing identity. Numerous surveys of Jewish sources from Alexandria have related to the importance of the Bible: for example, John J. Collins (2000) with emphasis on apologetic tendencies and John Barclay (1996) and Erich Gruen (1998, 2002) with emphasis on Jewish integration and humor in the diaspora. Kamesar (1994, 1995) launched a comparative approach to Philo's exegesis by contextualizing his methods in Hellenistic scholarship. Peder Borgen (1997) mapped Philo's different types of Bible interpretation in the different series of his works and contextualized his question-and-answer style in Hellenistic culture. Honigman (2003) interpreted the Letter of Aristeas as generally reflecting the spirit of Homeric scholarship, while Niehoff (2011, 19–37) compared key-passages of the letter to the Alexandrian scholia, which preserve Homeric scholarship, and concluded that the author rejects text criticism in Homeric style and instead protects the Jewish Bible against Homeric approaches. Finally, René Bloch (2011) contextualized all the Alexandrian-Jewish authors and their Bible interpretation in the lively Hellenistic debates about Greek myth.

Niehoff (2011) provides the first systematic analysis of Jewish Bible interpretation in Alexandria, covering the earlier exegetes from Demetrius and Aristobulus onward up to Philo, the most productive and best-preserved author. Niehoff argues that the Alexandrian Jews developed a highly sophisticated form of Bible exegesis, which went well beyond anything known from the land of Israel during the Second Temple period. While interpreters in the land of Israel either paraphrased the biblical stories (e.g., the book of Jubilees) or relied on divine revelation for their interpretation (see especially the pesher literature at Qumran), Alexandrian exegetes explicitly quoted verses and confronted textual problems contained in them. Demetrius is the first Jewish interpreter known to have raised questions about apparent contradictions between biblical verses as well as the verisimilitude of certain stories. Some stories did not seem plausible from a historical or scientific point of view and thus required an explanation. Both concerns are anchored in Homeric scholarship and are applied by Demetrius to the Jewish Scriptures. While some Homeric scholars, such as Aristarchus of Samothrace, solved such textual problems by emending the text, Demetrius offered literal solutions and preserved his canonical text. The Jewish exegete Aristobulus furthermore emerges as a literal interpreter, who treats problems of verisimilitude and solves some of them by recourse to metaphor. Finally, Niehoff (2011) analyzed Philo's numerous references to other interpreters and identified in them fragments of other voices from the Jewish community of Alexandria. Rich and diverse material is recovered in this way from Philo's writings, sometimes even quotations of whole passages from treatises of his colleagues. Such colleagues were remarkably receptive to text-critical scholarship in Homeric style and scrutinized the biblical text, offering emendations and suggesting sources that Moses had used when writing the Bible. The most illuminating example is found in the beginning of Philo's treatise *De confusione linguarum*, which preserves a precious fragment of an anonymous Jewish treatise comparing the biblical story to a similar narrative in Homer's *Odyssey*.

Philo himself provides the richest and most diverse evidence of Jewish Bible exegesis in Alexandria, as most of his voluminous work is devoted to an analysis of the books of Genesis and Exodus. We must initially distinguish between his different series of works, which approach the matter of Bible interpretation from completely different perspectives. The Allegorical Commentary belongs to the early stage of Philo's career and addresses highly educated colleagues in the Jewish community of Alexandria, while the *Quaestiones et solutiones in Genesin* and *Exodum* provides a summary for a broader audience and the Exposition of the Law, with its biographies of the patriarchs, turns to a Greco-Roman audience in the context of Philo's embassy to Rome. In each of his series Philo treats the Jewish scriptures as befits his audience. In the Allegorical Commentary, which ranges from the treatises called *Legum allegoriae* 1–3 to *De somniis* (vols. 1–5 in the Loeb edition), Philo systematically quotes verses, raises problems and then solves them by recourse to additional verses from other contexts and Platonic philosophy. Under his hands the biblical stories become narratives about the soul in its flight from the world to the divine realm. As this series addresses specialized readers in antiquity, it is also today the most difficult series of Philo's works, which requires patience and careful study. Such an investment of time, however, richly pays off, as Philo introduces the reader into an extremely interesting world of Bible interpretation, which seriously engages textual problems and offers allegorical solutions in a Platonic spirit. For example, Philo is already aware of the contradiction between Gen 11:31, where Abraham is said to be taken by his father Terah from Chaldea, and Gen 12:1, where God commands Abraham to leave Chaldea and go to the land of Israel. Philo says that "nobody versed in the Scriptures" will be oblivious to the difficulty of the different journeys mentioned in the two chapters and concludes that Gen 11:31 must not be taken as a "historical account" (*Migr.* 177; *Somn.* 1.52). According to Philo, Abraham's travel should instead be appreciated as a journey of the soul, which departs from the material realm as well as astrology and arrives at the spiritual realm, which implies faith in the one God (*Migr.* 43). Philo often uses verses from Psalms to reflect on the stories of Genesis from a more personal and spiritual perspective. Apart from the Torah, this book is the most frequently quoted in Philo's work and assumes the role of a spiritual key, thus significantly anticipating Paul's epistles, which also quote the Psalms more often than the Prophets and identify them as a universal canon (Niehoff 2020).

Philo's series *Quaestiones et solutiones in Genesin and Exodum* (Loeb supplementary vols. 1 and 2) are badly preserved in the original Greek and need to be supplemented by the Armenian translation made by the early church there. This series of works is easily accessible, as it is focused on the sequence of biblical verses and provides short answers without delving into secondary texts and associative thinking. Philo seems to have prepared here a handbook for students, who wanted to hear his opinion on the Bible, without having the time or the expertise to go into any depth (Niehoff 2011, 152–68; cf. different views of Sterling 1991). Given that Philo is far more reticent here to point to serious textual problems, it is possible that this handbook was also used in the synagogues of Alexandria.

Philo's Exposition of the Law ranges from his treatise *De opificio mundi*, which is mistakenly placed in the English translation in the first volume, through the biographies of Abraham, Moses and Joseph to the Decalogue and the *De specialibus legibus 1–4* (Loeb vols. 6–8). This series adopts a strikingly different approach. Rather than quoting biblical verses and problematizing them, Philo offers a broad narrative about the creation, the Israelite forefathers and the Jewish law (Niehoff 2011, 169–85). In his view, all these aspects are connected, because Jewish law is grounded in nature and anticipated by the moral lifestyle of the forefathers, which also accords with nature. In this series Philo presupposes no knowledge of Judaism and offers an ideal image of his religion to a non-Jewish audience, interested in learning more about the Jews who were at that time subject to public debates in connection with the pogrom in Alexandria and the embassy to the Roman emperor. Most interestingly, Philo arrives as an ambassador in Rome and realizes with remarkable speed what a Roman audience would find of interest. He is thus able to appeal to the philosophical sensitivities and values of Roman readers, arguing that Judaism is a religion ideally suited to the empire. One of Philo's strategies to render Judaism appealing and modern is to tell the story of the Israelite forefathers in the form of a biography. Assuming Roman notions of biography, especially Cicero's, Philo tells significant anecdotes of his heroes to highlight their moral choices and exemplify the values of his religion (Niehoff 2018a, 109–30). Remarkably, the biblical matriarchs also play a role in Philo's biographies and are equally dressed in Roman garb (Niehoff 2018a, 130–48). They emerge as loyal wives and enterprising sisters, who assist their families and enable their mobility in the world. This type of Bible interpretation is highly significant in the middle of the first century CE and anticipates the gospels, who have also been identified as a kind of biography and Plutarch's famous gallery of Greco-Roman heroes (Hägg 2012). Niehoff (2018a) moreover shows that Philo seriously addresses Roman Stoicism, using this branch of philosophy also to explain Jewish law as a system that orients the observer toward an ethical life style in accordance with nature.

Previous scholarship on Philo as an interpreter of biblical narratives and law was often based on the assumption of inner-Jewish discussions or an inward-turned biblical discourse. Following in the earlier tradition of Samuel Belkin (1936), Naomi Cohen (1985, 1987, 1995) interpreted Philo's legal interpretations in the light of rabbinic literature, arguing that he preserves orthodox halakah, which was only later put into writing in the land of Israel. This argument often relied on circular argumentation, using later traditions to reconstruct Philo and then Philo to prove the early date of later attested rabbinic traditions. In a similar spirit, Valentin Nikiprowetzky (1977, 1983) argued for the closed exegetical universe of Philo, stressing his question-and-answer style and ubiquitous references to biblical verses, even in treatises not directly commenting on the scriptures. This approach has made the valuable contribution of highlighting the importance of Bible interpretation for an overall appreciation of Philo's work but has overlooked both the diversity of Philo's series of works and his engagement of Homeric methods. His biblical universe can thus hardly be regarded as isolated. Sarah Pearce (2013a, 2013b) has followed Nikiprowetzky in stressing the biblical dimension of Philo's discussion of the commandments. Lutz Doering (1999) and Jutta Leonhardt (2001) contextualize Philo's interpretation of legal passages in inner Jewish debates.

3. "Either Plato Imitates Philo or Philo Imitates Plato": Jewish-Alexandrian Philosophy

This famous bon mot by Jerome (*Vir. ill.* 11), the fourth-century Christian Bible scholar, reflects the predominant impression of Philo as a Platonist. Philo explicitly quotes from Plato's dialogues, especially the *Theaetetus*, and echoes his ideas on numerous occasions throughout his voluminous oeuvre. Runia (1986, 2001) established the importance of Plato for a proper evaluation of Philo as a philosopher, giving special attention to the *Timaeus*, which left visible traces in Philo's *De opificio mundi* and other treatises. Runia (1993b) also addressed the question whether Philo belongs to the form of philosophy called Middle-Platonism, a Hellenistic development of Plato's thought, which anticipates Neoplatonism. Runia expressed an ambivalent position on this issue. While acknowledging Philo's indebtedness to Plato's ideas and the Platonic tradition more generally, he stresses that he was primarily a Bible interpreter and thus not really a member of any philosophical school. His thought is said to have revolved around the problems of the biblical text and did not seek philosophical consistency.

Runia's study of Philo's philosophy complements Harry Wolfson (1947), who initiated the scholarly discussion and enthusiastically identified Philo as the founder of Western theology. Wolfson offered a comprehensive interpretation of Philo's thought, including his philosophy of Jewish law (halakah), stressing Aristotelian elements, which he compared to rabbinic perspectives. In 1947 the phenomenon of Middle-Platonism was not yet on scholars' minds and was therefore overlooked by Wolfson. It is John Dillon (1977) who first highlighted and outlined the phenomenon of Middle-Platonism as a distinct movement, which needs to be appreciated on its own. In Dillon's analysis Philo emerged as the first extant author significantly contributing to our understanding of Middle-Platonism and anticipating Plutarch. Dillon not only saw Philo as fully integrated into Hellenistic philosophy, even as a central speaker of one of its schools, but also pointed to the hybridity of his thought and especially his simultaneous integration of Stoic elements. In other words, while Runia focuses exclusively on one philosophical tradition, namely, a rather pure form of Platonism, Dillon has shown the creative mixing of traditions characteristic of the Hellenistic period and Philo's work. In his view, Philo is a prime example of experimenting with both the strictly transcendental tradition of Platonism and the immanent views of the Stoa. Along similar lines, Gretchen Reydams-Schils (1999) stressed Philo's engagement of Stoic interpretations of Plato's *Timaeus*, showing that Philo was not only a reader of the original dialogue, but also a keen participant in its tradition of interpretation. This approach resonates well with the earlier study of the French scholar Emile Bréhier (1950), who identified numerous Stoic motifs in Philo's oeuvre. The work of this scholar may not have been broadly used, both because it was written in French and because he limited himself to pointing to Stoic motifs without investigating Philo's particular use of them. The debate about the place of Stoicism in Philo's philosophy resurfaced recently, when Carlos Lévy (2009) argued that Philo uses Stoic terms in a merely formal sense, while appropriating them for Jewish theology. The excellent collection of articles gathered by Francesca Alesse (2008) provides a panoramic view of the different philosophical schools and their possible impact on Philo.

A new perspective on Philo's philosophy has been offered by Niehoff (2018a), who points to a significant development in his thought. While at the beginning of his career Philo was committed to a distinctly Alexandrian form of Platonism, he later actively engaged Roman Stoicism to offer a new interpretation of Judaism and Jewish law. Niehoff shows that the early Philo embraced a stringent form of Platonic transcendentalism, which he developed into a negative theology. His emphasis on God's purely spiritual nature leads him even to disconnect him from the creation of the world and anticipates gnostic notions. Philo moreover introduces the idea of the Logos as a mediator between God and the world. At this point in his career, Philo mentions some Stoic ideas, such as living in accordance with nature or with one's own character but translates them into Platonic ideas. Most obviously, he dislikes the immanent approach of the Stoa, which identifies God in the world and man as the seat of morality. Later, however, when spending around three years in Rome as the head of the Jewish embassy, Philo discovered the attractiveness of Stoic ideas championed there. He begins to inscribe the Jewish tradition into Stoic language, arguing most notably that Jewish law is equivalent to the law of nature. He also emphasizes the individual personality of each of the biblical heroes, using them as exemplary figures in line with Stoic exemplary ethics.

4. Philo as a Historian

While Gruen (in this volume) has already sketched the historical events that shaped the diaspora experience, it is my task in this section to assess the role Philo played in modern scholarship as a historian of the ethnic violence in Alexandria in the summer of 38 CE. Philo writes as an eyewitness, who experienced the violence in his hometown and then headed the Jewish embassy to the Roman Emperor Gaius Caligula, which sought to confirm Jewish civil rights (38–41 CE). Some of the events that he covers are also reported, with significant variance in detail, by Josephus one generation later. One of the burning questions of modern scholarship is whether Philo is necessarily more reliable thanks to his participation in the events.

The best starting points to study Philo's involvement in the embassy and his subsequent historiography are still Mary Smallwood (1961), Pieter W. van der Horst (2003), and Andrew Harker (2008). While Smallwood offers the text of Philo's *Legatio ad Gaium* as well as a detailed historical commentary, Harker starts from the Egyptian martyr literature, which is also based on the experience of embassies to the emperor. Useful comparisons between Philo and Josephus as historians of the ethnic violence in Alexandria can be found in Per Bilde (1978) and Daniel Schwartz (1990). Bilde argues for the greater reliability of Josephus, as he uses sources deriving directly from Agrippa I, which enable him to provide a more realistic picture than Philo, who is rather eager to convey his theological image of an evil Roman emperor chastised by divine providence. Schwartz, on the other hand, generally accepts Philo's image of the crisis in Alexandria, including the highly negative image of Gaius Caligula.

Niehoff (2018a, 25–46) offers a new perspective on Philo as a historical writer, comparing his enigmatic style to that of the Second Sophistic (a movement of Greek intellectuals in the Roman Empire reviving Greek culture). Shifting the focus from the question of sources to the historian himself, Niehoff shows that Philo is consciously evasive in his style and introduces a playful dimension. He fashions himself as a pious leader in contrast to King Agrippa I, a highly successful and far more secular diplomat. Philo's negative image of Gaius Caligula is moreover investigated in the context of Claudius, his successor, under whom the *Legatio ad Gaium* was written. Seeing that the new emperor styled himself as a positive mirror image of his assassinated predecessor, Philo's rhetoric resonates well with that of Seneca and other intellectuals, who were all eager to disconnect themselves from Gaius and inscribe themselves into the new imperial language.

5. Philo on Women

Dorothy Sly (1990) and Daniel Boyarin (1993) raised poignant gender issues regarding Philo and initiated lively debates about his role in the emergence of Western misogyny. Both scholars concluded that Philo combined Greek stereotypes about women with a forceful appeal to biblical authority and thus created a highly influential form of misogyny. With increasing theoretical sophistication of feminist scholarship (on which see Françoise Mirguet, §4 in this volume), more nuanced views have been offered. Most recently, Niehoff (2017) suggested that Philo's views on women were not stable and do not amount to one essential position that can be judged either as misogynist or not. Instead, he changed his views with the changing of his circumstances and indicates the cultural embeddedness of discourses about women in antiquity. While the Allegorical Commentary at the beginning of his career devalues women as symbols of the material world, they appear in the Exposition of the Law as Roman matrons active in their partnerships and families and promoting pristine Jewish values.

Moreover, scholarship has generally moved away from an exclusive focus on Philo's image of biblical women and looked at other sites in his work where gender issues come into the foreground. Philo's treatise on the Therapeutae, a group of Jewish philosophers living as a philosophical community near Alexandria, has drawn special attention, because this group included educated women. As Philo is our only witness to this group, scholars have discussed to what extent his account *De vita contemplativa* is reliable, given that we cannot check it against other accounts. One of the ways of investigating this issue is to compare his description of the women among the Therapeutae with his views expressed in other treatises, where he clearly speaks for himself. Joan Taylor (2003, 2017) has argued most outspokenly for the general reliability of Philo's account and his positive attitude toward the Jewish women in the group, who were highly educated and participated in traditional Jewish Bible interpretation. Using comparative material about non-Jewish women philosophers from the surrounding Hellenistic culture, Taylor suggests that the image of the Jewish women fits the spirit of the time. Reading between the lines of Philo's account, she further argues that the women were even entitled to take their turn in presiding over the Bible study and lead the group of philosophers. Ross Kraemer (1989), by contrast, highlights Philo's resistance to gender equality and argues that his image of the women among the Therapeutae is not true in a strictly historical sense. In her view, Philo's account implies that the women had to compromise their femininity, including their reproduction, in order to lead a monastic philosophical life. Either way, Philo's treatise on the Therapeutae provides us with our earliest report about Jewish women philosophers, engaged in the quintessentially Jewish activity of Bible interpretation.

6. Work to Be Done: Alexandrian Judaism in Context

Alexandrian Judaism, especially Philo, deserves to be appreciated in the broader context of the Roman Empire. Moving beyond traditional reception history, which focuses on the transmission of Philo's works and their quotation by subsequent authors (Runia 1993a, 2016; Van den Hoek 2000; Sterling 1999, 2015, 2016; Cover forthcoming), we note that the development of Alexandrian Judaism throws important light on wider tendencies in the Roman Empire. Alexandrian Judaism deserves to be appreciated in these wider discourses as a paradigmatic example of hybrid identity negotiating different strands of tradition as well as the increasing intellectual impact of Rome.

Initially, Philo can be fruitfully studied in view of another Jewish author with a distinctly Roman orientation, namely, Josephus. While earlier studies focused on his sources and endeavored to reconstruct the events "as they really happened," Josephus has recently emerged as a first-century author writing in Rome for Roman audiences. The implications of his Roman citizenship, his networks in the capital and familiarity with Roman discourses as well as the Roman traits of his Judaism have been studied (Goodman 1994; Mason 2001, 2005, 2016a, 2016b; Barclay 2007; den Hollander 2014; and Mason in this volume). This paradigm shift in scholarship on Josephus is highly significant for further investigations into Philo, because his situation as a Greek-speaking Jew coming from Alexandria to Rome a generation earlier is in many respects strikingly similar. Following Sterling (2013) and Niehoff (2016, 2018b), further comparative studies on Philo and Josephus promise significant insights.

Rabbinic sources from late antique *Palaestina* also deserve to be analyzed in view of Alexandrian Judaism, because both Jewish communities were intimately connected to Mediterranean harbors and embedded in urban, Greco-Roman cultures (on Caesarea see Patrich 2011; Isaac 2011, 2017). Wilhelm Bacher (1891) and Dominique Barthélemy (1967) already pointed to the possibility that Philo was known in Caesarea not only by Origen, who brought his works from Alexandria to Caesarea and openly acknowledged him, but also by Rabbi Hoshaya, his contemporary. The implications of this insight are explored by Niehoff (2018c) and deserve further in-depth studies. Moreover, Philo's Roman perspective on Jewish law throws important new light on the rabbis' negotiation of Roman law following Caracalla's general grant of Roman citizenship in 212 CE, which has been explored by Boaz Cohen (1966), Hezser (2003), Natalie Dohrmann (2003, 2008, 2013), Yair Furstenberg (2018, 2019) and Niehoff (2019). More scholarship on Philo and the rabbis can further illuminate these aspects, which we are only beginning to understand.

Philo's significance for the study of early Christianity ought to be investigated beyond the question of direct quotations from his work. Philo is highly relevant to Christian authors writing in Greek on the Septuagint, engaging similar philosophical ideas and often acutely aware of Roman discourses, seeking to integrate their religion into the language of empire. Among the gospel writers Luke has been identified as the author with the most visible Roman orientation in his portraits of both Jesus and Paul (Harrill 2011, 2012). Moreover, Paul's letters and the early apologists have been analyzed with a view to the realia and discursive structures in the Roman Empire (Schott 2007; Watson 2007; Nasrallah 2010; Holloway 2017). Further comparative studies will illuminate both Alexandrian Judaism and early Christianity.

Finally, the study of the Greek Renaissance under the Roman Empire, called "the Second Sophistic" since Philostratus's influential work on these authors at the beginning of the third century CE, has recently been studied from new perspectives (Swain 1996; Schmitz 1997; Whitmarsh 2001, 2010, 2013; König, Uden, and Langlands 2020). It has become clear that Greek culture was entwined with Roman structures of power and discourses. Writers such as Plutarch and Lucian cannot be properly understood without addressing the question of their involvement in Roman discourses and their impact on their construction of Greek identity. Greek authors of this period were characterized by fragmented identities and diverse perspectives. Further comparative studies between Philo and the Second Sophistic promise to uncover additional aspects of both phenomena.

Bibliography

Alesse, Francesca, ed. 2008. *Philo of Alexandria and Post-Aristotelian Philosophy*. Studies in Philo of Alexandria 5. Leiden: Brill.

Amir, Yehoshua. 1988. "Authority and Interpretation of Scripture in the Writings of Philo." Pages 421–53 in *Mikra: Text, Translation, Reading and Interpretation of the Hebrew Bible in Ancient Judaism and Early Christianity*. Edited by M. J. Mulder. CRINT 2.2. Assen: Van Gorcum; Minneapolis: Fortress.

Bacher, Wilhelm. 1891. "The Church Father Origen and Rabbi Hoshaya." *JQR* 3:357–60.

Barclay, John M. G. 1996. *Jews in the Mediterranean Diaspora from Alexander to Trajan (323 BCE–117 CE)*. Edinburgh: T&T Clark.

———. 2007. *Flavius Josephus: Against Apion; Translation and Commentary*. Leiden: Brill.
Barthélemy, Dominique. 1967. "Est-ce Hoshaya Rabba qui censura le 'Commentaire Allégorique'? A partir des retouches faites aux citations bibliques, étude sur la tradition textuelle du Commentaire Allégorique de Philon." Pages 45–78 in *Philon d'Alexandrie: Lyon 11–15 Septembre 1966*. Paris: Centre National de la Recherche Scientifique.
Belkin, Samuel. 1936. *The Alexandria Halakah in Apologetic Literature of the First Century C.E.* Philadelphia: Jewish Publication Society.
Bilde, Per. 1978. "The Roman Emperor Gaius' Attempt to Erect His Statue in the Temple of Jerusalem." *ST* 32:67–93.
Birnbaum, Ellen. 1996. *The Place of Judaism in Philo's Thought*. BJS 290. Atlanta: Scholars Press.
Bloch, René S. 2011. *Moses und der Mythos: Die Auseinandersetzung mit der griechischen Mythologie bei den jüdisch-hellenistischen Autoren*. JSJSup 145. Leiden: Brill.
Borgen, Peder. 1997. *Philo of Alexandria: An Exegete of His Time*. NovTSup 86. Leiden: Brill.
Boyarin, Daniel. 1993. *Carnal Israel: Reading Sex in Talmudic Culture*. New Historicism 25. Berkeley: University of California Press.
Bréhier, Emile 1950. *Les idées philosophiques et religieuses de Philon d'Alexandrie*. 3rd ed. Études de philosophie médiévale 8. Paris: Vrin.
Calabi, Francesca. 2013. *Filone di Alessandria*. Pensatori 32. Rome: Carocci.
Cohen, Boaz. 1966. *Jewish and Roman Law: A Comparative Study*. 2 vols. New York: Jewish Theological Seminary.
Cohen, Naomi. 1985. "Agraphos Nomos in Philo's Writings: A New Examination" [Hebrew]. *Da'at* 15:5–20.
———. 1987. "The Jewish Dimension of Philo's Judaism—An Elucidation of *de Spec. Leg.* IV 132–150." *JJS* 38:165–86.
———. 1995. *Philo Judaeus: His Universe of Discourse*. BEATAJ 24. Frankfurt: Lang.
Collins, John J. 2000. *Between Athens and Jerusalem: Jewish Identity in the Hellenistic Diaspora*. Grand Rapids: Eerdmans.
Collins, Nina L. 2000. *The Library of Alexandria and the Bible in Greek*. VTSup 82. Leiden: Brill.
Colson, F. H., G. H. Whitaker, and Ralph Marcus. 1929–1987. *Philo of Alexandria*. LCL. Cambridge: Harvard University Press.
Cover, Michael B. Forthcoming. "The Road Less Travelled by: Mapping Philonic Influence on Origen's Writings."

Dillon, John. 1977. *The Middle Platonists: A Study of Platonism, 80 B.C. to A.D. 220.* London: Duckworth.

Doering, Lutz. 1999. *Schabbat: Sabbathalacha und -praxis im antiken Judentum und Urchristentum.* TSAJ 78. Tübingen: Mohr Siebeck.

Dohrmann, Natalie B. 2003. "The *Boundaries* of the Law and the Problem of Jurisdiction in Early Palestinian Midrash." Pages 83–103 in *Rabbinic Law in Its Roman and Near Eastern Context.* Edited by Catherine Hezser. TSAJ 97. Tübingen: Mohr Siebeck.

———. 2008. "Manumission and Transformation in Jewish and Roman Law." Pages 51–65 in *Biblical Interpretation and Cultural Exchange: Comparative Exegesis in Context.* Edited by Natalie B. Dohrmann and David Stern. Jewish Culture and Contexts. Philadelphia: University of Pennsylvania Press.

———. 2013. "Law and Imperial Idioms: Rabbinic Legalism in a Roman World." Pages 63–78 in *Jews, Christians and the Roman Empire: The Poetics of Power in Late Antiquity.* Edited by Natalie B. Dohrmann and Annette Yoshiko Reed. Philadelphia: University of Pennsylvania Press.

Fine, Steven. 1996. "From Meeting House to Sacred Realm: Holiness and the Ancient Synagogue." Pages 21–47 in *Sacred Realm: The Emergence of the Synagogue in the Ancient World.* Edited by Steven Fine. Oxford: Oxford University Press.

Fraser, M. P. 1972. *Ptolemaic Alexandria.* 3 vols. Oxford: Clarendon.

Furstenberg, Yair. 2018. "From Competition to Integration: The Laws of the Nations in Rabbinic Literature within Its Roman Context" [Hebrew]. *Dine Israel* 32:3–40.

———. 2019. "The Rabbis and the Roman Citizenship Model: The Case of the Samaritans." Pages 181–216 in *In the Crucible of Empire: The Impact of Roman Citizenship upon Greeks, Jews and Christians.* Edited by Katell Berthelot and Jonathan Price. Leuven: Peeters.

Geljon, Albert C., and David T. Runia. 2013. *Philo of Alexandria: On Cultivation.* Philo of Alexandria Commentary 4. Leiden: Brill.

Goodman, Martin. 1994. "Josephus as Roman Citizen." Pages 329–38 in *Josephus and the History of the Greco-Roman Period: Essays in Memory of Morton Smith.* Edited by Fausto Parente and Joseph Sievers. StPB 41. Leiden: Brill.

Grabbe, Lester L. 2008. *The Coming of the Greeks: The Early Hellenistic Period (335–175 BCE).* Vol. 2 of *A History of the Jews and Judaism in the Second Temple Period.* London: T&T Clark.

Gruen, Erich S. 1998. *Heritage and Hellenism: The Reinvention of Jewish Tradition*. HCS 30. Berkeley: University of California Press.

———. 2002. *Diaspora: Jews amidst Greeks and Romans*. Cambridge: Harvard University Press.

Hadas-Lebel, Mireille. 2012. *Philo of Alexandria: A Thinker in the Jewish Diaspora*. Translated by Robin Frechet. Studies in Philo of Alexandria 7. Leiden: Brill.

Hägg, Thomas. 2012. *The Art of Biography in Antiquity*. Cambridge: Cambridge University Press.

Harker, Andrew. 2008. *Loyalty and Dissidence in Roman Egypt: The Case of the Acta Alexandrinorum*. New York: Cambridge University Press.

Harrill, Albert J. 2011. "Paul and Empire: Studying Roman Identity after the Cultural Turn." *Early Christianity* 2:281–311.

———. 2012. *Paul the Apostle: His Life and Legacy in Their Roman Context*. Cambridge: Cambridge University Press.

Hezser, Catherine, ed. 2003. *Rabbinic Law in Its Roman and Near Eastern Context*. TSAJ 97. Tübingen: Mohr Siebeck.

———. 2016. "Mobility, Flexibility and the Diasporization of Palestinian Judaism." Pages 197–216 in *"Let the Wise Listen and Add to Their Learning" (Prov. 1.5): Festschrift for Günther Stemberger on the Occasion of His Seventy-Fifth Birthday*. Edited by Constanza Cordoni and Gerhard Langer. SJ 90. Berlin: de Gruyter.

Hoek, Annewies van den. 2000. "Philo and Origen: A Descriptive Catalogue of Their Relationship." *SPhiloA* 12:44–121.

Holladay, Carl R. 1983–1996. *Fragments from the Hellenistic Jewish Authors*. SBLTT 20, 30, 39, 40. 4 vols. Chico, CA: Scholars Press.

Hollander, William den. 2014. *Josephus, the Emperors, and the City of Rome: From Hostage to Historian*. AGJU 86. Leiden: Brill.

Holloway, Paul A. 2017. *Philippians*. Hermeneia. Minneapolis: Fortress.

Honigman, Sylvie. 2003. *The Septuagint and Homeric Scholarship in Alexandria: A Study in the Narrative of the Letter of Aristeas*. London: Routledge.

Horst, Pieter W van der. 2003. *Philo of Alexandria: Philo's Flaccus; The First Pogrom; Introduction, Translation, and Commentary*. Philo of Alexandria Commentary 2. Leiden: Brill.

Isaac, Benjamin. 2011. "Caesarea." *CIIP* 1:17–36.

———. 2017. "Latin Cities of the Roman Near East." Pages 257–84 in *Empire and Ideology in the Greco-Roman World: Selected Papers*. Edited by Benjamin Isaac. Cambridge: Cambridge University Press.

Kamesar, Adam. 1994. "Philo, Grammatike, and the Narrative Aggada." Pages 216–42 in *Pursuing the Text: Studies in Honor of Ben Zion Wacholder on the Occasion of His Seventieth Birthday*. Edited by John C. Reeves and John Kampen. JSOTSup 184. Sheffield: Sheffield Academic.

———. 1995. "Philo and the Literary Quality of the Bible: A Theoretical Aspect of the Problem." *JJS* 46:55–68.

———, ed. 2009. *The Cambridge Companion to Philo*. Cambridge Companions to Philosophy. Cambridge: Cambridge University Press.

Katz, Peter. 1950. *Philo's Bible: The Aberrant Text of Bible Quotations in Some Philonic Writings and Its Place in the Textual History of the Greek Bible*. Cambridge: Cambridge University Press.

König, Alice, James Uden, and Rebecca Langlands, eds. 2020. *Literature and Culture in the Roman Empire, 96–235 CE: Cross-Cultural Interactions*. Cambridge: Cambridge University Press.

Kraemer, Ross S. 1989. "Monastic Jewish Women in Greco-Roman Egypt: Philo Judaeus on the Therapeutrides." *Signs* 14:342–70.

———. 1998. *When Aseneth Met Joseph: A Late Antique Tale of the Biblical Patriarch and His Egyptian Wife, Reconsidered*. Oxford: Oxford University Press.

Kraft, Robert A., and George W. E. Nickelsburg, eds. 1986. *Early Judaism and Its Modern Interpreters*. BMI 2. Philadelphia: Fortress Press; Atlanta: Scholars Press.

Lapin, Hayim. 1999. "Rabbis and Cities in Later Roman Palestine." *JJS* 50:187–207.

———. 2000. "Rabbis and Cities: Some Aspects of the Rabbinic Movement in Its Greco-Roman Environment." Pages 51–80 in vol. 2 of *The Talmud Yerushalmi and Greco-Roman Culture*. Edited by Peter Schäfer and Catherine Hezser. TSAJ 79. 2 vols. Tübingen: Mohr Siebeck.

———. 2012. *The Rabbis as Romans: The Rabbinic Movement in Palestine, 100–400*. Oxford: Oxford University Press.

Leonhardt, Jutta. 2001. *Jewish Worship in Philo of Alexandria*. TSAJ 84. Tübingen: Mohr Siebeck.

Lévy, Carlos. 2009. "Philo's Ethics." Pages 146–72 in *The Cambridge Companion to Philo*. Edited by Adam Kamesar. Cambridge Companions to Philosophy. Cambridge: Cambridge University Press.

Mason, Steve. 2001. *Flavius Josephus: Life of Josephus; Translation and Commentary*. Leiden: Brill.

———. 2005. "Of Audience and Meaning: Reading Josephus' *Bellum Iudaicum* in the Context of a Flavian Audience." Pages 70–100 in *Josephus and Jewish History in Flavian Rome and Beyond*. Edited by Joseph Sievers and Gaia Lembi. JSJSup 104. Leiden: Brill.

———. 2016a. "Josephus as a Roman Historian." Pages 89–107 in *A Companion to Josephus*. Edited by Honora Howell Chapman and Zuleika Rodgers. BCAW. Oxford: Wiley Blackwell.

———. 2016b. "Josephus' Autobiography." Pages 59–74 in *A Companion to Josephus*. Edited by Honora Howell Chapman and Zuleika Rodgers. BCAW. Oxford: Wiley Blackwell.

Nasrallah, Laura S. 2010. *Christian Responses to Roman Art and Architecture: The Second-Century Church amid the Spaces of Empire*. Cambridge: Cambridge University Press.

Niehoff, Maren R. 1999. "Alexandrian Judaism in 19th Century *Wissenschaft des Judentums*: Between Modernity and Christianity." Pages 9–28 in *Jüdische Geschichte in hellenistisch-römischer Zeit: Wege der Forschung; vom alten zum neuen Schürer*. Edited by Aharon Oppenheimer. Schriften des Historischen Kollegs, Kolloquien 44. Munich: Oldenburg.

———. 2011. *Jewish Exegesis and Homeric Scholarship in Alexandria*. Cambridge: Cambridge University Press.

———. 2016. "Josephus and Philo in Rome." Pages 135–46 in *A Companion to Josephus*. Edited by Honora Howell Chapman and Zuleika Rodgers. BCAW. Oxford: Wiley Blackwell.

———. 2017. "Between Social Context and Personal Ideology: Philo's Changing Views of Women." Pages 187–203 in *Early Jewish Writings*. Edited by Eileen Schuller and Marie-Theres Wacker. BW 3.1. Atlanta: SBL Press.

———. 2018a. *Philo of Alexandria: An Intellectual Biography*. New Haven: Yale University Press.

———. 2018b. "Philo and Josephus Fashion Themselves as Religious Authors in Rome." Pages 83–103 in *Autoren in religiösen literarischen Texten der späthellenistischen und frühkaiserzeitlichen Welt: Zwölf Fallstudien*. Edited by Eve-Marie Becker and Jörg Rüpke. Culture, Religion, and Politics in the Greco-Roman World 3. Tübingen: Mohr Siebeck.

———. 2018c. "Colonizing and Decolonizing the Creation: A Dispute between Rabbi Hoshaya and Origen." Pages 113–29 in *Scriptures, Sacred Traditions, and Strategies of Religious Subversion: Studies in Discourse with the Work of Guy G. Stroumsa*. Edited by Moshe Blidstein,

Serge Ruger, and Daniel Stökl-Ben Ezra. STAC 112. Tübingen: Mohr Siebeck.

———. 2019. "A Hybrid Self: Rabbi Abbahu in Legal Debates in Caesarea." Pages 293–329 in *Self, Self-Fashioning and Individuality in Late Antiquity*. Edited by Maren R. Niehoff and Joshua Levinson. Culture, Religion, and Politics in the Greco-Roman World 4. Tübingen: Mohr Siebeck.

———. 2020. "Philo and Paul on the Psalms: Towards a Spiritual Notion of Scripture". *NovT* 62:392–415.

Nikiprowetzky, Valentin. 1977. *Le Commentaire de L'Ecriture chez Philon d'Alexandrie: Son caractère et sa portée; observations philologiques*. ALGHJ 11. Leiden: Brill.

———. 1983. "L'exégèse de Philon d'Alexandrie dans le De Gigantibus et le Quod Deus." Pages 5–75 in *Two Treatises of Philo of Alexandria*. Edited by David Winston and John M. Dillon. BJS 25. Chico, CA: Scholars Press.

Patrich, Joseph. 2011. *Studies in the Archaeology and History of Caesarea Maritima: Caput Judaeae, Metropolis Palaestinae*. AJEC 77. Leiden: Brill.

Paz, Yakir. 2012. "Re-scripturizing Traditions: Designating Dependence in Rabbinic Halakhic Midrashim and Homeric Scholarship." Pages 269–98 in *Homer and the Bible in the Eyes of Ancient Interpreters*. Edited by Maren R. Niehoff. JSRC 16. Leiden: Brill.

Pearce, Sarah J. 2013a. "Philo of Alexandria on the Second Commandment." Pages 49–76 in *The Image and Its Prohibition in Jewish Antiquity*. Edited by Sarah Pearce. JJSSup 2. Oxford: Journal of Jewish Studies.

———. 2013b. "Philo, On the Decalogue." Pages 989–1031 in *Outside the Bible: Ancient Jewish Writings Related to Scripture*. Edited by Louis H. Feldman, James L. Kugel, and Lawrence H. Schiffman. 3 vols. Philadelphia: Jewish Publication Society; Lincoln: University of Nebraska Press.

Rajak, Tessa. 2009. *Translation and Survival: The Greek Bible of the Ancient Jewish Diaspora*. Oxford: Oxford University Press.

Raup Johnson, Sara. 2004. *Historical Fictions and Hellenistic Jewish Identity: Third Maccabees in Its Cultural Context*. HCS 43. Berkeley: University of California Press.

Reydams-Schils, Gretchen. 1999. *Demiurge and Providence: Stoic and Platonist Readings of Plato's Timaeus*. Monothéismes et philosophie. Turnhout: Brepols.

Runia, David T. 1981. "Philo's *De Aeternitate Mundi*: The Problem of Interpretation." *VC* 3:105–51.

———. 1986. *Philo of Alexandria and the Timaeus of Plato*. Philosophia antiqua 44. Leiden: Brill.

———. 1987. "Further Observations on the Structure of Philo's Allegorical Treatises." *VC* 41:105–38.

———. 1993a. *Philo in Early Christian Literature: A Survey*. CRINT 3.3. Assen: Van Gorcum; Minneapolis: Fortress.

———. 1993b. "Was Philo a Middle Platonist? A Difficult Question Revisited." *SPhiloA* 5:124–33.

———. 2001. *Philo of Alexandria: On the Creation of the Cosmos according to Moses. Introduction, Translation and Commentary*. Philo of Alexandria Commentary 1. Leiden: Brill.

———. 2016. "Philo in Byzantium." *VC* 70:259–81.

Sänger, Patrick. 2019. *Die Ptolemäische Organisationsform politeuma: Ein Herrschaftsinstrument zugunsten jüdischer und anderer hellenischer Gemeinschaften*. TSAJ 178. Tübingen: Mohr Siebeck.

Schmitz, Thomas. 1997. *Bildung und Macht: Zur sozialen und politischen Funktion der zweiten Sophistik in der griechischen Welt der Kaiserzeit*. Zetemata 97. Munich: Beck.

Schott, Jeremy M. 2008. *Christianity, Empire, and the Making of Religion in Late Antiquity*. Divinations. Philadelphia: University of Pennsylvania Press.

Schwartz, Daniel R. 1990. *Agrippa I: The Last King of Judaea*. TSAJ 23. Tübingen: Mohr Siebeck.

Seland, Torrey. 2014. *Reading Philo: A Handbook to Philo of Alexandria*. Grand Rapids: Eerdmans.

Sly, Dorothy. 1990. *Philo's Perception of Women*. BJS 209. Atlanta: Scholars Press.

Smallwood, E. Mary. 1961. *Philonis Alexandrini Legatio Ad Gaium*. Leiden: Brill.

Sterling, Gregory. 1990. "Philo and the Logic of Apologetics: An Analysis of the Hypothetica." Pages 412–30 in *Society of Biblical Literature Seminar Papers 1990*. SBLSP 29. Atlanta: Society of Biblical Literature.

———. 1991. "Philo's Quaestiones: Prolegomena or Afterthought?" Pages 99–123 in *Both Literal and Allegorical: Studies in Philo of Alexandria's "Questions and Answers on Genesis and Exodus."* Edited by David M. Hay. BJS 232. Atlanta: Scholars Press.

———. 1999. "'The School of Sacred Laws': The Social Setting Philo's Treatises." *VC* 53:148–64.

———. 2010. "Philo." Pages 1063–70 in *The Eerdmans Dictionary of Early Judaism*. Edited by John J. Collins and Daniel C. Harlow. Grand Rapids: Eerdmans.

———. 2012a. "The Interpreter of Moses: Philo of Alexandria and the Biblical Text." Pages 415–35 in *A Companion to Biblical Interpretation in Early Judaism*. Edited by Matthias Henze. Grand Rapids: Eerdmans.

———. 2012b. "'Prolific in Expression and Broad in Thought': Internal References to Philo's *Allegorical Commentary* and *Exposition of the Law*." *Euphrosyne* 40:55–76.

———. 2013. "'A Man of Highest Repute': Did Josephus Know the Writings of Philo?" *SPhiloA* 25:101–13.

———. 2015. "The Theft of Philosophy: Philo of Alexandria and Numenius of Apamea." *SPhiloA* 27:71–85.

———. 2016. "Philo's School: The Social Setting of Ancient Commentaries." Pages 123–42 *Sophisten in Hellenismus und Kaiserzeit Orte, Methoden und Personen der Bildungsvermittlung*. Edited by Beatrice Wyss, Rainer Hirsch-Luipold, and Solmeng-Jonas Hirschi. STAC 101. Tübingen: Mohr Siebeck.

Swain, Simon 1996. *Hellenism and Empire: Language, Classicism, and Power in the Greek World, AD 50–250*. Oxford: Clarendon.

Taylor, Joan E. 2003. *Jewish Women Philosophers of First-Century Alexandria: Philo's "Therapeutae" Reconsidered*. Oxford: Oxford University Press.

———. 2017. "Real Women and Literary Airbrushing: The Women 'Therapeutae' of Philo's *De Vita Contemplativa* and the Identity of the Group." Pages 205–24 in *Early Jewish Writings*. Edited by Eileen Schuller and Marie-Theres Wacker. BW 3.1. Atlanta: SBL Press.

Watson, Francis. 2007. *Paul, Judaism, and the Gentiles*. Rev. ed. Grand Rapids: Eerdmans.

White, L. Michael, and G. Anthony Keddie. 2018. *Jewish Fictional Letters from Hellenistic Egypt: The Epistle of Aristeas and Related Literature*. WGRW 37. Atlanta: SBL Press.

Whitmarsh, Tim. 2001. *Greek Literature and the Roman Empire: The Politics of Imitation*. Oxford: Oxford University Press.

———, ed. 2010. *Local Knowledge and Microidentities in the Imperial Greek World*. Cambridge: Cambridge University Press.

———. 2013. *Beyond the Second Sophistic: Adventures in Greek Postclassicism*. Berkeley: University of California Press.
Wilson, Walter. 2010. *Philo of Alexandria: On the Virtues*. Philo of Alexandria Commentary 3. Leiden: Brill.
Wolfson, Harry A. 1947. *Philo: Foundations of Religious Philosophy in Judaism, Christianity, and Islam*. Cambridge: Harvard University Press.
Wright, Benjamin G., III. 2015. *The Letter of Aristeas to Philocrates or On the Translation of the Law of the Jews*. CEJL 8. Berlin: de Gruyter.

13

THINKING ABOUT SCRIPTURE
IN SECOND TEMPLE TIMES

JAMES KUGEL

Perhaps the most striking thing about scripture in the postexilic period and thereafter is the one most easily lost sight of. This was a time when, as never previously, ancient Israel's sacred writings were on peoples' minds. In biblical texts dated to this period, earlier scripture is frequently quoted and paraphrased, sometimes invoked to argue for a revolutionary new order or, on the contrary, cited to argue against such a change, indeed, to urge a return to the idealized form of life of an earlier day. Prophets still walked the streets of Jerusalem, but in the eyes of some, scripture itself was fast eclipsing the role of all such soothsayers and visionaries, as if God now spoke more reliably from the crumbling scrolls of ancient parchment than from the mouths of living human beings. Psalm 119, one of the latest psalms in our Bible and by far the longest, is a litany-like celebration of scripture, with verse after verse announcing the psalmist's devotion to God's "statutes," "laws," and "ordinances." At one point the psalmist exclaims: "How I love your teachings, I speak about them *all day long*" (Ps 119:97).[1] The Qumran community, proprietors of the Dead Sea Scrolls, had a similar outlook on scripture's role in daily life: "In a place where the Ten are [assembled], let there never be lacking someone expounding the Torah continuously, one man to another, *day and night* in turns. And let the [Council of the] Many be sure, for a third of *every night in the year*, to read from the Book and expound the law and pray together" (1QS VI, 6–8). People had always prayed to God, but alongside the unadorned "Help me!" there now appeared a new form of request:

---

1. Unless otherwise noted, all translations are mine.

"Help me in the same way that you helped So-and-so (a famous biblical figure)" (Newman 1999).

How did scripture come to be so important, indeed, the object of such devotion? Elsewhere in the ancient Near East, worship of the gods was still largely or exclusively centered on a temple or temples, as it had been for millennia. Inside the temple, sacrifices were regularly offered to assure the gods' favor and to hold the people's enemies at bay—an act that one scholar has aptly called the "care and feeding of the gods"? (Oppenheim 1977, 183). Israel, too, still had its temples, but at some point in the Second Temple period, in addition to sacrificing animals there came new forms of piety in which the sacred writings from Israel's past had a prominent part. From our modern perspective, we may lose sight of the utter strangeness of scripture's new role. But surely it was odd to suppose that reciting ancient *texts* could ever be considered a form of worship, as if they had anything in common with the offering of freshly killed animals sizzling on a sacred altar. How did this come about?

The answer begins well before the time of Ps 119's composition or the writings of the Dead Sea Scrolls community; it leads back to the period immediately following the collapse of the Neo-Babylonian Empire, when, according to the biblical account (Ezra 1:2–4), the Persian emperor Cyrus issued a decree allowing the Judeans who had been exiled to Babylon to return to their ancestral homeland.[2] Many historians have expressed doubts about aspects of the biblical picture (e.g., Becking 2006), suggesting that the account of the edict of Cyrus as well as the overall picture of Ezra 1–6 are of little historical value and that the actual numbers of returning Judeans as presented in Ezra 2 and Neh 7 are greatly exaggerated. Nevertheless, archaeological and other evidence support the claim that a steady trickle of returning immigrants began early in the Persian period (Lipschits 2003). These returnees constituted an immigrant elite that probably was at first separate from, and outnumbered by, the rural people of the land, those who had *not* been exiled. But it was the returnees who apparently had the support of the Persian hierarchy and who ultimately established the Judean temple-state (Japhet 2006; Horsley 2007, 19–23).

---

2. For simplicity's sake, I refer to that homeland as *Judea* throughout, though in different periods it was known in Hebrew as *Yehudah* or Aramaic *Yehud*, for a time as part of the Persian satrapy of Beyond the River (*Eber Nari* or *Abar Nahara*; cf. Ezra 4:11, Neh 2:9, etc.), later to become Greek *Ioudaia* and Latin *Iudaea*.

It seems likely that those returning to Judea were for the most part a self-selected group, and the very fact of their choosing to go back to their homeland may thus tell us something about their thinking. They were returning to a reality that most of them had never experienced firsthand but one whose memory had been preserved during their exile by word of mouth—and by scripture. Some, perhaps many, wished to return to Judea to reassume ownership of their ancestral property, but along with such material concerns came the desire to return to the way of life (real or imagined) that had been theirs before the Babylonian conquest. Such texts as the new covenant passage in Jer 31:31–34 and the public reading of the torah in Neh 8:1–12 are evidence, albeit idealized, of a postexilic desire to "do things right" the second time, a desire that came to focus on "the laws of your God" (Ezra 7:25–26), now sometimes referred to as "the *torah* ["teaching"] of God/the LORD" or "the *torah* of Moses" (see Beckwith 1990, 39–40 Lim 2013, 3.).

1. Scribes and Scribal Culture

For more than two centuries, biblical scholars have struggled to understand how, and in what stages, the Pentateuch came to be the book that we know today—without, however, reaching any apparent unanimity (see Dozeman, Schmid, and Schwartz 2011). No one doubts, however, that the Pentateuch included writings from Israel's distant past, some parts going back well before the Babylonian exile, and these must have been copied and handed down repeatedly. The sages (sometimes referred to as scribes, but they were no mere copying machines) who preserved and passed on these texts must have had a significant role in their achieving their final form. In recent years, therefore, scholars have increasingly focused attention on these anonymous scribes and the scribal culture in which they existed in Second Temple times (Davies 1998; Schniedewind 2004; Carr 2005, 2011; Van der Toorn 2007; Horsley 2007). The study of literacy and orality, and of the scribes who transmitted sacred texts, leads ultimately to what is a fundamental question raised by modern scholars: What was the very *idea of scripture* under which sages and scribes operated during most of the biblical period?

The answer is surprising. The evidence from Qumran and contemporary sources suggests that even in the second century BCE, and for centuries and centuries earlier, sacred texts were conceived to be fundamentally *malleable*. While many scriptural texts implied or asserted outright that their words had been dictated or inspired by God, this circumstance did not prevent later scribes or copyists from modifying the texts that they were copying, adding their own formulations or ideas to the received version, indeed, rearranging whole blocks of writing, and sometimes utterly changing the earlier text's intended meaning. To cite a few well-known examples: scholars have long recognized that the last twenty-seven chapters of the book of Isaiah cannot be dated to the eighth century BCE—the setting of many of the preceding chapters—but must be the work of a different writer or writers who lived almost a century and a half later. The reason for appending these chapters to an earlier form of the writings of Isaiah is unclear, but it should be noted that even the chapters preceding those last twenty-seven do not, by the current consensus, stem from a single hand; for example, the section known to scholars as the Isaiah Apocalypse in Isa 24–27 is now believed to postdate even the chapters added at the end of the book. Other parts of the book have been tied to the time of various events that occurred at the end of the eighth or the early seventh centuries. In short, our biblical book of Isaiah seems to be the end product of a series of multiple revisions and rearrangements (Blenkinsopp, 2006).

The case of Isaiah is hardly unique. The book of Jeremiah likewise bears witness to numerous editorial changes. Even before the discovery of the Dead Sea Scrolls, scholars had recognized that the book of Jeremiah in the Old Greek (Septuagint) text is about 13 percent shorter than the traditional Hebrew (Masoretic) text found in most Bibles today; moreover, the arrangement of some of the Septuagint's chapters and subunits was likewise found to be different (Janzen 1973; Tov 1981). For a time, some scholars chalked up the differences between these two versions to laziness on the part of the Septuagint translators, but the Dead Sea Scrolls have made it clear that the Septuagint translators were working with a different (and markedly shorter) Hebrew text. Most biblicists today believe that the Masoretic Text of Jeremiah is an expansion of the Septuagint version (rather than the Septuagint being a condensation of the MT). Either way, however, it seems clear that some of those who transmitted this sacred text did not allow its sanctity to prevent them from editing, rearranging, and changing its words; apparently, sanctity went along with malleability. Perhaps the most striking thing about the Jeremiah fragments discovered among the Dead Sea Scrolls is the fact that both the longer and shorter versions seem to have coexisted in the same library, or at least to have belonged to the same sectarian group. Nowadays, this circumstance might lead one to ask: If one version was, strictly speaking, the authoritative text, indeed, the word of God, then ought not the other to be declared inauthentic, some sort of of interloper? But apparently, such a conclusion was not foregone in those days. Malleability was still the rule at Qumran.

In fact, modern biblical scholars have concluded that this sort of malleability characterized the transmission of nearly every book in what would become the Hebrew Bible: Joshua, Judges, Samuel and Kings, the major prophets and the minor prophets, Psalms and Proverbs—all these and more underwent significant modifications by different hands in the course of their transmission (Fishbane 1985). Even the Pentateuch, which, as we have seen, was the central and authoritative text of Second Temple Judaism, was not immune to scribal intervention. In fact, a specific group of Pentateuchal fragments have profoundly troubled scholars with a seemingly simple question: what should we call them?

2. The Reworked Pentateuch

The fragments, identified as 4Q158 and 4Q364–367, seem to bear some similarity to the MT Pentateuch but are far from identical to it. They contain, for example, instances of harmonistic editing, changes aimed at avoiding apparent contradictions by copying one part of the Pentateuch and inserting it into another in order to keep the two perfectly in line with one another. But there are also cases that look like out-and-out invention (on all of these, see Zahn 2011). For example, 4Q158's narration of Jacob's wrestling with an angel (MT Gen 32:25–30) includes the words by which the angel blessed Jacob, words not given in any other version of the Pentateuch: "May the Lo[rd] make you fruitful [and numerous]; [May He grant you] knowledge and understanding and may He save you from all violence and [...] to this day and for generations to come." Perhaps these words were added because the received text had mentioned the fact that the angel had blessed Jacob (Gen 32:29) but did not quote the actual words of his blessing.

Another significant difference between the MT and these fragments occurs in 4Q365. According to the book of Exodus, after (or while) Moses had led the Israelites in singing a hymn to God (Exod 15:1–18), Miriam sang a song along with all the women. Its opening line, "Sing to the Lord, for He has gloriously triumphed; horse and rider He has cast into the sea" (Exod 15:21) matches almost perfectly the first line of the men's song. But there it stops; presumably, quoting this first line was intended to imply that the women sang the rest of Moses's song as well, in which case there would be no point in writing out the whole text a second time. But this is not how

4Q365 presents things. There, Miriam sings a quite different song, unfortunately one that has survived in very fragmentary form:

> You have put to shame [
> for the majesty [
> Great are You, O savior [
> Lost is the enemy's hope, and forg[otten
> They have perished in mighty waters [
> And exalt to the heights [
> who acts gloriously [

Was this an otherwise unknown hymn inserted (or perhaps composed) by the anonymous editor or copyist? Did the act of inserting it turn what had been a copy of the Pentateuch into something different, a new, variant composition? Where exactly is the dividing line between a particular recension of an existing text and the creation of a new one?

These questions have made it difficult for scholars to settle on a name for 4Q158 and 4Q364–367. At first, these fragments were referred to as an example of the "rewritten Bible." This term was borrowed from Géza Vermès's (1961) study of various nonbiblical texts—the book of Jubilees, the Aramaic biblical targumim, the Genesis Apocryphon, Josephus's *Antiquitates judaicae*, and others—all of which expand on or explicate the Hebrew Bible. In adopting the same name for the Qumran fragments, researchers were implying that these texts, like those studied by Vermès, were clearly *not* the Bible itself but some sort of rewriting, a retelling or paraphrasing of the Bible (indeed, "biblical paraphrase" was another early name proposed for 4Q158 [Allegro 1968]). More recently, rewritten Bible has been rejected as a way of referring to these Qumran texts: since there was no Bible, no authorized canon of scripture, at the time of the Dead Sea Scrolls, there was as yet no Bible to be rewritten. For the same reason, even the word rewritten came to be regarded as prejudicial, since this name might seem to imply that there already existed a fixed, agreed upon *text*, which was not yet the case, even if we limit our inquiry to the Pentateuch alone (see the discussion in Crawford 1999; 2008, 1–99). Thus, "*reworked* Pentateuch" came to be preferred by many, since it seemed noncommittal, implying *some* editorial changes without suggesting a massive rewriting (Tov and White [Crawford] 1994).

But was reworked still going too far? Could one person's reworked Pentateuch not simply be someone else's Pentateuch (Ulrich and VanderKam 1994; Ulrich 2002; Segal 2000)? After all, scholars had long been aware that the Samaritans (on whom, see Pummer 2007; Kartveit and Knoppers 2018) have their own version of the Pentateuch. This Samaritan Pentateuch (SP) contains numerous differences vis-à-vis the MT Pentateuch, including the harmonistic editing mentioned above (Weiss 1981; Sanderson 1986; Schattner-Rieser 2009; Crawford 2011). But such differences hardly indicate that the Samaritan Pentateuch is not *a* Pentateuch or even that it is on a different footing from the other versions we know, the MT and the Septuagint. These, along with Qumran fragments and other evidence, are all textual witnesses, and the evidence of each must be weighed in considering every single verse of the Pentateuch. As a matter of fact, some of the harmonistic editing evidenced in the SP is found as well in the Qumran reworked Pentateuch manuscripts—so perhaps we would do better to consider both as representing part of another text tradition of the Pentateuch, neither better or worse than the other Pentateuchs we know of. The question has been debated by various scholars, with some of them reversing their positions over recent years (Segal 2000; Crawford 2008; Zahn 2011).

3. The Idea of Authorship

All this leads back to the larger matter of malleability: How could this idea have ever gotten started? If, for some centuries, people had handed down texts from generation to generation, was not their whole purpose to preserve the original authors' words as exactly as possible? Indeed, was it not crucial to know that the very words of Isaiah or Jeremiah—God's chosen prophets—had been written down and passed along with the greatest exactitude, and that scribes of the Pentateuch had religiously followed the commandment of Deut 4:2, "You shall not add to what I am commanding you nor take anything away from it"?

In seeking to answer these questions nowadays, many scholars begin by cautioning against imposing modern ideas and standards onto the biblical world. Authorship, it is frequently pointed out, is a relatively new concept (Wyrick, 2004; Van der Toorn, 2007, 33–108). There certainly were people in ancient Israel whom we would call authors—sages and scribes who took memorable sayings, snatches of legends, and the like and turned them into continuous texts—but these people themselves probably had a somewhat different notion of their activity and social role than *author* might imply. In the words of one scholar, "Those who actually manufactured texts did not see themselves as authors. They did not pursue originality, and what they wrote was not, in their eyes, an expression of talent, but a manifestation of craftsmanship. They were scribes rather than authors" (Van der Toorn 2007, 51). As makers of literary artifacts, of scrolls and (later) of codices, they were not personally identified with the texts that they produced.

To be sure, finished texts often said quite unequivocally whose words they were: "These are the words that Moses spoke to all Israel," "The vision of Isaiah son of Amoz," "The proverbs of Solomon, son of David," and so forth. But even reading these titles as claims of authorship is somewhat misleading (Wyrick 2004, 80–110). Hindy Najman (2003) has put the matter most insightfully by speaking of "discourses that are inextricably linked to their founders." Nowadays, she explains, someone can profess to be a Marxist or a Freudian; people who do so are tacitly asserting that their ideas or actions are a faithful continuation of the founder's own ideas or actions. "Of course," she observes, "today such people make known their own names, under which they author books. But in some ancient cultures the way to continue or return to the founder's discourse was precisely to ascribe what one had said or written, not to oneself but rather to the founder" (12). This, as she has argued, was indeed the case with biblical and extrabiblical writings over a long period of time. In particular, the development of what she calls "Mosaic discourse" has a rich history, stretching from Deuteronomy to extrabiblical writings like the book of Jubilees (which claims to have been dictated by the "Angel of the Presence" to Moses on Mount Sinai) and the Temple Scroll (which, in a switch, presents God speaking in the first person and giving his own version of laws elsewhere attributed to Moses) and ultimately into rabbinic claims of a chain of their own authority stretching back to Mount Sinai. This being the case, the attribution of a specific piece of writing to a named historical figure was likely to be as malleable as the text itself: the name "Moses" may have first appeared in the Pentateuch, but Mosaic discourse certainly did not end there.

This phenomenon comes to the fore in the writings known to scholars as the biblical pseudepigrapha: writings from the late or postbiblical period that claim to be the work of Enoch or Ezra, Isaiah or Moses, but are in truth the writings of an anonymous scribe (among many recent treatments, see Van der Toorn 2007; Reed 2008; Stone 2011, 110–21, 383–92; Dimant 2014). There are many such pseudepigraphic texts, and they raise a fundamental question: Why? Why keep handing out these biblical pseudonyms, to the point of creating what looks like an epidemic of literary forgery, instead of having the real writers sign their own names to their works? But it seems most unlikely that these people had any kind of deceit in mind. Rather, the real writer of Jubilees saw himself as a faithful disciple and decipherer of Moses, a Mosaicist who could explain any oddity or obscurity in the Pentateuch and who carried its message further to speak to Jews in the second century BCE. It was no accident that he ascribed his book to Moses and, in his own eyes, no distortion either.

4. The Narrowing Funnel

Eventually all this stopped. Texts began to be viewed as the writings of their presumed *authors*, and the *authority* (these two words are connected) that such writings enjoyed came to depend on the perceived reliability of their works' attribution. This shift was gradual—pseudepigraphy continued well into the Common Era—but as the idea of authorship gained ground, the pluriformity of texts became increasingly restricted. What exactly had the real Isaiah or Moses said? Introducing a new word or two into an existing text may still have been possible, but the heavy-handed alterations of an earlier age no longer were.

Thus, one might compare the career of Israel's sacred writings to a kind of funnel, wide at the top—in, say, the sixth or the fifth century BCE, when almost anything in a revered text could still be rearranged or supplemented or otherwise changed—but then gradually narrowing to reach the second or first century BCE and beyond, until finally, at the funnel's very bottom, biblical texts came to be utterly fixed, with no further alterations possible. Malleability was gone forever.

Or was it? To imagine this funnel-like process of narrowing is actually misleading. Long before the modifications of the texts themselves had come to a halt (at the bottom of the funnel, for the most part by the end of the second century or so CE), ancient sages and scribes had devised another way of revising the received sacred works. They left the words of the text alone but changed their apparent meaning through a new, highly creative activity: scriptural interpretation.

5. Ancient Interpreters

Much has been written in recent years about different aspects of ancient interpretation (among many others: Fishbane 1985; Brooke 1985, 2002; Bernstein 2013; Henze 2012), but before getting to some of the details, it might be well to start with a few general observations. First, ancient biblical interpretation is an interpretation of verses. It is not that ancient interpreters were not interested in the overall significance of larger units, but their point of departure was never such matters as the Joseph story or the Torah's teachings about the divine punishment. Rather, interpreters always focused on a single verse or even a single word or phrase within it. The typical reason for this narrow focus was the existence of an apparent problem or question arising out of the verse. The interpreter's job was to answer such questions and more specifically to do so in such a way as to *defend* and *justify* the received text, smoothing out any perceived difficulties in it and thereby maintaining its perfection. Here are some examples of the problems interpreters were called upon to solve (all of them chosen from the book of Genesis):

(1) After Ham "saw his father's nakedness" and thereby sinned (Gen 9:22), why did Noah curse Ham's son Canaan instead of cursing Ham himself?
(2) Why did God need to *test* Abraham (Gen 22:1)? Did God not know in advance how the test would turn out?
(3) How could Lot's daughters commit such an egregious sin as sleeping with their father (Gen 19:33–35), and why were they not punished for it?
(4) If Potiphar's house was empty on the day that his wife tried to seduce Joseph (Gen 39:11), how could she "cry out to the members of her household" (Gen 39:14) when Joseph ran outside? Was the house empty or was it not?

And here are their answers (for all of these, Kugel 1998, 223, 301, 338–39, 449):

(1) Noah could not curse Ham because it says in Gen 9:1 that "God blessed Noah *and his sons*," and no human can undo a blessing from God. But if "sons" in this verse is understood to mean *only* his sons, this left Noah free to curse Canaan, who was Noah's grandson.
(2) God's testing of Abraham was somewhat like his testing of Job. Satan, the Bible relates, had challenged God to test Job's faithfulness (Job 1:11, 2:4), so interpreters theorized that Abraham's test may have similarly been the result of a challenge from Satan. Of course, Satan's challenge is not mentioned openly in the story of Abraham's test, but the narrative does begin with the innocent-looking phrase, "After these things" (Gen 22:1). Interpreters of

course knew that "things" in Hebrew (*debarim*) can also mean "words." They therefore suggested that the opening verse should be read as "After these *words* God tested Abraham" (Gen 22:1), the unstated words having presumably been spoken by Satan. Of course, God knew from the start how the test would turn out, but he nonetheless accepted Satan's challenge to prove Abraham's faithfulness—not just to Satan but to the whole world.

(3) Lot's elder daughter had said to her sister, "Our father is old, and *there is not a man on earth* to come in to us in the manner of the world" (Gen 19:31). The words "not a man on earth" did not merely mean "there's no eligible man around." It literally meant that the daughters believed that the rest of the world had been destroyed along with Sodom; since the only remaining male, their own father Lot, was already old, they had to act fast to save the human race.

(4) The text had indeed said the house was empty (Gen 39:11), but it did not say that Potiphar's wife had called out to her housemates immediately. She must have calmly waited for them to return home and then *summoned* them, not because she was in any danger but to ask for their help in falsely accusing Joseph. How do we know this? The narrative goes on to tell us what she "called out": "See! This Hebrew man was brought to *us* to dally with *us*!" (Gen 39:14). The plurals, interpreters said, are not an instance of the "royal we" but an indication that Potiphar's wife was asking the other ladies of the house to back up her story by accusing Joseph of having previously tried the same thing with them.

6. Exegetical Motifs

Interpretations of this sort are called exegetical motifs, brief explanations of, or expansions upon, a scriptural text whose details typically posed some sort of question. The above examples all seek to back up their interpretation with some proof from scripture, but this need not be the case. Sometimes ancient interpreters simply asserted the existence of something that was altogether absent from the text that they were explaining. They said, for example, that Cain killed his brother Abel by smashing his head with a stone. In truth, the Bible never says how Abel was killed. They said that Melchizedek, the king of Salem who greeted Abraham (Gen 14:18), was in reality Noah's son Shem. They said that Exod 16:29,

"Let no man go out of his place on the seventh day," did not mean that people were stuck at home on the Sabbath, only that they were not to go beyond the limits of their villages and towns. They said, "An eye for an eye" (Exod 21:24) really means "monetary compensation for an eye." And so forth. But whether or not such bits of exegesis were backed up with scriptural prooftexts, they came to be widely accepted. After all, the sages who transmitted them were the experts, the text scholars whose occupation earned them the highest praise (Sir 38:24–39:11). Who could dispute with them?

Thus, exegetical motifs circulated widely. They also moved about in different forms and literary genres; in fact, they are called *motifs* precisely because, like motifs in music and literature, they could easily be adopted from one composition and transferred to another. They appear as early as works dated to the third century BCE, and they continued to circulate well into the Middle Ages and beyond. They are found, for example, in the form of *quaestiones*, short lists of questions and their answers (apparently a form borrowed from Hellenistic commentaries on Homer), such as those in Philo's *Quaestiones et solutiones in Genesin* and *Quaestiones et solutiones in Exodum* (Topchyan and Muradyan 2013). Exegetical motifs are also attested in continuous, sometimes line-by-line, commentaries, such as the Qumran pesher 4Q252 Commentary on Genesis (Bernstein, 1994) or Philo's biblical commentaries (on which, see Feldman, Kugel, and Schiffman 2013). They appear in extensive retellings of scriptural narratives like 1 Enoch (Nickelsburg 2001, 29–30) or the book of Jubilees (Kugel 2012), in 1Q20 Genesis Apocryphon (Machiela 2009) or Josephus's *Antiquitates judaicae* (Feldman 2000, esp. 7–8 n. 22). They are evoked in catalogues of biblical heroes, such as Ben Sira's "Praise of the Fathers" (Sir 44–50) or Wis 10 (Enns 1997) or Stephen's speech in Acts 7 (Kugel 2004). They are found as well in prayers and liturgies that cite scripture, such as Judith's prayer in Jdt 9:2–4 (Newman 1999) or 4Q365 Prayer of Enosh (Kugel 1998b); and perhaps most commonly, they are alluded to—whether consciously or not is often hard to say—in passing remarks in contexts that have little to do with answering exegetical questions, compositions such as the account of the creation in 11QPs^a Hymn to the Creator (Kugel 1998a, 48–52) or the brief history of the Jews in Jdt 5:5–22 (Newman 1999, 123–38). Exegetical motifs were so widespread and so easily passed on that, in a very real sense, they soon came to be regarded as part of the text itself, with each motif recited alongside its proper verse (or sometimes the wrong verse!).

7. A Common Background

The sages and scribes who put forward interpretations of sacred scripture seem to have differed from one another in many respects—their social roles and political affiliations, their attitudes toward Hellenism and Greek culture, even the degree to which they were aware that they were transmitting interpretations (on incidental interpretation, see Barzilai 2007). Yet despite their great diversity, ancient interpreters all seem to have shared certain basic ideas about *how* sacred texts were to be approached. James Kugel (1998a) has tried to boil these down to four basic assumptions about scripture held by all ancient interpreters:

(1) Scriptural texts are often *cryptic*; when they say A, they often mean B.
(2) Although many scriptural texts relate events or pronouncements that belong to the distant past, they are intended not merely to recount the past but to give instructions to today's readers/listeners, and in this sense are fundamentally *relevant to us*.
(3) Scripture is also *utterly consistent, without repetitions, internal contradictions or mistakes of any kind*, indeed, containing nothing unnecessary or needlessly repetitive.
(4) Scripture ultimately *comes from God*, either directly dictated or given through prophetic inspiration.

How to explain the fact that ancient interpreters all seemed to have shared these same four assumptions? (They are all the more remarkable in that these are not the assumptions readers generally bring to the reading of *other*, nonscriptural texts.) These interpretive assumptions seem to have been inherited from an earlier stage, when Jewish sages first began to switch their attention from the age-old, international pursuit of wisdom—which included studying and learning by heart collections of wise sayings from the past—to their new occupation, searching Israel's scriptures for their God-given insights and instructions. In this new enterprise sages simply continued to apply the same methods that they had used in interpreting the wise sayings of their predecessors (see Kugel 2001, 1–26; 2017)

8. The Emergence of a Canon

Scripture's long march through the Second Temple period culminated in the emergence of a fixed body of sacred texts, the Hebrew Bible. This collection included, in addition to the Pentateuch, a varied group of other writings, large parts of which had survived from preexilic times. Handed down from generation to generation by Judean sages and scribes, they now became part of a defined entity, the Hebrew Bible.

Much has been written about the endpoint of this process, the moment when, in various religious communities, the contents of the sacred library of scripture came to be firmly established. (On this aspect of canonization, see the recent contributions of Ulrich [1999, 2000, 2010, 2015], the essays in McDonald and Sanders [2002], as well as VanderKam [2012], and Lim [2010 and 2013].) However, less attention has been paid to the long period that preceded this endpoint. The story of scripture's evolution during those years is wrapped up, once again, in Judea's scribal culture and its ancient biblical interpreters.

A canon is generally conceived to serve as "a norm that obligates a community" (VanderKam 2012, 50); it is "the definitive list of inspired, authoritative books which constitute the recognized and accepted body of sacred scripture" (Ulrich 2002, 29). If so, however, it is hard to see why the canonizers chose the writings that they chose. What sense did it make, for example, to include in this collection whole sections of the historical writings that run from Joshua through 2 Chronicles? Specifically, why expose readers to the details of Samson's amorous encounters with Delilah (or, for that matter, with the anonymous prostitute in Judg 16:1)? What could be the point of recounting the details of King David's violent and often morally questionable rise to power (Halpern 2001)? He could hardly be described as a model of piety, having, among other things, orchestrated the murder of his loyal servant Uriah in order to allow him then to marry Uriah's freshly widowed wife, Bathsheba. What of the spendthrift ways of David's son Solomon and his many wives? What are *any* of these narratives doing in a religious community's canon of sacred writings?

In truth, if Jews during most of the Second Temple period had been asked which of their texts constituted the "norm that obligates a community," their answer would undoubtedly have been: the laws of the Torah, Genesis through Deuteronomy. This was indeed Judaism's *regula vitae*. In the fourth century BCE, Hecataeus of Abdera (as cited by Josephus) mentions only "our laws" (that is, those of the Pentateuch) as Jewish scripture: "for the sake of these laws, naked and defenseless they [the Jews] face tortures and death in its most terrible form, rather than repudiate the faith of their forefathers" (Stern 1976). True, some of the narratives accompanying these laws may have appeared problematic, but the Pentateuch's body of divine commandments told people in great detail what to do and not to do, and this indeed constituted "a norm that obligates a community." It may be worthwhile here to recall the apocryphal book of Baruch's praise of the Torah, "the book of the commandments of God." Thanks to it, Baruch is able to say, "Happy are we, Israel, *for we know what is pleasing to God*" (Bar 4:4, emphasis added). Then what was the point of canonizing any other book?

Making a virtue of a necessity, some have argued that the portraits of Samson and Jephthah, David, Solomon, and others are an expression of the Hebrew Bible's particular genius, presenting its heroes "warts and all." But is this claim consistent with the idea of a biblical canon? It would be more accurate to say that most of the warts in the Bible's portraits of biblical heroes are there because the purpose for which these narratives were originally collected was not the purpose to which they were ultimately put. In other words, the canonizers were not starting from scratch. There already existed a body of texts that had been assembled for quite a different purpose, to recount the trials and triumphs of Israel's history. (On the origins and stages of the Deuteronomistic history scholars still disagree: see, inter alia, Cross 1973, 274–89; Halpern 1988; Knoppers and McConville 2000; Römer 2007.) The canonizers' mission was to continue this history's history's "good king, bad king" approach and to carry it further, where possible presenting the existing narratives as a series of lessons or stories with a moral (Barton 1986). The book of Ben Sira (also called Sirach or Ecclesiasticus) exemplifies this change. It concludes with a parade of figures from Israel's past, all of them essentially stick figures, people whose lives could be summed up and rated in a sentence or two. Similarly, the list of scriptural heroes in chapter 10 of the Wisdom of Solomon does not even mention its heroes' names: they are each called, simply, "the righteous one" (even Lot, in Wis 10:6).

This sort of reconfiguration is most clearly evidenced in the sages' rewriting of narrative portions of the Pentateuch. The story of Cain and Abel (Gen 4) was converted from an etiological tale intended to account for the nomadic Kenites' legendary cruelty to a tale of the good Abel (though he is never presented as such in the Pentateuch) and a Cain who was altogether evil, eventually construed to be the son of the devil on the basis of an exegetical motif arising from Gen 4:1 (1 John 3:10–12; Kugel 1989, 1998a). Abraham was refashioned as the altogether good founder of monotheism (though no such idea is found in the Hebrew Bible itself), thanks to an exegetical motif attached to Josh 24:2–3 (Levenson 2012). For the book of Jubilees, there was a simple lesson in the story of Dinah (Gen 34): "Do not marry non-Jews."

Israel's laws were likewise changed by ancient interpreters, for the most part to allow the emergent Bible to fit new standards and concerns. Thus, the legal principle of "an eye for an eye" (Exod 21:24) came to be modified as "monetary compensation for an eye" as reported in the writings of Josephus (*A.J.* 4:280) as well as in rabbinic halakah (b. B. Qam. 83b–84a). The prohibition (by then antiquated) of sacrificing one's offspring to the god Molech (Lev 18:21, 20:2–5) was transformed by clever exegesis into a prohibition of exogamy (Jub. 30.7–10; Targum Neophyti marginal note to Lev 20:2; and possibly 6Q15 [Damascus Document] frag. 5). Indeed, perhaps the most egregious revision was that of the scriptural prohibition of adding to or subtracting from God's words (Deut 4:2 and 10:11); it was silently disregarded, since adding and subtracting was exactly what ancient interpreters regularly did.

Biblical prophecies were also transformed, with passages taken out of context and given a new, timeless message. John Barton (1986) has identified four general themes embodied in such reinterpretations: prophecy became (1) ethical instruction, (2) prophetic foreknowledge of the (much later) time of the interpreter, (3) a demonstration of the divine plan in history, or (4) a lesson in theology or esoteric teaching.

Through all these efforts, Israel's ancient library was gradually transformed. The blemished heroes were still there, but with a few deft changes—such as the late addition of a new heading for Ps 51 (Childs 1971), which turned David into a *penitent* sinner, something he was not in 2 Sam 12—some of the most egregious cases could be mollified. More generally, the interpreters' own insistence that *all* these ancient texts contained lessons relevant to their own day succeeded in creating what would later be the canon of scripture, even if sometimes it would be a canon more in reputation than in fact (cf. Haran 1994–2002).

9. Summary

The Persian period marked the beginning of a new era, a time when Israel's ancient writings were becoming increasingly important in daily life. The laws of the Pentateuch were preeminent, a divinely given collection of do's and don'ts; along with them were collections of prophetic and other sacred writings from an earlier day. Learned scribes attached to the Jerusalem temple or the royal court preserved and copied such texts, in the process often changing their words and overall meaning to fit later circumstances. Such textual malleability reigned for some time, but gradually the nature of possible changes narrowed. Meanwhile, a new, highly creative style of interpreting scripture was emerging, based on four fundamental assumptions about *how* sacred texts were to be understood. (These assumptions probably reflect the ancient connection of literacy training with the copying and studying of wisdom sayings.) Thus, the scribes who in an earlier day had assembled and freely edited ancient writings now became the creative interpreters of writings considered virtually unchangeable—and sacred. For some time, the body of texts they interpreted remained relatively open, but toward the end of the Second Temple period, this body had become a specific set of approved books, the nascent biblical canon.

10. Transformations

For all their accomplishments in the Second Temple period, it would be wrong to imply that work of ancient interpreters ended with the final canonization. The full achievement of ancient biblical interpretation can be seen in the subsequent development of Jewish and Christian ways of reading. If ancient interpreters could turn Habakkuk's prophecies into a prediction of the Qumran sect's Teacher of Righteousness centuries later (1QpHab VII, 4), then it was only a short hop from there to early Christianity's typological reading of the offering of Isaac as a foreshadowing of the crucifixion centuries to come (Barn. 7:3, Irenaeus, *Haer.* 4.5.4; cf. Rom 8:31–32). This in turn led to the sanctioning of typological exegesis in general: thus, the doctrine of the Trinity was foreshadowed in the three strangers who came to visit Abraham (Gen 18:2), as well as in the trisagion of Isa 6:3 and in the three names of God in the Shema (Deut 6:4). A later saying described the principle succinctly: *Quod in vetere latet, in novo patet* ("What is hidden in the Old [Testament] is made clear in the New"). Likewise, if sacred scripture included Solomon's Song of Songs—which must have been intended to be read allegorically if it was included in the biblical canon—then that reading could move effortlessly from the Jewish allegory of God's love for Israel to Christianity's allegory of Christ and the church. Indeed, was this not a sanction for the allegorical reading of potentially anything in the Old Testament?

Rabbinic Judaism led to no less dramatic transformations. Most notably, the very notion of torah came to include two equally sacred texts, the written text of the Pentateuch and the rabbinic Oral Torah of interpretations and expansions (so called because it was originally transmitted only orally, from teacher to student). Undefined at first (m. Avot 1:1), this other torah came to include (in rabbinic doctrine and/or popular imagination) the contents of the Mishnah, the Jerusalem and Babylonian Talmuds, midrashic collections, Geonic rulings, and in some circles, even the medieval commentaries of Rashi and his contemporaries. The Torah's qualities of being cryptic, relevant, flawless, and divinely inspired were passed on to these previously altogether human compositions.

None of these transformations could have been imagined at the time of the return from Babylonian exile, when the Torah was simply "the book of the commandments of God." But in a real sense, it was the institutionalization of ancient biblical interpreters (at first as sages and scribes, then later as commentators and sermon-makers and liturgists, from the later Second Temple period and beyond) that led to all these later transformations, making of scripture a vibrant, living reality into the Middle Ages and beyond.

Bibliography

Allegro, John M. 1968. *Qumran Cave 4.1 (4Q158–4Q186)*. DJD 5. Oxford: Clarendon.

Barton, John. 1986. *Oracles of God: Perceptions of Ancient Prophecy in Israel after the Exile*. London: Darton, Longman & Todd.

Barzilai, Gabriel. 2007. "Incidental Biblical Exegesis in the Qumran Scrolls and Its Importance for the Study of the Second Temple Period." *DSD* 14:1–24.

Becking, Bob. 2006. "'We All Returned as One!' Critical Notes on the Myth of the Mass Return." Pages 3–18 in *Judah and the Judeans in the Persian Period*. Edited by Oded Lipschitz and Manfred Oeming. Winona Lake, IN: Eisenbrauns.

Beckwith, Roger T. 1990. "Formation of the Hebrew Bible." Pages 39–86 in *Mikra: Text, Translation, Reading and Interpretation of the Hebrew Bible in Ancient Judaism and Early Christianity*. Edited by M. J. Mulder. CRINT 2.2. Assen: Van Gorcum; Minneapolis: Fortress.

Bernstein, Moshe J. 1994. "4Q252: From Re-written Bible to Biblical Commentary." *JJS* 45:1–27.

———. 2013. *Reading and Re-reading Scripture at Qumran*. STDJ 107. 2 vols. Leiden: Brill.

Blenkinsopp, Joseph. 2006. *Opening the Sealed Book: Interpretations of the Book of Isaiah in Late Antiquity*. Grand Rapids: Eerdmans.

Brooke, George J. 1985. *Exegesis at Qumran: 4Q Florilegium in Its Jewish Context*. JSOTSup 29. Sheffield: JSOT Press.

———. 2002. "The Rewritten Law, Prophets, and Psalms: Issues for Understanding the Text of the Bible." Pages 31–40 in *The Bible as Book: The Hebrew Bible and the Judean Desert Discoveries*. Edited by E. Herbert and Emanuel Tov. London: British Library.

Carr, David M. 2005. *Writing on the Tablet of the Heart: Origins of Scripture and Literature*. New York: Oxford University Press.

Childs, Brevard. 1971. "Psalm Titles and Midrashic Exegesis." *JSS* 16:137–50.

Crawford, Sidnie White. 1999 "The 'Rewritten Bible' at Qumran: A Look at Three Texts." *ErIsr* 26:1–8.

———. 2008. *Rewriting Scripture in Second Temple Times*. SDSS. Grand Rapids: Eerdmans.

———. 2011. "The Pentateuch as Found in the Pre-Samaritan Texts and 4QReworked Pentateuch." Pages 123–36 in *Changes in Scripture: Rewriting and Interpreting Authoritative Traditions in the Second Temple Period*. Edited by Hanne von Weissenberger, Juha Pakkala, and Marko Marrrila. BZAW 419. Berlin: de Gruyter.

Cross, Frank Moore. 1973. *Canaanite Myth and Hebrew Epic: Essays in the History of the Religion of Israel*. Cambridge: Harvard University Press.

Davies, Philip R. 1998. *Scribes and Schools: The Canonization of Hebrew Scriptures*. LAI. Louisville: Westminster John Knox.

Dimant, Devorah. 2014. "Hebrew Pseudepigrapha at Qumran." Pages 89–103 in *Old Testament Pseudepigrapha and the Scriptures*. Edited by Eibert Tigchelaar. BETL 270. Leuven: Peeters.

Dozeman, Thomas B., Konrad Schmid, and Baruch J. Schwartz. 2011. *The Pentateuch: International Perspectives on Current Research*. FAT 78. Tübingen: Mohr Siebeck.

Enns, Peter. 1997. *Exodus Retold: Ancient Exegesis of the Departure from Egypt in Wis 10:15–21 and 19:1–9*. HSM 57. Atlanta: Scholars Press.

Feldman, Louis. 2000. *Flavius Josephus, Translation and Commentaries: Judean Antiquities; Books 1–4*. Leiden: Brill.

Feldman, Louis, James L. Kugel, and Lawrence H. Schiffman. 2013. *Outside the Bible: Ancient Jewish Writings Related to Scripture*. 3 vols. Philadelphia: Jewish Publication Society; Lincoln: University of Nebraska Press.

Fishbane, Michael. 1985. *Biblical Interpretation in Ancient Israel.* Oxford: Clarendon.

Halpern, Baruch. 1988. *The First Historians: The Hebrew Bible and History.* San Francisco: Harper & Row.

———. 2001. *David's Secret Demons: Messiah, Murderer, Traitor, King.* Grand Rapids: Eerdmans.

Haran, Menahem. 1994–2002. *The Biblical Collection* [Hebrew]. 4 vols. Jerusalem: Bialik.

Henze, Matthias, ed. 2012. *A Companion to Biblical Interpretation in Early Judaism.* Grand Rapids: Eerdmans.

Horsely, Richard. 2007. *Scribes, Visionaries, and the Politics of Second Temple Judea.* Louisville: Westminster John Knox.

Janzen, J. Gerald. 1973. *Studies in the Text of Jeremiah.* HSM 6. Cambridge: Harvard University Press.

Japhet, Sara. 2006. "The Concept of the Remnant in the Restoration Period: On the Vocabulary of Self-Definition." Pages 432–49 in *From the Rivers of Babylon to the Highlands of Judah: Collected Essays on the Restoration Period.* Winona Lake, IN: Eisenbrauns.

Kartveit, Magnar, and Gary Knoppers. 2018. *The Bible, Qumran, and the Samaritans.* SJ 104. Berlin: de Gruyter.

Knoppers, Gary, and J. Gordon McConville. 2000. *Reconsidering Israel and Judah: Recent Studies on the Deuteronomistic History.* SBTS 8. Winona Lake, IN: Eisenbrauns.

Kugel, James L. 1989. "Cain and Abel in Fact and Fable." Pages 167–90 in *Hebrew Bible or Old Testament? Studying the Bible in Judaism and Christianity.* Edited by Roger Brooks and John J. Collins. Notre Dame: University of Notre Dame.

———. 1998. *Traditions of the Bible: A Guide to The Bible as It Was at the Start of the Common Era.* Cambridge: Harvard University Press.

———. 1998a. "'4Q369: The Prayer of Enosh' and Ancient Biblical Interpretation." *DSD* 5:119–48.

———. 2001. *Studies in Ancient Midrash.* Cambridge: Harvard University Press.

———. 2004. "Stephen's Speech in Its Exegetical Context." Pages 206–18 in *From Prophecy to Testament: The Function of the Old Testament in the New.* Edited by Craig Evans. Peabody, MA: Hendrickson.

———. 2012. *A Walk through Jubilees: Studies in the Book of Jubilees and the World of Its Creation.* JSJSup 156. Leiden: Brill.

———. 2017. "Ancient Israelite Pedagogy." Pages 15–58 in *Pedagogy in Ancient Judaism and Early Christianity*. Edited by Karina Martin Hogan, Matthew J. Goff, and Emma Wasserman. EJL 41. Atlanta: SBL Press.
Levenson, Jon D. 2012. *Inheriting Abraham: The Legacy of the Patriarch in Judaism, Christianity, and Islam*. Princeton: Princeton University Press.
Lim, Timothy. 2010. "Authoritative Scriptures and the Dead Sea Scrolls." Pages 303–22 in *The Oxford Handbook of the Dead Sea Scrolls*. Edited by Timothy Lim and John J. Collins. New York: Oxford University Press.
———. 2013. *The Formation of the Jewish Canon*. ABRL. New Haven: Yale University Press.
Lipschits, Oded. 2003. "Demographic Changes in Judah between the Seventh and the Fifth Centuries BCE." Pages 323–76 in *Judah and the Judeans in the Neo-Babylonian Period*. Edited by Oded Lipschits and Joseph Blenkinsopp. Winona Lake, IN: Eisenbrauns.
Machiela, Daniel A. 2009. *The Dead Sea Genesis Apocryphon: A New Text and Translation with Introduction and Special Treatment of Columns 13–17*. STDJ 79. Leiden: Brill.
McDonald, Lee Martin, and James A. Sanders, eds. 2002. *The Canon Debate*. Peabody, MA: Hendrickson.
Najman, Hindy. 2003. *Seconding Sinai: The Development of Mosaic Discourse in Second Temple Judaism*. JSJSup 77. Leiden: Brill.
Newman, Judith Hood. 1999. *Praying by the Book: The Scripturalization of Prayer in Second Temple Judaism*. EJL 14. Atlanta: Scholars Press.
Nickelsburg, George W. E. 2001. *1 Enoch 1: A Commentary on the Book of 1 Enoch, Chapters 1–36; 81–108*. Hermeneia. Minneapolis: Fortress.
Oppenheim, A. Leo. 1977. *Ancient Mesopotamia: Portrait of a Dead Civilization*. Rev. ed. Chicago: University of Chicago Press.
Pummer, Reinhard. 2007. "The Samaritans and Their Pentateuch." Pages 237–69 in *The Pentateuch as Torah: New Models for Understanding Its Promulgation and Acceptance*. Edited by Gary Knoppers and Bernard M. Levinson. Winona Lake, IN: Eisenbrauns.
Reed, Annette Yoshiko. 2008. "Pseudepigraphy Authorship and the Reception of 'the Bible' in Late Antiquity." Pages 467–90 in *The Reception and Interpretation of the Bible in Late Antiquity: Proceedings of the Montréal Colloquium in Honour of Charles Kannengiesser, 11–13 October 2006*.

Edited by Lorenzo DiTomasso and Lucian Turcescu. BAC 6. Leiden: Brill.

Römer, Thomas. 2007. *The So-Called Deuteronomistic History: A Sociological, Historical and Literary Introduction*. 2nd ed. London: T&T Clark.

Sanderson, Judith. 1986. *An Exodus Scroll from Qumran: 4QpaleoExod and the Samaritan Tradition*. HSS 30. Atlanta: Scholars Press.

Schattner-Rieser, U. 2009. "Der samaritanische Pentateuch im Lichte der präsamaritanischen Qumrantexte." Pages 145–68 in *Qumran und der biblische Kanon*. Edited by Jörg Frey and Michael Becker. BThSt 92. Neukirchen-Vluyn: Neukirchener Verlag.

Schniedewind, William. 2004. *How the Bible Became a Book: The Textualization of Ancient Israel*. Cambridge: Cambridge University Press.

Segal, Michael. 2000. "4QReworked Pentateuch or 4QPentateuch?" Pages 391–99 in *The Dead Sea Scrolls Fifty Years after Their Discovery (1947–1997)*. Edited by Lawrence A. Schiffman, Emanuel Tov, James C. VanderKam, and Galen Marquis. Jerusalem: Israel Exploration Society.

Stern, Menahem. 1976. *Greek and Latin Authors on Jews and Judaism*. 3 vols. Jerusalem: Academy of Sciences and Humanities.

Stone, Michael E. 2011: *Ancient Judaism: New Visions and Views*. Grand Rapids, Eerdmans.

Toorn, Karel van der. 2007. *Scribal Culture and the Making of the Hebrew Bible*. Cambridge: Harvard University Press.

Topchyan, Aram, and Gohar Muradyan. 2013. "Questions and Answers in Genesis and Exodus." Pages 807–81 in *Outside the Bible: Ancient Jewish Writings Related to Scripture*. Edited by Louis Feldman, James L. Kugel, and Lawrence H. Schiffman. 3 vols. Philadelphia: Jewish Publication Society; Lincoln: University of Nebraska Press.

Tov, Emanuel. 1981. *The Text-Critical Use of the Septuagint in Biblical Research*. JBS 3. Jerusalem: Simor.

Tov, Emanuel, and Sidnie White [Crawford]. 1994. "Reworked Pentateuch." Pages 187–352 in *Qumran Cave 4.VIII: Parabiblical Texts Part 1*. Edited by Harold W. Attridge. DJD 13. Oxford: Clarendon.

Ulrich, Eugene. 1999. *The Dead Sea Scrolls and the Origins of the Bible*. SDSS. Grand Rapids: Eerdmans.

———. 2000. "The Qumran Scrolls and the Biblical Text." Pages 51–59 in *The Dead Sea Scrolls Fifty Years after Their Discovery (1947–1997)*. Edited by Lawrence A. Schiffman, Emanuel Tov, James C. VanderKam, and Galen Marquis. Jerusalem: Israel Exploration Society.

———. 2002. "The Notion and Definition of Canon." Pages 21–35 in *The Canon Debate*. Edited by Lee Martin McDonald and James A. Sanders. Peabody, MA: Hendrickson.

———. 2010. *The Biblical Qumran Scrolls: Transcriptions and Textual Variants*. VTSup 134. Leiden: Brill.

———. 2015. *The Dead Sea Scrolls and the Developmental Composition of the Bible*. VTSup 169. Leiden: Brill.

Ulrich, Eugene, and James C. VanderKam, eds. 1994. *The Community of the Renewed Covenant: The Notre Dame Symposium on the Dead Sea Scrolls*. CJAn 10. Notre Dame: University of Notre Dame Press.

VanderKam, James C. 2012. *The Dead Sea Scrolls and the Bible*. Grand Rapids: Eerdmans.

Vermès, Géza. 1961. *Scripture and Tradition in Judaism: Haggadic Studies*. StPB 4. Leiden: Brill.

Weiss, Richard. 1981. "Synonymous Variants in Divergences between the Samaritan and Masoretic Texts of the Pentateuch." Pages 63–189 in *Studies in the Text and Language of the Bible* [Hebrew]. Edited by Richard Weiss. Jerusalem: Magnes.

Wyrick, Jed. 2004. *The Ascension of Authorship: Attribution and Canon Formation in Jewish, Hellenistic, and Christian Traditions*. Harvard Studies in Comparative Literature 49. Cambridge: Harvard University Press

Zahn, Molly M. 2011. *Rethinking Rewritten Scripture: Composition and Exegesis in the 4QReworked Pentateuch Manuscripts*. STDJ 95. Leiden: Brill.

14
Testaments

ROBERT KUGLER

The number of early Jewish texts defined by their titles as "testaments" far exceeds the number that actually meet the generally accepted definition of the genre (Kugler 2010a, 2010b). So, a first task of this article on early Jewish testamentary literature is to address the (now mostly settled) question of genre. Since attending to the question of genre raises the question whether the texts assigned to the category share anything in common as a matter of substance, I address that as well in the opening section, offering in the bargain brief declarations of my own judgment as to the overall aim of each work. Following are discussions of the three texts that meet the genre standard—Testament of Moses, Testament of Job, and Testaments of the Twelve Patriarchs—that summarize their contents, the recent history of research, and the critical issues and substantive themes pertaining to them of greatest interest to a broad readership. The article concludes with brief comments on future directions for research on early Jewish testaments.

1. Genre and Other General Topics Related to Early Jewish Testaments

In the past, scholars have defined the genre testament in two ways—by the presence of formal literary features or by the nature of a text's content. The literary features normally assigned to the genre constitute a simple narrative framework: an introduction in which the testator gathers his family to hear a near-death speech, the speech itself, and a conclusion that narrates the speaker's death (Collins 1984, 325). Content definitions of the testamentary genre, though, are not so clear-cut. Candidates for the required content have included paraenesis (von Nordheim 1980), eschatological or apocalyptic discourse (Munck 1950), and paraenesis *and* eschatology together (Kolenkow 1975). The obvious difficulty with content as a defining trait of the genre, though, is that paraenesis, eschatological discourse, and combined paraenesis and eschatological discourse can and do take up residence in a variety of other genres defined by literary frameworks (e.g., Psalms of Solomon may be said to include eschatological discourse and paraenesis in the literary framework of psalmody). To be sure, while hortatory and eschatological-apocalyptic contents do appear in the testaments discussed in the following pages, still other kinds of content make a showing as well (e.g., the obvious biographical elements in Testaments of the Twelve Patriarchs and Testament of Job), providing still another indicator of the inadvisability of using content as the measure of the genre. Thus, most now rely on the presence of the narrative framework to declare a piece of early Jewish literature a testament, a view I endorse—which leaves us, as already noted, with just Testament of Moses, Testament of Job, and Testaments of the Twelve Patriarchs (see, however, Yoshiko Reed 2014, who puts the framework definition in question). Other texts dubbed testaments, including Testament of Adam, Testament of Abraham, Testament of Isaac, Testament of Jacob, and Testament of Solomon, simply lack the narrative framework of the genre, or are of uncertain provenance, appearing to be Christian in origin, or are later than the period covered by this volume.

Having set aside content as a defining trait of the testamentary genre, it is important to acknowledge that nonetheless the three works that fit the bill *do* still share a common substantive feature: with varying degrees of detail, each offers a roadmap for Jewish identity in the context to which it was addressed, and each does so through the same, widely used rhetorical device directly related to the genre that defines the three texts, pseudepigraphic speeches of figures revered among the Jews of the Greco-Roman world. As should be clear from the following, in my judgment Testament of Moses, although using Moses's authority to call recipients to faithful adherence to the laws God made known in the Torah, chiefly aimed to speak through no less illustrious figure than Moses the truth that Israel's enduring identity is that of God's people through God's *unilateral* election of the people; and Testament of Job, although acknowledging through the voice and experiences of Job that the changed circumstances of Jews in Egypt under Roman rule left them without means to attain wealth, status, and honor as they had under the Ptolemies, declares that God's abiding affinity was with them alone among peoples and in that they had from God inexhaustible, unassailable ascribed honor, status, and spiritual wealth, in this world and the one that lay beyond bodily death. For its part, Testaments of the Twelve Patriarchs also makes a bold claim about Jewish identity through pseudepigraphic speeches of revered figures, the sons of Jacob, but unlike the other two works that focus on embracing the fact of election as the core of Jewish identity, Testaments of the Twelve Patriarchs attach Jewish self-definition in the Greco-Roman world to an ethic of obedience to torah, embodying Stoic virtues and acknowledging God's affirmation of these ways of being in the person of Jesus—all of which the testaments treats as equal in practice. In short, though differing in the relative importance they place on ethics or election, all three testamentary works set out to achieve the same purpose: to define Jewishness in the Greco-Roman world through the authority of the heroes of Israel of old.

2. Testament of Moses

The Testament of Moses begins with Moses summoning Joshua to give him final instructions before he dies and concludes with what we take to be the beginning of the account of his death (the end of the sole surviving manuscript, a Latin palimpsest, breaks off before concluding): it is a testament. Yet Moses's message to Joshua also exhibits characteristics of an apocalypse (esp. Daniel; Collins 2016, 163). Like apocalypses, the testament offers assurance contrary to prevailing circumstances that the world is created for Israel (ch. 1); a special revelation of the history-as-future (chs. 2–8, from the exile to the Hasmoneans [ch. 8], with apparent references to Herod and his sons and the Roman commander Varus's assault on Jerusalem in 4 BCE [ch. 6]); portrayal of the end of history as the dawn of a heavenly kingdom inaugurated by an angelic figure and achieved on a supernatural level (chs. 9–10, Taxo and his sons and the *nuntius*); support for martyrdom in the face of persecution (ch. 9); and an appeal to its audience to lead pious lives as they await history's end (chs. 11–12).

The single, incomplete Latin manuscript of the testament was first published in 1861 by Antonio Ceriani. The identification of the Latin text as the Assumption of Moses instead of his testament remains an option for some. It was at first identified as the Assumption of Moses because of the quotation of 1:14 in Gelasius, *Hist. eccl.* 2.17.17, which identifies its source as the Assumption. But most agree, given its testamentary features, that it is the work known in antiquity as the Testament of Moses. Reference to a dispute over Moses's body between Michael and the devil in Jude 9 coheres with what Gelasius says of the Assumption of Moses in *Hist. eccl.* 2.21.7, an episode that is not featured in the surviving Latin text. Thus, the consensus is that the Latin text is the Testament of Moses, although it may have gone on to address Moses's lifting up, or the episode was left to a separate work echoed in Gelasius's comments and Jude 9. Johannes Tromp (1993, 115), however, retains "assumption" in the title, arguing that a genre defined in modernity need not dictate the title of an ancient work, and Norbert Hofmann (2000, 10) likewise retains "assumption."

The work's original language is unknown, even if it is clear that the Latin translated a Greek text. Tromp (1993, 85) has argued that the supposed Hebraisms used by R. H. Charles (1913, 410) and depended on by Abraham Schalit (1989) as evidence of a Hebrew text behind a hypothetical Greek text are explicable in others ways; so, while it is possible that the Greek was a free rendering of a Hebrew text, we have no way of proving that—any original language of the testament that preceded the (hypothetical) Greek version remains unknown.

The questions of the work's date and redaction are closely related. Given the apparent references to Herod and his sons in chapter 6, no one doubts that the present form is datable to the first century CE (or later). George Nickelsburg's (2005, 74–77, 247–48) argument that a first draft of the work dated to the crisis under Antiochus Epiphanes (ch. 8) was redacted to include references to the Hasmoneans, Herod, and Varus's attack on the land of Israel in 4 BCE (ch. 6) had achieved near-consensus by 1980. An alternative view is that the entire testament was composed at once in the early first century and that the author may or may not have had the specifics regarding Herod and the Varus campaign in mind when writing chapter 6 (Tromp 1993, 120–23; Hofmann 2000, 329; Priest 1985, 920–21; 1992, 920–21). John Priest (1992, 921; see also Tromp, 1993, 12–21) notes that the redactional history attributes "a logic to an apocalyptic author which is not altogether necessary." Another alternative to the consensus revives the nineteenth-century notion that the entire work is an early Christian composition and that Taxo is to be identified with Jesus (Israeli 2005, 747).

Taxo's identity and that of the *nuntius* in 10.2 also receive attention. Including Edna Israeli's suggestion, Taxo has been assigned a number of identities, real and symbolic. Seeing allusions in chapters 9–10 to a variety of cultic features enunciated in the Hebrew Bible and early Jewish literature, Mark Whitters (2010) argued that Taxo and the seven sons are a symbolic answer to the corrupted temple and its priesthood—they are pure priests who signal restored purity. Kenneth Atkinson (2006) identified Taxo as

Moses's successor and the final intercessor for Israel, and the *nuntius* of 10.2 as a priestly angel. Tromp (1990) argued that Taxo and the *nuntius* of 10.2 are the same—Taxo's vindication leads to the exaltation and ordination on high as priest, and then to the role of the avenger against Israel's enemies. Jan Willem van Henten (2003) argued that the *nuntius* of 10.2 may be read as Moses; 11.17 and 12.6 already suggest his role as a mediator, the function fits with 10.1–10, and some Qumran texts also present Moses as a mediator (4Q504 1 II, 8–11; 4Q374; 1Q22 IV; 4Q378 26; 4Q491; Van Henten 1987). John Collins (2016, 164) observed that Taxo may be understood as an antitype of Mattathias in 1 Macc 2 and an indication of the work's pacifist sensibilities: while both men are from priestly families, loyal to the law, loathe the impious ways of the gentiles, and encourage their sons to die rather than renounce their ways, Mattathias has five sons and Taxo has the perfect seven, and Mattathias takes vengeance through violence and Taxo trusts in God.

Another area of significant research is the testament's purpose, theology, and relationship to wider Jewish thought and movements. Priest (1992, 921) observed that in light of the rich diversity among Jews at the turn of the eras, attempts to affiliate the work with Essenes, Pharisees, or Maccabean-era Hasidim seek too much precision in assigning the text a community (yet Priest himself affiliated the text with the Hasidim). The trend recently has been toward assessing the theology of the work and drawing from that more tentative conclusions regarding its purpose and *general* affiliation. Many note the work's close alignment with Deuteronomic traditions, especially in the way its structure maps onto Deut 31–34 (Collins 2016, 161; see also Halpern-Amaru, 1994, 55–68; Hofmann 2000). Likewise, reliance on versions of the sin-exile-return pattern (chs. 2–4; chs. 5, 7, with the later addition of ch. 6) suggests a basic Deuteronomic outlook. Noting the resonances with Deuteronomy and its covenantal tradition, Collins (2016, 163) and Hofmann (2000, 329) align it with first century CE apocalypses like 4 Ezra and 2 Baruch. Collins (2016, 161–62) adds that its "theology might also be aptly described as covenantal nomism. Salvation comes through membership of the Jewish people and requires observance of the law. The pattern of sin and punishment is affirmed even in the face of persecution where the righteous are killed."

By contrast, without denying the importance of the Deuteronomic tradition of retributive justice to the testament and its view of Israel within a historical frame of reference, Betsy Halpern-Amaru draws attention to the echo of Gen 22:16–18; Exod 32:13 in the language of 3.9 to suggest that the testament also argues that ultimately "not intercession or covenantal nomism" but the "divine covenant and oath" that God made by himself assures Israel's future. On this reading the testament holds that the fulfillment of God's promise stands outside of history and apart from human action—it depends completely on God's faithfulness to God's covenant and oath, the fulfillment of which Moses assures Joshua will follow in due time, confirming the bookending declarations of the testament regarding Israel, creation, and the nations (1.12; 12.12; Halpern-Amaru 1994, 67–68; see also Kugler 2001a, 190–97).

3. Testament of Job

Testament of Job clearly meets the requirements of the genre: in chapter 1 Job summons his children to his side to hear his valedictory before he dies and chapters 52–53 narrate his death and the disposition of his body. The address that follows in chapters 2–44—an account of his life before his marriage to his children's mother, Dinah, daughter of Jacob and a reworking of material from the book of Job—gives the work its distinctive character. In the course of this lengthy speech he tells of the great wealth he possessed before Satan's attack and his use of it to serve the poor; Satan's attempts to defeat his patience in suffering by trickery through the manipulation of his maidservant and his first wife, Sitidos; Sitidos's death in poverty and shame; and his conversations with his friends who mistake his serenity in suffering as madness. Chapters 45–50 recount Job's bequeathal of his material inheritance to his sons and the spiritual-gift-bestowing bands God gave him in his suffering to his daughters and the expression of those gifts by the three women. In chapters 51–53 Nerios, Job's brother, narrates Job's death and the differing dispositions of his body and soul—the former is buried, the latter is taken away to the east by chariot by an otherworldly being—and gives a closing speech in praise of Job.

On most of the conventional issues associated with a Jewish pseudepigraphon preserved in Christian circles—the questions of Jewish or Christian origin, original language, textual history, and date and provenance—little has changed since 1980. Most agree with the Eckhard von Nordheim's (1980) judgment that the work was authored by a Jew. Given the certain affiliation between the testament and LXX Job established by Bernd Schaller (1980), a Greek original is assumed. As to textual history, the fragments of a papyrus codex containing parts of the testament in Coptic have been published (Schenke 2009, 2013, 2014; see also Römer 1989) and Maria Haralambakis (2012) (re)classified and described the Slavonic manuscript tradition. On date and provenance, suggestions have ranged from the very general to the very specific. At one end of the spectrum, Cees Haas (1989) argued that the treatment of the concept of perseverance in the text suggests a general Hellenistic-Jewish origin, and at the other end are the likes of Russell Spittler (1983, 834), who suggested that chapters 46–53 originated among Montanists; William Gruen, who argued for a second-century CE date at least for chapters 1–27 (relating Job's temple destruction to the destruction of the temple of Serapis in Alexandria and the Jewish revolt in 115–117 CE); and Robert Kugler and Richard Rohrbaugh (2004), who argue for an early Roman era, Egyptian provenance, citing the emphasis on trusting in ascribed over acquired honor as a response to the diminished opportunities Jews experienced in the transition from Ptolemaic to Roman rule. Most prefer the more cautious view that the text was likely formed "among Jews in Egypt in the first century BCE or first century CE" and certainly after about 150 BCE because of its dependence on LXX Job, before the fifth century CE, the rough date of the Coptic fragments, and probably before the third century, when Tertullian seemed to allude to 20:9 in *Pat.* 14.5 (Reed 2010, 816).

Scholarly positions on two other standard critical issues have likewise seen little change since 1980. Because of the differing portrayals of women in the testament—the negative portrayal of the maidservant in chapters 6–8 and Sitidos in 21–27 and 39–40 and the (apparently) positive depiction of Job's daughters in 46–53—some have argued that the testament is composite: Pieter van der Horst (1989) and Spittler (1983) both view chapters 46–53 as distinct from the rest of the work. Peter Nicholls (1982) less plausibly discerns four separate sources (and editorial seams at 28.1; 31.1; 45.4; 53.1), and Kierkegaard argues that the unique treatment of the figure of Satan in chapters 1–27 suggests that it was a distinct unit joined to two others (chs. 28–44; 45–53) to create the present work. Schaller (1979, 1989) argues for the unity of the text, and much of the recent work targeted at smaller issues in the testament implicitly or explicitly favors unity of composition (e.g., Kugler and Rohrbaugh 2004). On the question of genre, the nineteenth-century suggestion that the text be viewed as a midrash on the book of Job was echoed in the late twentieth century (Gorea 2007, 77; Wisse 2003, 35, 46–48) but was decisively critiqued and dismissed by Haralambakis (2012, 100–109), who also, less convincingly, rejects the testamentary assignment. The consensus remains that the text is best classified as a testament (von Nordheim 1980, 119–35; Collins 1984, 349–54).

Some have addressed the relationship of the testament to the biblical book of Job in its Hebrew or Greek forms. Schaller (1980) compiled a comprehensive list of the similarities between the different Greek texts of the testament and LXX Job that confirmed the reliance of the testament on the Septuagint version and demonstrated the usefulness of the testament's Greek manuscripts for tracking the history of the LXX Job. H.-M. Wahl (1994, 12) traced Elihu's transformation from the pious, spirit-driven speaker of the biblical book to an "instrument of evil" in the testament. Christopher Begg (1994) argued that the testament's treatment of the characters from the book of Job is meant to resolve a range of issues left open in the biblical work. Anathea Portier-Young (2013, 245) argued that the testament reworked aspects of LXX Job to show "readers a mystical path ... toward personal transformation" that allows them "to draw nearer to their heavenly inheritance, confident that heavenly glory surpasses all earthly wealth." Andrew Guffey (2017) argued that the testament looks to address the questions of theodicy left by the book of Job with an appeal to philosophical training in the Stoic-Cynic ideal of patient detachment, which equips one "to tolerate the dung-heap and to command the worms" and to "angelomorphic transformation and accession to a divine throne," "internalized apocalyptic," which negates the suffering itself (Portier-Young 2013, 232).

The topic most intensely studied in recent years is the uneven depiction of women in the testament. As noted, Van der Horst (1989, 113) suggested that the contrasting roles assigned to women indicates the text is composite and speculated that chapters 46–53 were associated with an ecstatic movement that gave women pride of place. By contrast, Susan Garrett (1993) argued that the negative portrait in chapters 1–45 and positive portrait in chapters 46–53 are of a piece and the work is from a single author: the first part portrays women as suffering because they are fixated on material reality, the things male authors charged women with fixating on in the Greco-Roman world; in the second part the daughters flourish precisely because they shed their feminine characteristics and became, in essence, manly. Kugler and Rohrbaugh (2004) argue that the testament uses women to underscore its central argument for Jews facing the transition from Ptolemaic to Roman rule in Egypt that acquired honor signaled by possessions and status is fleeting and relying on it leads to bitter disappointment (the maidservant and Sitidos), but honor ascribed by God is enduring (the daughters). Haralambakis (2010) reads the women through a gender studies lens to argue that, in fact, Job is the center of attention in the narrative and women play only a subordinate role to the text's goal of portraying Job as a "man in charge" who fulfills his masculine roles of father, husband, powerful king, wrestler, and benefactor to perfection—he is the ideal of masculinity throughout his ordeal, and the women in the text are merely instruments for achieving that goal. Nancy Klancher (2010) likewise reads the differing portraits of women as a key to understanding something of the work's view on masculinity, concluding that the women of the testament are meant to convey "specific constructs of male virtue" (213) and serve as mirrors of Job in his passage through life, and conversion in particular (see also Cason 2015a for a focus on Job and masculinity).

Some discussions of the women avoid the challenge of the different portraits by focusing solely on Sitidos (and Dinah) or the daughters. As to the daughters: Randall Chesnutt (1991, 125) argues that the spiritual insight of the daughters evinces high regard for women in the "real world of early Judaism." Rebecca Lesses (2007) reads chapters 46–53 as representative of an atypical tradition that assigns women the capacity to communicate with the heavenly realm. Peter Machinist (1997) addresses the daughters' inheritance, arguing that it aims to resolve the difficulty raised by Job 42:13–15, where the daughters receive an inheritance, contrary to the dominant biblical-legal standard of male-only inheritance. Jennifer Zilm (2013) links the multicolored bands Job gives his daughters with the Hebrew term *riqmah* in the Hebrew Bible and in Songs of Sabbath Sacrifice to suggest that they bestow the spiritual gift of angelic praise only while they are worn. Similarly, Heike Omerzu (2005) suggests that bands prepare the daughters to receive heavenly revelations. Angela Harkins (2014) draws on a series of connections she discerns among Job, Dinah, and fallen angels traditions to argue that the heavenly cords were to protect Job's daughters from sexual advances by heavenly beings. Robin Waugh (2014) argues that the testament is an early moment in the development of "profeminine patience literature" (cf. Shaw [1996, 281–84], who treats the women of the testament as feminized expressions of the patience tradition). As to Sitidos (and Dinah): Rehmann Sutter (1999) thinks that just as Jobab received a new name (Job), Sitidos did, too—Dina, her resurrection name after her passion. Michael Legaspi (2008, 71) says the testament combines two traditions about Job's wife—one evidenced in the rabbinic traditions, the Targum of Job and Pseudo-Philo, that Job's wife is Dinah, and the other, attested chiefly in the LXX, that she was a "wretched Arabian woman"—to clarify Job's background, answer questions about his relationship to Israel, and take up themes in the book of Job to legitimate the "role of women in Job's own moral athleticism." Reading Sitidos from a Bakhtinian perspective, Thomas Cason (2015a) argues that Job is in fact parasitic on her, letting her patience carry him through—his parasitism saves him, not his patience. John-Patrick O'Connor (2017) addresses the clothing changes Sitidos undergoes (Satan, too) in comparison with roughly contemporary texts to argue Sitidos's varying outerwear indicates her inward character.

A few other studies point to other lines of inquiry in studying the testament. Patrick Gray (2004) tackles the common assumption that the Epistle of James must have known the testament (cf. James 5:11), concluding that at least on source-critical matters, we must remain uncertain about the relationship between the two works. Haralambakis (2012) offers a structural analysis, narratological study, and reception history of the testament building especially from her work on the Slavonic textual traditions. Kugler (2016) has argued that the testament exhibits a dual anthropology as well as traces of dependence on documentary practices in Greco-Roman Egypt (2017).

As to a sense of the Testament's overall purpose in its context, unsurprisingly I find Kugler and Rohrbaugh's (2004) position, augmented by Kugler (2016), most persuasive: Job's account appeals to Jews in early Roman Egypt whose ability under the Ptolemies to acquire wealth and status—and honor—had been abruptly and decisively brought to an end with Roman rule; it argues that through God's election of the people of Israel and their descendants dispersed in places such as Egypt they had all the ascribed honor required to ensure them the elevated status that counts, that of standing before God as God's elect. So, although the Jews of Roman Egypt might suffer diminished material wellbeing, that most important portion of their being, merely held by the flesh, their souls, was bestowed in the here and now with highest honor and was destined to dwell after death with God (52:10).

4. Testaments of the Twelve Patriarchs

Each of the deathbed speeches of the sons of Jacob in the Testaments of the Twelve Patriarchs follows much the same pattern: it begins with the patriarch's summons to his children to his bedside; continues with his autobiographical reflections, moral exhortation, and future prediction; and concludes with an account of his death and burial. Seven patriarchs' autobiographical accounts rely on Genesis (Reuben [Gen 35:22]; Levi [Gen

34]; Judah [Gen 38] Issachar [Gen 49:14–15 LXX]; Zebulun [Gen 49:13]; Gad [Gen 37:2]; Joseph [Gen 39:6b–18]), and five depend on other sources and interpretive readings of Genesis (Simeon, Dan, Naphtali, Asher, and Benjamin). The autobiographical accounts trigger moral exhortation: right action equals pleasing God and opposing Beliar, keeping the twofold commandment to love God and one's neighbor, and avoiding traditional Greco-Roman vices. Individually the patriarchs' accounts address the pitfalls of failing to exercise self-control vis-à-vis strong drink (Judah), attractive women (Reuben; Judah), envy (Simeon), greed (Judah), falsehood (Dan), anger (Simeon; Gad), temptations to unjust violence (Simeon; Judah; Dan; Gad), and double-mindedness (Asher); they praise the virtues of zeal for the Lord (Levi), temperance and purity (Judah), simplicity of life (Issachar), merciful warm-heartedness (Zebulun), harmony with the natural order (Naphtali), single-mindedness (Asher), and chastity, endurance, and mercy (Joseph). The concluding eschatological sections exhibit a variety of forms, including sin-exile-return sections, Levi-Judah passages, ideal savior passages that look forward to a deliverer for Israel, and resurrection-of-the-patriarch passages.

In their present form, the Testaments of the Twelve Patriarchs are a Christian work: the future-oriented sections feature Christian eschatological expectations. At the same time, the composition includes material deriving from pre-Christian Jewish milieus (e.g., the biographies), as well as ideas and genres typical of Hellenistic philosophy (e.g., the ethical exhortation). Thus, with the exception of some interest in its ethics and piety, the focus of most scholarship devoted to the testaments up to the 1980s was on determining what led to this mix (Collins 1986, 276). Collins summarized the results of the effort up to the 1980s: textual criticism (especially reliance on early Armenian translations of the work) proved incapable of removing the Christian additions to get to a Jewish original; the Qumran-origins hypothesis had almost no adherents; Marinus de Jonge's (1953) position that the work is Christian in its present form and should be studied as such had gained strength, and yet the effort to recover the compositional history and circumscribe an earlier Jewish work in its various forms persisted. Little has changed. Significant work has been done to underscore the text-critical judgment; while the Qumran origins hypothesis has been decisively left behind, much has been done to better understand Qumran texts related to the Testaments; and de Jonge's position has won new adherents while others have carried on the effort to trace the history of the work's development from Jewish sources (or a complete collection of Jewish Testaments) to the Christian form we have. New developments include the revival of the nineteenth-century theory that the work was Jewish-Christian from its beginnings and an increase in studies that prescind from the question of origins to address features of the Testaments as a complete work.

Regarding text criticism, already before 1980 Michael Stone's (1969) work on the Armenian text had put into question the use of its minuses vis-à-vis the Greek text to isolate a pre-Christian-redaction form. He and Vered Hillel (2012) have since demonstrated that the minuses are most probably the result of a translator's increasing sloth as he progressed in his task and have nothing to do with confessional inclination. The text-critical path to a Jewish Testaments of the Twelve Patriarchs is illusory (*pace* DeSilva 2013, 24–29).

A focus of much scholarship on the testaments in recent decades has been to better understand the relationship between relevant Hebrew texts from Qumran and the testaments (on Midrash Wayissaʿu, a Hebrew text relating to Judah that survives only in a late form but is thought to reflect an earlier work, and the Hebrew Testament of Naphtali, see Hollander and de Jonge 1985, 25–27, 446–56). The echoes of Qumran texts in the Testaments of Judah (4Q538 and T. Jud. 12.11–12), Naphtali (4Q215 I, 2–5 and T. Naph. 1.11–12), and Joseph (4Q539 1 and 2 and T. Jos. 14.4–5; 15.1–17.2) are generally understood to indicate only that the authors of these texts knew similar or the same source materials independently of each other (Kugler 2001b, 28–30). Likewise, the testamentary texts related to Kohath and Amram, although perhaps related to the Levi material (see Reed 2014, 390–400), do not form any kind of precursor literary tradition to the Testaments (Drawnel 2010). The Qumran evidence for an early, Aramaic text concerning Levi, is a different case. Dating from the Hasmonean to early Herodian periods, seven manuscripts from Qumran (1Q21; 4Q213–214; Drawnel 2004; Greenfield, Stone, and Eshel 2004; de Jonge 1991, 244–62) give Aramaic texts parallel to parts of T. Levi 8–9; 11–14, as well as biographical, prayer, and wisdom speech texts unknown in the Greek testament. Medieval fragments of a Levi tradition from the Cairo Geniza and a Greek-language version of Levi's prayer, known from 4Q213a, inserted at T. Levi 2.3 in the Mount Athos manuscript of the Testaments supplement the Qumran evidence (see now the additional Cairo Geniza fragment in Bohak 2011). Although often close to the Greek Testament of Levi, this material is also so different from it as to guarantee a redactional history between the composition of the Qumran texts and the writing of the Testament of Levi. Kugler (1996; see contrastingly Stone 2002; 2003) posited a redactional history for a "Levi-Priestly tradition" but later renounced the trajectory, concluding that there were already multiple recensions of Aramaic Levi represented in the Qumran manuscripts and the Cairo Geniza fragments, making the reconstruction of an original Aramaic Levi document, let alone the construction of a precise trajectory from the Qumran manuscripts to the Testament of Levi impractical (Kugler 2008; see earlier Kugler 2001b, 30–31). By contrast, James Kugel (2010, 2013) has argued that the Aramaic material related to Levi from Qumran was the starting point for a full Hebrew Testaments of the Twelve Patriarchs and has addressed the relationship of the Qumran material to a Levi tradition in several publications (Kugel 1992, 1993, 2007, 2017a).

Through the 1990s two approaches to the related questions of the testaments' origin dominated discussion: They were first authored by Jews and were only later redacted to serve the interests of early Christians; alternatively, even though they include Jewish sources and there may have been a developmental-compositional history between the authoring of the sources and the completion of the present testaments, the present document is Christian and should be studied as such. A third position, that the testaments was a Jewish-Christian work from the beginning, has emerged in recent years.

Jarl Henning Ulrichsen and Kugel have posited a pre-Christian Testaments and its conversion to a Christian work. Ulrichsen (1991) posits a five-stage compositional history for the Testaments: a Jewish paraenetical work using Joseph as an ideal figure composed in Hebrew or Aramaic around 200 BCE in Palestine; the addition of most of the prophetic and eschatological-apocalyptic material between 160 and 100/63 BCE; before the turn of the era more Hebrew or Aramaic material of varied character was added; in the first century CE, more assorted material was added and the work was translated into Greek; and Christian elements were added beginning in the second century CE. Kugel (2010, 45–46; 2013, 1697–1703) posits a Hasmonean-era, Hebrew version that emphasized Levi and priesthood (Aramaic Levi), which was later redacted with pro-Judah passages that exalted kingship alongside the priesthood out of dissatisfaction with the Hasmoneans. A Greek translation followed around the turn of the eras, which also introduced aspects of Stoic philosophy. Following that Christian interpolations were introduced. (On his evidence for a pre-Christian, Hebrew version of the Testaments, see Kugel 2010; and for his view that the text may also have been augmented by later rabbinic thinkers, see Kugel 2017b.)

De Jonge staked out the major alternative to a Jewish origin and compositional history for the testaments in 1953. He argued that as we have it the work is a Christian text datable to the late second century CE. While he acknowledged that Christian authors used Jewish sources and that there might even have been a Jewish testaments at one time (Hollander and de Jonge 1985, 85), he thinks it is impossible to recover such a text, if it ever existed. Thus, he declared that, "our first and foremost task is to try to interpret the Testaments as they lie before us" (85; see further de Jonge 2003). Kugler (2001a) initially followed de Jonge in identifying the work as Christian, and Tom de Bruin (2015) also takes this view. Hillel (2013) and Graham Twelftree (2011) also exemplify the judgment that we do best to work with the Christian form.

A third approach (which revives a nineteenth-century position) to the origins of the testaments has emerged in recent years—to assign authorship to Jewish-Christians, believers who regarded both torah and Jesus to have enduring significance. Joel Marcus (2010) argues that the testaments arose from a late second- or early third-century Syrian Jewish-Christian community in dialogue with the community associated with the *Didascalia Apostolorum*. Marcus makes the case that the testaments charged its community with keeping the law's particulars (see, e.g., T. Jud. 26.1) in opposition to the *Didascalia*'s position that only the Decalogue was binding on followers of Jesus. Among those following Marcus in his general judgment, if not his assignment of the work to the specific context he suggests, are Philip Kurowski (2010) and Kugler (forthcoming).

In the last decades there have also been studies that leave aside the question of origins to address other matters. A number of studies are concerned with the interpretive moves authors of the testaments make, as well as their interpretive afterlife (e.g., Fisk 2000; Himmelfarb 1984; de Jonge 1991, 204–219, 221–32; Kugler 2012; Nisse 2017; Rosner 1992). Some concern themselves with the eschatology of the texts (Collins 2016, 165–75; Hollander 1995; de Jonge 1991, 164–79, 191–203). A fair number of studies address the ethics, piety, law, and paraenesis in the text (Berthelot 2003; Hollander 1995; de Jonge 1991, 277–89; 2002; 2004; Slingerland 1986; Thomas 2004). Others address a range of assorted issues in particular testaments (e.g., Baarda 1988, 1992; Hillel 2007; Hollander 1981; de Jonge 1991, 180–90, 290–300, 301–13; Kugel 1995; Mirguet 2014; Rosen-Zvi 2006). Some have ventured to address relatively unexplored issues raised by the testaments (e.g., von Gemünden 2016 on emotions and literary genres;

cf. Mirguet 2014; Pouchelle 2017 on education; Slingerland 1984 on the "Levitical hallmark").

Stepping back from the various specialized studies of specific aspects of the testaments to make a claim regarding the work's overall aim—as I have done for Testament of Moses and Testament of Job—the emerging view that it was a Jewish-Christian work (e.g., Marcus 2010) arguing for the coherence of following Jesus with living the life of an upright resident of the Roman world shaped by popular Stoic values, and, yes, living a fully torah-obedient life as a Jew (Kugler 2001b) seems most true to the contents of the work. The particular virtue of such a reading is its capacity to explain the work's considerable breadth of themes and genres and its numerous affinities with Hebrew scriptures, Greco-Roman popular philosophy, and rhetorical modes familiar to Jews, Christians, and pagans.

5. Future Directions

Annette Yoshiko Reed (2014) has started work on one promising avenue for future research, the prehistory of the testamentary genre. Equally intriguing is the question of why the genre seems to have all but disappeared so quickly after it emerged. On both questions, more attention to non-Jewish literature as source material might yield fresh insights. The same may be said for study of the known testaments, quite apart from the emergence and disappearance of the genre. Hollander and de Jonge (1985) made important progress in reading the Testaments of the Twelve Patriarchs in the wider Greco-Roman context, but much more remains to be done in this regard for all three testamentary works. Also to be encouraged is the emerging interest in treating topics and themes associated with the testaments that are unconnected to the traditional issues that have occupied scholarship for so long, such as the origin of the Testaments of the Twelve Patriarchs or the compositional coherence of the Testament of Job and the Testament of Moses. Especially promising are more studies that work to place the texts more securely in their own social, historical, and ideational worlds (e.g., Guffey 2017; Waugh 2014). And last, in keeping with the observations in section 1 above regarding the common purpose of the three representatives of the testamentary genre, much remains to be said about their contribution to the emergence of distinctive Jewish identities in the Greco-Roman world.

Bibliography

Atkinson, Kenneth. 2006. "Taxo's Martyrdom and the Role of the Nuntius in the 'Testament of Moses': Implications for Understanding the Role of Other Intermediary Figures." *JBL* 125:453–76.

Baarda, Tijtze. 1988. "Qehath—'What's in a Name?' Concerning the Interpretation of the Name 'Qehath' in the Testament of Levi 11:4–6." *JSJ* 19:215–29.

———. 1992. "The Shechem Episode in the Testament of Levi: A Comparison with Other Traditions." Pages 11–73 in *Sacred History and Sacred Text: A Symposium in Honour of A. S. van der Woude*. Edited by Jan Nicolaas Bremmer and Florentino García Martínez. CBET 5. Kampen: Kok Pharos.

Begg, Christopher. 1994. "Comparing Characters: The Book of Job and the Testament of Job." Pages 433–45 in *The Book of Job*. Edited by Willem A. M. Beuken. BETL 114. Leuven: Leuven University Press.

Berger, Peter L., and Thomas Luckmann. 1966. *The Social Construction of Reality: A Treatise in the Sociology of Knowledge*. Garden City, NY: Doubleday.

Berthelot, Katell. 2003. "Les parénèses de la charité dans les *Testaments des Douze Patriarches*." *MScRel* 60:23–39.

Bohak, Gideon. 2011. "A New Geniza Fragment of the *Aramaic Levi Document*." *Tarbiz* 79:373–83.

Bruin, Tom de. 2015. *The Great Controversy: The Individual's Struggle Between Good and Evil in the Testaments of the Twelve Patriarchs and in Their Jewish and Christian Contexts*. NTOA 106. Göttingen: Vandenhoeck & Ruprecht.

Cason, Thomas Scott. 2015a. "Job as Parasitic Grotesque: A Carnivalesque Reading of the Testament of Job." *Conversations with the Biblical World* 35:251–72.

———. 2015b. "Textual Cialis: Four Narratival Strategies for Repairing Disabled Masculinity in the Second Temple Tradition." *BibInt* 23:601–23.

Charles, R. H. 1913. *The Apocrypha and Pseudepigrapha of the Old Testament*. 2 vols. Oxford: Clarendon.

Chesnutt, Randall. 1991. "Revelatory Experiences Attributed to Biblical Women in Early Jewish Literature." Pages 107–25 in *"Women Like This": New Perspectives on Jewish Women in the Greco-Roman World*. Edited by Amy-Jill Levine. AJL 1. Atlanta: Scholars Press.

Collins, John J. 1984. "Testaments." Pages 325–55 in *Jewish Writings of the Second Temple Period: Apocrypha, Pseudepigrapha, Qumran Sectarian Writings, Philo, Josephus*. Edited by Michael E. Stone. CRINT 2.2. Philadelphia: Fortress; Leiden: Brill.

———. 1986. "The Testamentary Literature in Recent Scholarship." Pages 268–85 in *Early Judaism and Its Interpreters*. Edited by Robert A. Kraft and George W. E. Nickelsburg. BMI 2. Philadelphia: Fortress; Atlanta: Scholars Press.

———. 2016. *The Apocalyptic Imagination: An Introduction to Jewish Apocalyptic Literature*. 3rd ed. Grand Rapids: Eerdmans.

Desilva, David. 2013. "The *Testaments of the Twelve Patriarchs* as Witnesses to Pre-Christian Judaism: A Re-assessment." *JSP* 23:21–68.

Drawnel, Henryk. 2004. *An Aramaic Wisdom Text from Qumran: A New Interpretation of the Levi Document*. JSJSup 86. Leiden: Brill.

———. 2010. "The Initial Narrative of the 'Visions of Amram' and Its Literary Characteristics." *RevQ* 24:517–54.

Fisk, Bruce. 2000. "One Good Story Deserves Another: The Hermeneutics of Invoking Secondary Biblical Episodes in the Narratives of *Pseudo-Philo* and the *Testaments of the Twelve Patriarchs*." Pages 217–38 in *The Interpretation of Scripture in Early Judaism and Christianity: Studies in Language and Tradition*. Edited by Craig Evans. JSPSup 33. Sheffield: Sheffield Academic.

Garrett, Susan. 1993. "The 'Weaker Sex' in the Testament of Job." *JBL* 112:55–70.

Gemünden, Petra von. 2016. "Emotions and Literary Genres in the *Testaments of the Twelve Patriarchs* and the New Testament: A Contribution to Form History and Historical Psychology." *BibInt* 24:514–35.

Gorea, Maria. 2007. *Job, ses précurseurs et ses epigones ou comment faire du nouveau avec de l'ancien*. Orient & Mediterranée 1. Paris: de Boccard.

Gray, Patrick. 2004. "Points and Lines: Thematic Parallelism in the Letter of James and the 'Testament of Job.'" *NTS* 50:406–24.

Greenfield, Jonas C., Michael Stone, and Esther Eshel. 2004. *The Aramaic Levi Document: Edition, Translation, Commentary*. SVTP 19. Leiden: Brill.

Gruen, William. 2009. "Seeking a Context for the Testament of Job." *JSP* 18:163–79.

Guffey, Andrew. 2017. "Job and the 'Mystic's Solution' to Theodicy: Philosophical Paideia and Internalized Apocalypticism in the Testament of Job." Pages 215–39 in *Pedagogy in Ancient Judaism and Early Christi-*

anity. Edited by Karina Martin Hogan, Matthew J. Goff, and Emma Wasserman. EJL 41. Atlanta: SBL Press.

Haas, Cees. 1989. "Job's Perseverance in the *Testament of Job*. Pages 117–54 in *Studies in the Testament of Job*. Edited by Michael Knibb and Pieter van der Horst. SNTSMS 66. Cambridge: Cambridge University Press.

Halpern-Amaru, Betsy. 1994. *Rewriting the Bible: Land and Covenant in Post-Biblical Literature*. Valley Forge, PA: Trinity Press International.

Haralambakis, Maria. 2010. "'I Am Not Afraid of Anybody, I Am the Ruler of This Land': Job as Man in Charge in the *Testament of Job*." Pages 127–44 in *Men and Masculinity in the Hebrew Bible and Beyond*. Edited by Ovidiu Creangă. Bible in the Modern World 33. Sheffield: Sheffield Phoenix.

———. 2012. *The Testament of Job: Text, Narrative, and Reception History*. LSTS 80. London: Bloomsbury T&T Clark.

Harkins, Angela Kim. 2014. "A Fitting Inheritance for Job's Daughters in the Testament of Job." *Henoch* 36:64–85.

Henten, Jan Willem van. 1987. "Traditie en Interpretatie in Test.Mos. 9:1–10:10." *Summa Blad van de Theologische Faculteit van de Universiteit van Amsterdam* 19:18–29.

———. 2003. "Moses as Heavenly Messenger in Assumptio Mosis 10:2 and Qumran Passages." *JJS* 54:216–27.

Hillel, Vered. 2007. "Naphtali a Proto-Joseph in the Testaments of the Twelve Patriarchs." *JSP* 16:279–88.

———. 2013. *The Testaments of the Twelve Patriarchs: Structure, Source and Composition*. Lewiston, NY: Mellen.

Himmelfarb, Martha. 1984. "R. Moses the Preacher and the Testaments of the Twelve Patrarichs." *AJS Review* 9:55–78.

Hofmann, Norbert Johannes. 2000. *Die Assumptio Mosis: Studien zur massgültiger Überlieferung*. JSJSup 67. Leiden: Brill.

Hollander, Harm. 1981. *Joseph as an Ethical Model in the Testaments of the Twelve Patriarchs*. SVTP 6. Leiden: Brill.

———. 1995. "Israel and God's Eschatological Agent in the Testaments of the Twelve Patriarchs." Pages 91–104 in *Aspects of Religious Contact and Conflict in the Ancient World*. Edited by Pieter van der Horst. Utrechtse theologische reeks 31. Utrecht: Faculteit der Godgeleerheid, Universiteit Utrecht.

Hollander, Harm, and Marinus de Jonge. 1985. *The Testaments of the Twelve Patriarchs: A Commentary*. SVTP 8. Leiden: Brill.

Horst, Pieter van der. 1989. "Images of Women in the *Testament of Job*." Pages 93–116 in *Studies in the Testament of Job*. Edited by Michael Knibb and Pieter van der Horst. SNTSMS 66. Cambridge: Cambridge University Press.

Israeli, Edna. 2009. "'Taxo' and the Origins of the *Assumption of Moses*." *JBL* 128:735–57.

Jonge, Marinus de. 1953. *The Testaments of the Twelve Patriarchs: A Study of Their Text, Composition and Origin*. Assen: Van Gorcum.

———. 1991. *Jewish Eschatology, Early Christian Christology and the Testaments of the Twelve Patriarchs: Collected Essays*. VTSup 63. Leiden: Brill.

———. 2002. "The Two Great Commandments in the Testaments of the Twelve Patriarchs." *NovT* 44:371–92.

———. 2003. *Pseudepigrapha of the Old Testament as Part of Christian Literature: The Case of the Testaments of the Twelve Patriarchs and the Greek Life of Adam and Eve*. SVTP 18. Leiden: Brill.

———. 2004. "Sidelights on the Testaments of the Twelve Patriarchs from the Greek Catena on Genesis." Pages 303–17 in *Things Revealed: Studies in Early Jewish And Christian Literature in Honor of Michael E. Stone*. Edited by Esther Chazon, David Satran, and Ruth Clements. JSJSup 89. Leiden: Brill.

Kierkegaard, Bradford A. 2004. "Satan in the Testament of Job: A Literary Analysis." Pages 4–19 in Later Versions and Traditions. Volume 2 of *Of Scribes and Sages: Early Jewish Interpretation and Transmission of Scripture*. Edited by C. A. Evans. LSTS 51. London: T&T Clark.

Klancher, Nancy. 2010. "The Male Soul in Drag: Women-as-Job in the *Testament of Job*." *JSP* 19:225–45.

Kolenkow, A. B. 1975. "The Genre Testament and Forecasts of the Future in the Hellenistic Jewish Milieu." *JSJ* 6:57–71.

Kugel, James. 1992. "The Story of Dinah in the *Testament of Levi*." *HTR* 85:1–34.

———. 1993. "Levi's Elevation to the Priesthood in Second Temple Writings." *HTR* 86:1–64.

———. 1995. "Reuben's Sin with Bilhah in the Testament of Reuben." Pages 525–54 in *Pomegranates and Golden Bells: Studies in Biblical, Jewish, and Near Eastern Ritual, Law, and Literature in Honor of Jacob Milgrom*. Edited by David P. Wright, David Noel Freedman, and Avi Hurvitz. Winona Lake, IN: Eisenbrauns.

———. 2007. "How Old is the Aramaic Levi Document?" *DSD* 14:291–312.

———. 2010. "Some Translation and Copying Mistakes from the Original Hebrew of the Testaments of the Twelve Patriarchs." Pages 45–56 in *The Dead Sea Scrolls: Transmission of Traditions and Production of Texts*. Edited by Sarianna Metso, Hindy Najman, and Eileen Schuller. STDJ 92. Leiden: Brill.

———. 2013. "Testaments of the Twelve Patriarchs." Pages 1697–1855 in vol. 2 of *Outside the Bible: Ancient Jewish Writings Related to Scripture*. 3 vols. Edited by Louis Feldman, James Kugel, and Lawrence Schiffman. Philadelphia: Jewish Publication Society; Lincoln: University of Nebraska Press.

———. 2017a. "Simeon and Levi's Attack on Shechem, or: The Mystery of MS C of the Testaments of the Twelve Patriarchs." Pages 655–72 in vol. 1 of *Sibyls, Scriptures, and Scrolls: John Collins at Seventy*. Edited by Joel S. Baden, Hindy Najman, and Eibert J. C. Tigchelaar. JSJSup 175. 2 vols. Leiden: Brill.

———. 2017b. "With a Little Help from the Rabbis: The Testaments of the Twelve Patriarchs and Rabbinic Exegetical Traditions." Pages 139–56 in *The Faces of Torah: Studies in the Texts and Contexts of Ancient Judaism in Honor of Steven Fraade*. Edited by Michal Bar-Asher Siegal, Christine Hayes, and Tzi Novick. JSJSup 22. Göttingen: Vandenhoeck & Ruprecht.

Kugler, Robert. 1996. *From Patriarch to Priest: The Levi-Priestly Tradition from Aramaic Levi to Testament of Levi*. EJL 9. Atlanta: Scholars Press.

———. 2001a. "Testaments." Pages 189–213 in vol. 1 of *Justification and Variegated Nomism: A Fresh Appraisal of Paul and Second Temple Judaism*. 2 vols. Edited by D. A. Carson, Peter O'Brien, and Mark Seifrid. WUNT 2/140 Tübingen: J. C. B. Mohr.

———. 2001b. *Testaments of the Twelve Patriarchs*. Guides to the Apocrypha and Pseudepigrapha 2. Sheffield: Sheffield Academic.

———. 2008 "Whose Scripture? Whose Community? Reflections on the Dead Sea Scrolls Then and Now, by Way of *Aramaic Levi*." DSD 15:5–23.

———. 2010a. "Testaments." Pages 1294–97 in *The Eerdmans Dictionary of Early Judaism*. Edited by John J. Collins and Daniel C. Harlow. Grand Rapids: Eerdmans.

———. 2010b. "Patriarchs, Testaments of the Twelve." Pages 1031–33 in *The Eerdmans Dictionary of Early Judaism*. Edited by John J. Collins and Daniel C. Harlow. Grand Rapids: Eerdmans.

———. 2012. "The *Testaments of the Twelve Patriarchs*: A Not-So-Ambiguous Witness to Early Jewish Interpretive Practices." Pages 337–60 in *Companion to Biblical Interpretation in Early Judaism*. Edited by Matthias Henze. Grand Rapids: Eerdmans.

———. 2016. "On Anthropology and Honor in the Testament of Job." Pages 117–26 in *Dust of the Ground and Breath of Life (Gen 2:7): The Problem of a Dualistic Anthropology in Early Judaism and Christianity*. Edited by Jacques van Ruiten and George H. Van Kooten. TBN 20. Leiden: Brill.

———. 2017. "Of Echoes of Jewish Scriptures and Adaptations of Livestock Inventories in the Testament of Job." Pages 587–602 in *Reading the Bible in Ancient Traditions and Modern Editions: Studies in Memory of Peter W. Flint*. AJL 47. Atlanta: SBL Press.

———. Forthcoming. "The *Testament of the Twelve Patriarchs*." In *The Wiley Blackwell Companion to the Old Testament Apocrypha and Pseudepigrapha*. Edited by Randal Chesnutt. London: Wiley Blackwell.

Kugler, Robert, and Richard Rohrbaugh. 2004. "On Women and Honor in the Testament of Job." *JSP* 14:43–62.

Kurowski, Philip. 2010. *Der menschliche Gott aus Levi und Juda: Die "Testamente der zwölf Patriarchen" als Quelle judenchristlicher Theologie*. TANZ 52. Tübingen: Francke.

Legaspi, Michael. 2008. "Job's Wives in the Testament of Job: A Note on the Synthesis of Two Traditions." *JBL* 127:71–79.

Lesses, Rebecca. 2007. "Amulets and Angels: Visionary Experience in the Testament of Job and the Hekhalot Literature." Pages 49–74 in *Heavenly Tablets: Interpretation, Identity and Tradition in Ancient Judaism*. Edited by Lynn LiDonnici and Andrea Lieber. JSJSup 119. Leiden: Brill.

Machinist, Peter. 1997. "Job's Daughters and Their Inheritance in the Testament of Job and Its Biblical Congeners." Pages 67–80 in *The Echoes of Many Texts: Reflections on Jewish and Christian Traditions: Essays in Honor of Lou H. Silberman*. Edited by William G. Dever and J. Edward Wright. BJS 313. Atlanta: Scholars Press.

Marcus, Joel. 2010. "The Testaments of the Twelve Patriarchs and the *Didascalia Apostolorum*: A Common Jewish Christian Milieu?" *JTS* 61:596–626.

Mirguet, Françoise. 2014. "Emotional Responses to the Pain of Others in Josephus's Rewritten Bible and the Testament of Zebulun: Between Power and Vulnerability." *JBL* 133:838–57.

Munck, Johannes. 1950. "Discours d'adieu dans le Nouveau Testament et dans la littéreature biblique." Pages 155–70 in *Aux sources de la tradition chrétienne: Melanges offerts a M. Maurice Goguel a l'occasión de son soixante-dixieme anniversaire*. Edited by Pierre Menoud. Bibliotheque théologique. Neuchâtel: Delachaux & Nestlé.

Nicholls, Peter H. 1982. "The Structure and Purpose of the Testament of Job." PhD diss., Hebrew University.

Nickelsburg, George W. E. 2005. *Jewish Literature between the Bible and the Mishnah: A Historical and Literary Introduction*. 2nd ed. Minneapolis: Fortress.

Nisse, Ruth. 2017. "The Testaments of the Twelve Patriarchs in the Shadow of the Ten Lost Tribes." Pages 127–53 in *Jacob's Shipwreck: Diaspora, Translation, and Jewish-Christian Relations in Medieval England*. Ithaca, NY: Cornell University Press.

Nordheim, Eckhard von. 1980. *Die Lehre der Alten I: Das Testament als Literaturgattung im Judentum der hellenistisch-römischen Zeit*. ALGHJ 13. Leiden: Brill.

O'Connor, M. John-Patrick. 2017. "Satan and Sitis: The Significance of Clothing Changes in the Testament of Job. *JSP* 26:305–19.

Omerzu, Heike. 2005. "Women, Magic and Angels: On the Emancipation of Job's Daughters in the Apocryphal Testament of Job." Pages 85–103 in *Bodies in Question: Gender, Religion, Text*. Edited by Darlene Bird and Yvonne Sherwood. London: Routledge.

Portier-Young, Anathea. 2013. "Through the Dung-Heap to the Chariot: Intertextual Transformations in the *Testament of Job*." Pages 235–45 in *Reading Job Intertextually*. Edited by Katherine Dell and Will Kynes. LHBOTS 574. London: Bloomsbury.

Pouchelle, Patrick. 2017. "Discipline, Transmission, and Writing: Notes on Education in the Testaments of the Twelve Patriarchs." Pages 131–40 in *Second Temple Jewish "Paideia" in Context*. Edited by Jason Zurawski and Gabriele Boccaccini. BZNW 228. Berlin: de Gruyter.

Priest, John F. 1985. "Testament of Moses." *OTP* 1:919–34.

———. 1992. "Moses, Testament of." *ABD* 4:920–22.

Reed, Annette Yoshiko. 2010. "Job, Testament of." Pages 814–16 in *Eerdmans Dictionary of Early Judaism*. Edited by John J. Collins and Daniel C. Harlow. Grand Rapids: Eerdmans.

———. 2014. "Textuality between Death and Memory: The Prehistory and Formation of the Parabiblical Testament." *JQR* 104:381–412.

Römer, Cornelia. 1989. "P.Köln Inv Nr. 3221: Das Testament des Hiob in koptischer Sprache; ein Vorbericht." Pages 33–45 in *Studies in the Testament of Job*. Edited by Michael Knibb and Pieter van der Horst. SNTSMS 66. Cambridge: Cambridge University Press.

Rosen-Zvi, Ishay. 2006. "Bilhah the Temptress: 'The Testament of Reuben' and 'The Birth of Sexuality.'" *JQR* 96:65–94.

Rosner, B. 1992. "A Possible Quotation of Test. Reuben 5.5 in 1 Corinthians 6.18A." *JTS* 43:123–27.

Schalit, Abraham. 1989. *Untersuchungen zur Assumptio Mosis*. ALGHJ 17. Leiden: Brill.

Schaller, Bernd. 1979. *Das Testament Hiobs*. JSHRZ 3.3. Gütersloh: Gütersloher Verlagshaus.

———. 1980. "Das Testament Hiobs und die Septuaginta-Übersetzung des Buches Hiobs." *Bib* 61:377–406.

———. 1989. "Zur Komposition und Konzeption des Testaments Hiobs." Pages 46–92 in *Studies in the Testament of Job*. Edited by Michael Knibb and Pieter van der Horst. SNTSMS 66. Cambridge: Cambridge University Press.

Schenke, Gesa. 2009. *Das Testament des Iob*. Vol. 1 of *Das koptische Kölner Papyruskodex 3221*. Paderborn: Schonigh.

———. 2013. "The Testament of Job (Coptic Fragments): A New Translation and Introduction." Pages 160–75 in *Old Testament Pseudepigrapha: More Noncanonical Scriptures*. Vol. 1. Edited by Richard Bauckham, James R. Davila, and Alexander Panayotov. Cambridge: Cambridge University Press; Grand Rapids: Eerdmans.

———. 2014. "Neue Fragmente der Kölner Kodex 3221: Textzuwachs am koptischen Testament des Iob." *ZPE* 188:87–105.

Shaw, Brent. 1996. "Body/Power/Identity: Passions of the Martyrs." *JECS* 4:269–312.

Slingerland, Dixon. 1984. "The Levitical Hallmark within the Testaments of the Twelve Patriarchs." *JBL* 103:531–37.

———. 1986. "The Nature of *Nomos* (Law) Within the *Testaments of the Twelve Patriarchs*." *JBL* 105:39–48.

Spittler, Russell. 1983. "Testament of Job." *OTP* 1:829–68.

Stone, Michael. 1969. *The Testament of Levi: A First Study of the Armenian Manuscripts of the Testaments of the XII Patriarchs in the Convent of St. James, Jerusalem, with Text, Critical Apparatus, Notes and Translation*. Jerusalem. Saint James.

———. 2002. "Aramaic Levi in Its Contexts." *JSQ* 9:307–26.

———. 2003. "Aramaic Levi Document and Greek Testament of Levi." Pages 429–37 in *Emanuel: Studies in Hebrew Bible, Septuagint, and Dead Sea Scrolls in Honor of Emanuel Tov*. Edited by Shalom Paul, Robert A. Kraft, Lawrence H. Schiffman, and Weston W. Fields. VTSup 94. Leiden: Brill.

Stone, Michael, and Vered Hillel. 2012. *An "Editio Minor" of the Armenian Version of the Testaments of the Twelve Patriarchs*. Hebrew University Armenian Studies 11. Leuven: Peeters.

Sutter, Rehmann. 1999. "Das Testament Hiob: Hiob, Dina und ihre Töchter." Pages 465–73 in *Kompendium feministische Bibelauslegung*. Edited by Luise Schottroff. 2nd ed. Gütersloh: Gütersloher Verlagshaus.

Thomas, Johannes. 2004. "The Paraenesis of the Testaments of the Twelve Patriarchs: Between Torah and Jewish Wisdom." Pages 157–90 in *Early Christian Paraenesis in Context*. Edited by James Starr and Troels Engberg-Pedersen. BZAW 125. Berlin: de Gruyter.

Tromp, Johannes. 1990. "Taxo, Messenger of the Lord." *JSJ* 21:200–209.

———. 1993. *The Assumption of Moses: A Critical Edition with Commentary*. SVTP 10. Leiden: Brill.

Twelftree, Graham. 2011. "Exorcism and the Defeat of Beliar in the Testaments of the Twelve Patriarchs." *VC* 65:170–88.

Ulrichsen, Jarl Henning. 1991. *Die Grundschrift der Testamente der Zwölf Patriarchen: Eine Untersuchung zu Umfang, Inhalt, und Eigenart der ursprünglichen Schrift*. Stockholm: Almqvist & Wiksell.

Wahl, H.-M. 1994. "Elihu, Frevler oder Frommler? Die Auslegung des Hiobbuches (31–37) durch ein Pseudepigraphon (TestHi 41–43)." *JSJ* 25:1–17.

Waugh, Robin. 2014. "The Testament of Job as an Example of Profeminine Patience Literature." *JBL* 133:777–92.

Whitters, Mark. 2010. "Taxo and His Seven Sons in the Cave (Assumption of Moses 9–10)." *CBQ* 72:718–31.

Wisse, Maarten. 2003. *Scripture between Identity and Creativity: A Hermeneutical Theory Building upon Four Interpretations of Job*. Ars Disputandi Supplement 1. Utrecht: Ars Disputandi.

Zilm, Jennifer. 2013. "Multi-Coloured Like Woven Works: Gender, Ritual, Clothing and Praying with the Angels in the Dead Sea Scrolls and the Testament of Job." Pages 438–51 in *Prayer and Poetry in the Dead Scrolls and Related Literature: Essays in Honor of Eileen Schuller on the Occasion of Her Sixty-Fifth Birthday*. Edited by Jeremy Penner, Ken M. Penner, and Cecilia Wassen. STDJ 98. Leiden: Brill.

15
Narrative Literature

SYLVIE HONIGMAN

This chapter begins by tackling the question of how to define narrative literature. While the focus is on texts from the Hebrew Bible and early Jewish literature, this section also compares them with similar literary works that were produced in neighboring societies. After this, I will examine separately three texts considered to be central to the said category, namely, the books of Esther, Judith, and Tobit. The order in which they are discussed is determined by the number of publications that each text has respectively elicited since the 1980s.

1. Narrative Literature

1.1. What Is Narrative Literature?

Narrative literature is a label commonly assigned to a handful of texts included either in the Hebrew Bible or the Septuagint that tell a story involving unknown or marginal figures from the past, including women, in ways that might be deemed entertaining. In terms of their literary form and genre, they form a loose category, and some narratives are even embedded in longer works (e.g., Daniel; LXX 1 Esdras). Consequently, the corpus of texts defined as narratives (or similar labels) may vary. The core list includes: Esther, Dan 1–6, Judith, Tobit, and the Story of the Three Guards in 1 Esd 3:1–5:6. As court tales, scholars regularly add the Joseph story in Gen 37:2–48:22 and the Story of Ahikar (which was not Jewish but was popular among Jews; Humphreys 1973); as historical fiction, scholars add the Letter of Aristeas, 2 Maccabees, and 3 Maccabees (Johnson 2004, 9); as a novella, scholars add Joseph and Aseneth (Wills

2011); and as testaments (works written in an entertaining way contrasting with other works in the genre of the testaments), scholars add the Testament of Abraham, the Testament of Joseph, and the Testament of Job (Doran 1986).

Scholars disagree over the nature and function(s) of biblical narratives. Were they written merely for entertainment value, and if so, how did they eventually make their way into biblical canons? If not, how should we explain their otherwise incongruous light-hearted tone, and what therefore was their function? It should be noted from the outset that the very category of biblical narrative literature is pertinent only if we consider that the entertaining quality of the various works is their major defining feature. Conversely, if we consider that their entertainment value comes second to other agendas that the authors had, this category itself becomes problematic.

1.2. The Genesis of Narratives Included in the Biblical Corpus:
Oral and Written Elements

The light tone of the narratives is often attributed to their having originated in popular stories circulated in oral form (Morgan 2007, 3–5). In support of this popular origin, scholars point to formal features of the narratives, such as generic names ("Judith," literally "the Jewess"; the "Three Guards" in 1 Esdras), or they underscore the gross historical inaccuracies they contain (see below under Esther, Judith, and Tobit). Moreover, studies have shown that biblical narratives can be profitably analyzed by using typologies of folktale motifs, either with the Aarne-Thompson-Uther (ATU) classification system or with Vladimir Propp's typological ranking (Niditch and Doran 1977; Niditch 1987; Milne 1988; Soll 1988).

That said, we must distinguish between the presence of folktale motifs in certain works and the latter's textual history. Even though some elements in them may have originally been intended for oral consumption, they doubtless underwent alterations in the process of being written down. New elements were added (such as specifying regnal years or priestly material), while others were reworked or deleted. Moreover, some works that may seem like oral narratives may actually have been originally composed in writing (Niditch and Doran 1977, 182; Dimant 2017a).

Evidence that preexisting literary material was reused can be found in the parallels between biblical and nonbiblical compositions (on this phenomenon, see Selden 2010). For instance, passages from the Story of Ahikar have been traced to Tobit (1:21–22; 2:10; 11:18; 14:10); the story of

Vashti in Esther shows affinities with the Candaules story in Herodotus, *Hist.* 1.8 (Berlin 2001b, 8 n.16); the slaughter of the Jews' enemies in Esther may derive from the mythic transposition of the Assyrian royal ideology, according to which royal acts of revenge were carried out by gods (Dalley 2007). Narratives relating to a same character were furthermore gathered into collections and circulated in this form, and it has been argued that the stories in Dan 1–6 originated in such a compilation (Holm 2013).

1.3. Who Composed These Narratives?

Central to the issue of who composed the narratives is the question of self-referentiality. That is to say, to what extent does the story world mirror the actual social world of the author? Even if scholars nowadays assume that a gap of some kind invariably exists between text and author, disagreements abound regarding the degree of that gap. Four variables must be considered, and they affect not only the dating of a given work but also its interpretation: (1) the social identity of the author; (2) the time and (3) place in which he lived; and (4) the social sphere(s) in which the text was subsequently circulated. Regarding the issues of time and place, it may be worth noting that the device of casting a fictional world in the days of a past dynasty is well documented in ancient Egyptian literature (Holm 2013). This ploy is consistent with conservative societies, in which authority hinges on tradition. Likewise, the transposition of story worlds to foreign countries was a means to critique contemporary society without risking any direct references (Holm 2013).

Furthermore, in some cases texts and genres could also cross social boundaries. Court tales were in all likelihood originally composed within the royal entourage as part of the training curriculum of courtiers, that is, as a form of wisdom literature (Newsom 2014, 12–14). Their social function was to explore tensions between the king and his retinue, on the one hand, and between rival courtiers, on the other. However, this genre was eventually taken over by other classes of writers and adapted to serve additional functions. In some cases, court tales were combined with priestly (or, at least learned) material—apocalyptic visions in the book of Daniel, and the book of Ezra, LXX 1 Esdras—to form entirely new works. This reinterpretation may be read as self-referential (Collins 1985, 136, on Daniel) or allegorical. That is, the protagonists of the tale "come to personify the national hopes of the exiled Jews" (Henze 2001, 18). Allegorical readings have been proposed for Mordecai and Esther (Levenson 1997, 16), Daniel

(Henze 2001), and may also work for 1 Esdras. Contrastingly, Wills (1990) has argued that the court tales were circulated more widely outside the court and the temple, and that new works were composed among circles of lower social status.

1.4. Understanding the Entertainment Factor of the Narratives

If the entertaining slant of the narratives stems from their popular origin, why was this ingredient not edited out by the learned scribes when they combined them with learned material? What was its purpose?

In several studies, Lawrence Wills (e.g., 1995, 2011) promoted the view that levity in these works was an end per se, comparing them with Greco-Roman novels (see also Johnson 2004; Gruen 2016). In Wills's (2011) view, these works were popular primarily in a functional, not social way. That is, they had no institutionalized social use but were performed or read purely for entertainment. They fulfilled a vital, albeit informal social function precisely because of their relaxed tone. Notably, the popular genres actually reveal more about society's deeper concerns, "precisely … because [they] are… unprotected by [elitist] genre rules" (146). These Jewish novellas retained their novelistic nature until a late stage and were incorporated in biblical canons, first because their protagonists came to be revered as heroes of the faith and second because they filled in chronological gaps in biblical history.

In contrast, other scholars maintain that the entertaining tone of the works is there to further their sapiential or theological message. This is a subservient aspect of the text and not a key element of interpretation (see Whitmarsh 2013, 11–34). In Francis Macatangay's (2011) words, "stories have the incredible and uncanny ability to leave an indelible imprint on the human mind. Dry facts and statistical data are quickly forgotten, but anecdotes of human interest [are easily remembered]…. Hence, good stories make excellent vehicles for inculcating morals and reinforcing beliefs that the spinner of the tale thinks are of prime significance" (115).

Furthermore, evidence from neighboring cultures confirms that a lighter tone of narrative was not altogether incompatible with the social setting of the court or the temple and hence with a sapiential function. Proof of this social location comes from archaeological excavations in the temple of Tebtunis, Middle Egypt, which have yielded an extensive archive of literary texts of all kinds. Strikingly, 25 percent of the corpus altogether are tales, showing that the link between storytelling and the priestly circles remained strong well into imperial times. Likewise, it was a basic tenet for Greek theorists of rhetoric that pleasure (entertainment) and didactic purposes went hand in hand (Morgan 2007, 1–22).

1.5. The Multiple Functions of Narratives

Like Demotic narratives, biblical narratives have a loose literary form, borrowing from various genres at once. Hence, thematic eclecticism was the rule (Newsom 2007). We must assume that narratives were composed, read, and copied for multiple reasons and that the ways they were received and shared in antiquity were varied (Dieleman and Moyer 2010, 436), some of which are outlined as follows.

1.5.1. Wisdom

The affinities between court tales (the most common category of narratives) and wisdom literature are often pointed out (Niditch and Doran 1977, 182), yet in truth virtually all narratives contain sapiential elements. As the prominent part of the tales in the priestly library of Tebtunis suggests, these short self-contained narratives were indeed part of the sapiential training of scribes, alongside gnomic texts (Dieleman and Moyer 2010). As character-based stories, tales put the ethical virtues of the main protagonist(s) to test through a plot that pivots on a conflict with authorities—for instance, "Tobit's decision to bury the dead; Daniel's decision not to eat the king's food"; "Esther's decision to come unannounced before the king"; "Joseph's decision not to have sex with Potiphar's wife"; or "Job's decision to respond to loss with words of piety." "It is the character's decision to act on their virtue … that ultimately leads to the resolution of the conflict and the restoration of a harmonious world. The wisdom-didactic narratives are morally optimistic in their worldview and comedic in their structure" (Newsom 2014, 14).

1.5.2. A Lifestyle for Diaspora versus Subversion of Empire

Lee Humphreys (1973) read the court tales as sources providing guidelines on the "lifestyle for diaspora." Through their comedic structure and happy endings, they were designed to reassure diaspora Jews that, despite their predicament, they could successfully participate in the structures of empire without forswearing their identity as Jews.

More recently, scholars swayed by the influence of postcolonial studies have interpreted them instead as literature expressing a covert resistance to empire (Wills 1990; Newsom 2014, 15–18; Gruen 2016, 229–44). According to Wills (1990), the theme of the Jewish courtier in a foreign court reflects the perspective of a ruled ethnic, whereby one such community told stories of the cleverness of their own counselors in the multiethnic context of the foreign king's court. In this way, the narratives became a means for bolstering ethnic dignity and self-assertion.

Alongside these studies emphasizing imperial and identity politics, Matthias Henze (2001, 18–22) stresses that Jewish court tales invariably infuse the stock pattern of the court genre with a religious subtext. What is at play here is the conflict of authority between the foreign king and God. Moreover, the Jewish hero uses his access to the foreign king to save his people rather than for personal gain (Daniel; 1 Esdras).

1.5.3. The Assertion of Identity through History

A number of narratives have been categorized as historical fictions. According to Sara Raup Johnson (2004, 5), the authors of these works "manipulate and reshape traditions about the Jewish past in order to articulate a particular view of Jewish identity in the contemporary Hellenistic world." They modify "historical facts in service of a higher moral and aesthetic truth" to create compelling historical exempla (38, 41).

In Adele Berlin's (2001a, xxxv) view, historical references embedded in the narratives provided an "answer to the critical question of how a Jewish community in exile can see itself vis-à-vis the Israel of the Bible." Through thematic and verbal reference, the diaspora narratives were tied to earlier biblical stories that were already accepted as authoritative. For instance, since Mordecai was exiled with King Jeconiah, the book of Esther could pick up the story of Israel where the book of Kings left off. Likewise, Judith is also depicted as a judge of Israel (Wills 2011, 159).

The modern Western reader may be disconcerted by the gross chronological and historical inaccuracies found in virtually all the biblical narratives (for instance, Nebuchadnezzar is called a great Assyrian king in Jdt 1:1, and he converts to the God of Israel in Daniel). One way to dodge the problem is to attribute these misstatements to the allegedly popular origin of the tales, but this fails to explain why such inaccuracies were not put right when the tales were combined with learned material (as in Daniel). Moreover, the Demotic tales found in the priestly library of Tebtunis display similar inaccuracies

(Dieleman and Moyer 2010, 435–36). Rather, this feature is indicative of a certain way of making use of the past that historians of ancient Greece have dubbed "intentional history" (Foxhall, Gehrke, and Luraghi 2010). To understand this use of the past we must first remind ourselves that the way a society relates to time (past, present, and future) is culturally conditioned (Koselleck 1985; Hartog 2015). In modern Western societies the present is seen quite distinct from the past. This "regime of historicity" (Hartog 2015) is the precondition for any scientific historiography, whose aim is to scrupulously reconstruct an objective timeline. Once the past is thus objectivized, it may then be periodized, that is, itemized into a succession of fundamentally distinct empires. In contrast, for the ancients the present continued the past and prefigured the future (Koselleck 1985). What mattered for them was to show how the present was linked to the past in a meaningful way. This was effected by projecting the "elements of subjective, self-conscious self-categorization which construct the identity of a group as a group" onto key moments of the past that were pinpointed as critical elements worth remembering (Foxhall and Luraghi 2010, 9). For instance, Nebuchadnezzar converting to the God of Israel offers a vital precedent (exemplum) for a desideratum of the present. Moreover, the past that resembles the present cannot be itemized. Instead, it is thematized. What mattered was not that Nebuchadnezzar was a Babylonian but that both Nebuchadnezzar and the Assyrians were conquerors, for instance. Next, historical figures falling under the same thematic label were readily conflated in order to reinforce the chosen thematic category.

The comparative perspective—in particular Tim Whitmarsh's (2013) discussion of the nature and history of fiction in Greek literature in Hellenistic times and the discovery of tales in the Tebtunis library—arguably weakens the view that the biblical narratives were composed as entertainment literature. This theory also makes it puzzling as to why tales were combined with serious material in Daniel and 1 Esdras.

2. Esther, Judith, and Tobit

The rest of the chapter surveys specific works, starting with the books of Esther.

2.1. The Books of Esther

The story of Esther narrates how the eponymous Jewish orphan becomes queen of Persia, and how, when her kinsman Mordecai comes into conflict with Haman, he becomes the king's highest courtier. The ensuing attrition risks leading to the slaughter of the Jews across the Persian Empire. It is thanks to Esther's intervention that they are all spared, and the festival of Purim is instituted to commemorate this event. The scene is set in the royal court at Susa. The story exists in multiple versions and languages (Dorothy 1997, 13–16). The present overview covers the Masoretic Text (MT); the LXX; and the A-text (AT), a distinct Greek recension.

Recent decades have seen an increase of interest in MT Esther as a work of literature, thanks both to the use of Mikhail Bakhtin's (1984) analysis of carnivalesque literature and to the growing body of feminist scholarship, a surge of attention exemplified in a symposium (Crawford and Greenspoon 2003) and in volumes of collected articles (Brenner 1995, 1999). The Greek versions of Esther (LXX and AT) have ultimately garnered interest in their own right, enabling textual and literary comparisons between the various recensions. However, disagreements about the date and provenance of all the known versions remain.

2.1.1. Masoretic Text Esther as Carnivalesque Literature

Masoretic Text Esther combines a dramatic theme, the threat of the Jews' total annihilation, with an underlying comic tone. Kenneth Craig (1995) was the first to argue that the key to explain this contrast is to read the work as a case of carnivalesque literature. As a type of festival, carnival provides an escape from external, institutionalized oppressive forces. The celebration of the Purim festival contains carnivalesque elements (Berlin 2001a, xxi–xxii).

The vein of comedy in carnivalesque literature reflects the mood of the festival. As noted by Craig (1995, 52, 60–68), it is primarily characterized by the temporary, gleeful reversal of the daily social order. Accordingly, in Esther's narrative world two cultures are juxtaposed: the official Persian culture represented by king Ahasuerus and Haman, his vizier, and the unofficial lifestyle of Esther and Mordecai. As the informal culture vies with the official order of things, various symbols and places of power are lampooned (carnivalized) through various narrative devices. For instance, the Persian court becomes a place of revelry and bawdiness, and the king himself is portrayed as a fool. Other typical features of carnivalesque worlds are impersonation and deception (Mordecai bids Esther to conceal her Jewish identity), indulgence in food and drinking (the ten banquets of the book play an essential role in the plot; Berlin, 2001a, xvi), and sexual innuendo.

Likewise, the horrors of violence and death are often parodied in carnivalesque literature, here typified in the last chapters of Esther by the death of Haman and the massacre of the Jews' enemies. Another basic device is the pairing of opposites and reversals, as illustrated in the existential threat to the Jews and the about-turn that closes the narrative: Haman is hung on the gallows that he had intended for Mordecai, and those who plotted the slaughter of the Jews are themselves slain. Also consistent with the MT Esther's belonging to the carnivalesque genre is the frequent observation that it is the most secular of the biblical books (Craig 1995, 50, 136–40). In the wake of Craig's work, numerous scholars have explored further the function of the carnivalesque in MT Esther (e.g., Lacocque 2007).

2.1.2. Further Literary Readings

As new studies began to disclose the literary artistry and compositional sophistication of the book of Esther, the text began to emerge as a multifaceted work imbued with multiple messages (Fox 1991a, 157). However, these messages are allusive and their meaning must be inferred (Levenson 1997, 12).

Divergences of opinion pivot on the basic role of humor in the text. As the primary function of the work is to give legitimacy to the Purim festival—which is not mentioned in the Pentateuch—the mirth it contains primarily references the carnivalesque mood of the festival (Berlin 2001a, xv–xix). Furthermore, in the wake of Bakhtin's study several scholars point to the underlying social function of humor: It can be didactic and serve as a tool for deconstructing hegemony practices, shaping opinion, or changing attitudes (Craig 1995; see Brenner 1994). André Lacocque sees humor as liberating force, arguing that in MT Esther theocentrism shifts toward Judeocentrism. Humor here is close to irony and satire, that is, its subversive and potentially disruptive form. At the same time, according to Lacocque, levity in MT Esther was a way of dealing with an actual crisis, namely, the religious persecution of Antiochus IV Epiphanes.

Timothy Laniak (1998) analyzes how the anthropological categories of honor and shame inform MT Esther. Structurally, the work may be divided into four parts (chs. 1–2, 3–5, 6–7, and 8–10) applying the pattern of "challenge and honor" to Esther and Mordecai. After an initial period of favor, their honor is challenged through attacks threatening their lives. Subsequently, their fortunes are once more reversed through divine intervention, whereby they earn the utmost honor as leaders of their community. The moral of the tale is that while exile was a source of shame, honor could be regained in the very land of exile.

2.1.3. The Greek Recensions

Since Jerome, the six sections of LXX Esther that have no parallel in MT have been transmitted separately as Additions to Esther. In recent decades, the assumed distinction between a canonical text and interpolations came under critical scrutiny (Zsengellér 2010; Selden 2010). Whereas Cameron Boyd-Taylor (2015) upholds the traditional distinction, other scholars have begun to reassess the Greek versions of Esther in their integrity (Fox 1991b). In his commentary, Jon Levenson (1997) even merges MT and the LXX Additions. David Clines (1984) has produced the first English translation of the AT.

Studies of the Greek texts effected since the 1980s focus on both the textual and the literary aspects of the works. Although scholars agree that the LXX version was translated from a Hebrew text close to the MT (except for the six additions), Clines investigates the relationships between the MT and AT texts through the tools of redaction and literary criticism and establishes that the AT was translated from a Semitic *Vorlage* (prototype) distinct from the MT. In contrast with the previous consensus (restated in Fox 1991b), he identifies the AT as the earlier version, which was subsequently reworked to align it to the LXX, although this reworking was limited to the chapters following Esth 8:3 and to the LXX Additions.

Charles Dorothy (1997) compares the contents of the three versions through redaction criticism analysis and concludes that the redactor of AT supplemented a proto-AT text with material borrowed from the LXX, which he rewrote, whereas the redactor of the MT may have drawn from a proto-Esther text close to the proto-AT. However, the recensions differ in their respective thematic emphases, to the point that they belong to different genres. In contrast with the secular tone of MT, in LXX and AT religious notations abound, including prayers, references to God, and dramatic divine interventions. Moreover, LXX and AT are bookended by Mordecai's prophetic dream and its interpretation, and this dream frame repackages the rescue novella and festal etiology as the fulfillment of a prophetic revelation, transforming the figure of Mordecai into a prophet. Charles Harvey (2003) argues that this process of transformation in LXX and AT was a way to handle the ethical issues raised by its narrative.

2.1.4. Esther's Character (MT, LXX, and AT)

Earlier scholarship has tended to view Mordecai as the lead figure of the book, the one who devises the strategy of action, with Esther merely following his instructions. In recent decades, however, the role of Esther has been thoroughly reevaluated.

Paving the way for Esther's reinstatement was Sidnie White's (1989) article, in which she argues that the heroine's character and actions can only properly be appreciated by understanding the means of action effectively available to women of her society. By this standard Esther is the true pivot of the story. Michael V. Fox (1991a) shows that although the basic plot of the story draws on folktale motifs, the protagonists in Esther are not stock characters but evolve as the story progresses. This is particularly true of Esther herself, who moves from being a passive to an active element of the tale and finally emerging as an "authority" (1991a, 196–204). Whereas these studies focus principally on MT Esther, Linda Day (1995) investigates the substantial differences in the characterization of Esther between the MT, LXX, and AT texts. In the Greek versions, Esther displays strong affinities with the female protagonists of the Greek Hellenistic novels, whereas the protagonist of MT Esther has numerous facets of character and action in common with the biblical figure of Judith.

A fundamental trigger to the reappraisal of Esther's character came from gender and feminist studies, and numerous studies have shown that gender relationships are an important underlying element in the plot of MT Esther (Fox 1991a; Brenner 1995, 1999). The debate whether in acting to save her people Esther remains a conventional female character or defies gender constraints was substantially advanced by Rebecca Hancock's (2013) reappraisal of the place of women in patriarchy. In both the biblical and ancient Persian worlds, she argues, the political systems were structured on kinship rather than gender. Consequently, far from being confined to the domestic, private sphere, women of rank had access to monarchs and important political figures through their familial ties. Greek, Persian, and biblical sources attest that some women in the historical reality of Persia and Israel held positions as court counselors. The portrayal of Esther as a politically powerful woman is not exceptional and connects her to several biblical antecedents.

2.1.5. Textual History, Date, and Provenance

While the story of Esther itself is situated in the reign of the Persian King Xerxes I (486–465 BCE), the LXX version was translated in either 114 or 78/77 BCE, according to its postscript. The dating of MT Esther within this range remains controversial. In support of an early date, Berlin (2001a, xli–xlii, cf. xxx–xxxi) points to topical similarities with descriptions of the Persian Empire and Persian court contained in the Athenian literature of the fifth and fourth centuries BCE. Some scholars read the motif of the slaughter of the Jews as an echo of the religious persecution of Antiochus Epiphanes in the 160s (Wills 1995, 98–100; Lacocque 2007, 35; Macchi 2018), while Fox opines that, since the attitude to foreign rule in the work is largely positive, it must predate this crisis (1991a, 217–20). Meanwhile, the historical inaccuracies and thematic and stylistic affinities of the MT work with the Hellenistic novel led some scholars to point to a late Hellenistic dating, possibly later than the LXX translation (see Fox 1991a, 139–45).

Disagreement over the Greek versions hinges on their relative chronology and purported place of composition. Dorothy (1997) considers differences in style, vocabulary, and content: The manner of the LXX text is more detailed and matter-of-fact, lending the story a more detached, didactic slant, whose purpose is to document historical events and stress festal observance; therefore, the resulting text must have been intended for a hellenized diaspora audience. In contrast, he sees the style of the AT as more personal, dwelling on the characters' emotions, and stressing the role of divine providence in history. The text was tailored to foster communal identity in a more traditional, less hellenized community, possibly in Palestine. In contrast, Karen Jobes (1996) locates the LXX translation in Jerusalem, whereas she considers the AT as most likely the earliest Greek translation of the Esther story, possibly produced in Egypt.

2.2. The Book of Judith

As Toni Craven (2003) notes in her historiographical survey of the book of Judith, since the 1980s scholarly interest in this work has been intense, and the range of issues investigated continues to widen. The figure of the pious, wealthy, beautiful, and resourceful widowed woman who brings Israel's salvation by cutting off the head of Nebuchadnezzar's general Holofernes has been systematically dissected by means of literary critical tools and anthropological and gender analyses. Meanwhile, studies on the book's textual aspects have slowed, and therefore this topic is not covered here (Doran 1986; Corley 2015).

2.2.1. Literary Aspects

Craven's (1983) analysis of the work's composition has been widely accepted. According to her, each of the book's two parts (chs. 1–7 and 8–16) has a threefold chiasmic structure underlined by thematic repetition. The figure of Achior serves to tie the two sections together (Moore 1985, 59). That said, Barbara Schmitz (2105) argues that the work's structure is actually dual, which is devised to highlight different key facets of Judith's character: while the storyline itself depicts Judith as a femme fatale, the speeches and prayers instead portray her as a learned, wise, and pious woman. Jan Willem van Henten (1995) defends the basic coherence of Jdt 7–13, which delineates a time-frame of forty days, echoing the forty years of Exodus.

The book of Judith exploits the generic codes of historiography, both Jewish (such as historical and geographical inaccuracies; Moore 1985, 38–49; Esler 2002, 109–14) and Greek (Schmitz 2015, on speeches). Likewise, it is uncertain whether its storyline exploits genuine historical precedents or Greek literary models. In particular, Herodotus's *Historiae* are cited as shaping the story of the foreign invasion and of the figures of Nebuchadnezzar and Holofernes (Caponigro 1992; cf. Esler 2002, 119–20; Corley 1992, 26–27; Gera 2014, 57–78). According to Benedikt Eckhardt (2009), allusions to the Maccabean wars refer not to the events per se but to 1 Maccabees.

Several studies stress what they see as the fundamentally ironic tone of the work (Craven 1983; Moore 1985, 78–85; cf. Gruen 2002, 158–70). Esler (2002) speaks of "carnivalesque" playfulness, pointing to, in anthropological terms, the book's ludic treatment of history and the liminal status of its heroine. However, this interpretation raises problems, because in contrast with the book of Esther, Judith was never linked to a carnivalesque festival. Basing his approach on the similarities between the figure of Judith and those of the Maccabees in 1 Maccabees, Van Henten (1995) suggests that the work conveyed veiled criticism of the Hasmonean dynasty. This reading opens the possibility that the irony in Judith was intended as a form of parody, that is to say, the ludic aspects were subservient to an underlying political message.

2.2.2. The Character of Judith

Studies since the 1980s have shown that the figure of Judith draws on a variety of stock characters: female biblical prototypes (Crawford 2003, on Esther; White 1992, on Judg 4–5; cf. Rakel 1999, on Judith's song; cf. Gera 2014, 45–56; Corley 2015); female Greek templates (Van Henten 1995; Gera 2014, 65–72); and male biblical heroes, such as Moses (Van Henten 1995; Rakel 1999), David beheading Goliath (Esler 2002, 128–29), and Judas Maccabaeus beheading Nicanor (Moore 1985, 51). Feminist scholars characterize Judith as an "archetypal androgyne" who "transcends the male/female dichotomy" by combining the figures of the warrior and the femme fatale (Moore 1985, 65).

Anthropological studies have helped to solve the puzzle of a God-fearing heroine who tells untruths and commits murder. In Mediterranean cultures structured by the codes of honor and shame, individuals are bound by moral obligations to their social group, not to outsiders. It was therefore licit for Judith to use deceit as a means to safeguard the honor of the Israelites and God (Esler 2002, 132–35; deSilva 2006).

Gender scholars ponder whether Judith's character subverts patriarchal expectations of gender roles. While the feminist scholars well into the 1980s coopted Judith as subversive, opinions have since shown increasing caution (see the survey in Milne 2015). Philip Esler (2002, 137) stresses that as a widow with no father or son, Judith "represents a social anomaly of someone outside the usual male-controlled kinship patterns." In line with what he sees as the book's carnivalesque undertone, the disruption is only temporary, however (137–38). That said, by "letting [a woman] become an agent" in the masculine arena of war and by modeling her story on a variety of male paradigms, the author "reinvents what it means to be an Israelite" (135, 139). In Amy-Jill Levine's (1992a) view, Judith threatens gender boundaries, but this peril is ultimately averted through her reabsorption into her social group, albeit only upon her death and the subsequent distribution of her property.

2.2.3. Religious Aspects

Religious aspects come to the fore in the verbal statements in the speeches and prayers contained in the work and in the actions of the characters, primarily of Judith.

According to Thomas Hieke (1992), the book of Judith teaches torah by providing practical illustrations of how to adhere to the torah's commandments. Ora Brison (2015, 179) meanwhile argues that Judith's deeds must be understood through the prism of her religious persona; while "she embodies most of the religious and cultic roles in which the Israelite women may participate in the HB," her killing of Holofernes resembles ritual killings by zealots, such as Phinehas.

The book also provides crucial evidence for the practice of prayer (Newman 1999). Based on her analysis of the dual compositional structure of the book, Schmitz (2015) argues that the combination of the beautiful versus the learned and the pious aspects of Judith's portrayal advances a mode of action suggesting a new understanding of God's involvement in human history. Instead of God saving his people by direct intervention, we see Judith devising her own plan of action by drawing on her learning and pious education. Thus, prayers become "theological reflections that enable and support her saving actions" (174).

The episode of Achior's circumcision in Jdt 14 has been interpreted in various ways. Adolfo Roitman (1992) argues that the ideology of proselytism in the book is highlighted by the systematic thematic and functional parallels between Achior and Judith. As a righteous pagan and an Ammonite, Achior is the alter ego of a complete Jew by birth, and he perfects his condition through his conversion. According to Eckhardt (2009), the book offers a "counter-discourse" that subverts the legitimizing discourses of the Hasmoneans by quoting terms (such as Israel) and topics (such as circumcision) that are foregrounded in 1 Maccabees (the main literary vehicle of Hasmonean propaganda composed under John Hyrcanus), while altering—and possibly parodying—the political signification they have in 1 Maccabees.

2.2.4. Date, Original Language, and Provenance

Recent studies have established that the book of Judith was written between the end of John Hyrcanus's reign (135–104 BCE) and the Roman conquest (63 BCE). The higher date is bounded by the numerous intertextual references to 1 Maccabees and an implicit allusion to Hyrcanus's conquest of Samaria (Moore 1985, 51, 67–68; Corley 1992, 25). Carey Moore supports a dating "toward the end of the reign of John Hyrcanus I … or at the beginning of the reign of Alexander Janneus (103–78 BCE)." Tal Ilan

(1999, 150–51) speculates a chronological link between the reign of Queen Alexandra Salome (76–67 BCE) and the composition of the book.

The old consensus that the extant work was a translation of a Hebrew *Vorlage* has been reversed, and the view that Judith was originally composed in Greek has garnered wide support (Rakel 1999; Gera 2013; 2014, 79–94). The new consensus implies that Hebraisms in the text do not result from clumsy translation but are knowing imitations either of the Septuagint style (Corley 2015) or of the language of 1 Maccabees (Echkardt 2009). Most scholars situate the composition of Judith in Palestine.

2.3. The Book of Tobit

The book of Tobit recounts the sufferings of the righteous Tobit, who was exiled from Galilee to Nineveh, and of Sarah, his relative. Tobit's son Tobias marries Sarah, and both Tobit and Sarah are cured by the angel Raphael, whom God sends after hearing their prayers.

Research on Tobit since the 1980s went through two dramatic shifts. In the early 1980s scholarly interest in this work resumed. A seminal study was Irene Nowell's dissertation of 1983, in which she analyzes the narrative and literary fabric of the work through literary critical tools. The publication of Qumran fragments of the book in 1995 (Fitzmyer 2003) prompted a spate of new studies into the text's history and interpretation.

2.3.1. Text

The story of Tobit was transmitted in nine languages and multiple versions. The Qumran fragments bear witness to five Aramaic manuscripts and one in Hebrew (Fitzmyer 2003, 3–17; Stuckenbruck and Weeks 2015). Loren Stuckenbruck and Stuart Weeks (2015) survey the linguistic, literary, ideological, and exegetical differences between the three Greek recensions. Scholars nowadays debate whether simply to accept this pluriformity and its implications for our understanding of the work's message or attempt to unravel textual priorities (Perrin 2014, 118–20).

2.3.2. Composition History

In the 1980s, scholars disclosed folklore motifs in Tobit (Nowell 1983; Moore 1996, 11–14; Spencer 1999, 156–57). That said, William Soll (1989) concedes that the beginning and the end of the narrative sharply depart from the conventions of the fairy tale genre.

In recent decades, most scholars have accepted the integrity of the composition (Spencer 1999, 167–68). Macatangay (2011, 7–44) critically reviews the various aspects of the text that were taken to indicate redaction, before advancing literary and theological arguments evincing the work's coherence. In particular, all fourteen chapters of Tobit are attested in Qumran; although the story of Tobit ends in chapter 12, the last two chapters address the problem of the exile, and the personal salvation of Tobit vouches for God's eventual salvation of his people; and moreover, chapters 13–14 allude to certain narrative elements in the story of Joseph, which supplied a biblical model for the storyline of Tobit.

In line with the notion of a unified composition, the search for sources was gradually superseded by the view of a single author enriching his text with intertextual allusions to both Jewish (biblical and postbiblical) and non-Jewish traditions (like Ahikar; Macatangay 2011, 7–44; Perrin 2014, 121–28). Recent studies emphasize intertextual relationship with Genesis, Exodus, Job, and Psalms (Corley and Skemp 2005; Macatangay 2011). Thematic affinities with Ben Sira and the use of motifs commonly found in apocalyptic works have also been noted (Moore 1996, 21; Nickelsburg 1988).

Devorah Dimant (2017a) insists on the intertextual network between Tobit and Qumran Aramaic texts of the second century BCE (1 Enoch; Genesis Apocryphon), with bearings on the book's genre and place of composition.

2.3.3. Genre

The book of Tobit combines a variety of literary forms, and its genre has been alternatively defined as comedy (Wills 1995; McCracken 1995; see Pyper's 2006 critique), didactic journey story (Moore 1996, 21), or didactic fictional story (Macatangay 2011, 116–17). According to Macatangay, the core story recounting Tobias's journey in Tob 4–12 qualifies as a heroic tale, this core is framed in Tob 1–3 and 13–14 by Tobit's sayings. This mixture of tale and instruction is best described as a "sapiential novel" (118–20).

Dimant (2017ab) retorts that generically, Tobit belongs not with novels but with Qumran Aramaic works, which form a coherent corpus of text sharing distinct halakic prescriptions. The literary patterns of the patriarchal biographies and a court tale that are combined in it are documented in Qumran (see Genesis Apocryphon).

2.3.4. Message and Purpose

Most scholars agree that the purpose of Tobit is didactic and instructional. Like the book of Job, it explores the theme of the suffering of the righteous, and the Deuteronomic theology of reward for the just and punishment for the wicked underpins the work (Spencer 1999, 159–60). Micah Kiel (2012) objects that not all retributive theology is deuteronomistic; in this matter Tobit should be compared with Hellenistic works such as Ben Sira and 1 Enoch. Scholars have noted the work's vein of irony, in that readers know more than the characters themselves (Moore 1996, 24–26). But, of course, irony is not necessarily comic (Pyper 2006) and hence may be compatible with didacticism.

Using narrative criticism, Macatangay (2011) investigates the significance and function of the wisdom discourse in Tobit. The author, he notes, introduces practical instructions "at critical junctures … to serve as a kind of guide … in interpreting the narrative" (115). The intrinsic role of these prompts in the story is evidence that "the wisdom tradition of Israel became an essential avenue for shaping the identity of" Jews in the diaspora (5, 255–99).

Kinship is a central theme in Tobit. One school of scholars interprets the advocacy of endogamy as a concern to preserve ethnic boundaries in the conditions of life in the diaspora. This concern explains the differences in the representation of family life and ethnicity between Tobit and the stories from Genesis that influenced it (Pitkänen 2006). Rather than geography, the author inscribes Jewish identity in terms of bodies, thereby dissolving the boundaries between homeland and diaspora (Levine 1992b; 2015). In contrast, Dimant stresses that endogamy is a major theme in Qumran Aramaic works, which relates to priestly purity (2017a). Moreover, Tobit's biography is split between Galilee and Nineveh, and the religious duties he fulfills are different in each place. His behavior in Galilee is consistent with Qumran, not rabbinic halakah (2017b).

Alongside kinship relations, volumes of collected articles treat themes such as afterlife, food, prophecy, angelology, and demonology (Xeravits and Zsengellér 2005; Bredin 2006).

2.3.5. Date, Language, and Provenance

The prevailing view remains that the book of Tobit was composed in the late third or early second century BCE (prior to the Maccabean crisis). The

Qumran fragments dating between 100 BCE and 20 CE provide a *terminus ante quem* (Moore 1996, 40–42; Spencer 1999, 152; Perrin 2014, 113–15).

Despite discordant voices in support of Hebrew or Greek, the Qumran fragments have convinced most scholars since the 1980s that the original language of the book was Aramaic (Perrin 2014, 111–13). Affinities between the Aramaic of Tobit and contemporary Aramaic works from Qumran have been stressed (Fitzmeyer 2003, 25–27; Machiela and Perrin 2014).

Two opposed opinions have come to dominate scholarship regarding the work's place of composition. The long-held view that the work belongs to the Eastern diaspora remains popular (Perrin 2014, 115–116; Dimant 2017a, 174 n.10). Pointing to affinities between Tobit and Qumran Aramaic works in language, literary themes, and halakah, Dimant (2017a, 2017b) makes a strong case for a Judean origin.

3. Conclusion

A major shift in scholarship since the 1980s, gender and feminist studies have broadened the comprehension of female characters. Moreover, these studies have become increasingly sophisticated, moving away from the original notion that the Bible's female characters subvert patriarchal conventions toward a growing consensus that they nonetheless acted within the prescriptive gender roles of their society. Meanwhile, the use of increasingly sophisticated literary and linguistic tools has allowed major breakthroughs, notably the impact of Bakhtin's work on the book of Esther.

That said, the sharp disagreements about the works' time and place of composition is perplexing, and we have yet to properly assess the gap between the story world of the tales and the realities of the place and time in which the authors lived.

Equally important is the heterogeneous nature of biblical narratives. The very assumption that they form a separate genre hinges on premises that need to be examined afresh. First and foremost, humor is culturally conditioned, and we should be wary of supposing that ancient readers responded to the texts in the way we do now. Second, in the Greco-Roman world fiction became an autonomous genre of literature only in the second century CE (Whitmarsh 2013). With that in mind, is it really plausible that the biblical narratives were originally composed for the sake of entertainment? The book of Job is usually labeled by scholars as sapiential literature. For this reason, it offers an example that should spur new investigations into the generic ascription of other narrative works. Some of them might well qualify as narrativized wisdom, as opposed to gnomic wisdom.

Bibliography

Bakhtin, Mikhail. 1984. *Rabelais and His World*. Bloomington: Indiana University Press.

Berlin, Adele. 2001a. *Esther: The Traditional Hebrew Text with the New JPS Translation*. Philadelphia: Jewish Publication Society.

———. 2001b. "The Book of Esther and Ancient Storytelling." *JBL* 120:3–14.

Boyd-Taylor, Cameron. 2015. "Esther and Additions to Esther." Pages 203–21 in *T&T Clark Companion to the Septuagint*. Edited by James K. Aitken. London: Bloomsbury T&T Clark.

Bredin, Mark, ed. 2006. *Studies in the Book of Tobit: A Multidisciplinary Approach*. LSTS 55. London: T&T Clark.

Brenner, Athalya. 1994. "Who's Afraid of Feminist Criticism? Who's Afraid of Biblical Humour: The Case of the Obtuse Foreign Ruler in the Hebrew Bible." *JSOT* 63:38–55.

———, ed. 1995. *A Feminist Companion to Esther, Judith and Susanna*. FCB 7. Sheffield: Sheffield Academic.

———. 1999. *Ruth and Esther*. FCB 2/3. Sheffield: Sheffield Academic.

Brison, Ora. 2015. "Judith: A Pious Widow turned *Femme Fatale*, or More?" Pages 175–99 in *A Feminist Companion to Tobit and Judith*. Edited by Athalya Brenner and Helen Efthimiadis-Keith. FCB 2/20. London: Bloomsbury T&T Clark.

Caponigro, M. S. 1992. "Judith, Holding the Tale of Herodotus." Pages 47–59 in *"No One Spoke Ill of Her": Essays on Judith*. Edited by James C. VanderKam. EJL 2. Atlanta: Scholars Press.

Clines, David J. A. 1984. *Esther Scroll: The Story of the Story*. JSOTSup 30. Sheffield: JSOT Press.

Collins, John J. 1985. "Daniel and His Social World." *Int* 39:131–43.

Corley, Jeremy. 1992. "Imitation of Septuagintal Narrative and Greek Historiography in the Portrait of Holofernes." Pages 22–54 in *A Pious Seductress: Studies in the Book of Judith*. Edited by Geza G. Xeravits. DCLS 14. Berlin: de Gruyter.

———. 2015. "Judith." Pages 222–36 in *T&T Clark Companion to the Septuagint*. Edited by James K. Aitken. London: Bloomsbury T&T Clark.

Corley, Jeremy, and Vincent Skemp, eds. 2005. *Intertextual Studies in Ben Sira and Tobit: Essays in Honor of Alexander A. Di Lella*. CBQMS 38. Washington, DC: Catholic Biblical Association of America.

Craig, Kenneth. 1995. *Reading Esther: A Case for the Literary Carnivalesque*. LCBI. Louisville: Westminster John Knox.

Craven, Toni. 1983. *Artistry and Faith in the Book of Judith*. SBLDS 70. Chico, CA: Scholars Press.

———. 2003. "The Book of Judith in the Context of Twentieth-Century Studies of the Apocryphal/Deuterocanonical Books." *CurBR* 1:187–229.

Crawford, Sidnie White. 2003 "Esther and Judith: Contrasts in Character." Pages 61–76 in *The Book of Esther in Modern Research*. Edited by Sidnie White Crawford and Leonard J. Greenspoon. JSOTSup 380. London: T&T Clark.

Crawford, Sidnie W., and Leonard J. Greenspoon, eds. 2003. *The Book of Esther in Modern Research*. JSOTSup 380. London: T&T Clark.

Dalley, Stephanie. 2007. *Esther's Revenge at Susa: From Sennacherib to Ahasuerus*. Oxford: Oxford University Press.

Day, Linda M. 1995. *Three Faces of a Queen: Characterization in the Books of Esther*. JSOTSup 186. Sheffield: Sheffield Academic.

DeSilva, David A. 2006. "Judith as Heroine? Lies, Seduction and Murder in Cultural Perspective." *BTB* 36:55–61.

Dieleman, Jacco, and Ian S. Moyer. 2010. "Egyptian Literature." Pages 429–47 in *A Companion to Hellenistic Literature*. Edited by James J. Clauss and Martine Cuypers. Malden, MA: Wiley-Blackwell.

Dimant, Devorah. 2017a. "Tobit and the Qumran Aramaic Texts." Pages 173–92 in *From Enoch to Tobit: Collected Studies in Ancient Jewish Literature*. FAT 114. Tübingen: Mohr Siebeck.

———. 2017b. "The Book of Tobit and the Qumran Halakhah." Pages 193–212 in *From Enoch to Tobit: Collected Studies in Ancient Jewish Literature*. FAT 114. Tübingen: Mohr Siebeck.

Doran, Robert. 1986. "Narrative Literature." Pages 287–310 in *Early Judaism and Its Modern Interpreters*. Edited by Robert A. Kraft and George W. E. Nickelsburg. BMI 2. Altanta: Scholars Press; Philadelphia: Fortress.

Dorothy, Charles V. 1997. *The Books of Esther: Structure, Genre and Textual Integrity*. JSOTSup 187. Sheffield: Sheffield Academic.

Eckhardt, Benedikt. 2009. "Reclaiming Tradition: The Book of Judith and Hasmonean Politics." *JSP* 18:243–63.

Esler, Philip F. 2002. "Ludic History in the Book of Judith: The Reinvention of Israelite Identity?" *BibInt* 10:107–43.

Fitzmyer, Joseph A. 2003. *Tobit*. CEJL. Berlin: de Gruyter.

Fox, Michael V. 1991a. *Character and Ideology in the Book of Esther*. Columbia: University of South Carolina Press.

———. 1991b. *The Redaction of the Books of Esther: On Reading Composite Texts*. SBLMS 40. Atlanta: Scholars Press.

Foxhall, Lin, Hans-Joachim Gehrke, and Nino Luraghi. 2010. *Intentional History: Spinning Time in Ancient Greece*. Stuttgart: Steiner.

Foxhall, Lin, and Nino Luraghi. 2010. "Introduction." Pages 9–14 in *Intentional History: Spinning Time in Ancient Greece*. Edited by Lin Foxhall, Hans-Joachim Gehrke, and Nino Luraghi. Stuttgart: Steiner.

Gera, Deborah Levine. 2013. "Speech in the Book of Judith." Pages 413–23 in *XIV Congress of the IOSCS, Helsinki, 2010*. Edited by Melvin K. H. Peters. SCS 59. Atlanta: Society of Biblical Literature.

———. 2014. *Judith: Introduction, Translation and Commentary*. CEJL. Berlin: de Gruyter.

Gruen, Erich S. 2002. *Diaspora: Jews amidst Greeks and Romans*. Cambridge: Harvard University Press.

———. 2016. *The Construct of Identity in Hellenistic Judaism: Essays on Early Jewish Literature and History*. DCLS 29. Berlin: de Gruyter.

Hancock, Rebecca S. 2013. *Esther and the Politics of Negotiation: Public and Private Spaces and the Figure of the Female Royal Counselor*. Emerging Scholars. Minneapolis: Fortress.

Hartog, François. 2015. *Regimes of Historicity: Presentism and Experiences of Time*. New York: Columbia University Press.

Harvey, Charles D. 2003. *Finding Morality in the Diaspora? Moral Ambiguity and Transformed Morality in the Books of Esther*. BZAW 328. Berlin: de Gruyter.

Henze, Matthias. 2001. "The Narrative Frame of Daniel: A Literary Assessment." *JSJ* 32:5–24.

Henten, Jan Willem van. 1995. "Judith as Alternative Leader: A Rereading of Judith 7–13." Pages 224–52 in *A Feminist Companion to Esther, Judith and Susanna*. Edited by Athalya Brenner. FCB 7. Sheffield: Sheffield Academic.

Hieke, Thomas. 1992. "Torah in Judith: Dietary Laws, Purity and Other Torah Issues in the Book of Judith." Pages 97–110 in *A Pious Seductress: Studies in the Book of Judith*. Edited by Geza G. Xeravits. DCLS 14. Berlin: de Gruyter.

Holm, Tawny L. 2013. *Of Courtiers and Kings: The Biblical Daniel Narratives and Ancient Story-Collections*. EANEC 1. Winona Lake, IN: Eisenbrauns.
Humphreys, W. Lee. 1973. "A Life-Style for Diaspora: A Study of the Tales of Esther and Daniel." *JBL* 92:211–23.
Ilan, Tal. 1999. *Integrating Women into Second Temple History*. TSAJ 76. Tübingen: Mohr Siebeck.
Jobes, Karen H. 1996. *The Alpha-Text of Esther: Its Character and Relationship to the Masoretic Text*. SBLDS 153. Atlanta: Scholars Press.
Johnson, Sara Raup. 2004. *Historical Fictions and Hellenistic Jewish Identity: Third Maccabees in Its Cultural Context*. HCS 43. Berkeley: University of California Press.
Kiel, Micah D. 2012. *The "Whole Truth:" Rethinking Retribution in the Book of Tobit*. LSTS 82. London: T&T Clark.
Koselleck, Reinhart. 1985. *Futures Past: On the Semantics of Historical Time*. Cambridge: MIT Press.
Lacocque, André. 2007. *Esther Regina: A Bakhtinian Reading*. Rethinking Theory. Evanston, IL: Northwestern University Press.
Laniak, Timothy. 1998. *Shame and Honor in the Book of Esther*. SBLDS 165. Atlanta: Scholars Press.
Levenson, Jon D. 1997. *Esther: A Commentary*. OTL. Louisville: Westminster John Knox.
Levine, Amy-Jill. 1992a. "Sacrifice and Salvation: Otherness and Domestication in the Book of Judith." Pages 17–30 in *"No One Spoke Ill of Her": Essays on Judith*. James C. VanderKam. EJL 2. Atlanta: Scholars Press.
———. 1992b. "Diaspora as Metaphor: Bodies and Boundaries in the Book of Tobit." Pages 105–17 in *Diaspora Jews and Judaism: Essays in Honor of, and in Dialogue with, A. Thomas Kraabel*. Edited by J. A. Overman and Robert S. MacLennan. SFSHJ 41. Atlanta: Scholars Press.
———. 2015. "Redrawing the Boundaries: A New Look at 'Diaspora as Metaphor: Bodies and Boundaries in the Book of Tobit.'" Pages 3–22 in *A Feminist Companion to Esther, Judith and Susanna*. Edited by Athalya Brenner. FCB 7. Sheffield: Sheffield Academic.
Macatangay, Francis M. 2011. *The Wisdom Instructions in the Book of Tobit*. DCLS 12. Berlin: de Gruyter.
Macchi, Jean-Daniel. 2018. *Esther*. IECOT. Stuttgart: Kohlhammer.
Machiela, Daniel A., and Andrew B. Perrin. 2014. "Tobit and the Genesis Apocryphon: Toward a Family Portrait." *JBL* 133:111–32.

McCracken, David. 1995. "Narration and Comedy in the Book of Tobit." *JBL* 114:401–18.

Milne, Pamela J. 1988. *Vladimir Propp and the Study of Structure in Hebrew Biblical Narrative*. BLS 13. Sheffield: Sheffield Academic.

———. 2015. "What Shall We Do with Judith? A Feminist Reassessment of a Biblical 'Heroine.'" Pages 117–36 in *A Feminist Companion to Tobit and Judith*. Edited by Athalya Brenner and Helen Efthimiadis-Keith. FCB 2/20. London: Bloomsbury T&T Clark.

Moore, Carey A. 1985. *Judith: A New Translation with Introduction and Commentary*. AB 40B. Garden City, NY: Doubleday.

———. 1996. *Tobit: A New Translation with Introduction and Commentary*. AB 40A. New York: Doubleday.

Morgan, Teresa. 2007. *Popular Morality in the Early Roman Empire*. Cambridge: Cambridge University Press.

Newman, Judith H. 1999. *Praying by the Book: The Scripturalization of Prayer in Second Temple Judaism*. EJL 14. Atlanta: Scholars Press.

Newsom, Carol A. 2007. "Spying Out the Land: A Report from Genology." Pages 19–30 in *Bakhtin and Genre Theory in Biblical Studies*. Edited by Roland Boer. SemeiaSt 63. Atlanta: Society of Biblical Literature.

———. 2014. *Daniel: A Commentary*. OTL. Louisville: Westminster John Knox.

Nickelsburg, George W. E. 1988. "Tobit and Enoch: Distant Cousins with a Recognizable Resemblance." Pages 54–68 in *Society of Biblical Literature 1988 Seminar Papers*. SBLSP 27. Atlanta: Scholars Press.

Niditch, Susan. 1987. *A Prelude to Biblical Folklore: Underdogs and Tricksters*. New Voices in Biblical Studies. San Francisco: Harper and Row.

Niditch, Susan, and Robert Doran. 1977. "The Success Story of the Wise Courtier: A Formal Approach." *JBL* 96:179–93.

Nowell, Irene. 1983. "The Book of Tobit: Narrative Technique and Theology." PhD diss., Catholic University of America.

Perrin, Andrew B. 2014. "An Almanac of Tobit Studies: 2000–2014." *CurBR* 13:107–42.

Pitkänen, Pekka. 2006. "Family Life and Ethnicity in Early Israel and in Tobit." Pages 104–17 in *Studies in the Book of Tobit: A Multidisciplinary Approach*. Edited by Mark Bredin. LSTS 55. London: T&T Clark.

Pyper, Hugh. 2006. "'Sarah Is the Hero:' Kierkegaard's Reading of Tobit in Fear and Trembling." Pages 59–71 in *Studies in the Book of Tobit: A Multidisciplinary Approach*. Edited by Mark Bredin. LSTS 55. London: T&T Clark.

Rakel, Claudia. 1999. "'I Will Sing a New Song to My God:' Some Remarks on the Intertextuality of Judith 16.1–17." Pages 27–47 in *Judges: A Feminist Companion to the Bible*. Edited by Athalya Brenner. FCB 2/4. Sheffield: Sheffield Academic.

Roitman, Adolfo D. 1992. "Achior in the Book of Judith: His Role and Significance." Pages 31–45 in *"No One Spoke Ill of Her": Essays on Judith*. Edited by James C. VanderKam. EJL 2. Atlanta: Scholars Press.

Schmitz, Barbara. 2015. "The Function of the Speeches and Prayers in the Books of Judith." Pages 164–74 in *A Feminist Companion to Tobit and Judith*. Edited by Athalya Brenner-Idan and Helen Efthimiadis-Keith. FCB 2/20. London: Bloomsbury T&T Clark.

Selden, Daniel. 2010. "Text Networks." *Ancient Narrative* 8:1–24.

Soll, William. 1988. "Tobit and Folklore Studies, with Emphasis on Propp's Morphology." Pages 39–53 in *Society of Biblical Literature 1988 Seminar Papers*. SBLSP 27. Atlanta: Scholars Press.

———. 1989. "Misfortune and Exile in Tobit: The Juncture of a Fairy Tale Source and Deuteronomic Theology." *CBQ* 51:209–31.

Spencer, Richard A. 1999. "The Book of Tobit in Recent Research." *CurBS* 7:147–80.

Stuckenbruck, Loren, and Stuart Weeks. 2015. "Tobit." Pages 237–60 in *T&T Clark Companion to the Septuagint*. Edited by James K. Aitken. London: Bloomsbury T&T Clark.

White, Sidnie Ann. 1989. "Esther: A Feminine Model for Jewish Diaspora." Pages 161–77 in *Gender and Difference in Ancient Israel*. Edited by Peggy L. Day. Minneapolis: Fortress.

———. 1992. "In the Steps of Jael and Deborah: Judith as Heroine." Pages 5–16 in *"No One Spoke Ill of Her": Essays on Judith*. Edited by James C. VanderKam. EJL 2. Atlanta: Scholars Press.

Whitmarsh, Tim. 2013. *Beyond the Second Sophistic: Adventures in Greek Postclassicism*. Berkeley: University of California Press.

Wills, Lawrence M. 1990. *The Jew in the Court of the Foreign King: Ancient Jewish Court Legends*. HDR 26. Minneapolis: Fortress.

———. 1995. *The Jewish Novel in the Ancient World*. Myth and Poetics. Ithaca, NY: Cornell University Press.

———. 2011. "Jewish Novellas in a Greek and Roman Age: Fiction and Identity." *JSJ* 42:141–65.

Xeravits, Géza G., and Zsengellér, József, eds. 2005. *The Book of Tobit: Text, Tradition, Theology: Papers of the First International Conference on the*

Deuterocanonical Books, Pápa, Hungary, 20–21 May, 2004. JSJSup. 98. Leiden: Brill.

Zsengellér, József. 2010. "Addition or Edition? Deconstructing the Concept of Additions." Pages 1–15 in *Deuterocanonical Additions of the Old Testament Books*. Edited by Géza G. Xeravits and József Zsengellér. DCLS 5. Berlin: de Gruyter.

16

Jewish Historiography

STEVE MASON

[Everything] explicated by Jason of Cyrene in five volumes we shall try to digest in a single composition. Considering the flood of numbers and the difficulty facing those who want to immerse themselves in the stories of the *historia*..., we undertook to provide satisfaction for those who wish to read..., leaving the scrutiny of each detail to the composer [*to sungraphei*] while devoting *our* attention to the continuity of the sketches in this digest [*tes epitomes*].... Close inquiry, personally investigating subjects, and busying oneself with each separate part—they are proper for the author of the *historia*, whereas the person making the paraphrase [*ten metaphrasin*] must be allowed to aim for compression of language.
—2 Macc 2:23–32

The opportune moment now calls us to the demonstration from history [*epi ten apodeiksin tes historias*] of the temperate reasoning faculty.
—4 Macc 3:19–20

If it were possible for us to paint the *historia* of your piety on some surface, would those who saw it not shudder at seeing a mother of seven children endure diverse tortures, even death, for the sake of piety?
—4 Macc 17:7

1. Changing Frameworks

Those who write about human affairs have three tenses from which to choose. Given the perils of treating the future and the impossibility of describing the instant present, we naturally turn to the past. But if all writing about the human past counted as historiography, the term would be an empty signifier.

Scholars have confronted the potential chaos by offering us two rivers in which to paddle. The broader stream holds that every culture must reckon with its past and therefore each has its own way of doing history—whatever language they may use. For Johan Huizinga (1936, 5, 9), "History is always the imposition of form upon the past" or "the intellectual form in which a civilization renders account to itself of its past." This river is wide enough to carry along myths, epics, king lists, priestly annals, dynastic chronicles, and bardic tales: every ingredient of a national tradition (Hall 1991; Kraus 1999). Biblical scholar John Van Seters's (1983, 3) agreement that "history writing is a literate form of tradition" leads him to include biblical narrative. Indeed, it is common to label the Deuteronomistic narrative history, perhaps the first one (Halpern 1988; Halpern and Lemaire 2010) and thus the foundation of a Jewish historiography (Van Seters 1983, 1–7).

If the Bible inaugurates Jewish historiography, we might ask with Amram Tropper (2004) what became of it. Observing the ahistorical character of rabbinic tradition and doubting the Jewish bona fides of Greek-language corpora, Tropper sees Jewish historiography dissolving into the idealized chain of tradition that we find in Mishnah Avot, a shift he connects with the Second Sophistic movement. Robert Hall's (1991, 11) *Revealed Histories*, by contrast, examines Jewish (and Christian) works written by inspiration. He explores "the historical consciousness" of ancient Jews (13) under five heads: prophetic history, whether interpretive (Josephus's *Bellum judaicum*) or inspired (Jubilees); inspired historical sermons (Ezekiel, Liber Antiquitatum Biblicarum, Judith); apocalyptic world histories (in 1 Enoch, 2 Baruch, Apocalypse of Abraham); limited apocalyptic history (Daniel); and the classification-resistant 4 Ezra and Sibylline Oracles. The shoehorning required to unify Jewish historiography becomes clear when Hall describes Josephus's *Bellum judaicum* as "part of his prophetic mission" and "based on inspiration" (29–30), for Josephus alone dons the historian's mantle (below) while distinguishing history from prophecy (Feldman 1990).

The other conceptual stream is much narrower. It takes *historia* to be quintessentially Greek, framed by rhetorical education, and inconceivable without a vast supporting vocabulary for truth, accuracy, causation, psychological motives, testing, and proof (Bolin 1999; de Breucker 2012, 65–115, 683). Although Herodotus depended on local traditions (Luraghi 2001), *historia* was for him a critical investigation of the past animated by his character and political wisdom (Myres 1953, 9–10; Thomas 2000,

168–212). Mark Munn (2017) finds the conditions for history's birth in the need to eradicate false Athenian traditions at the time of the Peloponnesian war. Herodotus's concern to understand the Persian side would expose him to criticism for "love of barbarians" (Pseudo-Plutarch, *De Herodoti malignitate*). Thucydides, considered "the greatest of all history-writers" (Dionysius, *Thuc.* 2; cf. Josephus, *C.Ap.* 1.18) because he raised the standards for composing a tight narrative of the past (*sungrapho*, Thucydides, *P.W.* 1.1), likewise faced later criticism for lack of patriotism (Dionysius, *De Thucydide*).

Though very different writers, Herodotus and Thucydides established the historian's task as the analysis of events: identifying relations and true causes while fearlessly challenging tradition, narrow interest, and cherished belief. Thucydides composed a still-unmatched analysis of power and justice in interpolis relations, Polybius an account of constitutions and their health. These statesmen-writers considered history the best education for "political affairs" (*tas politikas prakseis*; Polybius, *Hist.* 1.1.2). Given that history expressed the author's unique character, he began with a proem to identify himself, his occasion for writing, and the basis of his authority (Marincola 1997, 128–74). History's driving idea of rigorous investigation of the human past, in spite of received tradition, would eventually be realized in the finally autonomous history departments of modern research universities (Bloch 1953, 20–23; Collingwood 1994, 9–21; Lowenthal 1997, 105–47; Beiser 2011, 1–25).

History's aura of astringent inquiry still comes through in 2 Maccabees (above), Josephus (*C. Ap.* 2.46), Tacitus (*Ann.* 1.1; *Hist.* 1.4), and later authors (Marincola, 1997, 158–74). Josephus assumes it when he castigates writers who "dare to call histories" works that lack rigor or balance (*B.J.* 1.2, 7). But 4 Maccabees reflects another use, which is implied by Josephus's censures and explicit in Lucian's *How History Ought to be Written* (160s CE). Namely, as histories proliferated and few consumers were in a position to assess the quality of research, history came to be evaluated only by such literary-rhetorical criteria as choice of subject matter, lucidity, proportion, style register, tone, artistry of speeches, and moral or patriotic concerns (e.g., Dionysius, *Thuc.* 1–3, 21, 50–51; cf. 4 Macc 17:7 above).

Ancient historiography was not so much a genre, then, as an undertaking broadly inspired by Herodotus and Thucydides, of any size or scope and whether in prose or verse (Farrell 2003; Conte and Most 1996; Marincola 1999; Marincola, Llewellyn-Jones, and Maciver 2012, 1–13). To be sure, history accumulated a range of commonplaces concerning truth, toil, and accuracy, which are best summarized—and satirized—in Lucian's essay (cf. Sextus Empiricus, *Math.* 1.248, 269). But writers of history were elite men who composed in all genres. Even when they chose *historia*, as a serious meal for statesmen, they seasoned the dish with geography, botany, philosophy, and rhetoric to make it memorable (Clarke 1999; Shahar 2004).

Scholars who view ancient historiography as a distinctive product of life in the Greek polis (city-state), as the impartial analysis of causes by an individual asserting rare political-moral acumen, do not include biblical narrative even if they date it late enough to be somehow influenced by Greek models (as Lemche 2000; Thompson 2000; Wesselius 2002).

Convention, in any case, permits a survey of Jewish historiography to leave biblical studies aside as a specialist field and focus on postbiblical literature. Here the candidates all survive in the Greek language and so offer at least the prospect of sharing the distinctive Greco-Roman conception of writing *historia*. Harold Attridge's (1986) chapter on Jewish historiography in this book's forerunner assumed the narrower definition. After identifying the works usually grouped as Jewish historiography, Attridge described the editions, translations, and other tools available for their study. When it came to their content, he was primarily interested in religious, theological, and apologetic tendencies. Since the Pharisees were then central in research, he discussed whether a given text was Pharisaic. He also touched on dating disputes, the identity of Alexander's Eupolemus, calendar problems in 1 Maccabees, Josephus's paragraph on Jesus (*A.J.* 18.63–64), and the historical value of Josephus's autobiography.

The present chapter builds on Attridge's foundation. The editions and tools he surveyed represented the mature work of the post-World War II generation. Together with the new investigations in rabbinic literature by Jacob Neusner and his students, the gathering Qumran Scrolls juggernaut, the fervent interest in apocalyptic and pseudepigraphical works, and E. P. Sanders's call for a wholesale reappraisal of Jewish-Christian relations (Udoh 2008), these tools were defining the field of early (not "late") Judaism—or "Judaisms"—now freed from tradition and placed on a publicly accessible, historical-philological foundation. Attridge's essay will not soon be supplanted. The same conditions that recommend a new *Early Judaism and Its Modern Interpreters* (Kraft and Nickelsburg 1986), however, suggest a new approach to historiography. These include changes in scholarly constituency, in academic interests, and in the material conditions of research.

As for material conditions, the digital revolution has changed everything. Whereas in the 1980s we were thrilled to pore over the new *Concordance to Flavius Josephus*, we now have online and desktop tools that instantly find all occurrences of roots and verbal collocations—in thousands of texts at once. The indispensable *Thesaurus Linguae Graecae* (stephanus.tlg.uci.edu), Packard Humanities Institute (latin.packhum.org), and desktop databases show how things have changed. Manuscripts that once required expensive travel to view are often examinable in high definition on portable devices. The desk piled with binding-stretched books has been replaced by a screen with tabbed PDFs. These riches can generate investigative problems that were unthinkable in the 1980s.

Scholarly constituencies have evolved in ways that may affect historiography more than other areas. The post–World War II research surveyed in *Early Judaism and Its Modern Interpreters* (Kraft and Nickelsburg 1986) focused on doing justice to ancient Judaism(s) as a subject of its own. The most notable shift in the past three decades has been the steady integration of ancient Jewish history into the Mediterranean scene. We see this, for example, in the work of scholars who won renown for contributions to Hellenistic-Roman history and then applied that background to the study of Judea and Judeans (Gruen 2002; Millar 2002–2006; Eck 2007). Historians interested in Roman provincial administration, military practice, religion, minority rights, or Hellenistic-Roman intellectual and literary culture generally, find Judea and its diaspora to be rich nodes. One index of this development is that Josephus's corpus, which until the mid-1990s had been largely ignored in studies of either Roman or Greek literature, is among the most frequently cited exemplars in John Marincola's (1997) famed *Authority and Tradition in Ancient Historiography*.

The growing integration of all ancient historiography—understood as the conscious writing of *historia*—has provided new vantage points from which to question traditional categories, even such cornerstones as religion and the subset Judaism, as distinct from Judean life in all its variety (Boyarin 2004; Mason 2007; Nongbri 2013; Barton and Boyarin 2017).

One could easily fill the space for this chapter with bibliography from the expanding universe generated by this big bang. The problem provides its own solution, however, because online searching has replaced obsolete printed lists. We turn instead to consider notable shifts in scholarly interest since 1986, beginning with problems of definition, category, and genre.

2. Jewish Historiography: Definitions and Parameters

To discuss ancient Jewish historiography, we must have some clarity about the terms Jewish and historiography. To begin with the latter: did the authors in question think they were doing the same kind of thing?

The three quotations at the head of this chapter highlight the problem. Few would call 4 Maccabees a history because the author presents it as an argumentative essay (1:1–2, 7, 13). Yet his programmatic sentence—promising a demonstration of, or monument to, history (*ten apodeiksin tes historias*)—recalls Herodotus's opening line (*Hist.* 1.1: *histories apodeksis hede*). The *historia* to be used by 4 Maccabees is not, however, Herodotus-like inquiry. To prove the supremacy of reasoning over suffering, this author exploits episodes from 2 Maccabees concerning famous Judeans who had endured lethal terrors rather than violate the laws of Moses.

In antiquity, the connection between rhetoric and past events was close. Rhetoricians expected orators to use the past (Villalba i Verneda 1986, 250–51; Woodman 1988; Suetonius, *Rhet.* 1). After the speech's introduction (*exordium*), the *narratio* invited audiences to rethink often familiar events from the perspective being argued (Cicero, *De or.* 2.18.80; Quintilian, *Inst.* 2.4.2–3; 4.2.1, 52–53; Josephus, *B.J.* 5.375–420). Quintilian urged writers not to get bogged down in details. They should take the accepted version of a story, or one that rested on credible authority, and focus their efforts on refashioning it for their purposes (*Inst.* 1.8.18). This approximates what 4 Maccabees does with 2 Maccabees. The author knows about *historia* and does not claim to be doing it.

Did he consider 2 Maccabees *historia*? Apparently so (DeSilva 2006, 111), although the author of 2 Maccabees did not. In this chapter's opening quotation, he insists that only Jason of Cyrene bore the historian's burden and refuses to let his digest, which draws out simpler lines from the historian's complex work, be judged by the same standard. When Daniel Schwartz (2008, 14) describes 2 Maccabees as a "history of the trials and tribulations of Jerusalem," he must be using history in the popular sense, for he sees the purpose of the surviving epitome as persuasive: to observe both Nicanor's Day and Hanukkah (7–10). Jonathan Goldstein's (2003, passim) tag, "the abridged history," is apt.

Nor is it clear that the author of 1 Maccabees, another staple of ancient Jewish historiography, intended Greek-style historiography. Most scholars think that our Greek text renders a lost Hebrew original, in which case one might not expect to find *historia*. But the evidence for a Hebrew source is meager and otherwise explainable (Yarrow 2006, 87), while the official documents of chapters 8 to 13 give the work a decidedly Greek cast. The author shows enough awareness of Greek literary culture (Bartlett 1998, 33) that he could have donned the historian's mantle if it had suited him. Instead he assumes a quasi-biblical authority, with a style reminiscent of Judges and Samuel (Bartlett 1998, 16), beginning *in medias res* with "And it came to pass that." He punctuates the story with Bible-like verse (1 Macc 1:23–28, 35–40; 2:6–13; 3:2–9) and diction that would be at home in apocalyptic literature. Successors of Alexander the Great multiply evils until the "sinful root" King Antiochus IV attracts "transgressors of the law" from the sons of Israel, and divinely chosen Hasmoneans (5:62) must deal righteous retribution (1:1–11). Robert Doran (1979, 113), rightly rejecting the old notion of a "tragic history" genre, paradoxically calls the work "a history of recent events filled with the theme of the epiphanic help of God," a description that exposes the distance from Greek *historia*. The same is true of Nils Martola's (1984) finding that the story is about correcting an imbalance—Jerusalem's intrusive Seleucid citadel—and David S. Williams's (2001) observations concerning the work's highly literary character.

If we did count 1 Maccabees as undeclared historiography, would not Virgil's *Aeneid*, Greco-Roman tragedy, much of the Bible, wisdom and apocalyptic literature, the Genesis Apocryphon, and Jubilees also qualify? The question is not whether such texts have historical *value*. They do—as do pottery fragments. Doron Mendels (1987) explored 1 Enoch, Daniel, Eupolemus, 1 Maccabees, Judith, Jubilees, and the Testaments of the Twelve Patriarchs to lay bare phases in the Hasmonean conception of the land. Daniel Harrington (1988) exposed the "anatomy" of the Hasmonean revolt using Daniel and 1 and 2 Maccabees. But the ancient texts reveal no effort to write *historia*, even or especially when they allow the term's implications.

Greco-Roman writers distinguished at least three related forms from *historia*, and these might help to explain some Jewish texts. First, military and political leaders would draft notes or memoirs (*hypomnemata, commentarii*) about events they experienced (Cicero, *Att.* 1.19; 2.1; *Fam.* 5.12). Even if they wrote these with literary skill, they considered them only material for later history (Plutarch, *Sull.* 23.2; *Luc.* 1.3; Josephus, *Vita* 342, 348). Josephus may have intended his autobiography as *hypomnemata* (note the cognate verb in *B.J.* 20.267), for he refers readers to his *Bellum judaicum* for detailed history (*Vita* 336, 362, 367). Second, the boundary between history and biography was fluid, since histories were largely biographical and the same men wrote both (e.g., Sallust, Tacitus, Josephus). Plutarch could distinguish his *Lives* from history (*Alex.* 1.2), but often he remarked on their historical character (*Thes.* 1.1-3; *Aem.* 1.1-5; *Dem.* 2.1; cf. Sallust, *Bell. Cat.* 4-5; *Bell. Jug.* 4). Finally, we have noticed the use of *historia* in speeches and argumentative essays. This model might explain not only the relationship of 2 and 4 Maccabees to Jason's history, but also that of Josephus's highly rhetorical essay *Contra Apionem* (Feldman and Levison 1996; Gerber 1997; Gruen 2005) to the elaborate history, *Antiquitates judaicae*, that it seeks to vindicate (*C. Ap.* 1.1, 54-55).

Philo of Alexandria (ca. 20 BCE-50 CE) is known for his allegorical exegesis, but we commonly peel off two of his works as histories: *Legatio ad Gaium* and *In Flaccum* (Royse 2009, 34, 53-55). Recounting Philo's experiences in 38 to 41 CE, these apparently once anchored a five-part series *De virtutibus* (Eusebius, *Hist. eccl.* 2.5.1; Smallwood 1961, 38-43). Did Philo consider these compositions histories? He knows the category *historia* but reserves it for authoritative ancient accounts by poets and historians, including Moses (*Cher.* 105; *Sacr.* 78; *Congr.* 15, 44; *Somn.* 1.52, 205; *Mos.* 2.46). By contrast, Philo's description of the *Legatio ad Gaium* as "what we saw and heard" (*Legat.* 349) suggests memoirs (*hypomnemata*) rather than *historia*, and a standard commentary on the work opens by saying: "The *Legatio* is an invective against Gaius, illustrated by various examples of that Emperor's outrageous behaviour" (Smallwood 1961, 3). Likewise, a recent commentary on the *In Flaccum* describes it as a story of divine revenge against a persecutor, the latter half being Philo's pure invention, and as a combination of theodicy, consolation, novel, and history (Van der Horst 2003, 1-4, 11-15).

If historiography requires definition, so does the *Jewish* in Jewish historiography. One option would be to include everything written on the Judeans, as did L. Cornelius Alexander of Miletus, nicknamed Polyhistor ("diversely learned/curious") by the ancients, in the first century BCE (Adler 2011). But this definition would encompass treatises by such hostile commentators as Nicolaus of Damascus, Manetho and the other writers targeted in Josephus's *Contra Apionem*, Philo of Byblos (Baumgarten 1981, 35-36), and Antonius Julianus (Minucius Felix, *Oct.* 33.4), not to mention later Christian authors. They all wrote *about* Jews for their own reasons but not what most consider Jewish history.

Polyhistor demands special attention because his *Peri Ioudaion* preserves paragraphs from the more shadowy inhabitants of the domain "Jewish historiography": Demetrius, Eupolemus, Pseudo-Eupolemus,

Artapanus, Cleodemus Malchus, Aristeas, Pseudo-Hecataeus, Theophilus, and Thallus (Holladay 1983). Polyhistor himself was a Greek grammarian and bibliophile (Suetonius, *Gramm.* 5), captured early in the Mithridatic wars and sent to Rome as a slave-tutor. In 81–80 BCE he received his freedom under L. Cornelius Sulla (Freudenthal 1874, 17–19; de Breucker 2012, 154–55). His *Peri Ioudaion* was one of perhaps two dozen ethnographic studies (on the Libyans, Egyptians, Babylonians, etc.) that he penned for contemporaries. He was better known for his strange tales pertaining to Greece and Rome than for the sketches of Eastern peoples (Pliny, *Nat.* 1.3c, 4c, 5c, 6c; cf. Adler 2011, 238–40). But after Eusebius (early 300s CE) decided to use his pastiche of otherwise lost Jewish authors, chiefly in the ninth book of *Praeparatio Evangelica*, these twice-mediated fragments survived to tantalize modern students.

Eusebius often stresses that he quotes Polyhistor verbatim, and scholars tend to suppose that he and Polyhistor were both "relatively accurate" in what they quoted (Holladay 1983, 8; cf. Freudenthal 1874, 3–16, 32–33). Eusebius's contextualizations, by contrast, are recognized as deceptive to the point of being sinister (Inowlocki 2006). He crafted his work to serve "a well-structured apologetic strategy," as "a formidable weapon and tool of control" for disseminating the gospel (Inowlocki 2011, 209, 216). There is no reason to think that the "bungler" Polyhistor had treated his Jewish sources any more transparently (Freudenthal 1874, 22–31; cf. Adler 2011, 225–26; Long 2013). The twice-refracted fragments, even if accurate in themselves, cannot reveal the aims, structures, and themes of the originals. Nor do they indicate that the Judean authors intended to write history. Demetrius looks more like an exegete (Freudenthal 1874, 35; but Holladay 1983, 54). Carl Holladay (1983) labels Eupolemus's fragments "history," as early Christian authors had but observes that his work repackages tradition to exude "a strongly patriotic, even nationalistic character" (96–99), while Artapanus's fragments resemble "popular romance" (190). We do not find conscious historiography in the texts that Polyhistor plundered for his ethnography of Judeans.

A second option, restricting Jewish historiography to histories written *by* Jews, would face other difficulties: the uncertain ethnicity of some authors; the question whether narratives that describe Roman legions, military campaigns, or internal Roman politics count as Jewish historiography because they are written by a Jewish author; and the paradox of a Jewish historian dependent on non-Jewish sources, as Josephus on Nicolaus. On the first question, Polyhistor's fragments of Eupolemus are now confidently (though speculatively) divided between a Judean Eupolemus and the Samarian Pseudo-Eupolemus—because of a reference to Mount Gerizim, though Polyhistor or Eusebius assumed them to be the work of one man. Likewise, the prophet Cleodemus Malchus, whom Josephus knew from Polyhistor (Josephus, *A.J.* 1.240), we guess to be Samarian (Holladay 1983, 58–59; Adler 2011, 234–35). Josephus, adding a wrinkle, thought that writers we consider Judean were gentiles (*B.J.* 1.17; *C. Ap.* 1.216–218; Gruen 2005).

A third option would admit as Jewish historiography only texts about the past that revealed a Jewish perspective, however defined. But as we have seen, Josephus's *Bellum judaicum* is so devoid of obvious biblical-Jewish coloring that it was long considered Flavian propaganda (Laqueur 1970 and Weber 1973 to Curran 2007, 77). Someone following that approach and this criterion might have to accept only the *Antiquitates judaicae* as Jewish historiography, though Josephus postures in *Bellum judaicum* as a Judean spokesman (*J.W.* 1.1–3). Having glanced at Josephus from various angles, we must now consider his work as such.

3. The Jewish Historian Flavius Josephus

A sentence beginning "the ancient Jewish historian" is nearly certain to continue with "Flavius Josephus." Josephus (37–ca. 100 CE) was a priest-aristocrat who surrendered during the Roman invasion of Galilee in 67 and, after Jerusalem's fall in 70, spent the balance of his life in Rome, where he composed four works in thirty volumes. These works are saturated with cognates of *historia* (128 times) and Thucydidean *syngrapho* (*B.J.* 1.2, 13, 18; 7.448; *A.J.* 1.1, 6, 29; 20.268), supported by the resonant language of truth (*aletheia* 271), accuracy (*akribeia* 135), and causation (*aitia* 334, *prophasis* 59, *aphorme* 61). He feels confident enough in his role as statesman-historian to flout the "laws of history" that bind less commanding authors (*B.H.* 1.11; 5.20; cf. Polybius, *Hist.* 38.4). He sees *historia* as a Greek activity but claims that present-day Greeks have lost the plot: Judeans have better ancient source material and a more robust commitment to truth-seeking (*C. Ap.* 1.7–27; cf. *B.J.* 1.13–16; *Vita* 40). Josephus's later reflections on his seven-volume *Bellum judaicum* and twenty-volume *Antiquitates judaicae* show him asking to be judged by history's highest standards (*Vita* 336–67; *C. Ap.* 1.1–5, 50–55).

The surge in Josephus research since Attridge (1986) makes even a partial summary impossible. For the manuscripts, history of reception, and many other matters, happily, readers can consult the expert essays in Honora Chapman and Zuleika Rodgers (2016). Compact introductions to his life and works include Tessa Rajak (2002), Per Bilde (1988, 13–122), Mireille Hadas-Lebel (1993), and Mason (2003, 1–211). Of the fundamental new resources, it must suffice to mention the (English) synopsis of the Greek and Slavonic *Bellum judaicum* (Leeming and Leeming 2003) and a range of translation and commentary projects in French (Nodet 1990–2010; Munnich 2017; Goldberg 2018), German (Labow 2005; Siegert 2008; Siegert, Schreckenberg, and Vogel 2001), Hebrew (Kasher 1996; Schwartz 2007; Ullmann 2009), Italian (Calabi 2007), Japanese (Hata 1977–1978, 1999–2002a, 1999–2002b), and English (Mason et al. 2000–; Hammond 2017). We shall keep our focus here on Josephus's way of writing history.

In the year that *Early Judaism and Its Modern Interpreters* (Kraft and Nickelsburg 1986) appeared, Pere Villalba i Varneda's (1986) *The Historical Method of Flavius Josephus* provided an unprecedented exploration of Josephus's approach to historical narration, first by subject (e.g., historical personalities, speeches, chronology, geography, wars) and then by literary device (e.g., ecphrasis, narrative anticipation), before taking up such personal elements as reasoning and paradox, ethical-philosophical reflection, eulogy and censure, proem and epilogue. His conclusion planted Josephus firmly within the Greco-Roman historiographical tradition.

How much remained to be explored, in spite of that work's imposing comprehensiveness, became clear in the numerous conference and other collected-essay volumes that followed (e.g., Feldman and Hata 1987, 1989; Parente and Sievers 1994; Siegert and Kalms 1998, 1999, 2002, 2003; Kalms 2000, 2001; Mason 1998, 2009; Sievers and Lembi 2005; Edmondson, Mason, and Rives 2005; Rodgers 2007; Pastor, Stern, and Mor 2011), not to mention the profusion of dissertations and monographs (below). The Josephus Seminar, inaugurated by the Society of Biblical Literature in 1999, remains vital today. I devote the remaining space to historiographical dimensions of this newly animated research.

One conspicuous absence is interest in the "lost Aramaic" precursor of Josephus's *Bellum judaicum*. Josephus claims in the proem of the extent work that he decided to "recast in the Greek language, for the Roman Empire, what [plural] I previously composed in the native [language] for the upper barbarians" (1.3)—meaning inhabitants of the Parthian Empire (1.6). Fusing this remark with a decontextualized comment from the middle of the work (*B.J.* 3.108), scholars used to infer that the Flavians commissioned Josephus to write an Aramaic account that would deter the Parthians from belligerent thoughts (Laqueur 1970, 125–28; Thackeray 1967, 127–29). The lost Aramaic not only seemed to explain the existence of the Greek *Bellum judaicum*, as translated propaganda; it undergirded Henry St.-John Thackeray's belief that Josephus, whom he imagined as a Pharisee from a backwater province, required slave-assistants to render his Aramaic in the sophisticated Greek we now read. Rajak (2002, 174–84, 233–36) demolished most of these assumptions. She argued that the lost Aramaic, which Josephus ignores in later reflections on *Bellum judaicum*'s composition, could have had little relationship to our Greek, that the Greek *Bellum judaicum* does not answer to the needs of propaganda, that Josephus must have had the skill to write decent Greek without help, and that the Parthians of the 70s needed no Judean to dissuade them from belligerence.

Rajak's brush-clearing exercise combined with a growing interest in Josephus as author to create the space for the studies of "Josephus and *x*" that constitute the new subdiscipline of Josephus research. Instead of using Josephus as a cipher for facts about Roman Judea or more interesting sources, scholars now try first to understand his complex corpus. Neither the lost Aramaic nor the hypothesized sources that once preoccupied researchers figure much in compositionally oriented studies of Josephus on: the war (Bilde 1979; Rajak 2002; Goodman 1987, 2007; Price 1992; McLaren 1998; Mason 2016); women (Halpern-Amaru 1988; Mayer-Schärtel 1995; Grüenfelder 2003; Ilan 2006); priesthood (Gussmann 2008); Pharisees (Mason 1991); Essenes (Finkbeiner 2010); *sicarii* (Brighton 2009); Samaritans (Egger 1986; Pummer 2009); King Herod (Toher 2003; Landau 2006); Jewish festivals/Passover (Colautti 2002; Siggelkow-Berner 2011); the emperors (Den Hollander 2014); or use of embedded letters (Olson 2010), speeches (below), spectacle, and drama (Chapman 1998; Price and Ullmann 2002).

The concern to understand Josephus's histories as intelligent compositions does not mark a turn toward solipsistic literary study. It is only the late-arriving realization of a principle long since applied to Livy, Tacitus, or Cassius Dio, as to biblical and New Testament texts: that we cannot responsibly use literary (or material) sources for historical purposes until we interpret them (Bloch 1953, 138–44; Collingwood 1994, 274–78). Application to Josephus was delayed by the tenacity with which he was viewed as a mere transmitter. Just as Neusner and Bruce Chilton (2009) insisted that exploration of the historical Pharisees await interpretation of each text that describes them, so Josephus researchers ask that the study of Herod, the

Essenes, or Masada await contextual understanding of Josephus's descriptions in his context.

As the Flavian-propaganda interpretation of *Bellum judaicum* dissolved, a new consensus formed around the idea that Josephus wrote to absolve his nation, especially himself and his priestly class, from war guilt. He deflected blame for all hostilities on a small band of rebels, who first provoked Roman harshness and then ignored priestly advice by violently responding (Rajak 2002, 78-83; Goodman 1987, 20-21; Bilde 1988, 77-78; S. Schwartz 1990, 15; Price, 1992, 32-33; McLaren 1998, 55-56; Mader 2000, 10-17). One might doubt, however, that Josephus's elaborate descriptions of priestly activity in the build-up to war, especially his own achievements as a general, somehow run counter to his literary aims. A different approach would allow these passages their full weight and understand *Bellum judaicum*'s aims in a less thesis-like way (Bilde 1979). One might rather see Josephus as trying to create an ethos, as a Judean statesman speaking to peers in other cultures. Such pervasive themes as the character of Judeans in warfare, polis-management in perilous times, reversals of fortune, and pollution and purity, would constitute the threads of his effort to communicate with kindred spirits in the established historiographical framework (Mason, 2016, 60-137).

How does Josephus engage that framework? Already in the 1920s, Thackeray noticed Josephus's many allusions to classical historians, from Thucydides to Sallust, though his assumptions forced him to attribute these to literary assistants. More holistic recent interpretations have credited Josephus with drawing inspiration for core concepts from Polybius (Eckstein 1990), Thucydides (Mader 2000), and Strabo (Shahar 2004). After Thucydides (*P.W.* 1.22.1) allowed that speeches could never be reported as they were given, they came to be seen as fields of rhetorical invention (Polybius, *Hist.* 12.25-25a.4f, 25i-26b; 12.25i.9; Dionysius, *Thuc.* 16-18). Polybius eschewed them for that reason (*Hist.* 36.1.1-7), but most historians took advantage of the opportunity for rhetorical display. Josephus's *Bellum judaicum* includes seven major set-piece orations plus many shorter ones (Villalba i Varneda 1986, 89-117; Runnalls 1997). How exactly they function is a matter of debate, depending on scholars' views of Josephus's philosophical-political models (Luz 1983; Ladouceur 1987), his ideological-persuasive aims (Saulnier 1991; Rajak 1991; Price 2008), and his view of Greek rhetoric (Mason 2011).

Two fundamental problems in Josephus research concern his use of sources and the relationship between his two histories, *Bellum judaicum* and *Antiquitates judaicae*. The problems are related, for in the half-century before 1920, scholars usually attributed the differences between *B.J.* 1–3 and *A.J.* 13–20, when they narrate the same events, to supposed new sources for the later work. Richard Laqueur (1970) undermined that general explanation (not denying some new sources) by showing that Josephus's *Vita* reworked episodes from his own past in ways that could not be attributed to sources. Laqueur ascribed the new framework and themes of *Antiquitates judaicae* to Josephus's changed circumstances and allegiances: moving from Roman propaganda in *Bellum judaicum* to rapprochement with Judaism in *Jewish Antiquities*. The idea that Josephus underwent some kind of *volte-face* between his two histories proved irresistible throughout the twentieth century (Cohen 1979; S. Schwartz 1990).

Attridge (1986, 326–27) argued that the two histories followed distinct historiographical schools: one Polybian and presentist, the other rhetorical and interested in antiquity. But the notion that distinct schools existed has crumbled along with modern skepticism about fixed genre boundaries (Feldman 1998a, 9–12; cf. Mason 1991, 376–83). Klaus-Stefan Krieger (1994) fused Laqueur's biographical approach with a new-style compositional reading of each work. Insisting that each episode be read in light of its narrative's context, he argued that *Bellum judaicum* was written for the western Jewish diaspora, as a postwar plea for cooperation with Rome, whereas *Antiquitates judaicae* was mainly for gentiles interested in Judaism. This view, however, requires downplaying evidence for *Bellum judaicum*'s assumption of a local gentile audience (1.1–9, 22, 110, 146, 152, 650; 2.42, 119–66, 170, etc.). Meanwhile, D. Schwartz (1990; 2013) revived source-critical solutions for many differences in the two works (cf. Ilan 1995; 2006; Bergmeier 1993; Collins 2009). More recently, he has taken a more Laqueurian approach, positing a profound change in Josephus's outlook. The Jerusalemite priest who wrote the *Bellum judaicum* came to express a diasporic outlook—more religious than national-territorial—in the *Antiquitates judaicae* (2007a, 18–22). Michael Tuval (2013) makes an elaborate case for this approach.

Other scholars (Bilde 1988, 121–22; Rajak 1998a) have found no great difficulty in reading the two histories as compatible in overarching theme and purpose. After all, Josephus claims that he had considered including the ancient past as a prologue to the *Bellum judaicum*, before deciding that this would ruin the symmetry of the war monograph (*B.J.* 1.18; *A.J.* 1.6–7). The later work claims to build directly on *Bellum judaicum* (1.1–8) and cites it several times, and Josephus's later reflection on both histories (*C.*

Ap. 1.53–56) reveals no qualms about his turn to the ancient past—since the Judeans' ancient records, composed by prophets, are uniquely reliable. Mason (1991) challenged a crucial premise of the *volte-face* view: that Josephus's *Antiquitates judaicae* and *Vita* promote the Pharisees (or Yavnean rabbis). The excavation of biblical substrata already in *Bellum judaicum* has further militated against the notion of abrupt change (Gray 1993; Mason 1994; Spilsbury 2003), as has the realization that even *Antiquitates judaicae*, though more obviously biblical in subject matter, translates core biblical themes into the Greco-Roman language of natural law, political constitutions, philosophy, virtue and vice, providence, and patronage (Attridge 1976; Halpern-Amaru 1981; Spilsbury 1998).

Researchers who find *Bellum judaicum* and *Antiquitates judaicae* compatible acknowledge their myriad differences but attribute these to the creative spirit encouraged in ancient rhetorical handbooks (*progymnasmata*). Much as Plutarch and the gospel writers rewrote source material as needed, Josephus evinces no anxiety about reconfiguring *Bellum judaicum*'s episodes to suit the new subject, structure, and themes of *Antiquitates judaicae*. What are these? Thackeray's argument that Josephus modeled his twenty-volume *Antiquitates judaicae* on the twenty-volume *Antiquitates romanae* by Dionysius of Halicarnassus has retained its appeal (Feldman 1998a, 7–8). Gregory Sterling (1992, 289–90) accepts it while proposing an older and more basic model. Like the Babylonian and Egyptian priests Berossus and Manetho, more than three centuries earlier, Josephus was engaging in "apologetic historiography," which is to say explaining an ancient oriental people's ways to the rest of the world in Greek language and categories.

Josephus's biblical paraphrase (*A.J.* 1–11) has continued to attract the lion's share of interest in the *Antiquitates judaicae*, though it cuts across Josephus's clear structuring of the work in two ten-volume halves (Bilde 1988, 91–92). *Antiquitates judaicae*'s moralizing approach, treating history as serial biography and passing judgment on each character in turn—an approach familiar from Hellenistic and especially Roman historiography (Otis 1967)—facilitated Louis Feldman's (1998a, 1998b) deep explorations of Josephus's use of biblical figures. Christopher Begg's (1993, 2000) analyses of the same material take a less personal approach, examining Josephus's presentation of the early and later monarchies and comparing it with other textual traditions.

Scholars usually study *Antiquitates judaicae*'s postbiblical material, not flagged as such by Josephus, piecemeal and according to their interests in the Letter of Aristeas (*A.J.* 12), the Hasmonean history or 1 Maccabees (13), King Herod (14–17), Mesopotamian Jewry (18; Rajak 1998b), or Roman affairs (18–19; Wiseman 2013). Efforts to read *A.J.* 12–20 as an integrated part of *Antiquitates judaicae* remain rare (Semenchenko 2002; Mason 2012).

4. Conclusion

Josephus's *Antiquitates judaicae* returns us to our starting point because it sits on both sides of the question, "What constitutes Jewish historiography?" On the one hand, Josephus views historiography as a Greek undertaking. This confident Judean priest takes up the challenge of beating the Greeks at their own game. On the other hand, the work's dependence on the prophet-written Bible, Aristeas, and 1 Maccabees suggest that he considered history not the only or perhaps the best way of knowing the distant past.

Bibliography

Adler, William. 2011. "Alexander Polyhistor's *Peri Ioudaiōn* and Literary Culture in Republican Rome." Pages 225–40 in *Reconsidering Eusebius: Collected Papers on Literary, Historical, and Theological Issues.* Edited by Sabrina Inowlocki and Claudio Zamagni. VCSup 107. Leiden: Brill.

Attridge, Harold W. 1976. *The Interpretation of Biblical History in the Antiquitates Judaicae of Flavius Josephus.* HDR 7. Missoula: Scholars Press.

———. 1986. "Jewish Historiography." Pages 311–43 in *Early Judaism and Its Modern Interpreters.* Edited by Robert A. Kraft and George W. E. Nickelsburg. BMI 2. Philadelphia: Fortress; Atlanta: Scholars Press.

Bartlett, John R. 1998. *1 Maccabees.* Guides to Apocrypha and Pseudepigrapha. Sheffield: Sheffield Academic.

Barton, Carlin, and Daniel Boyarin. 2017. *Imagine No Religion: How Modern Abstractions Hide Ancient Realities.* New York: Fordham University Press.

Baumgarten, Albert I. 1981. *The Phoenician History of Philo of Byblos.* EPRO 89. Leiden: Brill.

Begg, Christopher T. 1993. *Josephus' Account of the Early Divided Monarchy (AJ 8, 212–420): Rewriting the Bible.* BETL 108. Leuven: Leuven University Press.

———. 2000. *Josephus' Story of the Later Monarchy (AJ 9, 1–10,185)*. BETL 145. Leuven: Leuven University Press.
Beiser, Frederick C. 2011. *The German Historicist Tradition*. Oxford: Oxford University Press.
Bergmeier, Roland. 1993. *Die Essener-Berichte des Flavius Josephus: Quellenstudien zu den Essenertexten im Werk des judischen Historiographen*. Kampen: Kok Pharos.
Bilde, Per. 1979. "The Causes of the Jewish War According to Josephus." *JSJ* 10:179–202.
———. 1988. *Flavius Josephus between Jerusalem and Rome: His Life, His Works and Their Importance*. JSPSup 2. Sheffield: Sheffield Academic.
Bloch, Marc. 1953. *The Historian's Craft*. Translated by Peter Putnam. New York: Random House.
Bolin, Thomas M. 1999. "History, Historiography, and the Use of the Past in the Hebrew Bible." Pages 113–140 in *The Limits of Historiography: Genre and Narrative in Ancient Historical Texts*. Edited by Christina Shuttleworth Kraus. MnS 191. Leiden: Brill.
Boyarin, Daniel. 2004. *Border Lines: The Partition of Judaeo-Christianity*. Divinations. Philadelphia: University of Pennsylvania Press.
Breucker, Geurt E. E. de. 2012. "De *Babyloniaca* van Berossos van Babylon: Inleiding, editie en commentaar." PhD diss., University of Groningen.
Brighton, Mark. 2009. *The Sicarii in Josephus's Judean War: Rhetorical Analysis and Historical Observations*. EJL 27. Atlanta: Society of Biblical Literature.
Calabi, Francesca. 2007. *Flavio Giuseppe: In Difesa degli Ebrei (Contro Apione)*. Genoa: Marietti.
Chapman, Honora H. 1998. "Spectacle and Theater in Josephus's *Bellum Judaicum*." PhD diss., Stanford University.
Chapman, Honora H., and Zuleika Rodgers, eds. 2016. *A Companion to Josephus*. BCAW. Chichester: Wiley Blackwell.
Clarke, Katherine. 1999. *Between Geography and History: Hellenistic Constructions of the Roman World*. Oxford Classical Monographs. Oxford: Clarendon.
Cohen, S. J. D. 1979. *Josephus in Galilee and Rome: His Vita and Development as a Historian*. Columbia Studies in the Classical Tradition 8. Leiden: Brill.
Colautti, Federico M. 2002. *Passover in the Works of Josephus*. JSJSup 75. Leiden: Brill.

Collingwood, R. G. 1994. *The Idea of History*. Edited by Jan van der Dussen. Rev. ed. Oxford: Oxford University Press.

Collins, John J. 2009. "Josephus on the Essenes: The Sources of His Information." Pages 51–72 in *A Wandering Galilean: Essays in Honour of Seán Freyne*. Edited by Zuleika Rodgers. JSJSup 132. Leiden: Brill.

Conte, Gian Biagio, and Glenn W. Most. 1996. "Genre." Pages 630–31 in *Oxford Classical Dictionary*. Edited by Simon Hornblower and Anthony Spawforth. 3rd ed. Oxford: Oxford University Press.

Curran, John R. 2007. "The Jewish War: Some Neglected Regional Factors." *CW* 101:75–91.

DeSilva, David A. 2006. *4 Maccabees: Introduction and Commentary on the Greek Text in Codex Sinaiticus*. Septuagint Commentary. Leiden: Brill.

Doran, Robert. 1979. "2 Maccabees and 'Tragic History.'" *HUCA* 50:107–14.

Eck, Werner. 2007. *Rom und Judaea: Fünf Vorträge zur römischen Herrschaft in Palaestina*. Tria Corda 2. Tübingen: Mohr Siebeck.

Eckstein, Arthur M. 1990. "Josephus and Polybius: A Reconsideration." *ClAnt* 9:175–208.

Egger, Rita. 1986. *Josephus Flavius und die Samaritaner: Eine terminologische Untersuchung zur Identitätsklärung der Samaritaner*. NTOA 4. Göttingen: Vandenhoeck & Ruprecht; Fribourg: Universitätsverlag.

Edmondson, Jonathan, Steve Mason, and James B. Rives, eds. 2005. *Flavius Josephus and Flavian Rome*. Oxford: Oxford University Press.

Farrell, Joseph. 2003. "Classical Genre in Theory and Practice." *New Literary History* 34:383–408.

Feldman, Louis H. 1990. "Prophets and Prophecy in Josephus." *JTS* 41:386–422.

———.1998a. *Josephus's Interpretation of the Bible*. Berkeley: University of California Press.

———.1998b. *Studies in Josephus' Rewritten Bible*. JSJSup 58. Leiden: Brill.

Feldman, Louis H., and Gohei Hata, eds. 1987. *Josephus, Judaism, and Christianity*. Detroit: Wayne State University Press.

———. 1989. *Josephus, the Bible, and History*. Detroit: Wayne State University Press.

Feldman, Louis H., and John R. Levison, eds. 1996. *Josephus' Contra Apionem: Studies in Its Character and Context with a Latin Concordance to the Portion Missing in Greek*. AGJU 34. Leiden: Brill.

Finkbeiner, Douglas P. 2010. "The Essenes according to Josephus: Exploring the Contribution of Josephus' Portrait of the Essenes to His Larger Literary Agenda." PhD diss., University of Pennsylvania.
Freudenthal, Jacob. 1874. *Hellenistische Studien I: Alexander Polyhistor und die von ihm erhaltenen Reste jüdischer und samaritanischer Geschichtswerke*. Breslau: Grass, Barth & Co. (Friedrich).
Gerber, Christine. 1997. *Ein Bild des Judentums für Nichtjuden von Flavius Josephus: Untersuchungen zu seiner Schrift Contra Apionem*. AGJU 40. Leiden: Brill.
Goldberg, Sylvie-Anne. 2018. *Flavius Josèphe: Contra Apion*. Classiques en poche 119. Paris: Les Belles Lettres.
Goldstein, Jonathan A. 1983. *II Maccabees: A New Translation with Introduction and Commentary*. AB 41A. New York: Doubleday.
Goodman, Martin. 1987. *The Ruling Class of Judaea: The Origins of the Jewish Revolt against Rome AD 66–70*. Cambridge: Cambridge University Press.
———. 2007. *Rome and Jerusalem: The Clash of Ancient Civilizations*. London: Lane.
Gray, Rebecca. 1993. *Prophetic Figures in Late Second Temple Jewish Palestine: The Evidence from Josephus*. Oxford: Oxford University Press.
Gruen, Erich S. 2002. *Diaspora: Jews amidst Greeks and Romans*. Cambridge: Harvard University Press.
———. 2005. "Greeks and Jews: Mutual Misperceptions in Josephus' *Contra Apionem*." Pages 31–51 in *Ancient Judaism in Its Hellenistic Context*. Edited by Carol Bakhos. JSJSup 95. Leiden: Brill.
Grünenfelder, Regula. 2003. *Frauen an den Krisenherden: Eine rhetorisch-politische Deutung des Bellum Judaicum*. Münster: LIT.
Gussmann, Oliver. 2008. *Das Priesterverständnis des Flavius Josephus*. TSAJ 124. Tübingen: Mohr Siebeck.
Hadas-Lebel, Mireille. 1993. *Flavius Josephus: Eyewitness to Rome's First-Century Conquest of Judea*. Translated by Richard Miller. New York: Macmillan.
Hall, Robert G. 1991. *Revealed Histories: Techniques for Ancient Jewish and Christian Historiography*. JSPSup 6. Sheffield: JSOT Press.
Halpern, Baruch. 1988. *The First Historians: The Hebrew Bible and History*. San Francisco: Harper & Row.
Halpern, Baruch, and André Lemaire, eds. 2010. *The Books of Kings: Sources, Composition, Historiography and Reception*. VTSup 129. Leiden: Brill.

Halpern-Amaru, Betsy. 1981. "Land Theology in Josephus' *Jewish Antiquities*." *JQR* 71:201–29.

———. 1988. "Portraits of Biblical Women in Josephus' *Antiquities*." *JJS* 39:143–170.

Hammond, Martin. 2017. *The Jewish War*. Introduction and notes by Martin Goodman. Oxford: Oxford University Press.

Harrington, Daniel J. 1988. *The Maccabean Revolt: Anatomy of a Biblical Revolution*. OTS 1. Wilmington, DE: Glazier.

Hata, Gohei. 1977–1978. *Vita; Against Apion* [Japanese]. 2 vols. Tokyo: Yamamotoshoten.

———. 1999–2002a. *Josephus, Jewish War* [Japanese]. 3 vols. Tokyo: Chikuma Gakugeibunko.

———. 1999–2002b. *Josephus, Antiquities of the Jews* [Japanese]. 6 vols. Tokyo: Chikuma Gakugeibunko.

Holladay, Carl R., ed. 1983. *Historians*. Vol. 1 of *Fragments from Hellenistic Jewish Authors*. SBLTT 20. Chico, CA: Scholars Press.

Hollander, William den. 2014. *Josephus, the Emperors, and the City of Rome: From Hostage to Historian*. AGJU 86. Leiden: Brill.

Horst, Pieter W. van der. 2003. *Philo's Flaccus: The First Pogrom*. Philo of Alexandria Commentary 2. Leiden: Brill.

Huizinga, Johan H. 1936. "A Definition of the Concept of History." Pages 1–10 in *Philosophy and History: Essays Presented to Ernst Cassirer*. Edited by Raymond Klibansky and H. J. Paton. Oxford: Clarendon.

Ilan, Tal. 1995. *Jewish Women in Greco-Roman Palestine: An Inquiry into Women and Status*. TSAJ 44. Tübingen: Mohr Siebeck.

———. 2006. *Silencing the Queen: The Literary Histories of Shelamzion and Other Jewish Women*. TSAJ 115. Tübingen: Mohr Siebeck.

Inowlocki, Sabrina. 2006. *Eusebius and the Jewish Authors: His Citation Technique in an Apologetic Context*. AJEC 64. Leiden: Brill.

———. 2011. "Eusebius' Construction of a Christian Culture in an Apologetic Context: Reading the *Praeparatio Evangelica* as a Library." Pages 199–223 in *Reconsidering Eusebius: Collected Papers on Literary, Historical, and Theological Issues*. Edited by Sabrina Inowlocki and Claudio Zamagni. VCSup 107. Leiden: Brill.

Kalms, Jürgen U., ed. 2000. *Internationales Josephus-Kolloquium: Aarhus 1999*. MJSt 6. Münster: LIT.

———. 2001. *Internationales Josephus-Kolloquium: Amsterdam 2000*. MJSt 10. Münster: LIT.

Kasher, Aryeh, ed. 1996. *Flavius Josephus, Against Apion: A New Translation with Introduction and Commentary* [Hebrew]. 2 vols. Jerusalem: Zalman Shazar Center for Jewish History and the Historical Society of Israel.

Kraft, Robert A., and George W. E. Nickelsburg, eds. 1986. *Early Judaism and Its Modern Interpreters*. BMI 2. Philadelphia: Fortress; Atlanta: Scholars Press.

Kraus, Christina S., ed. 1999. *The Limits of Historiography: Genre and Narrative in Ancient Historical Texts*. MnS 191. Leiden: Brill.

Krieger, Klaus-Stefan. 1994. *Geschichtsschreibung als Apologetik bei Flavius Josephus*. TANZ 9. Tübingen: Francke.

Labow, Dagmar, ed. 2005. *Contra Apionem, Buch I: Einleitung, Text, textkritischer Apparat, Übersetzung und Kommentar*. BWANT 167. Stuttgart: Kohlhammer.

Ladouceur, David J. 1987. "Josephus and Masada." Pages 95–113 *Josephus, Judaism, and Christianity*. Edited by Louis H. Feldman and Gohei Hata. Detroit: Wayne State University Press.

Landau, Tamar. 2006. *Out-Heroding Herod: Josephus, Rhetoric, and the Herod Narratives*. AJEC 63. Leiden: Brill.

Laqueur, Richard. 1970. *Der jüdische Historiker Flavius Josephus: ein biographischer Versuch auf neuer quellenkritischer Grundlage*. Darmstadt: Wissenschaftliche Buchgesellschaft.

Leeming, Henry, and Katherine Leeming, with Lyubov Osinkina, eds. 2003. *Josephus' Jewish War and Its Slavonic Version: A Synoptic Comparison*. AGJU 46. Leiden: Brill.

Lemche, Niels P. 2000. "Good and Bad in History: the Greek Connection." Pages 127–40 in *Rethinking the Foundations: Historiography in the Ancient World and in the Bible; Essays in Honour of John Van Seters*. Edited by Steven L. McKenzie and Thomas Römer. BZAW 294. Berlin: de Gruyter.

Long, A. A. 2013. "The Eclectic Pythagoreanism of Alexander Polyhistor." Pages 139–59 in *Aristotle, Plato and Pythagoreanism in the First Century BC: New Directions for Philosophy*. Edited by Malcolm Schofield. Cambridge: Cambridge University Press.

Lowenthal, David. 1997. *The Heritage Crusade and the Spoils of History*. Cambridge: Cambridge University Press.

Luraghi, Nino, ed. 2001. *The Historian's Craft in the Age of Herodotus*. Oxford: Oxford University Press.

Luz, Menahem. 1983. "Eleazar's Second Speech on Masada and Its Literary Precedents." *RMP* 126:25–43.
Mader, Gottfried. 2000. *Josephus and the Politics of Historiography: Apologetic and Impression Management in the Bellum Judaicum.* MnS 205. Leiden: Brill.
Marincola, John. 1997. *Authority and Tradition in Ancient Historiography.* Cambridge: Cambridge University Press.
———. 1999. "Genre, Convention and Innovation in Greco-Roman Historiography." Pages 281–324 in *The Limits of Historiography: Genre and Narrative in Ancient Historical Texts.* Edited by Christina Shuttleworth Kraus. MnS 191. Leiden: Brill.
Marincola, John, Lloyd Llewellyn-Jones, and Calum Maciver, eds. 2012. *Greek Notions of the Past in the Archaic and Classical Eras: History without Historians.* Edinburgh Leventis Studies 6. Edinburgh: Edinburgh University Press.
Martola, Nils. 1984. *Capture and Liberation: A Study in the Composition of the First Book of Maccabees.* AAAbo.H 63. Åbo: Åbo Akademi.
Mason, Steve. 1991. *Flavius Josephus on the Pharisees: A Composition-Critical Study.* StPB 39. Leiden: Brill.
———. 1994. "Josephus, Daniel, and the Flavian House." Pages 161–91 in *Josephus and the History of the Greco-Roman Period: Essays in Memory of Morton Smith.* Edited by Fausto Parente and Joseph Sievers. StPB 41. Leiden: Brill.
———, ed. 1998. *Understanding Josephus: Seven Perspectives.* JSPSup 32. Sheffield: Sheffield Academic.
———. 2003. *Josephus and the New Testament.* 2nd ed. Peabody, MA: Hendrickson.
———. 2007. "Jews, Judaeans, Judaizing, Judaism: Problems of Categorization in Ancient History." *JSJ* 38:457–512.
———. 2009. *Josephus, Judea, and Christian Origins: Methods and Categories.* Peabody, MA: Hendrickson.
———. 2011. "Speech-making in Ancient Rhetoric, Josephus, and Acts: Messages and Playfulness. Part I." *Early Christianity* 2:445–67.
———. 2012. "The Importance of the Latter Half of Josephus's *Judaean Antiquities* for his Roman Audience." Pages 129–53 in *Pentateuchal Traditions in the Late Second Temple Period: Proceedings of the International Workshop in Tokyo, August 28–31, 2007.* Edited by Akio Moriya and Gohei Hata. JSJSup 158. Leiden: Brill.

———. 2016. *A History of The Jewish War, A.D. 66–74*. New York: Cambridge University Press.
Mason, Steve, et al., eds. 2000–. *Flavius Josephus: Translation and Commentary*. Leiden: Brill.
Mayer-Schärtel, Bärbel. 1995. *Das Frauenbild des Josephus: Eine sozialgeschichtliche und kulturanthropologische Untersuchung*. Stuttgart: Kohlhammer.
McKenzie, Steven L., and Thomas Römer, eds. 2000. *Rethinking the Foundations: Historiography in the Ancient World and in the Bible; Essays in Honour of John Van Seters*. BZAW 294. Berlin: de Gruyter.
McLaren, James S. 1998. *Turbulent Times? Josephus and Scholarship on Judaea in the First Century*. JSPSup 29. Sheffield: Sheffield Academic.
Mendels, Doron. 1987. *The Land of Israel as a Political Concept in Hasmonean Literature: Recourse to History in Second Century B.C. Claims to the Holy Land*. TSAJ 15. Tübingen: Mohr Siebeck.
Millar, Fergus. 2002–2006. *Rome, the Greek World, and the East*. 3 volumes. Edited by Hannah M. Cotton and Guy M. Rogers. Studies in the History of Greece and Rome. 3 vols. Chapel Hill: University of North Carolina Press.
Munn, Mark. 2017. "Why History? On the Emergence of Historical Writing." Pages 2–23 in *Ancient Historiography on War and Empire*. Edited by Timothy Howe, Sabine Müller, and Richard Stoneman. Oxford: Oxbow.
Munnich, Olivier. 2017. *Flavius Josèphe: Guerre des Juifs; Livre V*. Classiques en poche 118. Paris: Les Belles Lettres.
Myres, John L. 1953. *Herodotus: Father of History*. Oxford: Clarendon.
Neusner, Jacob, and Bruce Chilton, eds. 2007. *In Quest of the Historical Pharisees*. Waco, TX: Baylor University Press.
Nodet, Étienne, ed. 1990–2010. *Flavius Josèphe, les Antiquités Juives: Introduction et texte, traduction et notes*. Paris: Cerf.
Nongbri, Brent. 2013. *Before Religion: A History of a Modern Concept*. New Haven: Yale University Press.
Olson, Ryan S. 2010. *Tragedy, Authority, and Trickery: The Poetics of Embedded Letters in Josephus*. Hellenic Studies 42. Cambridge: Harvard University Press.
Otis, Brooks. 1967. "The Uniqueness of Latin Literature." *Arion* 6:185–206.
Parente, Fausto, and Joseph Sievers, eds. 1994. *Josephus and the History of the Greco-Roman Period: Essays in Memory of Morton Smith*. StPB 41. Leiden: Brill.

Pastor, Jack, Pnina Stern, and Menahem Mor, eds. 2011. *Flavius Josephus: Interpretation and History*. JSJSup 146. Leiden: Brill.

Price, Jonathan J. 1992. *Jerusalem under Siege: The Collapse of the Jewish State, 66–70 C.E.* BSJS 3. Leiden: Brill.

———. 2008. "The Failure of Rhetoric in Josephus' *Bellum Judaicum*." *Ramus* 36:6–24.

Price, Jonathan J., and Lisa Ullmann. 2002. "Drama and History in Josephus." *Scripta Classica Israelica* 21:97–111.

Pummer, Reinhard. 2009. *The Samaritans in Flavius Josephus*. TSAJ 129. Tübingen: Mohr Siebeck.

Rajak, Tessa. 1991. "Friends, Romans, Subjects: Agrippa II's Speech in Josephus's 'Jewish War.'" Pages 122–34 in *Images of Empire*. Edited by Loveday Alexander. JSOTSup 122. Sheffield: JSOT Press.

———. 1998a. "The *Against Apion* and the Continuities in Josephus's Political Thought." Pages 222–46 in *Understanding Josephus: Seven Perspectives*. Edited by Steve Mason. JSPSup 32. Sheffield: Sheffield Academic.

———. 1998b. "The Parthians in Josephus." Pages 309–24 in *Das Partherreich und seine Zeugnisse: The Arsacid Empire; Sources and Documentation*. Edited by Josef Wiesehöfer. Historia 122. Stuttgart: Steiner.

———. 2002. *Josephus: The Historian and His Society*. 2nd ed. London: Duckworth.

Rodgers, Zuleika, ed. 2007. *Making History: Josephus and Historical Method*. JSJSup 110. Leiden: Brill.

Royse, James R. 2009. "The Works of Philo." Pages 32–64 in *The Cambridge Companion to Philo*. Edited by Adam Kamesar. Cambridge Companions to Philosophy. Cambridge: Cambridge University Press.

Runnalls, Donna. 1997. "The Rhetoric of Josephus." Pages 737–54 in *Handbook of Classical Rhetoric in the Hellenistic Period 330 BC–AD 400*. Edited by Stanley E. Porter. Leiden: Brill.

Saulnier, Christiane. 1991. "Flavius Josèphe et la propagande flavienne." *RB* 98:199–221.

Schwartz, Daniel R. 1990. *Agrippa 1: The Last King of Judea*. TSAJ 23. Tübingen: Mohr Siebeck.

———. 2007. *Life of Josephus: Introduction, Translation, Commentary* [Hebrew]. Between Bible and Mishnah. Jerusalem: Yad Ben-Zvi.

———. 2008. *2 Maccabees*. CEJL. Berlin: de Gruyter.

———. 2013. *Reading the First Century: On Reading Josephus and Studying Jewish History of the First Century*. WUNT 300. Tübingen: Mohr Siebeck.

Schwartz, Seth. 1990. *Josephus and Judaean Politics*. Columbia Studies in the Classical Tradition 18. Leiden: Brill.
Semenchenko, Lada. 2002. "Hellenistic Motifs in the *Jewish Antiquities* of Flavius Josephus" [Russian]. PhD diss., Russian Academy of Sciences.
Shahar, Yuval. 2004. *Josephus Geographicus: The Classical Context of Geography in Josephus*. TSAJ 98. Tübingen: Mohr Siebeck.
Siegert, Folker, ed. 2008. *Über die Ursprünglichkeit des Judentums (Contra Apionem)*. SIJD 6. 2 vols. Göttingen: Vandenhoeck & Ruprecht.
Siegert, Folker, and Jürgen U. Kalms, eds. 1998. *Internationales Josephus-Kolloquium, Münster 1997: Vorträge aus dem Institutum Judaicum Delitzschianum*. Münsteraner judaistische Studien 2. Münster: LIT.
―――, eds. 1999. *Internationales Josephus-Kolloquium, Brussel 1998*. Münsteraner judaistische Studien 4. Münster: LIT.
―――, eds. 2002. *Internationales Josephus-Kolloquium Paris 2001: Studies on the Antiquities of Josephus = études sur les Antiquités de Josèphe*. Münsteraner judaistische Studien 12. Münster: LIT.
―――, eds. 2003. *Internationales Josephus-Kolloquium Dortmund 2002: Arbeiten aus dem Institutum Judaicum Delitzschianum*. Münsteraner judaistische Studien 14. Münster, LIT.
Siegert, Folker, Heinz Schreckenberg, and Manuel Vogel, eds. 2001. *Aus meinem Leben (Vita)*. Tübingen: Mohr Siebeck.
Sievers, Joseph, and Gaia Lembi, eds. 2005. *Josephus and Jewish History in Flavian Rome and Beyond*. JSJSup 104. Leiden: Brill.
Siggelkow-Berner, Birke. 2011. *Die jüdischen Feste im Bellum Judaicum des Flavius Josephus*. WUNT 2/306. Tübingen, Mohr Siebeck.
Smallwood, E. Mary. 1961. *Philonis Alexandrini Legatio ad Gaium*. Leiden: Brill.
Spilsbury, Paul. 1998. *The Image of the Jew in Flavius Josephus' Paraphrase of the Bible*. TSAJ 69. Tübingen: Mohr Siebeck.
―――. 2003. "Flavius Josephus on the Rise and Fall of the Roman Empire." *JTS* 54:1–24.
Sterling, Gregory E. 1992. *Historiography and Self-Definition: Josephos, Luke-Acts, and Apologetic Historiography*. NovTSup 64. Leiden: Brill.
Thackeray, Henry St.-John. 1967. *Josephus: The Man and the Historian*. New York: Ktav.
Thomas, Rosalind. 2000. *Herodotus in Context: Ethnography, Science and the Art of Persuasion*. Cambridge: Cambridge University Press.
Thompson, Thomas L. 2000. "Tradition and History: The Scholarship of John van Seters." Pages 9–22 in *Rethinking the Foundations: Historiog-*

raphy in the Ancient World and in the Bible; Essays in Honour of John Van Seters. Edited by Steven L. McKenzie and Thomas Römer. BZAW 294. Berlin: de Gruyter.

Toher, Mark. 2003. "Nicolaus and Herod in the *Antiquitates Judaicae*." HSCP 101:427–47.

Tropper, Amram. 2004. "The Fate of Jewish Historiography after the Bible." *History and Theory* 43:179–97.

Tuval, Michael. 2013. *From Jerusalem Priest to Roman Jew: On Josephus and the Paradigms of Ancient Judaism.* WUNT 2/357. Tübingen: Mohr Siebeck.

Udoh, Fabian E., ed. 2008. *Redefining First-Century Jewish and Christian Identities: Essays in Honor of Ed Parish Sanders.* CJAn 16. Notre Dame: University of Notre Dame Press.

Ullmann, Lisa, ed. 2009. *The War of the Jews against the Romans* [Hebrew]. Jerusalem: Carmel.

Van Seters, John. 1983. *In Search of History: Historiography in the Ancient World and the Origins of Biblical History.* New Haven: Yale University Press.

Weber, Wilhelm. 1973. *Josephus und Vespasian: Untersuchungen zu dem Jüdischen Krieg des Flavius Josephus.* Hildesheim: Olms.

Villalba i Varneda, Pere. 1986. *The Historical Method of Flavius Josephus.* ALGHJ 19. Leiden: Brill.

Wesselius, Jan Wim. 2002. *The Origin of the History of Israel: Herodotus's Histories as Blueprint for the First Books of the Bible.* JSOTSup 345. London: Sheffield Academic.

Williams, David S. 2001. "Recent Research in 1 Maccabees." *CurBS* 9:169–84.

Wiseman, T. P. 2013. *The Death of Caligula: Josephus Ant. Iud. xix 1–273, Translation and Commentary.* Liverpool: Liverpool University Press.

Woodman, A. J. 1988. *Rhetoric in Classical Historiography: Four Studies.* London: Croom Helm.

Yarrow, Liv M. 2006. *Historiography at the End of the Republic: Provincial Perspectives on Roman Rule.* Oxford Classical Monographs. Oxford: Oxford University Press.

17
APOCALYPTIC LITERATURE

MATTHIAS HENZE

In their introduction to the first edition of *Early Judaism and Its Modern Interpreters*, the volume editors Robert Kraft and George Nickelsburg (1986, 18) singled out the study of apocalypticism as "the most prolific and intensive area in the renewed study of early Judaism," calling it "a microcosm of the field as a whole." The impression is echoed by John Collins (1986, 345), who opens his entry on "Apocalyptic Literature" in the same volume on a similar note: "No aspect of Judaism in the Hellenistic period has received more extensive scholarly attention than apocalyptic literature."

The 1970s and early 1980s saw an unprecedented number of publications that transformed the modern study of apocalyptic literature. In 1970, Klaus Koch published his small but influential book *Ratlos vor der Apokalyptik* (*Clueless about Apocalyptic*), an intentionally polemical pamphlet addressed to his Old and New Testament colleagues, whom he challenges to reexamine their prejudices against apocalyptic texts. Biblical theology needs to pay greater attention to the history of Israel's religion, Koch claims. Only then will scholars realize the significance of apocalypticism as a religious movement at the turn of the Common Era (1970, 115–19; 1982). That Koch's little book inaugurated a new era of study is suggested by the fact that a great many studies to this day continue to use it as their point of entry into the discussion.

Paul Hanson made several important contributions to the apocalyptic debate in the 1970s, most prominently with his seminal monograph *The Dawn of Apocalyptic* (1975; see also Cross 1969). Addressing the question of

---

My sincere thanks to Rodney A. Werline and Benjamin G. Wright III for reading and commenting on an earlier draft of this essay.

the origins of apocalypticism in ancient Israel, Hanson argues that the roots of apocalyptic eschatology are found in Israel's postexilic prophets of the late sixth and early fifth century BCE. The transition from prophetic to apocalyptic eschatology was gradual. Hanson (1975, 27–31) calls Second Isaiah's prophecy "proto-apocalyptic" and the oracles in Zech 9–10 and Isa 24–27 "early apocalyptic." Philipp Vielhauer's (1975, 485–528; also 1964) book *Geschichte der urchristlichen Literatur* (*History of Early Christian Literature*) devotes a chapter to early Christian apocalypses. Vielhauer (1975, 485–94) recognizes the Jewish origin of the genre apocalypse and begins with a form-critical description of the most pertinent Jewish texts. In 1976, Michael Stone published his classic essay "List of Revealed Things in the Apocalyptic Literature." Responding to a tendency in the field to define apocalypticism primarily in terms of eschatology, Stone shows that apocalyptic literature is about much more than end time speculations. He points out that a number of early Jewish apocalypses include strikingly similar lists of secrets revealed to the visionary. These lists are concerned with a range of subjects related to astronomy, meteorology, uranology, and cosmology (1976, 414). In the 1970s, John J. Collins directed a working group at the Society of Biblical Literature whose charge was to identify and define the genre apocalypse and to determine which texts should be called apocalypses (Collins 1979).

In 1979, an international colloquium on apocalypticism met in Uppsala, Sweden. The proceedings, published in 1983 by David Hellholm under the title *Apocalypticism in the Mediterranean World and the Near East*, include no fewer than thirty-five contributions by the leading scholars in the field (see also Collins and Charlesworth 1991). The significance of the Uppsala meeting as a milestone in the scholarly understanding of early Jewish apocalyptic literature can hardly be overstated. In 1982, Christopher Rowland's *The Open Heaven* appeared. Like Stone, Rowland wants to correct the approach to apocalypses that overly focuses on the eschatological aspects. Instead, Rowland argues that apocalypses are "as much involved in the attempt to understand things as they are now as to predict future events" (1982, 2). Two years later, in 1984, Collins published the first edition of his *Apocalyptic Imagination* that soon became a classic introduction to Jewish apocalyptic literature, now in its third edition (2016; see Crawford et al. 2018). James Charlesworth's two-volume *The Old Testament Pseudepigrapha* (*OTP*), published in 1983 and 1985, made some of the key apocalypses and related texts easily accessible in English translation. And in 1986, the first edition of *Early Judaism and Its Modern Interpreters* came out (Kraft and Nickelsburg 1986).

In short, the 1970s and early 1980s mark a watershed moment in modern apocalyptic research (on the history of scholarship, see DiTommaso 2007a, 2007b; Yarbro Collins 2011; de Villiers 2018). The questions these scholars asked and the discourse they framed gave shape to the rapidly growing field of apocalyptic studies. The Uppsala volume captures this moment particularly well (Hellholm 1983). While the study of apocalyptic literature has made substantial advances since then, the basic framework of the scholarly discourse has remained largely intact and continues to set the terms for the discussion. In this essay, I focus on five central issues of the debate: the question of genre; the function and social location of Jewish apocalypses; the significance of the discovery of the Dead Sea Scrolls; Jewish apocalypticism, Jesus, and Paul; and apocalypticism and early Jewish mysticism. I close with a brief look at some of the most recent avenues of research that are particularly promising for the future of apocalyptic research.

1. The Apocalyptic Genre

1.1. What Is an Apocalypse?

When in the 1970s scholars began to identify the defining features of an apocalypse as a distinct form of literature, semantic confusion prevailed. Since *Apokalyptik* is a noun in German, the word *apocalyptic* was also used as a noun in Anglophone scholarship (it continues to be used as such mostly in British scholarship). But what exactly is apocalyptic? How is one to differentiate semantically between the literary genre, the apocalyptic world view(s), and the historical movements? In a short yet influential article, Hanson (1976, 28–31) suggested that apocalypticism, which he understood as a "system of thought produced by visionary movements," operates on three distinct, albeit interrelated levels: the *apocalypse*, understood as a literary genre; *apocalyptic eschatology*, which Hanson defines as "a religious perspective, a way of viewing divine plans in relation to mundane realities" that can be found in a variety of literary genres; and *apocalypticism*, a "symbolic universe in which an apocalyptic movement codifies its identity and interpretation of reality." Hanson rightfully emphasizes that all definitions must remain flexible, since what is being defined is "not a static system, but a phenomenon characterized by movement." This call for flexibility, grounded in the recognition that not all apocalypses are alike and that literary genres evolve over time, became critically important in the genre debate.

The Apocalypse Group at the Society of Biblical Literature, working in the 1970s under the leadership of Collins, defined apocalypse as "a genre of revelatory literature with a narrative framework, in which a revelation is mediated by an otherworldly being to a human recipient, disclosing a transcendent reality which is both temporal, insofar as it envisages eschatological salvation, and spatial insofar as it involves another, supernatural world" (Collins 1979, 9). The group also divided apocalypses into two groups: apocalypses of the historical type that include an extended, panoramic view of history, and apocalypses that feature an otherworldly journey (14–15).

For other scholars, this definition is too restrictive and places too much emphasis on the eschatological future. For Rowland, for example, not eschatological expectations but the disclosure of knowledge is the central aspect of apocalyptic literature. Rowland (1985) emphasizes that apocalypses are a form of revelatory literature. By unveiling the divine mysteries, apocalypses make God's will intelligible: "To speak of apocalyptic, therefore, is to concentrate on the theme of the direct communication of the heavenly mysteries in all their diversity" (14). These two definitions, that of the Society of Biblical Literature working group with its emphasis on eschatology, and Rowland's definition with his focus on revelation, highlight two central aspects of Jewish apocalypticism, its horizontal and its vertical dimensions (for more definitions of the apocalypse, see Stone 1984, 383–84; Davies 1989; Bauckham 2001, 135; and Grabbe 2003, 129–30).

The influential and often-quoted definition of the Society of Biblical Literature working group has been widely discussed. Working within the parameters of biblical form criticism, the team focused on the form and content of Jewish apocalypses. Notably absent are any references to the function of apocalypses and their social location. The omission was intentional, as Collins (2015, 13–14) explains: the group felt that the question of function is better discussed for each text separately. Also absent from the analysis in the mid-1970s are any concerns for the rhetorical dimensions of the apocalyptic discourse, such as language and tone (see Carey and Bloomquist 1999; Newsom 2014), as well as any theoretical considerations regarding literary genres and genre theory in general.

The latter aspect was taken up by Carol Newsom (2005) in an important article. Newsom's intention is not to criticize the work of the Apocalypse Group, let alone to propose an alternative definition. Rather, as she often does in her work, Newsom looks beyond the boundaries of biblical studies, surveys some recent developments in genre theory in other humanistic and social-scientific disciplines, and wonders how these insights might beneficially be applied to the apocalyptic genre. The Society of Biblical Literature working group understood its task as one of definition and classification: They compiled lists of distinctive features possessed by apocalypses and determined the boundaries of the genre. But lists and classifications are necessarily binary and static, whereas genres are dynamic and change over time. Invoking the work of Alastair Fowler, Newsom (2005, 439) employs a memorable metaphor: "The classification approach tends to treat genres as though they were pigeonholes, when in fact genres are more like pigeons."

Literary critics and psychologists have explored alternative ways of thinking about genre. One theory that is especially promising for apocalyptic studies is prototype theory from the field of cognitive psychology. Instead of claiming that there are certain definitive features that must be shared by all members of a group, prototype theory holds that there are significant variations among the members. Some members are prototypes, meaning they are more typical. Newsom uses the example of robins and sparrows as prototypes of birds, whereas others may be more peripheral, such as ostriches and penguins, and thus occupy a somewhat marginal status in the same group. Newsom (2005, 443) comments: "One of the advantages of prototype theory is that it provides a way for bringing together what seems so commonsensical in classificatory approaches, while avoiding their rigidity.... As applied to genre categories, prototype theory would require an identification of examples that are prototypical and an analysis of the privileged properties that establish the sense of typicality" (see also Collins 2014, 1–5; 2015b, 12–13; for the related discussion of wisdom as a literary genre, see Wright's article in this volume; and Najman and Popović 2010).

1.2. Related Types of Texts and Genres

Apocalypses are by definition multigeneric, meaning that they are collages of several literary genres. They may include narratives, revelatory dialogues and oracles, prayers and doxologies, symbolic visions, dreams and dream interpretations, historical reviews and prophecies, cosmic journeys, oral testaments, epistles, and so on. Traditionally, scholars have distinguished between a text's *Rahmengattung*, the generic framework or macrogenre— in our case the apocalypse—and the multiple microgenres that together constitute the apocalypse. This distinction is still useful. Alternatively, however, we might think of apocalypses as generic hybrids that deploy the literary features of more than one genre, without privileging one genre over the others. It should also be noted that, like many biblical books, apocalypses can be assigned to more than one genre: to say that a text is an apocalypse does not exclude the possibility that it can simultaneously be grouped with texts of a different genre (Collins 2015, 6–7).

Several genres of early Jewish literature are closely related to the apocalypse, to the point that the boundaries between them are porous and genres become compatible. One of these genres is the testament. In his groundbreaking commentary on 1 Enoch, for example, George Nickelsburg (2001, 24) speculates "whether chaps. 6–11 [of 1 Enoch] were present in the first form of the Enochic testament." Similarly, leaning on the work of W. D. Davies, Markus Bockmuehl (1997, 24 n. 2) points out that "the most common genre in 'apocalyptic literature' may well be that of *testament* rather than apocalypse" (emphasis original; see also Portier-Young 2011, 391–94). Another genre closely related to the apocalypse is the oracle, best known from the Sibylline Oracles. Like the testament, it, too, has obvious similarities with the apocalypse. Finally, in the late 1990s and early 2000s, the Wisdom and Apocalypticism in Early Judaism and Early Christianity Group at the Society of Biblical Literature reexamined the relationship between wisdom and apocalypticism by shifting the focus to the social context (Wright and Wills 2005; also Knibb 2009; Horsley and Tiller 2012; Goff 2014). Pointing to the shared social matrix of wisdom texts and apocalypses, Nickelsburg (2005, 20) writes, "The entities usually defined as sapiential and apocalyptic often cannot be cleanly separated from one another because both are the products of wisdom circles."

A significant number of early Jewish texts share the literary features of more than one genre. The book of Jubilees, for example, has been called a classic example of rewritten Bible, though it remains unclear whether rewritten Bible is actually a literary genre. Others have proposed that Jubilees should be considered an apocalypse. In his recent seminal commentary on Jubilees, James VanderKam (2018, 20–21) points out that Jubilees does, in fact, match the definition of an apocalypse of the Society of Biblical Literature working group rather closely. At the same time, there are other aspects in Jubilees, such as the lack of interest in the eschatological future, that make Jubilees "a marginal member of the genre" at best. Another text that includes prophecies of great suffering and hence might be called an apocalypse is the Testament of Moses. Stone (1984, 419) writes: "Of the extant testaments, this [Testament of Moses] is closest to an apocalyptic vision of the historical type."

1.3. The Apocalypse—Still a Useful Genre?

Genre analysis has made invaluable contributions to apocalyptic studies and remains vital today. It has sharpened our eye for how apocalypses work as literary artifacts, while laying bare the limits of genre attribution. Apocalypse remains a useful genre. Yet, two problems prevail. The first is rigidity. When classifications and definitions are applied too rigorously and binary distinctions between belonging and not belonging are used to assign texts to static groups, the explanatory benefit of genre analysis is lost. Second, the term apocalypse has become overly fraught. In modern parlance it connotes disaster and catastrophe. Scholars use the term with increasing reluctance, feeling the need to explain exactly what they mean. As so often, Stone (1976, 443) was well ahead in the discussion when he wrote over forty years ago: "It may perhaps be suggested that the terms 'apocalyptic' and 'apocalypticism' be abandoned altogether." Stone sums up the sentiment of many scholars today, who would rather avoid the term apocalypse altogether. At present, it is far from clear, however, what other term, if any, might take its place.

2. The Function and Social Location of Jewish Apocalypses

2.1. Function

Critics of the Society of Biblical Literature working group definition were quick to point out that it says nothing about the purpose or function of apocalyptic texts. In a subsequent *Semeia* volume on early Christian apocalypses edited by Adela Yarbro Collins (1986, 7), the definition was amended and a clause added that an apocalypse is "intended to interpret present, earthly circumstances in light of the supernatural world of the future, and to influence both the understanding and the behavior of the audience by means of divine authority." This addition, too, does not fully address the function of an apocalypse, or at least it does so in a fairly abstract manner.

The main challenge is that early Jewish apocalypses were written over a significant period of time—roughly from the third century BCE to the late first century CE—by different authors and in different contexts, so that there simply cannot be a single definition or location that covers their diverse functions (Stone 1984, 433–35). It has often been claimed that apocalypses are crisis literature, written in a specific historical situation and "intended for a group in crisis with the purpose of exhortation and/or consolation by means of divine authority" (Hellholm 1986, 27; Daschke 2010 emphasizes the aspect of mourning in apocalyptic literature; Najman 2014 reads 4 Ezra as a "reboot" after the destruction of Jerusalem). While it is true that some apocalypses respond to a specific crisis—whether historical or ethnic/religious, imagined or real—this is hardly true of all apocalypses. The Enochic Astronomical Book (1 En. 72–82) of the third century BCE, for example, is preoccupied with cosmological speculations, the movements of the sun, moon, and stars, and the calendar, not with loss or devastation. Daniel 7–12, written during the Maccabean Revolt (167–164 BCE), comes closest to crisis literature. Indeed, early proponents of the crisis hypothesis saw Daniel as paradigmatic of all apocalypses, presumably because of its biblical status (the fact that Daniel was seen as normative was problematic, because it skewed the study of other apocalypses). Second Baruch and 4 Ezra, both written in the late first century CE, respond to the fall of Jerusalem to the Romans. But this is only one, and hardly the dominant aspect of these rather complex texts, and it should not be overemphasized to the detriment of other important aspects in the two apocalypses (see also Tigchelaar 1996, 263–65). A single explanation of the function of the diverse apocalyptic texts will not do.

2.2. Social Location

While it is unlikely that function can or even should become part of the genre definition, function *is* tied to the question of the socioreligious matrix of Jewish apocalypses. An early and influential voice in this debate was Hanson. Making his case that the origins of apocalyptic eschatology are found in sixth-century BCE prophecy, Hanson (1975, 1976) distinguishes between two groups in postexilic Judea: the "Hierocratic Party of the Zadokites," which he identifies with Ezek 40–48, Haggai, and Zech 1–8, and "the Visionaries," whom Hanson finds behind Zech 9–14 and Isa 56–66. The texts of the hierocratic circles closest resemble early Jewish apocalypses, whereas "the dawn of apocalyptic" is to be found in the prophecies of the visionaries. Underlying Hanson's (1976, 30) hypothesis of two distinct, protoapocalyptic groups are a number of assumptions about early Jewish apocalypticism that proved to be influential and that were widely shared at the time: that behind each apocalypse stands a group, a social movement or small conventicle; that apocalypses are "a protest of the apocalyptic community against dominant society," from which the group feels alienated and marginalized; and that apocalypses create a "symbolic counter-universe," their own theological flights of fancy, whose aim it is to provide the group with a sense of identity and a vision of its ultimate vindication.

A principle difficulty with determining the social setting of Jewish apocalypses is that apocalypses are pseudepigraphic writings set in a fictitious environment. Apocalyptic texts provide precious little indication of their original location. Some scholars have turned to social-scientific models and have used sociological and anthropological studies to determine the texts' original social locations. Hanson (1975, 211–20) himself had already enlisted the help of Max Weber, Karl Mannheim, and Ernst Troeltsch. Two programmatic articles, both published in 1989, seek to recover the social setting of Jewish apocalypses. Lester Grabbe (1989) uses anthropological studies of millennial movements, specifically the example of Handsome Lake, a prophet from the Seneca Indians in the early nineteenth century, as comparative evidence. Grabbe directly disputes some of Hanson's theses, arguing that not all apocalypses come from conventicles, that apocalypses do not necessarily respond to a crisis, and that their apocalyptic worldviews are not necessarily different from what have already become widespread beliefs (see also Grabbe 2003). While Grabbe's corrections of some stereotypes about apocalyptic literature are important, the compatibility of the ancient Jewish texts and modern anthropological models remains methodologically problematic.

Philip Davies (1989) is equally critical of some common assumptions, including Hanson's. Davies maintains that early Jewish apocalypses do not derive from prophecy or from wisdom circles of the kind of "the court-based worldly instruction of Proverbs" (260), nor were they written in conventicles. Instead, Davies contends, apocalypses are the products of scribes. This is not the literature of a persecuted minority. To the contrary, these are texts of the established priesthood and of highly educated circles of scribes:

> The social background of apocalyptic writing thus furnished is more fully described and precisely documented by the activity of political "establishment" and culturally cosmopolitan *scribes* than of visionary "counter-establishment" *conventicles*.... What determines the production of apocalyptic literature is not a millenarian posture nor a predicament of

persecution, though these may be contributory factors. It is scribal convention. (Davies 1989, 263 [emphasis original]; see also 1993)

Davies's insistence that we think of apocalypses as scribal products is important and challenges monolithic views of who scribes in early Judaism were. What is more, wisdom texts are also associated with scribes. The conclusion that the social locations of apocalypses are varied and diverse, and that wisdom literature, too, is of scribal origin, means that scribal circles were diverse and variously located.

More recently, Philip Esler (2014) has applied social-scientific approaches to Jewish apocalyptic literature. Surveying different ways in which biblical scholars have incorporated social-scientific research into their work since the 1970s, Esler himself focuses on social identity theory to argue that what Jewish apocalypses such as 1 Enoch and Daniel respond to is not an attack on religion but a real threat to Judean ethnicity: "The dominant question that arises is the extent to which ancient Judeans of the Mediterranean world regarded the major problem they faced not as religious persecution by an evil empire, whether Seleucid or Roman … but as a threat to the survival of their Judean ethnic group" (136). Esler thus appeals to social-scientific studies to argue that, when reading Jewish apocalypses, greater attention needs to be paid to matters of ethnic identity.

2.3. Empire: Apocalypse as Resistance Literature

In the early 2010s, two monographs read early Jewish apocalypses as resistance literature to imperial hegemony and domination. Richard Horsley (2010, 3) observes that virtually all apocalypses of the late Second Temple period "focus on oppressive imperial rule and also, in many cases, on resistance to the point of martyrdom." This leads Horsley to read apocalypses "as expressions and explanations" of imperial resistance. More specifically, Horsley contends that apocalypses are the products of circles of learned Judean scribes. Scribes were highly trained guardians of the sacred traditions. It was their primary task to serve both as intellectual and legal advisors to the priestly aristocracy in charge of the temple and as administrators in the imperial regimes. When collaboration between the priests and the regime became too close and threatened the traditional Judean way of life, some of the scribes objected, appealed to divine sovereignty, and devised "tactics of protest and defiance" (195).

Anathea Portier-Young (2011, 2014) has written the most sophisticated and systematic account of apocalypses as resistance literature. Focusing on the first historical apocalypses, Daniel, the Apocalypse of Weeks (1 En. 93.1–10 + 91.11–17), and the Book of Dreams (1 En. 83–90), Portier-Young carefully investigates exactly *how* the apocalypses resisted empire. The monograph consists of three parts. Part 1, "Theorizing Resistance," a discussion of the meaning of hegemony, domination, and resistance, provides the theoretical framework for the book. Whereas Horsley is uncomfortable with the genre apocalypse and would rather replace genre analysis with historical analysis, Portier-Young (2011, xxii) embraces "the literary genre apocalypse as resistant counterdiscourse." In part 2, "Seleucid Domination in Judea," Portier-Young moves from theory to history and documents the era of Seleucid rule in Judea from 200 BCE to 167 BCE. In particular, she describes the various means by which the Seleucid kings established their domination and asserted and maintained their power. This is a masterful analysis of Seleucid hegemony and a convincing rereading of Antiochus's edict and persecution. Part 3, "Apocalyptic Theologies of Resistance," reads the three Jewish apocalypses as resistant discourse. The resistance to empire in these texts is not merely an exercise in rhetoric. Rather, Portier-Young (2011, xxiii) finds in all three texts a "creative interplay between theology, hermeneutics, and ethics, or, put another way, between the framework of belief, practices of reading, and the shaping of resistant action" (on the politics of time reckoning in apocalyptic literature as a form of resistance to the Seleucid Empire, see the important book by Kosmin 2018, 137–86).

While many questions remain about the social matrices of Jewish apocalypses forty years after the groundbreaking work of Hanson, our grasp of the apocalyptic texts has advanced considerably. At the center of these advances stands the recognition that early Jewish apocalypses are heterogeneous, written by diverse social movements to fulfill multiple functions. In the words of Lorenzo DiTommaso (2010, 464), "while apocalypticism might correlate to typical societal contexts, it could not be restricted to a single social movement or milieu … the element of social setting cannot define either the genre or the worldview." Few scholars today will assert that all apocalypses are the literary products of socially marginalized conventicles, that their diverse worldviews are by definition incompatible with more traditional ways of thinking, or that all apocalypses are resistance literature (on the latter, see Portier-Young 2014, 154–56). Heterogeneous Jewish apocalypses cannot be reduced to a single setting or function, just as apocalypses do not stem from a single apocalyptic movement or reflect a single worldview. The questions of their social origin, location, and purpose will have to be addressed on a text-by-text basis.

3. Jewish Apocalypticism and the Dead Sea Scrolls

As the Dead Sea Scrolls were beginning to be published during the first few decades after their discovery, hopes were high that the newly discovered texts would provide "the solution to all the problems that had vexed scholarship in the field of apocalypticism" (García Martínez 2007, 195). Indeed, such initial hopes were not unfounded. It soon became clear that the scrolls include the oldest known manuscripts of some of the most important Jewish apocalypses, including Daniel, 1 Enoch, and Jubilees, that a wealth of other, hitherto unknown apocalyptic texts had been found among the scrolls, that the sectarian texts themselves frequently use apocalyptic language and motifs, and that the community behind the scrolls was an apocalyptic group—small, secluded, and guided by its own sectarian teachings, a community just as proponents of the apocalyptic conventicles hypothesis had long hypothesized (García Martínez 2007, 196). But the euphoric pan-Qumranism of the 1950s and 1960s was short lived. Speaking about the significance of the scrolls for apocalyptic research at the Uppsala Colloquium, Hartmut Stegemann (1983, 495) opens with the somewhat sobering observation that apocalypticism specialists of his time fall into two camps: those who remain hopeful that the scrolls might turn out to be "eine Art Wundermedizin" ("a sort of miracle medicine") for our understanding of Jewish apocalypticism, and those who have been disillusioned by the lack of new insights the scrolls have yielded so far.

Today few will dispute that the Dead Sea Scrolls have contributed immeasurably to our understanding of early Jewish apocalypticism (see Schofield's article in this volume). Three areas in which the scrolls have been invaluable stand out: Qumran as an apocalyptic community; apocalyptic texts discovered at Qumran; and apocalyptic topics and motifs in the scrolls that are also attested in Jewish apocalypses.

3.1. The Qumran Community: An Apocalyptic Community

Stegeman (1983, 525–26) concludes his Uppsala essay with the contention that, in spite of the numerous apocalyptic texts found among the scrolls, the Qumran community was not an apocalyptic movement, and, indeed, that it did not show much interest in things apocalyptic. The evidence, now fully published, suggests otherwise. Focusing primarily on the Damascus Document, "its claim to special revelation, use of periodization, dualism, and eschatology," and, to a lesser degree, on the War Scroll (1QM) and the Community Rule (1QS), Collins (1997, 284–85) argues that the Qumran community stems from "the same general milieu as the apocalyptic movements" and hence should be considered an apocalyptic movement. Florentino García Martínez (1992) concurs. The study of the Qumran community and the study of Jewish apocalypses mutually inform each other, as one illuminates the other: Jewish apocalypses teach us about the very ideas that gave rise to the scrolls community in the first place, and studying the scrolls is necessary for a proper understanding of Jewish apocalypses, even for texts like 4 Ezra that were written after the destruction of the Qumran settlement (García Martínez 1992, x–xi).

The exact nature of the Qumran community continues to attract attention. In his important recent monograph on secret groups in ancient Judaism, Stone (2018, 119–39) argues that, rather than calling the Qumran community a sect (so Baumgarten 1997, and many others), we should think of it as a secret society, one of several in Second Temple times that cultivated certain esoteric traditions of learning and practice whose circulation was forbidden. Studying the implementation and secret transmission of this knowledge provides much insight into the inner workings and social structure of the group.

3.2. Apocalyptic Texts from Qumran

One of the more surprising aspects of the Qumran community is that, even though it was an apocalyptic community, its members do not appear to have composed any new apocalypses (Collins 1997, 9–11). Yet, in addition to the copies of known apocalypses discovered among the scrolls, there are a significant number of texts that, even though they may not fall under the genre apocalypse, include apocalyptic language and traditions. It is also noteworthy that a large number of these texts are written in Aramaic: of the over ninety Aramaic manuscripts discovered among the scrolls, about two-thirds include apocalyptic material (so DiTommaso 2010, 456; already García Martínez 1992).

A significant number of scrolls can be said to be apocalyptic, or at least to include apocalyptic elements. These include the Daniel texts: the manuscripts of the biblical book, as well as the so-called Pseudo-Daniel texts (4Q243–245), and a short composition known as the Son of God text or the Apocryphon of Daniel (4Q246). The Enoch texts: included are manuscripts of the Book of the Watchers, the Similitudes, the Astronomical Book, and the Epistle, plus several copies of the Book of Giants. The Jubilees texts: the fragments of the book of Jubilees and the so-called Pseudo-Jubilees texts (4Q225–227); and numerous other compositions, such as the New Jerusalem texts (1Q32; 2Q24; 4Q554–555; 5Q15; 11Q18); the Aramaic Levi Document (1Q21; 4Q213–214); the Visions of Amram (4Q543–549); and the Messianic Apocalypse (4Q521). Three of the main rulebooks from Qumran are not apocalypses but include apocalyptic ideas: the War Scroll (1QM), the Community Rule (1QS; particularly the Instruction on the Two Spirits in 1QS III, 13–IV, 24), and the Damascus Document (CD).

3.3. Apocalyptic Topics and Motifs

The Qumran documents frequently employ apocalyptic topics, motifs, and language that are also found in early Jewish apocalyptic texts outside the Qumran community (Collins 1997; García Martínez 1998; Frey 2007).

3.3.1. The Origin of Evil

The different explanations in Jewish apocalypses for the origin of evil is a telling example of the heterogeneity of apocalyptic texts. The Enochic tradition focuses on the myth of the fallen angels (Gen 6:1–4), whose most elaborate account is found in the Book of the Watchers (1 En. 1–36). For 4 Ezra, by contrast, the evil inclination stems from Adam and his "evil heart" (4 Ezra 3.21–22; cf. 2 Bar. 54; Rom 5). The covenanters from Qumran were familiar with the Watchers story (CD II, 15–16), but their main explanation of the origin of evil is found in the dualistic Instruction on the Two Spirits (1QS III, 13–IV, 24), which teaches that all human beings are under the influence of the Prince of Light and the Angel of Darkness.

3.3.2. Messianism

The expectation of an eschatological agent of God, a descendant of David who will appear at the end of time to establish a kingdom of peace, is widely attested in Jewish apocalypses. As in the case of the origin of evil, expectations differ significantly from text to text. The Enochic Book of

Parables (1 En. 37–71) expects an ideal ruler figure, designated the Son of Man and Chosen One (1 En. 48; 52). Fourth Ezra includes several messianic passages with different sets of messianic expectations, even within the same text (4 Ezra 7.26–44; 11.1–12.36; 13.1–56). Some Jewish apocalypses, such as the Apocalypse of Weeks (1 En. 93.1–10; 91.11–17), do not mention a messianic figure at all. The scrolls also frequently refer to messianic figures, most notably in the Messianic Apocalypse (4Q521) and the Son of God text (4Q246). Some core sectarian documents appear to refer to two eschatological figures of deliverance instead of one, the Messiah of Israel and the Messiah of Aaron (1QS IX, 11; CD XXII, 23; XIV, 1 9; XIX, 10; XX, 1).

3.3.3. The Periodization of History

The division of the passage of time into distinct segments is *the* defining feature of apocalypses of the historical type. One of the oldest Jewish apocalypses, the Enochic Apocalypse of Weeks (1 En. 93.1–10, 91.11–17), divides all of history into ten periods or weeks. Daniel 2 and 4 introduce the schema of the four kingdoms, and Dan 9 speaks of seventy weeks of years. Baruch's elaborate vision of the cloud alternates between good and evil periods in the history of Israel that spans from Adam's transgression to the messianic age (2 Bar. 53–74). In the scrolls, we find periodizations of history in the opening columns of the Damascus Document, as well as in some of the exegetical texts, such as the Pesher on the Periods (4Q180–181) and the Melchizedek text (11Q13 [11QMelchizedek]).

3.3.4. The Eschatological War and the Expectation of an End

The concept of the periodization of time is predicated on the notion that history unfolds based on a predetermined divine plan. It also assumes that, just as time had a definitive beginning (Gen 1), so it is aimed toward a definitive end. Jewish apocalypses of the historical type are united in their belief that the end will not be abrupt but will consist of a sequence of events, though exactly *how* the end-time drama will unfold differs from text to text. The Qumran community believed that it was living at "the end of days." Several scrolls speak of the end (1QS IV, 18–19; 1QpHab VII) in terms of a great cosmic upheaval. None does so in more graphic terms than the War Scroll (1QM), a dramatic account of the eschatological war and final victory of the Sons of Light over all evildoers.

3.3.5. The Resurrection of the Dead

Another stock motif in the final drama is the expectation that the dead will rise again. Daniel 12:1–3 promises everlasting life to a group called "the wise." Similarly, the Epistle of Enoch announces that "the righteous will rise from the sleep" (1 En. 90.10; also 1 En. 104.1–6). The most explicit account of the gradual transformations of the resurrected in Jewish apocalypses is found in 2 Baruch (2 Bar. 49–52). Resurrection language is also used in the scrolls (e.g., 1QS IV, 11–14; XI, 5–8; 1QH^a XIX, 6–17), though it is not clear whether these passages refer to the afterlife, or whether resurrection language at Qumran is used to describe the actual life in the community: joining the Qumran group is the equivalent of rising from the dead. It is difficult to avoid the impression that the ambiguity is deliberate.

3.3.6. Communion with the Heavenly World

Jewish apocalypses show great interest in angels and demons. The texts give them names and tell of their origins, their ranks, their activities, and, if they are evil, of their ultimate demise. In the Book of the Watchers, for example, Enoch ascends into heaven into the heavenly throne room, where he witnesses the ongoing worship of God (1 En. 14; cf. Dan 7). The community at Qumran, too, was keenly aware of the heavenly worship. A cycle of liturgies known as the Songs of the Sabbath Sacrifice (4Q400–407) expresses the hope of the covenanters to be present in the heavenly temple and to participate in the ongoing angelic service (also 1 QS XI, 7–8; 1QH^a XI, 19–21).

Early Jewish apocalypses share a set of theological concerns and literary motifs that could be summarized under the umbrella term apocalyptic eschatology. Even our most cursory look at the texts shows their remarkable diversity and richness. The scrolls give witness of yet another community that was shaped by many of the same apocalyptic beliefs and practices, and, like each of the apocalypses, gives them its own interpretation. In the words of Florentino García Martínez (2007, 199), "the cluster of ideas appearing in the sectarian scrolls ... represents a genuine apocalyptic tradition, connected with, but different from, other apocalyptic traditions."

4. Jewish Apocalypticism and Christian Origins

Another group that exhibits signs of the influence of apocalypticism is the movement initiated by Jesus and his followers. This movement was

Jewish and possessed a high degree of eschatological expectation that the kingdom of God was close at hand. The exact relationship between Jewish apocalypticism and Christian origins has recently become the subject of several studies, as scholars have increasingly sought to understand Jesus and the Jesus Movement in the context of, rather than in opposition to, the Judaism of first century Israel. Methodological concerns have played a major role in the debate over the last two decades (on Christian origins, see Doering's article in this volume).

4.1. Jesus: An Apocalyptic Prophet?

The case that Jesus was an apocalyptic prophet was already made a century ago by Johannes Weiss (1863–1914) and, more forcefully, by Albert Schweitzer (1875–1965; on the history of scholarship, see Allison 1999; Murphy 2012, 281–305; Yarbro Collins 2014; Paget 2017). In the latter half of the twentieth century, however, a number of scholars came to reject the idea of an apocalyptic Jesus—so much so that Koch famously chided his New Testament colleagues for their "angestrengte[s] Bemühen, Jesus vor der Apokalyptik zu retten" ("forced effort to save Jesus from apocalypticism") (Koch 1970, 55–90; also Frey 2016). Skepticism still prevails today (for the voices of Marcus Borg, John Dominic Crossan, and Stephen Patterson, all skeptics of an apocalyptic Jesus, see Miller 2001; also Kloppenborg and Marshall 2005).

The most ardent contemporary proponents of the hypothesis that Jesus was an apocalyptic prophet are Dale Allison (1998; 2001) and Bart Ehrman (1999). Allison deliberately does not make Jesus's apocalyptic sayings a cornerstone of his argument, nor does he try to reconstruct the earliest layers of the Jesus tradition, as any such attempt is necessarily hypothetical. Instead, Allison relies on circumstantial evidence: Jesus was baptized by John the Baptist, an apocalyptic prophet; Jesus's earliest followers proclaimed that the end was near, and they interpreted Jesus's resurrection as the first in a sequence of eschatological events that were beginning to unfold; and apocalyptic thinking was widespread in first-century Judaism. To claim, therefore, that Jesus did not have a strong apocalyptic orientation would entail a major discontinuity (Allison 2001, 20–24).

Unlike Allison, Ehrman builds his case by relying heavily on the dating of the sources, and Jesus's apocalyptic teachings figure prominently in Ehrman's reconstruction. Ehrman asserts that older sources tend to be more reliable than later sources. The oldest sources of Jesus we have

(Q, Mark, Matthew, and Luke) all describe an apocalyptic Jesus, whereas the later sources (John and Thomas) do not. Moreover, later sources tend to deapocalypticize Jesus's message, a trend that continues well into the second century CE. Ehrman (1999, 139) thus concludes that "Jesus himself must have been a Jewish apocalypticist" and that Jesus's deeds and other teachings fit well within an apocalyptic context.

4.2. The Apocalyptic Paul

Paul's letters, too, include ample apocalyptic language and motifs. Paul did not write an apocalypse, but his theology is distinctly apocalyptic in character and deploys many core concepts of Jewish apocalyptic eschatology. In 1 Thess 4, for example, Paul writes of Jesus's return in the language of apocalyptic expectations; 1 Cor 15 is an elaborate treatise on the resurrection of the dead, a recurring theme in Jewish apocalypses; and in Rom 8 Paul contrasts "the sufferings of this present time" with "the glory to be revealed to us" (Rom 8:18), invoking a common topos in Jewish apocalypticism, the expectation of an imminent end (de Boer 1998).

Over the last two decades, scholarship on the so-called apocalyptic Paul has sought to define the meaning of apocalyptic in the context of Pauline theology: Why are we justified to call Paul's theology apocalyptic, what does the label apocalyptic mean in Pauline studies, and how should we study Paul, the apocalyptic thinker? It is not Paul's indebtedness to Jewish apocalypticism that is in question but the precise nature of Paul's own apocalyptic eschatology and its significance for his theology. The editors of a recent volume on the apocalyptic Paul, Ben Blackwell, John Goodrich, and Jason Maston (2016, 3–21), divide Pauline scholars into two groups: the eschatological invasion group they associate with Weiss, Schweitzer, Rudolf Bultmann and the like, and the unveiled fulfillment group that follows Rowland and stresses Paul's mystical experiences. While such binary models may seem simplistic, the distinction uncovers some principle differences in contemporary readings of Paul's apocalyptic imagination.

4.3. Jewish Apocalypses and the Origins of Christianity

The surge of interest over the last couple of decades in the apocalyptic orientation of Jesus and Paul has given us a new way of looking at the old texts. It has significantly advanced our understanding of the teachings of

Jesus and Paul, and it has further underscored the significance of Jewish apocalypticism for the origins of Christianity. Of course, this does not exclude other influences: Paul, for example, made ample use of Hellenistic rhetoric and philosophy. There is also a range of apocalyptic issues, well known from Jewish apocalypses, that are absent from the New Testament (Stone 2011, 29). But it is evident that Jewish apocalypticism provides an important framework for studying the origins of Christianity (Yarbro Collins 2014, 338; Frey 2006).

As scholars are increasingly becoming aware of the heterogeneity of early Jewish apocalypses and of the diverse scribal circles behind them, the label *apocalyptic worldview* appears imprecise and calls for specification. It is also no longer enough to work exclusively with New Testament texts when trying to uncover the apocalyptic Jesus or Paul. Apocalyptic texts in the New Testament need to be interpreted within the wider context, and as part of the large corpus of early Jewish apocalypses (Stuckenbruck 2013, 2014) and not in contrast to it (Tilly 2012, 88–96). Only a close, comparative reading of the New Testament with Jewish apocalypses will enable us to gain a more precise understanding of the kind of apocalyptic teachings and practices that gave birth to and shaped early Christianity.

5. Jewish Apocalypticism and Mysticism

5.1. A Continuous Tradition of Jewish Mysticism?

The idea that Jewish mysticism, and more specifically *merkabah* mysticism, the first fully developed system of Jewish mysticism, has deep roots in the apocalyptic literature of the late Second Temple period was initially proposed by Gershom Scholem (1995) in the first half of the twentieth century. In his seminal work *Major Trends in Jewish Mysticism*, first published in 1941, Scholem argues that "the main subjects of the later Merkabah mysticism already occupy a central position in this oldest esoteric literature" of early Judaism. Scholem mentions in passing the books of 1 Enoch, 4 Ezra, and the Apocalypse of Abraham, albeit without offering a close reading of any specific passages, and maintains that there are "subterranean but effective, and occasionally traceable, connections" between these apocalypses and the later works of the *merkabah* and *hekhalot* literature (40–43; see Lieber's article in this volume). In brief, Scholem argues that there is a single, continuous tradition of Jewish mysticism, a religious movement that reaches back to the late Second Temple era. This mystic tradition, with its own distinct features, can be further subdivided into three distinct stages, each associated with a particular historical period:

> The anonymous conventicles of the old apocalyptics; the Merkabah speculation of the Mishnaic teachers who are known to us by name; and the Merkabah mystics of late and post-Talmudic times, as reflected in the literature which has come down to us. We are dealing here with a religious movement of distinctive character. (Scholem 1995, 43; see also Schäfer 2009, 1–33; Reed 2013; Boustan and McCullough 2014)

Scholem's hypothesis of a single, unbroken tradition that originated in the late Second Temple period with "the old apocalyptics," continued in the time of the Mishnah with "the Mishnaic teachers," and culminated in the *hekhalot* literature of the late and post-Talmudic era under "the Merkabah mystics," has attracted several supporters. One of them is Ithamar Gruenwald. Gruenwald investigates in great detail the mystical elements in apocalyptic writings, such as the vision report of the heavenly throne room in 1 En. 14 and 71, whose scriptural origins he finds in texts like Isa 6, Ezek 1, and Dan 7. Gruenwald (2014, 68–110) also finds similar visions of the *merkabah* in texts like the Ascension of Isaiah and the New Testament book of Revelation.

Recently, scholars have sought to underscore the significance and place of the Dead Sea Scrolls in the early history of Jewish mysticism. The argument is that some of the scrolls describe a (liturgical) communion with the angels. The scrolls also include accounts of an ascent into heaven that culminates in a vision of God in the heavenly throne room, like the communion with the angels, a motif that resurfaces again in *hekhalot* literature. Philip Alexander (2006, vii), for example, downplays the significance of the early apocalyptic texts for any attempt to trace the origins of Jewish mysticism and instead points to Qumran, claiming that "there was mysticism at Qumran" (see also Davila 2010; Collins 2018). In particular, Alexander singles out the Songs of the Sabbath Sacrifice as the earliest version of a heavenly journey that bears great affinity to what is found again much later in the *hekhalot* texts (for a sharp criticism of Alexander's position, see Schäfer 2009, 152–53).

5.2. From Continuity to Differences

In recent decades, scholars have started to take aim at Scholem's powerful paradigm of a continuous mystic tradition. Criticism is coming from various angles. One has to do with definition. What exactly do we mean when we speak of "early Jewish mysticism"? Traditionally, mysticism has been seen as a particular form of the religious life that strives to attain a mystical union, or *unio mystica*, of the individual with the divine. In this reading, mysticism denotes a particular religious experience, "a private, interiorized, and unmediated encounter with the divine" (Boustan and McCullough 2014, 87). The problem is that experiences, by definition, remain inaccessible to the outsider and largely resist critical analysis. In the end, it may well prove impossible to determine whether the texts are literary creations or whether they testify to an actual mystical experience. Another problem with definition is that Jewish mysticism has taken on many different forms and expressions over time. Peter Schäfer (2009, 354), one of the leading critics of Scholem's paradigm of a linear development, stresses the great "variety of sources, motifs, and emphases" and states: "in a certain sense we must be capable of bearing the polymorphic and even chaotic evidence that our sources confront us with." This leads Schäfer to state categorically at the outset of his investigation into the origins of Jewish mysticism, "Any attempt to define mysticism in a way that allows the definition to be generally accepted is hopeless" (2009, 1).

Beyond finding the right definition, there is a larger methodological issue that continues to divide Scholem's followers and critics. Scholem's quest for origins and continuity in Jewish mysticism, and particularly his desire to postulate a link between the early Jewish apocalypses and the *hekhalot* texts, is propelled by his desire to emphasize commonalities across different time periods and divergent literary corpora. In other words, Scholem wants to find links and see connections where others see differences. Few will deny common patterns and motifs, but not everybody finds in them evidence of continuous developments and historical trajectories. A case in point is Martha Himmelfarb's (1993) work on the ascent narratives in Jewish and Christian apocalypses. Himmelfarb surveys a wide variety of texts—the Book of the Watchers, the Testament of Levi, 2 Enoch, the Similitudes of Enoch, the Apocalypse of Zephaniah, the Apocalypse of Abraham, the Ascension of Isaiah, and 3 Baruch—works Himmelfarb dates from the third century BCE to the second century CE. In her analysis, differences prevail. Himmelfarb clearly sees lines of continuity, for example, with regard to the Book of the Watchers and its "powerful influence even on works with interests quite distant from its own" (46). And yet, her careful reading of the texts reveals significant variations between textual corpora and even among the early Jewish apocalypses themselves (Boustan and McCullough 2014, 93).

6. Outlook

Scholarship on apocalyptic literature has gone unabated since the 1970s and early 1980s. Over the last couple of decades, a number of exciting and promising new avenues of research have opened up. Many of these new initiatives are the result of greater interdisciplinary collaboration, a willingness to break out of academic silos, to rethink the old models and vocabulary, and the desire to look beyond the Second Temple period (on new methodologies, see Werline's article in this volume).

6.1. Temporality and Spatiality

Apocalyptic temporality is the subject of several recent innovative studies. This promising new interest in apocalyptic notions of time and temporality largely responds to two trends in Jewish studies: one, represented by Sacha Stern and others, that claims that early Judaism did not have an abstract concept of time, or, if it did, that it is inferior to that of biblical prophecy; and the other, widespread in apocalyptic studies still today, that employs traditional binaries of linear/circular, historic/mythic, and *chronos/ kairos* when thinking about time. As a counterpoint, several recent studies contend that apocalyptic texts, including the Dead Sea Scrolls, attest to sophisticated concepts of time, and that the conventional binaries are insufficient to characterize the complex understandings and diverse experiences of time in apocalyptic writings. Jonathan Ben-Dov (2016, 301–2) argues compellingly that the Qumran community is keenly interested in the here and now and that their sense of time is geared toward "producing a very 'thick' present." Devorah Dimant (2009, 2013) investigates diverse views on time and temporality in the scrolls and apocalyptic writings. Matthias Henze (2011, 278–93; 2012; 2018) reexamines the vocabulary of time in later apocalypses (see Bundvad 2014).

Equally promising is the recent work on spatiality in apocalyptic literature. "Apocalyptic literature is preoccupied with space, especially transcendent and otherwise not immediately available space," writes Kelley Coblentz Bautch (2016, 276). To understand the use of space in apocalyptic literature as a cultural construct, scholars have turned to spatial theory for help. The work of Henri Lefebvre (1991) and Edward Soja (1996) has been especially influential. It distinguishes between three kinds of spaces: space as empirical reality, space as imagined and represented, and space as a lived reality (Lefebvre 1991; Soja 1996; Lied 2008). The work of Mikhail Bakhtin, and especially his category of the *chronotope*, or "time-space," shows how closely intertwined temporality and spatiality are and how fruitful these categories can be for our reading of apocalyptic literature (Newsom 2005, 449; Coblentz Bautch 2016, 279).

6.2. Apocalypses through the Centuries

Another emerging field of study is driven by the desire to extend the chronological borders of apocalyptic studies and no longer be confined by the chronological limits of the Second Temple period. This new interest to follow the apocalypses through the centuries takes several forms. One concerns the history of the manuscripts. Liv Ingeborg Lied studies the transmission of apocalyptic texts. Thinking of manuscripts as artifacts and reading them with the help of proper codicological methods, Lied (Lundhaug and Lied 2017, and her essay in this volume) insists not only on taking the lives of the manuscripts seriously, but to make the manuscripts the point of entry into the study of early Jewish texts. Manuscript history is part of the reception history of the apocalypses. It has long been recognized that Jewish apocalypses were transmitted, used, interpreted, and rewritten by Christian churches over the centuries. Much greater attention needs to be paid to the transmission history of the apocalypses in the diverse language traditions of the Eastern and Western churches. This important work will require significant collaboration between Second Temple scholars, philologists, codicologists, medievalists, and cultural historians. In addition to the texts themselves, apocalyptic tropes and traditions disseminate across cultural, linguistic, and religious boundaries and take on lives of their own. The work to trace these traditions is only beginning (DiTommaso 2005; Reed 2005; Stone 2011, 1–30; Reeves and Reed 2018).

Bibliography

Alexander, Philip. 2006. *Mystical Texts: Songs of the Sabbath Sacrifice and Related Manuscripts*. LSTS 61. London: T&T Clark.

Allison, Dale C. 1998. *Jesus of Nazareth: Millenarian Prophet*. Minneapolis: Fortress.

———. 1999. "The Eschatology of Jesus." Pages 267–302 in *The Origins of Apocalypticism in Judaism and Early Christianity*. Vol. 1 of *The Encyclopedia of Apocalypticism*. Edited by John J. Collins. New York: Continuum.

———. 2001. "Jesus Was an Apocalyptic Prophet." Pages 17–29 in *The Apocalyptic Jesus: A Debate*. Edited by Robert J. Miller. Santa Rosa, CA: Polebridge.

Bauckham, Richard. 2001. "Apocalypses." Pages 135–87 in *The Complexities of Second Temple Judaism*. Vol. 1 of *Justification and Variegated Nomism*. Edited by D. A. Carson, Peter T. O'Brien, and Mark A. Seifrid. WUNT 2/140. Tübingen: Mohr Siebeck; Grand Rapids: Baker Academic.

Baumgarten, Albert I. 1997. *The Flourishing of Jewish Sects in the Maccabean Era: An Interpretation*. JSJSup 55. Leiden: Brill.

Ben-Dov, Jonathan. 2016. "Apocalyptic Temporality: The Force of the Here and Now." *HeBAI* 5:289–303.

Blackwell, Ben C., John K. Goodrich, and Jason Maston, eds. 2016. *Paul and the Apocalyptic Imagination*. Minneapolis: Fortress.

Bockmuehl, Markus N. A. 1997. *Revelation and Mystery in Ancient Judaism and Pauline Christianity*. Grand Rapids: Eerdmans.

Boer, Martinus C. de. 1998. "Paul and Apocalyptic Eschatology." Pages 345–83 in *The Origins of Apocalypticism in Judaism and Early Christianity*. Vol. 1 of *The Encyclopedia of Apocalypticism*. Edited by John J. Collins. New York: Continuum.

Boustan, Ra'anan, and Patrick G. McCullough. 2014. "Apocalyptic Literature and the Study of Early Jewish Mysticism." Pages 85–103 in *The Oxford Handbook of Apocalyptic Literature*. Edited by John J. Collins. Oxford: Oxford University Press.

Bundvad, Mette. 2014. "Defending the Concept of Time in the Hebrew Bible." *SJOT* 28:280–97.

Carey, Greg, and L. Gregory Bloomquist, eds. 1999. *Vision and Persuasion: Rhetorical Dimensions of Apocalyptic Discourse*. St. Louis: Chalice.

Coblentz Bautch, Kelley. 2016. "Spatiality and Apocalyptic Literature." *HeBAI* 5:273–88.

Collins, John J. 1979. "Introduction: Towards the Morphology of a Genre." *Semeia* 14:1–20.

———. 1984. *The Apocalyptic Imagination: An Introduction to the Jewish Matrix of Christianity*. New York: Crossroad.

———. 1986. "Apocalyptic Literature." Pages 345–70 in *Early Judaism and Its Modern Interpreters*. Edited by Robert A. Kraft and George W. E. Nickelsburg. BMI 2. Philadelphia: Fortress; Atlanta: Scholars Press.

———. 1997. *Apocalypticism in the Dead Sea Scrolls*. London: Routledge.

———. 2014. "What Is Apocalyptic Literature?" Pages 1–16 in *The Oxford Handbook of Apocalyptic Literature*. Edited by John J. Collins. Oxford: Oxford University Press.

———. 2015. "Introduction: The Genre Apocalypse Reconsidered." Pages 1–20 in *Apocalypse, Prophecy, and Pseudepigraphy: On Jewish Apocalyptic Literature*. Grand Rapids: Eerdmans.

———. 2016. *The Apocalyptic Imagination: An Introduction to Jewish Apocalyptic Literature*. 3rd ed. Grand Rapids: Eerdmans.

———. 2018. "Is There Mysticism in the Dead Sea Scrolls?" Pages 61–80 in *Apocalypticism and Mysticism in Ancient Judaism and Early Christianity*. Edited by John J. Collins, Pieter G. R. Villiers, and Adela Yarbro Collins. Ekstasis 7. Berlin: de Gruyter.

Collins, John J., and J. H. Charlesworth, eds. 1991. *Mysteries and Revelations: Apocalyptic Studies since the Uppsala Colloquium*. JSPSup 9. Sheffield: JSOT Press.

Crawford, Sidnie White, and Cecilia Wassen, eds. 2018. *Apocalyptic Thinking in Early Judaism: Engaging with John Collins' The Apocalyptic Imagination*. JSJSup 182. Leiden: Brill.

Cross, Frank M. 1969. "New Directions in the Study of Apocalyptic." Pages 157–65 in *Apocalypticism*. Edited by Robert W. Funk. New York: Herder & Herder.

Daschke, Dereck. 2010. *City of Ruins: Mourning the Destruction of Jerusalem through Jewish Apocalypse*. BibInt 99. Leiden: Brill.

Davies, Philip R. 1989. "The Social World of Apocalyptic Writings." Pages 251–71 in *The World of Ancient Israel: Sociological, Anthropological and Political Perspectives*. Edited by Ronald E. Clements. Cambridge: Cambridge University Press.

———. 1993. "Reading Daniel Sociologically." Pages 345–61 in *The Book of Daniel in the Light of New Findings*. Edited by A. S. van der Woude. BETL 106. Leuven: Leuven University Press.

Davila, James R. 2010. "Exploring the Mystical Background of the Dead Sea Scrolls." Pages 433–54 in *The Oxford Handbook of the Dead Sea Scrolls*. Edited by Timothy H. Lim and John J. Collins. Oxford: Oxford University Press.

Dimant, Devorah. 2009. "Exegesis and Time in the Pesharim from Qumran." *REJ* 168:373–93.

———. 2013. "*4 Ezra* and *2 Baruch* in Light of Qumran Literature." Pages 31–61 in *Fourth Ezra and Second Baruch: Reconstruction after the*

Fall. Edited by Matthias Henze and Gabriele Boccaccini. JSJSup 164. Leiden: Brill.

DiTommaso, Lorenzo. 2005. *The Book of Daniel and the Apocryphal Daniel Literature*. SVTP 20. Leiden: Brill.

———. 2007a. "Apocalypses and Apocalypticism in Antiquity (Part I)." *CurBR* 5:235–86.

———. 2007b. "Apocalypses and Apocalypticism in Antiquity (Part II)." *CurBR* 5:367–432.

———. 2010. "Apocalypticism and the Aramaic Texts from Qumran." Pages 451–83 in *Aramaic Qumranica: Proceedings of the Conference on the Aramaic Texts from Qumran in Aix-en-Provence, 30 June–2 July 2008*. Edited by Katell Berthelot and Daniel Stöckel Ben Ezra. STDJ 94. Leiden: Brill.

Ehrman, Bart D. 1999. *Jesus: Apocalyptic Prophet of the New Millennium*. Oxford: Oxford University Press.

Esler, Philip E. 2014. "Social-Scientific Approaches to Apocalyptic Literature." Pages 123–44 in *The Oxford Handbook of Apocalyptic Literature*. Edited by John J. Collins. Oxford: Oxford University Press.

Frey, Jörg. 2006. "Die Apokalyptik als Herausforderung der neutestamentlichen Wissenschaft. Zum Problem: Jesus und die Apokalyptik." Pages 23–94 in *Apokalyptik als Herausforderung neutestamentlicher Theologie*. Edited by Michael Becker and Markus Öhler. WUNT 2/214. Tübingen: Mohr Siebeck.

———. 2007. "Die Bedeutung der Qumrantexte für das Verständnis der Apokalyptik im Frühjudentum und im Urchristentum." Pages 11–62 in *Apokalyptik und Qumran*. Edited by Jörg Frey and Michael Becker. Paderborn: Bonifatius.

———. 2016. "Jesus und die Apokalyptik." Pages 85–158 in *Von Jesus zur neutestamentlichen Theologie: Kleine Schriften II*. Edited by Benjamin Schliesser. WUNT 368. Tübingen: Mohr Siebeck.

García Martínez, Florentino. 1992. *Qumran and Apocalyptic: Studies On the Aramaic Texts from Qumran*. STDJ 9. Leiden: Brill.

———. 1998. "Apocalypticism in the Dead Sea Scrolls." Pages 162–92 in *The Origins of Apocalypticism in Judaism and Christianity*. Vol. 1 of *The Encyclopedia of Apocalypticism:* Edited by John J. Collins. New York: Continuum.

———. 2007. *Qumranica Minora I: Qumran Origins and Apocalypticism*. Edited by Eibert J. C. Tigchelaar. STDJ 63. Leiden: Brill.

Goff, Matthew. 2014. "Wisdom and Apocalypticism." Pages 52–68 in *The Oxford Handbook of Apocalyptic Literature*. Edited by John J. Collins. Oxford: Oxford University Press.

Grabbe, Lester L. 1989. "The Social Setting of Early Jewish Apocalypticism." *JSP* 4:27–47.

———. 2003. "Prophetic and Apocalyptic: Time for New Definitions–And New Thinking." Pages 107–33 in *Knowing the End from the Beginning: The Prophetic, the Apocalyptic and Their Relationships*. Edited by Lester L. Grabbe and Robert D. Haak. JSPSup 46. London: T&T Clark.

Gruenwald, Ithamar. 2014. *Apocalyptic and Merkavah Mysticism*. 2nd ed. AJEC 90. Leiden: Brill.

Hanson, Paul D. 1975. *The Dawn of Apocalyptic: The Historical and Sociological Roots of Jewish Apocalyptic Eschatology*. Philadelphia: Fortress.

———. 1976. "Apocalypticism." Pages 28–34 in *The Interpreter's Dictionary of the Bible: Supplemental Volume*. Edited by Keith R. Crim. Nashville: Abingdon.

Hellholm, David, ed. 1983. *Apocalypticism in the Mediterranean World and the Near East: Proceedings of the International Colloquium on Apocalypticism. Uppsala, August 12–17, 1979*. Tübingen: Mohr Siebeck.

———. 1986. "The Problem of Apocalyptic Genre and the Apocalypse of John." *Semeia* 36:13–64.

Henze, Matthias. 2011. *Jewish Apocalypticism in Late First Century Israel: Reading Second Baruch in Context*. TSAJ 142. Tübingen: Mohr Siebeck.

———. 2012. "*4 Ezra* and *2 Baruch*: Literary Composition and Oral Performance in First-Century Apocalyptic Literature." *JBL* 131:181–200.

———. 2018. "Dimensions of Time in Jewish Apocalyptic Thought: The Case of 4 Ezra." Pages 13–34 in *Figures of Ezra*. Edited by Jan N. Bremmer, Veronika Hirschberger, and Tobias Nicklas. Studies in Early Christian Apocrypha 13. Leuven: Peeters.

Himmelfarb, Martha. 1993. *Ascent to Heaven in Jewish and Christian Apocalypses*. New York: Oxford University Press.

Horsley, Richard A. 2010. *Revolt of the Scribes: Resistance and Apocalyptic Origins*. Minneapolis: Fortress.

Horsley, Richard A., and Patrick Tiller. 2012. *After Apocalyptic and Wisdom: Rethinking Texts in Context*. Eugene, OR: Cascade.

Kloppenborg, John S., and John W. Marshall, eds. 2005. *Apocalypticism, Anti-Semitism and the Historical Jesus*. JSNTSup 275. London: T&T Clark.

Knibb, Michael A. 2009. "Apocalyptic and Wisdom in 4 Ezra." Pages 271–88 in *Essays on the Book of Enoch and Other Early Jewish Texts and Traditions*. SVTP 22. Leiden: Brill.

Koch, Klaus. 1970. *Ratlos vor der Apokalyptik: Eine Streitschrift über ein vernachlässigtes Gebiet der Bibelwissenschaft und die schädlichen Auswirkungen auf Theologie und Philosophie*. Gütersloh: Gütersloher Verlagshaus Mohn.

———. 1982. "Einleitung." Pages 1–31 in *Apokalyptik*. Edited by Klaus Koch and Johann Michael Schmidt. Wege der Forschung 365. Darmstadt: Wissenschaftliche Buchgesellschaft.

Kosmin, Paul J. 2018. *Time and Its Adversaries in the Seleucid Empire*. Cambridge: Harvard University Press.

Kraft, Robert A., and George W. E. Nickelsburg, eds. 1986. *Early Judaism and Its Modern Interpreters*. BMI 2. Philadelphia: Fortress; Atlanta: Scholars Press.

Lefebvre, Henri. 1991. *The Production of Space*. Oxford: Blackwell.

Lied, Liv Ingeborg. 2008. *The Other Lands of Israel: Imaginations of the Land in 2 Baruch*. JSJSup 129. Leiden: Brill.

Lundhaug, Hugo, and Liv Ingeborg Lied. 2017. "Studying Snapshots: On Manuscript Culture, Textual Fluidity, and New Philology." Pages 1–19 in *Snapshots of Evolving Traditions: Jewish and Christian Manuscript Culture, Textual Fluidity, and New Philology*. Edited by Liv Ingeborg Lied and Hugo Lundhaug. TUGAL 175. Berlin: de Gruyter.

Miller, Robert J., ed. 2001. *The Apocalyptic Jesus: A Debate*. Santa Rosa, CA: Polebridge.

Murphy, Frederick J. 2012. *Apocalypticism in the Bible and Its World: A Comprehensive Introduction*. Grand Rapids: Baker Academic.

Najman, Hindy. 2014. *Losing the Temple and Recovering the Future: An Analysis of 4 Ezra*. New York: Cambridge University Press.

Najman, Hindy, and Mladen Popović, eds. 2010. *Rethinking Genre: Essays in Honor of John J. Collins*. DSD 17.

Newsom, Carol A. 2005. "Spying Out the Land: A Report from Genology." Pages 437–50 in *Seeking Out the Wisdom of the Ancients: Essays Offered to Honor Michael V. Fox on the Occasion of His Sixty-Fifth Birthday*. Edited by Ronald L. Troxel, Kelvin G. Friebel, and Dennis R. Magary. Winona Lake, IN: Eisenbrauns.

———. 2014. "The Rhetoric of Jewish Apocalyptic Literature." Pages 201–17 in *The Oxford Handbook of Apocalyptic Literature*. Edited by John J. Collins. Oxford: Oxford University Press.

Nickelsburg, George W. E. 2001. *1 Enoch 1: A Commentary on the Book of 1 Enoch, Chapters 1–36; 81–108*. Hermeneia. Minneapolis: Fortress.
———. 2005. "Wisdom and Apocalypticism in Early Judaism: Some Points for Discussion." Pages 17–37 in *Conflicted Boundaries in Wisdom and Apocalypticism*. Edited by Benjamin G. Wright III and Lawrence M. Wills. SymS 35. Atlanta: Society of Biblical Literature.
Paget, James Carleton. 2017. "Das 'Gottesreich' als eschatologisches Konzept: Johannes Weiß und Albert Schweitzer." Pages 55–66 in *Jesus Handbuch*. Edited by Jens Schröter and Christine Jacobi. Tübingen: Mohr Siebeck.
Portier-Young, Anathea. 2011. *Apocalypse against Empire: Theologies of Resistance in Early Judaism*. Grand Rapids: Eerdmans.
———. 2014. "Jewish Apocalyptic Literature as Resistance Literature." Pages 145–62 in *The Oxford Handbook of Apocalyptic Literature*. Edited by John J. Collins. Oxford: Oxford University Press.
Reed, Annette Yoshiko. 2005. *Fallen Angels and the History of Judaism and Christianity: The Reception of Enochic Literature*. Cambridge: Cambridge University Press.
———. 2013. "Rethinking (Jewish-)Christian Evidence for Jewish Mysticism." Pages 349–77 in *Hekhalot Literature in Context: Between Byzantium and Babylonia*. Edited by Ra'anan Boustan, Martha Himmelfarb, and Peter Schäfer. TSAJ 153. Tübingen: Mohr Siebeck.
Reeves, John C., and Annette Y. Reed. 2018. *Enoch from Antiquity to the Middle Ages, Volume I: Sources from Judaism, Christianity, and Islam*. Oxford: Oxford University Press.
Rowland, Christopher. 1982. *The Open Heaven: A Study of Apocalyptic in Judaism and Early Christianity*. London: SPCK.
Schäfer, Peter. 2009. *The Origins of Jewish Mysticism*. Tübingen: Mohr Siebeck.
Scholem, Gershom. 1995. *Major Trends in Jewish Mysticism*. New York: Schocken Books.
Soja, Edward. 1996. *Thirdspace: Journeys to Los Angeles and Other Real-and-Imagined Places*. Malden, MA: Blackwell.
Stegemann, Hartmut. 1983. "Die Bedeutung der Qumranfunde für die Erforschung der Apokalyptik." Pages 495–530 in *Apocalypticism in the Mediterranean World and the Near East: Proceedings of the International Colloquium on Apocalypticism. Uppsala, August 12–17, 1979*. Edited by David Hellholm. Tübingen: Mohr Siebeck.

Stone, Michael E. 1976. "Lists of Revealed Things in the Apocalyptic Literature." Pages 414–52 in *Magnalia Dei: The Mighty Acts of God: Essays on the Bible and Archaeology in Memory of G. Ernest Wright*. Edited by Frank Moore Cross, Werner E. Lemke, and Patrick D. Miller. Garden City, NY: Doubleday. Repr. as pages 378–418 in Michael E. Stone, *Selected Studies in the Pseudepigrapha with Special Reference to the Armenian Tradition*. SVTP 9. Leiden: Brill, 1991.

———. 1984. "Apocalyptic Writings." Pages 383–441 in *Jewish Writings of the Second Temple Period: Apocrypha, Pseudepigrapha, Qumran Sectarian Writings, Philo, Josephus*. Edited by Michael E. Stone. CRINT 2.2. Assen: Van Gorcum; Philadelphia: Fortress.

———. 2011. *Ancient Judaism: New Visions and Views*. Grand Rapids: Eerdmans.

———. 2018. *Secret Groups in Ancient Judaism*. Oxford: Oxford University Press.

Stuckenbruck, Loren T. 2013. "Overlapping Ages at Qumran and 'Apocalyptic' in Pauline Theology." Pages 309–26 in *The Dead Sea Scrolls and Pauline Literature*. Edited by Jean-Sébastien Rey. STDJ 102. Leiden: Brill.

———. 2014. "Posturing 'Apocalyptic' in Pauline Theology: How Much Contrast with Jewish Tradition?" Pages 240–56 in *The Myth of Rebellious Angels: Studies in Second Temple Judaism and New Testament Texts*. WUNT 335. Tübingen: Mohr Siebeck.

Tigchelaar, Eibert J. C. 1996. *Prophets of Old and the Day of the End: Zechariah, the Book of Watchers and Apocalyptic*. OTS 35. Leiden: Brill.

Tilly, Michael. 2012. *Apokalyptik*. Tübingen: Francke.

VanderKam, James C. 2018. *Jubilees: A Commentary in Two Volumes*. Hermeneia. Minneapolis: Fortress.

Vielhauer, Philipp. 1964. "Einleitung." Pages 407–27 in *Neutestamentliche Apokryphen II: Apostolisches, Apokalypsen und Verwandtes*. Edited by Edgar Hennecke and Wilhelm Schneemelcher. 3rd ed. Tübingen: Mohr Siebeck.

———. 1975. *Geschichte der urchristlichen Literatur: Einleitung in das Neue Testament, die Apokryphen und die apostolischen Väter*. Berlin: de Gruyter.

Villiers, Pieter G. R. de. 2018. "Apocalypses and Mystical Texts: Investigating Prolegomena and the State of Affairs." Pages 7–59 in *Apocalypticism and Mysticism in Ancient Judaism and Early Christianity*. Edited

by John J. Collins, Pieter G. R. de Villiers, and Adela Yarbro Collins. Ekstasis 7. Berlin: de Gruyter.
Wright, Benjamin G., III, and Lawrence M. Wills, eds. 2005. *Conflicted Boundaries in Wisdom and Apocalypticism*. SymS 35. Atlanta: Society of Biblical Literature.
Yarbro Collins, Adela. 1986. "Introduction: Early Christian Apocalypticism." *Semeia* 36:1-11.
———. 2011. "Apocalypse Now: The State of Apocalyptic Studies Near the End of the First Decade of the Twenty-First Century." *HTR* 104: 447-57.
———. 2014. "Apocalypticism and Christian Origins." Pages 326-39 in *The Oxford Handbook of Apocalyptic Literature*. Edited by John J. Collins. Oxford: Oxford University Press.

Appendix: Apocalypses in Early Judaism

1. Apocalypses according to John J. Collins (2016, 8)

Otherworldly Journeys: Apocalypse of Zephaniah, Testament of Abraham, 3 Baruch, Testament of Levi 2-5, 2 Enoch, Book of the Watchers (1 En. 1-36), Similitudes of Enoch (1 En. 37-71), Astronomical Book (1 En. 72-82), Apocalypse of Abraham

Historical Apocalypses: 2 Baruch, 4 Ezra, Jubilees, Apocalypse of Weeks (1 En. 93:1-10; 91:11-17), Animal Apocalypse (1 En. 85-90), Daniel

2. Apocalypses according to Christopher Rowland (1985, 15)

Daniel, Revelation, 1 Enoch, 2 Enoch, Jubilees, 2 Baruch, 3 Baruch, 4 Ezra, Apocalypse of Abraham, Testament of Abraham, Testaments of Levi and Naphtali (from the Testaments of the Twelve Patriarchs), Ascension of Isaiah, Shepherd of Hermas, 3 Enoch

18
WISDOM LITERATURE

BENJAMIN G. WRIGHT III

The study of wisdom literature in early Judaism has come a long way since the essay in *Early Judaism and Its Modern Interpreters* in 1986 (Mack and Murphy 1986). To begin with, Burton Mack's and Roland Murphy's structure of the piece—an introduction of two pages followed by sections on each book/writer included in the category—could not possibly work in 2020. In the early 1980s, very few of the wisdom texts discovered at Qumran had been published, and those that were known received no attention in the essay in *Early Judaism and Its Modern Interpreters* (Kraft and Nickelsburg 1986). Additionally, the article has little theoretical/methodological orientation, and almost of necessity what theoretical comments Mack and Murphy include are grounded in, and to a degree contrasted with, the study of the wisdom texts in the Hebrew Bible.

Second, Mack's and Murphy's assessment of what constitutes wisdom literature as a category and the texts comprised within it highlights the difficulty of deciding what, in fact, wisdom literature was/is, and their remarks about the category wisdom cast a broad net, leading to some idiosyncratic choices:

> These several writings have little in common and *do not compose a corpus of literature* either as a traditional collection or manifestations of a single or coherent tradition of Jewish thought. They are taken together here as documents that, in one way or another, evidence early Jewish thought in the Hellenistic and early Roman eras. In this encounter, reflections upon Judaism's own traditions of wisdom occurred, and various attempts were made to conceptualize wisdom both as a mode and as an object of perception or thought. Such conceptualizations could be related to Hellenistic philosophical categories and used to interpret other aspects of the

Jewish religious tradition—its Torah, its cultus, its history, and its ethic. (Mack and Murphy 1986, 371, emphasis added)

Mack and Murphy go on to argue that contemporary Hebrew Bible scholarship had begun to problematize the category of wisdom, and so any presumed connections of Second Temple texts with the three traditional wisdom books of the Old Testament made little sense, especially, since these three—Proverbs, Job, and Qohelet—are so disparate from one another. Mack and Murphy justified using the category wisdom, however, since they understood it as an

> "intellectual tradition" ... within which individual sages were enabled to collect and transmit a proverbial wisdom, reflect upon its assumptions about human experience of the nature and adequacy of these assumptions. These assumptions concerned the trustworthiness of an ethico-religious ordering of the world and human affairs. The questions had to do with the limitations of human knowledge to grasp fully this ordering, especially when confronted by human suffering or experience which required theodicy. (Mack and Murphy 1986, 371–72)

They contended that the works they treated still would find continuity with the Hebrew Bible wisdom books in the use of speech forms also found there. At the same time, they recognized the differences, particularly the use of new literary forms. Yet, although they rejected wisdom literature as defined by a corpus of texts, their replacement of it with an intellectual tradition did not resolve the problem. Very few scholars, even those who work with the broadest definition of wisdom literature, would grant that texts like the Letter of Aristeas or Aristobulus qualify as wisdom literature; for example, one would be hard pressed to see the author of Aristeas as a sage who collected proverbial wisdom and used it to "reflect upon its assumptions about human experience of the nature and adequacy of those assumptions," despite the fact that the symposium section resembles some types of wisdom. In fact, Mack and Murphy devote only two full paragraphs to Aristeas, never justifying its inclusion in the chapter.

In the years since 1986, scholarly interest in early Jewish wisdom literature has seen a rapid rise, and just about every one of the points that Mack and Murphy appealed to in their short introduction has been contested in the scholarship on wisdom literature. Part of the reason for this increased interest and contestation stems from the publication of a corpus of texts that have been labeled wisdom discovered among the Dead Sea

Scrolls. Aside from 4Q184 (the so-called Wiles of the Wicked Woman) and 4Q185 (4QSapiential Work), both published by John Allegro in 1968 in *Qumran Cave 4.I (4Q158–4Q186)* (DJD 5), most of these texts had not yet been published in 1986 and neither Mack and Murphy's article nor Jerome Murphy O'Connor's *Early Judaism and Its Modern Interpreters* chapter, "The Judean Desert," which focused mainly on the history of the discovery, the major sectarian texts from cave 1 and cave 4, and CD, mention wisdom texts from Qumran at all. Indeed 4QInstruction, perhaps the most well-known Qumran wisdom text, published in (DJD 34), did not appear until 1999. (1Q26, a copy of Instruction consisting of four small fragments, had been published in Barthélemy and Milik 1955 [DJD 1], titled simply "un apocryphe.") Yet in the years that followed *Early Judaism and Its Modern Interpreters* (Kraft and Nickelsburg 1986), as with so many other types of early Jewish literature, the scrolls provided a jump-start to scholarly research in the wisdom literature of early Judaism. (For detailed discussion of the history of scholarship on the Qumran wisdom texts, see Goff 2009, 2018.)

Given the current state of the study of early Jewish wisdom literature, then, I will focus on the significant critical issues and approaches that have emerged over the past thirty to thirty-five years, such as wisdom as a literary genre, wisdom in relation to apocalyptic, wisdom and prophecy/revelation, and the social location of the producers of wisdom. In an appendix, I list those texts most often included in the category.

1. Biblical and Nonbiblical Wisdom

The ongoing and persistent distinction in much contemporary scholarship between biblical and nonbiblical texts has constituted a major obstacle to the study of early Jewish wisdom literature, and it reflects the prioritization of Bible as a normative category for analysis of ancient wisdom. For example, studies of Israelite and Jewish wisdom literature often focus on the three biblical texts—Proverbs, Qoheleth, and Job—perhaps with the inclusion of Ben Sira and Wisdom of Solomon. Indeed, Mack and Murphy (1986, 371) explicitly note that their designation of early Jewish wisdom "assumes some continuity with the wisdom literature of the Hebrew Bible." In general, if other texts come into play at all in these studies, they do not receive the same degree of analysis. Either they are compared to the biblical books in order to highlight how problematic the category is, or they are relegated almost to afterthoughts. So, for example, Stuart Weeks's (2010) short volume, *An Introduction to the Study of Wisdom Literature*, contains detailed chapters on Proverbs (twenty-four pages), Job (twenty-two pages), and Ecclesiastes (thirteen pages), and a chapter entitled "Other Jewish Wisdom Literature" (twenty-one pages) that covers wisdom psalms, the Wisdom of Ben Sira, Bar 3:9–4:4, the Wisdom of Solomon, and wisdom at Qumran. In a volume edited by Mark Sneed (2015c), *Was There a Wisdom Tradition?*, only one essay (Schellenberg 2015) devotes significant attention to Ben Sira or Wisdom of Solomon, and the Qumran texts are mentioned on two pages in the entire volume. If we are to talk at all meaningfully about wisdom literature in ancient Judaism, two desiderata are (1) widespread recognition that Jewish wisdom texts destabilize the traditional category of wisdom as it has been framed and defined by Proverbs, Qoheleth, and Job, and (2) a more thoroughgoing integration of the other early Jewish wisdom texts with those that are part of the Jewish and Christian canons. As of 2020, for instance, there does not yet exist an introduction to wisdom literature that treats the biblical wisdom texts, Ben Sira, Wisdom of Solomon, the Qumran wisdom texts, and Pseudo-Phocylides on an equal footing. Leo Perdue (2008) and Sneed (2015b) come closest, but even in these introductions Proverbs, Job, and Ecclesiastes take pride of place. Sneed does not mention Pseudo-Phocylides, for instance, and Perdue barely does more than mention it. Some scholars have begun to engage in such integrative study. As one example, Samuel Adams (2008), writing on the act-consequence nexus so often found in wisdom texts, examines Egyptian instructions, Proverbs, Ecclesiastes, Ben Sira, and 4QInstruction as equal participants in this discourse. A volume in the Oxford Handbook series devoted to wisdom literature that will give more equal treatment of all of these texts is scheduled to appear in 2020 (Kynes, forthcoming).

2. Genre

So how should an interpreter distinguish wisdom literature from other types of texts, especially in light of the publication of texts from Qumran (see Goff 2009)? James Crenshaw's (1998) definition of wisdom as a genre, based on the traditional wisdom books of the Hebrew Bible, in which he argues for a marriage of form and content has been the usual starting point for recent discussions:

> The conclusion reached from this multifaceted approach to defining wisdom is that formally, wisdom consists of proverbial sentence or

instruction, self-evident intuitions about mastering life for human betterment, gropings after life's secrets with regard to innocent suffering, grappling with finitude, and quest for truth concealed in the created order and manifested in a feminine persona. When a marriage between form and content exists, there is wisdom literature. (Crenshaw 1998, 11)

Numerous critiques have demonstrated the deficiencies in Crenshaw's definition, focusing particularly on its fusing of form and content and its relationship to form-critical assumptions (Collins 1997b, 278–80 [responding to the first edition]; Goff 2010, 295–96; Weeks 2010, 142–43; Sneed 2011). Nevertheless, scholars have not reached any agreement about what constitutes wisdom as a category, and some have even argued for dispensing with the category altogether. Discussions about the viability of the category have, again, generally taken place within broader theoretical discussions on genre genealogy and genre theory within biblical studies and the study of early Judaism. These approaches tend to abandon older idea of genres as consisting of lists of essential taxonomic features. To cite two examples, the volume edited by Roland Boer (2007) contains articles devoted primarily to Mikhail Bakhtin's theoretical approach to genre, as well as some contributions that apply Bakhtin's perspectives to specific biblical genres (e.g., apocalyptic) and books (e.g., Daniel, Lamentations, Matthew, John). *Dead Sea Discoveries* 17, edited by Hindy Najman and Mladen Popović (2010), specifically addresses genre theory and early Jewish texts such as the Hodayot, pesharim, the Epistle of Enoch, 4QInstruction, and the so-called rewritten-Bible texts in addition to wisdom literature.

Although critical of proposals for the generic category of wisdom, John Collins (1997a, 1997b) does not appear to want to jettison the idea altogether. He expresses reservations about calling wisdom literature a genre per se, calling it a "macro-genre, in the sense that it holds together a cluster of related forms" (1997b, 266) or "by certain family resemblances rather than by a constant essence" (1997a, 1). The idea of family resemblance has some benefits because this recognizes the inherent looseness of the category without attributing to it essential characteristics or essences (Sneed 2015a, 59; Dell 2015; Cheung 2015). Another aspect of the difficulty of defining wisdom as a genre is that, as Collins (2010) points out, genres mark literary conventions, and often arguments for wisdom as a genre range beyond the literary.

Other scholars appeal to prototype theory, which draws on models of how people create cognitive categories. Benjamin Wright has proposed four central properties that function together as an idealized cognitive model of wisdom literature (Newsom 2007, 2010 on theory; Wright 2010 on wisdom and apocalyptic; Williamson 2010 on the pesharim). One of the benefits of prototype theory is that rather than a list of features that includes or excludes particular texts, categories (and thus, genres) radiate from central and typical exemplars out to other examples that sit more on the periphery. Categories consist of a constellation of properties that are related in what Michael Sinding has called an "idealized cognitive model" (see Newsom 2007, 25; Wright 2010, 265–66). So, for example, Wright (2010, 270) has proposed four central properties that make up an idealized cognitive model of wisdom: "(1) instruction or pedagogical form and intent that articulates (2) a concern for pursuing or acquiring wisdom (or its equivalent) through study and learning, which exhibits (3) an engagement with earlier sapiential tradition (perhaps in conjunction with other authoritative sources), resulting in (4) an interest in or concern for practical ethics or behavior."

Some scholars who have serious doubts about wisdom as a genre appeal to higher-level markers, such as worldview, to preserve a corpus of texts that can be called wisdom without having to argue that wisdom constitutes a literary genre. Concentrating on the core five wisdom texts (Proverbs, Qoheleth, Job, Ben Sira, and Wisdom of Solomon), Annette Schellenberg (2015, 116) argues that they share a series of concerns that might be called a worldview, although she notes that "this word might be too grandiose." Other scholars have maintained that wisdom texts engage in a sapiential discourse that holds them together, although this term is used in very different ways. Collins (2010) sees discourse as a literary form that wisdom texts take, as opposed to narrative, for example, and he proposes as a starting point that "wisdom literature is discursive, non-narrative, literature that takes the form either of direct address, or of ostensibly factual assertion" (400–401).

Matthew Goff (2010, 299), who wants to keep wisdom as a literary category, includes participation in sapiential discourse as one of two primary characteristics of wisdom, which involves both appropriation of older traditions and their reconfiguration: "Such compositions [i.e., wisdom texts] were written in a way that is characterized ... by engagement with the traditional wisdom of Israel as exemplified by Proverbs." He also sets aside the descriptors "pedagogical" or "instructional" in favor of "noetic," by which he means that "wisdom texts foster in their intended addressees a desire to search for understanding of the world" (298). Stuart

Weeks (2010, 143) calls wisdom a "mode of discourse" that "existed within a complicated and interconnected literary culture, where other texts could certainly share aspects of that discourse whilst retaining a strong attachment to other types and traditions of writing," and Sneed's (2011, 71) assessment that wisdom is a "mode of literature that is only loosely homogenous" looks to be a variant on the idea of discourse as the way to delimit wisdom. Whereas most of these discussions have focused on texts more traditionally regarded as wisdom, Hindy Najman (2017) has broadened the conversation by expressly moving beyond genre discussions to identifying a wider concept of a "discourse of wisdom." Relying on Walter Benjamin, she develops the idea of a "semantic constellation" that would encompass a group of terms that one could expect might appear in a text. The relationships among these terms might be flexible, but "the *iterability* of the network suggests that we are dealing with a specific worldview or family of worldviews" (2017, 464 [emphasis original]). Conceptualized in this way, texts as seemingly disparate as 4QInstruction and the treatises of Philo participate in this wisdom discourse.

Will Kynes has taken the most pessimistic position on the hope for defining a wisdom genre. In Kynes's (2016, 2018a, 2018b) view, the category wisdom is an invention of nineteenth century biblical scholarship that has outlived any usefulness it might have had, and its vague definition has allowed scholars to inject almost any meaning into it, ultimately finding wisdom everywhere—what he terms "pansapientialism." Kynes (2018a, 149–50) argues for pursuing what he calls an "intertextual network approach," which he argues provides a better representation of "the wholeness of life in antiquity," on the one hand, and "transcends the limiting subjectivity of a solitary viewpoint," on the other. Yet the intertextual network in which Kynes locates wisdom is explicitly canonical, and it remains to be seen how much texts such as Ben Sira, Pseudo-Phocylides, or Instruction complicate his arguments.

Carol Newsom (2010) has pointed out that one can take several different approaches to genre, and the approach that one adopts depends very much on what questions one wants to ask. Thus, as she writes, "In any particular instance of genre study, several approaches may be in play in a complementary fashion" (247). As she demonstrates in her usual incisive manner, for the Hodayot one might approach genre through intertextual comparison, classification, social function and cultural know-how, and/or modes of perception (Newsom 2010). In the current state of the discussion, it does not appear as if the question of wisdom as a genre will be resolved in the terms that it has been set out thus far, and the conversation, which has been robust and productive, will likely continue.

3. The Qumran Wisdom Texts

Qumran wisdom texts have still not been fully integrated into broader discussions on wisdom, which remain dominated by biblical wisdom. Only in the mid-1990s did the wisdom texts from Qumran begin to find their way into scholarly discussions—even before the official publication of the most extensive fragments of Instruction, the largest of the Qumran wisdom texts, which came in 1999 (e.g., Van der Woude 1995; Caquot 1996; Harrington 1994, 1996; for a partial reedition of the text, see Tigchelaar 2001). Due to their fragmentary conditions, scholars of the scrolls often disagreed on exactly which texts ought to be considered sapiential and what characteristics of wisdom these texts exhibited. (See below on the contributions made by the increased study of these texts and the appendix for a list of the most frequently identified Qumran wisdom texts.) Subsequent studies of the corpus of Qumran wisdom texts have made them more widely available (Lange 2002; Strugnell 2002; Goff 2007; Kampen 2011). Still, to the extent that these texts in many respects look quite different from the biblical wisdom books, they have had an increasingly significant impact that has begun to reshape discussions of early Jewish wisdom.

4. The Contribution of Early Jewish Wisdom Texts

Not only have the wisdom texts of early Judaism had an increasing impact on debates about whether wisdom ought to be considered a genre, they have also contributed to our understanding of early Jewish literature more broadly, in particular their relationship with apocalyptic and torah.

4.1. Wisdom and Apocalyptic

In 1960, Gerhard von Rad in his *Theologie des Alten Testaments* proposed that apocalyptic emerged out of wisdom. As Collins noted in 1993, von Rad's thesis had not gained general acceptance (Collins 2001, 369 n. 2; Goff 2014, 57–60). At the same time that he pointed to scholars who had engaged the relationship between wisdom and apocalyptic, including himself, Collins (2001, 370) wrote, "Attempts to generalize the relationship between the two categories, however, encounter severe problems, and should, arguably, be abandoned." Yet, Collins did not abandon looking at wisdom and apocalyptic texts together. In fact, his comment above comes in an introduction to an article in which he examined the origins of evil in Ben Sira and several Dead Sea texts. He also discusses the influence of apocalyptic on the Wisdom of Solomon (Collins 1997a, 183–85; see also Burkes 2002). The title of von Rad's book points to one aspect of the difficulty that Collins highlights, though. Much of the early comparisons of wisdom and apocalyptic focused on theology or ideology. So, for example, apocalyptic literature was seen to have much more in common with mantic wisdom than with more traditional wisdom such as that found in Proverbs, particularly with respect to eschatology, which played a large role in the comparisons. (On mantic wisdom generally, see Bohak 2016.) Of course, the Qumran wisdom texts that did engage in eschatological/apocalyptic thinking that much more closely approached apocalyptic texts had not yet been studied very thoroughly and for the most part were not taken into account.

At about the same time, a consultation (later to become a group) began at the Society of Biblical Literature Annual Meetings, on wisdom and apocalypticism in early Judaism and early Christianity. In the first session in 1994, George Nickelsburg (2005, 19) set out an agenda for the group, which included an emphasis on thinking about "the social and cultural realities that gave rise to and are reflected in the relevant primary sources: institutions, offices, roles, and functions that resulted in Jewish sapiential and apocalyptic literature and made use of it." For a volume that collected representative papers from the group in its first decade (Wright and Wills 2005), Sarah Tanzer (2005) reflected on what had happened in the interim to Nickelsburg's initial questions and points for discussion. She concluded by noting the continuing problems of definition and compartmentalization:

> Certainly many of the same stumbling blocks remain in trying to understand the interrelationship of wisdom and apocalypticism in early Judaism, and although we have been wary of dichotomizing tendencies in the past, much current research has led to different (but still somewhat dichotomizing) ways of defining the divide between the various types of wisdom and the differing perspectives of the scribes who produced it. (49)

As stumbling blocks, Tanzer points particularly to the lack of an agreed upon definition of wisdom as a genre, whether or not one can speak of a wisdom worldview, a lack of distinctiveness of wisdom as a category, since wisdom is found in different genres, the tendency to dichotomize between wisdom and apocalyptic, and the difficulty of determining the social location of wisdom and apocalyptic. Although scholars have paid significant attention to these issues in the years since Tanzer's response to Nickelsburg, the Wisdom and Apocalypticism Group of the Society of Biblical Literature continues working, and many of these same questions and issues remain on the table.

In the early 2000s, study of the Qumran wisdom texts had begun in earnest. One text in particular, Instruction (earlier called Sapiential Work A), seemed to upset all the categories, since it contained traditional, practical advice about money, parents, and women, for example. Yet it had a decidedly apocalyptic orientation with the addressee being admonished to study the *raz nihyeh*, "the mystery that is to be." This text, the largest wisdom text from Qumran, became one of the centerpieces of scholarly debate on the relationship between wisdom and apocalyptic (see Goff 2009, 386–88; 2013 and the literature cited there). Of particular interest was the mysterious *raz nihyeh*, the mystery that is to be/come, on which the addressee of Instruction is admonished to study, gaze upon, and meditate upon. Its contents remain a topic of discussion, although most scholars agree that it is a comprehensive repository of knowledge that encompasses the mysteries of creation and God's role in history along with knowledge of how to live a life pleasing to God (Kampen 2011, 46–50). Goff (2013, 15) points out that in 4Q417 1 I, 8–9, the *raz nihyeh*, functions in creation in a way analogous to Wisdom in Prov 8:22–31. Due to its melding of traditional wisdom with a clearly apocalyptic orientation, Instruction has played a significant role in reshaping the contours of the study of wisdom in the Second Temple period.

In light of the ways that some Qumran wisdom texts exhibited eschatological and apocalyptic characteristics together with the eschatological character of the Qumran Yahad, the Fifty-First Colloquium Biblicum Lovaniense in 2002 devoted its sessions to "Wisdom and Apocalypticism, both in the Dead Sea Scrolls and in the Biblical Tradition" (García Martínez 2003, xi). The articles in the resulting volume, while focusing mostly on Qumran, highlight the same issues as earlier discussions of wisdom and apocalyptic: the dilemma of definitions; how to relate wisdom and apocalyptic; social location; and theology. The volumes edited by Wright and Wills (2005) and García Martínez (2003) offer a good sense of where the scholarly debates stood in first decade of the twenty-first century.

4.2. Wisdom and Torah

The relationship of wisdom and law in the Hebrew Bible has received significant examination, which particularly focused on passages like Deut 4:5–7, where Israel is called a "wise and discerning people" because the people possess an entire law of just "statutes and ordinances." Joseph Blenkinsopp (1995, 151) argued that "in its earliest stages, Israelite law could be seen as a specialization of clan wisdom." However, as Jack T. Sanders (2001, 122) notes, "Since the Jewish people of the early second-temple period possessed a variety of religious traditions, it was not a foregone conclusion that the Mosaic Torah would become a dominant force." In order to explain how Mosaic torah achieved its dominance in Judaism, Sanders (2001, 130) appealed to Peter Berger's and Thomas Luckmann's concept that Berger would call the "sacred canopy," a symbolic universe that authorizes an "institutional world," which becomes experienced as "objective reality." Sanders, who treats Ben Sira, the Qumran wisdom texts, and Wisdom of Solomon, sketched a picture in which two sacred canopies, wisdom and law, competed with one another, and their collision resulted in law being absorbed into the sapiential sacred canopy. According to Sanders, the increasing authority of the Mosaic torah, and its rising dominance, presented the wisdom tradition with a life or death choice: "The wisdom tradition, faced—as are all living entities eventually—with the choice of accommodating or dying, accommodated. The older sacred canopy absorbed the newer, but it did not become identical with it. The wisdom school absorbed the Mosaic Torah in such a way as to maintain what our authors took to be the essential elements of the sapiential tradition" (2001, 135). Thus, although Sanders does not put it this way, by taking Mosaic torah into the older wisdom tradition, ironically the sages became enablers of the growing dominance of torah.

While not all scholars would agree with Sanders's reconstruction of a life-and-death struggle between wisdom and torah/law, it clearly is the case that early Jewish wisdom texts accepted torah as one source from which wisdom might be derived. Perhaps the most dramatic development that brings wisdom and torah into relationship is the idea that divine wisdom can be found in the torah. The parade example is Ben Sira 24:23—"All these things [i.e., what has gone before about wisdom] are the book of the covenant of the Most High God, a law that Moses commanded us, an inheritance for the assemblies of Jacob"—although the idea also emerges in Bar 3:9–4:4, 4Q185, and 4Q525. This brief statement together with Sir

17:1–14 has prompted differing assessments about how wisdom and torah relate both in Ben Sira and in early Judaism more generally and whether wisdom is given to Israel or to all humanity. (For a general discussion of the various positions on Ben Sira, see Wright 2013, 157–65.) Is torah subsumed under wisdom (e.g., Collins 1997a, 55; Sanders 2001)? Or is it the other way around (e.g., Sheppard 1980; Kister 2004, 16)? Is Mosaic torah only a partial revelation of a more universal wisdom (Marböck 2006)? Or has it always been intended for all humanity (Reiterer 2004)? Are there two apportionments of wisdom, one for Israel and one for all people (Goering 2009)? However these relationships are ultimately assessed, in chapter 24 Ben Sira argues that the Wisdom who was present at creation and whom God sent to dwell in Zion and serve in the temple has found embodiment in the "book of the covenant of the Most High God." He thus creates a pedagogical triangulation of acquiring wisdom, fulfilling the law, and fearing God as the goal for his students (Wright 2013). While these texts bring into relationship the mythic (divine wisdom) and the legal (torah, commandments, statutes, and ordinances), both end up serving the interests of the sage's pedagogical agenda.

Thus, wisdom literature increasingly has been studied for the way that these texts understand and interpret the torah, both in its specifics and as a concept (e.g., Sheppard 1980; Kister 2004). Wisdom texts participate in an active and dynamic engagement with torah, although they exhibit great diversity in their approaches to and uses of torah (Brooke 2002). In some cases, such as Instruction, one finds halakic exegesis that depends directly on biblical legal strictures, even if the text is not quoted, as we see in 4Q418 103 II, 7–9, which exegetes the law against mixed things in Lev 19:19 and Deut 22:9. In other cases, a text might allude to a specific legal notion without directly exegeting it, as we see in Sir 23:23 on the adulterous woman who "has disobeyed the law of the Most High." The Sentences of Pseudo-Phocylides has numerous admonitions that relate to the law in its Greek translation, the Septuagint. In other instances, wisdom texts make more general exhortations to lead a moral life, for the addressee to "keep the commandments" (Sir 1:26), to "keep her statutes" (*ḥōqîm*, 4Q525 I, 1), or to "walk in the (T)torah of the Most High" (4Q525 II, 3–4). Early Jewish wisdom texts also exegete the narratives contained in the torah for use in paranesis. Prime examples can be found in Sir 16:6–10, Wis 10:1–11:20, or 4Q185 1–2 I.

As the status of the Mosaic torah rose in the Second Temple period, then, the sages who produced wisdom literature could not ignore it. In this respect, Sanders was correct. Yet, whether we capitalize the term, as Torah, or not, as torah=teaching, we find in the wisdom texts an engagement with (T)torah as a concept, an icon, or as an authoritative set of texts to be exegeted, a move that pervades wisdom throughout the Second Temple period.

4.3. Wisdom and Revelation

Most early Jewish wisdom texts evince a desire for the addressee to acquire wisdom. For some, the mechanism for gaining wisdom evokes the language of inspiration or revelation. This revelatory inspiration can be attributed to the sage's direct connection to wisdom or to what is gained through the process of study, especially of authoritative texts and/or creation. While we do not see the kind of supernatural revelation through otherworldly mediators characteristic of apocalyptic texts, wisdom texts nonetheless can frame insight as revelation. Wisdom herself might serve as a mediator who reveals divine knowledge to the sage, the language often taking the form of revealing the secrets of Wisdom (of her equivalent in the case of Instruction).

Just how many of these texts appeal to revelation is not clear, since many of the Qumran texts are fragmentary, which renders many questions unanswerable. Perhaps some of them connected wisdom with revelation or prophecy, but two texts, Instruction and Ben Sira, have revelation as important themes, and another, Wisdom of Solomon, suggests that the knowledge of divine secrets comes by revelation/inspiration.

In Instruction the idea of revelation is bound up with the *raz nihyeh* (see above). In 1QS XI, 3–4, the *raz nihyeh* refers to supernatural revelation; God discloses (*ptḥ*) "the light of my heart the mystery that is to be." The knowledge contained in the *raz nihyeh*, then, is framed as revelation (Goff 2009, 380), and the *mevin*, the understanding one, gains this revelatory knowledge through study and contemplation rather than through any angelic mediator or heavenly journey. Similarly, in 4QMysteries (4Q299, 4Q300) the *raz nihyeh* is connected with wisdom (1Q27 1 I, 1–7) in a text that "shows the intermingling of both sapiential and prophetic origin" (Kister 2004, 46). Wisdom, then, as it is related to the *raz nihyeh*, takes on a revelatory cast.

Ben Sira employs the idea of revelation or inspiration in more than one way. First, Wisdom reveals "her secrets" to those who pursue her (Sir 4:18). Since Wisdom can be found in the created order, the teaching of the sages, and the torah, all of these are potential sources where Wisdom might reveal those secrets (Aitken 1999, 192–93; Wright 2012, 234–35). In each case, the mechanism might be different: observing the created order, listening to the sages, and studying the torah. Standing between Wisdom and those seeking her is the sage, who serves as an "inspired mediator" (Beentjes, 2012, 222). Ben Sira has a direct connection to Wisdom, which he articulates via the extensive metaphor of water in chapter 24, and in 39:6, if the sage petitions God and God is willing, the sage will "be filled with a spirit of understanding" and "pour forth words of wisdom of his own." Moreover, Ben Sira speaks about his own teaching in the language of prophecy (Sir 24:33): "I will again pour out teaching like prophecy [Gk; in prophecy (Syriac)], and leave it to all future generations." Perdue (2005, 153) has argued that Ben Sira sees himself as standing "in succession to the long line of prophets," but whether he is an heir to the prophets or an inspired mediator of Wisdom revealed, the sage's knowledge and wisdom gets framed with the language of revelatory inspiration.

In the Wisdom of Solomon, we find hints of a notion of revelation or inspiration. Shannon Burkes (2002) has pointed out that 2:22 refers to the secrets of God that the wicked do not know, and in Solomon's prayer for wisdom in chapter 7, he claims to have learned "all things, both what is secret and what is manifest, for Wisdom, the fashioner of all things taught [*edidaksen*] me." Burkes suggests that "the secret knowledge that he learned was something that could be known only through revelation" (36).

4.4. Greek Wisdom and *Paideia*

In the Hellenistic world, Jewish sages took advantage of Greek wisdom in various ways. Elisa Uusimäki (2017, 23) argues that the sage "in the sense of an exemplar or a teacher emulated by his pupils is not explicit until Hellenistic Judaism." Uusimäki locates this conception of the sage in the Greek world largely in philosophical sources that discuss the model sage that can be traced back to Plato. She reads Jewish wisdom against the backdrop of Greek philosophy as spiritual exercises, building on earlier explorations of the quest for perfection in ancient Jewish texts (Najman 2010a, 2010b). Uusimäki's analysis extends beyond Greek-language texts to those written in Semitic languages. Scholars have shown how Jewish wisdom texts have drawn on a range of Greek philosophical ideas and texts, particularly Platonic and Stoic ideas, the most prominent cases being the Wisdom of Solomon and 4 Maccabees.

Hellenistic Jews adopted widely Greek forms of literature, and gnomic poetry fit well with the goals of wisdom literature. The Sentences of Pseudo-Phocylides is a pseudepigraphic Jewish work dating from the first century BCE to the first century CE that purports to be from the sixth century BCE gnomic poet Phocylides of Miletus. Its author engages in imitation (*mimesis*), even down to writing in old Ionic, the dialect of Greek in which Phocylides wrote (Wilson 2005). A later text (of uncertain date), likely in Syriac, the Sentences of the Syriac Menander, claims to give wisdom from the famed Greek playwright of the fourth century BCE (Monaco 2013). In each of these cases, in order to articulate their wisdom, Jewish authors followed a widespread tactic among Jewish writers in the Hellenistic period of adopting the personae of famous Greek figures.

In this vein, recent scholarship has renewed its interest in the relationship between Jewish education in the Hellenistic and Roman periods and Greek *paideia*. While Alexandria was the center of Hellenistic learning in the Eastern Mediterranean during this period, Jews from a wide variety of locations engaged Greek educational resources, and some wisdom texts offer evidence of sages who engaged Greek *paideia*. Two recent volumes of essays provide a good state of the question with respect to Jews and Greek *paideia*, including wisdom literature (Hogan, Goff, Wasserman 2017; Zurawski and Boccaccini 2017).

4.6. The Social Location of the Producers of Wisdom

Since the publication of *Early Judaism and Its Modern Interpreters* (Kraft and Nickelsburg 1986), scholars across many disciplines have thought about the social location of ancient writers and the production of ancient texts, particularly the location and practices of ancient scribes. That is, wisdom texts, like all other texts, were produced by particular people in specific historical and social circumstances. Studies by Christine Schams (1998), David Carr (2005), Karel van der Toorn (2007), and Richard Horsley (2007) have generated much discussion among scholars of wisdom literature. The move to focus on the social locations and worlds of those who produced wisdom literature has been something of a response to older scholarship that highlighted the timelessness, and thus the acontextual or ahistorical character, of wisdom. As Perdue (2008, 1) writes, "The wisdom tradition cannot be understood apart from the larger social history of the cultures in which it took root and flourished."

Within the area of wisdom literature, an increased interest in the social location of those who produced and copied wisdom texts was the original focus of the Wisdom and Apocalypticism Group of the Society of Biblical Literature (Wright and Wills 2005). Within that group and elsewhere, the relationship between those scribes who produced wisdom and those who produced apocalyptic was an early focus. Randall Argall (1995), for example, concluded that those who produced the early Enoch books and the Jerusalemite sage Ben Sira were rivals who contended over basic ideas. In some cases, they displayed very similar approaches and in others quite a difference. Horsley (2007) widens the lens to think more broadly about scribal groups in Second Temple Jerusalem, where various scribal groups jockeyed for power and position. For Horsley, a sage such as Ben Sira plays a significant role in understanding these dynamics. Instruction has also become a focus of attention over the location of the sage, given the persistent emphasis in the text on the *mevin*'s poverty. Is it actual or metaphorical or both (Goff 2013, 23–26 and the bibliography there)?

For wisdom literature, asking these questions has resulted in important insights into ancient Jewish scribal culture. As scholarship on early Judaism continues to focus on the social realities of ancient Jews, the question of where the sages and other producers of early Jewish wisdom fit in those landscapes will undoubtedly remain an important focus.

5. Jewish Wisdom in the Hellenistic and Roman Periods

Menahem Kister (2004, 45) has pointed out that in the Second Temple period "wisdom conventions, forms and concepts are subsumed ... under a new system, far removed from those of the biblical wisdom literature." In this short statement, he has put his finger on an important point. Whether it is Ben Sira or Instruction or Wisdom of Solomon or Pseudo-Phocylides, the range of possibilities for Jewish wisdom has exploded earlier conceptions of what constituted wisdom literature. The texts from the Dead Sea showed that previously known texts, such as Ben Sira or Wisdom of Solomon, were typical, if anything can be called typical, of early Jewish wisdom rather than atypical. The study of these texts, although the bibliography has become enormous, remains in its early stages, primarily because of the timing of the publication of all the Qumran texts. Now that much of the initial work has been done on them, scholars can move to next steps, as we have seen happening in some of the studies highlighted in this article. What exactly wisdom is, if it is a thing or not, remains one actively debated question among many. The fact that this essay could not proceed along the same lines as the earlier *Early Judaism and Its Modern Interpreters* article (Mack and Murphy 1986) testifies to the way that the study of wisdom literature has blossomed over the last thirty to forty years.

Bibliography:

Adams, Samuel L. 2008. *Wisdom in Transition: Act and Consequence in Second Temple Instructions.* JSJSup 125. Leiden: Brill.
Aitken, James K. 1999. "Apocalyptic, Revelation and Early Jewish Wisdom Literature." Pages 181–93 in *New Heaven and New Earth: Prophecy and the Millennium; Essays in Honour of Anthony Gelston.* Edited by P. J. Harland and C. T. R. Hayward. VTSup 77. Leiden: Brill.
Allegro, John. 1986. *Qumran Cave 4.I (4Q158–4Q186).* DJD 5. Oxford: Clarendon.
Argall, Randal A. 1995. *1 Enoch and Sirach: A Comparative Literary and Conceptual Analysis of the Themes of Revelation, Creation, and Judgment.* EJL 8. Atlanta: Scholars Press.
Barthélemy, Dominique, and Józef T. Milik. 1955. *Qumran Cave 1.* DJD 1. Oxford: Clarendon.
Beentjes, Pancratius C. 2012. "What about Apocalypticism in the Book of Ben Sira?" Pages 207–27 in *Congress Volume: Helsinki, 2010.* Edited by Martti Nissinen. VTSup 148. Leiden: Brill.
Blenkinsopp, Joseph. 1995. *Wisdom and Law in the Old Testament: The Ordering of Life in Israel and Early Judaism.* Rev. ed. Oxford: Oxford University Press.
Boer, Roland. 2007. *Bakhtin and Genre Theory in Biblical Studies.* SemeiaSt 63. Atlanta: Society of Biblical Literature.
Bohak, Gideon. 2016. "Manuals of Mantic Wisdom from the Dead Sea Scrolls to the Cairo Genizah." Pages 191–216 in *Tracing Sapiential Traditions in Ancient Judaism.* Edited by Hindy Najman, Jean-Sébastien Rey, and Eibert J. C. Tigchelaar. JSJSup 174. Leiden: Brill.
Brooke, George J. 2002. "Biblical Interpretation in the Wisdom Texts from Qumran." Pages 201–20 in *The Wisdom Texts from Qumran and the Development of Sapiential Thought.* Edited by Charlotte Hempel, Armin Lange, and Hermann Lichtenberger. BETL 159. Leuven: Peeters.
Burkes, Shannon. 2002. "Wisdom and Apocalypticism in the Wisdom of Solomon." *HTR* 95:21–44.

Caquot, André. 1996. "Les textes de sagesse de Qoumrân (aperçu préliminaire)." *RHPR* 76:1–34.
Carr, David M. 2005. *Writing on the Tablet of the Heart: Origins of Scripture and Literature*. Oxford: Oxford University Press.
Cheung, Simon Chi-Chung. 2015. *Wisdom Intoned: A Reappraisal of the Genre "Wisdom Psalms."* LHBOTS 613. London: Bloomsbury T&T Clark.
Collins, John J. 1997a. *Jewish Wisdom in the Hellenistic Age*. OTL. Louisville: Westminster John Knox.
———. 1997b. "Wisdom Reconsidered, in Light of the Scrolls." *DSD* 4:265–81.
———. 2001. "Wisdom, Apocalypticism and the Dead Sea Scrolls." Pages 369–83 in *Seers, Sibyls and Sages in Hellenistic-Roman Judaism*. Edited by John J. Collins. JSJSup 54. Leiden: Brill.
———. 2010. "Epilogue: Genre Analysis and the Dead Sea Scrolls." *DSD* 17:389–401.
Crenshaw, James L. 1998. *Old Testament Wisdom: An Introduction*. Rev. ed. Louisville: Westminster John Knox.
Dell, Katherine. 2015. "Deciding the Boundaries of 'Wisdom': Applying the Concept of Family Resemblance." Pages 145–60 in *Was There a Wisdom Tradition: New Perspectives in Israelite Wisdom Studies*. Edited by Mark R. Sneed. AIL 23. Atlanta: SBL Press.
García Martínez, Florentino. 2003. *Wisdom and Apocalypticism in the Dead Sea Scrolls and in the Biblical Tradition*. BETL 168. Leuven: Peeters.
Goering, Greg Schmidt. 2009. *Wisdom's Root Revealed: Ben Sira and the Election of Israel*. JSJSup 139. Leiden: Brill.
Goff, Matthew J. 2007. *Discerning Wisdom: The Sapiential Literature of the Dead Sea Scrolls*. VTSup 116. Leiden: Brill.
———. 2009. "Recent Trends in the Study of Early Jewish Wisdom Literature: The Contribution of 4QInstruction and Other Qumran Texts." *CurBR* 7:376–416.
———. 2010. "Qumran Wisdom Literature and the Problem of Genre." *DSD* 17:286–306.
———. 2013. *4QInstruction*. WLAW 2. Atlanta: Society of Biblical Literature.
———. 2014. "Wisdom and Apocalypticism." Page 52–68 in *The Oxford Handbook of Apocalyptic Literature*. Edited by John J. Collins. Oxford: Oxford University Press.

———. 2018. "Wisdom." Pages 449–56 in *The T&T Clark Companion to the Dead Sea Scrolls*. Edited by George J. Brooke and Charlotte Hempel. London: Bloomsbury T&T Clark.

Harrington, Daniel J. 1994. "Wisdom at Qumran." Pages 137–52 in *The Community of the Renewed Covenant: The Notre Dame Symposium on the Dead Sea Scrolls*. Edited by Eugene Ulrich and James C. VanderKam. CJAn 10. Notre Dame: University of Notre Dame Press.

———. 1996. *Wisdom Texts from Qumran*. Literature of the Dead Sea Scrolls. London: Routledge.

Hogan, Karina Martin, Matthew Goff, and Emma Wasserman, eds. 2017. *Pedagogy in Ancient Judaism and Early Christianity*. EJL 41. Atlanta: SBL Press.

Horsley, Richard A. 2007. *Scribes, Visionaries and the Politics of Second Temple Judea*. Louisville: Westminster John Knox.

Kampen, John. 2011. *Wisdom Literature*. ECDSS. Grand Rapids: Eerdmans.

Kister, Menahem. 2004. "Wisdom Literature and Its Relation to Other Genres: From Ben Sira to Mysteries." Pages 13–47 in *Sapiential Perspectives: Wisdom Literature in Light of the Dead Sea Scrolls: Proceedings of the Sixth International Symposium of the Orion Center for the Study of the Dead Sea Scrolls and Associated Literature, 20–22 May, 2001*. Edited by Gregory E. Sterling and Ruth A. Clements. STDJ 51. Leiden: Brill.

Kraft, Robert A., and George W. E. Nickelsburg, eds. 1986. *Early Judaism and Its Modern Interpreters*. BMI 2. Philadelphia: Fortress; Atlanta: Scholars Press.

Kynes, Will. 2016. "The Nineteenth-Century Beginnings of 'Wisdom Literature' and Its Twenty-first-Century End?" Pages 83–108 in *Perspectives on Israelite Wisdom: Proceedings of the Oxford Old Testament Seminar*. Edited by John Jarick. LHBOTS 618. London: Bloomsbury T&T Clark.

———. 2018a. *An Obituary for "Wisdom Literature": The Birth, Death, and Textual Reintegration of a Biblical Corpus*. Oxford: Oxford University Press.

———. 2018b. "The 'Wisdom Literature Category: An Obituary." *JTS* 69:1–24.

———. Forthcoming. *The Oxford Handbook of Wisdom and Wisdom Literature*. Oxford: Oxford University Press.

Lange, Armin. 2002. "Die Weisheitstexte aus Qumran: Eine Einleitung." Pages 3–30 in *The Wisdom Texts from Qumran and the Development of Sapiential Thought*. Edited by Charlotte Hempel, Armin Lange, and Hermann Lichtenberger BETL 159. Leuven: Peeters.

Mack, Burton L., and Roland E. Murphy. 1986. "Wisdom Literature." Pages 371–410 in *Early Judaism and Its Modern Interpreters*. Edited by Robert A. Kraft and George W. E. Nickelsburg. BMI 2. Philadelphia: Fortress; Atlanta: Scholars Press.

Marböck, Johannes. 2006. *Weisheit und Frömmigkeit: Studien zur alttestamentlichen Literatur der Spätzeit*. ÖBS. Frankfurt: Lang.

Monaco, David Gregory. 2013. *The Sentences of the Syriac Menander: Introduction, Text and Translation, and Commentary*. Gorgias Studies in Classical and Late Antiquity. Piscataway, NJ: Gorgias.

Murphy-O'Connor, Jerome. 1986. "The Judean Desert." Pages 119–56 in *Early Judaism and Its Modern Interpreters*. Edited by Robert Kraft and George W. E. Nickelsburg. BMI 2. Philadelphia: Fortress; Atlanta: Scholars Press.

Najman, Hindy. 2010a. "The Quest for Perfection in Ancient Judaism." Pages 219–34 in *Past Renewals: Interpretive Authority, Renewed Revelation and the Quest for Perfection in Jewish Antiquity*. JSJSup 53. Leiden Brill.

———. 2010b. "Text and Figure in Ancient Jewish *Paideia*." Pages 243–56 in *Past Renewals: Interpretive Authority, Renewed Revelation and the Quest for Perfection in Jewish Antiquity*. JSJSup 53. Leiden Brill.

———. 2017. "Jewish Wisdom in the Hellenistic Period: Towards the Study of a Semantic Constellation." Pages 459–72 in *Is There a Text in This Cave? Studies in the Textuality of the Dead Sea Scrolls in Honour of George J. Brooke*. Edited by Ariel Feldman, Maria Cioată, and Charlotte Hempel. STDJ 119. Leiden: Brill.

Najman, Hindy, and Mladen Popović. 2010. *Rethinking Genre: Essays in Honor of John J. Collins*. DSD 17.

Newsom, Carol A. 2007. "Spying Out the Land: A Report from Genology." Pages 19–30 in *Bakhtin and Genre Theory in Biblical Studies*. Edited by Roland Boer. SemeiaSt 63. Atlanta: Society of Biblical Literature.

———. 2010. "Pairing Research Questions and Theories of Genre: A Case Study of the Hodayot." *DSD* 17:241–259.

Nickelsburg, George W. E. 2005. "Wisdom and Apocalypticism in Early Judaism: Some Points for Discussion." Pages 17–37 in *Conflicted Boundaries in Wisdom and Apocalyptic*. Edited by Benjamin G. Wright III and Lawrence M. Wills. SymS 35. Atlanta: Society of Biblical Literature.

Perdue, Leo G. 2005. "Ben Sira and the Prophets." Pages 132–54 in *Intertextual Studies in Ben Sira and Tobit: Essays in Honor of Alexander A. Di Lella, O.F.M.* Edited by Jeremy Corley and Vincent Skemp. CBQMS 38. Washington, DC: Catholic Biblical Association of America.

———. 2008. *The Sword and the Stylus: An Introduction to Wisdom in the Age of Empires.* Grand Rapids: Eerdmans, 2008.

Rad, Gerhard von. 1960. *Theologie des Alten Testaments.* 2 vols. Munich: Kaiser.

Reiterer, Friederich V. 2004. "Neue Akzente in der Gesetzesvorstellung: תורת חיים bei Ben Sira." Pages 851–71 in *Gott und Mensch im Dialog: Festschrift für Otto Kaiser zum 80. Geburtstag.* Edited by Markus Witte. BZAW 345. 2 vols. Berlin: de Gruyter.

Sanders, Jack T. 2001. "When Sacred Canopies Collide: The Reception of the Torah of Moses in the Wisdom Literature of the Second-Temple Period." *JSJ* 32:121–36.

Schams, Christine. 1998. *Jewish Scribes of the Second Temple Period.* JSOTSup 291. Sheffield: Sheffield Academic.

Schellenberg, Annette. 2015. "Don't Throw the Baby Out with the Bathwater: On the Distinctness of the Sapiential Understanding of the World." Pages 115–44 in *Was There a Wisdom Tradition: New Perspectives in Israelite Wisdom Studies.* Edited by Mark R. Sneed. AIL 23. Atlanta: SBL Press.

Sheppard, Gerald T. 1980. *Wisdom as a Hermeneutical Construct: A Study in the Sapientializing of the Old Testament.* BZAW 151. Berlin: de Gruyter.

Sneed, Mark R. 2011. "Is the 'Wisdom Tradition' a Tradition?" *CBQ* 73:50–71.

———. 2015a. "'Grasping after the Wind': The Elusive Attempt to Define and Delimit Wisdom." Pages 39–67 in *Was There a Wisdom Tradition? New Perspectives in Israelite Wisdom Studies.* Edited by Mark R. Sneed. AIL 23. Atlanta: SBL Press.

———. 2015b. *The Social World of the Sages: An Introduction to Israelite and Jewish Wisdom Literature.* Minneapolis: Fortress.

———, ed. 2015c. *Was There a Wisdom Tradition? New Perspectives in Israelite Wisdom Studies.* AIL 23. Atlanta: SBL Press.

Strugnell, John. 2002. "The Smaller Hebrew Wisdom Texts Found a Qumran: Variations, Resemblances, and Lines of Development." Pages 31–60 in *The Wisdom Texts from Qumran and the Development of Sapi-*

ential Thought. Edited by Charlotte Hempel, Armin Lange, and Hermann Lichtenberger. BETL 159. Leuven: Peeters.

Strugnell, John, Daniel J. Harrington, and Torleif Elgvin. 1999. *Sapiential Texts, Part 2: Cave 4.XXIV.* DJD 34. Oxford: Clarendon.

Tanzer, Sarah J. 2005. "Response to George Nickelsburg, 'Wisdom and Apocalypticism in Early Judaism.'" Pages 39–49 in *Conflicted Boundaries in Wisdom and Apocalyptic.* Edited by Benjamin G. Wright III and Lawrence M. Wills. SymS 35. Atlanta: Society of Biblical Literature.

Tigchelaar, Eibert J. C. 2001. *To Increase Learning for the Understanding Ones: Reading and Reconstructing the Fragmentary Early Jewish Sapiential Text 4QInstruction.* STDJ 44. Leiden: Brill.

Toorn, Karel van der. 2007. *Scribal Culture and the Making of the Hebrew Bible.* Cambridge: Harvard University Press.

Uusimäki, Elisa. 2017. "The Rise of the Sage in Greek and Jewish Antiquity." *JSJ* 49:1–29.

Weeks, Stuart. 2010. *An Introduction to the Study of Wisdom Literature.* T&T Clark Approaches to Biblical Studies. London: T&T Clark.

Williamson, Robert, Jr. 2010. "Pesher: A Cognitive Model of the Genre." *DSD* 17:307–331.

Wilson, Walter T. 2005. *The Sentences of Pseudo-Phocylides.* CEJL. Berlin: de Gruyter.

Woude, A. S. van der. 1995. "Wisdom at Qumran." Pages 244–56 in *Wisdom in Ancient Israel: Essays in Honour of J.A. Emerton.* Edited by John Day, Robert P. Gordon, and Hugh G. M. Williamson. Cambridge: Cambridge University Press.

Wright, Benjamin G., III. 2010. "Joining the Club: A Suggestion about Genre in Early Jewish Texts." *DSD* 17:289–314.

———. 2012. "Conflicted Boundaries: Ben Sira, Sage and Seer." Pages 229–53 in *Congress Volume: Helsinki, 2010.* Edited by Martti Nissinen. VTSup 148. Leiden: Brill.

———. 2013. "Torah and Sapiential Pedagogy in the Book of Ben Sira." Pages 157–86 in *Wisdom and Torah: The Reception of "Torah" in the Wisdom Literature of the Second Temple Period.* Edited by Berndt U. Schipper and D. Andrew Teeter. JSJSup 163. Leiden: Brill.

Wright, Benjamin G., III, and Lawrence M. Wills, eds. 2005. *Conflicted Boundaries in Wisdom and Apocalypticism.* SymS 35. Atlanta: Society of Biblical Literature.

Zurawski, Jason M., and Gabriele Boccaccini, eds. 2017. *Second Temple Jewish "Paideia" in Context.* BZNW 228. Berlin: de Gruyter.

Appendix: Early Jewish Texts Labeled as Wisdom Literature

For discussion of the small fragments among the Dead Sea Scrolls often thought to be parts of wisdom texts, see Lange 2002, 3–9; and Strugnell 2002.

1Q 26; 4Q415–418, 418a, 423 (Instruction/Musar le-Mevin)
1Q 27; 4Q299–301 (Book of Mysteries)
4Q184 (Wiles of the Wicked Woman)
4Q185 (4QSapiential work)
4Q298 (Words of the Maskil to the Sons of Dawn)
4Q420–421 (Ways of Righteousness)
4Q424 (Instruction-like Composition B)
4Q525 (Beatitudes)
11Q5 XVIII, 1–16 = Psalm 154 (Syriac)
11Q5 26 (Hymn to the Creator)
Aramaic Levi Document
Baruch 3:9–4:4
CD II (Treatise on the Two Spirits)
4 Maccabees
Pirke Avoth
Psalm 19, 119
The Sentences of Pseudo-Phocylides
The Sentences of the Syriac Menander (?)
Targumim to Job (4Q157, 11Q10 [11QtgJob])
Tobit
The Wisdom of Ben Sira
The Wisdom of Solomon

19
EARLY JEWISH PRAYER

DANIEL K. FALK AND ANGELA KIM HARKINS

Since the 1980s, scholarship on early Jewish prayer has developed dramatically to become an energetic subfield of research in its own right. The change is readily apparent by contrasting the state of research on early Jewish prayers and hymns in the early 1980s as described in the surveys by James Charlesworth in the first edition of *Early Judaism and Its Modern Interpreters* (1986, but covering research up to 1981) and David Flusser (1984) with the state of the field today. In broad terms, there is now a much richer corpus of data that is more certainly relevant to the practice of prayer—mostly from the Dead Sea Scrolls—and there is now a much wider range of questions and approaches being brought to the study of early Jewish prayer. This article will focus on describing the major developments since these two surveys and evaluate directions for further research. Special attention will be devoted to new approaches and questions.

1. Definition of Prayer

At the beginning it is necessary to consider what it is that one seeks to learn when studying prayer. Many studies of prayer in ancient texts turn out not to be primarily interested in prayer per se, but in mining texts related to prayer in order to learn about something else: theology, ideology, literature, social structure, group identity, and so on. For example, study of prayer in Philo or Josephus can be a means of examining the views and rhetoric of Philo and Josephus, and the prayers in the books of Maccabees may be analyzed as literary devices to further the narrative. These are legitimate objects of investigation, of course, but it is important to acknowledge that while textual analysis of a prayer embedded in a narrative may yield information about literary motifs, the *Tendenz* of the author, and so on, it is inadequate as a study of prayer as a practice, even if such literary prayers probably do reflect practice in some way. Herein lies the central problem in studying ancient prayer: the vast majority of evidence is in the form of texts, and the major avenue of investigation is textual analysis of structure, themes, and ideas. However, prayer is not merely a text. In Judaism it generally involves performative action in a social context with an intended effect for the person and/or community, and so a holistic study of prayer requires diverse approaches from the social, psychological, and behavioral sciences.

Definitions of prayer vary as a result of their focus on whether prayer is primarily a text or a practice. Prayer may be defined broadly as an act of communication with a deity initiated by a human. This moves the focus from textual form to function and includes intention and significance; that is, prayer is "performed with the purpose of getting results from or in the interaction of communication" (Malina 1980, 215). As an act, nonverbal aspects such as place, time, and gesture are equally meaningful. The verbal part of prayer may be prose or poetry, and although often addressed to God in the second person this is not an essential feature: prayers may also be indirect or combine direct and indirect speech. There are numerous terms for Jewish prayer in ancient Hebrew (e.g., *tefillah, teḥinnah, berakah, mizmor, shir, tehillah, todah, hodah*) and Greek sources (e.g., *euche, proseuche, deesis, aitema, psalmos, hymnos*, and *ode*), but these are not used consistently as technical terms (Schuller 1998), and scholars vary in their terminology. The terms psalm and hymn will be used here respectively for poetic prayer in general and poetic praise in particular.

2. Sources of Prayer

Until the mid-1980s (e.g., Reventlow 1986), the Hebrew Psalter still dominated much of the scholarship on early Jewish prayer, both as the predominant corpus of prayer in Second Temple Judaism and as providing the major analytical categories in terms of form criticism and hypothetical cultic settings in isolation from the literary context. Moshe Greenberg (1983), however, directed scholarly attention to the prose prayers embedded in narratives, arguing on the basis of patterns similar to interpersonal speech that these are not merely a literary convention, but reflect actual prayer practice of popular religion. Acknowledging this shift, both Samuel Balentine (1993) and Patrick Miller (1994) focused on prose prayers in their studies of biblical prayer, and both looked to narrative context as clues to the character of prayer and its literary and theological functions. The turn to focus on prose prayers is also apparent in a number of other monographs from the 1990s and on (e.g., Werline 1998; Newman 1999; Boda 1999; Bautch 2003). With regard to biblical prayer, it should be added that insufficient attention has been given to prayer in the Septuagint as a product of the Greek-speaking Jewish community in Egypt.

There has been a significant increase in attention to prayers and psalms embedded in various Jewish writings from the Second Temple period among the deuterocanonical literature and throughout the writings of Philo and Josephus (Egger-Wenzel and Corley 2004; McDowell 2006; Matlock 2012; Van der Horst and Newman 2008; Leonhardt-Balzer, 2001; Jonquière, 2007). Most of these are compositions of the authors to serve literary functions, by developing themes and characterization of figures in the text to whom the prayers are attributed. Study of them reveals more about the theology and rhetorical purposes of the authors than about general Jewish piety. Nevertheless, it is likely that they bear some verisimilitude to prayer practice.

The New Testament and early Christian sources provide some evidence for Jewish prayer (cf. Wick 2002). Much of the literature, however, is primarily focused on theological concerns, with two problematic tendencies (Bradshaw 2002): (1) reading the prayer of Jesus and early Christians against Judaism (and the Greco-Roman world) to emphasize the uniqueness of Christian prayer and (2) assuming continuity with a developed Jewish liturgy retrojected from later sources.

Rabbinic sources may contain some authentic data about prayer practices in the Second Temple period, but these must be used with extreme caution (Reif 2004). There is an increasing recognition that rabbinic literature reflects complex social realities and competition and for rhetorical purposes often retrojects liturgical practices onto times of the temple (Langer 2018).

The most significant development has come from the large increase in prayer material from the Dead Sea Scrolls published in the 1980s and 1990s. The corpus now includes more than a hundred different prayers and at least a hundred different previously unknown psalms and fills several large volumes of the official series Discoveries in Judaean Desert (Baillet 1982 [DJD 7]; Eshel et al. 1998 [DJD 11]; Chazon et al. 1999 [DJD 29]; Stegeman, Schuller, and Newsom 2009 [DJD 40]), and parts of several further volumes (esp. García Martínez, Tigchelaar, and Van der Woude 1998 [DJD 23]; Baumgarten et al. 1999 [DJD 35]). These include scrolls of prayers for calendrical occasions (festivals, Sabbaths, days of the month, days of the week), various ad hoc occasions including ritual purification, exorcism, and possibly a marriage ritual, as well as collections of prayers and psalms of uncertain use (Nitzan 1994; Falk 1999; Chazon 1998; Schuller 2004; Davila 2000). Due to the fragmentary nature of these scrolls, some of the collections are still poorly understood. More work is needed on improving reconstructions and clarifying the relationships among different versions or recensions of some prayers and collections (Falk 2010). Moreover, since these scrolls represent the only examples of actual liturgical manuscripts dating from the Second Temple period, the materiality of these artifacts requires further attention (Falk 2014).

3. Development of Jewish Liturgy

Until the last two decades, studies on early Jewish prayer were primarily concerned with historical and theological questions and employed traditional methods of literary and historical-critical analysis. In particular, a major concern was to plot the origins and development of various features of the later synagogue liturgy and Christian liturgies. Most starkly, the quest is for the missing links between the situation in the Hebrew Bible, which prescribes no laws about prayers of the people, and the rabbinic theory of prayer as a regulated religious obligation of the community, as attested in the Mishnah (Reif 1993, 1–87).

There are three main models in current scholarship for explaining the development of Jewish liturgy, differing on the degree of continuity they find between prayer practices of the Second Temple period and the statutory liturgy of the later synagogue. The first model finds direct continuity, positing that the main elements of the synagogue liturgy—especially the Amidah and the Shema—originated early in the Second Temple period. Using philological analysis of medieval rites and the evidence of Talmudic debates, scholars of the nineteenth and early twentieth century sought to reconstruct the earliest forms of prayers (see Reif 1993, 1–21). Thematic and verbal similarities to rabbinic prayers in Ben Sira and other early Jewish works were seen as evidence of early prototypes, and the publication of the Dead Sea Scrolls provided further fodder. Most prominently, Moshe Weinfeld claimed to identify reflections of various synagogue prayers among the Dead Sea Scrolls (see Reif 2004, 447).

A second model posits diverse popular prayer practices that developed in various settings during the Second Temple period. Some of the stereotyped themes and formulations from these prayers were adopted and standardized in the rabbinic liturgy, which developed gradually over centuries. This is especially associated with the form-critical research of Joseph Heinemann (1977) and is the dominant model in recent scholarship on the early development of Jewish liturgy (Reif 1993; Langer 2018).

A third model proposes a sharp discontinuity and finds its most detailed expression in a series of Hebrew articles by Ezra Fleischer (see summary and bibliography in Langer 1999). Fleischer argued forcefully that the rabbinic liturgy was a novel form of worship introduced in the decades following the destruction of the temple in 70 CE. At its heart was the entirely new conception of communal prayer as a religious obligation to compensate for the loss of the temple, and this required *de novo* fixed formulations for prayers. Thus, he rejected the idea of precedents to the rabbinic liturgy in the Second Temple period.

The Dead Sea Scrolls are critical to the debate among these models, as they provide the only known examples of clearly liturgical communal prayers dating from the Second Temple period. The full publication of the scrolls has rendered the first model unsustainable, since the abundant corpus of prayers failed to produce a single example that could be regarded as an early version of one of the later synagogue prayers. Between the remaining two models, the prayers in the Dead Sea Scrolls are either examples of the common stock of diverse prayer traditions from the Second Temple period that contributed to the development of the later synagogue liturgy, as Heinemann argued, or they represent the limited practice of a sectarian group estranged from temple worship and thus are effectively irrelevant to the development of prayer in Judaism more broadly, as Fleischer argued. Research on the liturgical scrolls found at Qumran, however, has shown that these prayers are of diverse origin and a significant number cannot be dismissed as sectarian prayers (Chazon 1998; Falk 1998). Thus, the evidence suggests that various prayer practices were developing in the Second Temple period among pious groups and that these had some influence on the later synagogue liturgy (Chazon 2012). In particular, continuities include stereotyped motifs and language, a scripturalizing style and vocabulary, clusters of petitions, a tendency toward scripted prayer and consistent patterns of framing prayers with blessings (see Chazon 1998; Nitzan 1994; Falk 1998; Reif 2004; Langer 2018). Beyond such generalities, however, much remains unclear, and the evidence from the Dead Sea

Scrolls has yet to be fully integrated into a comprehensive study of early Jewish prayer.

4. Penitential Prayer

In the 1990s and 2000s, penitential prayer became a major category of sustained investigation, starting with a series of published dissertations dedicated to exploring the emergence of penitential prayer as a distinct genre in the postexilic period. Rodney Werline (1998) traced how the Deuteronomic ideology of repentance in Deut 4 and 28–30 was transformed in the exilic period into a theory of penitential prayer as seen in 1 Kgs 8 and further developed into a religious institution for alleviating sin in the postexilic period. Employing linguistic analysis, comparison of literary forms, and redaction criticism, he explored how penitential traditions are reinterpreted on the basis of different historical experiences in the postexilic period by analyzing three groups of texts: Dan 9:1–27 and Bar 1:15–3:8; prayers from penitential reform movements (Qumran, Jubilees, 1 Enoch, Testament of Moses, Testaments of the Twelve Patriarchs); and prayers addressing the problem of theodicy (Tob 3:1–6; Pr Azar; 3 Macc 2:1–20; prayers in LXX Esther; Psalms of Solomon). Mark Boda (1999) executed a detailed tradition-historical analysis of the prayer in Neh 9:5b–37. Like Werline, he noted that the scriptural tradition is reshaped for the needs of the contemporary community. Whereas Werline recognized only minimal influence of the Levitical traditions, Boda demonstrated that the Deuteronomistic traditions were significantly transformed by Ezekielian and Priestly traditions. In contrast, Richard Bautch (2003) traced the roots of the development to the preexilic psalms of communal lament on the basis of form-critical analysis of Isa 63:7–64:11, Ezra 9:6–15, and Neh 9:6–37. He argued these were transformed into a new genre of penitential prayer in the postexilic period as confession of sin and historical recital replaced complaint. As a *Sitz im Leben* for these prayers, he hypothesized liturgies of repentance with little actual evidence. In perhaps an overly linear view, he also argued that some later prayers (Prayer of Manasseh, 4Q504 Words of the Luminaries, and 1 Macc 2) show a waning prominence of confession of sin in the Hellenistic and Roman periods in favor of recital of divine attributes as a motivation.

These and other monographs on early Jewish prayer (Falk, 1998; Newman, 1999) sparked a three-year Consultation on Penitential Prayer at the Society of Biblical Literature (2003–2005) that produced three volumes of essays treating the origins and development of penitential prayer in Second Temple Judaism and its lasting impact in Jewish and Christian liturgy (Boda, Falk, and Werline, 2006-2008). This rich scholarly dialogue highlighted important areas of convergence, in particular that there is a significant corpus of prose prayers with penitential motifs that are deserving of sustained attention on their own apart from form-critical research focused on the psalter (Gunkel 1967; Mowinckel 1962; Westermann 1981).

Beyond agreement on a core of four texts, however (Ezra 9:6-15; Neh 1:5-11; 9:6-37; and Dan 9:4-19), and some other texts regularly grouped with them (e.g., Bar 1:15-3:8; Prayer of Azariah; Tob 3:1-6; 3 Macc 2:1-10; 4Q504 Words of the Luminaries), it became increasingly clear that it was difficult to draw up a list of texts that formed a discrete classification or to define a set of distinctive shared characteristics. With many texts in various ways positioned at the definitional borders, it could even be questioned how helpful it really is to study penitential prayer as a distinct classification or whether it is more meaningful to investigate the various ways that penitential motifs and practices are employed in various prayers.

The study of penitential prayers highlighted the limited usefulness of form-critical analysis. Although it helped to identify prominent motifs and structures in penitential prayers, the diversity in form and function makes it questionable whether these constitute a distinct *Gattung*. In particular, the Dead Sea Scrolls provide for the first time concrete evidence of liturgical settings for prayers with confession of sin, including prayers for days of the week (4Q504 [4QDibHam]), festivals (1Q34+34bis; 4Q507; 4Q508; 4Q509+4Q505), purification rituals (4Q414, 4Q512), an annual covenant ceremony (1QS I, 18-II, 23), and others with unspecified setting (e.g., 4Q393, 1QH^a IV, 21-28; 1QS X-XI). But these are diverse in their employment of confession and penitential motifs, and none of them correspond well to the pattern derived from the core four texts. Moreover, the covenant ceremony in 1QS I, 18-II, 23 shows that confession of sin and language of the penitential tradition can function in ritual that serves to reinforce group boundaries (e.g., Falk 1998, 219-26).

Tradition-critical studies have been successful in defining many of the scriptural influences on penitential prayer—especially a combination of Deuteronomic and priestly traditions—but it is questionable whether these traditions should be plotted in a linear trajectory. Again, the diversity of employments of penitential language may point rather to a more complex use of traditions for different purposes in divergent social groups.

The limitations of such traditional historical-critical approaches encouraged new approaches that are more synchronic in orientation and draw on a broader arsenal of methods and insights from the human sciences, such as ritual studies, speech-act theory, rhetoric and identity formation, and so on. These focus particularly on the functions of prayer as practice rather than text and pay more attention to what prayer does rather than what ideas and developments its reflects. The shift is evident in Werline's modified definition of penitential prayer adopted for the Consultation on Penitential Prayer mentioned above: "Penitential prayer is a direct address to God in which an individual, group, or an individual on behalf of a group confesses sins and petitions for forgiveness *as an act of repentance*" (Werline 2007, 209; italics indicates addition in contrast to Werline 1998, 2).

5. Prayer and Scripture

The relationship of prayer and scripture has provoked increasingly sophisticated research questions. There are studies that identify and classify the use of scripture in a particular prayer text as a key to its meaning and purpose. Boda (1999, 1), for example, indicated that the goal of his tradition-historical analysis of Neh 9 was "to discern who was responsible for this composition and how tradition was being used by those responsible for it" and concluded that the prayer dates to the early restoration period in Judah, closely associated with Zechariah. He noted that the use of three tradition complexes (creation-Abraham-exodus; wilderness-Sinai; conquest-life in the land) show devotion to a Pentateuch much like the canonical form, but also that the scriptural tradition was reshaped for the needs of the contemporary community. His conclusion that "we see a community praying the tradition" (197), however, begs a crucial question: do we really see a community praying in this text? To what degree does Neh 9 reflect actual prayer practices of a community or rather the rhetoric of a literary text? At any rate, the focal point of Boda's analysis is on the composition and what this tells us about the author and his community.

The impact of scripture on the development of prayer practice runs throughout Werline's (1998) study of the penitential prayer traditions and Bilhah Nitzan's (1994) study of prayers and psalms from Qumran, as well as various studies that examine scriptural allusions and interpretive traditions (Hughes 2006). Even more specifically, Judith Newman (1999) has examined the ways that the extensive reuse and interpretation of scripture contributed to the shaping of prayer and the remarkable growth of prayer in the Second Temple period. She analyzes Neh 9, Jdt 9, and 3 Macc 2 to illustrate different ways that prayers are shaped by scripture: the use of scripture in telling history, the typological use of a scriptural episode, and a didactic use of examples of good and bad behavior. Although these texts are all embedded in narratives, she argues that they reflect to some degree actual prayer practice in the Second Temple period, "in particular *the ways in which and the degree to which they are scripturalized*" (1999, 205; emphasis original). Moreover, she notes that a "rhetorical shift occurs when scripture is prayed," for example, the adoption of the divine voice (206). Thus, although the analysis is literary, the study seeks to uncover the genetic relationship between scripture and prayer (cf. Chazon 2006).

In her most recent book, Newman (2018) has flipped the question to examine how the practice of prayer contributed to the formation of scripture. Drawing on insights from cognitive neurosciences and social sciences, she argues that embodied practices of prayer helped transform texts into scripture in five ways: the formation of the self; prompting revelation; providing "a communal model of an ideal prayer leader, one who has ingested and can reenact the tradition"; formation of the community; and a symbiotic relationship between the performance of prayer and the textualization of prayer (18–19; cf. 142–43). By turning the light on the "liturgical body" (both communal and individual) as the living context for the formation of scripture, Newman has brought prayer to the fore in a way that will provoke much new research.

6. Biblical Prayer Collections from the Dead Sea Scrolls

A significant number of psalms manuscripts were discovered among the Qumran caves. The best-preserved psalms scroll is known as the Great Psalms Scroll (11Q5 [11QPsª]), which is dated to the mid-first century CE and is approximately thirteen feet long. Scroll 11Q5 contains the majority of psalms from Ps 90 onward (books 4 and 5) and as many as eight nonbiblical psalms, including the psalm from Sir 51:13–30 and three of the Five Apocryphal Psalms of David known from the Syriac psalter (i.e., Pss 151, 154, 155). Scroll 11Q5 also contains four heretofore unknown psalms: "Plea for Deliverance" (XIX), "Apostrophe to Zion" (XXII, 1–15), "Hymn to the Creator" (XXVI, 9–15), and a remarkable composition known as "David's Composition" (XXVII, 1–11), which functions as an epilogue to the collection. This text attributes as many as 4,050 different songs to David, describing them as the result of prophetic inspiration. This is followed by Ps 151, which is also marked by Davidic themes, thereby casting a strong Davidic character to the entire collection.

Qumran Psalms manuscripts invite comparison with later forms of the biblical Psalter known from the MT, LXX, and Syriac textual traditions. The language of *biblical* is used here to mark a corpus of writing that is identifiable to scholars today; the term is certainly anachronistic for the people of the Second Temple period. Studies applying classic historical-critical approaches like redaction criticism to the psalter in light of the Qumran data argued in favor of a model of progressive canonization of the five smaller collections of psalms in which the first three books of psalms achieved stability by the time of the late Second Temple period (Wilson 1985). Since 11Q5 was preserved reasonably well, it attracted notable attention from scholars who sought to understand its relationship to the order and arrangement seen in other known psalters. Scholars early on argued strenuously that this should be recognized as a scriptural and authoritative collection for the Qumran movement, even though it did not resemble a known biblical psalter (Sanders 1974; Flint 1997, 202–27).

While some thirty-six manuscripts of psalms have been identified among the Qumran scrolls and speak to the importance of these texts, it is not at all clear that each manuscript contained complete copies of the psalters that came to be known as the MT, LXX or the Syriac. Some manuscripts (4Q83, 4Q84, 4Q87, 4Q94, 4Q96 [4QPs$^{a, b, e, m, o}$]) bear some resemblance to the biblical psalter known from the MT, but other psalms manuscripts reflect considerable variability in order and arrangement. Manuscripts like 11Q5 and 4Q88 [4QPs^f] not only provide scholars with important information about variant forms of the psalter during this time; they, along with the other psalms manuscripts, also have helped to raise key questions about the relationship of these different Qumran psalters to the Hebrew, Greek, and Syriac Textus Receptus and about the formation of prayer collections (Flint 1997; Willgren 2016). Perhaps the most notable change in the past forty years is the growing realization of the undue influence of our modern printing-press culture and an awareness of academia's intellectual bias toward the MT psalter. In addition to arguing in favor of the pluriformity of the literary edition of the collection, new scholarship has made especially noteworthy advances that challenge how scholars had previously conceptualized collections attributed to pseudonymous figures like David (Mroczek 2016).

7. Nonbiblical Prayer Collections from the Dead Sea Scrolls

Prayer collections such as the Cave 1 Hodayot scroll (1QH^a) brought new energy to the study of early Jewish prayer in the twentieth century. Early investigations read this collection in light of the biblical psalms, which were themselves understood primarily via form criticism. Eileen Schuller (1998) has raised important questions about the inadequacy of these known biblical forms for categorizing the diverse formal features of the nonbiblical compositions known as the Hodayot. In the past forty years, scholars have examined anew the Qumran Hodayot (Thanksgiving Hymns), one of the first Cave 1 scrolls to be published in the 1940s. In spite of this scroll's complicated history of material reconstruction (Harkins 2018), the publication of an affordable study edition means that this collection of prayers will continue to attract attention in the years to come (Schuller and Newsom 2012).

From the start, 1QH^a was read predominantly as literature and understood as autobiographical prayers, which favored a kind of historicizing analysis. Early scholars argued that some of the best-preserved sections of the scroll, columns X–XVII or so, were authored by the Teacher of Righteousness known from other Qumran texts, primarily CD and 1QpHab. This well-established view continued to have adherents but ultimately proved to be deeply problematic. Now that all the scrolls have been edited and published, it is clear that the teacher has very little textual support, scarcely mentioned in the giant trove of texts (Stuckenbruck 2007). The great majority of scholarship on the teacher hymns of 1QH^a reflects a typical, but problematic, disciplinary drive to use Second Temple prayers as data for historical reconstruction. The desire to reconstruct a historical person behind the "I" in the teacher hymns ultimately confuses vivid first-person speech with a genuine autobiographical voice and reflects how deeply entrenched modern biblical approaches are in idealized, Romantic understandings of authorship (Harkins 2012b).

Interest in the well-preserved sections of the teacher hymns and a concern to reconstruct a historical teacher led to the neglect of other aspects of the Hodayot scroll. The optimism with which scholars understood our ability to recover the historical context of Second Temple prayers took a turn in the 1980s with the first publications of the Cave 4 scrolls. The publication of these Cave 4 manuscripts had been eagerly awaited because they were thought to contain key information about the group's origins. Along with the publication of the most fragmentary and plentiful cave came a new (healthy) skepticism toward historically dominant approaches and our ability to recover a historical Teacher of Righteousness. Clear evidence of this change in attitude can be seen for the first time in discussions of Qumran scroll 4QMMT and the Cave 4 copies of the pesharim that were historicizing commentaries on biblical prophetic texts (Hempel 2013, 5).

With the publication of the Cave 4 Hodayot manuscripts (4Q427–4Q432) in the 1990s, scholars became aware of a remarkable composition known popularly as the Self-Glorification Hymn (Schuller 1999; Eshel 1999). Four copies of the Self-Glorification Hymn were identified in two versions: a long version (4Q427 [4QH^a] 7; 4Q431 [4QH^e] 1 [=4Q471b]; 1QH^a XXV, 34–XXVII, 3) and a short version (4Q491c) that may have been part of a War Scroll text (García Martínez 2007). This text describes a speaker in the heavenly realm, even higher than the angels. Scholars continue to debate the identity of the speaker of this stunning text, with the dominant views being the Teacher of Righteousness or the eschatological high priest. The text also generated studies that sought to trace continuity between forms of Second Temple mysticism and later forms of Judaism (Alexander 2006). The remarkable otherworldly and heavenly orientation of this psalm has exerted very little impact on the study of the Hodayot collection, largely because the Cave 4 manuscripts in which this composition was found had been published long after studies of 1QH^a had become well established. While the Self-Glorification Hymn generated much interest, it is most often encountered amid discussions of other non-Hodayot texts that speak of liturgical or eschatological matters, and regrettably it has not been well-integrated into the larger scholarly understanding of the Hodayot themselves.

Like the Cave 4 Hodayot that were published in the 1990s, other significant noncanonical psalm collections from this cave give further evidence of the rich diversity of prayers known from the Qumran discovery. One of the ongoing debates surrounding these apocryphal psalms collections is the relationship between the texts and the Qumran movement. While some of these have been closely associated with the Qumran movement from the start, other texts have disputed relationships with the Qumran group. The Songs of the Sage (two copies: 4Q510, 4Q511) have long been associated with the Qumran movement based on the appearance of some sectarian imagery and language: "*yaḥad*," "sons of light," and "men of the covenant" (Nitzan 1994, 235–37). The collection includes prayers for the sage (*maskil*) to "frighten and terrify evil spirits." Another collection (4Q434–4Q438) of nonbiblical prayers is known as Barkhi Nafshi because their resemblance to the biblical thanksgiving psalms 103 and 104 (Weinfeld and Seely 1999, 255). Even though these scrolls lack explicit sectarian language, the Discoveries in the Judaean Desert editors of the scroll presumed a Qumranic identification based on the late dating, full orthographic style, and general thematic resemblance to the Hodayot (Weinfeld and Seely 1999). Others remain unpersuaded and argue strongly that this is not a sectarian text, but that the prayer's language and imagery speak to an experience that could have been readily appropriated by the Qumran group (Brooke 2000). Mika Pajunen (2013, 66–70) asks if there is a discernable rationale for bringing these prayers—but not the biblical Barkhi Nafshi in Pss 103–104—into a single collection. These nonbiblical Barkhi Nafshi prayers share common themes and concerns by rehearsing past experiences in a way that anticipates future events. According to Pajunen, this type of identification of the group with the collective experiences of the past is a perspective that is not shared by the biblical Barkhi Nafshi psalms in the MT psalter, thus accounting for why the two groups of Barkhi Nafshi prayers were not combined into a single collection (69–70). As is true of many of the Cave 4 scrolls, 4Q434–4Q438 are extremely fragmentary, making it difficult to draw definitive conclusions about the precise contents of any given collection.

All of these Cave 4 prayer collections were categorized as apocryphal psalms—terminology that is seen as problematic today because it presumes an anachronistic understanding of canon. Other scrolls that routinely fall under the rubric of apocryphal psalms include 4Q380 and 4Q381 (4QNon-Canonical Psalms A and B). These psalms lack explicit Qumranic language, thus leading Schuller (2006) to date them prior to the movement, as early as the Persian or Hellenistic period, on linguistic grounds. This early group of prayers shows a strong influence from Deuteronomistic theology and contains prayers that are pseudepigraphically attributed to biblical prophets and different Judean kings: Obadiah, Manasseh, and a man-of-God. Another scroll, 11Q11 (11QapocrPs), consists of three heretofore unknown compositions for exorcism (I, 1–10; II, 1–V, 3; V, 4–VI, 3), which appear alongside a fourth exorcistic psalm, Ps 91 (VI, 4–14). Scholars reconstructed the name of David near the beginning of psalms one and two, but only the third psalm shows a clear and unambiguous reference to David (Puech 2000; Sanders 1997). While the fourth text, Ps 91, is not associated with David in the MT, it is associated with him in the LXX and appears with the superscription, "An Ode to David." The psalm references several dangers (e.g., the terror of the night, the plague, various monsters) and describes the speaker's deliverance from them. The collection concludes with the directive, "and they shall answer: Amen Amen," a clear indication of ritual use. Reading this scroll in light of the Great Psalms Scroll (11Q5), some argued in favor of understanding the exorcistic psalms collection in 11Q11 as the Davidic psalms referenced in 11Q5 as David's four psalms "for the afflicted" (Puech 2000; Sanders 1997), while others argued that the fragmentary scroll gives inconclusive evidence for only four compositions since more may have been in the scroll. Additional unresolved questions about 11Q11 have to do with the function of the scroll in the life of the group. Some scholars favor expanding the narrow understanding that 11Q11 was used only for exorcisms, proposing instead that this prayer collection functioned calendrically (Maier 1992). It is also possible to combine these views and argue that the apotropaic prayers in 11Q11 were recited on specific intercalary days (Eshel 2003). Exorcistic prayer collections like those found in 11Q11, along with texts like 4Q560 and 4Q510–511 (4QSongs of the Sage[a, b]), speak well to the performative aspects of prayers during the Second Temple period and their apotropaic function. While the Songs of the Sage are a nonbiblical prayer collection commonly identified as Qumranic based on its language and terminology, several of the Cave 4 prayer collections do not show overt signs of sectarian language or theology, thereby raising important questions about how these collections functioned at Qumran.

8. Other Early Jewish Nonbiblical Prayer Collections

The study of nonbiblical prayer collections pseudonymously attributed to the biblical king Solomon, the Odes of Solomon and the Psalms of Solomon, has notably increased in recent years. The Odes of Solomon are a collection of forty-two compositions that were highlighted in Charlesworth's (1986) essay in the first edition of the *Early Judaism and Its Modern Interpreters* (Kraft and Nickelsburg 1986). Study of this prayer collection has experienced a resurgence in the past forty years, as is evident in Michael Lattke's (2009) Hermeneia commentary, which synthesizes much of this recent work. Several studies examine the collection and its relationship to other biblical genres, including its pseudonymous attribution to Solomon (Franzmann 1991; Novak 2012). Closely associated with the Odes of Solomon in both the Greek and Syriac manuscript traditions is another collection of eighteen psalms known as the Psalms of Solomon, which is dated to Pompey's first-century BCE conquest of Jerusalem (e.g., Ps. Sol. 8.15–18). Scholarship on the Psalms of Solomon is driven by a historical interest in the late Second Temple period and also philological interest in the Greek and Aramaic of these prayers. The Psalms of Solomon have also been the subject of recent research symposia and edited volumes (Bons and Pouchelle 2015; Atkinson, Keddie and Pouchelle 2021), with new questions about the ritual and possible liturgical use of these texts being raised (Werline 2015, 2017). The proceedings of the third international meeting on the Psalms of Solomon held at Aix-Marseille University are forthcoming.

9. Disciplinary Shifts toward the Study of Religion

Since the first *Early Judaism and Its Modern Interpreters* (Kraft and Nickelsburg 1986), a significant disciplinary shift has taken place in the field of religious studies that had become increasingly critical of the undue prioritization of disembodied religious thought—namely doctrines or theological teachings—choosing instead to highlight alternative ways of understanding religion through practices and actions. Two major developments emerged as a result of this welcome change. The first is the expansion of methods used for studying early Jewish prayers resulting from the turn to the body and material culture. The second is an increased interest in the function of prayers and their effects on individuals and groups. Even so, a full understanding of the most basic questions about how these texts were experienced by the people of the past remains to be constructed.

9.1. The Body and Other Material Considerations

The turn to the body in religious studies has highlighted new approaches that have begun to gain traction in the study of prayer. Scholars are increasingly interested in how these prayers relate to the people of the past and have applied emotion-studies, sociological, anthropological, and cognitive-science-based approaches to these prayers (e.g., Jokiranta 2017; Reif and Egger-Wenzel 2015). As first-person writings, early Jewish prayers can be profitably analyzed as performative texts, along with a constellation of approaches associated with liturgy, worship, and ritual. Heightened attention to the body has also opened up a space to consider the lived experience of religion, including: the embodied mind, perceptions of spatiality, locomotion, and the senses; aspects of gender and sexuality; social and political contexts; and other material conditions (e.g., McDowell 2006; Harkins 2012a).

The scripturalizing language found in Second Temple prayers (Newman 1999) draws on the emotional impact of foundational experiences from a narrative past in order to ritually reconstitute them in the present moment. The scripted emotions and other ritual practices accompanying these texts allow for a performative staging that ultimately works to cultivate long-lasting religious dispositions and piety that can far exceed the moments of the ceremony itself. In the case of Second Temple prayers that use ritual mourning practices, the state of rumination that can be achieved can also have other long-lasting effects, including making presence from absence (Harkins 2017). Narrative prayers can also be said to have a propaedeutic function (cf. Gordley 2011), to teach about foundational events to groups after the exile, and to cultivate desired emotional dispositions so that a ritual preparedness can be achieved. Studies of the role of emotions in ancient ritual highlight the importance of staging and underscore how rituals aim to achieve a multisensory and immersive effect (Lieber 2015). Imaginative processes participate in how the reading process can achieve a simulation of physical bodyliness. Reading, in other words, is an activity that presumes mimetic bodily responses. Today, scholars acknowledge that the cognitive processes involved in imaginative reading are complex bodily ones, and the same is true for the activity of praying.

The move from seeing prayers as historical or literary writings to recognizing them as ritual texts has only just begun in recent years. Ritual studies have long understood reenactment as the imitative performance of key actions and behaviors. It is also the case that prayers cultivate emotional predispositions that may be preparatory for certain ritual experiences (Harkins 2012a). Furthermore, ritual studies have pushed scholars away from overdetermined understandings of people in the past, embracing a greater appreciation for the ways in which individuals experience prayers and religious practices in a multiplicity of ways. Michael Swartz (1997, 153) rightly notes that ritual reading is a far more complex bodily experience than most text-based scholars realize. The recovery of the body's role in performative dimensions of reading and praying is part of the larger disciplinary move away from the Cartesian dualism that bifurcates the mind and body.

One noteworthy conclusion of these new broad-based inquiries is an appreciable awareness of the complexity of ancient people and the realization that the models of Judaism (e.g., Greek-speaking Judaism; Semitic-speaking Judaism) which had long governed how scholars imagined the Second

Temple period actually *masked* important features of living, flesh-and-blood communities.

9.2. The Formation of Group and Individual Identity

Recent inquiry into how prayers shape social identity during the postexilic period and beyond constitutes a significant and promising line of study (Gerhards, Doeker, and Evenbauer 2003; Brooke 2017; Brettler 2017). This push to analyze the effects of prayers on the individuals and groups who prayed them can be situated alongside a complementary concern to understand how prayer might help explain aspects of the experience of religion in general. The relationship between group and individual identity has also been raised in the study of prayer texts. Carol Newsom's *Self as Symbolic Space* (2004) is an important marker of this tension. One of Newsom's driving questions is to investigate how prayer functions to form identity and construct the self. Her book is a pioneering study of the rhetorical function of prayers at Qumran. By turning away from historical questions and moving toward questions of experience, Newsom opened the door to larger unexplored topics like the application of ritual studies to early Jewish prayers (Arnold 2006; Harkins 2012a) and the examination of the larger religion of the people of the scrolls (Collins 2012). These studies of ritual approaches have also opened the door to new studies of the cognitive effects of ritually performing prayer on the people who pray them. In addition to asking questions about the horizontal effect of prayer on the groups who pray them, scholars have also begun asking about the vertical effects of prayer of making otherworldly realia accessible to the practitioner (Alexander 2006; Harkins 2012a). In the case of early Jewish prayers, this includes a realization that ritually experiencing otherworldly realia like angelic beings and heavenly spaces were important considerations for the authors of these texts.

The turn to the self that characterizes the late twentieth century is informed by changes in the social sciences and manifest in recent studies of early Jewish prayers that focus on the individual practitioner and his/her experiences. While theorized institutional models describe religion in antiquity on a grand scale, they tend to overdetermine the effect of rituals on groups. For example, earlier studies of prayers spoke of how prayers construct monolithic and uniform communities in the past, such as the one constructed by scholars of the psalms who had assumed that the "I" predictably represents the *entire* people of Israel. Such a democratizing approach to the "I" in the psalms appeals to our expectations of what ideal egalitarian groups are like, but effectively removes any diversity and (conveniently) reduces ancient Israel to a single, uncomplicated experience. Scholars are right to reject simplistic top-down views of religious systems and practices. Even though it is more difficult, it is worthwhile to recover the lived experience of religion—individual experiences and the oftentimes-fluid nature of identity that happens within a larger pluralistic cultural context (Satlow 2008). This move to complicate historiographical models raises important questions about the commonplace conceptualization of a monolithic Qumran community, which prevailed at the time of the first publication of *Early Judaism and Its Modern Interpreters* (Kraft and Nickelsburg 1986), and favors, instead, a significantly more diverse and pluriform understanding of the Qumran movement.

10. Conclusions

The most important developments in the study of early Jewish prayer over the past several decades have come from two areas. First, the full publication of the Dead Sea Scrolls—especially the fragmentary prayer manuscripts from Cave 4—has introduced a trove of new data for early Jewish prayer. Second, the growing skepticism about our ability to recover history from prayer texts has led to the welcome broadening of methodological approaches beyond the traditional historical-critical approaches of source, form, and redaction criticism. Methods from religious studies have introduced important new questions and perspectives: What did these texts do to the ancient reader, and how did these texts contribute to the persistence of this kind of religion? The study of prayers is becoming recognized as an opportunity to investigate the complexities of the lived experience of religion—complexities that are part of flesh-and-blood experiences. The shift to the individual and the phenomenological experiences of the body that has happened steadily in the social sciences during the last forty years has only recently emerged in the study of early Jewish prayers and offers promising new insights.

Bibliography

Alexander, Philip S. 2006. *Mystical Texts: Songs of the Sabbath Sacrifice and Related Manuscripts.* LSTS 61. London: T&T Clark.

Arnold, Russell C. D. 2006. *The Social Role of Liturgy in the Religion of the Qumran Community*. STDJ 60. Leiden: Brill.
Atkinson, Kenneth, G. Anthony Keddie, and Patrick Pouchelle, eds. 2021. *The Psalms of Solomon: Texts, Contexts, and Intertexts*. Atlanta: SBL Press.
Baillet, Maurice. 1982. *Qumrân grotte 4.III (4Q482–4Q520)*. DJD 7. Oxford: Clarendon.
Balentine, Samuel E. 1993. *Prayer in the Hebrew Bible: The Drama of Divine-Human Dialogue*. OBT. Minneapolis: Augsburg Fortress.
Baumgarten, Joseph, et al. 1999. *Qumran Cave 4.XXV: Halakhic Texts*. DJD 35. Oxford: Clarendon.
Bautch, Richard J. 2003. *Developments in Genre Between Post-exilic Penitential Prayers and the Psalms of Communal Lament*. AcBib 7. Atlanta: Society of Biblical Literature.
Boda, Mark J. 1999. *Praying the Tradition: The Origin and the Use of Tradition in Nehemiah 9*. BZAW 277. Berlin: de Gruyter.
Boda, Mark J., Daniel K. Falk, and Rodney A. Werline, eds. 2006–2008. *Seeking the Favor of God*. 3 vols. EJL 21–23. Atlanta: Society of Biblical Literature.
Bons, Eberhard, and Patrick Pouchelle. 2015. *The Psalms of Solomon: Language, History, Theology*. EJL 40. Atlanta: SBL Press.
Bradshaw, Paul F. 2002. *The Search for the Origins of Christian Worship: Sources and Methods for the Study of Early Liturgy*. 2nd ed. Oxford: Oxford University Press.
Brettler, Marc Zvi. 2017. "Those Who Pray Together Stay Together: The Role of Late Psalms in Creating Identity." Pages 279–304 in *Functions of Psalms and Prayers in the Late Second Temple Period*. Edited by Mika S. Pajunen and Jeremy Penner. BZAW 486. Berlin: de Gruyter.
Brooke, George J. 2000. "Body Parts in Barkhi Nafshi and the Qualifications for Membership of the Worshipping Community." Pages 79–94 in *Sapiential, Liturgical and Poetical Texts from Qumran: Proceedings of the Third Meeting of the International Organization for Qumran Studies, Published in Memory of Maurice Baillet*. Edited by Daniel K. Falk, Florentino García Martínez, and Eileen M. Schuller. STDJ 35. Leiden: Brill.
———. 2017. "Praying History in the Dead Sea Scrolls: Memory, Identity, Fulfilment." Pages 305–19 in *Functions of Psalms and Prayers in the Late Second Temple Period*. Edited by Mika S. Pajunen and Jeremy Penner. BZAW 486. Berlin: de Gruyter.

Charlesworth, James H. 1986. "Jewish Hymns, Odes, and Prayers (Ca. 167 B.C.E.–135 C.E.)." Pages 411–36 in *Early Judaism and Its Modern Interpreters*. Edited by Robert A. Kraft and George W. E. Nickelsburg. BMI 2. Philadelphia: Fortress; Atlanta: Scholars Press.

Chazon, Esther G. 1998. "Hymns and Prayers in the Dead Sea Scrolls." Pages 244–70 in vol. 1 of *The Dead Sea Scrolls after Fifty Years: A Comprehensive Assessment*. Edited by Peter W. Flint and James C. VanderKam. 2 vols. Leiden: Brill.

———. 2006. "Scripture and Prayer in 'the Words of the Luminaries.'" Pages 25–41 in *Prayers That Cite Scripture: Biblical Quotation in Jewish Prayers from Antiquity through the Middle Ages*. Edited by James L. Kugel. Cambridge: Harvard University Press.

———. 2012. "Liturgy before and after the Temple's Destruction: Change or Continuity?" Pages 371–92 in *Was 70 CE a Watershed in Jewish History? On Jews and Judaism Before and After the Destruction of the Second Temple*. Edited by Daniel R. Schwartz and Zeev Weiss. AJEC 78. Leiden: Brill.

Chazon, Esther, et al. 1999. *Qumran Cave 4.XX. Poetical and Liturgical Texts, Part 2*. DJD 29. Oxford: Clarendon.

Collins, John J. 2012. "Prayer and the Meaning of Ritual in the Dead Sea Scrolls." Pages 69–85 in *Prayer and Poetry in the Dead Sea Scrolls and Related Literature: Essays in Honor of Eileen Schuller on the Occasion of Her Sixty-Fifth Birthday*. Edited by Jeremy Penner, Ken M. Penner, and Cecilia Wassen. STDJ 98. Leiden: Brill.

Davila, James R. 2000. *Liturgical Works*. ECDSS. Grand Rapids: Eerdmans.

Egger-Wenzel, Renate, and Jeremy Corley, eds. 2004. *Prayer from Tobit to Qumran: Inaugural Conference of the ISDCL at Salzburg, Austria, 5–9 July 2003*. DCLY 2004. Berlin: de Gruyter.

Eshel, Esther. 1999. "Self-Glorification Hymn." Pages 421–35 in *Qumran Cave 4.XX. Poetical and Liturgical Texts, Part 2*. Edited by Esther Chazon et al. DJD 29. Oxford: Clarendon.

———. 2003. "Apotropaic Prayers in the Second Temple Period." Pages 69–88 in *Liturgical Perspectives: Prayer and Poetry in Light of the Dead Sea Scrolls; Proceedings of the Fifth International Symposium of the Orion Center for the Study of the Dead Sea Scrolls and Associated Literature, 19–23, January, 2000*. Edited by Esther G. Chazon, Ruth Clements, and Avital Pinnick. STDJ 48. Leiden: Brill.

Eshel, Esther, et al. 1998. *Qumran Cave 4.VI: Poetical and Liturgical Texts, Part 1*. DJD 11. Oxford: Clarendon.

Falk, Daniel K. 1998. *Daily, Sabbath, and Festival Prayers in the Dead Sea Scrolls*. STDJ 27. Leiden: Brill.
——. 1999. "Prayer in the Qumran Texts." Pages 852–76 in *The Early Roman Period*. Edited by William Horbury, W. D. Davies, and John Sturdy. CHJ 3. Cambridge: Cambridge University Press.
——. 2010. "The Contribution of the Qumran Scrolls to the Study of Ancient Jewish Liturgy." Pages 617–51 in *The Oxford Handbook of the Dead Sea Scrolls*. Edited by Timothy H. Lim, and John J. Collins. Oxford: Oxford University Press.
——. 2014. "Material Aspects of Prayer Manuscripts at Qumran." Pages 33–87 in *Literature or Liturgy? Early Christian Hymns and Prayers in Their Literary and Liturgical Context in Antiquity*. Edited by Clemens Leonhard and Hermut Löhr. WUNT 2/363. Tübingen: Mohr Siebeck.
Flint, Peter W. 1997. *The Dead Sea Psalms Scrolls and the Book of Psalms*. STDJ 17. Leiden: Brill.
Flusser, David. 1984. "Psalms, Hymns and Prayers." Pages 551–77 in *Jewish Writings of the Second Temple Period: Apocrypha, Pseudepigrapha, Qumran, Sectarian Writings, Philo, Josephus*. Edited by Michael E. Stone. CRINT 2.2. Philadelphia: Fortress; Assen: Van Gorcum.
Franzmann, Majella. 1991. *The Odes of Solomon: An Analysis of the Poetical Structure and Form*. NTOA 20. Fribourg: Universitätsverlag; Göttingen: Vandenhoeck & Ruprecht.
García Martínez, Florentino. 2007. "Old Texts and Modern Mirages: The 'I' of Two Qumran Hymns." Pages 105–25 in *Qumranica Minora*. Edited by Florentino García Martínez and Eibert J. C. Tigchelaar. Leiden: Brill.
García Martínez, Florentino, Eibert J. C. Tigchelaar, and Adam S. van der Woude. 1998. *Qumran Cave 11.II: (11Q2–18, 11Q20–31)*. DJD 23. Oxford: Clarendon.
Gerhards, Albert, Andrea Doeker, and Peter Evenbauer, eds. 2003. *Identität durch Gebet: Zur gemeinschaftsbildenden Funktion institutionalisierten Betens in Judentum und Christentum. Studien zu Judentum und Christentum*. Paderborn: Schöningh.
Gordley, Matthew E. 2011. "Didactic Hymns in the Dead Sea Scrolls." Pages 231–68 in *Teaching through Song in Antiquity: Didactic Hymnody among Greeks, Romans, Jews, and Christians*. WUNT 2/302. Tübingen: Mohr Siebeck.
Greenberg, Moshe. 1983. *Biblical Prose Prayer as a Window to the Popular Religion of Ancient Israel*. Taubman Lectures in Jewish Studies. Berkeley: University of California Press.

Gunkel, Hermann. 1967. *The Psalms: A Form-Critical Introduction*. FBBS 19. Philadelphia: Fortress.
Harkins, Angela K. 2012a. *Reading with an "I" to the Heavens: Looking at the Qumran Hodayot through the Lens of Visionary Traditions*. Ekstasis 3. Berlin: de Gruyter.
———. 2012b. "Who Is the Teacher of the Teacher Hymns? Re-Examining the Teacher Hymns Hypothesis Fifty Years Later." Pages 449–67 in *A Teacher for All Generations: Essays in Honor of James C. VanderKam*. Edited by Eric F. Mason, Alison Schofield, and Samuel I. Thomas. JSJSup 153. 2 vols. Leiden: Brill.
———. 2017. "The Function of Prayers of Ritual Mourning in the Second Temple Period." Pages 80–101 in *Functions of Psalms and Prayers in the Late Second Temple Period*. Edited by Mika S. Pajunen and Jeremy Penner. BZAW 486. Berlin: de Gruyter.
———. 2018. "Another Look at the Cave 1 Hodayot: Was CH I Materially Part of the Scroll 1QHodayot^a?" *DSD* 25:185–216.
Heinemann, Joseph. 1977. *Prayer in the Talmud: Forms and Patterns*. SJ 9. Berlin: de Gruyter.
Hempel, Charlotte. 2013. *The Qumran Rule Texts in Context: Collected Studies*. TSAJ 154. Tübingen: Mohr Siebeck.
Horst, Pieter W. van der, and Judith H. Newman. 2008. *Early Jewish Prayers in Greek*. CEJL. Berlin: de Gruyter.
Hughes, Julie A. 2006. *Scriptural Allusions and Exegesis in the Hodayot*. STDJ 59. Leiden: Brill.
Jokiranta, Jutta. 2017. "Towards a Cognitive Theory of Blessing: Dead Sea Scrolls as Test Case." Pages 25–47 in *Functions of Psalms and Prayers in the Late Second Temple Period*. Edited by Mika S. Pajunen and Jeremy Penner. BZAW 486. Berlin: de Gruyter.
Jonquière, Tessel M. 2007. *Prayer in Josephus*. AGJU 70. Leiden: Brill.
Kraft, Robert A., and George W. E. Nickelsburg, eds. 1986. *Early Judaism and Its Modern Interpreters*. BMI 2. Philadelphia: Fortress; Atlanta: Scholars Press.
Langer, Ruth. 1999. "Revisiting Early Rabbinic Liturgy: The Recent Contributions of Ezra Fleischer." *Prooftexts* 19:179–94.
———. 2018. "New Directions in Understanding Jewish Liturgy." Pages 147–73 in *Early Judaism: New Insights and Scholarship*. Edited by Frederick E. Greenspahn. Jewish Studies in the Twenty-First Century. New York: New York University Press.

Lattke, Michael. 2009. *The Odes of Solomon: A Commentary*. Hermeneia. Minneapolis: Fortress.

Leonhardt-Balzer, Jutta. 2001. *Jewish Worship in Philo of Alexandria*. TSAJ 84. Tübingen: Mohr Siebeck.

Lieber, Laura Suzanne. 2015. "Theater of the Holy: Performative Elements of Late Ancient Hymnography." HTR 108:327–55.

Maier, Johann. 1992. "Shîrê 'Ôlat hash-Shabbat: Some Observations on Their Calendric Implications and on Their Style." Pages 543–60 in *The Madrid Qumran Congress: Proceeding of the International Congress on the Dead Sea Scrolls, Madrid, 18–21 March, 1991*. Edited by Julio C. Trebolle Barrera and Luis Vegas Montaner. Leiden: Brill.

Malina, Bruce J. 1980. "What Is Prayer?" *TBT* 18:214–20.

Matlock, Michael D. 2012. *Discovering the Traditions of Prose Prayers in Early Jewish Literature*. LSTS 81. London: T&T Clark.

McDowell, Markus. 2006. *Prayers of Jewish Women: Studies of Patterns of Prayer in the Second Temple Period*. WUNT 2/211. Tübingen: Mohr Siebeck.

Miller, Patrick D. 1994. *They Cried to the Lord: The Form and Theology of Biblical Prayer*. Minneapolis: Fortress.

Mowinckel, Sigmund. 1962. *The Psalms in Israel's Worship*. New York: Abingdon.

Mroczek, Eva. 2016. *The Literary Imagination in Jewish Antiquity*. Oxford: Oxford University Press.

Newman, Judith H. 1999. *Praying by the Book: The Scripturalization of Prayer in Second Temple Judaism*. EJL 14. Atlanta: Scholars Press.

———. 2018. *Before the Bible: The Liturgical Body and the Formation of Scriptures in Early Judaism*. Oxford: Oxford University Press.

Newsom, Carol A. 2004. *The Self as Symbolic Space: Constructing Identity and Community at Qumran*. STDJ 52. Leiden: Brill.

Nitzan, Bilhah. 1994. *Qumran Prayer and Religious Poetry*. STDJ 12. Leiden: Brill.

Novak, Michael A. 2012. "The Odes of Solomon as Apocalyptic Literature." *VC* 66:527–50.

Pajunen, Mika S. 2013. *The Land to the Elect and Justice for All: Reading Psalms in the Dead Sea Scrolls in Light of 4Q381*. JAJSup 14. Göttingen: Vandenhoeck & Ruprecht.

Puech, Émile. 2000. "Les Psaumes davidiques du rituel d'exorcisme (11Q11)." Pages 160–81 in *Sapiential, Liturgical and Poetical Texts from Qumran: Proceedings of the Third Meeting of the International Organi-*

zation for Qumran Studies, Published in Memory of Maurice Baillet.* Edited by Daniel K. Falk, Florentino García Martínez, and Eileen M. Schuller. STDJ 35. Leiden: Brill.

Reif, Stefan C. 1993. *Judaism and Hebrew Prayer: New Perspectives on Jewish Liturgical History*. Cambridge: Cambridge University Press.

———. 2004. "Prayer in Early Judaism." Pages 439–64 in *Prayer from Tobit to Qumran: Inaugural Conference of the ISDCL at Salzburg, Austria, 5–9 July 2003*. Edited by Renate Egger-Wenzel and Jeremy Corley. DCLY 2004. Berlin: de Gruyter.

Reif, Stefan C., and Renate Egger-Wenzel, eds. 2015. *Ancient Jewish Prayers and Emotions: A Study of the Emotions Associated with Prayer in the Jewish and Related Literature of the Second Temple Period and Immediately Afterwards*. DCLS 26. Berlin: de Gruyter.

Reventlow, Henning. 1986. *Das Gebet im Alten Testament*. Stuttgart: Kohlhammer.

Sanders, James A. 1974. "Cave 11 Surprises and the Question of Canon." Pages 37–51 in *The Canon and Masorah of the Hebrew Bible*. Edited by S. Z. Leiman. New York: Ktav.

———. 1997. "Non-Masoretic Psalms (4Q88 = 4QPs^f, 11Q5 = 11QPs^a, 11Q6 = 11QPs^b)." Pages 155–215 in *Pseudepigraphic and Non-Masoretic Psalms and Prayers*. Vol. 4a of *The Dead Sea Scrolls: Hebrew, Aramaic, and Greek Texts with English Translations*. Edited by James H. Charlesworth and Henry W. L. Rietz. PTSDSSP. Tübingen: Mohr Siebeck; Louisville: Westminster John Knox.

Satlow, Michael L. 2008. "Beyond Influence: Toward a New Historiographic Paradigm." Pages 37–53 in *Jewish Literatures and Cultures: Context and Intertext*. Edited by Anita Norich and Yaron Z. Eliav. BJS 349. Providence, RI: Brown Judaic Studies.

Schuller, Eileen M. 1998. "The Use of Biblical Terms as Designations for Non-Biblical Hymnic and Prayer Compositions." Pages 207–22 in *Biblical Perspectives: Early Use and Interpretation of the Bible in Light of the Dead Sea Scrolls*. Edited by Michael E. Stone and Esther G. Chazon. STDJ 28. Leiden: Brill.

———. 1999. "Hodayot." Pages 69–254 in *Qumran Cave 4.XX. Poetical and Liturgical Texts, Part 2*. Edited by Esther G. Chazon et al. DJD 29. Oxford: Clarendon.

———. 2004. "Prayer at Qumran." Pages 411–28 in *Prayer from Tobit to Qumran: Inaugural Conference of the ISDCL at Salzburg, Austria, 5–9*

July 2003. Edited by Renate Egger-Wenzel and Jeremy Corley. DCLY 2004. Berlin: de Gruyter.

———. 2006. "Prayers and Psalms from the Pre-Maccabean Period." *DSD* 13:306–18.

Schuller, Eileen. M., and Carol A. Newsom. 2012. *The Hodayot (Thanksgiving Psalms): A Study Edition of 1QH^a*. EJL 36. Atlanta: Society of Biblical Literature.

Stegemann, Hartmut, Eileen Schuller, and Carol Newsom. 2009. *1QHodayot^a, with Incorporation of 1QHodayot^b and 4QHodayot^{a-f}*. DJD 40. Oxford: Clarendon.

Stuckenbruck, Loren T. 2007. "The Teacher of Righteousness Remembered: From Fragmentary Sources to Collective Memory in the Dead Sea Scrolls." Pages 75–94 in *Memory in the Bible and Antiquity: The Fifth Durham-Tübingen Research Symposium (Durham, September 2004)*. Edited by Stephen C. Barton, Loren T. Stuckenbruck, and Benjamin G. Wold. WUNT 212. Tübingen: Mohr Siebeck.

Swartz, Michael. 1997. "Ritual about Myth about Ritual: Towards an Understanding of the Avodah in the Rabbinic Period." *JJTP* 6:135–55.

Weinfeld, Moshe, and David Seely. 1999. "Barkhi Nafshi." Pages 255–334 in *Qumran Cave 4.XX: Poetical and Liturgical Texts, Part 2*. Edited by Esther Chazon et al. DJD 29. Oxford: Clarendon.

Werline, Rodney A. 1998. *Penitential Prayer in Second Temple Judaism: The Development of a Religious Institution*. EJL 13. Atlanta: Scholars Press.

———. 2007. "Reflections on Penitential Prayer: Definition and Form." Pages 209–25 in *The Development of Penitential Prayer in Second Temple Judaism*. Vol. 2 of *Seeking the Favor of God*. Edited by Mark J. Boda, Daniel K. Falk, and Rodney A. Werline. EJL 22. Atlanta: Society of Biblical Literature.

———. 2015. "The Formation of the Pious Person in the Psalms of Solomon." Pages 133–54 in *The Psalms of Solomon: Language, History, Theology*. Edited by Eberhard Bons and Patrick Pouchelle. EJL 40. Atlanta: SBL Press.

———. 2017. "The Imprecatory Features of *Psalms of Solomon* 4 and 12." Pages 48–62 in *Functions of Psalms and Prayers in the Late Second Temple Period*. Edited by Mika S. Pajunen and Jeremy Penner. BZAW 486. Berlin: de Gruyter.

Westermann, Claus. 1981. *Praise and Lament in the Psalms*. Atlanta: John Knox.

Wick, Peter. 2002. *Die urchristlichen Gottesdienste: Entstehung und Entwicklung im Rahmen der frühjüdischen Tempel-, Synagogen- und Hausfrömmigkeit.* BWANT 8. Stuttgart: Kohlhammer.

Willgren, David. 2016. *The Formation of the "Book" of Psalms: Reconsidering the Transmission and Canonization of Psalmody in Light of Material Culture and the Poetics of Anthologies.* FAT 2/88. Tübingen: Mohr Siebeck.

Wilson, Gerald H. 1985. *The Editing of the Hebrew Psalter.* SBLDS 76. Chico, CA: Scholars Press.

Part 4
The Afterlife of Early Judaism

20
Early Judaism and Rabbinic Judaism

ISHAY ROSEN-ZVI

1. Rabbis and Pharisees

Classical scholarship identified the rabbis as the heirs of the Pharisees, who disappeared from our sources after the destruction of the temple in 70 CE (Grabbe 1992; for the general debate whether or not the year 70 CE should be considered a watershed in Jewish history, see the articles gathered in Schwartz and Weiss 2011).[1] This identification satisfied a scholarly need to provide some kind of genealogy for the rabbis, who entered the arena almost ex nihilo after the destruction of the temple. Faced with the resounding historical success of the rabbinic movement in the fourth and fifth centuries, scholars searched for their predecessors and alighted upon the Pharisees. The identification was not groundless, however, but relied on three legs. The first was the similarity between the rabbinic and the Pharisaic halakah as well as both groups' self-perception as interpreters of the law. The second was that certain named individuals are prevalent in rabbinic literature that Josephus (Hillel, Rabban Gamaliel and Rabban

---

1. Since one cannot possibly cover in such a limited space the abundance of scholarly studies on rabbinic literature, I have followed these guidelines: Limiting myself to studies in the last three decades, I give precedence, especially in fields dense with bibliography, to most recent works particularly those that include bibliography to previous studies. I try to mark developments without discrediting old scholarship and without falling into triumphalism. I will elaborate in those areas that are least accessible to scholars from other areas. This is the reason I concentrate on compositions and texts rather than on themes and dwell specifically on text-centered and philologically driven studies. For more comprehensive surveys, see, e.g., Katz 2006; Safrai and Tomson 2006; Ben Eliyahu et al. 2012.

Shim'on b. Gamaliel) and Acts (Gamaliel) identify as Pharisees. The third is a continuity between the anti-Sadducean (and a group known in the Mishnah and Tosefta as the Boethusians, who might be the Essenes; see, e.g., m. Menah. 10:3; t. Kip. 10:8) path of the Pharisees, as depicted in both the New Testament and the rabbinic polemics. Additionally, because the rabbis are distant and critical of priests, especially the Sadducees, it stands to reason that they should be considered an outgrowth of the other large temple-era group, the Pharisees. However, as Morton Smith (1967; Neusner 1971; S. Cohen 1984; see, however, D. R. Schwartz 1983) and his students emphasized, there is a danger of circular reasoning here, for the narration of the Pharisees by Josephus as rabbinic-like scholars and leaders might be, in fact, affected by the rise of the rabbinic movement after the destruction.

Some scholars undermine the connection between temple-era Pharisees and postdestruction rabbis (Furstenberg 2016, 8–10; Schremer 2018, 561–63). The rabbis of the Mishnah never identify themselves as Pharisees, and references to a group by this name in Tannaitic literature are far from being unanimously positive (Neusner 1971). Albert Baumgarten (1983, 426) argues that the name *Pharisees* was a self-adopted moniker ("specifiers"), which hostile groups read in a derogatory sense ("separatists"). Some Tannaitic sources seem to follow the derogatory interpretation. While the term sometimes refers there to a specific group, similar to the Pharisees mentioned by Josephus and the gospels, as the opposition to the Sadducees (e.g., m. Yad. 3:6–8), in other places it is not used as a proper name, but rather refers to separatists in general (e.g., t. Sotah 15:11, t. Ber. 3:28). Ellis Rivkin (1969) justly warned against identifying all the occurrences of *perushim* with the Pharisees, especially when they are coupled with heretics, ascetics, or sectarians, or when they are opposed to "the people of the land," *am ha-aretz*. Shaye Cohen (1984) offered a stimulating compromise: the early rabbis were indeed the Pharisees' heirs, but they concealed this fact so not to be seen as partisans.

These questions about the Pharisees and the rabbis gained a fresh perspective upon the publication of fragments from a document known as Miqṣat Ma'aśê ha-Torah (4QMMT), found among the Dead Sea Scrolls. In a pioneering study of the document, Jacob Sussman (1989) showed that some of the disputes listed in the work are narrated in the Mishnah as disputes between Pharisees and Sadducees and that it is exactly the opinions the Mishnah attributes to the latter that 4QMMT actively espouses. The connections between Pharisees and rabbis are not straightforward, however. Thus, while Rabban Johanan b. Zakkai defends the pharisaic position in m. Yad. 4:6, he does not identify himself with them (Furstenberg 2012b).

Based on the general assumption of a continuation between Pharisees and rabbis, more recent studies attempted to reconstruct specific Pharisaic legislation from rabbinic literature, using source-critical methods to distinguish between older and newer layers. This was done especially with regard to purity legislation, on which we have a lot of material from all generations of the Tannaim (Shemesh 2009; Noam 2010; Furstenberg 2016). These scholars also offered criteria to determine, in every case of a legal difference between rabbinic literature and Qumranic works, whether the reason for the legal difference is a synchronic sectarian dispute, or a diachronic development in the postdestruction Jewish communities (Noam 2010, 353–59; Shemesh 2009, 3–7). The use of rabbinic literature as a gateway to the world of the Pharisees is predicated on an understanding that rabbinic literature is multilayered and that early traditions are preserved and reinterpreted by later layers but are not replaced. The result of this trend is far-reaching, as it effectively made social history both dependent on and secondary to literary and source criticism. Recent scholars have thus concentrated most of their efforts not on identifying hints of the historical Pharisees but on isolating various sources of Tannaitic traditions themselves, a change which allowed for a more fine-grained view of both continuity and change. But the criteria for source-criticism of the Mishnah are far from simple, and the methodological tools require sharpening (Furstenberg 2012a; Rosen-Zvi 2015b).

2. The Tannaitic Revolution

Regardless of the Pharisaic hypothesis, identifying early traditions in the Mishnah led scholars to examine the early phases of Tannaitic halakah. But lacking explicit attributions—for most of the Mishnah is anonymous—and since clear linguistic markers for antiquity are also rare, scholars tended to use content and genre as chronological markers, particularly tagging temple-related units as early. More recent scholarship, however, showed that various chapters and tractates considered authentic representatives of the temple and its cult are in fact products of deliberate formation in the Tannaitic study house. The rabbis were continuing to discuss temple-related matters, long after the temple was destroyed, as both a legal exercise and a place for theological speculations. The temple, in other words, was good to think with long after it was gone (Rosen-Zvi 2012a, 239–54).

Jacob Neusner (1981), in his vast oeuvre, shifted the focus from the sources of the Mishnah to its final form as a unified composition. This approach though, also has its drawbacks, (S. Cohen 1983). The Mishnah is a stratified work, and later strata do not obliterate the early ones (Zlotnick 1988). Furthermore, an editorial process similar to ones known from the contemporary world was foreign to the world of the rabbis (Elman 2004). In recent years a middle way has emerged. Instead of mining it for older traditions from the times of the temple, scholars have begun to evaluate rabbinic literature in its postdestruction setting, while at the same time being attuned to its different layers and gradual development in the Tannaitic academy (*beit midrash*) (for a review see Rosen-Zvi 2008).

Shaye Cohen (2007) offered a new classification for the sources of the Mishnah: (1) biblical verses; (2) Greco-Roman or Mesopotamian legal traditions (for the latter see Ayali-Darshan 2013; Milgram 2016); (3) customs observed by the general Jewish population; (4) temple-era traditions, both about the temple itself, and the workings of the high court (Sanhedrin); (5) priestly traditions; (6) laws of the pious and other sectarian sources. Cohen then concluded that most of the Mishnah does not harken from any of these sources, but rather was created in the Tannaitic study houses in Judaea and the Galilee. A different type of classification of Mishnaic laws, based on style and rhetoric rather than sources, was offered by Moshe Simon-Shoshan (2012). He showed that, contrary to previous scholarship (e.g., Frankel 2005), there is no dichotomous division between law and narrative in the Mishnah, but rather legal narratives are an integral component of the halakic conversation. They are, furthermore, but one extreme of a sequence of levels of narrativity in presenting the law, which range from direct apodictic instructions to complex exempla narratives.

There is no consensus in recent scholarship (on nineteenth-century discussions, see C. Gafni 2011) as to the causes of the birth and growth of the rabbinic study house after the temple's destruction and the new modes of scholarship that emerged from this: the Mishnah, legal debate arranged topically, and Midrash, exegesis arranged according to the order of the Pentateuch. Some have attributed this growth to the need to organize early traditions in the chaotic state of postdestruction Judea (Albeck 1959; cf. Schremer 2010). Others have pointed to the destruction as a harbinger of a *conceptual* shift, which compelled the Tannaim to offer a broad vision for a better world (Kraemer 2006, 313) or to shut themselves in their study houses in an attempt to build a textual replacement for the disappointing world outside (Neusner 1983). Still others have read the Mishnah as an attempt to create a unified halakah to counter sectarianism (Goldberg 1987) or as a foil to Christian polemics, with an emphasis on the antiquity of its law (Yuval 2011). Lastly, some have pointed to the Mishnah as an organic development, a need to organize and archive the quickly growing body of knowledge (Naeh 2005). All these suggestions are quite speculative by nature, point to different aspects of the Mishnah, and are not mutually exclusive.

3. The Redaction and the Oral Transmission of the Mishnah

New trends in scholarship are also apparent on the question of the redaction of the Mishnah in the third-century. Chanoch Albeck (1959) and Jacob N. Epstein (2000) debated whether the Mishnah was meant to be an anthology or a law book. More recent scholars have begun to examine new directions in order to break down this dichotomy. Such is the attempt to connect the Mishnah to the first redacted Roman law books in the second century (Elman 2004). Another direction emphasizes the didactic dimensions of the Mishnah's redaction, in which other, nonlegal, considerations are employed in redaction (Goldberg 1987; Alexander 2006). Yet another is an attempt to separate the redaction of the Mishnah from its reception. While the Mishnah was created as an anthology, the first generations of the Amoraim transformed it into a law book. They achieved this goal by employing rules of precedence developed in the study house of R. Yohanan, thus making it possible to decide the actual halakah from the undecided debated recorded in the Mishnah (Brandes 2002).

The Mishnah is the epitome of one of the most original and peculiar concepts of rabbinic culture: Oral Torah (*torah she-beal pe*). But, before we can discuss the ideology behind this concept, the very technology of oral transmission should be examined. Saul Lieberman (1950) was the first to suggest that a work could be published orally, by making one version mandatory, and teaching it to all reciters in the various study houses. However, Lieberman left open the possibility that the Mishnah was *also* written, in notes and on writing tablets, with no formal standing. That door was closed by Sussman (2005) in a detailed study in which he conclusively proved that the Mishnah existed only in an oral form. There is not any evidence in rabbinic literature that the Mishnah was known in any written mode of transmission. Even for cases of doubt or dispute, the Talmuds never mention that rabbis checked a written copy of Mishnah in order to decide upon a reading. Scholars also turned to orality studies to understand the Mishnah better (Jaffee 2001; Alexander 2006). Moulie Vidas (2017) has shown that while the Mishnah was *transmitted* orally, its earliest audiences talked about it as a book, possibly as an effect of contemporaneous Hellenistic and Christian written cultures. This bookish sensitivity without books may explain the scholarly reluctance to accept its oral-only nature.

The rabbis insistence on keeping their own work oral while inhabiting a scholastic culture centered on a canon of books is somewhat paradoxical; four main reasons for this have been advanced. First, Martin Jaffee (2001, 142–52) connects rabbinic orality to Hellenistic philosophical approaches, according to which wisdom must be passed orally, as a living tradition, from student to teacher. Hellenistic suspicion of writing, however, did not preclude the production of many written works, so it is unclear how this ethos would have had this kind of impact on the rabbis. Second, Israel Yuval (2011; cf. Bregman 2004) reads the orality of the Mishnah as a polemic against the nascent Christian movement. Since the written torah is shared by both Jews and Christians, the rabbinic torah needs to be kept unwritten to maintain Jewish distinctiveness. It is questionable, however, whether we can ascribe such polemic already to the early rabbis. Third, Natalie Dohrmann (2015) reads this penchant for orality as an anti-Roman statement. Roman law was focused on documents and publication. The Tannaim create an alternative legal system in which laws are oral and kept under the imperial radar. However, it is unclear why writing, quite common in prerabbinic Jewish circles, would be marked specifically as Roman. Finally, after all that has been said on the matter since the publication of Sussman's "Oral Law" (2005), his own explanation still seems to me the simplest and the most convincing. The Mishnah needs to remain oral in order to mark its difference from the torah. There is only one kind of book in the Tannaitic academy: the holy books of scripture.

4. Tannaitic Halakah in Comparative Contexts

The comparandum of choice for Tannaitic halakah has shifted in the past two decades from Hellenistic (Lieberman 1942, 1950; Daube 1943; Fischel 1973) to Roman materials. This shift is connected to a conceptual change from thinking about cultural contexts in a scholastic mode to considering them through political lenses, specifically through the lens of the empire. Roman contexts feature not only in local studies on the sources of rabbinic laws (see, e.g., B. Cohen 1966; Dohrmann 2008; Milgram 2016), but also with regard to legal imagery (Tropper 2005), conceptualization (Moscovitz 2002, 163–200), rhetoric (Hidary 2018), and transmission (Hezser 2007).

Joshua Burns (2017) suggested reading these phenomena against the Constitutio Antoniniana, which granted Roman citizenship to all inhabitants of the empire in 212 CE, forcing Roman judges to contend with Jewish law. Yair Furstenberg (2018) claimed that similarities in the rhetorical terms and legal structures may betray a secondary shaping of the rabbinic law in ways comprehensible to Roman jurists, especially in areas of personal status, in which Roman authorities had special interest. Rabbinic legalistic discourse itself—much more developed and dense than anything known in prerabbinic halakah (Halbertal 2013)—was also read against the backdrop of Roman legalism (Dohrmann 2015). Hayim Lapin (2012) extended this trend further, claiming that the rabbis are to be read as a typical Roman provincial elite.

Scholars have questioned this trend on both the level of the details as well as of the big picture. Some asked whether Roman law did in fact affect rabbinic halakah, and if so how much (Katzoff 1989). Others asked how typically Roman were in fact the rabbis. The Mishnah is, after all, not a very typical provincial work. It avoids any attempt to adjudicate its role alongside the empire or its local authorities, instead presenting an entire independent legal world, replete with a king and a Sanhedrin, civil and criminal law, which is binding on Jews everywhere (S. Schwartz 2009; Rosen-Zvi 2016).

5. Midrash and Prerabbinic Biblical Interpretation

One of the oldest questions concerning the formation of rabbinic law is whether rabbinic legislation should be perceived as an actual product of biblical interpretation, as was the mainstay since the advent of *Wissenschaft des Judenthums* (Harris 1995), or whether it stems from an ancient oral tradition, which was only later superimposed upon scripture (Epstein 1955, 501–15; Albeck 1959 40–62). Following the seminal work of Ephraim Urbach (1958), many scholars tend to date Midrashic exegesis later than the study of freestanding halakic tradition (Herr 1979; Schremer 2001; Noam 2008).

Recently, these larger questions have given way to more specific discussions of the connections between midrash and the various modes of biblical interpretation in the Second Temple period.

5.1. Qumran

While some scholars point to various midrashic techniques in the halakic works from Qumran (Mandel 2001; Noam 2002; 2010, 330–36; Werman and Shemesh 2011, 51–71) others are more skeptical regarding this comparison. Steven Fraade (2011a) emphasized that halakic works from Qumran are arranged topically, like the Mishnah, or as rewritten scripture. Furthermore, the fact that Qumranic midrash is revealed only through comparative scholarly work, must itself be accounted for. Fraade (2011c; cf. Brooke 2009) questioned also the validity of early studies of pesher literature that read it as an early form of midrash (Hartog 2017). The comparisons between these phenomena, telling in and of itself, did not yield a genetic connection and did not assist us in reconstructing the historical origins of Midrash.

5.2. Paul

Midrash was often used to identify the underpinnings of Paul's biblical interpretation. Paul's freedom in verse quotation and usage of scripture was traditionally understood against the backdrop of the epistolary genre (Longenecker 1999). In a series of papers Menahem Kister (2007a, 2007b, 2010, 2014), suggested that Paul was not simply manipulating his audience but was engaging in sophisticated exegesis, in a manner similar to midrash. This opened the door to a new, more informed comparison between Paul's use of scripture with the rabbinic midrash; two radical attempts to form a holy community through radical (re)readings of scripture (Fisch 2018).

These debates are related to a more basic question of how to define midrash. Is it unique to rabbinic literature? Is it a literary genre that appears in various eras or a historically contingent phenomenon? Should it be viewed as a hermeneutic approach? (Teugels 2004; Bakhos 2006).

James Kugel (1998) was a pioneer of reading postbiblical literature as biblical exegesis. While the interpretive achievements of this paradigm are indisputable, scholars have questioned the methodology behind this endeavor (Reeves 2010; Lambert 2016). Hindy Najman (2003, 2010) and Eva Mroczek (2015) critiqued the assumptions behind reading Second Temple literature against the backdrop of the Bible, which reduced this rich and varied literature into an auxiliary material to the canon in the making (Satlow 2014; Collins 2017). Furthermore, the concept of interpretation in these works "seems to have expanded beyond exegesis, becoming a broader umbrella term for the use of or allusion to tropes, characters, symbols and expressions that also appear in biblical texts" (Mroczek 2016, 7–8).

Especially problematic is the use of rabbinic midrash as a key to understanding earlier literatures. For it implies a canonical, closed, and hierarchical model, in which a closed text is explicitly interpreted by professional interpreters who understand themselves as subjects of the interpreted texts. Scholars have suggested that rabbinic literature is to be considered the first Jewish culture centered around a biblical canon, the one, indispensable book (Sussman 2005; Dohrmann 2015). It is not the set number of books that was the cornerstone of the canonization project (Darshan 2007) but the nature of the rabbinic hermeneutic project itself, which was unprecedently radical and total. Although various scrolls of biblical books were not physically bound or stitched together in any way, the rabbis *conceptually* transformed their library of books into one whole book. The rabbis refuse to see their holy writ as part of a collection of books, instead forming an image of a single book (named simply thus, *sefer*). They have done so, as Dohrmann (2015) convincingly argues, by two complementary moves. On the one hand, they united all the books of their canon through the intertextual practice of midrash while at the same time dismissed all the other books from the study house. (The term *sefarim hitsonim* used by the rabbis for apocrypha refers to this process; see, e.g., m. Sanh. 10:1.) On the other hand, the rabbis maintained their own legislation and traditions in an exclusive oral form, thus maintaining the Bible as the only book in the study house.

Paul Mandel (2017) questions the adequacy of interpretation as an organizing principle with regard to rabbinic literature itself. The root *drš*, he argues, denotes, both in Qumran and in early rabbinic literature, preaching and teaching, not interpretation, as is commonly read. The latter meaning is an innovation of the generation of Rabbi Akiva in the second half of the second century. Although some of Mandel's readings are debatable, the study is an important corrective against wholesale attributions of interpretive motives to ancient literature.

6. Tannaitic Midrashic Compilations

In recent years, Menahem Kahana and his students have expanded the number of Tannaitic midrashic texts at our disposal. Kahana (2005) published all known Geniza fragments of halakic midrashim (excluding those of the Sifra, which will be published separately). These fragments (available now on the internet: http://www.jewishmanuscripts.org) often offer significantly better readings than those of the medieval manuscripts preserved in European libraries.

Kahana (1999b) also published a study of the two Mekiltot on the Amalek pericope (Exod 17:8–16). He showed that the two Mekiltot on Exodus, which originate from different midrashic schools, diverge only in their legal material, while the haggadic material is similar, and must thus been derived from a shared source, perhaps a circle of *ba'alei haggadah* (on which see Hirshman 2005). This material too was reworked by the midrashic schools. However, the version in the Mekilta of Rabbi Ishmael is less reworked and thus closer to the original than that of the Mekilta of Rabbi Shim'on. Kahana collected and summarized the scholarship on the field, and the findings of his own work in Kahana 2006. He also published a critical edition and commentary on Sifre Numbers (2011).

Side by side with the philological research, the study of midrashic hermeneutic also flourished in the last three decades. The harbinger of this revolution was Daniel Boyarin's (1990) *Intertextuality and the Reading of Midrash*. For Boyarin, the rabbinic reader reads the Torah not only as a finite text, a one-time collection of commandments and tales (*parole*) but as a lexicon of quotations (*langue*), from which the homilist can create and re-create new tales, almost without end. Midrashic interpretation is not readily apparent from the verse, but it is also not created by the homilist. Instead it is achieved by the reading of different versions in conjunction. The act of de- and recontextualization is the key to understanding how an innovative midrashic interpretation is made. Fraade (1991, and his programmatic essay 2011b) analyzed the idea of torah and its interpretation in the Tannaitic midrash Sifre Deuteronomy and discussed the complex relationship created between the work's interpretive, ideological, and rhetorical contexts. Christine Hayes (1997) pointed to similar models of intertextuality in the study of the Mishnah in the Babylonian Talmud. Moshe Halbertal (1997) discussed the hermeneutic assumptions of some Tannaitic legal homilies, and ascribed their divergence from the simple readings to their ideological and moral commitments. Taking a different tack, David Henshke (1994) read various Tannaitic legal opinions, seemingly far-fetched and divorced from scripture, as a result of a harmonistic hermeneutic, which is committed to solving repetitions and contradictions in the verses. In the introduction to his edition of the Tannaitic work *Seder Olam*, Chaim Milikowsky (2013) offers a mapping of various kinds of Tannaitic hermeneutics.

The study of midrashic hermeneutic moved lately to the legal contexts as well. While early work on the halakic parts of the Tannaitic midrashim busied itself with methods of reading mainly in order to distinguish between the schools of R. Akiva and R. Ishmael (Hoffmann 1888; Epstein 1955, 501–15), contemporary scholarship tackles them as an end in themselves. Scholars have studied various midrashic techniques and terms in order to decode their hermeneutic assumptions (Rosen-Zvi 2014). Azzan Yadin-Israel (2004) dedicated a monograph to Ishmaelian legal hermeneutics, arguing that it is guided and limited by cues in the text itself, which is conceived as the guide to its own interpretation. In a later book, on the hermeneutics of the midrashim of the school of R. Akiva, Yadin-Israel (2015) claims that the Akivan work Sifra applies a "hermeneutic of camouflage," presenting itself as a work of interpretation while in fact simply iterating traditions found in the Mishnah (but see Gvaryahu 2016).

Besides hermeneutics, are there also ideological differences between the two Tannaitic houses of R. Akiva and R. Ishmael? Marc Hirshman (1999) reconstructed the universalist tendency of the school of R. Ishmael, according to which the torah is meant for "all inhabitants of the world." Kahana (1999a) too argued, based on a comparing of statements in the two midrashic works on Deuteronomy, that the Ishmaelian Mekilta to Deuteronomy takes a more universalistic approach. Both studies however concentrate on haggadic statements and narratives only. I (Rosen-Zvi 2011) argued that the two Tannaitic schools reveal a different anthropology: *yetzer ha-ra* (the evil inclination) a quasi-demonic being that pulls people to sin, originated in the school of R. Ishmael, while the school of R. Akiva speaks only of a more neutral *yetzer*, which is neutral and decidedly undemonic in nature.

The comparative aspect of midrash has also recently been expanded significantly. In the Hellenistic context, Yakir Paz (2016) exposed significant connections between midrashic techniques and terms and counterparts in Alexandrian Homeric scholia, which predate them by several hundred years. These techniques are not found at Qumran and so cannot be accounted for as early Jewish traditions (for the search for Hellenistic background for the biblical interpretation at Qumran, see Hartog 2017). Paz (2012) further argues for a genetic model, in which Alexandrian methods were adopted by the rabbis, perhaps mediated by Alexandrian Jews (Niehoff 2011). In the Christian context, too, there is a recognition of the need to shift from polemic to comparative midrash, which focuses on textual conceptions and ideas of homiletics (Kister 2013).

Yonah Frankel shook the field of haggadic hermeneutics in the 1970s when he first read haggadic stories as high literature, using methods developed by new criticism (see the papers collected in Frankel 2001; unfortunately, none of his highly influential works were translated into English). In subsequent decades others methods and tools were added to the pallet. Eli Yassif (1999), Galit Hasan-Rokem (2000), and Dina Stein (2012) applied revamped techniques from the field of folklore and folk literature to haggadic stories. Joshua Levinson (2005) analyzed the complex relationship between narrative and commentary in the midrashic narrative, and noted the rise of narrativity with its internal logic, independently of midrashic reasoning, in the Babylonian Talmud. Barry Wimpfheimer (2011) and Boyarin (2009) cast doubt on the sharp distinction between halakah and haggadah in the Babylonian Talmud, presenting them instead as part of a unified dialectic move.

7. The Talmuds

The Palestinian Talmud (Yerushalmi) has always suffered from some neglect in comparison to its Babylonian (Bavli) counterpart. The text of the Yerushalmi is now available in a new edition according to its single complete manuscript (Sussmann 2001; for an evaluation of the edition, see Naeh 2002; for a collection of all the Geniza fragments of the Yerushalmi, see Sussmann 2020). Two reference works on Yerushalmi terminology have also been published (Moscovitz 2009; Assis 2010). A series of articles, published in three volumes, was dedicated to *The Talmud Yerushalmi and Greco-Roman Culture* (Schäfer and Hezser 1998–2002). Cahterine Hezser (1993; cf. Keshet 2008) published a study of the haggadah in Yerushalmi Nezikin.

The Yerushalmi is famously short, abrupt, and cryptic, but the reasons for that, especially in comparison to the expansive Bavli, are debated. Uzi Liebner (2009) showed that late fourth-century Galilee suffered from a population decline. Perhaps this explains the rushed redaction of the Yerushalmi.

With regard to the Bavli, too, a central innovation of recent years is electronic text. All known witnesses of the Bavli are now available in a dynamic online synoptic edition, with images of the manuscripts and genizah fragments, on the Friedberg Genizah Project (http://www.jewishmanuscripts.org; the basis of the Friedberg database is Sussmann 2012, on which see Reif 2014). Important studies of individual genizah fragments were published by Yoav Rosenthal (2003, 2007) and his students; more are in preparation now.

A series of new scholarly trends in the study of the Bavli makes this work a focal point of contemporary scholarly interest. Yaakov Elman (e.g.. 2005, 2009) reintroduced the Sassanian context to the study of the Bavli and others followed (Herman 2012; Secunda 2014; Kiel 2016; see also the studies collected in Bakhos and Shayegan 2010; Gabbay and Secunda 2014). Syrian Christianity is another context against which rabbinic literature, and especially the Bavli, has been newly reconsidered, especially in regard to narratives (e.g., Rubenstein 2017), polemic (Bar-Asher Siegal 2017), and individual traditions (Kalmin 2014). Various studies are devoted to the analysis of Bavli haggadah in relation to its earlier and more original Palestinian parallels (Rubenstein 2003), and to a discussion of the role of haggadah in the Bavli as a whole (Boyarin 2009; Wimpfheimer 2011; Wasserman 2017).

The building blocks of the Babylonian Talmud are discursive units of give and take called *sugiot* (sg. *sugia*). In the 1970s Shamma Friedman (1977) and David Weiss Halivni (2013; this is a translation of his programmatic introductions to his Hebrew critical commentary series, *Mekorot u-massorot* 1968–2012) precipitated a paradigm shift in the study of the Babylonian *sugia*, according to which the *sugia* is a product of a late redactional stratum. Peeling this stratum away reveals the early and authentic sources of the *sugia*. New scholarship, however, reads the *sugia* as a complex redacted entity that foils attempts at higher criticism. Attempts to reconstruct early phases of the *sugiot* were thus replaced in recent scholarship with analyses of the sophisticated literary and rhetorical devices used in the Talmudic *sugiot* (Vidas 2014; Septimus 2017).

8. Rabbis and Others

Tannaitic literature features but a few dialogues with others. The Mishnah (Yad. 4:6–8) offers a series of polemics between Sadducees and Pharisees (as well as with one "Galilean heretic"). Other Tannaitic texts offer a number of dialogues between rabbinic patriarchs of the Gamaliel family and Roman officials and laypeople (Hirshman 1999, ch. 10; Schremer 2010; Gvaryahu 2012; see, most famously, the visit of the two *strateotai* in Rabban Gameliel's study house in Sifre Deut 344 and parallels). Amoraic literature, on the other hand, is rich with anecdotes of encounters between rabbis and Roman officials, gentiles, heretics (*minim*), matrons, and prostitutes. Scholars debate whether these dialogues should be read as history or as rhetoric. The former method led to intense polemic as to the identity of the heretics in the sources, and especially the question of their relationship to Christians (Boyarin 2012 vs. Marcus 2009). Sussman's stance (Sussman 1989, 54 n. 176), that there are various kinds of heretics and that the sources do not present a unified *min* or a systematic heresiology, has become mainstream (e.g., Miller 1993).

Reading rabbinic-other dialogues as rhetoric understands them as projections of the rabbis own anxieties on others (Goodman 1996; Hayes 1998). Richard Kalmin (1994) noticed a shift from early sources, which treat *minim* as a real threat, to later ones, which treat them mostly as a joke. He debates whether this difference reflects different realities or different coping mechanisms. Recent work tend to treat the Tannaitic sources as more reliable historical information, and later sources, especially in the Babylonian Talmud (Hayes 1998), as products of an internal discourse, deployed for rhetorical purposes (I. Gafni 1997, 33 n. 20; Burns 2012, 140 n. 45).

More generally, rabbinics as a field has become increasingly closer to the study of contemporary nonrabbinic Jewish literature. Unlike the comparative studies marked in the paragraphs above, these studies do not seek, generally speaking, genetic connections, but rather try to read the rabbis as part and parcel of their broader environment. Various studies compared rabbinic literature to targumim (Shin'an 1985, 1991, 1992; Fraade 1992, 1998, 2006), liturgical poetry, *piyyut* (Elizur 1992; Münz-Manor 2006), magic (Bohak 2008), and *hekhalot* literature (Boustan 2005, 2011; Vidas 2014, 167–202). Milikowsky (2013, 15–17) suggested that *Seder Olam* is a protorabbinic work, which was created to oppose Jewish-Hellenistic historiography. Vered Noam (2003) published a new edition of The Scroll of Fasting, with a commentary focused on the relationship of the scholia to this early work to rabbinic literature. A new collaborative work by Noam and Tal Ilan (2017) explores parallel traditions in Josephus and rabbinic literature. It reads them not as genetically related but rather as two adaptation of a single oral corpus of early Pharisaic narratives.

9. Body, Gender, Sexuality in Rabbinic Literature

The field in which we witness the most radical change in scholarly sensitivity in recent years is that of gender studies (and related areas of body and sexuality.) Several monographs from the beginning of the 1990s (esp. Biale 1992; Boyarin 1993) marked a watershed in the study of rabbis and sexuality. These studies not only grafted the rabbis into the history of sexuality by examining their corporal and sexual ethos (Seidman 1994) but actively presented them as carnal and prosexuality and contrasted them with ascetic tendencies that rejected sexuality (or allowed it for procreative aim only). The rabbis were compared to Jewish Hellenistic writers like Philo, who is said to have loathed the body and its appetite (for a critique of this reading see Winston 1998), as well as to the disgust over human carnality and its contrast to divine grace found in sectarian texts like the Thanksgiving Scroll from Qumran (Sekki 1987). The most popular contrast, however, was with early Christian asceticism and monasticism, against the light of which rabbinic statement in favor of marriage and sex were read (Schremer 2003).

Scholars also contextualized the rabbis' attitudes toward sexuality as part of the larger picture of rabbinic anthropology, emphasizing the basic monism at the background of their conception of the body (Goshen-Gotstein 1994). If the classic Stoic attitude was labeled as a combination of cosmological and anthropological monism (everything is physical and rational) with ethical dualism (bodily appetites are base and should be restrained if not extinguished altogether; see Inwood 1985), the rabbinic attitude can be portrayed as the exact opposite: anthropological dualism (humans are constructed of body and soul) combined with ethical monism (no contrast between these parts; no negation of the body; no identification of the evil inclination with it; see Rosen-Zvi 2012b).

Others, however, questioned the common antiascetic narrative and presented a more complex picture (Fraade 1986). Based on a broader definition of ascetic practice, influenced mainly by Piere Hadot's and Michel Foucault's studies of Hellenistic and Roman *askesis*, they identified similar practices in rabbinic texts (Levinson 1998; Satlow 2003; Diamond 2004). Some argued that the rabbinic legislation on purities (*taharot*) and sacrifices (*kodashim*), which give unprecedented place to the mental state of the actors, should be also read as part of the Hellenistic *askesis* (Levinson 2012; Balberg 2014; but see Rosen-Zvi 2015a).

New sensitivities to problems of gender economy led to novel readings of rabbinic sources. While some feminist readings looked for different attitudes toward women in rabbinic sources (Hauptman 1998; Baskin 2002), others moved to the question of representations and constructions of sexual identity and roles themselves (Boyarin 1997; Fonrobert 2000; Kattan Gribetz 2013; Balberg 2014; see an analysis of two competing readings of the narrative in m. Nid. 8:3 in Rosen-Zvi 2005).

10. Summary

The last three decades saw the gap between the field of rabbinics and the study of Second Temple Judaism becoming smaller. This was achieved by two complementary moves. First, various studies looked for the origins of rabbinic practices, both legal and hermeneutic, in various Second Temple texts (Qumran, Philo, Paul, Josephus, etc.). At the same time, the rabbis were read side-by-side with and compared to all sorts of non- and prerabbinic literatures (targum and synagogue liturgy, magic and mysticism, historiography, pesharim and allegorical commentaries) and groups (Jewish Hellenism, sectarianism, Pharisees, Hasidism, early Christians, etc.), with no explicit genetic goal, but rather in order to see the rabbis in less isolation. Some recent studies read early rabbinic legal compositions as an integral part of the general Roman legalistic discourse. This latter move produced, however, some concern from forced comparisons that prevent us from acknowledging unique phenomena in rabbinic literature.

Two central areas that saw significant paradigm shifts in the last decades are midrashic hermeneutic and the study of the Babylonian *sugia*. The studies of body and gender as well as the constructions of self and other were also thoroughly transformed in recent years. In most other areas, however, a less heroic, more accumulative advance can be detected. New electronic databases have provided us with better texts and textual tools. Various kinds of research, such as that of midrashic terminology, were made possible in large scale due to easy computerized searches. We are also more adept and careful with eking history out of literary materials. Comparative studies, based on better texts and textual sensitivity, offer the most exciting promise. Greek, Latin, Syriac, and Persian materials allow us to take rabbinic literature out of the secluded study house and back into the streets of the late ancient cities and markets.

Bibliography

Albeck, Chanoch. 1959. *Introduction to the Mishnah* [Hebrew]. Jerusalem: Bialik.

Alexander, Elizabeth Shanks. 2006. *Transmitting Mishnah: The Shaping Influence of Oral Tradition*. New York: Cambridge University Press.

Assis, Moshe. 2010. *A Concordance of Amoraic Terms Expressions and Phrases in the Yerushalmi* [Hebrew]. 3 vols. New York: Jewish Theological Seminary of America.

Ayali-Darshan, Noga. 2013. "The Origin and Meaning of the Crimson Thread in the Mishnaic Scapegoat Ritual in Light of an Ancient Syro-Anatolian Custom." *JSJ* 44:530–52.
Bakhos, Carol. 2006. "Method(ological) Matters in the Study of Midrash." Pages 161–87 in *Current Trends in the Study of Midrash*. JSJSup 106. Leiden: Brill.
Bakhos, Carol, and M. Rahim Shayegan. 2010. *The Talmud in Its Iranian Context*. TSAJ 135. Tübingen: Mohr Siebeck.
Balberg, Mira. 2014. *Purity, Body, and Self in Early Rabbinic Literature*. Berkeley: University of California Press.
Bar-Asher Siegal, Michal. 2017. "Matthew 5:22: The Insult 'Fool'; and the Interpretation of the Law in Christian and Rabbinic Sources." *RHR* 234:5–23.
Baskin, Judith. 2002. *Midrashic Women: Formations of the Feminine in Rabbinic Literature*. Hanover: Brandeis University Press.
Baumgarten, Albert I. 1983. "The Name of the Pharisees." *JBL* 102:411–28.
Biale, David. 1992. *Eros and the Jews: From Biblical Israel to Contemporary America*. New York: Basic Books.
Bohak, Gideon. 2008. *Ancient Jewish Magic*. New York: Cambridge University Press.
Boustan, Ra'anan S. 2005. *From Martyr to Mystic: Rabbinic Martyrology and Making of Merkavah Mysticism*. TSAJ 112. Tübingen: Mohr Siebeck.
———. 2011. "Rabbinization and the Making of Early Jewish Mysticism." *JQR* 101:482–501.
Boyarin, Daniel. 1990. *Intertextuality and the Reading of Midrash*. ISBL. Bloomington: Indiana University Press.
———. 1993. *Carnal Israel: Reading Sex in Talmudic Culture*. Berkeley: University of California Press.
———. 1997. *Unheroic Conduct: The Rise of Heterosexuality and the Invention of the Jewish Man*. Berkeley: University of California Press.
———. 2009. *Socrates and the Fat Rabbis*. Chicago: University of Chicago Press.
———. 2012. "Once Again Birkat Hamminim Revisited." Pages 91–106 in *La Croisée Des Chemins Revisitée: Quand l'Eglise et la Synagogue se sont-elles distinguées? Actes du colloque de Tours 18–19 Juin 2010*. Edited by Simon Claude Mimouni and Bernard Pouderon. Paris: Cerf.
Brandes, Yehudah. 2002. "The Beginnings of the Rules of Halakhic Adjudication" [Hebrew]. PhD diss., Hebrew University of Jerusalem.

Bregman, Marc. 2004. "Mishnah and LXX as Mystery: An Example of Jewish-Christian Polemic in the Byzantine Period." Pages 333–42 in *Continuity and Renewal: Jews and Judaism in Byzantine-Christian Palestine*. Edited by Lee I. Levine. Jerusalem: Dinur Center; Yad Ben Zvi.

Brooke, George J. 2009. "From Bible to Midrash: Approaches to Biblical Interpretation in the Dead Sea Scrolls by Modern Interpreters." Pages 1–19 in *Northern Lights on the Dead Sea Scrolls: Proceedings of the Nordic Qumran Network 2003–2006*. Edited by Anders Klostergaard Petersen et al. STDJ 80. Leiden: Brill.

Burns, Joshua Ezra. 2012. "The Relocation of Heresy in a Late Ancient Midrash, or: When in Rome, Do as the Romans Do." *JSQ* 19:129–47.

———. 2017. "Roman Law in the Jewish House of Study: Constructing Rabbinic Authority after the Constitutio Antoniniana." Pages 293–307 in *Faces of Torah: Studies in the Texts and Contexts of Ancient Judaism in Honor of Steven Fraade*. Edited by Michal Bar Asher Siegal, Christine Hayes, and Tzvi Novick. JAJSup 22. Göttingen: Vandenhoeck & Ruprecht.

Cohen, Boaz. 1966. *Jewish and Roman Law: A Comparative Study*. New York: Jewish Theological Seminary of America.

Cohen, Shaye J. D. 1983. "Jacob Neusner, Mishna, and Counter-Rabbinics: A Review Essay." *Conservative Judaism* 37:48–63.

———. 1984. "The Significance of Yavneh: Pharisees, Rabbis, and the End of Jewish Sectarianism." *HUCA* 55:27–53.

———. 2007. "The Judean Legal Tradition and the Halakhah of the Mishnah." Pages 121–43 in *The Cambridge Companion to the Talmud and Rabbinic Literature*. Edited by Charlotte E. Fonrobert and Martin S. Jaffee. Cambridge: Cambridge University Press.

Collins, John J. 2017. *The Invention of Judaism: Torah and Jewish Identity from Deuteronomy to Paul*. Taubman Lectures in Jewish Studies 7. Oakland: University of California Press.

Darshan, Guy. 2007. "Twenty-Four or Twenty-Two Books of the Bible and the Homeric Corpus" [Hebrew]. *Tarbiz* 77:5–22.

Daube, David. 1943. "Civil Law of the Mishnah: The Arrangement of the Three Gates." *Tulane Law Review* 18:351–407.

Diamond, Eliezer. 2004. *Holy Men and Hunger Artists: Fasting and Asceticism in Rabbinic Culture*. Oxford: Oxford University Press.

Dohrmann, Natalie B. 2008. "Manumission and Transformation in Jewish and Roman Law." Pages 51–65 in *Jewish Biblical Interpretation and Cultural Exchange: Comparative Exegesis in Context*. Edited by Natalie

B. Dohrmann and David Stern. Jewish Culture and Contexts. Philadelphia: University of Pennsylvania Press.

———. 2015. "Can 'Law' Be Private? The Mixed Message of Rabbinic Oral Law." Pages 187–216 in *Public and Private in Ancient Mediterranean Law and Religion*. Edited by Clifford Ando and Jörg Rüpke. RVV 65. Berlin: de Gruyter.

Eliyahu, Eyal ben, Yehudah Cohn, Fergus Millar, and Philip S. Alexander, eds. 2012. *Oxford Handbook of Jewish Literature from Late Antiquity, 135–700 CE*. Oxford: Oxford University Press.

Elizur, Shulamit. 1992. "Mi-piyyut le-midrash." Pages 383–97 in vol. 2 of *Rabbi Mordechai Breuer Jubilee Volume*. 2 vols. Edited by Moshe Bar-Asher. Jerusalem: Academon.

Elman, Yaakov. 2004. "Order, Sequence, and Selection: The Mishnah's Anthological Choices." Pages 53–80 in *The Anthology in Jewish Literature*. Edited by David Stern. Oxford: Oxford University Press.

———. 2005. "The Other in the Mirror: Iranians and Jews View One Another; Questions of Identity, Conversion, and Exogamy in the Fifth-Century Iranian Empire, Part One." *Bulletin of the Asia Institute* 19:15–25.

———. 2009. "Middle Persian Culture and Babylonian Sages: Accommodation and Resistance in the Shaping of Rabbinic Legal Tradition." Pages 165–97 in *The Cambridge Companion to the Talmud and Rabbinic Literature*. Edited by Charlotte E. Fonrobert and Martin S. Jaffee. Cambridge: Cambridge University Press.

Epstein, Jacob N. 1955. *Prolegomena ad litteras tannaiticas: Mishna, Tosephta et Interpretationes Halachicas* [Hebrew]. Edited by E. Z. Melammed. Tel Aviv: Magnes; Jerusalem: Dvir.

———. 2000. *Introduction to the Text of the Mishnah* [Hebrew]. 3rd ed. Jerusalem: Magnes.

Fisch, Yael. 2018. "Paul's Interpretation of Scripture and the (Pre-)History of Midrash" [Hebrew]. PhD diss., Tel-Aviv University.

Fischel, Henry Albert. 1973. *Rabbinic Literature and Greco-Roman Philosophy: A Study of Epicurea and Rhetorica in Early Midrashic Writings*. StPB 21. Leiden: Brill.

Fonrobert, Charlotte. 2000. *Menstrual Purity: Rabbinic and Christian Reconstruction of Biblical Gender*. Contraversions. Stanford: Stanford University Press.

Fraade, Steven. 1986. "Ascetical Aspects of Ancient Judaism." Pages 253–88 in *Jewish Spirituality: From the Bible through the Middle Ages*. Edited by Arthur Green. World Spirituality 13. New York: Crossroad.

———. 1991. *From Tradition to Commentary: Torah and Its Interpretation in the Midrash Sifre to Deuteronomy*. SUNY Series in Judaica. Albany: State University of New York Press.

———. 1992. "Rabbinic Views on the Practice of Targum, and Multilingualism in the Jewish Galilee of the Third–Sixth Centuries." Pages 253–86 in *The Galilee in Late Antiquity*. Edited by Lee I. Levine. New York: Jewish Theological Seminary of America.

———. 1998. "Scripture, Targum, and Talmud as Instruction: A Complex Textual Story from the Sifra." Pages 109–22 in *Hesed Ve-Emet; Studies in Honor of Ernest S. Frerichs*. Edited by Jodi Magness and Seymour Gitin. BJS 320. Atlanta: Scholars Press.

———. 2006. "Locating Targum in the Textual Polysystem of Rabbinic Pedagogy." *BIOSCS* 39:69–91.

———. 2011a. "Looking For Legal Midrash At Qumran." Pages 145–67 in *Legal Fictions: Studies of Law and Narrative in the Discursive Worlds of Ancient Jewish Sectarians and Sages*. JSJSup 147. Leiden: Brill.

———. 2011b. "Moses and the Commandments: Can Hermeneutics, History, and Rhetoric Be Disentangled?" Pages 477–99 in *Legal Fictions: Studies of Law and Narrative in the Discursive Worlds of Ancient Jewish Sectarians and Sages*. JSJSup 147. Leiden: Brill.

———. 2011c. "Rabbinic Midrash and Ancient Jewish Biblical Interpretation." Pages 399–426 in *Legal Fictions: Studies of Law and Narrative in the Discursive Worlds of Ancient Jewish Sectarians and Sages*. JSJSup 147. Leiden: Brill.

Frankel, Yonah. 2001. *Sipur ha-agadah, aḥdut shel tokhen ve-tsurah: Kovets mehkarim*. Tel Aviv: Ha-kibbutz ha-meuchad.

———. 2005. "Ha-Aggadah Sheba-Mishnah." *Mehkerei Talmud* 3:683–55.

Friedman, Shamma. 1977. "A Critical Study of Yevamot X with a Methodological Introduction" [Hebrew]. Pages 275–441 in vol. 1 of *Texts and Studies: Analecta Judaica*. Edited by Hayim Zalman Dimitrovsky. 2 vols. New York: Jewish Theological Seminary of America.

Furstenberg, Yair. 2012a. "Early Redactions of Purities: Re-Examination of Mishnah Source-Criticism" [Hebrew]. *Tarbiz* 80:507–37.

———. 2012b. "'We Rail Against You, Pharisees': The Creation of the Pharisaic Worldview in the Mishnah" [Hebrew]. Pages 283–311 in *Halakhah: Explicit and Implied Theoretical and Ideological Aspects*. Edited by Avinoam Rosenack. Jerusalem: Van Leer.

———. 2016. *Purity and Community in Antiquity: Traditions of the Law from Second Temple Judaism to the Mishnah* [Hebrew]. Jerusalem: Magnes.

———. 2018. "The Rabbis and the Roman Citizenship Model: The Case of the Samaritans." Pages 181–216 in *In the Crucible of Empire: The Impact of Roman Citizenship upon Greeks, Jews and Christians*. Edited by Katell Berthelot and Jonathan J. Price. Interdisciplinary Studies in Ancient Culture and Religion 21. Leuven: Peeters.

Gabbay, Uri, and Shai Secunda. 2014. *Encounters by the Rivers of Babylon: Scholarly Conversations between Jews, Iranians, and Babylonians in Antiquity*. TSAJ 160. Tübingen: Mohr Siebeck.

Gafni, Chanan. 2011. *The Mishnah's Plain Sense: A Study of Modern Talmudic Scholarship*. Sifriyat "Helal Ben-Ḥayim" [Hebrew]. Tel Aviv: Hakibbutz ha-meuchad.

Gafni, Isaiah. 1997. *Land, Center and Diaspora: Jewish Constructs in Late Antiquity*. JSPSup 21. Sheffield: Sheffield Academic.

Goldberg, Abraham. 1987. "The Mishna—A Study Book of Halakha." Pages 211–62 in *The Literature of the Sages, First Part: Oral Tora, Halakha, Mishna, Tosefta, Talmud, External Tractates*. Edited by Shmuel Safrai and Peter J. Tomson. CRINT 2.3a. Assan: Van Gorcum; Philadelphia: Fortress.

Goodman, Martin. 1996. "The Function of 'Minim' in Early Rabbinic Judaism." Pages 501–10 in *Geschichte, Tradition, Reflexion: Festschrift für Martin Hengel zum 70. Geburtstag*. Edited by Hubert Cancik. Tübingen: Mohr Siebeck.

Goshen-Gottstein, Alon. 1994. "The Body as Image of God in Rabbinic Literature." *HTR* 87:171–95.

Grabbe, Lester L. 1992. *Judaism from Cyrus to Hadrian*. 2 vols. Minneapolis: Fortress.

Gvaryahu, Amit. 2012. "A New Reading of the Three Dialogues in Mishnah Avodah Zarah." *JSQ* 19:207–29.

———. 2016. Review of Review of *Scripture and Tradition: Rabbi Akiva and the Triumph of Midrash*, by Azzan Yadin-Israel. *Shofar* 34:139–41.

Halbertal, Moshe. 1997. *Interpretative Revolutions in the Making* [Hebrew]. Jerusalem: Magnes.

———. 2013. "The History of Halakhah and the Emergence of Halakhah" [Hebrew]. *Diné Israel* 29:1–23.

Halivni, David. 2013. *The Formation of the Babylonian Talmud*. Oxford: Oxford University Press.

Harris, Jay Michael. 1995. *How Do We Know This? Midrash and the Fragmentation of Modern Judaism.* Albany: State University of New York Press.

Hartog, Pieter B. 2017. *Pesher and Hypomnema: A Comparison of Two Commentary Traditions from the Hellenistic-Roman Period.* STDJ 121. Leiden: Brill.

Hasan-Rokem, Galit. 2000. *Web of Life: Folklore and Midrash in Rabbinic Literature.* Contraversions. Stanford: Stanford University Press.

Hauptman, Judith. 1998. *Rereading the Rabbis: A Woman's Voice.* Boulder: Westview.

Hayes, Christine E. 1997. *Between the Babylonian and Palestinian Talmuds: Accounting for Halakhic Difference In Selected Sugyot from Tractate Avodah Zarah.* New York: Oxford University Press.

———. 1998. "Displaced Self-Perceptions: The Deployment of Mînîm and Romans in b. Sanhedrin 90b–91a." Pages 249–89 in *Religious and Ethnic Communities in Later Roman Palestine.* Edited by Hayim Lapin. Bethesda: University Press of Maryland.

Henshke, David. 1994. "The Rabbis' Approach to Biblical Self-Contradictions" [Hebrew]. *Sidra* 10:39–55.

Herman, Geoffrey. 2012. *A Prince without a Kingdom: The Exilarch in the Sasanian Era.* TSAJ 150. Tübingen: Mohr Siebeck.

Herr, M. D. 1979. "Continuum in the Chain of Torah Transmission." *Zion* 44:43–56.

Hezser, Catherine. 1993. *Form, Function and Historical Significance of Rabbinic Story in Yerushalmi Neziqin.* TSAJ 137. Tübingen: Mohr Siebeck.

———. 2007. "Roman Law and Rabbinic Legal Compostition." Pages 144–64 in *The Cambridge Companion to the Talmud and Rabbinic Literature.* Edited by Charlotte E. Fonrobert. Cambridge University Press: Cambridge.

Hidary, Richard. 2018. *Rabbis and Classical Rhetoric: Sophistic Education and Oratory in the Talmud and Midrash.* Cambridge: Cambridge University Press.

Hirshman, Marc. 1999. *"Torah for the Entire World": A Universal Strand in Tannaitic Literature and Its Relationship to Gentile Wisdom* [Hebrew]. Tel-Aviv: Ha-kibbutz ha-meuchad.

———. 2005. "What Is the Place of Aggada and Who Were the Baalei Aggada?" [Hebrew]. *Mehkerei Talmud* 3:190–208.

Hoffmann, David. 1888. *Zur Einleitung in Die Halachischen Midrashim.* Beitrage Zum Jahresbericht Des Rabbiner-Seminars Zu Berlin 5647. Berlin: Driesner.

Inwood, Brad. 1985. *Ethics and Human Action in Early Stoicism*. Oxford: Clarendon.
Jaffee, Martin S. 2001. *Torah in the Mouth: Writing and Oral Tradition in Palestinian Judaism 200 BCE–400 CE*. New York: Oxford University Press.
Kahana, Menahem. 1999a. "The Attitude toward Gentiles in the Tannaic and Amoraic Periods" [Hebrew]. *Et ha-daʾat* 3:22–36.
———. 1999b. *The Two Mekhiltot of the Amalek Portion: The Originality of the Version of the Mekhila of Rabbi Ishmael with Respect to the Mehilta of Rabbi Shimon ben Yohai* [Hebrew]. Jerusalem: Magnes.
———. 2005. *Kitei Midreshei Halakhah Min Ha-Genizah*. Jerusalem: Magnes.
———. 2006. "The Halakhic Midrashim." Pages 3–107 in *The Literature of the Sages Part 2: Second part: Midrash and Targum, Liturgy, Poetry, Mysticism, Contracts, Inscriptions, Ancient Science and the Languages of Rabbinic Literature* [Hebrew]. Edited by Shemuel Safrai and Peter J. Tomson. CRINT 2.3b. Assen: Van Gorcum; Philadelphia: Fortress.
———. 2011. *Sifre on Numbers: An Annotated Edition* [Hebrew]. 5 vols. Jerusalem: Magnes.
Kalmin, Richard. 1994. "Christians and Heretics in Rabbinic Literature of Late Antiquity." *HTR* 87:155–69.
———. 2014. *Migrating Tales: The Talmud's Narratives and Their Historical Context*. Berkeley: University of California Press.
Kattan Gribetz, Sarit. 2013. "Conceptions of Time and Rhythms of Daily Life in Rabbinic Literature, 200–600 C.E." PhD diss., Princeton University.
Katz, Steven T., ed. 2006. *The Late Roman-Rabbinic Period*. CHJ 4. Cambridge: Cambridge University Press.
Katzoff, R. 1989. "Sperber's *Dictionary of Greek and Latin Legal Terms in Rabbinic Literature*: A Review-Essay." *JSJ* 20:195–206.
Keshet, Lia. 2008. "The Aggada in the Talmud Yerushalmi" [Hebrew]. PhD diss., Hebrew University of Jerusalem.
Kiel, Yishai. 2016. *Sexuality in the Babylonian Talmud: Christian and Sasanian Contexts in Late Antiquity*. New York: Cambridge University Press.
Kister, Menahem. 2007a. "Romans 5:12–21 against the Background of Torah-Theology and Hebrew Usage." *HTR* 100:391–424.
———. 2007b. "'In Adam': 1 Cor 15:21–22; 12:27 in Their Jewish Setting." Pages 685–90 in *Flores Florentino: Dead Sea Scrolls and Other Early*

Jewish Studies in Honour of Florentino García Martínez. Edited by Anton Hilhorst, Emile Puech, and Eibert J. C. Tigchelaar. JSJSup 122. Leiden: Brill.

———. 2010. "'First Adam' And 'Second Adam' In 1 Cor 15:45–49 in the Light of Midrashic Exegesis and Hebrew Usage." Pages 351–66 in *The New Testament and Rabbinic Literature.* Edited by Reimund Bieringer. JSJSup 136. Leiden: Brill.

———. 2013. "Allegorical Interpretations of Biblical Narratives in Rabbinic Literature, Philo, and Origen: Some Case Studies." Pages 133–83 in *New Approaches to the Study of Biblical Interpretation in Judaism of the Second Temple Period and in Early Christianity.* Edited by Gary A. Anderson, Ruth Clement, and David Safran. STDJ 106. Leiden: Brill.

———. 2014. "Body and Sin: Romans and Colossians in Light of Qumran and Rabbinic Texts." Pages 171–208 in *the Dead Sea Scrolls and Pauline Literature.* Edited by Jean-Sébastien Rey. STDJ 102. Leiden: Brill.

Kraemer, David. 2006. "The Mishnah." Pages 299–315 in *The Late Roman-Rabbinic Period.* Edited by Steven T. Katz. CHJ 4. Cambridge: Cambridge University Press.

Kugel, James. 1998. *Traditions of the Bible: A Guide to the Bible as It Was at the Start of the Common Era.* Cambridge: Harvard University Press.

Lambert, David. 2016. "How the 'Torah of Moses' Became Revelation: An Early, Apocalyptic Theory of Pentateuchal Origins." *JSJ* 47:22–54.

Lapin, Hayim. 2012. *Rabbis as Romans: The Rabbinic Movement in Palestine, 100–400 CE.* Oxford: Oxford University Press.

Levinson, Joshua. 1998. "Athlete of Faith and Fatal Fictions" [Hebrew]. *Tarbiz* 68:61–86.

———. 2005. *Twice Told Tale: A Poetics of the Exegetical Narrative in Rabbinic Midrash* [Hebrew]. Jerusalem: Magnes.

———. 2012. "From Narrative Practice to Cultural Poetics: Literary Anthropology and the Rabbinic Sense of Self." Pages 345–67 in *Homer and the Bible in the Eyes of Ancient Interpreters.* Edited by Maren Niehoff. JSRC 16. Leiden: Brill.

Lieberman, Saul. 1942. *Greek in Jewish Palestine: Studies in the Life and Manners of Jewish Palestine in the II–IV Centuries C.E.* New York: Jewish Theological Seminary of America.

———. 1950. *Hellenism in Jewish Palestine; Studies in the Literary Transmission, Beliefs and Manners of Palestine in the I Century B. C. E.–IV Century C.E.* Texts and Studies of the Jewish Theological Seminary of America 18. New York: Jewish Theological Seminary of America.

Liebner, Uzi. 2009. "Settlement Patterns in the Eastern Galilee: Implications Regarding the Transformation of Rabbinic Culture in Late Antiquity." Pages 269–95 in *Jewish Identities in Antiquity: Studies in Memory of Menahem Stern*. Edited by Lee I. Levine and Daniel R. Schwartz. TSAJ 130. Tübingen: Mohr Siebeck.

Longenecker, Richard N. 1999. *Biblical Exegesis in the Apostolic Period*. 2nd ed. Grand Rapids: Eerdmans; Vancouver: Regent College Publishing.

Mandel, Paul. 2001. "Midrashic Exegesis and Its Precedents in the Dead Sea Scrolls." *DSD* 8:149–68.

———. 2017. *The Origins of Midrash: From Teaching to Text*. JSJSup 180. Leiden: Brill.

Marcus, Joel. 2009. "Birkat Ha-Minim Revisited." *NTS* 55:523–51.

Milgram, Jonathan S. 2016. *From Mesopotamia to the Mishnah: Tannaitic Inheritance Law in Its Legal and Social Contexts*. TSAJ 164. Tübingen: Mohr Siebeck.

Milikowsky, Chaim Joseph. 2013. *Seder Olam: Critical Edition with Introduction and Commentary* [Hebrew]. 2 vols. Jerusalem: Yad Ben-Zvi.

Miller, Stuart. 1993. "The 'Minim' of Sepphoris Reconsidered." *HTR* 86:377–402.

Moscovitz, Leib. 2002. *Talmudic Reasoning: From Casuistics to Conceptualization*. TSAJ 89. Tübingen: Mohr Siebeck.

———. 2009. *The Terminology of the Yerushalmi: The Principal Terms* [Hebrew]. Jerusalem: Magnes.

Mroczek, Eva. 2015. "The Hegemony of the Biblical in the Study of Second Temple Literature." *JAJ* 6:2–35.

———. 2016. *The Literary Imagination in Jewish Antiquity*. Oxford: Oxford University Press.

Münz-Manor, Ophir. 2006. "All About Sarah: Questions of Gender in Yannai's Poems on Sarah's (and Abraham's) Barrenness." *Prooftexts* 26:344–74.

Naeh, Shlomo. 2002. "'Talmud Yerushalmi' of The Academy of the Hebrew Language" [Hebrew]. *Tarbiz* 71:569–603.

———. 2005. "Ummanut Ha-Zikaron: Mivnim shel Zikaron ve-Tavniyyot shel Tekst Be-Sifrut Hazal." *Mehkerei Talmud* 3:543–89.

Najman, Hindy. 2003. *Seconding Sinai: The Development of Mosaic Discourse in Second Temple Judaism*. JSJSup 77. Leiden: Brill.

———. 2010. "Reconsidering Jubilees: Prophecy and Exemplarity." Pages 189–204 in *Past Renewals: Interpretative Authority, Renewed Revela-*

tion and the Quest for Perfection in Jewish Antiquity. Edited by Hindy Najman. JSJSup 53. Leiden: Brill.

Neusner, Jacob. 1971. *The Rabbinic Traditions about the Pharisees before 70*. Leiden: Brill.

———. 1981. *Judaism, the Evidence of the Mishnah*. Chicago: University of Chicago Press.

———. 1983. *Ancient Israel after Catastrophe: The Religious World View of the Mishnah*. Charleston: University Press of Virginia.

Niehoff, Maren. 2011. *Jewish Exegesis and Homeric Scholarship in Alexandria*. Cambridge: Cambridge University Press.

Noam, Vered. 2002. "Beit Shammai and the Sectarian Halakha" [Hebrew]. *Madaei Hayahadot* 41:45–67.

———. 2003. *Megillat Taʿanit: Versions Interpretations History* [Hebrew]. Jerusalem: Yad Ben-Zvi.

———. 2008. "The Dual Strategy of Rabbinic Purity Legislation." *JSJ* 39:471–512.

———. 2009. "The Stirrings of Midrash Halakh at Qumran" [Hebrew]. *Diné Israel* 26–27:3–26.

———. 2010. *From Qumran to the Tannaitic Revolution: Conceptions of Impurity* [Hebrew]. Jerusalem: Yad Ben-Zvi.

Noam, Vered, and Tal Ilan. 2017. *Between Josephus and Hazal* [Hebrew]. Bein mikra le-mishnah. Jerusalem: Yad Ben-Zvi.

Paz, Yakir. 2012. "Re-Scripturizing Traditions: Designating Dependence in Rabbinic Halakhic Midrashim and Homeric Scholarship." Pages 269–98 in *Homer and the Bible in the Eyes of Ancient Interpreters*. Edited by Maren Niehoff. JSRC 16. Leiden: Brill.

———. 2016. "From Scribes to Scholars: Rabbinic Biblical Exegesis in Light of the Homeric Commentaries" [Hebrew]. PhD diss., Hebrew University of Jerusalem.

Reeves, John C. 2010. "Problematizing the Bible … Then and Now." *JQR* 100:139–52.

Reif, Stefan C. 2014. "Some Reflections on the Publication of a New Thesaurus of Talmudic Manuscripts." *JQR* 104:601–12.

Rivkin, Ellis. 1969. "Defining the Pharisees: The Tannaitic Sources." *HUCA* 40–41:205–49.

Rosenthal, Yoav. 2003. "Babylonian Talmud, Tractate Kareitot: A Study of Its Textual Traditions" [Hebrew]. PhD diss., Hebrew University of Jerusalem.

---. 2007. "On the Early Form of Bavli Moʿed Qatan 7b–8a" [Hebrew]. *Tarbiz* 77:45–69.
Rosen-Zvi, Ishay. 2005. "Misogyny and Its Discontents." *Prooftexts* 25:217–227.
---. 2008. "Orality, Narrative, Rhetoric: New Directions in Mishnah Research." *AJSR* 32:235–49.
---. 2011. *Demonic Desires: "Yetzer Hara" and the Problem of Evil in Late Antiquity*. Philadelphia: University of Pennsylvania Press.
---. 2012a. *The Mishnaic Sotah Ritual: Temple, Gender and Midrash*. Translated by Orr Scharf. JSJSup 160. Leiden; Boston: Brill.
---. 2012b. *Body and Soul in Ancient Judaism* [Hebrew]. Tel Aviv: Modan.
---. 2014. "Structure and Reflectivity in Tannaitic Legal Homilies, Or: How to Read Midrashic Terminology." *Prooftexts* 34:271–301.
---. 2015a. "The Mishnaic Mental Revolution: A Reassessment." *JJS* 66:36–58.
---. 2015b. "Mishnah." In *The Oxford Encyclopedia of the Bible and Law*. Edited by Brent Strawn. 2 vols. Oxford: Oxford University Press.
---. 2016. "Rabbis and Romanization: A Review Essay." Pages 218–45 in *Jewish Cultural Encounters in the Ancient Mediterranean and Near Eastern World*. Edited by Mladen Popovic, Myles Schoonover, and Marijn Vandenberghe. JSJSup 178. Leiden: Brill.
Rubenstein, Jeffrey L. 2003. *The Culture of the Babylonian Talmud*. Baltimore: Johns Hopkins University Press.
---. 2017. "Hero, Saint, and Sage: The Life of R. Elazar b. R. Shimon in Pesiqta de Rab Kahana 11." Pages 509–28 in *The Faces of Torah: Studies in the Texts and Contexts of Ancient Judaism in Honor of Steven Fraade*. Edited by Michal Bar Asher Segal, Christine Hayes, and Tzi Novick. JAJSup 22. Göttingen: Vandenhoeck & Ruprecht.
Safrai, Shemuel, and Peter J. Tomson, eds. 2006. *The Literature of the Sages Part 2: Second Part: Midrash and Targum, Liturgy, Poetry, Mysticism, Contracts, Inscriptions, Ancient Science and the Languages of Rabbinic Literature*. CRINT 2.3b. Assen: Van Gorcum; Philadelphia: Fortress.
Satlow, Michael L. 2003. "'And on the Earth You Shall Sleep': 'Talmud Torah' and Rabbinic Asceticism." *JR* 83:204–25.
---. 2014. *How the Bible Became Holy*. New Haven: Yale University Press.
Schäfer, Peter, and Catherine Hezser. 1998–2002. *The Talmud Yerushalmi and Graeco-Roman Culture*. TSAJ 71, 79, 93. Tübingen: Mohr Siebeck.

Schremer, Adiel. 2001. "'[T]he[y] Did Not Read in the Sealed Book': Qumran Halakhic Revolution and the Emergence of Torah Study in Second Temple Judaism." Pages 105–26 in *Historical Perspectives: From the Hasmoneans to Bar Kokhba in Light of the Dead Sea Scrolls*. Edited by David M. Goodblatt, Daniel R. Schwartz, and Avital Pinnick. STDJ 37. Leiden: Brill.

———. 2003. *Male and Female He Created Them: Jewish Marriage in Late Second Temple, Mishnah and Talmud Periods*. Jerusalem: Merkaz Zalman Shazar.

———. 2010. *Brothers Estranged: Heresy, Christianity, and Jewish Identity in Late Antiquity*. Oxford: Oxford University Press.

———. 2018. "The Sages in Palestinian Jewish Society of the Mishnah Period: Torah, Prestige and Social Standing" [Hebrew]. Pages 553–81 in *The Classic Rabbinic Literature of Eretz Israel: Introductions and Studies*. Edited by David Rozenthal et al. Jerusalem: Yad Ben Zvi.

Schwartz, Daniel R. 1983. "Josephus and Nicolaus on the Pharisees." *JSJ* 14:157–71.

Schwartz, Daniel R., and Zeev Weiss, eds. 2011. *Was 70 CE a Watershed in Jewish History? On Jews and Judaism before and after the Destruction of the Second Temple*. AJEC 78. Brill: Leiden.

Schwartz, Seth. 2009. *Were the Jews a Mediterranean Society? Reciprocity and Solidarity in Ancient Judaism*. Princeton: Princeton University Press.

Secunda, Shai. 2014. *The Iranian Talmud: Reading the Bavli in Its Sasanian Context*. Divinations. Philadelphia: University of Pennsylvania Press.

Seidman, Naomi. 1994. "Carnal Knowledge: Sex and the Body in Jewish Studies." *JSocS* 1:115–46.

Sekki, Arthur. 1987. "The Meaning of Ruach at Qumran." PhD diss., University of Wisconsin-Madison.

Septimus, Zvi. 2017. "Revisiting the Fat Rabbis." Pages 418–56 in *Talmudic Transgressions: Engaging the Work of Daniel Boyarin*. Edited by Charlotte Fonrobert, Ishay Rosen-Zvi, Aharon Shemesh, and Moulie Vidas. JSJSup 181. Leiden: Brill.

Shemesh, Aharon. 2009. *Halakhah in the Making: The Development of Jewish Law from Qumran to the Rabbis*. Taubman Lectures in Jewish Studies 6. Berkeley: University of California Press.

Shin'an, Avigdor. 1985. "The 'Palestinian' Targums—Repetitions, Internal Unity, Contradictions." *JJS* 36:72–87.

———. 1991. "'Targumic Additions' in Targum Pseudo-Jonathan." *Text* 16:139–55.

———. 1992. "The Aramaic Targum as a Mirror of Galilean Jewry." Pages 241–51 in *The Galilee in Late Antiquity*. Edited by Lee I. Levine. New York: Jewish Theological Seminary of America.

Simon-Shoshan, Moshe. 2012. *Stories of the Law: Narrative Discourse and the Construction of Authority in the Mishnah*. New York: Oxford University Press.

Smith, Morton. 1967. "Goodenough's Jewish Symbols in Retrospect." *JBL* 86:53–68.

Stein, Dina. 2012. *Textual Mirrors: Reflexivity, Midrash, and the Rabbinic Self*. Divinations. Philadelphia: University of Pennsylvania Press.

Sussmann, Yaakov. 1989. "The History of Halakah and the Dead Sea Scrolls—Preliminary Observations on Miqṣat Ma'ase Ha-Torah (4QMMT)" [Hebrew]. *Tarbiz* 59:11–76.

———. 2001. "Introduction" [Hebrew]. Pages 9*–37* in *Talmud Yerushalmi according to Ms. Or. 4720 (Scaliger 3)*. Jerusalem: Academy of the Hebrew Language.

———. 2002. *Ginze Yerushalmi*. Jerusalem: Yad Ben Zvi.

———. 2005. "Oral Law: The Power of the Jot and Tittle" [Hebrew]. *Mehkerei Talmud* 3:209–384.

———. 2012. *Thesaurus of Talmudic Manuscripts* [Hebrew]. 3 vols. Jerusalem: Yad Ben-Zvi.

Teugels, Lieve M. 2004. *Bible and Midrash: The Story of "The Wooing of Rebekah" (Gen. 24)*. CBETS 35. Leuven: Peeters.

Tropper, Amram. 2005. "Roman Contexts in Jewish Texts: On 'Diatagma' and 'Prostagma' in Rabbinic Literature." *JQR* 95:207–27.

Urbach, Ephraim E. 1958. "The Derasha as a Basis of the Halakah and the Problem of the Soferim" [Hebrew]. *Tarbiz* 27:166–82.

Vidas, Moulie. 2014. *Tradition and the Formation of the Talmud*. Princeton: Princeton University Press.

———. 2017. "A Place of Torah." Pages 23–73 in *Talmudic Transgressions: Engaging the Work of Daniel Boyarin*. Edited by Charlotte Fonrobert, Ishay Rosen-Zvi, Aharon Shemesh, and Moulie Vidas. JSJSup 181. Leiden: Brill.

Wasserman, Mira. 2017. *Jews, Gentiles, and Other Animals: The Talmud after the Humanities*. Divinations. Philadelphia: University of Pennsylvania Press.

Werman, Cana, and Aharon Shemesh. 2011. *Revealing the Hidden: Exegesis and Halakah in the Qumran Scrolls* [Hebrew]. Jerusalem: Bialik.

Wimpfheimer, Barry S. 2011. *Narrating the Law: A Poetics of Talmudic Legal Stories*. Divinations. Philadelphia: University of Pennsylvania Press.

Winston, David. 1998. "Philo and the Rabbis on Sex and the Body." *Poetics Today* 19:41–62.

Yadin-Israel, Azzan. 2004. *Scripture as Logos: Rabbi Ishmael and the Origins of Midrash*. Divinations. Philadelphia: University of Pennsylvania Press.

———. 2012. "Concepts of Scripture in the Schools of Rabbi Akiva and Rabbi Ishmael." Pages 47–63 in *Jewish Concepts of Scripture: A Comparative Introduction*. Edited by Benjamin D. Sommer. New York: New York University Press.

———. 2015. *Scripture and Tradition: Rabbi Akiva and the Triumph of Midrash*. Divinations. Philadelphia: University of Pennsylvania Press.

Yassif, Eli. 1999. *The Hebrew Folktale: History, Genre, Meaning*. Translated by Jacqueline S. Teitelbaum. Folklore Studies in Translation. Bloomington: Indiana University Press.

Yuval, Israel J. 2011. "The Orality of Jewish Oral Law: From Pedagogy to Ideology." Pages 237–60 in *Judaism, Christianity, and Islam in the Course of History: Exchange and Conflicts* Edited by Lothar Gall and Dietmar Willoweit. Schriften des Historischen Kollegs 82. Munich: Oldenbourg.

Zlotnick, Dov. 1988. *The Iron Pillar, Mishnah: Redaction, Form, and Intent*. Jerusalem: Bialik.

21
EARLY JUDAISM AND MYSTICISM

ANDREA LIEBER

> The first phase in the development of Jewish mysticism before its crystallization in the mediaeval Kabbalah is also the longest. Its literary remains are traceable over a period of almost a thousand years, from the first century B.C. to the tenth A.D., and some of its important records have survived. In spite of its length, and notwithstanding the fluctuations of the historical process, there is every justification for treating it as a single distinct phase.
> —Gershom Scholem, *Major Trends in Jewish Mysticism*

1. Introduction

When Gershom Scholem published *Major Trends in Jewish Mysticism* in 1941, he was not the first scholar to explore the intersection of mysticism and early Judaism. In fact, Scholem's work built on decades of previous research by intellectual leaders of *Wissenschaft des Judentums* such as Heinrich Graetz (1846) and Moritz Friedländer (1898), who had long observed that Judaism's ancient esoteric traditions might shed light on the development of medieval kabbalah and the gnostic traditions that were so intertwined with the development of Christianity. Yet, it was Scholem's bold assertion in *Major Trends* that kabbalah developed from a singular chain of esoteric traditions spanning from the Second Temple era through the late rabbinic period that has exercised the greatest influence in shaping the field of early Jewish mysticism as an area of scholarly inquiry. Scholem's claim that kabbalah had its roots in antiquity established historical authenticity for the medieval traditions that would occupy the center of his own research for decades to come. This provocative thesis also launched a research agenda for generations of scholars seeking to fill the gaps in Scholem's sweeping narrative and to understand better the chain of tradition that linked Jewish mysticism to antiquity.

In the seventy years since the publication of *Major Trends*, Scholem's legacy has played an outsized role in shaping the conversation around early Jewish mysticism. Even as critics challenge many of the assumptions at the heart of his work, Scholem's categories still remain the starting point for most scholarly discussions of this material. However, a growing sensitivity to the cultural complexity of prerabbinic Judaism and the fluidity of what scholars once considered discrete categories of identity in antiquity, as well as increased engagement with methodological trends in the study of religion, have impacted the trajectory of this research. One of the important contributions of the original *Early Judaism and Its Modern Interpreters* (Kraft and Nickelsburg 1986) volume in the 1980s was to acknowledge the way new research methods, new literary discoveries, and new insights into complex social and cultural fabric of early Judaism had come to impact scholarship in the field. Given that the study of early Judaism and mysticism was quite robust at the time of its publication (indeed, the 1980s saw the publication of some of the field's most influential works), it is curious that there was no chapter in the original volume dedicated to research on Jewish mysticism. The intervening thirty years have seen early Jewish esotericism become an important area of concentration for students of Jewish and Christian origins. It remains a highly diverse field of study that in many ways is still wrestling with the impact of Scholem's legacy. Indeed, the quest for a grand narrative that places Judaism's esoteric traditions in relation to Christianity, gnosticism, or rabbinic culture continues to cause controversy among leading scholars.

The enthusiasm inspired by Scholem's work also underlies its challenges. Given what we know today about the complexity and fluidity of religious and cultural identity during the formative period of early Judaism, it is difficult to take seriously the idea of a single, unbroken chain of tradition transmitted over many centuries and across wide geographical boundaries. Scholem's invitation to consider Jewish mysticism's first phase as encompassing nearly one thousand years of literary evidence ignited interest among a wide array of scholars across multiple fields. Experts in Second Temple history, apocalyptic and pseudepigraphic literature, Philo, early church fathers such as Origin and Clement of Alexandria, Nag Hammadi and gnostic literature, New Testament, Dead Sea Scrolls, and early rabbinic literature have all joined this ongoing scholarly conversation, making it a challenge to define the chronological and textual parameters of study. As a result, questions related to definition, authorship, influence, dating, and provenance have defined the field as much as efforts to discern meaning behind the obscure traditions that stand at the center of the literary evidence.

In this essay, I summarize the history of scholarship on mysticism and early Judaism, beginning with the very basic question of how to define early Jewish mysticism. I then review the key avenues of research that continue to drive the field today, namely, how the corpus of Jewish mystical traditions intersects with the study of rabbinic Judaism, the Dead Sea Scrolls, early Christianity, and gnosticism. Due to the diversity of perspectives at the table, the wide range of primary sources that are brought to bear on this subject and the long history of scholarship reaching back to the nineteenth century, my discussion is not exhaustive but seeks to introduce the enduring questions that have defined the field with an emphasis on scholarly contributions since the 1980s.

2. Delimiting the Sources

The term *mysticism* as it is used in the context of early Judaism refers to the varied ways in which the authors of ancient Jewish texts expressed their desire to know a reality beyond the human realm, to experience direct connection with a transcendent God, and to acquire esoteric knowledge. Scholem viewed early Jewish mysticism as a postbiblical phenomenon influenced by the highly syncretic landscape of the Second Temple era, citing Persian, Egyptian, or Hellenistic cultural influence as formative elements. The pseudepigraphic and apocalyptic narratives of the Second Temple period, such as 1 and 2 Enoch, Apocalypse of Abraham, 2 Baruch, Testament of Levi, and Ascension of Isaiah are replete with visions of an anthropomorphic God, tales of heavenly ascent, revelation of hidden secrets, angelic adjurations, and transformative divine encounters. In this literature, divine prophecy is reinterpreted with heavenly ascent emerging as a new model for mediating the divine/human realms. The apocalyptic seer is often portrayed as a quasi-angelic mediator figure positioned between the realm of divine beings and the human realm, suggesting a cosmic and eschatological dualism that has important implications for the emergence of ancient Jewish messianism.

Similar motifs also appear in the work of Philo of Alexandria (Goodenough 1969; Schäfer 2009, 154–74). Philo's description of the Therapeutae (*Contempl.* 1–2) portrayed this sectarian group as an ancient community whose practices and ideology represents a mystical expression of Jewish asceticism with important parallels among the Qumran sectarian documents. Philo's exegetical and philosophical writing is infused with a body-soul dualistic worldview that reflects his synthesis of Greek and Jewish thought. While Philo does not talk about embodied heavenly ascent, his writing provides evidence of philosophical speculation about the divine realm that may have influenced the development of mystical traditions in the Hellenistic period. He developed a dualistic notion of the body and soul in which the soul separates from the body in its ascension to heaven and experiences God in an experience of ecstatic vision. Scholars point specifically to Joseph and Aseneth as a pseudepigraphic work in which Aseneth's spiritual/angelic transformation is influenced by such ideas.

The Dead Sea Scrolls are also a rich source for exploring early Jewish mysticism. The gradual publication of the scrolls beginning the 1960s ignited an exciting wave of new research that focused on the scrolls' affirmation of a pronounced eschatological dualism and the appearance of angelic mediator-figures and cultic symbolism. In particular, works such as Songs of the Sabbath Sacrifice and the Thanksgiving Scroll (Alexander 2006; Gruenwald 2014; Schiffman 1982; Fletcher-Louis 2002; Elior and Louvish 2004) have been well studied for their place in the landscape of early Jewish mystical literature.

Because many of the same motifs persist in gnostic, rabbinic, and early Christian writings, the canon of texts brought to bear on the study of early Jewish mysticism reaches well into late antiquity. When read against the esoteric traditions of the Second Temple era, later rabbinic traditions about the four who entered *pardes*, Paul's report of ascending to the third heaven and gnostic traditions of heavenly mediation and cosmic dualism suggest thematic commonalities, thus extending the timeline of early Jewish mysticism to include this later material.

Scholem's understanding of the development of early Jewish mysticism relied heavily on his study of *hekhalot* literature, a collection of esoteric writings preserved in medieval manuscripts and concerned with speculation about ascent to heaven and visions of the divine throne. While the *hekhalot* manuscripts themselves are clearly medieval, dating to the twelfth century, their pseudepigraphic narrative places them in a rabbinic context, purporting to be the words of sages from the Tannaitic Palestine. Based on a handful of references in rabbinic literature, Scholem was convinced of an early provenance for this material, dating it approximately to the third century CE. For many scholars today, the *hekhalot* corpus is, in fact, synonymous with early Jewish mysticism, as evidenced by prominence of *hekhalot* research among recent publications.

Scholem emphasized the centrality of visionary experiences in *hekhalot* narratives and saw their preoccupation with certain biblical motifs, such as the heavenly ascent of Enoch, the throne imagery in Isa 6, and the chariot vision of Ezek 1, as an important connection to the ancient apocalypses. Like the apocalypses, the *hekhalot* narratives imagine the possibility of an open heaven and are concerned with the revelation of hidden knowledge and the mediation of heaven and earth. While Scholem prioritized the visionary dimension of the *hekhalot* corpus, later scholars, such as Peter Schäfer (1981, 1984, 1992, 2009), James Davila (2001, 2002, 2013a, 2031b), and Michael Swartz (1994, 1996, 2011, 2013, 2018) turned instead to the adjurational elements of these texts, linking their study to research on Jewish magical traditions in antiquity. As Gideon Bohak (2008) notes in his history of Jewish magic, the majority of sources for Jewish magic date to a later provenance of approximately fifth to sixth century. Despite the paucity of primary sources reflecting magical praxis during the Second Temple period, the Sibylline Oracles, the Septuagint, Book of the Watchers, and Jubilees reference prohibited magical practices that are sometimes associated with demonic forces. While such prohibitions suggest that magical rites were practiced in some form, the lack of material evidence suggests that perhaps those remnants did not survive.

Some scholars challenge the idea that early Jewish mysticism begins in a postbiblical milieu, seeking instead to identify traditions of esotericism in the Hebrew Bible itself. Rachel Elior (1997), Schäfer (2009), and Elliot Wolfson (1994b, 17–28) each begin their exploration of early Jewish mysticism with Ezekiel's prophetic vision of the chariot-throne, the interpretation of which plays a central role in later sources, but which in and of itself might be viewed as a mystical text of sorts. Ezekiel's ability to see God is an important precursor to the apocalyptic interest in heavenly ascent. Indeed, Martha Himmelfarb's 1993 *Ascent to Heaven* opens with a discussion of the way the Book of the Watchers in 1 Enoch draws on motifs contained in Ezekiel's vision. Seth Sanders's (2017) interesting work on the Neo-Assyrian period makes the case that the mythic persona of Enoch as it appears in the Judean and Hellenistic apocalypses is best understood by looking at Mesopotamian traditions about the mythic scribal figure Adapa.

This push and pull over where early Jewish mysticism began is directly related to efforts to articulate a clear story line about the origins of these traditions, yet the complexity of the texts and their contexts simply resists definition. There are important biblical precedents for direct experience of God. Moses's ascent on Mount Sinai to receive the torah, Ezekiel's chariot vision, and the traditions surrounding the figure of Enoch, who becomes a model for heavenly ascent, since there is no accounting of his death, after he "walked with God" in the Genesis narrative (Gen 5:24). The priestly tradition of the high priest's entry into the inner sanctum of the temple also provides important material for the mystical imagination in early Jewish esoteric writings.

It appears that the early interpreters of biblical theophanies saw these recorded experiences as paradigmatic. After all, if the study of mysticism is concerned with a tradition's experiential dimension, why wouldn't the many biblical theophanies and prophetic narratives also be read as mystical? Looking to the biblical world, sacrifice and cultic ritual emerge as the predominant modes for encountering the divine. The detailed descriptions of the tabernacle and the Jerusalem temple present a well-articulated scheme for mediating the presence of God through sacrificial ritual, and the idea of a heavenly temple that parallels the earthly temple exists even in preexilic biblical sources. Why should an adept's appearance before the heavenly throne be considered mystical while the entry of the high priest into the holy of holies is not?

3. Defining Early Jewish Mysticism

Categorizing any ancient source as mystical raises critical questions that have been at the center of scholarly debates for decades. In the preface to his important work on mysticism, Bernard McGinn (1991, xiv) wrote, "There can be no direct access to experience for the historian. Experience as such is not a part of the historical record. The only thing left to the historian or the historical theologian is the evidence, largely in the form of written records, left to us by Christians of former ages." If all we have are the written records of Jewish mysticism, are these textual artifacts a doorway to understanding the experiential dimension of ancient Jewish practice? Are these esoteric narratives primarily literary in nature, reflecting the rich imagination of their ancient authors, or do they preserve a record of ritual practices that were experienced among the communities that produced them? What might be at stake in imagining an experiential core at the heart of these traditions? Who produced them and what function did they serve in their relationship to the so-called normative traditions of rabbinic Judaism? These questions drove scholarly inquiry throughout the twentieth century and continue to animate scholarly conversation today.

Applied to the study of early Judaism, mysticism is an analytical framework that has been useful in categorizing esoteric practices described in the ancient literature. However, it is important to acknowledge that mysticism is a contested term in the study of religion. As a modern construct developed in the nineteenth century and projected back onto ancient sources, the lens of mysticism carries intellectual baggage. As April DeConick (2006, 2) has noted, mysticism is an etic, rather than an emic word. It is not a term that ancients used to describe their religious experiences, but it is rather "a modern typology, contemporary analytic vocabulary that we are imposing on the ancients in order to investigate their religiosity." In a recent discussion of the place of apocalyptic literature in the study of Jewish mysticism, Ra'anan Boustan and Patrick McCullough (2014, 87; see also Huss 2015; and Reed 2013) consider the "ideological assumptions embedded within the category of 'mysticism'" and the resultant limits of its utility as a comparative tool. The understanding of mysticism as a "private, interiorized and unmediated encounter with the divine" projects Christian ideals about individual piety onto its subject, thereby making it an inappropriate lens for studying esoteric phenomena across cultures.

Having internalized post-Enlightenment Protestant notions of mysticism, *Wissenschaft* thinkers like Graetz (1846) viewed mystical expressions of Judaism as a foil for the legalistic rationalism of rabbinic Judaism. In this view, Jewish esotericism appears as a dark undercurrent that started among the Essenes and could be traced straight through to modern Hasidism, finding expression in Christianity along the way. This framework, which positioned Judaism as overly concerned with legalism and Christianity with religious feeling, shaped Graetz's thinking in ways that feel problematic to the contemporary scholar. Yet, the portrait of Judaism as inherently nonmystical or antithetical to mysticism persists. As recently as 2009, Christopher Rowland and Christopher Morray-Jones (2009, 4) noted their surprise that the word mysticism might be used in connection with Judaism, "which gives the impression of being concerned more with mundane, practical issues rather than reliance on experience of the otherworldly."

Scholem understood mysticism as a key developmental stage in the historical expression of Jewish religion; he is perhaps most celebrated for legitimating the careful study of Jewish mystical texts in historical context at a time when the irrationality of these highly symbolic and mythical traditions caused many scholars to dismiss them as aberrant. As his contemporaries were moving toward the comparative study of mysticism as a lens to cut across categories like Jewish or Christian (e.g., Otto 1932), Scholem insisted on the particularity of Jewish mysticism, ironically affirming it as unique in its very essence. While Western esotericism privileged union with the divine, or *unio mystica*, as the primary goal of the mystical adept, Scholem argued forcefully that this concept was entirely absent from Jewish tradition. He categorically rejected any notion of mystical union that resulted in the ecstatic merging of self with the divine presence and viewed this as evidence of Jewish mysticism's essential uniqueness.

Instead, Scholem pointed to the vision of an anthropomorphic God enthroned in the heavenly temple as the culminating element of early Jewish mysticism. The prominence of this motif among the apocalypses led him to conclude "without a doubt" that the earliest Jewish mysticism was what he called "throne-mysticism," in which the mystical adept "is not absorbed in contemplation of God's true nature, but in the perception of God's appearance on the throne as described by Ezekiel and cognition of the mysteries of the celestial throne-world" (1941, 78). It was precisely in the heavenly throne visions of the apocalypses that Scholem saw the most significant link between the ancient material and the *hekhalot* manuscripts, which were ascribed to rabbinic sages and featured narratives of heavenly ascent and visions of an enthroned, anthropomorphic divine being. Scholem based his early dating of the *hekhalot* texts on several key passages in rabbinic literature and understood *merkabah* traditions to have developed out of rabbinic culture, viewing the apocalyptic narratives as important antecedents. In asserting the throne vision at the center of Jewish mystical traditions, he pointed scholars toward the importance of exegetical traditions around Isaiah, Daniel, and Ezekiel, but also highlighted the need to explore other related motifs: heavenly ascent, magical adjuration, angelic transformation, and divine dualism.

In one of the first comprehensive challenges to Scholem's method, Moshe Idel's (1988, 27–29) *Kabbalah: New Perspectives* critiqued Scholem's lack of theoretical sophistication in his view of mysticism and his overemphasis on the textual and doctrinal dimensions of Judaism's mystical traditions. Idel challenged Scholem's wholesale rejection of *unio mystica* and argued that there is in fact a strain of ecstatic practice characteristic of Jewish mysticism that Scholem deliberately ignored in his reading (10–16). As a phenomenologist heavily influenced by Mircea Eliade, Idel believed that the literary evidence at the heart of Scholem's study was merely the tip of the iceberg, concealing a rich tradition of ecstatic religious experience that in his mind was the essence of Jewish mysticism. He saw Scholem as overly focused on what he termed "theosophic" dimensions of Jewish mysticism, to the exclusion of its ecstatic elements, in which *unio mystica* does play a significant role. While Idel's work did not emphasize mystical traditions in early Judaism, his ideas were important in opening the door to new scholarship that would focus on ecstatic practices in the ancient sources, particularly as expressed in the traditions of the *merkabah*, or heavenly chariot/throne. For example, Adam Afterman's (2016) recent study of *unio mystica* in medieval Jewish sources continues Idel's line of reasoning and contends that language of mystical union originates in an early Jewish context with Philo of Alexandria as part of his attempt to synthesize Middle Platonism with Hellenistic Jewish thought.

Wolfson (1993) articulated a middle ground between the positions of Scholem and Idel in his discussion of heavenly transformation of the mystical adept as an alternative expression of *unio mystica* in early Jewish sources. Informed by discussions of angelic transformation in apocalyptic ascent narratives (Himmelfarb 1993), Wolfson (1994a, 186) observed that a variety of sources portray the human being's ability to cross the boundaries of space and time and join the heavenly realm through participation in the angelic liturgy in a standing position or through enthronement, which entails taking a seated posture. The idea of angelic transformation of the human adept is central also to the work of Andrei Orlov (2005), who has studied this motif extensively as it appears in the Enoch and Metatron traditions. The recent work of Michael Schneider (2012, 2017) pursues the theme of apotheosis as an expression of priestly mysticism in the Wisdom of Ben Sira, 4 Ezra, and other Hellenistic sources.

4. Intersections

Given the longevity of research on early Judaism and mysticism, there is surprising consistency in the questions that have occupied scholars for the past several decades. In this section, I explore three general avenues of inquiry, namely, the exploration of early mysticism in relation to normative rabbinic Judaism, to Qumran materials and related discourse about the Jerusalem temple, and to early Christianity and gnosticism. These avenues are not silos; there is intersection among them, and there are scholars whose work attempts to explore them all.

4.1. Early Jewish Mysticism and Rabbinic Judaism

There are two regularly cited examples from rabbinic literature to support the close relationship between *hekhalot* literature and rabbinic Judaism. The responsum of eleventh century rabbinic sage, Hai Gaon, which records physical instructions for achieving a mystical vision of the inner chambers of the heavenly *hekhal*, was an important proof text for Scholem and continues to serve as scaffolding for arguments that see the *hekhalot* traditions as aligned with normative rabbinic culture. Likewise, the story of the four rabbinic sages who entered *pardes* contained in the Babylonian Talmud, Hag. 14b, stands at the heart of discussions about whether the practice of mystical speculation represents a normative or sectarian practice. Given the commonalities shared between *hekhalot* and rabbinic literatures, debate has centered around questions that tend to affirm a binary division between mystical Judaism and normative Judaism. Are the mystical traditions attested in the *hekhalot* sources a product of rabbinic culture and authority? Or, conversely, do they represent a challenge to the hierarchies and ideas that structure the rabbinic worldview? Scholem theorized that *hekhalot* texts derived from the Tannaitic period; thus, he understood mysticism as an integral and formative aspect of rabbinic Judaism, influenced by the apocalyptic traditions. Indeed, as Boustan (2011, 484) has put it, "in Scholem's view, Hekhalot literature constituted the ecstatic-esoteric dimension of rabbinic tradition and thus served as the dynamic beating heart of a law-centered rabbinism."

Ithamar Gruenwald followed Scholem's lead in exploring mystical elements of apocalyptic literature as an important antecedent to the *hekhalot* traditions. Gruenwald's *Apocalyptic and Merkavah Mysticism* was published in 1980 and revised in a second edition released in 2014. In this work, Gruenwald delivered thorough textual analysis to support Scholem's contention that the *merkabah* traditions were of rabbinic origin and could be linked directly to mystical traditions that derived specifically from the postbiblical apocalypses. Gruenwald also affirmed Scholem's view that the apocalypses represent a departure from the biblical worldview. He wrote, "Mystical visions had their antecedents in biblical literature. However, the manners in which these visions are described in apocalyptic, and the place they occupy there, make it clear that a new religious mood and interest prevails in these books" (68).

Ira Chernus's (1982) *Mysticism in Rabbinic Judaism* focused on the importance of biblical interpretation in rabbinic culture as a key to understanding rabbinic mysticism. Analyzing midrashim from the Tannaitic and Amoraic periods, Chernus argued that the rabbis used midrash to legitimate a new form of religious experience. Drawing on the biblical motif of the Sinai revelation, the rabbis saw the ecstatic vision of the divine as a means of continued revelation. Chernus suggested as well that this understanding served simultaneously to reinforce the centrality of the Mosaic law, the interpretation of which is of course central to the rabbinic project.

Gruenwald's 2014 revised version of *Apocalyptic and Merkavah Mysticism* issues a call for the use of ritual theory in understanding the adjurational material in *hekhalot* texts. Naomi Janowitz took this approach in her 1989 *Poetics of Ascent,* drawing on linguistic and anthropological methods to understand the theory of language employed in Ma'aseh Merakvah. Analyzing the use of magical names and formulae as performative speech, she explored how this literary work might have functioned as a ritual text. In this perspective, she departed from Scholelm and Gruenwald who read the text as reports of experiences that already happened. Davila took a similar approach in his 2001 work, *Descenders to the Chariot,* where he applied the model of shamanism to consider passage of the *hekhalot* adept from one realm to another. Davila (2013a) continued this work in his *Ritual in the Hekhalot Literature,* where he argued that the *hekhalot* texts are a user manual for controlling angels toward the end of gaining esoteric knowledge. In contrast to Schäfer and David Halperin, Davila was insistent that the ritual practices described in the *hekhalot* corpus were intended to be used and put into practice. Rebecca Lesses (1995, 1998, 2007, 2013a, 2013b) and Swartz (1996) also look to ritual theory to make sense of the magical praxes contained in these texts. An important contribution of Lesses's work is her attention to gender in studying ritual practices in the context of early Jewish mysticism.

In contrast to Gruenwald and Chernus, who supported Scholem's basic contention that the *hekhalot* material predates the rabbis, David Halperin's (1984) *Faces of the Chariot* proposed a counter view to Scholem's early dating of the *hekahlot* texts that anchored a completely different understanding of the rabbis's relationship to these esoteric traditions. Halperin argued that the earliest form of *ma'aseh merkabah* referenced in Tannaitic sources is purely exegetical in nature and does not match up with the ecstatic practices narrated in the *hekhalot* texts. Halperin posited a late Amoraic, Babylonian context for the *hekhalot* literature, which undermines Scholem's thesis. Halperin (1984, 442) argued that *hekhalot* texts represent the imaginative work of the *amei haaretz,* the common folks, who challenged rabbinic authority. He read the stories of ascent as rabbinic pretenders, successfully ascending to heaven as an act of rebellion. An important element of Halperin's work is his view that these texts were primarily exegetical, presenting an interpretation of the Mosaic ascent upon Sinai coupled with Ezekiel's vision of the chariot/throne (11–37). Halperin is aligned with Schäfer in identifying the theurgic and adjurational elements of the *hekhalot* texts as primary, contrasted with Scholem who saw the visionary material as central.

Schäfer's (1981) publication of the *Synopse zur Hekhalot Literatur* represents a critical turning point in the study of early Jewish mysticism, specifically as it relates to rabbinic tradition. The *Synopse* presented the *hekhalot* material as macroforms organized by synoptic parallels, rather than as a critical edition of the texts. This strategy effectively exposed the fragmentary nature of the material, revealing inconsistencies and a lack of coherence that challenged many of Scholem's claims. The fragmentary nature of the manuscripts called into question the notion that these sources represent discrete literary works that might be attributed to authors. A departure from the publication of critical editions of a single work, such as Hekhalot Zutarti or Ma'aseh Merkabah, the *Synopse* is rather a compilation of textual units published as parallels to highlight the composite nature of the corpus, revealing similar motifs among manuscript traditions, but also showing important variants. Schäfer's work demonstrated that the motifs Scholem and subsequent authors like Gruenwald had emphasized were not necessarily the most significant motifs in the corpus. Specifically, Schäfer contends that the macroforms do not suggest that vision of an enthroned God in the heavenly temple is really such a prominent motif; rather, careful study of the *Synopse* suggests that adjurations and ritual practices emerge as the central preoccupation of this literature.

The *Synopse* highlighted the complexity of the *hekhalot* manuscripts and showed that the texts themselves resist any attempt at understanding them as a singular, unified tradition. Schäfer's work also inspired scholarship that placed the literary development of the texts at the center. This turn poses a challenge to those scholars who rely on the early dating of the *hekhalot* material to ground arguments about the interconnection of *merkabah* mysticism with the esoteric traditions of the Second Temple and early Christian eras. Indeed, one of the most persistent divisions in the field is the divide between those scholars who remain committed to the early dating of this material and those who view the material as a product of the early Middle Ages. Critics of Schäfer's work, including an early review by Elior in 1987, noted that his presentation of seven manuscripts was selective and did not include the entirety of the *hekhalot* material. This criticism has been revived today by Daniel Abrams (1996), who argues that Schäfer's selective publication of the manuscripts skews the portrayal of what constitute the main thematic elements of the corpus.

Boustan (2011, 482) points to a tendency among scholars to oversimplify the relationship between *hekhalot* literature and rabbinic Judaism, viewing them either as two distinct forms of Judaism (normative and sectarian) or complementary aspects of a single tradition. In an effort to break through the limitations of this binary view, Boustan argues for a more nuanced approach to understanding the "imperfectly intersecting terrains" of rabbinic and *hekhalot* literatures that privileges historical context over phenomenological readings.

4.2. Early Jewish Mysticism, Qumran, and the Jerusalem Temple

The question of mysticism at Qumran has been well studied by scholars of early Judaism and early Christianity. From the time Songs of the Sabbath Sacrifice was published in 1960 (Strugnell), parallels with *hekhalot* texts were noted by scholars including Lawrence Schiffman (1982), James Baumgarten (1988), Bilhah Nitzan (1994), and Davila (1996). Given the centrality of temple imagery to many early Jewish mystical sources and the prominence of cultic symbolism throughout Qumran material, an important focus of the scholarly discussion concerns the place of the ancient priesthood in the imagination of early Jewish mystics. Might the mystical narratives about ascent to and enthronement in a heavenly temple derive from an ancient priestly tradition, or are they an imaginative interpretation that draws on priestly narratives of the Hebrew Bible? Perhaps the heavenly temple represents a polemical critique of the contemporary priesthood and was created to affirm a place where true, pure worship of God is conducted. Or, could the image of a heavenly temple be a creative response to the destruction of the earthly temple, enabling an exiled people to access God outside the confines of Jerusalem? The Dead Sea Scrolls provide fertile ground for the consideration of such questions.

The heavenly temple as it appears in mystical literature is staffed by angels and the occasional mystic rather than priests; in place of the ark and altar, one finds God's anthropomorphic figure enthroned between the cherubim. The heavenly temple, like the earthly one, is the place where God's presence dwells and the place where God can be encountered. Mystical ascent to the temple represents a heroic quest for ultimate knowledge of God, a dream-like experience in which the mystic risks self-annihilation. Crispin Fletcher-Louis (2002) found ample evidence among the scrolls to support his theory of "angelmorphic humanity," according to which the perfected state of the human being is its angelic form.

Elior's epic work, *The Three Temples*, originally published in 1992 in Hebrew and translated into English in 2004, engages deeply with Qumran sources in tracing the trope of a heavenly chariot-throne to the sectarian polemics surrounding the priesthood during the Second Temple period (233–35). In line with both Scholem and Gruenwald, Elior argues for an early date to the *hekhalot* corpus, placing the traditions amid the sectarian conflicts of the Second Temple period. Indeed, Elior's ambitious narrative reaches all the way back to the destruction of the First Temple, linking priests deposed in 587 BCE during the Babylonian conquest to both the Zadokite priests who lost power to the Hasmonean priests in the second century BCE and the priestly circles who lost control in 70 CE during the Roman conquest. Elior mines the symbolism of the temple in both its earthly and heavenly manifestations through the eyes of disempowered priests who, having lost power on earth, imagine regaining their divine connection through heavenly service. In her analysis, Elior explores the relationship between ritual and ideology as an interpretive key for reading these perplexing sources.

4.3. Early Jewish Mysticism, Early Christianity, and Gnosticism

Finally, where does early Jewish mysticism stand in relation to emerging Christianity? Can Jewish esotericism be seen as a formative element for ideas about an embodied, hypostatic divine messiah who mediates between heaven and earth, or do efforts to understand Christianity as an expression of Jewish mysticism reflect theological biases that shape the way modern scholars read these ancient sources? Might early Christianity find its roots in a secret, esoteric variety of Judaism that was suppressed by rabbinic legalism? The notion that esoteric narratives of the ancient apocalypses represent a truer, more enduring, and authentic Judaism that ultimately found expression in esoteric varieties of Christianity is read by some contemporary scholars as a reiteration of classic stereotypes that position Judaism as a religion of law in contrast to Christianity as a religion of the heart (Reed 2013; Boustan and Sanzo 2017; Huss 2015).

Scholem's (1961) identification of the *hekhalot* traditions as a form of Jewish gnosticism situated the study of this material precisely amid the study of Christian origins and affirmed the possibility of a pre-Christian gnosticism. The identification of gnostic motifs in Jewish literature of the Second Temple and early rabbinic periods has fueled conversation around gnosticism and its relationship to Jewish mysticism. Though the textual evidence points to gnosticism as a post-Christian phenomenon, generations of modern scholars have looked to this era and its literary productions in search of a pre-Christian form of gnostic thought. If a distinctively Jewish tradition of gnosis could be identified among the diverse sectarian literature of the Second Temple period, then the prevalence of Hebrew/Aramaic names and biblical references in gnostic literature could be more clearly understood as emerging from an early Jewish or Jewish-Christian milieu. While recent scholarly consensus has shifted away from the notion of a Jewish provenance for gnosticism, the common elements shared by Jewish and gnostic sources raise unanswered questions about how ideas were circulated, received, and transmitted in antiquity.

A number of important scholarly works on early Christian mysticism look to Jewish sources, particularly the apocalyptic and *hekhalot* materials, to make sense of Christian esoteric traditions. Alan Segal's (1990) *Paul the Convert*, which analyzes Paul's reported ascent to the third heaven in light of *hekhalot* traditions of heavenly ascent, is a prime example. Morray-Jones (1993) expanded Segal's argument about Paul to develop his own interpretation of Paul's self-disclosed mystical experience as an example of *merkabah* mysticism. DeConick's (1996, 28–39) treatment of the Gospel of Thomas emphasized the influence of early Jewish mysticism on Thomas's theological outlook. The extensive works of Orlov (2005, 2007, 2009, 2011, 2017a, 2017b) built from the understanding that Jewish mystical traditions played a formative role in developing Christian esotericism.

Scholarship on divine mediators has been of particular interest to those interested in antecedents to Christianity, finding the embodied, enthroned imagery of God to be a prototype for traditions about Christ as the embodied Son of God. It is the apocalyptic seer who mediates the mythic dualities, sometimes literally or metaphorically, through an ascent into the heavens. The seer stands in between heaven and earth, communicating with God typically through an angelic divine mediator. The identity of the angelic mediator figure is a topic of great interest to scholars of both gnosticism and early Christianity, who see them as an antecedent of the gnostic demiurge or as a prefiguration of Jesus's status as both human and divine. An important point of contrast with the gnostic apocalypses is that the dualism of the Jewish sources is not in and of itself a theological dualism, in that the overall worldview of Jewish apocalyptic literature remains decidedly monotheistic. This line of inquiry has important significance for questions about Christian theology and the location of a hypostatic, angelic being with human qualities in the literature of ancient Judaism. In addition, rabbinic discourse about the two powers heresy, which Segal (1977) showed to be an important foil for the rabbinic definition of monotheism, was theorized as supporting evidence for a pre-Christian gnostic tradition.

5. Conclusion

In William James's classic lectures of 1902, *Varieties of Religious Experience*, he described the ineffability of mystical experience. In James's (2008, 532–33) understanding, a defining characteristic of the mystical is that it "defies expression … no adequate report of its contents can be given in words." It is therefore a great paradox that the study of early Jewish mysticism is concerned almost entirely with words—ancient texts that preserve mysterious narratives which often seem to conceal more than they reveal. If mystical experiences are inherently ineffable, is it no wonder that the study of these textual traditions continue to raise more questions than they answer? Despite McGinn's (1991) caveat that there can "be no direct access to experience for the historian," scholars of early Judaism continue to mine textual evidence in search of the experiential. While there may be ongoing disagreement about the precise path that leads from the esoteric traditions of the Second Temple period to the development of kabbalah, or the precise role these ideas play in the emergence of rabbinic Judaism and early Christianity, the scholarly conversation continues to engage generations of new scholars interested in solving this puzzle.

Current studies seek to push even further on the categories that have historically defined the field. For example, Swartz's (2018, 1–2) recent work takes a functional approach to the study of ancient magic and mysticism that prioritizes the commonalities of these phenomena rather than considering them as two distinct areas of inquiry. In doing so, he collapses the distinction between magical texts as expressions of isolated, individual practice and mysticism as the expression of a movement or a group. Swartz presents magic and mysticism as two sides of the same coin, with magic expressing the desire to bring heavenly powers down to earth and mysticism expressing the human desire to ascend to heaven. The artifacts of both magic and mysticism represent expressions of cultural creativity that Swartz reads as technologies that negotiate "between the values and world-views of their cultures and the texture of everyday life" (22). These technologies took the form of literary and artistic productions and physical practices that we must interpret with a view toward their cultural and historical context. For Swartz (2011, 257–77), this means a renewed attention to the ritual dimension of the texts and their liturgical context in relation to classical *piyyutim*, or liturgical poetry, typically dated between the fifth and eighth century Palestine. Swartz's work suggests that reading magical and mystical texts in light of these somewhat later sources opens new areas for analysis.

Annette Reed's (2013, 358–59) study of the Pseudo-Clementine Homilies, a fourth-century Syrian text typically categorized as a Jewish-Christian work, argues that the study of early Jewish mysticism would benefit from expanding the contextual sources to include Christian material, including Jewish-Christian literature of late antiquity. Reed reaches back into scholarship of the nineteenth century, exploring insights found in the work of those *Wissenschaft* thinkers eschewed by Scholem, such as Graetz. Using the Pseudo-Clementines as an example, she shows that this complex text does not conform to any of the modern scholarly narratives about the history of Jewish mysticism, even though it does seem to preserve a snapshot of some "strands of ideas in the course of development" (376). Like Swartz, Reed's work challenges future scholars to attend to a more fluid and complex understanding of the categories that have shaped academic inquiry up until now.

While many pioneers of scholarship on early Jewish mysticism operated within complicated academic and religious frameworks that led them to hypotheses that may seem reductive and oversimplified today, recent studies seek to make visible the theological blind spots of earlier scholarship with a view toward a more nuanced understanding of the religious worldview of early Judaism. As the next generation of scholars takes up these issues, challenging received narratives and breaking down categories that have heretofore shaped the field, it will be important to pay attention to the new assumptions and frameworks scholars project onto their subject. As Reed (2013, 377) noted, looking back at the critical insights eclipsed by narratives imposed by previous scholarship should "give us pause when tempted by the triumphalism of the scholarly construction of new meta-narratives about 'mysticism' in each generation."

Bibliography

Abrams, Daniel. 1996. "Critical and Post-critical Textual Scholarship of Jewish Mystical Literature: Notes on the History and Development of Modern Editing Techniques." *Kabbalah* 1:17–71.

Afterman, Adam. 2016. *"And They Shall Be One Flesh": On the Language of Mystical Union in Judaism*. JJTPSup 26. Leiden: Brill.

Alexander, Philip S. 2006. *The Mystical Texts: Songs of the Sabbath Sacrifice and Related Manuscripts*. LSTS 61. London: T&T Clark.

Baumgarten, James M. 1988. "The Qumran Sabbath Shirot and Rabbinic Merkabah Traditions." *RevQ* 13:199–213.

Bohak, Gideon. 2008. *Ancient Jewish Magic: A History*. Cambridge: Cambridge University Press.

Boustan, Ra'anan S. 2011. "Rabbinization and the Making of Early Jewish Mysticism." *JQR* 101:482–501.

Boustan, Ra'anan S., and Patrick McCullough. 2014. "Apocalyptic Literature and the Study of Early Jewish Mysticism." Pages 85–103 in *The Oxford Handbook of Apocalyptic Literature*. Edited by John J. Collins. Oxford: Oxford University Press.

Boustan, Ra'anan S., and Joseph Emanuel Sanzo. 2017. "Christian Magicians, Jewish Magical Idioms, and the Shared Magical Culture of Late Antiquity." *HTR* 110:217–40.

Chernus, Ira. 1982. *Mysticism in Rabbinic Judaism: Studies in the History of Midrash*. SJ 11. Berlin: de Gruyter.

Davila, James R. 1996. "The 'Hodayot' Hymnist and the Four Who Entered Paradise." *RevQ* 17:457–78.

———. 2001. *Descenders to the Chariot: The People Behind the Hekhalot Literature*. JSJSup 70. Leiden: Brill.

———. 2002. "The Macrocosmic Temple, Scriptural Exegesis, and the Songs of the Sabbath Sacrifice." *DSD* 9:1–19.

———. 2013a. *Hekhalot Literature in Translation: Major Texts of Merkavah Mysticism*. JJTPSup 20. Leiden: Brill.

———. 2013b. "Ritual in the Hekhalot Literature." Pages 449–66 in *Practicing Gnosis: Ritual, Magic, Theurgy and Liturgy in Nag Hammadi, Manichean and Other Ancient Literature; Essays in Honor of Birger A. Pearson*. Edited by April D. DeConick, Gregory Shaw, and John D. Turner. NHMS 85. Leiden: Brill.

DeConick, April, D. 1996. *Seek to See Him: Ascent and Vision Mysticism in the Gospel of Thomas*. VCSup 33. Leiden: Brill.

———. 2006. "What Is Early Jewish and Christian Mysticism?" Pages 1–24 in *Paradise Now: Essays on Early Jewish and Christian Mysticism*. Edited by April D. DeConick. SymS 11. Atlanta: Society of Biblical Literature.
Elior, Rachel. 1987. "The Concept of God in Hekhalot Mysticism/ייחודה של התופעה הדתית בספרות ההיכלות דמות האל והרחבת גבולות ההשגה." *Meḥḳere Yerushalayim be-maḥashevet Yiśraʾel/Jerusalem Studies in Jewish Thought* 1–2:13–64.
———. 1997. "From Earthly Temple to Heavenly Shrines: Prayer and Sacred Song in the Hekhalot Literature and Its Relation to Temple Traditions." *JSQ* 4:217–67.
Elior, Rachel, and David Louvish. 2004. *The Three Temples: On the Emergence of Jewish Mysticism*. Oxford: Littman Library of Jewish Civilization.
Fletcher-Louis, Crispin. 2002. *All the Glory of Adam: Liturgical Anthropology in the Dead Sea Scrolls*. STDJ 42. Leiden: Brill.
Friedländer, Moritz. 1898. *Der Vorchristliche-Jüdische Gnosticismus*. Göttingen: Vandenhoeck & Ruprecht.
Goodenough, Erwin R. 1969. *By Light, Light; The Mystic Gospel of Hellenistic Judaism*. Amsterdam: Philo Press, 1969.
Graetz, Heinrich. 1846. *Gnostizismus und Judentum*. Krotoschin: Monasch.
Gruenwald, Ithamar. 1980. *Apocalyptic and Merkavah Mysticism*. AGJU 14. Leiden: Brill.
———. 2014. *Apocalyptic and Merkavah Mysticism*. AJEC 90. 2nd ed. Leiden: Brill.
Halperin, David J. 1980. *The Merkabah in Rabbinic Literature*. AOS 62. New Haven: American Oriental Society.
———. 1981. "Origen, Ezekiel's Merkabah, and the Ascension of Moses." *Church History* 50:261–75.
———. 1984. *Faces of the Chariot: Jewish Responses to Ezekiel's Vision*. TSAJ 16. Tübingen: Mohr Siebeck.
———. 1988. "Ascension or Invasion: Implications of the Heavenly Journey in Ancient Judaism." *Religion* 18:47–67.
Himmelfarb, Martha. 1993. *Ascent to Heaven in Jewish and Christian Apocalypses*. New York: Oxford University Press.
Huss, Boaz. 2015. "Jewish Mysticism: The Invention of an Unbroken Jewish Tradition." *Conference on Jewish Studies* 8:19–29.
Idel, Moshe. 1988. *Kabbalah: New Perspectives*. New Haven: Yale University Press.
James, William. 2008. *The Varieties of Religious Experience: A Study in Human Nature*. Waiheke Island: Floating Press.

Janowitz, Naomi. 1989. *The Poetics of Ascent: Theories of Language in a Rabbinic Ascent Text*. Albany: State University of New York Press.

Kraft, Robert A., and George W. E. Nickelsburg, eds. 1986. *Early Judaism and Its Modern Interpreters*. BMI 2. Philadelphia: Fortress; Atlanta: Scholars Press.

Lesses, Rebecca. 1995. "The Adjuration of the Prince of the Presence: Performative Utterance in a Jewish Ritual." Pages 185–206 in *Ancient Magic and Ritual Power*. Edited by Paul Mirecki and Marvin Meyer. RGRW 129. Leiden: Brill.

———. 1998. *Ritual Practices to Gain Power: Angels, Incantation and Revelation in Early Jewish Mysticism*. HTS 44. Harrisburg, PA: Trinity Press International.

———. 2007. "Amulets and Angels: Visionary Experience in the 'Testament of Job' and the Hekhalot Literature." Pages 49–74 in *Heavenly Tablets: Interpretation, Identity and Tradition in Ancient Judaism*. Edited by Lynn LiDonnici and Andrea Lieber. JSJSup 119. Leiden: Brill.

———. 2013a. "Image and Word: Performative Ritual and Material Culture in the Aramaic Incantations Bowls." Pages 377–408 in *Practicing Gnosis: Ritual, Magic, Theurgy and Liturgy in Nag Hammadi, Manichean and Other Ancient Literature; Essays in Honor of Birger A. Pearson*. Edited by April D. DeConick, Gregory Shaw, and John D. Turner. NHMS 85. Leiden: Brill.

———. 2013b. "Women and Gender in the Hekhalot Literature." Pages 279–312 in *Hekhalot Literature in Context: Between Byzantium and Babylonia*. Edited by Ra'anan Boustan, Martha Himmelfarb, and Peter Schäfer. TSAJ 153. Tübingen: Mohr Siebeck.

McGinn, Bernard. 1991. *The Foundations of Mysticism*. Vol. 1 of *The Presence of God*. New York: Crossroad.

Morray-Jones, Christopher. 1993. "Paradise Revisited (2 Cor 12:1–12): The Jewish Mystical Background of Paul's Apostolate." *HTR* 86:177–292.

Nitzan, Bilhah. 1994. "Harmonic and Mystical Characteristics in Poetic and Liturgical Writings from Qumran." *JQR* 85:163–83.

Orlov, Andrei. 2005. *The Enoch-Metatron Tradition*. TSAJ 107. Tübingen: Mohr Siebeck.

———. 2007. *From Apocalypticism to Merkabah Mysticism Studies in the Slavonic Pseudepigrapha*. JSJSup 114. Leiden: Brill.

———. 2009. "Arboreal Metaphors and the Divine Body Traditions in the Apocalypse of Abraham." *HTR* 102:439–51.

———. 2011. *Dark Mirrors Azazel and Satanael in Early Jewish Demonology*. Albany: State University of New York Press.

———. 2017a. *The Greatest Mirror: Heavenly Counterparts in the Jewish Pseudepigrapha*. Albany, New York: State University of New York Press.

———. 2017b. *Yahoel and Metatron: Aural Apocalypticism and the Origins of Early Jewish Mysticism*. TSAJ 169. Tübingen: Mohr Siebeck.

Otto, Rudolph. 1932. *Mysticism East and West: A Comparative Analysis of the Nature of Mysticism*. Translated by Bertha L. Bracey and Richenda C. Payne. New York: Macmillan.

Reed, Annette Yashiko. 2013. "Rethinking (Jewish-)Christian Evidence for Jewish Mysticism." Pages 349–77 in *Hekhalot Literature in Context: Between Byzantium and Babylonia*. Edited by Ra'anan Boustan, Martha Himmelfarb, and Peter Schäfer. TSAJ 153. Tübingen: Mohr Siebeck.

Rowland, Christopher, and Christopher Morray-Jones. 2009. *The Mystery of God: Early Jewish Mysticism and the New Testament*. CRINT 12. Leiden: Brill.

Sanders, Seth L. 2017. *From Adapa to Enoch: Scribal Culture and Religious Vision in Judea and Babylon*. TSAJ 167. Tübingen: Mohr Siebeck.

Schäfer, Peter. 1981. *Synopse zur Hekhalot Literatur*. TSAJ 2. Tübingen: Mohr Siebeck.

———. 1984. "New Testament and Hekhalot Literature: The Journey into Heaven in Paul and in Merkabah Mysticism." *JJS* 35:19–35.

———. 1992. *The Hidden and Manifest God: Some Major Themes in Early Jewish Mysticism*. Albany: State University of New York Press.

———. 2009. *The Origins of Jewish Mysticism*. Princeton: Princeton University Press.

Schiffman, Lawrence. 1982. "Merkabah Speculation at Qumran: The 4Q Serekh Shirot 'Olat ha-Shabbat." Pages 15–47 in *Mystics, Philosophers and Politicians: Essays in Jewish Intellectual History in Honor of A. Altmann*. Edited by J. Reinharz and D. Swetschinski. Durham: Duke University Press.

Schneider, Michael. 2012. *The Appearance of the High Priest: Theophany, Apotheosis and Binitarian Theology from Priestly Tradition of the Second Temple Period through Ancient Jewish Mysticism* [Hebrew]. Los Angeles: Cherub Press.

———. 2017. "Seventy Names and Seventy Books: Fourth Ezra and Hekhalot Literature." *Jewish Studies* 52:1–34.

Scholem, Gershom. 1941. *Major Trends in Jewish Mysticism*. New York: Schocken Books.

———. 1961. *Jewish Gnosticism, Merkabah Mysticism, and Talmudic Tradition*. 2nd ed. New York: Jewish Theological Seminary of America.

Segal, Alan F. 1977. *Two Powers in Heaven: Early Rabbinic Reports about Christianity and Gnosticism*. SJLA 25. Leiden: Brill.

———. 1990. *Paul the Convert: The Apostolate and Apostasy of Saul the Pharisee*. New Haven: Yale University Press.

Strugnell, John. 1960. "The Angelic Liturgy at Qumran: 4QSerek Shirot 'Olat Hashshabba." Pages 318–45 in *Congress Volume: Oxford 1959*. VTSup 7. Leiden: Brill.

Swartz, Michael D. 1994. "'Like the Ministering Angels': Ritual and Purity in Early Jewish Mysticism and Magic." *AJSR* 19:135–68.

———. 1996. *Scholastic Magic: Ritual and Revelation in Early Jewish Mysticism*. Princeton: Princeton University Press.

———. 2011a. "*Piyut* and Heikhalot: Recent Research and Its Implications for the History of Ancient Jewish Liturgy and Mysticism." Pages 263–81 in *The Experience of Jewish Liturgy: Studies Dedicated to Menachem Schmeltzer*. Edited by Debra Reed Blank. BRLJ 31. Leiden: Brill.

———. 2013. "Mystics without Minds? Body and Soul in Merkavah Mysticism." Pages 33–43 in *Meditation in Judaism, Christianity and Islam*. Edited by Halvor Eifring. London: Bloomsbury.

———. 2018. *The Mechanics of Providence: The Workings of Ancient Jewish Magic and Mysticism*. TSAJ 172. Tübingen: Mohr Siebeck.

Wolfson, Elliot R. 1993. "'Yeridah La-Merkabah': Typology of Ecstasy and Enthronement in Ancient Jewish Mysticism." Pages 13–44 in *Mystics of the Book: Themes, Topics, and Typologies*. Edited by Robert A. Herrera. New York: Lang.

———. 1994a. "Mysticism and the Poetic-Liturgical Compositions from Qumran: A Response to Bilhah Nitzan." *JQR* 85:185–202.

———. 1994b. *Through a Speculum That Shines: Vision and Imagination in Medieval Jewish Mysticism*. Princeton: Princeton University Press.

22
Early Judaism and Early Christianity

LUTZ DOERING

A chapter on early Judaism and early Christianity is an addition and innovation in the second edition of *Early Judaism and Its Modern Interpreters*. In the years around the rough terminus for the consideration of scholarship in the first edition (1980; see Kraft and Nickelsburg 1986), a number of fresh approaches to early Judaism began to appear in the scholarship on the New Testament and early Christianity. These approaches partly responded to changes in the study of early Judaism after the discovery of the Dead Sea Scrolls, which led to an appreciation of variegation in Second Temple Judaism. This essay will initially summarize these changes and then cover scholarship in the following areas: the historical Jesus and early Jewish texts and traditions, Paul's place in early Judaism, the study of early Judaism and further aspects of early Christianity, and the so-called parting of the ways between Judaism and Christianity.

1. Research on Multiform Early Judaism and Its Relevance for Early Christianity

The discovery of the Dead Sea Scrolls in the caves of Qumran is arguably the most important manuscript find for the study of early Judaism (see Alison Schofield's essay in this volume). Their impact on New Testament research is charted by Jörg Frey (2006), who distinguishes four periods: (1) an initial phase and premature assumptions (1947–ca. 1955), (2) the Qumran fever and the foundational discussion of material then available (ca. 1955–1970), (3) a period of stagnation (ca. 1970–1991), and (4) a new Qumran springtime (since 1991). In period (2), much relevant discussion took place, including "messianism and eschatology, baptism and the Last

Supper, ideas of the Spirit and dualism and predestination, the Christian use of the Scriptures, and the organization of the Early Church" (Frey 2006, 413–14). At the time, however, the majority of New Testament scholars continued to see the background to early Christianity in Hellenistic Judaism, the Greco-Roman world, or gnosticism. In addition, the Qumran finds available were dominated by texts from Cave 1, and scholarship tended to think of the Qumran community as a small sect "out there" in the desert. After the period of stagnation (3), which at least saw increased interest in legal matters with the publication of the Temple Scroll and initial reports about 4QMMT, it has been since the complete release of all texts, including the Cave 4 manuscripts, from 1991 onward that the variegated evidence of the Qumran scrolls, pointing to different kinds of texts and social groups (sectarian, nonsectarian, and perhaps protosectarian), has been fully appreciated. A number of cul-de-sacs have been identified; thus, no serious scholar today identifies Christian figures in Qumran texts or claims the presence of Christian texts for Cave 7. More recently, the marginalization of the Yahad has been given up, and it has begun to be seen as a more widespread and variegated group in Second Temple Judaism (Collins 2010a). Hence, Qumran texts are now set into a circumspect conversation with early Christian texts, with parallels being carefully established and bounded by comparison with other early Jewish and also Greco-Roman texts. This leads to a traditiohistorically more viable context for the New Testament, (e.g., Brooke 2005; Frey 2006; Kuhn 2006; or the studies in García Martínez 2009; or Rey 2014).

Another area is the study of the so-called Old Testament Apocrypha and Pseudepigrapha. While Pseudepigrapha studies had already been *en vogue* in the early twentieth century, it was only after the discovery of the Qumran scrolls that a more apposite context could be established for the Pseudepigrapha attested there (e.g., 1 Enoch and Jubilees). The upsurge in Pseudepigrapha (and also Apocrypha) studies since the 1970s, with collections and translations of primary texts, and latterly also major commentaries, has had a firm impact on the study of early Christianity (*OTP*; Charlesworth 1985; Bauckham, Davila, and Panayotov 2013; Commentaries on Early Jewish Literature; Hermeneia series; and Jüdische Schriften aus hellenistisch-römischer Zeit). The apocryphal and pseudepigraphal works point to different varieties of Judaism for the period between the fourth century BCE and the second century CE, which are difficult to locate socially or to align with any of the known sects of early Judaism. They are especially relevant for the interpretation of theological tropes and beliefs in the New Testament, such as Son of Man, messiah, kingdom of God, angelology, eschatological judgment, resurrection and afterlife, or rewards and punishments. Importantly, there are close intertextual links between some New Testament texts and some of the pseudepigraphal ones (e.g. Jude 14–15, quoting 1 En. 1.9; Jude 9 referring the lost end of the Assumption [or Testament] of Moses; or 1 Pet 3:19–20, probably alluding to 1 En. 10.11–15), while the Apocrypha have become part of the Christian Bible in its various versions. That Christians also handed down the Pseudepigrapha and partly reworked them shows that they could fit Christian agendas well. Study of these texts by New Testament scholars was fostered by the Society for New Testament Studies Pseudepigrapha seminar 1976–1983 (Charlesworth 1985), and scholars like George Nickelsburg (2003, 2006 [1st ed. 1972]), Michael Stone (2011), and Robert Kraft (2009) are notable for their wide-ranging and stimulating contributions on the Pseudepigrapha and their relevance for early Christianity. More recently, the meetings of the Enoch Seminar have highlighted the role of Enochic writings, their relation to other early Jewish texts, and their significance for early Christianity (Boccaccini 2007; Stuckenbruck and Boccaccini 2016; Boccaccini and Segovia 2016).

Equally important for understanding early Christianity are revisionist trends in the study of rabbinic literature and ancient Jewish historiography that question the previously held view of Pharisaism, constructed from rabbinic literature, as the normative Judaism of the period in which Christianity began. According to the revised approaches, the Pharisees were a prominent yet still minority group within Palestinian society known for their concern with table-fellowship and purity (Neusner 1973) and engaged in controversy with the relatively smaller sects of Sadducees and Essenes (Stemberger 1991). Shaye Cohen (1984) suggests that the significance of Yavneh (the place of the academy founded by R. Johanan b. Zakkai) lay in the internalization of debate. The direct and exclusive continuity between Pharisees and rabbis has been questioned (see, e.g., Stemberger 1991, 129–35), and the rabbis themselves now tend to be seen as initially constituting a circle of like-minded scholars rather than as controlling Jewish society (Hezser 1997). In short, early Judaism has come to be appreciated as variegated, and it has become difficult to pitch Jesus and early Christians "against the normative Judaism" of their time. While the editors of the first edition of *Early Judaism and Its Modern Interpreters* (Kraft and Nickelsburg 1986) went so far as to suggest that "it might be more appropriate to speak of early Judaisms" (2), such a notion is in danger of losing sight of the integrating aspects of the varieties of early Judaism. Nevertheless, the perception of variegation is important and allows us to understand how Christianity originated and initially developed within early Judaism, as shown presently.

2. The Historical Jesus and Second Temple Judaism

Much of the new quest for the historical Jesus inaugurated by Ernst Käsemann (1954 [ET 1964]) had been motivated by theological concerns and had emphasized the distinctiveness of Jesus over against Judaism, as witnessed by the prominence of the criterion of double dissimilarity *from Judaism* and the early church for the identification of authentic Jesus traditions. In contrast, a new trend that came to be called the Third Quest (the term was coined by N. T. Wright [Neill and Wright 1987, 379]) has invested a sustained effort in elucidating Jesus's social and religious context and hence his place within late Second Temple Judaism. Anticipated by Jewish scholars such as David Flusser (1968 [revised ET 2007]) and Géza Vermes (1973), who understood Jesus as a Galilean Jew, this trend can be characterized by a use of first-century sources, especially Josephus, the Dead Sea Scrolls, and apocalyptic literature, and a willingness to see the complex pluriformity of early Judaism (Wright 1996, 84–85). The Third Quest emerged within Anglophone scholarship around 1980 but has since become the dominant paradigm of Jesus research worldwide. The majority of European and some North American scholars involved in the quest follow Albert Schweitzer in assuming that Jesus expected the imminent coming of the kingdom of God. A number of predominantly North American scholars, however, privileging noncanonical Christian sources (e.g., the Gospel of Thomas) and/or working with a layered concept of Q in which the earliest layer is allegedly sapiential and noneschatological, view Jesus as a Cynic teacher retaining considerable (e.g., Crossan 1991) or very limited (e.g., Mack 1988) Jewish garb. However, as Gerd Theissen and Annette Merz comment, "the 'noneschatological' Jesus seems to have more Californian than Galilean local colouring" (1997, 29 [ET 1998, 11]). Closely connected with the Jesus Seminar, the noneschatological Jesus appears to have receded to the background in the past few years. Recent archaeological work, moreover, has shown beyond doubt the predominantly Jewish character of first-century Galilee (J. Reed 2000; Chancey 2002; Fiensy and Strange 2014–2015).

The most substantive attempts by individual scholars to locate Jesus in Second Temple Judaism thus far have been those of E. P. Sanders (1985,

1990, 1–96), Wright (1992, 1996)—inserting Jesus, in different ways, into Israel's "restoration eschatology"—as well as John Meier (1991–2016). Theissen and Merz (1997 [ET 1998]) provide an initial summary of this quest and pose methodological questions, in particular as to the continued use of the criterion of double dissimilarity (not least by Meier), which they suggest should be replaced with a search for "double plausibility," that is, regarding both Jesus's fit into a Jewish context and the effects Jesus's ministry had on the development of early Christianity. More recent collaborative efforts have yielded impressive summaries of the quest (Holmén and Porter 2011 [4 vols.]; Schröter and Jacobi with Nogossek 2017). Meanwhile, the criteria in Jesus research more generally have come under methodological scrutiny (e.g., Keith and Le Donne 2012), and several attempts have been made to establish memory in Jesus research, either on the assumption of "informal controlled tradition" (Dunn 2003b, referring to the work of K. Bailey [205–10]) or as a hermeneutical paradigm centering on the Jesus images of the (Synoptic) Gospels (Schröter in Schröter and Jacobi, with Nogossek 2017, 112–24).

In studies influenced by the Third Quest, Jesus is typically located within the political context of first-century Palestine and within the religious context of first-century Judaism (e.g., see contributions to Holmén and Porter 2011; Schröter and Jacobi, with Nogossek 2017). Third Quest scholars compare and partly contrast Jesus with anti-Roman rebels, messianic pretenders, and sign prophets (see Horsley with Hanson 1999 on the social profiles of these movements). Jesus's calling of disciples is seen as both inspired by Israelite prophets and, in its inclusion of tax collectors and sinners (Mark 2:13–17 par.), as undermining the values of the religious elites. His calling of *twelve* disciples is symbolically connected with the restoration of Israel, though interpretations thereof differ in detail. Jesus's proclamation of the kingdom of God can be related to Jewish expectations, while the temporal structure and the role Jesus assigns to himself in the coming of the kingdom distinguish his message from that of his contemporaries. His healings and exorcisms are viewed in the context of prophetic miracles and Jewish discourses on demonic powers. His practice of table-fellowship with the marginalized—leading to the accusation of being a "glutton and wine-bibber" (Luke 7:34)—can be explained as an anticipation of the eschatological banquet expected in a variety of Jewish traditions. Jesus's addressing God as Father is less distinct from Jewish ways of speaking about and with God than scholars like Joachim Jeremias (1966 [ET 1967]) claimed. On the other hand, Jesus's parables, while generally belonging with a Jewish mode of narration, have no precise equivalent in Second Temple Judaism. Jesus's ethic, which centers round the love commandment, "is a Jewish ethic" (Theissen and Merz 1997, 350 [ET 1998, 394]).

A related field that has particularly benefited from the close study of early Jewish sources is Jesus and halakah. Contrary to the view held by Käsemann (1954, 146–47 [ET 1964, 40]), that "Jesus felt himself in a position to override, with an unparalleled and sovereign freedom, the words of the Torah and the authority of Moses," scholars more recently have argued that, later developments of the material in the gospels notwithstanding, Jesus engages in the halakic debates of his Jewish contemporaries. Suffice it to point to three examples. First, far from abrogating the Sabbath commandment, Jesus inserts his healing on the Sabbath into Jewish discourses on life saving while pointing to the creational character of the Sabbath as serving human beings (Mark 2:27–28; 3:4 par.; Doering 1999, 409–32, 441–57). Second, although Jesus's apparently general prohibition of divorce (Mark 10:2–9 par.) stands out within ancient Judaism, one hinge of his argument—that God created humankind "male and female" (Gen 1:27)—is invoked for related issues (probably polygyny) in CD-A IV, 20–21 (e.g., Doering 2009; for the wider treatment of the topic in the Jesus tradition and Paul, which includes the slightly different aspect of remarriage after divorce [Mark 10:10–12; 1 Cor 7:11], see Loader 2012, 240–92). Third, in Mark 7:14–23 Jesus might reject the Pharisaic innovation of mandatory hand washing, retaining the older view that hands cannot defile food in a way that would render a human being consuming it unclean; only in *this* respect, "he declared all foods clean" (Mark 7:15; Furstenberg 2008; cf. Poirier 1996; for the wider context see Kazen 2002). The reference to creation in some of these debates may point to a more realistic notion of law held by Jesus, as it prevails, mutatis mutandis, also in Qumran texts (Kazen 2013); in the Jesus tradition, it can be viewed in the context of an *Endzeit-Urzeit* correspondence in which primordial conditions are restored in the eschaton (Doering 2009).

While interpretations of Jesus's temple action and temple saying differ in detail, there is now a tendency to compare them with the expectation of an eschatological temple in certain early Jewish texts such as Jubilees or the Temple Scroll (e.g., Sanders 1985, 61–76; Wright 1996, 405–28) or to view them in the context of prophetic criticism of the temple and its establishment (e.g., Evans 1997). Moreover, many scholars see a connection between the temple action and Jesus's death. Jesus's passion is evaluated within the social, political, legal, and religious context of first-century Judea (e.g., Theissen and Merz 1997, 387–410 [ET 1998, 440–69]).

3. Paul's Place in Early Judaism

The question of Paul's place in Judaism had been reopened after World War II by two very different contributions. One was Rudolf Bultmann's *Theology of the New Testament* (Bultmann 1953 [ET 1952–1955]; the first German installment appeared in 1948). Bultmann followed the placement of Paul within the Hellenistic thought world proposed by the Göttingen history of religions school (e.g., Bousset) at the beginning of the twentieth century. Moreover, his Lutheran and existentialist approach took its cue from anthropology and described faith as a change from a merited—and hence misguided—existence to one that is given as a free gift. As a result, Paul's Jewishness receded to the background, and Judaism in general became a cipher for "natural humanity" in its attempt to secure its existence through merit ("works"). The second book was W. D. Davies's *Paul and Rabbinic Judaism* (1948). In it, Davies argued for Paul's proximity to rabbinic Judaism; in fact, he was a Pharisee who believed the messiah had arrived. There are problems with this view due to the monolithic and anachronistic picture of Judaism built on later (rabbinic) sources and insufficient attention to Paul's critique of the law and Jewish lifestyle. However, with the discovery of the Dead Sea Scrolls and the intensification of scholarship on early Judaism in the postwar period (see above), time was ripe for a more nuanced placement of Paul in early Judaism.

Following the critique of the Lutheran introspective interpretation by Krister Stendahl (1960), it was Sanders's *Paul and Palestinian Judaism* (1977) that can be seen as a watershed in Pauline studies of the last decades, and this led the way to what has come to be known as the New Perspective on Paul (first so labeled by Dunn in 1983; see Dunn 2008, 99–120). In this book, Sanders forcefully attacks the negative view of Judaism as a religion of works righteousness. The central notion in Sanders's proposal is "covenantal nomism": all major segments of early Judaism (except for, says Sanders, the author of 4 Ezra) agree that the covenant is a divine gift and that the torah is not to be kept in order to *earn* covenant membership but rather to *express* it. In short, law-keeping is not about "getting in" but about "staying in." Comparing "patterns of religion," Sanders claims that Paul's pattern is structurally analogous to that of "common Judaism" (a term Sanders would elaborate on later; see Sanders

1992), but that he replaced the covenant by faith in Christ. In fact, what is wrong with Judaism for Paul is that "it is not Christianity" (Sanders 1977, 552). Other scholars developed the New Perspective further. James Dunn (2008) regards circumcision, food laws, and the Sabbath not only as identity markers but also as boundary markers aimed at upholding Israel's special status vis-à-vis the gentiles, and these national boundaries Paul targets with the term "works of the law" (e.g. Gal 2:16), and he rejects them for his gentile believers—a notion Dunn also perceives as present in 4QMMT. To critics of his thesis, Dunn has responded that "works of the law" are not *limited* to these legal issues but that these are in fact in focus in Galatians (213–15, 413–17). Wright (2013), in a recent summary of his thinking on Paul, develops the thesis that Paul, like many other early Jewish figures (including Jesus), thought about Israel as being in a real or metaphorical exile, awaiting the fulfillment of the covenantal blessings: a new exodus, God's coming to his temple, and a new creation. For Wright, Paul's theology is structured by layered, concentric narratives: The outer one extends from creation to new creation; embedded in it is the narrative of Abraham's family, and at its core lies the story of the messiah Jesus fulfilling the faithfulness that Israel was unable to accomplish (for a critical assessment of a narrative approach to Pauline theology see Longenecker 2002). Francis Watson (rev. ed. 2007), also critical of the Lutheran Paul, suggests that Paul turned to the gentile mission only after his message had been rejected by fellow Jews. Watson employs a "sociological approach" (thus the subtitle of the 1st ed. 1986) and argues that Paul has transformed his mission from a reform movement to a "sect," with salvation requiring membership therein. Paul's message aims at legitimizing "the social reality of sectarian Gentile Christian communities in which the law was not observed" (2007, 345). In the revised edition (2007), Watson suggests that his view points "beyond the New Perspective."

Indeed, since the late 1990s the New Perspective has received sustained criticism, particularly as regards the notion of covenantal nomism and a perceived loss of depth in Pauline theology. Critics have pointed out that both early Judaism and Paul's theology were more complex than New Perspective scholars assume (Carson, Seifrid, and O'Brien 2001, 2004), that retribution remains fundamental in Judaism (Avemarie 1996, for rabbinic texts), and that the individual's stance before God, dependent on obedience, is more important in early Judaism than the New Perspective allows for (Gathercole 2002). For some, a Lutheran interpretation of Paul is therefore not to be dismissed outright, though the distorted image of Judaism as a religion of work righteousness is untenable (e.g., Westerholm 2004). In Germany, the mainland of the Lutheran interpretation, reception of the New Perspective was initially hesitant (for early criticism see e.g. Hengel and Stuhlmacher in Hengel and Heckel 1991). Since then, however, German-speaking scholars have adopted (mainly with reference to Sanders and Dunn) important insights of the New Perspective, particularly as to an appropriate account of early Judaism, though often putting the emphasis within Paul's theology different from Anglophone scholars and yielding original contributions to the debate (see, e.g., Bachmann and Woyke 2005; Maschmeier 2010; Wolter 2011 [ET 2015]; Frey 2012; evaluation in Gathercole 2013).

In addition, individual aspects relevant for Paul's relationship with Judaism have been studied in recent years: his self-presentation as Hebrew and Israelite (Niebuhr 1992), his adaptation of Jewish halakah in his teaching to gentiles (Tomson 1990), his indebtedness to early Jewish argumentation and interpretation (a rich area of study, see, e.g., Frey 2000; Kuhn 2006; Kister 2007; Tiwald 2008; Rey 2014; Cover 2015), alternatively reframed as a multisided dialogue between Paul and Jewish authors (e.g., Watson 2004; Maston 2010), as well as Paul's role in the development of a Christian letter practice building on *both* Greco-Roman *and* Jewish epistolary cultures (Doering 2012).

The most recent phase of the Paul debate is marked by contradictory tendencies. While some scholars proceed along the lines of the (now neither new nor uniform) New Perspective (e.g., Wright 2013), and the "old" approaches continue to attract evangelicals in particular, others attempt to preserve insights of the New Perspective regarding Jewish theologies while showing how and why Paul differs; thus, John Barclay (2015) argues that while grace features in all varieties of first-century Judaism, Paul differs from most varieties in proclaiming an *incongruous* gift that calls for a response. Yet others engage in what has come to be called the Radical New Perspective or, perhaps more appropriately, an approach seeing Paul within Judaism. Forerunners of this approach in North America were Lloyd Gaston (1987), Stanley Stowers (1994), and John Gager (2000), who argued that Paul addressed gentiles only, not Jews, so that his critique of law does not affect the latter. Paul within Judaism scholars both sharpen the sociological approach and wish to avoid what is perceived, even in the proposals of the New Perspective, as continued supersessionism. Instead, Paul is here seen as remaining completely within Judaism. For most of the scholars identifying with this trend (e.g., the contributors to Nanos and Zetterholm

2015) this means that he does not problematize torah obedience for Jewish believers in Christ. In contrast, "Paul's instructions are specifically about what is appropriate *for non-Jews* who turn to God through Jesus Christ" (Nanos and Zetterhom 2015, 146, emphasis original). It remains debated how best to describe these believing non-Jews: Christians is anachronistic; they are like, but also unlike, Godfearers—or, as Paula Fredriksen (2017, 74) puts it, they can be described as "ex-pagan pagans." Within a scenario of eschatological restoration "the nations join *with* Israel, but they do not *join* Israel" (Fredriksen 2010, 243, emphasis original). Matthew Thiessen (2016) argues that Paul was in fact an "ethnic essentialist" who, much like the author(s) of Jubilees, does not accept the possibility of gentiles converting to Judaism by circumcision; hence, their participation *had* to be effected by other means (similarly Hayes 2015, 141–51). On the other hand, critics of the newest approach(es) have asked whether Paul's criticism of the law can really be construed as limited to non-Jews (Wedderburn 2005) and whether Paul's construction of his gentiles-in-Christ as Abraham's seed does not challenge the eschatological model "that requires the distinction between non-Jews and Jews to be maintained," as typically proposed by Paul within Judaism scholars (Donaldson 2015, 298).

4. The Study of Early Judaism and Further Aspects of Early Christianity

One area for which the importance of Jewish traditions for early Christianity has been underlined in recent decades is the area of messianism and Christology. Scholarship on early Jewish messianism was significantly advanced by John Collins (2010b [1st ed. 1995]), who moved away from the focus on the term messiah and conceptually considered royal, priestly, and prophetic notions of messianism emerging from the Dead Sea Scrolls and other early Jewish texts. Moreover, while previous New Testament research attempted to emphasize the novelty of Christology over against Jewish monotheism, recent research has suggested that early Judaism developed binitarian tendencies in which an exalted figure appears alongside God and that these tendencies are relevant for the understanding and early development of early Christology. In this context, the Son of Man of Dan 7, of the Similitudes of Enoch (1 En. 37–71), and of 4 Ezra 13 plays an important role. Against the collective interpretation of the Son of Man of Dan 7:13 *en vogue* in earlier research, this figure is increasingly identified with the archangel Michael (see Collins 2016, 122–33; Koch 2007; Schäfer 2017,

25–30; though contrast Boyarin 2012b). In the Similitudes of Enoch, the Son of Man is exalted to a God-like position, and the concluding chapters 1 En. 70–71, somewhat surprisingly, describe Enoch's apotheosis. While this might not necessarily be taken as anticipating the Christian notion of God incarnate (Boyarin 2012a, 85; for criticism, see Schäfer 2017, 52–60), the role of the Similitudes of Enoch—now often dated to the early or mid-first century CE (Collins 2016, 221)—for an historical understanding of New Testament Christology is seen more positively now (cf. Boccaccini 2007). Despite its slightly later date (around 100 CE), 4 Ezra with its combination of the Son of Man figure and the messiah is also indicative of a trend in early Judaism relevant for the New Testament. Klaus Koch (1993) suggested that this "two stage" messianology, with the distinction between a preliminary activity, often ascribed to the messiah, and a strictly eschatological one belonging to the new eon, often associated with the Son of Man, is also suggestive for New Testament passages like Rom 1:3–4 or Mark 14:62 as well as the distinction between "Christ" and "Son of Man" language. Furthermore, the identification of wisdom with the Logos in sapiential literature (e.g. Wis 7:22–30; 9:4–11) and the elevation of the Logos in Philo (e.g., *Conf.* 146–147; *QG* 2.62) are now taken as indicative of early Jewish binitarian tendencies akin to, rather than different from, for example, Johannine Christology (Schäfer 2017, 31–39, 69–71). Moreover, Paul's notion of Christ has now come to be seen not as contrasting with but corresponding to early Jewish messiah language (Novenson 2012). While some scholars see the honorific language of Jewish messianism as instrumental to the emergence of Christ-devotion (Horbury 1998) or even go as far as to assume Jewish worship of other figures besides God (e.g., conceptualized as "divine humanity" as God's image by Fletcher-Louis 1999), others deem worship to Christ a Christian innovation, claiming that such worship is withheld from the exalted figures in early Judaism (e.g., Hurtado 2003). More generally, recent study of Jewish apocalypticism has shed new light on the Synoptic Gospels, Paul's letters, and Revelation (summarized in Collins 2016, 321–51). In particular, Nickelsburg's (2006; 1st ed. 1972) study of resurrection and immortality and Loren Stuckenbruck's (2014) work on evil and demons have opened up new avenues for research on these topics in early Christianity.

Overall, recent New Testament scholarship tends to be less antithetical in its comparison of early Jewish and New Testament traditions. Thus, while it is acknowledged that the double love command of the Synoptic Gospels is without exact counterpart in early Jewish sources, the relevance of summaries of the attitude toward God and human beings in Hellenistic Jewish texts (Philo, Testament of the Twelve Patriarchs) is affirmed (e.g., Berger 1972; Berthelot 2004). The prevalent research methodology is not to assume genealogical dependence but rather to create a conversation between these texts, while in a few cases reception is still deemed possible. One such area is the reception of scripture: New Testament authors, especially Paul (e.g., Lincicum 2010), John (Menken 2015), and Hebrews (Docherty 2009), are now typically set within their early Jewish context without any leveling of their particularities. This pertains also to the text forms of the scriptures received by early Christian authors, which are placed within the debate about the Septuagint/Old Greek and its (Jewish) recensions and revisions (e.g., Kraus and Karrer, with Meiser 2010; de Vries and Karrer 2013). In addition, several authors have studied the reception and appropriation of Jewish festivals in early Christianity (e.g., Ulfgard 1998; Weiss 2003; Stökl Ben Ezra 2003; Felsch 2011; Wheaton 2015), pointing also to ruptures in early Christian celebration of festivals (Leonhard 2017). Others have probed the ways in which Jewish halakah lay at the foundation of Christian ethics (e.g., Bockmuehl 2000). A further field is epistolography, where the study of Greco-Roman practices has recently been supplemented by a consideration of Jewish letter writing, which shows formal and pragmatic similarities (e.g., communication with communities, diaspora letters; Doering 2012). Another approach is to compare one author or group of witnesses with the New Testament. Thus, Steve Mason (2003) shows the relevance of the study of Josephus for the New Testament, Reimund Bieringer et al. (2010) that of rabbinic literature.

5. The Parting of the Ways between Judaism and Christianity

An area of intensive debate over the past decades has been the question of when and how Christianity parted ways with Judaism. The metaphor of the parting of the ways replaced an older model, according to which Christianity was perceived as Judaism's daughter religion, and instead assumes a process in the shape of a Y: out of a common entity, two distinct religions emerge, rabbinic Judaism and Christianity. An early study establishing this notion was James Parkes (1934), who suggested that, after the initial clash in the conflicts of Jesus and the earliest church, the outcome of the first Jewish war set the scene for the development to follow (for the influence of Parkes, see Burns 2016, 19–25). Both the Pharisaic precursors of the rabbis and the Jewish Christians are said to have fled Jerusalem, the former to Yavneh, the latter to Pella. But the destruction of Jerusalem and the temple was interpreted by the Jewish Christians differently, as the "departure of the scepter from Israel," and they consequently strengthened their links with gentile Christians. The parting of the ways thus took place in the Yavnean period (70–135 CE), when the Pharisaic sages regrouped as rabbis and excluded the Jewish Christians through the insertion of the Birkat Haminim ("blessing [i.e., cursing] of the heretics") into the Eighteen Benedictions. The Jewish Christians, in turn, could not accept the (other) Jews' embrace of another messiah and hence refused to support the Bar Kokhba revolt, while the Jews, though divided on Bar Kokhba, were agreed on refusing Christ as messiah (Parkes 1934, 77–79).

Parkes allowed that some had come to a separation "much earlier, even as Paul and other Jewish apostles had done" (79). Such a view is still found among some recent scholars. Thus, Udo Schnelle (2005, 159–70; expanded in 2014, 160–74) views the designation of the Christ-believers in Antioch as *christianoi* around 40 CE as indicative of their beginning to be perceived as distinct from Jews. According to Schnelle, this development was conceptually strengthened by Paul's mission to the gentiles and led to the separation of the predominantly gentile congregations in Rome from the Jewish community by the end of the 50s CE. Within this approach, the mission to the gentiles is seen as leading the church out of Judaism. Hence, Ulrich Luz (2007, 54–55) thinks the Matthean community, despite its "Jewish-Christian" roots, "no longer belongs to the Jewish synagogue"; Matthew's Gospel, with its emphasis of the gentile mission (Matt 28:18–20), provides the response to the rejection of Jesus by the majority of Israel. More recently, however, scholars have justly questioned whether there was already Christianity distinct from Judaism during the times of either Paul (see, e.g., Wolter 2011, 23 [ET 2015, 23–24]) or Matthew (see, e.g., Konradt 2007 [ET 2014]).

The importance of Yavneh, the Birkat Haminim, and the Bar Kokhba revolt for the parting is emphasized in numerous studies (from a Judaic studies perspective see Schiffman 1985). In his monograph on the partings (*sic*) of the ways, Dunn (1991) initially adopted such a general scheme as well, with some emphasis on the series of rifts until the eventual parting. Another volume edited by Dunn (1992) pointed to somewhat more variegation in the parting, both in scholars' opinions and in the varieties of Christianity under discussion. Thus, Philip Alexander (1992, 1–25) suggested a somewhat later parting because the rabbis still seemed to interact with Jewish-Christian *minim*. Dunn (1992, 177–211) himself argued that Acts, Matthew, and John, despite their anti-Jewish statements, do not imply that the parting was completed, as Judaism was itself being redefined at the time of their writing. Nevertheless, it seemed that for the Epistle of Barnabas and Justin Martyr the parting had already occurred, though they were still in contact with Jews (Horbury 1992, 315–45). Hence, this volume suggested that while the period 70–135 CE was "of particular importance for 'the parting of the ways,'" the latter "was very 'bitty,' long drawn out and influenced by a range of social, geographical, and political as well as theological factors" (Dunn 1992, 368, 367).

Since then, the firmness of the parting of the ways and even the usefulness of the metaphor have been questioned. Poignantly, the title of Adam Becker and Annette Yoshiko Reed's book (2003) claimed that the ways "never parted," though in fact the contributions to this volume tend to take the fourth century CE as the period from which Judaism and Christianity appear distinct from one another. Particularly notable for revisiting the issue is the work of Judith Lieu and Daniel Boyarin (acknowledged in the 2nd ed. of Dunn's monograph [2003a, xii, xxii–xxiii]). Lieu (1996; 2002, 11–29; 2004) points to the ongoing engagement between Jews and Christians, with no firm boundaries in the second century, and emphasizes the rhetorical function of patristic discourses of the Other, which suggests the ongoing existence of social ties, however undesirable they may seem to these writers. Boyarin (2004) claims that "Judaeo-Christianity," as he calls it, "partitioned" only in the fourth century, when Judaism was created as a counterpart of Christianity in the heresiological discourses of both proto-orthodox Christians and rabbinic Jews, and within the political context of a Christianized Roman Empire. Incidentally, these debates also raise questions regarding the distinction between "early" Judaism and rabbinic Judaism, as the process of the parting appears to comprise both. Moreover, they call for more attention to Jewish Christianity, which tends to be sidelined by older scholarly accounts (for critical evaluation, see Reed 2018). Also, the temple destruction in 70 CE was hardly a firm watershed that could be used to distinguish early from subsequent Judaism (see Schwartz and Weiss, with Clements 2012).

More recently, there have been several moderating voices, in part again suggesting evidence for some earlier partings of ways. Developing observations by Martin Goodman (e.g., 1992, 27–38) that changes in the administration of the *fiscus Judaicus* under Nerva in 96 CE implied a religious definition of who was a Jew, Marius Heemstra (2010) argues that this change was decisive, since from now on Jewish Christians could be regarded as no longer being Jewish. Daniel Stökl Ben Ezra (2009), generally sympathetic to blurred boundaries and ongoing interaction, nevertheless suggests that a comparison of the typical contents of an early Jewish library (i.e., Qumran) and Christian books from second- and third-century Egypt (as attested to in the Leuven Database of Ancient Books) shows some divergence in the inclusion of group-specific books, which is higher for the Christian side. Hence it is questionable "to speak of Christianity as a *Jewish* group or as a form of *Judaism* from the late second century onward at the latest, at least in Egypt" (171–72, emphasis original). Moreover, Cohen (2018) summarizes his general endorsement of the older view that Jews and Christians formed separate communities already in the first half of the second century. At the same time, the editors of a volume appearing in the same year as Cohen's contribution suggest a nonlinear approach to the parting of the ways, moving away from imagining it in a Y shape: "Jews who did not believe in or follow Jesus and Jews and gentiles who did believe in Jesus forged numerous partings, some minor and some major, some temporary and some irrevocable, some local and some, eventually, more widespread" (Baron, Hicks-Keeton, and Thiessen 2018, 3). It thus emerges more clearly now than ever that parting was an extended and variegated process, depending on place, time, and perspective.

6. Conclusion

In the past four decades or so, early Judaism—now perceived as more variegated—has been considered increasingly and in various productive ways to illuminate early Christianity. Major foci of study have been Jesus and Paul in their respective Jewish contexts, various tradition-historical links or material similarities with early Christianity, and the question of the parting of the ways. The strong antagonism between early Judaism and early Christianity assumed in some earlier scholarship has largely been abandoned. Not only does early Judaism shed light on early Christianity, but the same could also be said vice versa: Given the Jewishness of most New Testament texts, they can be read as early Jewish literature; moreover, there are ongoing discussions on how (Jewish) Christians may have informed the early rabbis (e.g., Burns 2016; and, considering also much later periods, Yuval 2006). The debate on the parting of the ways has in fact highlighted the question on when and how Judaism and Christianity can be distinguished from one another, and this debate is likely to continue.

Bibliography

Alexander, Philip S. "'The Parting of the Ways' from the Perspective of Rabbinic Judaism." Pages 1–25 in *Jews and Christians: The Parting of the Ways A.D. 70 to 135; The Second Durham-Tübingen Research Symposium on Earliest Christianity and Judaism (Durham, September, 1989)*. Edited by James D. G. Dunn. WUNT 66. Tübingen: Mohr Siebeck.

Avemarie, Friedrich. 1996. *Tora und Leben: Untersuchungen zur Heilsbedeutung der Tora in der frühen rabbinischen Literatur*. TSAJ 55. Tübingen: Mohr Siebeck.

Bachmann, Michael, and Johannes Woyke, eds. 2005. *Lutherische und Neue Paulusperspektive: Beiträge zu einem Schlüsselproblem der gegenwärtigen exegetischen Diskussion*. WUNT 182. Tübingen: Mohr Siebeck.

Barclay, John M. G. 2015. *Paul and the Gift*. Grand Rapids: Eerdmans.

Baron, Lori, Jill Hicks-Keaton, and Matthew Thiessen, eds. 2018. *The Ways That Often Parted: Essays in Honor of Joel Marcus*. ECL 24. Atlanta: SBL Press.

Bauckham, Richard, James R. Davila, and Alexander Panayotov. 2013. *Old Testament Pseudepigrapha: More Noncanonical Scriptures*. Vol. 1. Grand Rapids: Eerdmans.

Becker, Adam H., and Annette Yoshiko Reed. eds. 2003. *The Ways That Never Parted: Jews and Christians in Late Antiquity and the Early Middle Ages*. TSAJ 95. Tübingen: Mohr Siebeck.

Berger, Klaus. 1972. *Die Gesetzesauslegung Jesu, Teil 1: Markus und Parallelen*. WMANT 40. Neukirchen-Vluyn: Neukirchener Verlag.

Berthelot, Katell. 2004. *L'"humanité de l'autre homme" dans la pensée juive ancienne*. JSJSup 87. Leiden: Brill.

Bieringer, Reimund, Florentino García Martínez, Didier Pollefeyt, and Peter Tomson, eds. 2010. *The New Testament and Rabbinic Literature*. JSJSup 136. Leiden: Brill.

Boccaccini, Gabriele, ed. 2007. *Enoch and the Messiah Son of Man: Revisiting the Book of Parables*. Grand Rapids: Eerdmans.

Boccaccini, Gabriele, and Carlos A. Segovia, eds. 2016. *Paul the Jew: Rereading the Apostle as a Figure of Second Temple Judaism*. Minneapolis: Fortress.

Bockmuehl, Markus. 2000. *Jewish Law in Gentile Churches: Halakhah and the Beginning of Christian Public Ethics*. Edinburgh: T&T Clark.

Boyarin, Daniel. 2004. *Border Lines: The Partition of Judaeo-Christianity*. Divinations. Philadelphia: University of Pennsylvania Press.

———. 2012a. *The Jewish Gospels: The Story of the Jewish Christ.* New York: New Press.

———. 2012b. "Daniel 7, Intertextuality, and the History of Israel's Cult." *HTR* 105:139–62.

Brooke, George J. 2005. *The Dead Sea Scrolls and the New Testament.* Minneapolis: Fortress.

Bultmann, Rudolf. 1953. *Theologie des Neuen Testaments.* Tübingen: Mohr Siebeck.

———. 1952–1955. *Theology of the New Testament.* Translated by Kendrick Grobel. 2 vols. London: SCM.

Burns, Joshua Ezra. 2016. *The Christian Schism in Jewish History and Jewish Memory.* New York: Cambridge University Press.

Carson, D. A., Peter T. O'Brien, and Mark A. Seifrid, eds. 2001, 2004. *Justification and Variegated Nomism.* 2 vols. WUNT 2/140, 181. Tübingen: Mohr Siebeck.

Chancey, Mark A. 2002. *The Myth of a Gentile Galilee.* SNTSMS 118. Cambridge: Cambridge University Press.

Charlesworth, James H. 1985. *The Old Testament Pseudepigrapha and the New Testament: Prolegomena for the Study of Christian Origins.* SNTSMS 54. Cambridge: Cambridge University Press.

Cohen, Shaye J. D. 1984. "The Significance of Yavneh: Pharisees, Rabbis, and the End of Jewish Sectarianism." *HUCA* 55:27–53.

———. 2018. "The Ways That Parted: Jews, Christians, and Jewish Christians." Pages 307–39 in *Jews and Christians in the First and Second Century: The Interbellum 70–132 CE.* Edited by Joshua J. Schwartz and Peter J. Tomson. CRINT 15. Leiden: Brill.

Collins, John J. 2010a. *Beyond the Qumran Community: The Sectarian Movement of the Dead Sea Scrolls.* Grand Rapids: Eerdmans.

———. 2010b. *The Scepter and the Star: Messianism in Light of the Dead Sea Scrolls.* 2nd ed. Grand Rapids: Eerdmans.

———. 2016. *The Apocalyptic Imagination: An Introduction to Jewish Apocalyptic Literature.* 3rd ed. Grand Rapids: Eerdmans.

Cover, Michael. 2015. *Lifting the Veil: 2 Corinthians 3:7–18 in Light of Jewish Homiletic and Commentary Traditions.* BZNW 210. Berlin: de Gruyter.

Crossan, John Dominic. 1991. *The Historical Jesus: The Life of a Mediterranean Jewish Peasant.* San Francisco: HarperCollins.

Davies, W. D. 1948. *Paul and Rabbinic Judaism: Some Rabbinic Elements in Pauline Theology.* London: SPCK.

Docherty, Susan E. 2009. *The Use of the Old Testament in Hebrews: A Case Study in Early Jewish Bible Interpretation*. WUNT 2/260. Tübingen: Mohr Siebeck.

Doering, Lutz. 1999. *Schabbat: Sabbathalacha und -praxis im antiken Judentum und Urchristentum*. TSAJ 78. Tübingen: Mohr Siebeck.

———. 2009. "Marriage and Creation in Mark 10 and CD 4–5." Pages 133–63 in *Echoes from the Caves: Qumran and the New Testament*. Edited by Florentino García Martínez. STDJ 85. Leiden: Brill.

———. 2012. *Ancient Jewish Letters and the Beginnings of Christian Epistolography*. WUNT 298. Tübingen: Mohr Siebeck.

Donaldson, Terence L. 2015. "Paul within Judaism: A Critical Evaluation from a 'New Perspective' Perspective." Pages 277–301 in *Paul within Judaism*. Edited by Mark D. Nanos and Magnus Zetterholm. Minneapolis: Fortress.

Dunn, James D. G. 1991. *The Partings of the Ways: Between Christianity and Judaism and Their Significance for the Character of Christianity*. London: SCM.

———, ed. 1992. *Jews and Christians: The Parting of the Ways A.D. 70 to 135; The Second Durham-Tübingen Research Symposium on Earliest Christianity and Judaism (Durham, September, 1989)*. WUNT 66. Tübingen: Mohr Siebeck.

———. 2003a. *The Partings of the Ways: Between Christianity and Judaism and Their Significance for the Character of Christianity*. 2nd ed. London: SCM.

———. 2003b. *Jesus Remembered*. Christianity in the Making 1. Grand Rapids: Eerdmans.

———. 2008. *The New Perspective on Paul*. Rev. ed. Grand Rapids: Eerdmans.

Evans, Craig A. 1997. "From 'House of Prayer' to 'Cave of Robbers': Jesus' Prophetic Criticism of the Temple Establishment." Pages 417–42 in *The Quest for Context and Meaning: Studies in Intertextuality in Honor of James A. Sanders*. Edited by Craig A. Evans and Shemaryahu Talmon. BIS 28. Leiden: Brill.

Felsch, Dorit. 2011. *Die Feste im Johannesevangelium: Jüdische Tradition und christologische Deutung*. WUNT 2/308. Tübingen: Mohr Siebeck.

Fiensy, David A., and James R. Strange, eds. 2014–2015. *Galilee in the Late Second Temple and Mishnaic Periods*. 2 vols. Minneapolis: Fortress.

Fletcher-Louis, Crispin H. T. 1999. "The Worship of Divine Humanity as God's Image and the Worship of Jesus." Pages 112–128 in *The Jewish*

Roots of Christological Monotheism: Papers from the St. Andrews Conference on the Historical Roots of the Worship of Jesus. Edited by Carey C. Newman, James R. Davila, and Gladys S. Lewis. JSJSup 63. Leiden: Brill.

Flusser, David. 1968. *Jesus: Mit Selbstzeugnissen und Bilddokumenten dargestellt*. Reinbek: Rowohlt.

―――. 2007. *The Sage from Galilee: Rediscovering Jesus' Genius*. Revised by R. Steven Notley. Grand Rapids: Eerdmans.

Fredriksen, Paula. 2010. "Judaizing the Nations: The Ritual Demands of Paul's Gospel." *NTS* 56:232–52.

―――. 2017. *Paul: The Pagans' Apostle*. New Haven: Yale University Press.

Frey, Jörg. 2000. "The Notion of 'Flesh' in 4QInstruction and the Background of Pauline Usage." Pages 197–226 in *Poetical, Liturgical and Sapiential Texts: Proceedings of the Third Meeting of the International Organization for Qumran Studies, Oslo, 1998; Published in Memory of Maurice Baillet*. Edited by Daniel K. Falk, Florentino García Martínez, and Eileen M. Schuller. STDJ 35. Leiden: Brill.

―――. 2006. "The Impact of the Dead Sea Scrolls on New Testament Interpretation: Proposals, Problems, and Further Perspectives." Pages 407–61 in *The Scrolls and Christian Origins*. Vol 3 of *The Bible and the Dead Sea Scrolls*. Edited by James H. Charlesworth. Waco, TX: Baylor University Press.

―――. 2012. "The Jewishness of Paul." Pages 57–96 in *Paul: Life, Setting, Work, Letters*. Edited by Oda Wischmeyer. London: T&T Clark.

Furstenberg, Ya'ir. 2008. "Defilement Penetrating the Body: A New Understanding of Contamination in Mark 7.15." *NTS* 54:176–200.

Gager, John G. 2000. *Reinventing Paul*. New York: Oxford University Press.

García Martínez, Florentino, ed. 2009. *Echoes from the Caves: Qumran and the New Testament*. STDJ 85. Leiden: Brill.

Gaston, Lloyd. 1987. *Paul and the Torah*. Vancouver: University of British Columbia Press.

Gathercole, Simon. 2002. *Where Is Boasting: Early Jewish Soteriology and Paul's Response in Romans 1–5*. Grand Rapids: Eerdmans.

―――. 2013. "Deutsche Erwiderungen auf die 'New Perspective': Eine anglophone Sicht." Pages 115–53 in *Die Theologie des Paulus in der Diskussion: Reflexionen im Anschluss an Michael Wolters Grundriss*. Edited by Jörg Frey and Benjamin Schließer. BThS 140. Neukirchen-Vluyn: Neukirchener Verlag.

Goodman, Martin. 1992. "Disapora Reactions to the Destruction of the Temple." Pages 27–38 in *Jews and Christians: The Parting of the Ways*

A.D. 70 to 135; *The Second Durham-Tübingen Research Symposium on Earliest Christianity and Judaism (Durham, September, 1989).* Edited by James D. G. Dunn. WUNT 66. Tübingen: Mohr Siebeck.

Hayes, Christine E. 2015. *What's Divine about Divine Law: Early Perspectives.* Princeton: Princeton University Press.

Heemstra, Marius. 2010. *The Fiscus Judaicus and the Parting of the Ways.* WUNT 2/277. Tübingen: Mohr Siebeck.

Hengel, Martin, and Ulrich Heckel, eds. 1991. *Paulus und das antike Judentum: Tübingen-Durham-Symposium im Gedenken an den 50. Todestag Adolf Schlatters (†19. Mai 1938).* WUNT 58. Tübingen: Mohr Siebeck.

Hezser, Catherine. 1997. *The Social Structure of the Rabbinic Movement in Roman Palestine.* TSAJ 66. Tübingen: Mohr Siebeck.

Holmén, Tom, and Stanley E. Porter, eds. 2011. *Handbook for the Study of the Historical Jesus.* 4 vols. Leiden: Brill.

Horbury, William. 1992. "Jewish-Christian Relations in Barnabas and Justin Martyr." Pages 315–45 in *Jews and Christians: The Parting of the Ways A.D. 70 to 135; The Second Durham-Tübingen Research Symposium on Earliest Christianity and Judaism (Durham, September, 1989).* Edited by James D. G. Dunn. WUNT 66. Tübingen: Mohr Siebeck.

———. 1998. *Jewish Messianism and the Cult of Christ.* London: SCM.

Horsley, Richard A., with John S. Hanson. 1999. *Bandits, Prophets, and Messiahs: Popular Movements at the Time of Jesus.* Harrisburg, PA: Trinity Press International.

Hurtado, Larry W. 2003. *Lord Jesus Christ: Devotion to Jesus in Earliest Christianity.* Grand Rapids: Eerdmans.

Jeremias, Joachim. 1966. "Abba." Pages 15–67 in Jeremias, *Abba: Studien zur neutestamentlichen Theologie- und Zeitgeschichte.* Göttingen: Vandenhoeck & Ruprecht.

———. 1967. "Abba." Pages 11–65 in Jeremias, *The Prayers of Jesus.* SBT 6. London: SCM.

Käsemann, Ernst. 1954. "Das Problem des historischen Jesus." *ZTK* 51:125–53.

———. 1964. "The Problem of the Historical Jesus." Pages 15–47 in Käsemann, *Essays on New Testament Themes.* Translated by W. J. Montague. SBT 41. London: SCM.

Kazen, Thomas. 2002. *Jesus and Purity Halakhah: Was Jesus Indifferent to Impurity?* ConBNT 38. Stockholm: Almqvist & Wiksell.

———. 2013. *Scripture, Interpretation, or Authority? Motives and Arguments in Jesus' Halakic Conflicts.* WUNT 320. Tübingen: Mohr Siebeck.

Keith, Chris, and Anthony Le Donne, eds. 2012. *Jesus, Criteria, and the Demise of Authenticity*. London: T&T Clark.
Kister, Menahem. 2007. "Romans 5:12–21 against the Background of Torah-Theology and Hebrew Usage." *HTR* 100:391–424.
Koch, Klaus. 1993. "Messias und Menschensohn: Die zweistufige Messianologie der jüngeren Apokalyptik." *JBTh* 8:73–102.
———. 2007. "Der 'Menschensohn' in Daniel." *ZAW* 119:369–85.
Konradt, Matthias. 2007. *Israel, Kirche und die Völker im Matthäusevangelium*. WUNT 215. Tübingen: Mohr Siebeck.
———. 2014. *Israel, Church, and the Gentiles in the Gospel of Matthew*. Waco, TX: Baylor University Press.
Kraft, Robert A. 2009. *Exploring the Scripturesque: Jewish Texts and Their Christian Contexts*. JSJSup 137. Leiden: Brill.
Kraft, Robert A., and George W. E. Nickelsburg, eds. 1986. *Early Judaism and Its Modern Interpreters*. BMI 2. Philadelphia: Fortress; Atlanta: Scholars Press.
Kraus, Wolfgang, and Martin Karrer, with Martin Meiser, eds. 2010. *Die Septuaginta—Texte, Theologien, Einflüsse: 2. Internationale Fachtagung veranstaltet von Septuaginta Deutsch (LXX.D), Wuppertal 23.–27.7.2008*. WUNT 252. Tübingen: Mohr Siebeck.
Kuhn, Heinz-Wolfgang. 2006. "The Impact of Selected Qumran Texts on the Understanding of Pauline Theology." Pages 153–85 in *The Bible and the Dead Sea Scrolls, Volume III: The Scrolls and Christian Origins*. Edited by James H. Charlesworth. Waco, TX: Baylor University Press.
Leonhard, Clemens. 2017. "Celebrations and the Abstention from Celebrations of Sacred Time in Early Christianity." Pages 265–86 in *The Construction of Time in Antiquity: Ritual, Art, and Identity*. Edited by Jonathan Ben-Dov and Lutz Doering. New York: Cambridge University Press.
Lieu, Judith M. 1996. *Image and Reality: The Jews in the World of the Christians in the Second Century*. Edinburgh: T&T Clark.
———. 2002. *Neither Jew nor Greek? Constructing Early Christianity*. Edinburgh: T&T Clark.
———. 2004. *Christian Identity in the Jewish and Graeco-Roman World*. Oxford: Oxford University Press.
Lincicum, David. 2010. *Paul and the Early Jewish Encounter with Deuteronomy*. WUNT 2/284. Tübingen: Mohr Siebeck.
Loader, William. 2012. *The New Testament on Sexuality*. Grand Rapids: Eerdmans.

Longenecker, Bruce W., ed. 2002. *Narrative Dynamics in Paul: A Critical Assessment*. Louisville: Westminster John Knox.

Luz, Ulrich. 2007. *Matthew 1–7: A Commentary*. Rev. ed. Hermeneia. Minneapolis: Fortress.

Mack, Burton L. 1988. *A Myth of Innocence: Mark and Christian Origins*. Philadelphia: Fortress.

Maschmeier, Jens-Christian. 2010. *Rechtfertigung bei Paulus: Eine Kritik alter und neuer Paulusperspektiven*. BWANT 189. Stuttgart: Kohlhammer.

Mason, Steve. 2003. *Josephus and the New Testament*. 2nd ed. Grand Rapids: Baker Academic.

Maston, Jason. 2010. *Divine and Human Agency in Second Temple Judaism and Paul*. WUNT 2/297. Tübingen: Mohr Siebeck.

Meier, John P. 1991–2016. *A Marginal Jew: Rethinking the Historical Jesus*. 5 vols. ABRL. New York: Yale University Press.

Menken, Maarten J. J. 2015. *Studies in John's Gospel and Epistles: Collected Essays*. CBET 77. Leuven: Peeters.

Nanos, Mark D., and Magnus Zetterholm, eds. 2015. *Paul within Judaism: Restoring the First-Century Context to the Apostle*. Minneapolis: Fortress.

Neill, Stephen, and Tom Wright 1987. *The Interpretation of the New Testament 1861–1986*. 2nd ed. Oxford: Oxford University Press.

Neusner, Jacob. 1973. *From Politics to Piety: The Emergence of Pharisaic Judaism*. Englewood Cliffs, NJ: Prentice-Hall.

Nickelsburg, George W. E. 1972. *Resurrection, Immortality, and Eternal Life in Intertestamental Judaism*. HTS 26. Cambridge: Harvard University Press.

———. 2003. *Ancient Judaism and Christian Origins: Diversity, Continuity, and Transformation*. Minneapolis: Fortress.

———. 2006. *Resurrection, Immortality, and Eternal Life in Intertestamental Judaism*. Exp. ed. HTS 26. New Haven: Harvard University Press.

Niebuhr, Karl-Wilhelm. 1992. *Heidenapostel aus Israel: Die jüdische Identität des Paulus nach ihrer Darstellung in seinen Briefen*. WUNT 62. Tübingen: Mohr Siebeck.

Novenson, Matthew V. 2012. *Christ among the Messiahs: Christ Language in Paul and Messiah Language in Ancient Judaism*. Oxford: Oxford University Press.

Parkes, James W. 1934. *The Conflict of the Church and the Synagogue: A Study in the Origins of Antisemitism*. London: Soncino.

Poirier, John C. 1996. "Why Did the Pharisees Wash Their Hands?" *JJS* 47:217–33.

Reed, Annette Yoshiko. 2018. *Jewish-Christianity and the History of Judaism*. TSAJ 171. Tübingen: Mohr Siebeck.

Reed, Jonathan L. 2000. *Archaeology and the Galilean Jesus: A Re-examination of the Evidence*. Harrisburg, PA: Trinity Press International.

Rey, Jean-Sébastien, ed. 2014. *The Dead Sea Scrolls and Pauline Literature*. STDJ 102. Leiden: Brill.

Sanders, E. P. 1977. *Paul and Palestinian Judaism: A Comparison of Patterns of Religion*. London: SCM.

———. 1985. *Jesus and Judaism*. London: SCM.

———. 1990. *Jewish Law from Jesus to the Mishnah: Five Studies*. London: SCM; Philadelphia: Trinity Press International.

———. 1992. *Judaism: Practice and Belief, 63 BCE–66 CE*. London: SCM; Philadelphia: Trinity Press International.

Schäfer, Peter. 2017. *Zwei Götter im Himmel: Gottesvorstellungen in der jüdischen Antike*. Munich: Beck.

Schiffman, Lawrence H. 1985. *Who Was a Jew? Rabbinic and Halakhic Perspectives on the Jewish-Christian Schism*. Hoboken, NJ: Ktav.

Schnelle, Udo. 2005. *Apostle Paul: His Life and Theology*. Translated by M. Eugene Boring. Grand Rapids: Baker Academic.

———. 2014. *Paulus: Leben und Denken*. 2nd ed. Berlin: de Gruyter.

Schröter, Jens, and Christine Jacobi, with Lena Nogossek, eds. 2017. *Jesus Handbuch*. Tübingen: Mohr Siebeck.

Schwartz, Daniel R., and Zeev Weiss, with Ruth Clements, eds. 2012. *Was 70 CE a Watershed in Jewish History? On Jews and Judaism before and after the Destruction of the Second Temple*. AGJU 78. Leiden: Brill.

Stemberger, Günter. 1991. *Pharisäer, Sadduzäer, Essener*. SBS 144. Stuttgart: Katholisches Bibelwerk.

Stendahl, Krister. 1963. "The Apostle Paul and the Introspective Conscience of the West." *HTR* 56:199–215.

Stökl Ben Ezra, Daniel. 2003. *The Impact of Yom Kippur on Early Christianity: The Day of Atonement from Second Temple Judaism to the Fifth Century*. WUNT 163. Tübingen: Mohr Siebeck.

———. 2009. "Weighing the Parts: A Papyrological Perspective on the Parting of the Ways." *NovT* 51:168–86.

Stone, Michael E. 2011. *Ancient Judaism: New Visions and Views*. Grand Rapids: Eerdmans.

Stowers, Stanley K. 1994. *A Rereading of Romans: Justice, Jews, and Gentiles*. New Haven: Yale University Press.
Stuckenbruck, Loren T. 2014. *The Myth of Rebellious Angels: Studies in Second Temple Judaism and New Testament Texts*. WUNT 335. Tübingen: Mohr Siebeck.
Stuckenbruck, Loren T., and Gabriele Boccaccini, eds. 2016. *Enoch and the Synoptic Gospels: Reminiscences, Allusions, Intertextuality*. EJL 44. Atlanta: SBL Press.
Theissen, Gerd, and Annette Merz 1997. *Der historische Jesus: Ein Lehrbuch*. 2nd. ed. Göttingen: Vandenhoeck & Ruprecht.
———. 1998. *The Historical Jesus: A Comprehensive Guide*. London: SCM.
Thiessen, Matthew. 2016. *Paul and the Gentile Problem*. Oxford: Oxford University Press.
Tiwald, Markus. 2008. *Hebräer von Hebräern: Paulus auf dem Hintergrund frühjüdischer Argumentation und biblischer Interpretation*. HBS 52. Freiburg im Breisgau: Herder.
Tomson, Peter J. 1990. *Paul and the Jewish Law: Halakha in the Letters of the Apostle to the Gentiles*. CRINT 3.1. Assen: Van Gorcum; Minneapolis: Fortress.
Ulfgard, Håkan. 1998. *The Story of Sukkot: The Setting, Shaping, and Sequel of the Biblical Feast of Tabernacles*. BGBE 34. Tübingen: Mohr Siebeck.
Vermes, Géza. 1973. *Jesus the Jew: A Historian's Reading of the Gospels*. London: Collins.
Vries, Johannes de, and Martin Karrer, eds. 2013. *Textual History and the Reception of Scripture in Early Christianity/Textgeschichte und Schriftrezeption im frühen Christentum*. SCS 60. Atlanta: Society of Biblical Literature.
Watson, Francis. 1986. *Paul, Judaism, and the Gentiles: A Sociological Approach*. SNTSMS 56. Cambridge: Cambridge University Press.
———. 2004. *Paul and the Hermeneutics of Faith*. London: T&T Clark.
———. 2007. *Paul, Judaism, and the Gentiles: Beyond the New Perspective*. Rev. ed. Grand Rapids: Eerdmans.
Wedderburn, A. J. M. 2005. "Eine neuere Paulusperspektive?" Pages 46–64 in *Biographie und Persönlichkeit des Paulus*. Edited by Eve-Marie Becker and Peter Pilhofer. WUNT 187. Tübingen: Mohr Siebeck.
Weiss, Herold. 2003. *A Day of Gladness: The Sabbath among Jews and Christians in Antiquity*. Columbia: University of South Carolina Press.
Westerholm, Stephen. 2004. *Perspectives Old and New: The "Lutheran" Paul and His Critics*. Grand Rapids: Eerdmans.

Wheaton, Gerry. 2015. *The Role of Jewish Feasts in John's Gospel.* SNTSMS 162. Cambridge: Cambridge University Press.
Wolter, Michael. 2011. *Paulus: Ein Grundriss seiner Theologie.* Neukirchen-Vluyn: Neukirchener Verlag.
———. 2015. *Paul: An Outline of His Theology.* Translated by Robert L. Brawley. Waco, TX: Baylor University Press.
Wright, N. T. 1992. *The New Testament and the People of God.* Christian Origins and the Question of God 1. London: SPCK.
———. 1996. *Jesus and the Victory of God.* Christian Origins and the Question of God 2. London: SPCK.
———. 2013. *Paul and the Faithfulness of God.* 4 parts in 2 vols. Christian Origins and the Question of God 4. London: SPCK.
Yuval, Israel Jacob. 2006. *Two Nations in Your Womb: Perceptions of Jews and Christians in Late Antiquity and the Middle Ages.* Translated by Barbara Harshav and Jonathan Chipman. Berkeley: University of California Press.

23
THE TRANSMISSION HISTORY OF THE APOCRYPHA AND PSEUDEPIGRAPHA

LIV INGEBORG LIED

The attention given to the transmission history of the texts categorized in scholarship as apocrypha and pseudepigrapha and the traditions associated with them is a relatively recent phenomenon. With some important exceptions, the focused study on the continuing lives of these texts and traditions beyond the centuries in which they are assumed to have originated can be traced back no further than the 1990s. The fact that the topic was not covered by any dedicated essay in the first edition of *Early Judaism and Its Modern Interpreters* (Kraft and Nickelsburg 1986) reflects this general situation in scholarship.

The study of the transmission of apocryphal and pseudepigraphal texts and traditions is currently a growing interest, and for good reasons. These texts and the traditions associated with them lived long and fascinating lives. They moved across religious communities and cultural spheres, they migrated from one language to another, they continued to be copied for centuries, they evolved as they circulated, and they mattered to the people who engaged with them. This essay aims to show how scholars have made sense of these complex historical and literary processes, focusing on some select, major, discourses in the field, and allowing for some reflections on potential ways forward.

I am grateful to Maria Cioată, Martha Himmelfarb, Matthew P. Monger, Lorenzo DiTommaso, Michael Stone, the Biblical Studies Colloquium at the University of Gothenburg, and the editors for their invaluable input and assistance.

1. Setting the Stage

This essay deals with scholarship on texts that have commonly been identified as apocrypha and pseudepigrapha. The term *apocrypha* is used differently in various academic fields, as well as by different religious communities. In this essay, I apply the term in the way it is commonly used by scholars of early Jewish writings to refer to texts that were part of the Greek Old Testament used by early Christian communities, but which are not found in the Hebrew Bible as we know it. The term *pseudepigrapha* has been in use in Western scholarship from the early eighteenth century onward (Fabricius 1713, 1722, 1723). It refers to texts that were part of neither the Hebrew Bible nor the Apocrypha, but which contain narratives about figures and events known from the Hebrew Bible/Old Testament and which are typically assumed to originate in the Jewish Second Temple period. The use of these categories in scholarship is widely debated, and rightfully so. The categorizations are conventional and etic in nature. They are not precise descriptions of discrete collections of texts, and both categories are defined negatively, that is, by *what they are not* (see Stone 2006b; Piovanelli 2007; Reed 2009; Stuckenbruck 2011; Burke and Piovanelli 2015; and Lim in the present volume for an overview of the larger complexity).

There are two reasons why I still retain the categorization in the present essay and consider it important to discuss precisely these two categories of texts together. First, the categories apocrypha and pseudepigrapha have ordered large parts of the scholarly discourse on the texts categorized as such, particularly in the Protestant West. As the later discussion will show, this does not mean that the categorization necessarily represents the texts in their differing historical contexts in a fruitful way. However, since this is an essay about *scholarship*, and not about the texts and traditions themselves, the categorization that has structured major parts of the scholarly conversation matters. Second, although both categories of texts have predominantly been transmitted in Christian communities, scholars have traditionally explored the texts categorized as apocrypha and pseudepigrapha as early and Jewish (emblematically, Kautzsch 1900; Charles 1913; Oesterley 1935). This means that scholarship on the transmission of apocrypha and pseudepigrapha share several challenges and see many of the same debates.

This essay concerns the transmission of texts and traditions. In this essay, I apply the term *text* when I talk about a writing or a book, that is, a discrete, identifiable and relatively substantial block of literary contents

(Stone 2006a). We come across texts either as discrete layout units in surviving manuscripts or in the shape of cultural conceptions of identifiable books. I apply the term *traditions* to refer to selections and expressions of a memorialized past (Reed 2015). Unlike texts, traditions are normally not found in self-contained accounts but are typically integrated into other works (see Macaskill with Greenwood 2013). When the term traditions appears in this essay, it refers to entities such as circulating stories and narrative clusters, paraphrases or interpretative solutions, as well as motifs and tropes. Traditions may be traced both in verbal (written and oral) and graphic works. Although the interest in visual arts has increased rapidly in recent years, scholarship on the transmission of apocryphal and pseudepigraphal traditions has privileged verbal expressions. The dominant focus in this essay on the transmission of verbal expressions in literary texts reflects this focus in the research literature.

I will apply the term *transmission* in a broad sense to talk about the interconnected cultural practices of preservation, mediation, and transformation of texts and traditions. When we turn our attention from the origins and early contexts of apocryphal and pseudepigraphal texts and traditions to their transmission, we direct our gaze toward an ongoing, and potentially multilinear, process of cultural engagement. This process may include—but neither presumes nor privileges—any given point of origin (Breed 2014). This means that processes of text production and text transmission may overlap. Likewise, the transmission process is in principle without end. To make this survey analytically stringent, though, this essay focuses on transmission of texts and traditions in *manuscript cultures*. Manuscript cultures are cultures in which texts were copied by hand, textual artifacts were relatively rare, texts were less streamlined than in a print culture and where textualization was only one technology of memorization among others (see Nichols 1990; Lied and Lundhaug 2017). It is important to keep in mind that a substantial proportion of the manuscripts that once included apocryphal and pseudepigraphal texts and traditions are assumedly lost. Furthermore, some of the practices that once involved these texts and traditions, such as oral transmission or learning narratives by heart, did not necessarily leave discernible traces for scholars to explore.

Ideally, this essay should include scholarship on the transmission of the Apocrypha and the Pseudepigrapha in religious communities beyond Judaism and Christianity. The exclusion of Muslim and Manichean engagement is artificial and unfortunate but necessary to make the essay manageable (see, however, Reeves 1992, 1999; Wasserstrom 1994; Pregill 2008; Crone 2016; Segovia 2017; Reed and Reeves 2018).

2. A Brief History of Scholarship: Four Major Approaches

The last two decades have seen a marked rise in interest in the study of the transmission of early Jewish texts and traditions, the Apocrypha and the Pseudepigrapha included. This increased attention to transmission history owes much to a general turn toward transmission, or reception, in wider circles of humanistic scholarship and the integration of these perspectives in research on early Jewish and Christian literatures. The interest in the transmission of texts and traditions is also fed by the wider attention to issues pertaining to technologies of memorization, such as text production, engagement and circulation; scribal-, book- and reading cultures; orality, aurality, memory and performance; as well as studies of manuscripts and art.

Some seminal publications by scholars specializing in the Apocrypha and the Pseudepigrapha have also been vital to the increased attention to transmission history. A contribution that is often invoked as its point of departure is Marinus de Jonge's book *The Testaments of the Twelve Patriarchs: A Study of Their Text, Composition and Origin*, originally published in 1953. In the preface to the second edition of this book, published in 1975, de Jonge reflects on the development of his research record since the first publication of the book. He pinpoints the change of focus from original composition to later transmission and thus illustrates some of the emerging shifts in the late twentieth century that would lead to more studies of transmission history. By the mid-1970s, more pioneering scholarship had been conducted, prominently by Michael E. Stone (e.g., 1986, 1991, 2006b) and Robert A. Kraft (e.g., 1976, 1994, 2001, 2009). Kraft's name is emblematically associated with methodological discussion of pseudepigraphal texts in Christian transmission. With his double focus on early Jewish literature and Armenian studies, Stone published a wide range of books and articles that became crucial to the exploration of the transmission of the Apocrypha and Pseudepigrapha.

Since the late-1990s, a wide group of scholars has made advancements to the way we understand the long lives of these texts and traditions. The same period also saw the organization of seminars and conferences that became generative spaces for communal debate (e.g., at the Society for New Testament Studies, Society of Biblical Literature, European Association of

Biblical Studies, and the Enoch Seminar). Special issues in journals and collaborative publication initiatives also offered a venue for the production of new knowledge about their history.

2.1. First Approach: The Long Life and Circulation of a Discrete Writing

Four main approaches have dominated the study of the transmission of the Apocrypha and the Pseudepigrapha. The first approach, which accounts for a substantial part of the studies, explores *the long life of a particular, identifiable writing* across linguistic and cultural divides. These studies show how specific texts circulated throughout history, how different communities engaged with them, and how these texts have both affected and been affected by these encounters. Typically, scholars have paid most attention to the texts that have either enjoyed a particularly wide transmission or been known in the Christian West for a long time, such as 4 Ezra/2 Esdras, the Testament of the Twelve Patriarchs, 1 Enoch, and Jubilees (e.g., Bergren 1996; de Jonge 2003; Hogan 2013; Stuckenbruck 2013; Himmelfarb 2016; Reed and Reeves 2018). Studies of the transmission history of Jubilees, for instance, show that this text was already circulating (in whole and in parts) and evolving in Hebrew in the first centuries BCE. Narratives known to us today as parts of this book were employed by Christian chronographers writing in Greek and Syriac in late antiquity. A Latin manuscript preserves parts of Jubilees in conjunction with other texts ascribed to Moses; Jubilees is referred to and paraphrased by Arabic sources; excerpts are part of Greek exegetical manuscripts; and the book is regularly part of medieval Ethiopic biblical manuscripts (e.g., Fabricius 1713; Rönsch 1874; Adler 1986–1987, 2003; VanderKam 2009; Reed 2015; Erho and Stuckenbruck 2013; Monger 2018; Hanneken 2019; Coogan forthcoming).

2.2. Second Approach: Exploring the Receiving Environments

The second major approach is the engagement with apocryphal and pseudepigraphal texts and traditions *in specific linguistic or cultural contexts, putting the receiving environments center stage*. From a bird's-eye view, the totality of these studies shows how these texts and traditions were known, copied, and applied by a wide range of communities, extending from old Irish in the north (e.g., Dumville 1973; Murdoch 1976, 2009) to Ethiopic communities in the south (Cowley 1988; Erho and Stuckenbruck 2013). These studies illustrate how the texts were used in specific historical contexts and point out how varied the reception could be at different times. Some of these studies show how although texts may be apocryphal or pseudepigraphal to the scholars who study them today; they may have been, for instance, biblical to one or more of the communities that engaged them in late antiquity and the Middle Ages. This is so for most texts categorized as apocryphal, as well as for texts such as 1 Enoch and Jubilees, which Ethiopic Christians probably understood as biblical. Other studies have highlighted the importance of specific linguistic contexts, such as the Greek, which has played a key mediating role in the history of transmission of the texts (e.g., Denis 1970; Stuckenbruck 2011). Other linguistic contexts, such as the Slavonic, are important because they preserve the only surviving or the most reliable witnesses of texts such as 2 Enoch and the Apocalypse of Abraham (e.g., Roddy 2001; Orlov 2009; Kulik and Minov 2016; DiTommaso and Böttrich 2011). The exploration of many of the cultural contexts that preserved and engaged the Apocrypha and Pseudepigrapha is still in an early phase. This is the situation for Coptic and Arabic transmission (but see, e.g., Graf 1944; Frankfurter 1996; Hjälm 2015). Other linguistic spheres have received more focused attention, often due to the efforts of individual scholars, but much work remains to be done. This is the case, for instance, for the Syriac (e.g., Brock 1979; Bundy 1991) and the Armenian (e.g., Stone 2006a).

2.3. Third Approach: Focus on the Media

The third approach in the history of research is the *focus on the media—the (material) forms that mediated apocryphal and pseudepigraphal texts and traditions*—primarily manuscripts and visual media, as well as oral storytelling. Although scholars have always paid attention to the manuscripts that preserve the texts in their capacity as text witnesses, the exploration of manuscript transmission *as reception* is still in an early phase. Such studies explore the texts as intrinsic parts of the manuscripts that contain them, seeing them as part of the fabric of the receiving contexts (e.g., Stone 1999; Miltenova [in Dimitrova 2010]; Gutman and Van Peursen 2011; Cioată 2012; Lied 2016). These studies pinpoint, for instance, the variety of collections in which they were included, the various formats in which the texts were copied, and how their names sometimes changed, inviting questions as to how those who came across these texts in the manuscripts may have identified them. Other studies explore traces of engagement by active readers that are still visible on the manuscript pages to explore how those who came across the texts in the manuscript context would have used them (e.g., Stuckenbruck and Erho 2018).

The last few decades have shown that the transmission of apocryphal and pseudepigraphal texts and traditions was multimedial. Apocryphal and pseudepigraphal materials were transmitted in graphic representations, such as in icons and frescos, manuscript illuminations and numismatic materials (e.g., Bailey 2010; Newman 2015; Gutman and Van Peursen 2011; Badalanova Geller 2017). Likewise, texts and traditions are likely to have been circulating in both oral and written form, often as interconnected and overlapping expressions (e.g., Reed and Reeves 2018). Texts were read aloud in public settings, heard and memorized, sometimes enacted, expressed in prayer or, as in the case of Judith, in musical form (e.g., Harness 2010). Due to the relatively high rates of illiteracy, the limited distribution of inscribed texts and the general importance of visual and oral/aural modes of communication throughout late antiquity and the Middle Ages, these forms of mediations were probably vital to the circulation of, and engagement with, apocryphal and pseudepigraphal traditions.

2.4. Fourth Approach: Exploring the Circulation of Traditions Associated with the Apocrypha and the Pseudepigrapha

The fourth approach to the history of transmission of the Apocrypha and the Pseudepigrapha is the study of the circulation of, and creative engagement with, *traditions*, most commonly *motifs, themes, figures, and narrative clusters associated with these texts*. For a long time, identifying citations from, and paraphrases of, apocryphal and pseudepigraphal texts in other literary texts was a common way of studying parallels or dependence (see, Fabricius 1713; Migne 1856–1858; Lawlor 1897; James 1920). These studies focused either on the source texts, tracing the origin of a tradition, or the receiving texts, exploring how traditions matter in new blends. By way of example, several studies have looked at the usages of traditions known (to us) from 1 Enoch in Jude and the Testaments of the Twelve Patriarchs, among Christian chronographers and patristic authors, and in apotropaic, esoteric, and commentary literature (e.g., Nickelsburg 1983; Adler 1989; VanderKam 1996; Boccaccini 2014; Reed 2005; Reed and Reeves 2018; Asale 2020). Another major focus is the interest in the engagement with exemplary figures and the narratives built around them. Numerous publications have addressed the continuing interest in, and development of, figures such as Adam, Eve, Melchizedek, Baruch, Judith, and Enoch, which can be traced back to knowledge of traditions found in apocryphal and pseudepigraphal accounts (e.g., Vanderkam 1996; Nickelsburg and Collins 1980; J. E. Wright 2003; Böttrich 2016; Gera 2010; Minov 2015; Adler 2018). Finally, several studies have traced the engagement with motifs or thematic clusters down through the centuries, displaying how they circulated and developed across cultural and linguistic contexts. Parts of this research have focused on the cultural dynamics that shaped their transmission, for instance, and importantly, in terms of folk tales or legends (e.g., Ginzberg 1909–1938; Yassif 1988, 2016; Kugel 1997; Badalanova Geller 2017). Other contributions have explored the longer life of particular expressions associated with apocryphal and pseudepigraphal traditions. Examples include studies of the lost tribes (e.g., James 1920) and (the disappearance of) the ark of the covenant (e.g., Milikowsky 2015). One of the most frequently explored story clusters is the widely distributed and evolving narratives about (fallen) angels and giants (Stuckenbruck 2007; Reed 2005, 2009). They appear in various shapes and with interconnected thematic emphases, such as preexisting angels (Granat 2015) and illicit angelic instruction (Reed 2014), or with a focus on Semihaza and Azazel (Reed 2001, 2005).

3. Three Major Debates

Three important debates have shaped and continue to shape the history of scholarship on the transmission of apocryphal and pseudepigraphal texts and traditions.

3.1. The Dynamics of Christian and Jewish Transmission: Continuity, Rupture, Reentry?

The first debate concerns some of the major dynamics of the transmission of these texts and traditions—their preservation in Christian communities and their (assumed) reentry into Jewish circles in the Middle Ages. Why did Christians continue to copy and engage the Apocrypha and the Pseudepigrapha? Why are copies of and references to the Apocrypha and the Pseudepigrapha relatively rare in Jewish sources up until the sixth/seventh century, and why did the situation assumedly change at the end of the period of the classical rabbinic literature?

As noted initially, the Apocrypha and the Pseudepigrapha were preserved throughout late antiquity and the early Middle Ages predominantly by Christians (e.g., Ginzberg 1909–1938; James 1920; Kraft 1975, 1994,

2009; Herr 1990; De Jonge 2003; Davila 2005; DiTommaso 2008; Stuckenbruck 2011; Stone 2011; Kulik et al. 2019). As De Jonge (2003) has suggested, a major reason for the preservation of these texts and traditions is probably the high regard and important functions of the Old Testament among Christians. However, it is also evident that the Christian transmission history of the Apocrypha and the Pseudepigrapha is complex and that it is intertwined with the history of the Old Testament in various ways.

For one, apocryphal and pseudepigraphal texts were copied as books in a variety of manuscripts. They appear in Old Testament codices of various formats. Apocryphal books are sometimes found as a discrete collection of writings. More often, though, individual apocryphal and pseudepigraphal writings were interspersed among, or attached to, other Old Testament books (Stuckenbruck 2011; Borchardt 2018). For instance, the Prayer of Manasseh appears in some Syriac manuscripts after Chronicles (Gutman and Van Peursen 2011), as do 2 Baruch and 4 Ezra in others (Lied 2016). The Testaments of the Twelve Patriarchs was copied after Genesis or after the Pentateuch in several Armenian manuscripts (Stone 2006a). Texts such as the Testament of Job, 3 Baruch, and Joseph and Aseneth are also found in hagiographical, homiletical, and miscellaneous collections (Harlow 1996; Burchard 2010; Miltenova [in Dimitrova 2010]; Cioată 2012). The identification of the collections that preserve apocryphal and pseudepigraphal books gives us one indication as to how discrete texts may have been perceived and how they may have been used. In some contexts, consequently, some texts have served as biblical books, while in other contexts they may have been understood, for instance, as saints' lives.

Importantly, the relationship between the Apocrypha, the Pseudepigrapha and the Old Testament should not be imagined exclusively as a relationship between fixed, written, and bound books and collections (Reed 2005; Mroczek 2016; Najman 2017). The transmission of these texts and traditions took place in cultural environments that were soaked in a multimedial and developing biblical narrative. That narrative was known through educational practices, worship contexts, legends, and lore, and it would be present through literary, graphic, and oral media. A major reason why the apocryphal and pseudepigraphal traditions were relevant to Christian communities was that they provided more information about key Old Testament figures, narratives, and events. They filled in lacunae in a comprehensive biblical storyline, adding information where the biblical accounts were meager, and as such they contributed to the evolving storyline in the communities that engaged with them (Reeves 1999; Bauckham

2008). One example of such use of apocryphal and pseudepigraphal traditions is found in Christian historiographical accounts. These traditions were probably included because they provided information about periods that were important to the Christian *historia sacra*, for instance, the antediluvian period. As pointed out above, narratives associated with Jubilees and 1 Enoch circulated as parts of Greek and Syriac chronographies (Adler 1989). Likewise, traditions associated with Melchizedek became part of Slavonic historiographical accounts, the so-called *palaea* literature (Böttrich 2011; Adler 2015, 2018).

Certain Christian ritual events and reading practices also served the continued relevance of apocryphal and pseudepigraphal traditions. The celebration of days of commemoration dedicated to exemplary biblical figures, such as Baruch, would warrant narratives associated with these figures being read in public settings (Bogaert 1969). Commentary and interpretative practices paved the way for the use of an extract of Jubilees in a Greek catena to Genesis, a manuscript containing a chain of exegetical extracts aiding the interpretation of Genesis (Coogan forthcoming). A variety of pseudepigraphal and apocryphal traditions also appears in the broadly distributed genre of question and answer texts (Miltenova 2004; Stone 2016).

It should be noted that many apocryphal and pseudepigraphal texts have been preserved in monastic circles (see Lied and Stuckenbruck 2019). Some of the texts clearly enjoyed a broader circulation, and it is possible that the large amount of texts found in monastic keeping attests, first and foremost, to their capacity for offering optimal survival conditions. Nevertheless, we cannot rule out the possibility that the circulation of many of these texts was always predominantly monastic and that monastic readers have thus been among their primary readers.

This brief sketch of scholarship confirms that the communities that preserved and engaged with apocryphal and pseudepigraphal texts and traditions throughout late antiquity and the early Middle Ages were primarily Christian. Many scholars hold that apocryphal and pseudepigraphal texts were generally not transmitted in Jewish communities in that period—at least not in rabbinic circles (e.g., Reeves 1999; Adelman 2009; Stuckenbruck 2011; Kister et al 2015; Himmelfarb 2019). Up until the sixth or seventh century, that is, the period of the classical rabbinic literature, the traces of apocryphal and pseudepigraphal *texts* in the surviving rabbinic literature are meager. *Traditions* associated with apocryphal and pseudepigraphal materials are present, though, but probably circulating and developing independently of the writings from which they were drawn (Yassif 1988; Kister et al 2015; Himmelfarb 2019). An intriguing exception is Ben Sira, which is both explicitly mentioned and cited in classical rabbinic literature (Labendz 2006; B. Wright 2018).

However, judging by the surviving source materials—and noting that our knowledge is restricted by what has survived—the situation changed at the end of the period of the classical rabbinic literature. The Cairo Genizah contained manuscript fragments of, for instance, Ben Sira, Aramaic Levi, the Testament of Naphtali, the Ladder of Jacob, the Prayer of Manasseh, and Tobit. This indicates that these texts were copied and circulating in Jewish milieus, roughly, at the turn of the millennium and onward (e.g., Leicht 1996; Fröhlich 2002; Bauckham, Davila, and Panayotov 2013). At this time, a larger repertoire of these texts, or excerpted portions of these texts, resurface in Jewish transmission. A broader range of traditions associated with both apocryphal and pseudepigraphal texts is found in rabbinic literature, in midrash, piyyut, in *hekhalot* literature, and in amulets and incantation bowls (e.g., Reeves 1999; Edrei and Mendels 2007; Davila 2013; Kister 2012; Kister et al. 2015; Wollenberg 2017; Himmelfarb 2019; Reed forthcoming).

How have scholars understood the Jewish transmission of apocryphal and pseudepigraphal texts and traditions? A long-standing hypothesis is that the texts continued to survive for centuries in select Jewish milieus and that this might explain, for instance, the appearance of the fragmented texts found in the Cairo Genizah (Geiger 1911; Albeck 1940; cf., Stone 1996a, 1996b). Another hypothesis holds that these texts and traditions reemerged in Jewish circles as the period of the classical rabbinic literature came to an end. How this happened remains debated (see Ballaban 1994; Reeves 1999; Adelman 2009). The reemergence could have been caused by a medieval manuscript find. Such finds are reported in late antique and medieval literary sources, for instance by Origen and by the patriarch Timothy I (Reeves 1999). Another suggestion is that the Jewish reemergence is the result of contact, intersections with and (back-)borrowing from neighboring communities (Himmelfarb 1994; Reeves 1999). There are many indications of cross-community sharing and interaction in the Middle Ages. Both people and manuscripts traveled. Christians, Jews, and Muslims coexisted in many areas, such as in Syro-Palestine, Spain, and Mesopotamia, and were likely to share both traditions and texts (e.g., Himmelfarb 1994; Reeves 1999; Edrei and Mendels 2007). Christian converts may also have translated texts (back) into Hebrew, and they may have brought literary traditions with them into Jewish milieus (Himmelfarb 1984; Gutman and Van Peursen 2011).

Some scholars have flagged the methodological challenges of this debate. As Stone (2019) and Martha Himmelfarb (2016, 2019) have pointed out, much remains unknown about the transmission of pseudepigraphal and apocryphal texts and traditions in medieval Jewish literature, intellectual circles, and society. New evidence may surface and change the current impression. Furthermore, it is unlikely that any single explanation will explain all aspects equally well. The hypotheses are not mutually exclusive and we should consider a broader set of alternatives along the survival-hiatus continuum (Kister et al 2015). As several scholars have pointed out, it is also important to remember that the simplistic categories "Jewish" and "Christian" may not serve as fruitful labels for the various individuals, groups, and communities that engaged with apocryphal and pseudepigraphal texts and traditions (e.g., De Jonge 1975; Satran 1995; Becker and Reed 2003; Reed 2009, 2015; Reed and Reeves 2018).

3.2. The Circulating Entity: Between Book and Stubborn Multivalence

The research literature that explores the Apocrypha and the Pseudepigrapha shows that scholars generally tend to imagine these texts as books, typically assumed to be copied correspondingly as identifiable layout units in extant manuscripts. This is how the major collections that have made the Apocrypha and the Pseudepigrapha available to modern readers throughout the last few centuries have represented them (e.g., Migne 1856–1858; Kautzsch 1900; Charles 1913; *OTP*; Sparks 1984; Bauckham, Davila, and Panayotov 2013). This is also how they were typically presented in the research literature published during the twentieth century. However, as a result of the increased interest in processes of transmission, the media and the cultural contexts that shaped them, scholars have responded to, and increasingly challenged, the dominant imagination of the circulating the Apocrypha and the Pseudepigrapha as books (Mroczek 2016). What is the *object* that is being transmitted and how do we conceptualize and imagine entities that are moving and changing?

One response to the dominant imagination draws on studies of the manuscripts that preserve the texts. Scholars have mapped the ways in which apocryphal and pseudepigraphal texts were copied, pointing out the bewildering variety of literary shapes and textual forms found in the manuscripts (e.g., Weeks, Gathercole, and Stuckenbruck 2004; Stone 2015; Lied 2015, 2017; DiTommaso 2005, 2019). Indeed, apocryphal and pseudepigraphal texts are sometimes copied as books, but often, as is the case, for instance, with the medieval Hebrew Tobit, they appear in a variety of shapes that differ from one another, sometimes significantly (Cioată 2017). Books may grow, as is the case with 4 Ezra, which at some point merged with 5 and 6 Ezra into the literary unit 2 Esdras, well known from the Vulgate (Bergren 1996). Sometimes, the transformation is so substantial that it may become more meaningful to talk about literary clusters or plural books rather than to represent the variance in terms of a singular book (e.g., Stone 2011).

Often, the Apocrypha and the Pseudepigrapha were not copied in their entirety, but in the form of autonomously circulating excerpted parts or as summaries (e.g., Yassif 1997; Stuckenbruck 2011; Lied 2013). Sometimes narratives associated with, or excerpted from, the texts, such as the story about the Maccabean mother and the seven sons, were copied on their own. Other smaller text units, such as prayers and epistles, were at times also copied autonomously (Gutman and Van Peursen 2011; Lied 2017). In other words, the manuscripts suggest that the book format is only one of many ways in which the Apocrypha and the Pseudepigrapha circulated. Representing all these shapes in terms of a book may easily create a biased view as to how these materials were perceived in the historical contexts that engaged with them.

Another response to the dominance of the book model is found in the research literature that explores the transmission of apocryphal and pseudepigraphal traditions, that is, accounts of the various shapes that are integrated into, and transmitted as parts of, other works. Many of these studies display the high degree of creativity involved and the corresponding difficulty in trying to identify any one-to-one dependence on a source text. As, for instance, the circulating narratives associated with Abraham, Melchizedek, and Judith show, popular storylines, narrative clusters, and motifs assume many shapes, they blend with other traditions and they evolve as they circulate (Bauckham 2008; Böttrich 2010; Gera 2010; Adler 2018). Annette Yoshiko Reed (2015) refers to this situation as "stubbornly multivalent" and warns about the risk of reification of literary entities that were flexible and evolving. Hence, these circulating and evolving narratives are neither fruitfully grasped in terms of clear-cut dependence on a former source text nor fruitfully imagined as part of a traceable, uniform, trajectory of a discrete, self-contained book.

An important outcome of these recent research contributions to the complexity of the transmission is that they challenge the scholarly imagination of texts and traditions assumed to be early and invite us to consider the nature of the source materials that provide access to them. As, among others, Lorenzo DiTommaso (2019) has pointed out, these texts are "*received* works, having been embroidered, reworked, and adapted to their later cultural settings" (emphasis original). In other words, the manuscript sources scholars apply to explore assumed early texts, often represented as books, are likely to have been transformed in transmission. We have access to diachronic products, often shaped over centuries, in broken trajectories, and as William Adler (2018) has argued, their development has typically been intertwined with their receiving contexts.

3.3. The Provenance Debate: Origins, Transmission and Back Again?

As pointed out in the introductory part of this essay, the dominant focus in scholarship on apocryphal and pseudepigraphal texts to date has been the earliest period of their existence, concentrating on processes of textual composition, authorship, and their originating milieus. Indeed, a major motivation for studying the Apocrypha and the Pseudepigrapha has been their potential for providing information about Second Temple Judaism and Christian origins. A debate, sometimes referred to as "the provenance debate," has addressed the tension that arises between this dominant scholarly interest in exploring pseudepigraphal texts as early Jewish products and the fact that these texts were predominantly transmitted by late antique and medieval Christian communities. Manuscripts dating to the time of the assumed origin of the texts are rare, which means that scholars do not have direct access to the texts as they were to those who first produced them. The access to the early texts and their producers is dependent on the surviving manuscripts and the communities that produced and preserved the manuscripts.

The debate is emblematically connected to the oeuvres of De Jonge, Stone, and Kraft. In the mid-1970s, Kraft explored the preservation of pseudepigrapha among Christians in two papers: "The Multiform Jewish Heritage of Early Christianity" (1975) and "The Pseudepigrapha in Christianity" (1976, published in 1994). In these papers, as well as in a series of later publications, Kraft (1994, 2001, 2009) addressed the methodological risks involved in the hasty scholarly use of Christian manuscript materials for distilling information about early Jewish texts without first exploring their significance as sources to Christian interests and activities. Kraft (2001, 372) summarizes his position in a much quoted passage: "I call this the 'default' position—sources transmitted by way of Christian communities are 'Christian' whatever else they may also prove to be."

A number of publications have heeded this call, creating cumulative effects in the field. Its effects can be seen, first, in the study of individual texts. The debate about the Testament of the Twelve Patriarchs is longstanding and exemplary. This text is now generally treated as a Christian, late antique text (de Jonge 1953, 2003). Similar debates have been raised—with various outcomes—about the Apocalypse of Elijah (Frankfurter 1993), the Lives of the Prophets (Satran 1995), the Ascension of Isaiah (Bettiolo and Norelli 1995), the Greek Life of Adam and Eve (de Jonge and Tromp 1997), 2 Baruch (Lied 2016), 3 Baruch (Harlow 1996, 2001; Himmelfarb 2016; Collins 2019), 4 Baruch (De Jonge 2000), Joseph and Aseneth (Kraemer 1998) and 1 Enoch (e.g., Knibb 2001). Second, the call has also ignited a general debate about the provenance of pseudepigraphal texts (e.g., Davila 2005). At the time of writing this essay, several views are simultaneously in sway. Some scholars challenge Kraft's "default position," arguing that each case must be explored individually (Bauckham 2008; Stuckenbruck 2011; Collins forthcoming).

Although generally acknowledged in the debates about the provenance of these texts, it is worth noting that the methodological warning championed by De Jonge, Stone, and Kraft has had a relatively marginal effect on editorial practices. With some notable exceptions, the focus remains on the early text; the manuscripts produced in later centuries are still valued primarily as witnesses to that text, and the text is still often represented as a singular, discrete unit (see, for example, Bauckham, Davila, and Panayotov 2013).

It is not without a touch of irony that the provenance debate—one of the debates that has produced the most knowledge about the *transmission* of the Pseudepigrapha—is in fact a debate about their *origins*. This fact frames the presentation of transmission. Sometimes, the transmission is explicitly construed as a problem of Christian additions and adaptions that need to be known in order to be overcome before a proper investigation of origins can take place (Van Henten and Schaller 2001). At other times, the discourse on origins is invoked to argue the relevance of a study of transmission, since the history of transmission has not necessarily been seen as interesting in its own right. For better or for worse, the writing of transmission history may then end up being framed by the major discussion points of a discipline geared toward understanding the origins of these texts and traditions (Davila 2005; De Jonge 2003).

As illustrated by the research contributions discussed in this essay, this is where scholarship on transmission history can make a difference. The current overview shows, first, that apocryphal and pseudepigraphal texts lived long lives, and second, that they typically continued to evolve as they circulated. If we assume, as many of the scholars mentioned in this essay do, that text production and text transmission overlap and that transmission is a continuing process without any clear beginning or end, we could see texts as diachronic and moving entities. Throughout their long lives, they would probably be equally at home in many communities—Jewish, Christian, or other. Such a discursive position would allow phases other than the assumed earliest phase of the life of a text to equally influence our judgment about what the text "is." What it was at given points in time, and what it became as the text circulated, would be equally interesting, valid and worthy of study.

4. Concluding Remarks

In summation, this essay has presented four major approaches to the history of transmission of apocryphal and pseudepigraphal texts and traditions. Scholars have focused on the paths of circulation of individual texts; the environments that received and engaged with them; the (material) forms that shaped their mediation; and the transmission and transformation of traditions associated with the Apocrypha and the Pseudepigrapha in later literature, art, and lore. The essay has also traced three major debates that have shaped scholarship on the transmission of these texts and traditions. The first debate explores the reasons for the continuing Christian copying of, and engagement with, the Apocrypha and the Pseudepigrapha during late antiquity and the Middle Ages, and their apparent reappearance in Jewish transmission only after the sixth/seventh century. The second debate concerns the shape of their circulation and challenges the scholarly imagination of the circulating units. The third and final debate addresses the question of the provenance of the Pseudepigrapha in particular and the importance ascribed to knowledge of the transmission of these texts in order to deal with the provenance question in a methodologically sound manner.

Two issues in particular deserve more attention in the years to come. First, as the research covered in this essay shows, the materials that provide access to apocryphal and pseudepigraphal texts and traditions are the *received* materials. With some exceptions, the majority of the manuscript sources we use when we study apocryphal and pseudepigraphal texts were produced by late antique and medieval Christian communities. The copies preserved in these manuscripts show that the texts have evolved. The extent of creative engagement by later transmitters varies, but the texts have sometimes changed to a relatively large degree. In other words, we generally base our study of apocryphal and pseudepigraphal texts and traditions on manuscripts produced by other and later communities than the ones that are commonly ascribed ownership of the literary texts, and the shapes of the texts available to us are the results of centuries of combinations of faithful copying and creative adaption. As some of the major voices in the debate about the transmission of these texts have stressed, we could fruitfully dedicate more attention to the investigation of the texts *as received texts*. Such an approach would be beneficial both to scholars who wish to apply manuscript copies as witnesses to earlier texts and to those who want to know more about the engagement with the texts in the receiving context.

Second, the focus on origins has served as a dominant discursive gravitational point in the disciplines dealing with the Apocrypha and the Pseudepigrapha. This means that many of the guiding hypotheses, interpretative frames, and categorizations in these fields were developed to better understand the earliest contexts of the texts and traditions. As we trace the long lives of apocryphal and pseudepigraphal texts and traditions, or pause on specific contexts of later engagement, they challenge us to move beyond the traditionally held limits of academic disciplines focusing on early Jewish literatures and to make the study of apocryphal and pseudepigraphal texts and traditions a matter of broader, interdisciplinary, humanistic concern. When we do, we may discover that the discourses that have framed the study of these texts as early Jewish texts may not necessarily be equally fruitful when exploring later periods. We may realize that the categories apocrypha and pseudepigrapha employed by scholars of early Judaism may not constitute fruitful categories to scholars focusing on later periods of Christian engagement. The divides between Pseudepigrapha, Apocrypha, New Testament/Christian Apocrypha, or the Bible for that matter, would be brought into play since these categories do not fruitfully grasp the diverse and fluctuating understanding of the texts and traditions in later centuries (Junod 1983; DiTommaso and Böttrich 2011; Burke and Piovanelli 2015; Stone 2018; Cioată 2019). In such an investigation of the longer lives of these texts and traditions, scholars trained in the wider spectrum of humanistic disciplines could even invite modern interpreters of early Judaism to study historical contexts where these texts were neither pseudepigrapha nor apocrypha.

Bibliography

Adelman, Rachel. 2009. *The Return of the Repressed: Pirqe De-Rabbi Eliezer and the Pseudepigrapha*. JSJSup 140. Leiden: Brill.

Adler, William. 1986–1987. "Abraham and the Burning of the Temple of Idols: Jubilees' Traditions in Christian Chronography." *JQR* 77:95–117.

———. 1989. *Time Immemorial: Archaic History and Its Sources in Christian Chronography from Julius Africanus to George Syncellus*. Dumbarton Oaks Studies 26. Washington, DC: Dumbarton Oaks.

———. 2003. "Reception History of the Book of Jubilees: A Prime Example." Paper presented at the Seminar on Christian Origins. Philadelphia, PA, March 13.

———. 2015. "Parabiblical Traditions and Their Use in the *Palaea Historica*." Pages 1–39 in *Tradition, Transmission, and Transformation from Second Temple Literature through Judaism and Christianity in Late Antiquity: Proceedings of the Thirteenth International Symposium of the Orion Center for the Study of the Dead Sea Scrolls and Associated Literature*. Edited by Menahem Kister, Hillel I. Newman, Michael Segal, and Ruth A. Clemens. STDJ 113. Leiden: Brill.

———. 2018. "The Story of Abraham and Melchizedek in the *Palaea Historica*." Pages 47–63 in *The Embroidered Bible: Studies in Biblical Apocrypha and Pseudepigrapha in Honour of Michael E. Stone*. Edited by Lorenzo DiTommaso, Matthias Henze, and William Adler. SVTP 26. Leiden: Brill.

Albeck, Hanoch. 1940. *Midrash Breshit Rabbati* [Hebrew]. Jerusalem: Mekize Nirdamim.

Asale, Bruk Ayele. 2020. *1 Enoch as Christian Scripture: A Study in the Reception and Appropriation of 1 Enoch in Jude and the Ethiopian Orthodox Tewahǝdo Canon*. Eugene, OR: Wipf & Stock.

Badalanova Geller, Florentina. 2017. "Clandestine Transparencies: Retrieving the Book of Jubilees in Slavia Orthodoxa (Iconographic, Apocryphal and Folklore Witnesses)." *Judaïsme ancien/Ancient Judaism* 5:183–279.

Bailey, Elizabeth. 2010. "Judith, Jael and Humilitas in the Speculum Virginum." Pages 275–90 in *The Sword of Judith: Judith Studies across the*

Disciplines. Edited by Kevin R. Brine, Elena Ciletti, and Henrike Lähnemann. Cambridge: Open Book.

Ballaban, Steven A. 1994. "The Enigma of the Lost Second Temple Literature: Routes of Recovery." PhD diss., Hebrew Union College.

Bauckham, Richard J. 2008. "The Continuing Quest for the Provenance of Old Testament Pseudepigrapha." Pages 9–29 in *The Pseudepigrapha and Christian Origins: Essays from the Studiorum Novi Testamenti Societas*. Edited by Gerbern S. Oegema and James H. Charlesworth. London: T&T Clark.

Bauckham, Richard J., James R. Davila, and Alexander Panayotov, eds. 2013. *Old Testament Pseudepigrapha: More Noncanonical Scriptures*. Vol 1. Grand Rapids: Eerdmans.

Becker, Adam H., and Annette Yoshiko Reed, eds. 2003. *The Ways That Never Parted: Jews and Christians in Late Antiquity and the Early Middle Ages*. TSAJ 95. Tübingen: Mohr Siebeck.

Bergren, Theodore A. 1996. "Christian Influence on the Transmission History of 4, 5, and 6 Ezra." Pages 102–27 in *Jewish Traditions in Early Christian Literature: The Jewish Apocalyptic Heritage in Early Christianity*. Edited by William Adler and James VanderKam. CRINT 3.4. Assen: Van Gorcum; Minneapolis: Fortress.

Bettiolo, Paolo, and Enrico Norelli. 1995. *Ascensio Isaiae: Textus, Commentarius*. CCSA 7–8. 2 vols. Turnhout: Brepols.

Boccaccni, Gabriele. 2014. "History of Research." http://www.4enoch.org/wiki4/index.php?title=Category:Enochic_Studies.

Bogaert, Pierre-Maurice. 1969. *Apocalypse de Baruch: Introduction, traduction du Syriaque et commentaire*. 2 vols. SC 144–145. Paris: Cerf.

Borchardt, Francis. 2018. "How Bel and the Serpent Went from Addition to Edition of Daniel." *CBQ* 80:409–28.

Böttrich, Christfried. 2010. *Weisheitliche, magische und legendarische Erzählungen: Geschichte Melchisedeks*. JSHRZ 1. Gütersloh: Gütersloher Verlagshaus.

———. 2011. "'Die Geschichte Melchisedeks' (histMelch) im slavischen Kulturkreis." Pages 159–200 in *Old Testament Apocrypha in the Slavonic Traditions: Continuity and Diversity*. Edited by Lorenzo DiTommaso and Christfried Böttrich. TSAJ 140. Tubingen: Mohr Siebeck.

———. 2016. "Melchizedek among Russian Saints: The History of Melchizedek between Jews and Slavs." Pages 373–90 in *The Bible in Slavic Tradition*. Edited by Alexander Kulik, Catherine Mary MacRobert, Svetlina

Nikolova, Moshe Taube, and Cynthia M. Vakareliyska. Studia Judaeoslavica 9. Leiden: Brill.

Breed, Brennan W. 2014. *Nomadic Text: A Theory of Biblical Reception History.* ISBL. Bloomington: Indiana University Press.

Brock, Sebastian P. 1979. "Jewish Traditions in Syriac Sources." *JJS* 30:212–32.

Bundy, David. 1991. "Pseudepigrapha in Syriac Literature." Pages 745–65 in *Society of Biblical Literature 1991 Seminar Papers.* SBLSP 30. Atlanta: Scholars Press.

Burchard, Christoph. 2010. *A Minor Edition of the Armenian Version of "Joseph and Aseneth."* Hebrew University Armenian Studies 10. Leuven: Peeters.

Burke, Tony, and Pierluigi Piovanelli, eds. 2015. *Rediscovering the Apocryphal Continent: New Perspectives on Early Christian and Late Antique Apocryphal Texts and Traditions.* WUNT 349. Tübingen: Mohr Siebeck.

Charles, R. H. 1913. *The Apocrypha and Pseudepigrapha of the Old Testament.* 2 vols. Oxford: Clarendon.

Cioată, Maria (Haralambakis). 2012. *The Testament of Job: Text, Narrative and Reception History.* LSTS 80. London: T&T Clark.

———. 2017. "Medieval Hebrew Tellings of Tobit: 'Versions' of the Book of Tobit or New Texts?" Pages 334–67 in *Is There a Text in This Cave? Studies in the Textuality of the Dead Sea Scrolls in Honour of George J. Brooke.* Edited by Ariel Feldman, Maria Cioată, and Charlotte Hempel. STDJ 119. Leiden: Brill.

———. 2019. "'Apocrypha' and 'Pseudepigrapha' as 'Popular Literature': Moses Gaster's Contributions in Conversation with Current Debates." *Scripta & E-Scripta* 19:205–63.

Collins, John J. 2019. "Pseudepigrapha between Judaism and Christianity." Pages 309–30 in *The Old Testament Pseudepigrapha: Fifty Years of the Pseudepigrapha Section at the SBL.* Edited by Matthias Henze and Liv Ingeborg Lied. EJL 50. Atlanta: SBL Press.

Coogan, Jeremiah. Forthcoming. "The Reception of Jubilees in a Fifth Century Catena of Genesis." *ZAC.*

Cowley, Roger W. 1988. *Ethiopian Biblical Interpretation: A Study in Exegetical Tradition and Hermeneutics.* University of Cambridge Oriental Publications 38. Cambridge: Cambridge University Press.

Crone, Patricia. 2016. "The *Book of Watchers* in the Qur'ān." Pages 183–218 in *The Qur'ānic Pagans and Related Matters.* Vol. 1 of *Collected Studies in Three Volumes*. Edited by Hanna Siurua. 3 vols. Islamic History and Civilization 129. Leiden: Brill.

Davila, James R. 2005. *The Provenance of the Pseudepigrapha: Jewish, Christian, or Other*. JSJSup 105. Leiden: Brill.

———. 2013. *Hekhalot Literature in Translation: Major Texts of Merkavah Mysticism*. JJTPSup 20. Leiden: Brill.

Denis, Albert-Marie. 1970. *Apocalypsis Henochi Graece: Fragmenta pseudepigraphorum quae supersunt graeca*. PVTG 3. Leiden: Brill.

Dimitrova, M. 2010. "Selected Publications of Anissava Miltenova." *Scripta & E-Scripta* 8–9:495–507.

DiTommaso, Lorenzo. 2005. *The Book of Daniel and the Apocryphal Daniel Literature*. SVTP 20. Leiden: Brill.

———. 2008. "Pseudepigrapha Research and Christian Origins after the *OTP*." Pages 30–50 in *The Pseudepigrapha and Christian Origins: Essays from the Studiorum Novi Testamentum Societas*. Edited by Gerbern S. Oegema and James H. Charlesworth. Jewish and Christian Texts in Contexts and Related Studies 4. New York: T&T Clark.

———. 2019. "The Pseudepigrapha and Manuscript Research in the Digital Age." Pages 231–62 in *The Old Testament Pseudepigrapha: Fifty Years of the Pseudepigrapha Section at the SBL*. Edited by Matthias Henze and Liv Ingeborg Lied. EJL 50. Atlanta: SBL Press.

DiTommaso, Lorenzo, and Christfried Böttrich, eds. 2011. *Old Testament Apocrypha in the Slavonic Traditions: Continuity and Diversity*. TSAJ 140. Tübingen: Mohr Siebeck.

DiTommaso, Lorenzo, Matthias Henze, and William Adler, eds. 2018. *The Embroidered Bible: Studies in Biblical Apocrypha and Pseudepigrapha in Honour of Michael E. Stone*. SVTP 26. Leiden: Brill.

Dumville, D. N. 1973. "Biblical Apocrypha and the Early Irish: A Preliminary Investigation." *Proceedings of the Royal Irish Academy* 73:299–338.

Edrei, Arye, and Doron Mendels. 2007. "A Split Jewish Diaspora: Its Dramatic Consequences." *JSP* 16:91–137.

Erho, Ted M., and Loren T. Stuckenbruck. 2013. "A Manuscript History of Ethiopic Enoch." *JSP* 23:87–133.

Fabricius, Johann A. 1713. *Codex Pseudepigraphus Veteris Testamenti*. Hamburg: Felginer.

———. 1722. *Codex Pseudepigraphus Veteris Testamenti*. 2nd ed. Hamburg: Felginer.

———. 1723. *Codicis Pseudepigraphi Veteris Testamenti Volumen Alterum*

Accedit Josephi Veteris Christiani Auctoria Hypomnesticon. Hamburg: Felginer.

Frankfurter, David. 1993. *Elijah in Upper Egypt: The Apocalypse of Elijah and Early Egyptian Christianity.* Studies in Antiquity and Christianity. Minneapolis: Fortress.

———. 1996. "The Legacy of Jewish Apocalypses in Early Christianity: Regional Trajectories." Pages 129–200 in *The Jewish Apocalyptic Heritage in Early Christianity.* Edited by James VanderKam and William Adler. CRINT 3.4. Assen: Van Gorcum; Minneapolis: Fortress.

Fröhlich, Ida. 2002. "The Dead Sea Scrolls and Geniza Studies." Pages 61–67 in *David Kaufmann Memorial Volume: Papers Presented at the David Kaufmann Memorial Conference, November 29 1999.* Edited by Éva Apor. Budapest: Library of the Hungarian Academy of Sciences.

Geiger, Abraham. 1911. *Judaism and Its History: In Two Parts.* New York: Bloch.

Gera, Deborah L. 2010. "The Jewish Textual Traditions." Pages 23–40 in *The Sword of Judith: Judith Studies across the Disciplines.* Edited by Kevin R. Brine, Elena Ciletti, and Henrike Lähnemann. Cambridge: Open Book.

Ginzberg, Louis. 1909–1938. *The Legends of the Jews.* Translated by Henrietta Szold and Paul Radin. 6 vols. Philadelphia: Jewish Publication Society.

Graf, Georg. 1944. *Die Übersetzungen.* Vol. 1 of *Geschichte der christlichen arabischen Literatur.* Studi e testi. Vatican City: Biblioteca apostolica Vaticana.

Granat, Yehoshua. 2015. "No Angels before the World? A Preexistence Tradition and Its Transformation from Second Temple Literature to Early Piyyut." Pages 69–92 in *Tradition, Transmission, and Transformation from Second Temple Literature through Judaism and Christianity in Late Antiquity: Proceedings of the Thirteenth International Symposium of the Orion Center for the Study of the Dead Sea Scrolls and Associated Literature.* Edited by Menahem Kister, Hillel I. Newman, Michael Segal, and Ruth A. Clemens. STDJ 113. Leiden: Brill.

Gutman, Ariel, and Wido van Peursen. 2011. *The Two Syriac Versions of the Prayer of Manasseh.* Gorgias Eastern Christian Studies 30. Piscataway, NJ: Gorgias.

Hanneken, Todd R. 2019. "The Book of Jubilees in Latin." Pages 31–34 in vol. 2C of *The Textual History of the Bible.* Edited by Frank Feder and Matthias Henze. Leiden: Brill.

Harlow, Daniel C. 1996. *The Greek Apocalypse of Baruch (3 Baruch) in Hellenistic Judaism and Early Christianity.* SVTP 12. Leiden: Brill.

———. 2001. "The Christianization of Early Jewish Pseudepigrapha: The Case of 3 Baruch." *JSJ* 32:416–44.

Harness, Kelley. 2010. "Judith, Music, and Female Patrons in Early Modern Italy." Pages 371–85 in *The Sword of Judith: Judith Studies across the Disciplines.* Edited by Kevin R. Brine, Elena Ciletti, and Henrike Lähnemann. Cambridge: Open Book.

Henten, Jan Willem van, and Berndt Schaller. 2000. "Christianization of Ancient Jewish Writings." *JSJ* 32:369–70.

Herr, David Moshe. 1990. "Les raisons de la conservation des restes de la Littérature juive de l'Epoque du Second Temple." *Apocrypha* 1:219–30.

Himmelfarb, Martha. 1984. "R. Moses the Preacher and the Testaments of the Twelve Patriarchs." *AJSR* 9:55–78.

———. 1994. "Some Echoes of Jubilees in Medieval Hebrew Literature." Pages 115–41 in *Tracing the Threads: Studies in the Vitality of the Jewish Pseudepigrapha.* Edited by John C. Reeves. EJL 6. Atlanta: Scholars Press.

———. 2016. "*3 Baruch* Revisited: Jewish or Christian Composition, and Why It Matters." *ZAC* 20:41–62.

———. 2019. "Rabbinic and Post-Rabbinic." Pages 431–48 in *Oxford Guide to Early Jewish Texts and Traditions in Christian Transmission.* Edited by Alexander Kulik, Gabriele Boccaccini, Lorenzo DiTommaso, David Hamidovic, and Michael E. Stone. Oxford: Oxford University Press.

Hjälm, Miriam L. 2015. "The Christian Arabic Book of Daniel: Extant Versions, Canonical Constellations, and Relation to the Liturgical Practice, with an Appendix of 'The Song of the Three Young Men.'" *CCO* 12:115–78.

Hogan, Karina M. 2013. "The Preservation of 4 Ezra in the Vulgate: Thanks to Ambrose, not Jerome." Pages 381–402 in *Fourth Ezra and Second Baruch: Reconstruction after the Fall.* Edited by Matthias Henze and Gabriele Boccaccini. Leiden: Brill.

James, Montague R. 1920. *The Lost Apocrypha of the Old Testament: Their Titles and Fragments.* London: SPCK.

Jonge, Marinus de. 1953. *The Testaments of the Twelve Patriarchs: A Study of Their Text, Composition and Origin.* Assen: Van Gorcum.

———. 1975. *The Testament of the Twelve Patriarchs: A Study of Their Text Composition and Origin.* 2nd ed. Assen: Van Gorcum.

———. 2000. "Remarks in the Margin of the Paper 'The Figure of Jeremiah in the Paralipomena Jeremiae' by J. Riaud." *JSP* 22:45–49.
———. 2003. *Pseudepigrapha of the Old Testament as Part of Christian Literature: The Case of the Testaments of the Twelve Patriarchs and the Greek Life of Adam and Eve.* SVTP 18. Leiden: Brill.
Jonge, Marinus de, and Johannes Tromp. 1997. *The Life of Adam and Eve and Related Literature.* Guides to Apocrypha and Pseudepigrapha. Sheffield: Sheffield Academic.
Junod, Éric. 1983. "Apocryphes du NT ou apocryphes Chrétiens anciens? Remarques sur la désignations d'un corpus et indications bibliographiques sur les instruments de travail récents." *ETR* 58:409–21.
Kautzsch, Emil, ed. 1900. *Die Apokryphen and Pseudepigraphen des Alten Testaments.* 2 vols. Tübingen: Rothstein.
Kister, Menachem. 2012 "Ancient Material in *Pirqe De-Rabbi Eli'Ezer*: Basilides, Qumran, the *Book of Jubilees*." Pages 69–93 in *"Go Out and Study the Land" (Judges 18:2): Archaeological, Historical and Textual Studies in Honor of Hanan Eshel.* Edited by Aren M. Maeir, Jodi Magness, and Lawrence H. Schiffman. JSJSup 148. Leiden: Brill.
———. 2015. "Preface." Pages vii–xii in *Tradition, Transmission, and Transformation from Second Temple Literature through Judaism and Christianity in Late Antiquity: Proceedings of the Thirteenth International Symposium of the Orion Center for the Study of the Dead Sea Scrolls and Associated Literature.* STDJ 113. Leiden: Brill.
Knibb, Michael A. 2001. "Christian Adoption and Transmission of Jewish Pseudepigrapha: The Case of 1 Enoch." *JSJ* 32:396–415.
Kraft, Robert A. 1975. "The Multiform Jewish Heritage of Early Christianity." Pages 174–99 in *Christianity, Judaism and Other Greco-Roman Cults: Studies for Morton Smith at Sixty, Part Three; Judaism Before 70.* Edited by Jacob Neusner. SJLA 12. Leiden: Brill.
———. 1976. "The Pseudepigrapha in Christianity." Paper presented at the Annual Meeting of the Society for New Testament Studies, Duke University. Durham, NC, August.
———. 1994. "The Pseudepigrapha in Christianity." Pages 55–86 in *Tracing the Threads: Studies in the Vitality of the Jewish Pseudepigrapha.* Edited by John C. Reeves. EJL 6. Atlanta: Scholars Press.
———. 2001. "The Pseudepigrapha and Christianity, Revisited: Setting the Stage and Framing Some Central Questions." *JSJ* 32:371–95.
———. 2009. *Exploring the Scripturesque: Jewish Texts and Their Christian Contexts.* JSJSup 137. Leiden: Brill.

Kraft, Robert A., and George W. E. Nickelsburg, eds. 1986. *Early Judaism and Its Modern Interpreters*. BMI 2. Philadelphia: Fortress; Atlanta: Scholars Press.

Kraemer, Ross Shepard. 1998. *When Aseneth Met Joseph: A Late Antique Tale of the Biblical Patriarch and His Egyptian Wife, Reconsidered*. New York: Oxford University Press.

Kugel, James L. 1997. *The Bible as It Was*. Cambridge: Harvard University Press.

Kulik, Alexander, and Sergey Minov. 2016. *Biblical Pseudepigrapha in Slavonic Traditions*. Oxford: Oxford University Press.

Kulik, Alexander, Gabriele Boccaccini, Lorenzo DiTommaso, David Hamidovic, and Michael E. Stone, eds. 2019. *A Guide to Early Jewish Texts and Traditions in Christian Transmission*. Oxford: Oxford University Press.

Labendz, Jenny R. 2006. "The Book of Ben Sira in Rabbinic Literature." *AJSR* 30:347–92.

Lawlor, H. J. 1897. "Early Citations from the Book of Enoch." *Journal of Philology* 25:164–225.

Leicht, Reimund. 1996. "A Newly Discovered Hebrew Version of the Apocryphal 'Prayer of Manasseh.'" *JSQ* 3:359–73.

Lied, Liv Ingeborg. 2013. "Nachleben and Textual Identity: Variants and Variance in the Reception History of 2 Baruch." Pages 403–28 in *Fourth Ezra and Second Baruch: Reconstruction after the Fall*. Edited by Matthias Henze and Gabriele Boccaccini. JSJSupp 164. Leiden: Brill.

———. 2015. "Text—Work—Manuscript: What Is an Old Testament Pseudepigraphon?" *JSP* 25:150–65.

———. 2016. "2 Baruch and the Syriac Codex Ambrosianus (7a1): Studying Old Testament Pseudepigrapha in Their Manuscript Context." *JSP* 26:67–107.

———. 2017. "Between 'Text Witness' and 'Text on the Page': Trajectories in the History of Editing the Epistle of Baruch." Pages 272–96 in *Snapshots of Evolving Traditions: Jewish and Christian Manuscript Culture, Textual Fluidity, and New Philology*. Edited by Liv Ingeborg Lied and Hugo Lundhaug. TUGAL 175. Berlin: de Gruyter.

Lied, Liv Ingeborg, and Hugo Lundhaug, eds. 2017. *Snapshots of Evolving Traditions: Jewish and Christian Manuscript Culture, Textual Fluidity, and New Philology*. TUGAL 175. Berlin: de Gruyter.

Lied, Liv Ingeborg, and Loren Stuckenbruck. 2019. "The Pseudepigrapha and Their Manuscripts." Pages 203–30 in *The Old Testament Pseude-

pigrapha: Fifty Years of the Pseudepigrapha Section at the SBL. Edited by Matthias Henze and Liv Ingeborg Lied. EJL 50. Atlanta: SBL Press.

Macaskill, Grant, with Eamon Greenwood. 2013. "Adam Octipartite/Septipartite: A New Translation and Introduction." Pages 3–21 in vol. 1 of *Old Testament Pseudepigrapha: More Noncanonical Scriptures*. Edited by Richard J. Bauckham, James R. Davila, and Alexander Panayotov. Grand Rapids: Eerdmans.

Migne, Jacques-Paul. 1856–1858. *Dictionnaire des Apocryphes, Ou, Collection de tous les Livres Apocryphes relatifs à l'Ancient et au Nouveau Testament*. 2 vols. Turnhout: Brepols.

Milikowsky, Chaim 2015. "Where Is the Lost Ark of the Covenant? The True History (of the Ancient Tradtions)." Pages 208–30 in *Tradition, Transmission, and Transformation from Second Temple Literature through Judaism and Christianity in Late Antiquity: Proceedings of the Thirteenth International Symposium of the Orion Center for the Study of the Dead Sea Scrolls and Associated Literature*. Edited by Menahem Kister, Hillel I. Newman, Michael Segal, and Ruth A. Clemens. STDJ 113. Leiden: Brill.

Miltenova, Anasava. 2004. *Erotapokriseis: Съчинения от кратки въпроси и отговори в старобългарскаталитература*. Sofia: Damian Iakov.

Minov, Sergey. 2015. "Satan's Refusal to Worship Adam: A Jewish Motif and Its Reception in Syriac Christian Tradition." Pages 230–71 in *Tradition, Transmission, and Transformation from Second Temple Literature through Judaism and Christianity in Late Antiquity: Proceedings of the Thirteenth International Symposium of the Orion Center for the Study of the Dead Sea Scrolls and Associated Literature*. Edited by Menahem Kister, Hillel I. Newman, Michael Segal, and Ruth A. Clemens. STDJ 113. Leiden: Brill.

Monger, Matthew P. 2018. "The Many Forms of Jubilees: A Reassessment of the Manuscript Evidence from Qumran and the Lines of Transmission of the Parts and Whole of Jubilees." *RevQ* 30:191–211.

Mroczek, Eva. 2016. *The Literary Imagination in Jewish Antiquity*. New York: Oxford University Press.

Murdoch, Brian O. 1976. *The Irish Adam and Eve Story From Saltair Na Rann: Volume 2, Commentary*. Dublin: Dublin Institute for Advanced Studies.

———. 2009. *The Apocryphal Adam and Eve in Medieval Europe: Vernacular Translations and Adaptations of the Vita Adae et Evae*. Oxford: Oxford University Press.

Najman, Hindy. 2017. "Ethical Reading: The Transformation of the Text and the Self." *JTS* 68:507–29.

Newman, Hillel. 2015. "Stars of the Messiah." Pages 272–303 in *Tradition, Transmission, and Transformation from Second Temple Literature through Judaism and Christianity in Late Antiquity: Proceedings of the Thirteenth International Symposium of the Orion Center for the Study of the Dead Sea Scrolls and Associated Literature*. Edited by Menahem Kister, Hillel I. Newman, Michael Segal, and Ruth A. Clemens. STDJ 113. Leiden: Brill.

Nichols, Stephen G. 1990. "The New Philology: Introduction; Philology in a Manuscript Culture." *Speculum* 65:1–10.

Nickelsburg, George W. E., and John J. Collins, eds. 1980. *Ideal Figures in Ancient Judaism: Profiles and Paradigms*. SCS 12. Chico, CA: Scholars Press.

Oesterley, W. O. E. 1935. *An Introduction to the Books of the Apocrypha*. London: SPCK.

Orlov, Andrei A. 2009. *Selected Studies in the Slavonic Pseudepigrapha*. SVTP 23. Leiden: Brill.

Piovanelli, Pierluigi. 2007. "In Praise of 'the Default Position', or Reassessing the Christian Reception of the Jewish Pseudepigraphic Heritage." *NedTT* 61:233–50.

Pregill, Michael. 2008. "Isra'iliyyat, Myth, and Pseudepigraphy: Wahb b. Munabbih and the Early Islamic Versions of the Fall of Adam and Eve." *JSAI* 34:215–84.

Reed, Annette Yoshiko. 2001. "From Asael and Šemihazah to Uzzah, Azzah, and Azael: 3 Enoch 5 (§§7–8) and the Jewish Reception-History of 1 Enoch." *JSQ* 8:105–36.

———. 2005. *Fallen Angels and the History of Judaism and Christianity: The Reception of Enochic Literature*. Cambridge: Cambridge University Press.

———. 2009. "The Modern Invention of 'Old Testament Pseudepigrapha.'" *JTS* 60:403–36.

———. 2014. "Gendering Heavenly Secrets? Women, Angels, and the Problem of Misogyny and Magic." Pages 108–51 in *Daughters of Hecate: Women and Magic in Antiquity*. Edited by Kimberly Stratton and Dayna S. Kalleres. Oxford: Oxford University Press.

———. 2015. "Retelling Biblical Retellings: Epiphanius, the Psuedo-Clementines, and the Reception-History of Jubilees." Pages 304–21 in *Tradition, Transmission, and Transformation from Second Temple Literature through Judaism and Christianity in Late Antiquity: Proceedings of the Thirteenth International Symposium of the Orion Center for the Study of the Dead Sea Scrolls and Associated Literature*. Edited by Menahem Kister, Hillel I. Newman, Michael Segal, and Ruth A. Clemens. STDJ 113. Leiden: Brill.

———. Forthcoming. "Fallen Angels and the Afterlives of Enochic Traditions in Early Islam." In *Early Islam: The Sectarian Milieu of Late Antiquity? Proceedings of the Fourth Nangeroni Meeting*. Edited by Guillaume Dye. Chicago: Oriental Institute of the University of Chicago.

Reed, Annette Yoshiko, and John C. Reeves. 2018. *Sources from Judaism, Christianity and Islam*. Vol. 1 of *Enoch from Antiquity to the Middle Ages*. Oxford: Oxford University Press.

Reeves, John C. 1992. *Jewish Lore in Manichaean Cosmogony: Studies in the Book of Giants Traditions*. HUCM 14. Cincinnati: Hebrew Union College Press.

———. 1999. "Exploring the Afterlife of Jewish Pseudepigrapha in Medieval Near Eastern Religious Traditions: Some Initial Soundings." *JSJ* 30:148–77.

Roddy, Nicolae. 2001. *The Romanian Version of the Testament of Abraham: Text, Translation, and Cultural Context*. EJL 19. Atlanta: Society of Biblical Literature.

Rönsch, Hermann. 1874. *Das Buch der Jubiläen oder die kleine Genesis*. Leipzig: Reisland.

Satran, David. 1995. *Biblical Prophets in Byzantine Palestine: Reassessing the Lives of the Prophets*. SVTP 11. Leiden: Brill.

Segovia, Carlos. 2017. "'Those on the Right' and 'Those on the Left'! Rereading Qur'ān 56.1–56 (and the Founding Myth of Islam) in Light of Apocalypse of Abraham 21–2." *Oriens Christianus* 100:227–40.

Sparks, H. F. D. 1984. "Preface." Pages ix–xviii in *The Apocryphal Old Testament*. Edited by H. F. D. Sparks. Oxford: Oxford University Press.

Stone, Michael E. 1986. "Categorization and Classification of Apocrypha and Pseudepigrapha." *AbrN* 24:167–77.

———. 1991. "Methodological Issues in the Study of the Text of the Apocrypha and Pseudepigrapha." Pages 124–30 in *Selected Studies in Pseudepigrapha And Apocrypha: With Special Reference to the Armenian Tradition*. SVTP 9. Leiden: Brill.

———. 1996a. "The Testament of Naphtali." *JJS* 47:311–21.

———. 1996b. "The Genealogy of Bilhah." *DSD* 3:20–36.

———. 1999. "Two Armenian Manuscripts and the Historia sacra." Pages 21–36 in *Apocryphes Arméniens: Transmission—traduction—création—iconographie*. Edited by Valentina Clazolari Bouvier, Jean-Daniel Kaestli, and Bernard Outtier. Lausanne: Éditions du Zèbre.

———. 2006a. "The Book(s) Attributed to Noah." *DSD* 13:4–23.

———. 2006b. "The Armenian Apocryphal Literature: Translation and Creation." Pages 105–37 in vol. 1 of *Apocrypha, Pseudepigrapha and Armenian Studies*. Edited by Michael E. Stone. OLA 145. 2 vols. Leuven: Peeters.

———. 2011. *Ancient Judaism: New Visions and Views*. Grand Rapids: Eerdmans.

———. 2015. "The Reception and Reworking of Abraham Traditions in Armenian." Pages 343–59 in *Tradition, Transmission, and Transformation from Second Temple Literature through Judaism and Christianity in Late Antiquity: Proceedings of the Thirteenth International Symposium of the Orion Center for the Study of the Dead Sea Scrolls and Associated Literature*. Edited by Menahem Kister, Hillel I. Newman, Michael Segal, and Ruth A. Clemens. STDJ 113. Leiden: Brill.

———. 2016. *Armenian Apocrypha Relating to Angels and Biblical Heroes*. EJL 45. Atlanta: SBL Press.

———. 2019. "Early Days of the Society of Biblical Literature Pseudepigrapha Group: Pseudepigrapha Studies in the Second Half of the Twentieth Century." Pages 59–78 in *The Old Testament Pseudepigrapha: Fifty Years of the Pseudepigrapha Section at the SBL*. Edited by Matthias Henze and Liv Ingeborg Lied. EJL 50. Atlanta: SBL Press.

Stuckenbruck, Loren T. 2007. *1 Enoch 91–108*. CEJL. Berlin: de Gruyter.

———. 2011. "Apocrypha and Septuagint: Exploring the Christian Canon." Pages 177–201 in *Die Septuaginta und das frühe Christentum—The Septuagint and Christian Origins*. Edited by Scott Caulley and Hermann Lichtenberger. WUNT 277. Tübingen: Mohr Siebeck.

———. 2013. "The Book of Enoch: Its Reception in Second Temple Judaism and in Christianity." *Early Christianity* 1:7–40.

Stuckenbruck, Loren T., and Ted Erho. 2018. "EMML 8400 and Notes on the Reading of Hēnok in Ethiopia." Pages 125–29 in *Bible as Notepad: Tracing Annotations and Annotation Practices in Late Antique and Medieval Biblical Manuscripts*. Edited by Liv Ingeborg Lied and Marilena Maniaci. Manuscripta Biblica 3. Berlin: de Gruyter.

VanderKam, James C. 1996. "1 Enoch, Enochic Motifs, and Enoch in Early Christian Literature." Pages 33–101 in *The Jewish Apocalyptic Heritage in Early Christianity*. Edited by James C. VanderKam and William Adler. CRINT 3.4. Assen: Van Gorcum; Minneapolis: Fortress.

———. 2009. "The Manuscript Traditions of Jubilees." Pages 3–21 in *Enoch and the Mosaic Torah: The Evidence of the Book of Jubilees*. Edited by Gabriele Boccaccini and Giovanni Ibba. Grand Rapids: Eerdmans.

Wasserstrom, Steven M. 1994. "Jewish Pseudepigrapha in Muslim Literature: A Bibliographical and Methodological Sketch." Pages 87–114 in *Tracing the Threads: Studies in the Vitality of the Jewish Pseudepigrapha*. Edited by John C. Reeves. EJL 06. Atlanta: Scholars Press.

Weeks, Stuart, Simon Gathercole, and Loren Stuckenbruck. 2004. *The Book of Tobit: Texts from the Principal Ancient and Medieval Traditions; with synopsis, concordances, and annotated texts in Aramaic, Hebrew, Greek, Latin, and Syriac*. FSBP 3. Berlin: de Gruyter.

Wollenberg, Rebecca. 2017. "The Dangers of Reading as We Know It: Sight Reading as a Source of Heresy in Classical Rabbinic Literature." *JAAR* 85:709–45.

Wright, Benjamin G. 2018. "A Character in Search of a Story: The Reception of Ben Sira in Early Medieval Judaism." Pages 377–96 in *Wisdom Poured Out Like Water': Studies in Jewish and Christian Antiquity in Honor of Gabriele Boccaccini*. Edited by J. Harold Ellens, Isaac W. Oliver, Jason von Ehrenkrook, James Waddell, and Jason M. Zurawski. DCLS 38. Berlin: de Gruyter.

Wright, J. Edward. 2003. *Baruch Ben Neriah: From Biblical Scribe to Apocalyptic Seer*. Studies on Personalities of the Old Testament. Columbia: University of South Carolina Press.

Yassif, Eli. 1988. "Traces of Folk Traditions of the Second Temple Period in Rabbinic Literature." *JSJ* 39:212–33.

———. 1997. "The Hebrew Narrative Anthology in the Middle Ages." Translated by Jacqueline S. Teitelbaum. *Prooftexts* 17:153–75.

Appendix

This annotated bibliography consists of three parts: bibliographies, primary sources, and secondary sources. The publications listed below appeared in between 1986, the publication year of the first edition of *Early Judaism and Its Modern Interpreters*, and 2019.

1. Bibliographies

DiTommaso, Lorenzo. *A Bibliography of Pseudepigrapha Research 1850–1999*. JSPSup 39. Sheffield: Sheffield Academic, 2001. An exhaustive bibliography of modern research on the Pseudepigrapha.

Haelewyck, Jean-Claude. *Clavis Apocryphorum Veteris Testamenti*. Corpus Christianorum. Turnhout: Brepols, 1998. A list of 277 Old Testament pseudepigrapha, with brief bibliographies and notes on each entry.

2. Primary Sources:
Editions, English Translations, and Anthologies

Baukham, Richard, James Davila, Alex Panayotov, eds. *Old Testament Pseudepigrapha: More Noncanonical Scriptures*. Vol. 1. Grand Rapids: Eerdmans, 2013. Intended to complement James Charlesworth's *Old Testament Pseudepigrapha*, this first of a projected two-volume collection includes several previously unpublished or newly translated texts, and, at the same time, expands the chronological boundaries of the traditional understanding of Old Testament Pseudepigrapha.

Charlesworth, James H., ed. *The Old Testament Pseudepigrapha*. 2 vols. Garden City, NY: Doubleday, 1983–1985. Repr., Peabody, MA: Hendrickson, 2010. A classic collection of the Old Testament Pseudepigrapha in English translation, with brief introductions to each text.

Feldman, Louis H., James L. Kugel, and Lawrence H. Schiffman, eds. *Outside the Bible: Ancient Jewish Writings Related to Scripture*. 3 vols. Lincoln: University of Nebraska Press; Philadelphia: The Jewish Publication Society, 2013. A massive collection of late- and postbiblical Jewish texts in annotated English translation, including portions of the Dead

Sea Scrolls, the Septuagint, the Apocrypha and Pseudepigrapha, Philo, and Josephus.

García Martínez, Florentino, and Eibert J. C. Tigchelaar, *The Dead Sea Scrolls Study Edition*. 2 vols. New York: Brill, 1997–1998. A new transcription and English translation of the nonbiblical texts from Qumran, arranged by serial number from Cave 1 to Cave 11, intended primarily for classroom use.

Nickelsburg, George W. E., and Michael E. Stone, eds. *Early Judaism: Texts and Documents on Faith and Piety*. Rev. ed. Minneapolis: Fortress, 2009. A heavily annotated collection of portions of early Jewish texts, arranged by topic.

Nickelsburg, George W. E., and James C. VanderKam. *1 Enoch: A New Translation; Based on the Hermeneia Commentary*. Minneapolis: Fortress, 2004. The most up-to-date English translation, with introduction, of 1 Enoch.

Parry, Donald W., and Emanuel Tov. *The Dead Sea Scrolls Reader*. 2nd ed. 2 vols. Leiden: Brill, 2014. An edition of all nonbiblical Qumran texts, arranged by literary genre, with English translations on facing pages, and brief bibliographies.

Pietersma, Albert, and Benjamin G. Wright III, eds. *A New English Translation of the Septuagint: And the Other Greek Translations Traditionally Included under That Title*. New York: Oxford University Press, 2007. The first English translation of the Septuagint in a century and a half.

Schiffmann, Lawrence H. *Texts and Traditions: A Source Reader for the Study of Second Temple and Rabbinic Judaism*. Hoboken, NJ: Ktav, 1998. A broad collection of Jewish texts, from the Hebrew Bible, a variety of early Jewish texts, the Mishnah, and the Talmud.

Stone, Michael E., and Matthias Henze. *4 Ezra and 2 Baruch: Translations, Introductions, and Notes*. Minneapolis: Fortress, 2013. English translations, with introductions, of two closely related Jewish apocalypses.

Vermes, Géza, *The Complete Dead Sea Scrolls in English*. Rev. 50th anniversary ed. London: Penguin, 2011. An acclaimed translation of the nonbiblical scrolls, edited with an introduction and notes by one of the early leading scrolls scholars.

3. Secondary Sources

3.1. The History, Language, Literature, and Culture of Early Judaism

Barclay, John M. G. *Jews in the Mediterranean Diaspora: From Alexander to Trajan (323 BCE to 117 CE)*. Edinburgh: T&T Clark, 1996. A comprehensive study of the Jewish communities in the Mediterranean diaspora and their diverse literatures.

Bickerman, Elias Joseph. *The Jews in the Greek Age*. Cambridge: Harvard University Press, 1988. A history of the Jews in the Hellenistic period, written by one of the leading scholars of Greco-Roman history and the Hellenistic world in the twentieth century.

Cohen, Shaye J. D. *The Beginnings of Jewishness: Boundaries, Varieties, Uncertainties*. HCS 31. Berkeley: University of California Press, 1999. An exposition of the various definitions of Jewish identity, and particularly of the boundaries between Jews and non-Jews, from the formative period of Judaism in the second century BCE to the fifth century CE.

———. *From the Maccabees to the Mishnah*. 3rd ed. Louisville: Westminster John Knox, 2014. A classic textbook on the history of Judaism, its practices and beliefs, institutions, and literatures, from the Maccabean Revolt in the 160s BCE to the Mishnah in the late second century CE, in its third edition.

Collins, John J. *The Apocalyptic Imagination: An Introduction to Jewish Apocalyptic Literature*. 3rd ed. Grand Rapids: Eerdmans, 2016. A classic introduction to early Jewish apocalyptic literature, covering the history of modern scholarship, as well as the most important Jewish apocalypses (the Enochic apocalypses, Daniel, the Testaments, the Dead Sea Scrolls, 4 Ezra, 2 Baruch, the Apocalypse of Abraham, and the Sibylline Oracles) and early Christian apocalypses.

———. *Jewish Wisdom in the Hellenistic Age*. OTL. Louisville: Westminster John Knox, 1997. A study of Jewish wisdom literature (Ben Sira, Wisdom of Solomon, the Sentences of Pseudo-Phocylides, and the Dead Sea Scrolls) in the Hellenistic period.

———. *The Scepter and the Star: Messianism in Light of the Dead Sea Scrolls*. 2nd ed. Grand Rapids: Eerdmans, 2010. A comprehensive overview of messianic beliefs found in the Hebrew Bible and in early Jewish writings, including the Dead Sea Scrolls, the Psalms of Solomon, Jubilees, the Testament of the Twelve Patriarchs, and the Similitudes of Enoch.

Collins, John J., and Daniel C. Harlow, eds. *Early Judaism: A Comprehensive Overview.* Grand Rapids: Eerdmans, 2012. A collection of fifteen articles, written by the leading experts in the field, on the history, archaeology, and literature of early Judaism.

Coogan, Michael D., ed. *The Oxford History of the Biblical World.* New York: Oxford University Press, 2001. A collection of twelve articles on the history of ancient Israel, from the Bronze Age to the Roman period.

Davies W. D., and Louis Finkelstein, eds. *The Cambridge History of Judaism.* 8 vols. Cambridge: Cambridge University Press, 1984–2018. A detailed history of Judaism in eight volumes, from the Persian period to the modern world. Significant for our purposes: *The Persian Period* (vol. 1); *The Hellenistic Age* (vol. 2); *The Early Roman Period* (vol. 3); and *The Late Roman-Rabbinic Period* (vol. 4).

Denis, Albert-Marie, and Jean-Claude Haelewyck, eds. *Introduction à la littérature religieuse judéo-hellénistique: Pseudépigraphes de l'Ancien Testament.* 2 vols. Turnhout: Brepols, 2000. The most detailed introduction to the Apocrypha and Pseudepigrapha currently available, written by a formidable group of international scholars (in French).

Docherty, Susan. *The Jewish Pseudepigrapha: An Introduction to the Literature of the Second Temple Period.* Minneapolis: Fortress, 2015. A concise and accessible introduction to early Jewish texts from the late Second Temple period (ca. 250 BCE–100 CE) not included in the Hebrew Bible.

Feldman, Louis H. *Jew and Gentile in the Ancient World: Attitudes and Interactions from Alexander to Justinian.* Princeton: Princeton University Press, 1993. A history of various contacts between Jews and non-Jews, as well as of the prejudices against and attractions to the Jews in the Hellenistic and Early Roman periods, written by a leading authority.

Goodman, Martin, ed. *Jews in a Graeco-Roman World.* New York: Oxford University Press, 1998. A collection of sixteen articles on various aspects of the cultural and religious history of the Jews in the Greco-Roman world, including hellenization, social integration, as well as the similarities and differences between Jews, Greeks, and Romans.

Grabbe, Lester L. *An Introduction to Second Temple Judaism: History and Religion of the Jews in the Time of Nehemiah, the Maccabees, Hillel, and Jesus.* London: Bloomsbury, 2010. A concise introduction to early Judaism, its history and literatures.

Greensphan, Frederick E. ed. *Early Judaism: New Insights and Scholarship.* New York: New York University Press, 2018. A collection of nine essays by the foremost scholars on the transition from Second Temple to early Rabbinic Judaism, divided into two groups, "Early Diversity" (Second Temple) and "Emerging Normativity" (Rabbinic Judaism), intended for a general readership.

Gruen, Erich. *Diaspora: Jews amidst Greeks and Romans.* Cambridge: Harvard University Press, 2002. A study of the Jewish diaspora among Greeks and Romans, with particular attention to Jewish works, biblical and postbiblical, that were either written in the diaspora or are employing a diaspora setting for the creation of historical fiction.

———. *Heritage and Hellenism: The Reinvention of Jewish Tradition.* HCS 30. Berkeley: University of California Press, 1998. A detailed investigation of the interactions between Jews and Greeks in antiquity, and, more precisely, of how Jewish writers expressed their identity in ways borrowed from Greek culture, written by one of the leading scholars on Hellenistic Judaism.

Harrington, Daniel J. *Invitation to the Apocrypha.* Grand Rapids: Eerdmans, 1999. A concise and accessible introduction to the Old Testament Apocrypha or deuterocanonical books, written for a student audience.

Henze, Matthias, ed. *A Companion to Biblical Interpretation in Early Judaism.* Grand Rapids: Eerdmans, 2012. A collection of eighteen essays on various forms of biblical interpretation in early Judaism, ranging from the Hebrew Bible to the beginnings of rabbinic Judaism.

Horbury, William. *Jewish War under Trajan and Hadrian.* Cambridge: Cambridge University Press, 2014. An investigation of the two Jewish upheavals against Rome, the first during the last years of Trajan (115–117 CE), and the second, led by Bar Kokhba, during Hadrian's reign (132–135 CE).

Ilan, Tal. *Integrating Women into Second Temple History.* Peabody, MA: Hendrickson, 2001. A study on the place of women in early Judaism as documented in a variety of sources, including biblical and apocryphal books (Esther, Judith, Susanna, Ben Sira), the Judean desert papyri, and rabbinic literature.

Kugel, James L. *Traditions of the Bible: A Guide to the Bible as It Was at the Start of the Common Era.* Cambridge: Harvard University Press, 1998. A rich anthology of early interpretations, Jewish and Christian, of the stories found in the Torah, compiled and explained by the premier scholar on the premodern history of biblical interpretation.

Kugel, James L., and Rowan A. Greer. *Early Biblical Interpretation*. Philadelphia: Westminster, 1986. One of the first books that appeared on the subject of early biblical interpretation in early Judaism (Kugel) and early Christianity (Greer) written specifically for a student audience.

Kulik, Alexander, Gabriele Boccaccini, Lorenzo DiTommaso, David Hamidovic, and Michael E. Stone, eds. *The Oxford Guide to Early Jewish Texts and Traditions in Christian Transmission*. New York: Oxford University Press, 2019. A collection of twenty-six articles that investigate the problems of the preservation, reception, and transformation of Second Temple Jewish texts and traditions in diverse Christian milieus through the late medieval era.

Lied, Ingeborg Liv, and Hugo Lundhaug, eds. *Snapshots of Evolving Traditions: Jewish and Christian Manuscript Culture, Textual Fluidity, and New Philology*. TUGAL 175. Berlin: de Gruyter, 2017. Drawing on insights from new philology, the thirteen essays in this collection direct our attention to the lives of the manuscripts and the fluidity of the textual transmission in a manuscript culture.

Magness, Jodi. *The Archaeology of Qumran and the Dead Sea Scrolls*. SDSS. Grand Rapids: Eerdmans, 2002. An authoritative account of the site of Qumran, home of the group that left us the Dead Sea Scrolls, its archaeology, and modern controversies.

Mulder, Martin Jan, and Harry Sysling, eds. *Mikra: Text, Translation, Reading and Interpretation of the Hebrew Bible in Ancient Judaism and Early Christianity*. Peabody, MA: Hendrickson, 2004. A classic collection of authoritative studies on the Hebrew Bible, its versions (Greek, Aramaic, Latin), and the early history of biblical interpretation in the Dead Sea Scrolls, early Jewish writings, Philo, Josephus, and early Christian authors (the New Testament and church fathers).

Neusner, Jacob. *Judaism When Christianity Began: A Survey of Belief and Practice*. Louisville: Westminster John Knox, 2002. A concise introduction to the beliefs and practices of rabbinic Judaism during its formative period, arguing that we need to think of Judaism in the plural ("Judaisms").

Nickelsburg, George W. E. *Jewish Literature between the Bible and the Mishnah*. 2nd ed. Minneapolis: Fortress, 2005. A classic introduction to the Jewish literature from the late Second Temple period to the second century CE, including the Apocrypha (Baruch, Judith, 1 and 2 Maccabees, etc.), Pseudepigrapha (1 and 2 Enoch, the Sibylline Oracles, etc.), Philo, Josephus, and several Dead Sea Scrolls.

Rajak, Tessa. *The Jewish Dialogue with Greece and Rome: Studies in Cultural and Social Interaction*. AGJU 48. Leiden: Brill, 2001. A collection of twenty-seven essays on various aspects of Judaism in the Greco-Roman world, such as Judaism and Hellenism, Josephus, the Jewish diaspora, and Jewish epigraphy.

———. *Translation and Survival: The Greek Bible in the Ancient Jewish Diaspora*. Oxford: Oxford University Press, 2009. A study underscoring the significance of the Greek Bible, arguing that without it there would have been no Western Jewish diaspora and no Christianity.

Reed, Annette Yoshiko. *Fallen Angels and the History of Judaism and Christianity: The Reception of Enochic Literature*. New York: Cambridge University Press, 2005. An innovative study that considers the early history of Jewish-Christian relations through a focus on the traditions about the fallen angels, from the Second Temple period through late antiquity and the early Middle Ages.

Rowland, Christopher. *The Open Heaven: A Study of Apocalyptic in Judaism and Early Christianity*. Eugene, OR: Wipf & Stock, 2002. An early, classic introduction to apocalyptic literature, arguing that apocalyptic literature is primarily concerned with the disclosure of heavenly secrets and less so with speculations about the world to come.

Sanders, E. P. *Judaism: Practice and Belief, 63 BCE–66 CE*. Minneapolis: Fortress, 2016. A classic work on common Judaism, that is, Judaism as a functioning religion in the early Roman period, with particular attention to the religious practices and observances of the common people (sacrifices, tithes and taxes, legal debates, etc.).

Schäfer, Peter. *Judeophobia: Attitudes toward the Jews in the Ancient World*. Cambridge: Harvard University Press, 1997. A study of the origins of anti-Semitism in the ancient world, identifying Hellenistic Egypt as the generating source, with roots extending back into Egypt's pre-Hellenistic history.

Schiffman, Lawrence H. *From Text to Tradition: A History of Second Temple and Rabbinic Judaism*. Hoboken, NJ: Ktav, 1991. A broad, text-based study of ancient Judaism, covering the Persian and Hellenistic periods, early Christianity, the Jewish revolts, the Mishnah, and the Talmuds.

Simkovich, Malka Z. *Discovering Second Temple Literature: The Scriptures and Stories That Shaped Early Judaism*. Lincoln: University of Nebraska Press; Philadelphia: Jewish Publication Society, 2018. An introduction to Second Temple Judaism, with particular attention to the manuscript evidence, the diversity of Jewish life, and the various Jewish groups, sects, and authors.

Stone, Michael, ed. *Jewish Writings of the Second Temple Period: Apocrypha, Pseudepigrapha, Qumran Sectarian Writings, Philo, Josephus*. CRINT 2.2. Assen: Van Gorcum; Philadelphia: Fortress, 1984. An early, classic collection of fourteen essays on the diverse literature of the late Second Temple period, organized by authors (Philo, Josephus), genres (wisdom literature, testaments, psalms, hymns, and prayers), and collections (gnostic literature, Dead Sea Scrolls).

Toorn, Karel van der. *Scribal Culture and the Making of the Hebrew Bible*. Cambridge: Harvard University Press, 2007. A tribute to the scribes of the Second Temple period, particularly from 500 to 200 BCE, the literary elite who produced the Hebrew Bible.

Tov, Emanuel. *Textual Criticism of the Hebrew Bible*. 3rd ed. Minneapolis: Fortress, 2012. The third edition of this authoritative textbook and reference work on textual criticism of the Hebrew Bible includes new perspectives and insights on the biblical text gained from the Dead Sea Scrolls.

VanderKam, James C. *An Introduction to Early Judaism*. Grand Rapids: Eerdmans, 2001. A concise and accessible introduction to early Judaism, divided into three parts: a historical overview, a brief introduction to the most important writings, organized by genre, and a description of the Jewish leaders, groups, and institutions.

VanderKam, James C., and Peter Flint, *The Meaning of the Dead Sea Scrolls: Their Significance for Understanding the Bible, Judaism, Jesus, and Christianity*. San Francisco: HarperSanFrancisco, 2002. A balanced and authoritative introduction to the Dead Sea Scrolls, the history of their discovery, the manuscripts, their meaning and significance, and the modern controversies.

Vriezen, Theodoor Christian, and A. S. van der Woude, eds. *Ancient Israelite and Early Jewish Literature*. Leiden: Brill, 2005. An English translation of the tenth revised edition of *De literatuur van oud-Israël*, an authoritative introduction to the Hebrew Bible and early Jewish writings.

Williams, Margaret H. *Jews among Greeks and Romans: A Diasporan Sourcebook*. Baltimore: Johns Hopkins University Press, 1998. A collection of primary texts in English translation on various aspects of

Jewish life outside the land of Israel, from the fourth century BCE to the fifth century CE.

3.2. Concordances, Dictionaries, Encyclopedias, and Handbooks

Abegg, Martin, James Bowley, Edward Cook, eds. *The Dead Sea Scrolls Concordance*. 3 vols. Leiden: Brill, 2003–2016. A concordance of all Dead Sea Scrolls (vol. 1), an index to the Hebrew, Aramaic, and Greek texts of the nonbiblical, non-Qumran Judean Desert documents (vol. 2), and a keyword-in-context concordance (vol. 3).

Brooke, George J., and Charlotte Hempel, eds. *T&T Clark Companion to the Dead Sea Scrolls*. London: T&T Clark, 2019. An encyclopedia on the background and contexts of the scrolls, the methods of reading them, the most important scrolls, types of literature, and central themes.

Collins, John J., ed. *The Oxford Handbook of Apocalyptic Literature*. Oxford: Oxford University Press, 2014. A collection of twenty-eight articles, divided into five parts: contexts, social function, literary features, theology, and contemporary forms of apocalypticism.

Collins, John J., and Daniel C. Harlow, eds. *The Eerdmans Dictionary of Early Judaism*. Grand Rapids: Eerdmans, 2010. A major reference work to early Judaism, covering all aspects of Judaism roughly from the fourth century BCE to the second century CE.

Collins, John J., Bernard McGinn, and Stephen J. Stein, eds. *The Encyclopedia of Apocalypticism*. 3 vols. New York: Continuum, 1998. A broad overview of apocalyptic literature across the ages, organized chronologically: the origins of apocalypticism in Judaism and Christianity (vol. 1), apocalypticism in Western history and culture (vol. 2), and apocalypticism in the modern period and contemporary age (vol. 3).

Cook, Edward M. *Dictionary of Qumran Aramaic*. Winona Lake: Eisenbrauns, 2015. A dictionary of the Aramaic texts from the Dead Sea Scrolls.

Denis, Albert-Marie. *Concordance Grecque des Pseudépigraphes d'Ancien Testament: Concordance, Corpus des Texts, Indices*. Louvain-la-Neuve: Université catholique de Louvain, 1987. A concordance of the Greek Old Testament Pseudepigrapha.

———. *Concordance Latine des Pseudepigraphes d'Ancien Testament.* Turnhout: Brepols, 1993. A concordance of the Latin Old Testament Pseudepigrapha.

Feder, Frank, and Matthias Henze, eds. *The Deuterocanonical Scriptures.* Vol. 2 of *Textual History of the Bible.* 3 vols. Leiden: Brill, 2019–2020. A comprehensive and detailed analysis of the textual history, textual character, translation techniques, manuscripts, history of research, and importance of each textual witness for each of the deuterocanonical books.

Goodman, Martin, Jeremy Cohen, and David Jan Sorkin, eds. *The Oxford Handbook of Jewish Studies.* Oxford: Oxford University Press, 2002. A collection of thirty-nine essays on a wide range of topics, from the ancient to the modern period.

Haelewyck, Jean-Claude. *Clavis Apocryphorum Veteris Testamenti.* Corpus Christianorum. Turnhout: Brepols, 1998. A list of 277 Old Testament pseudepigrapha, with brief bibliographies and notes on each entry.

Kynes, Will, ed., *The Oxford Handbook of Wisdom and Wisdom Literature.* Oxford: Oxford University Press, 2020. A collection of thirty-seven essays, divided into six parts: the concept of wisdom, related cultures, wisdom in the modern world, the category of wisdom, wisdom and related literatures, and specific wisdom texts.

Levine, Amy-Jill, and Marc Zvi Brettler, eds. *The Jewish Annotated New Testament.* 2nd ed. Oxford: Oxford University Press, 2017. The first Jewish annotated New Testament of its kind. The annotations and essays seek to situate the New Testament in the context of first- and second-century CE Judaism.

Lim, Timothy H., and John J. Collins, eds. *The Oxford Handbook of the Dead Sea Scrolls.* Oxford: Oxford University Press, 2010. Thirty essays, divided into eight parts: archaeology, Jewish history, sectarianism, biblical texts and interpretation, religious themes, Christianity, post-Qumran Judaism, and new approaches to the scrolls.

Neusner, Jacob, and William Scott Green, eds. *Dictionary of Judaism in the Biblical Period: 450 BCE to 600 CE.* Peabody, MA: Hendrickson, 1996. A reference work with over 3,300 entries, ranging from the Hebrew Bible, early Jewish literature, the Dead Sea Scrolls, the Mishnah, and the Talmud.

Schiffman, Lawrence H., and James C. VanderKam, eds. *Encyclopedia of the Dead Sea Scrolls.* 2 vols. New York: Oxford University Press, 2000. A comprehensive and authoritative encyclopedia of the Dead Sea

Scrolls, edited by two of the world's foremost experts fifty years after the discovery of the scrolls.

Stuckenbruck, Loren T., and Daniel M. Gurtner, eds. *T&T Clark Encyclopedia of Second Temple Judaism*. 2 vols. New York: T&T Clark, 2019. With well over six hundred entries written by four hundred contributors, this encyclopedia covers a broad range of topics about Judaism from the fourth century BCE to the second century CE.

Toorn, Karel van der, Bob Becking, and Pieter W. van der Horst, eds. *Dictionary of Deities and Demons in the Bible*. 2nd ed. Leiden: Brill; Grand Rapids: Eerdmans, 1999. A dictionary of more than four hundred names of gods, angels, spirits, and demons mentioned in the Bible, in the apocryphal writings, and in Israel's neighboring civilizations.

4. Digitial Resources

4.1. Online Bibliographies

Biblical Bibliographies: https://www.cjconroy.net. A collection of bibliographies, mostly on the Hebrew Bible.

The Center for the Study of Christianity at the Hebrew University of Jerusalem: http://www.csc.org.il/db/browse.aspx?db=SB. A comprehensive bibliography on Syriac Christianity.

The National Library of Israel: https://web.nli.org.il/sites/NLI/english/Pages/default.aspx. A general index of books and articles on Jewish Studies from the National Library of Israel.

Oxford Bibliographies: http://www.oxfordbibliographies.com/. Bibliographies on a variety of topics, including early Judaism.

Regesta Imperii: http://opac.regesta-imperii.de/lang_en/. A free and comprehensive online bibliography of medieval literature, maintained by the Academy of Science and Literature in Mainz, Germany.

Syriac Resources online: http://syri.ac. An online annotated bibliography of Syriac resources.

4.2. Software

Accordance: https://www.accordancebible.com. A digital library application for the study of the Bible and related texts for Windows, Mac, iOS, and Android.

Logos: https://www.logos.com. Logos Bible Software is a digital library application for the study of the Bible and related texts for Windows, Mac, iOS, and Android.

4.3. General Databases

Ancient Jew Review: http://www.ancientjewreview.com/resources. A web journal devoted to the study of early Judaism.
Coptic Scriptorium: https://copticscriptorium.org. Digital research tools for the study of Coptic language and literature.
Digital Syriac Corpus: https://syriaccorpus.org. A curated digital repository of encoded texts written in classical Syriac.
The Slavonic Pseudepigrapha Projects: https://www.marquette.edu/maqom/pseudepigrapha.html. Digital research tools for the study of the Pseudepigrapha preserved and transmitted in Slavonic.
Spertus Institute for Jewish Learning and Leadership: https://www.spertus.edu/jewish-studies-learning-resources. A database for resources on the Hebrew Bible, rabbinic Judaism, and contemporary Judaism.

4.4. Early Jewish Writings

Early Jewish Writings: http://www.earlyjewishwritings.com. A collection of Jewish documents from antiquity (Hebrew Bible, apocrypha, pseudepigrapha, Philo, Josephus), with translations, introductions, and links.
The Online Critical Pseudepigrapha: http://ocp.tyndale.ca. A publication of electronic editions of the best critical texts of the Old Testament pseudepigrapha and related literature,

4.5. Dead Sea Scrolls

The Dead Sea Scrolls Digital Project: http://dss.collections.imj.org.il. The Israel Museum in Jerusalem, Israel, makes five scrolls digitally available.
The Leon Levy Dead Sea Scrolls Digital Library: https://www.deadseascrolls.org.il. A free online digital library of the Dead Sea Scrolls, maintained by the Israel Antiquities Authority (IAA).
Orion Center: http://orion.mscc.huji.ac.il. An up-to-date bibliography of modern scholarship on the Dead Sea Scrolls and other Second Temple

literature, maintained by the Orion Center at the Hebrew University in Jerusalem.

4.6. Rabbinic Literature

The Bar Ilan Responsa Project: https://www.responsa.co.il. A large electronic collection of rabbinic literature, including the Hebrew Bible and its principal commentaries, the Talmuds, Midrash, Zohar, etc. (subscription required).

Corpus Tannaiticum, the Mishnah: http://mishna.huma-num.fr. An *editio critica minor* of the Mishnah, based on the oldest complete manuscripts.

Digital Mishnah: https://www.digitalmishnah.org. A digital version of the Mishnah.

Sefaria: https://sefaria.org. An open library of digital rabbinic texts.

4.7. Manuscripts

Cambridge Digital Library: Cairo Genizah: https://cudl.lib.cam.ac.uk/collections/genizah/1. The Taylor-Schechter Cairo Genizah Collection at Cambridge University Library is the world's largest single collection of medieval Jewish manuscripts.

The Friedberg Jewish Manuscript Society: https://fjms.genizah.org. A collection of several sites that contain Genizah fragments, various medieval Jewish manuscripts, and early printings (subscription required).

Hill Museum and Manuscript Library: http://hmml.org. An online resource for the study of manuscript cultures, housed at Saint John's University.

Jubilees: http://jubilees.stmarytx.edu. The Jubilees Palimpsest Project.

Ktiv: http://web.nli.org.il/sites/NLIS/en/ManuScript/. An international collection of digitized Hebrew manuscripts and the National Library of Israel.

4.8. Inscriptions, Artifacts, and Lectionaries

Inscriptions of Israel/Palestine (IIP): https://library.brown.edu/iip/index. A freely accessible collection of all published inscriptions and their English translations from Israel/Palestine from ca. 500 BCE to 640 CE.

Israel Antiquities Authority (IAA): http://www.antiquities.org.il/t/PeriodsList_en.aspx. Archaeological objects from the Israel Antiquities Authority.

The Levantine Ceramics Project (LCP): https://www.levantineceramics.org. An open website focused on ceramics produced in Israel/Palestine from ca. 5500 BCE to 1920 CE.

Thesaurus Antiquorum Lectionariorum Ecclesiae Synagogaeque (ThALES): http://www.lectionary.eu. A large database of medieval Jewish and Christian lectionaries.

Contributors

Lutz Doering, Professor of New Testament and Ancient Judaism and Director of the Institutum Judaicum Delitzschianum, Westfälische Wilhelms-Universität Münster, Münster, Germany

Philip F. Esler, Portland Chair in New Testament Studies, University of Gloucestershire, Cheltenham, UK

Daniel K. Falk, Chaiken Family Chair in Jewish Studies, The Pennsylvania State University, University Park, Pennsylvania

Erich S. Gruen, Wood Professor Emeritus, The University of California at Berkeley, Berkeley, California

Todd R. Hanneken, Saint Mary's University, San Antonio, Texas

Angela Kim Harkins, Boston College School of Theology and Ministry, Brighton, Massachusetts

Matthias Henze, Isla Carroll and Percy E. Turner Professor of Hebrew Bible and Early Judaism, Rice University, Houston, Texas

Sylvie Honigman, Professor in Ancient History, Tel Aviv University, Tel Aviv, Israel

Pieter W. van der Horst, Professor Emeritus, Utrecht University, Utrecht, The Netherlands

James Kugel, Professor Emeritus, Bar-Ilan University, Ramat-Gan, Israel, and Harry M. Starr Professor Emeritus of Classical and Modern Hebrew Literature, Harvard University, Cambridge, Massachusetts

Robert Kugler, Paul S. Wright Professor of Christian Studies, Lewis & Clark College, Portland, Oregon

Andrea Lieber, Sophia Ava Asbell Chair in Judaic Studies, Dickinson College, Carlisle, Pennsylvania

Liv Ingeborg Lied, Norwegian School of Theology, Religion and Society, Oslo, Norway

Timothy H. Lim, Professor of Hebrew Bible & Second Temple Judaism, The University of Edinburgh, Edinburgh, UK

Steve Mason, Distinguished Professor of Ancient Mediterranean Religions and Cultures, University of Groningen, Groningen, The Netherlands

Eric M. Meyers, Bernice and Morton Lerner Distinguished Emeritus Professor in Judaic Studies, Duke University, Durham, North Carolina

Françoise Mirguet, Arizona State University, Tempe, Arizona

Maren R. Niehoff, Max Cooper Professor of Jewish Thought, The Hebrew University of Jerusalem, Jerusalem, Israel

Ishay Rosen-Zvi, Tel Aviv University, Tel Aviv, Israel

Alison Schofield, Associate Professor of Religious and Judaic Studies, University of Denver, Denver, Colorado

Chris Seeman, Walsh University, North Canton, Ohio

Rodney A. Werline, Leman and Marie Barnhill Endowed Chair in Religious Studies, Barton College, Wilson, North Carolina

Benjamin G. Wright III, University Distinguished Professor, Lehigh University, Bethlehem, Pennsylvania

Ancient Sources Index

Hebrew Bible/Old Testament

Genesis	157, 282, 287, 369, 575
1	160, 419
1–3	101
1:27	270, 546
3:19	52
4	319
4:1	319
5:4	524
6:1–4	418
9:1	314
9:22	314
11:31	287
12:1	287
14:18	315
18:2	321
19:31	315
19:33–35	314
22:1	314–15
22:16–18	333
32:25–30	309
32:29	309, 320, 340
34	320, 338–39
35:22	105, 338
37:2	339
37:2–48:22	353
39:11	314–15
39:14	315
49:13	339
49:14–15 [LXX]	339
50:10	52

Exodus	157, 282, 287, 369
15	101
15:1–18	309
15:21	309
16:29	315
17:8–16	498
19:24	160
21:24	316
23:7	270
31:24	320
32:13	333

Leviticus	157
12:3	52
15	52
18:13	270
18:21	320
19:19	448
20:2	320
20:2–5	320
23:20	52

Numbers	
24:17	270
25:10–13	24

Deuteronomy	77, 156–57, 159–60, 265, 312
4:2	311, 320
4:5–7	447
6:4	321
6:4–5	52
6:7	52
6:8–9	52
10:11	320
11:20	52
22:9	448

ANCIENT SOURCES INDEX: HEBREW BIBLE/OLD TESTAMENT

Deuteronomy (cont.)	
23:24	270
Joshua	267, 270
6:26	270
24:2–3	319
Judges	267, 309
4–5	366
16:11	318
Ruth	267
1 and 2 Samuel	258, 267
1 Samuel	309
25:26, 31, 33	270
10–11	157
2 Samuel	309
1 and 2 Kings	258, 267, 309
2 Kings	
2:35	55
22	265
1 and 2 Chronicles	159, 219, 267, 575
1 Chronicles	318
6:1–15	24
Ezra-Nehemiah	219, 267
Ezra	355
9	128
9:6–15	466
Nehemiah	
2:9	306
7	306
8	220, 269
9	468–69
9:5b–37	466
9:6–37	466–67

Esther	100, 106, 133, 156, 267, 269, 353–55, 358–61
1–2	361
3–5	361
6–7	361
8:3	362
8–10	361
Proverbs	309
1–9	160, 166
8:22–31	446
15:8	271
Job	267, 336, 370–71, 439–40, 442
[LXX]	336
1:11	314
2:4	314
42:13–17	337
Psalms	77, 157, 161, 267, 309, 369, 439–40, 442, 445
19	459
82:1	271
90	469
91	469
119	305–6, 459
119:97	305
Ecclesiastes/Qoheleth	268, 272, 439, 440, 442
Song of Songs	267–68, 272, 321
Isaiah	8–9, 147, 157, 161, 267, 308, 526
6	523
6:3	308
24–27	308
40:5	240, 308
56–66	412
63:7–64:11	466
Jeremiah	267, 308
31:31–34	307
Lamentations	267, 441

Ezekiel	267–68, 526	12:10	271
1	424, 526		
11:16	220	Apocrypha/Deuterocanonical Books	
40–48	412		
40:46	24	Tobit	118, 157, 257–58, 353–54, 359, 577, 579
43:19	24		
		1–3	369
Twelve Minor Prophets	267	1:21–22	354
		2:10	354
Hosea	161	3:1–6	466
		11–18	354
Micah	161	11:18	354
		12	369
Nahum	161	13–14	369
		14:10	354
Habakkuk	159		
		Judith	257–58, 385, 573
Zephaniah	161	1–7	365
		1:1	358
Haggai	218–19, 268	4:9–11	52
		5:5–22	316
Zechariah	218–19, 268, 468	7–13	365
1–8	412	9	127
9–14	412	9:2–4	316
		14	367
Malachi	218, 268, 270		
		Esther, Additions to	11, 257–58
Daniel	9, 118, 123, 127, 133, 157, 166, 267, 271, 355, 358–59, 380, 385 414, 416, 435, 441, 526	Wisdom of Solomon	127, 257–58, 440, 442, 447, 450, 452, 459
1	125	7	450
1–6	353, 355	7:22–30	551
2	419	9:4–11	551
4	419	10	316, 319
7	133, 424, 550	10:1–11:20	448
7–12	412	10:6	319
7:13	550		
8:26	258	Sirach	97, 101, 104, 123, 130, 157, 257–58, 267–68, 319, 440, 442–43, 445, 447, 449, 452, 459, 464, 527, 577
9	130, 419		
9:1–27	466		
9:4–19	467	Prologue	262
9:25–26	271	1:26	448
11:32	271	4:18	449
12:4	258	16:6–10	448
12:9–10	258	17:1–14	448

Sirach (cont.)		2 Maccabees	258, 353, 381, 384–85
23:23	448	2:13–15	265
24	448, 450	2:14	265
24:23	447	2:14–15	153
25:24	105	2:21	5
38:24–39:11	316	2:23–32	379
39:1–3	262	3	29
44–50	316	6:8–9	28
51:13–30	469	8:1	5
		8:27	51
Baruch	128, 257–58	14:38	5
1:1–3:8	130		
1:15–3:8	466–67	1 Esdras	258, 268, 353–54, 466
3:9–4:4	440, 447, 459	3:1–5:6	353
4:4	319		
		Prayer of Manasseh	258, 575, 577
Letter of Jeremiah	157, 257		
		Psalm 151	258
Daniel, Additions to	11, 257–58		
Susanna	268	3 Maccabees	80, 258–59, 353
3	52	2	469
Prayer of Azariah	466–67	2:1–10	467
		2:1–20	466
1 Maccabees	69–70, 127, 258, 268, 365,		
367–68		2 Esdras	258
1:1–11	385		
1:23–28	385	4 Maccabees	80, 105–6, 258, 381, 384,
1:35–40	385	450, 459	
1:56	265	1:1–2	384
2	333	1:7	384
2:6–13	385	1:13	384
2:54	24	3:19–20	379
3:2–9	384	4:26	5
5:62	385	17:7	379
7:14	24		
8	32	Inscriptions and Papyri	
10:61–65	23		
11:20–27	23	Acta Alexandrinorum	31
13:27–29	223	154–159	73
14:14	23		
14:27–49	24	Babatha archive	48
14:41	25		
15:14–24	78	*Beth She'arim*	
15:21	23	2.141	195
		2.147	195

ANCIENT SOURCES INDEX: INSCRIPTIONS AND PAPYRI   617

2.148	195	1.BS5–7	196
2.162	198	1.BS5–9, 17–25	196
2.172	196	1.BS20	196
2.194	198	1.BS22	196
		1.Cre3	195
Corpus Inscriptionum Iudaeae/Palestinae		1.Dal3	187
1.9	194	1.Mac1	194
2176	196	1.Thr3	195
2180	196	2.168	197
2191	196	2.5a	187
2196	196	2.8–21	186
		2.14	190, 197
Corpus Papyrorum Judaicarum		2.25	195
1:xvii–xx	187	2.43	195
1.1–5	209	2.236	198
1.25–26	208		
1.28–30	208	*Jewish Inscriptions of Graeco-Roman Egypt*	
1.39	208	22	194
1.48–111	208	84	193
1.126	208	117	194
1.130	208		
1.131	208	*Jewish Inscriptions of Western Europe*	
1.132	208	1.22	193
1.142–149	209	1.36	193
1.151	209	1.53	195
2.144	208	1.59	195
2.409	208	1.62	195
2.414	208	1.72	195
2.415	208	1.86	193
2.422	208	1.163	193, 195
2.424	208	2.103	198–99
3.43–56	187	2.212	193
4.557	210	2.240	193
		2.251	195
Corpus Papyrorum Raineri		2.271	193
18.7–9, 11	209	2.502	193
		2.281	193
Herakleopolis Papyri	30	2.542	195
		2.564	193
Inscriptiones Judaicae Orientis		2.576	193
1.Ach42	196	2.577	195
1.Ach42–45	190, 196	2.584	194
1.Ach43	196		
1.Ach44	196	P.Murabba'ât	
1.Ach45	196	20.3	52

ANCIENT SOURCES INDEX: INSCRIPTIONS AND PAPYRI

P. Yadin 2
   10.5   52

Theodotus   51

Urkunden des Politeuma der Juden von Herakleopolis
   1–20   210
   4, 5   208

Dead Sea Scrolls

4Q286–290 (4QBer^{a-e})   125

4Q510–511 (4QShir^{a-b})   149

Ages of Creation (4Q180)   161

Apocryphon of David (2Q22)   258

Apocryphon of Jeremiah (4Q383–385; 4Q387; 4Q389)   160

Apocryphon of Moses (4Q375–377)   160
   1Q22   269
   1Q29   269
   2Q21   269
   4Q375   269
   4Q376   269
   4Q408   269

Aramaic Levi Document (1Q21; 4Q213–214)   418, 341, 577

Barkhi Nafshi (4Q434–438)   168, 473

Beatitudes   166
   4Q525   160

Catena (4Q177/4QCatena^a)
   2, 9–10   166

Commentary on Genesis A (4Q252)   161, 167

Communal Confession (4Q393)   467

Consolations (4Q176)   156

Copper Scroll (3Q15)   151

Damascus Document (CD)   119–22, 124, 126, 149, 153, 155, 163, 167, 269
   I, 1–11   154
   III, 20–IV, 4   24
   IV, 20–21   270, 546
   V, 8–9   270
   IX, 9–10   270
   IX, 20–21   271
   XII, 23–XIII, 1   167
   XIII, 7   154
   XIV, 7   154
   XIV, 19   167
   XVI, 1–3   270
   XVI, 6   270
   XVII, 19–21   270
   XIX, 10–11   167
   4Q266–273   164
   4Q270
      I, 13–15   98
   5Q12   164
   6Q15   164

Deuteronomy (4Q41/4QDeuteronomy^n)   160

Exodus (4Q22/4QpaleoExod^m)   160

Ezra (4Q117)   269

Festival Prayers
   1Q34+34bis   467
   4Q507   467
   4Q508   467
   4Q509+4Q505   467

Florilegium (4Q174)   161, 167
   I, 14–15   166
   II, 3   271

Genesis Apocryphon (1Q20)   9, 160, 258, 269

Halakhah A and B (4Q251; 4Q264)   161

Hodayot (1QH^a)   10, 121, 125–26, 128, 130, 165, 272, 471, 472
   IV, 21–28   467
   X–XVII   471
   XXV, 34–XXXVII, 3   472
   4Q433   165
   4Q433a   165
   4Q440   165

Instruction
   1Q26   165
   4Q415–418a   165
   4Q418   156, 272
   4Q423   165

Jeremiah
   4Q70/4QJer^a   158
   4Q71/4QJer^b   158
   4Q72/4QJer^c   158
   4Q72a/4QJer^d   158

Joshua (4QJosh^a)   159

Jubilees (2Q20)   160

Melchizedek (11Q13)   161, 166
   1; 2i; 3i; 4 II, 18   271
   I, 10   271

Mezuzah (8Q4)   149

Miqṣat Maʿaśê ha-Torah (4QMMT)   149, 155, 161–62, 166, 472, 542, 548
   4Q397
     14–21, 15   270

Miscellaneous Rules (4Q265)   154, 161

Mysteries   166
   1Q27   156

Mysteries^{a–b} (4Q299–300)   156

New Jerusalem   148

Ordinances (4Q159; 4Q513–514)   161

Pesher   119, 272, 286
   1QpHab
     VII, 1–5   269
     VII, 3–5   159
     VII, 6–13   166
     VII, 10–12   152
     XI, 2–4   161
   4QpIsa^a   167

Psalms
   1Q16/1QpPs   271
   4Q83   470
   4Q84   470
   4Q87   470
   4Q88 (4QPs^f)   470
   4Q94)   470
   4Q96 (4QPs^{a, b, e, m, o})   470
   4Q171/4QpPsalms^a   162, 271
   4Q173/4QpPsalms^b   271
   4Q380, 4Q381/4QNon-Canonical Psalms A and B   473
   Psalms Scroll (11Q5/11QPs^a)   149, 156, 261, 271, 316, 469–70, 474
     XIX   469
     XXII, 1–15   469
     XXVI, 9–15   469
     XXVII, 1–11   469
   Apocryphal Psalms (11Q11)   473–74
     I, 1–10   473
     II, 1–V, 3   473
     V, 4–VI, 3   473
   Syriac Psalms
     Ps 151   469, 470
     Ps 154   469
     Ps 155   469

Pseudo-Ezekiel (4Q3853–388; 4Q391)   160

Pseudo-Jubilees (4Q225–227)	160
Pseudo-Moses (4Q385–390)	160

Reworked Pentateuch
4Q158	270
4Q364–367	270

Ritual of Marriage (4Q502)	154
Ritual of Purification (4Q414, 4Q512)	467

Rule of the Community (1QS) 11, 125–26, 149, 152, 163, 167, 269
I, 5–6	152
I, 7	152
I, 18–23	154
I, 18–II, 23	467
II, 19–23	154
III–IV	125
IV, 4–6	154
IV, 6–8	166
IV, 11–14	166
V, 2, 9	24
V, 2–3	154
V, 3–4	152
V, 15	270
VI, 1	155
VI, 1–25	154
VII, 3	154
VIII, 2	152
VIII, 5–7	169
VIII, 10	152
IX, 10–11	167
X–XI	467
4Q256/4QS^b	163
4Q258/4QS^d	163
4Q259/4QS^e	156, 163

Rule of the Congregation (1Q28a/1QSa) 149, 166, 167
I, 2, 24	24
I, 11	97

Samuel
4QSam^a	157
4QSam^c	152

Self-Glorification Hymn
4Q427 [4QH^a] 7	472
4Q431 [4QH^e] 1 [=4Q471b]	472
1QH^a XXV, 34–XXXVII, 3	472

Songs of the Sabbath Sacrifices (4Q400–407; 11Q17)	165, 169
Songs of the Sage (4Q510, 4Q511, 4Q560)	472, 474
Targum Job (11Q10)	160

Temple Scroll (11Q19) 148, 151, 156, 160–61, 268, 270, 542, 546
LVII, 11–15	25–26
4Q524	270
11Q19	270
11Q20	270

Testimonia (4Q175)	152, 161
21–23	270
Tohorot (4Q274)	161

War Scroll (1QM) 155, 166, 167
4Q491	
17, 4	271

Wiles of the Wicked Women (4Q184)	105, 160, 166
Words of the Luminaries (4Q504–506)	124, 160, 165
4Q504 (4QDibHam)	466, 467

Josephus and Philo

Josephus, *Antiquitates Judaicae*
1–11	393
1.214	52

1.6–7	392	Josephus, *Bellum Judaicum*	268, 380, 390, 391
6.68–69	157		
6.426–427	86	1–13	392
9.291	60	1.1	35
10.35	267	1.2	388
12	394	1.1–3	388
12–20	394	1.1–8	392
12.164–176	222	1.1–9	392
12.230–233	222	1.6	389
12.323	265	1.13	388
13	394	1.13–16	388
13–20	392	1.17	388
13.62–72	78	1.18	388
13.171	54	1.22	392
13.254	57	1.62	57
13.318	25	1.107–119	98
13.417	98	1.110	392
13.430	98	1.146	392
13.431	98	1.152	392
14–17	394	1.160	154
14.57	79	2.20–22	34
14.110	86	2.42	392
14.117	29	2.80–91	34
14.185–246	73	2.117	34
14.185–267	29	2.119	54
14.238–240	76	2.119–161	102
14.256–267	73	2.119–66	392
15.219	98	2.162	54
15.237	98	2.164	54
15.417	60	2.170	392
16.43	79	3.108	389
16.160–178	29, 73	2.247	265
16.164	265	4.560–563	103
17.299–314	34	5.375–420	384
17.355	34	6.199–219	106
18	394	6.354	265
18.2	34	7.148	265
18.11	54	7.150	265
18.63–64	382	7.162	265
18.65–84	74		
19.278–312	29	Josephus, *Contra Apionem*	58–59, 386
20.224–51	24	1.1	386
20.247	26	1.1–4	267
20.264	192	1.1–5	388
		1.11	52

1.18	381	177	287
1.34–36	265		
1.37–38	266	Philo, *De opificio mundi*	288, 290
1.38–41	261, 267		
1.42	268	Philo, *De sacrificiis Abelis et Cain*	
1.50–55	388	78	386
1.53–56	393		
1.54–55	386	Philo, *De somniis*	287
1.216–218	388	1.52	287, 386
2.46	381	1.205	386
2.184–189	22	2.127	79
2.201	98		
		Philo, *De specialibus legibus*	288
Josephus, *Vita*	392	1.1–2	83
1.6	265	1.69	86
10	54	1.200	102
40	336, 385, 388	1.201	104
342	385	2.168	86
348	385	3.37–38	102
362	385		
367	385	Philo, *De vita contemplativa*	100, 293
		1–2	521
Philo, *De Abrahamo*		21–22	56
93	99	60	102
135–136	102		
245–246	99	Philo, *De vita Mosis*	
		1.1	104
Philo, *De cherubim*		1.158	104
105	386	2.46	386
		2.215–216	79
Philo, *De confusione linguarum*	287		
146–147	551	Philo, *Hypothetica*	51
		7.1	102
Philo, *De congressu eruditionis gratia*		7.11–13	79
15	386		
44	386	Philo, *In Flaccum*	30, 386
		1–101	72
Philo, *De decalogo*		17, 29	30
121–131	102	56	31
Philo, *De fuga et inventione*		Philo, *Legatio ad Gaium*	30, 292, 386
51	103, 104	118	104
		143	225
Philo, *De migratione Abrahami*		150	282
43	288	155–156	86

155–157	74	2 Baruch	6, 125, 333, 380, 412, 425, 435, 521, 575, 581
156	79		
156–57	51	20.3–4	258–59
158	76	49–52	420
216	86	53–74	419
319–320	99	54	418
349	386	87.1	259

Philo, *Legum allegoriae*   99, 287

		2 Enoch	435, 521, 572
2.74	104	30.10	105
3.68	104		
3.222–224	104	2 Esdras	571, 579

Philo, *Questiones et solutiones in Exodum*   287, 288, 316

		3 Baruch	425, 435, 575, 581
1.7	102	4 Baruch	581

Philo, *Questiones et solutiones in Genesin*   287, 288, 316

4 Ezra   6, 121, 123, 132, 272, 333, 380, 412, 417, 423, 435, 527, 547, 551, 571, 575, 579

2.62	551		
3.3	104	3.21–22	418
3.47	102	7.26–44	419
3.48	102	11.1–12.36	419
3.49	52	12.37	258
		13	550
Pseudepigrapha		14.5	258
		14.45–48	258, 261

1 Enoch   9, 11, 53, 118, 122–23, 125, 157, 166, 269–71, 380, 385, 414, 416, 423, 466, 521, 542, 571–73, 576, 581

1–36	47, 53, 126, 418, 435, 523	5 Ezra	579
1.1–2	269		
1.9	157, 543	6 Ezra	579
6–11	410		
10.11–15	543	Ahiqar	353, 354, 369
12–36	125		
37–71	419, 435, 550	Apocalypse of Abraham	380, 435, 521, 572
48.52	419	Apocalypse of Elijah	581
70–71	551		
72–82	412, 435	Apocalypse of Zephaniah	425, 435
83–90	133		
85–90	415, 435	Ascension of Isaiah	425, 435, 521, 581
93.1–10	133, 415, 419, 435		
91.11–17	133, 415, 419, 435	Assumption of Moses	543

624   ANCIENT SOURCES INDEX: PSEUDEPIGRAPHA

Greek Life of Adam and Eve	581	Testament of Abraham	330, 354, 435
7.1	105		
14.2	105	Testament of Asher	339
17.1–2	105		
31–42	105	Testament of Dan	339
Joseph and Aseneth	11, 80, 99, 283, 353,	Testament of Gad	339
	522, 575, 581		
15.1	103	Testament of Isaac	330
24.7, 25.8	103		
		Testament of Job	329–30, 334, 337, 575
Jubilees	9, 99, 123, 127, 156, 157, 160,	1–27	335
	268–71, 286, 310, 312, 316, 385, 410,	1–45	336
	416, 466, 435, 542, 546, 550, 571–72,	6–8	335
	576	15–50	334
Prologue	269	18.4	103
30.7–10	320	20.8	103
32.13–15	337	20.9	335
		21–27	335
Ladder of Jacob	577	28–44	335
		28.1	335
Letter of Aristeas	80, 223, 262, 268, 282,	39–40	335
	283, 284, 286, 394, 438	45.4	335
1–11, 300–321	81	46–53	335, 336, 337
		51–53	334
Lives of the Prophets	581	52–53	335
		52.10	338
Odes of Solomon	474, 475	53.1	335
Psalms of Solomon	80, 131, 330, 466,	Testament of Joseph	339
	474, 475	14.4–5	340
17	23	15.1–17.2	340
Pseudo-Philo	9, 99, 337, 380	Testament of Judah	339
11.8	51	12.11–12	340
		26.1	342
Pseudo-Phocylides	440, 443, 451, 452,		
	459	Testament of Levi	338, 428, 435, 521
		2–5	435
Sibylline Oracles	80, 410, 527	2.3	340
1.42	105	8–9	340
		11–14	340
Syriac Menander	459		
		Testament of Moses	329–31, 410–11, 466
Testament of Adam	330	1	331

1.2	334	14:62	551
2-4	333		
2-8	331	Luke	295, 422
3.9	333	7:4-5	197
5	333	7:34	545
6	331, 332, 333	17:16	60
7	333	17:18	60
8	331, 332		
9	331	John	422, 441, 554
9-10	331, 332		
10.1-10	333	Acts	554
10.2	332, 333	2:1-11	86
11-12	331	7	316
11.17	333	17-19	78, 79
12.6	333	18:2	74

Testament of Naphtali 339, 340, 435, 577
   1.11-12   340

Testament of Reuben   338, 339
   3.11-15   105
   5.1   105
   5.6-7   105

Testament of Simeon   339

Testament of Solomon   330

Testament of the Twelve Patriarchs 329-31, 385, 466, 552, 571, 573, 575, 581

New Testament

Matthew	422, 441, 554
28:18-20	553
Mark	422
2:13-17	545
2:27-28	546
3:4	546
6:1-6	51
6:21	47
7:14-23	546
7:15	546
10:2-9	546

Romans	
1:3-4	551
5	418
8:31-32	321
8	422
8:18	422
1 Corinthians	
5	422
14	424
2 Corinthians	130
Galatians	2:16
1 Thessalonians	
4	428
James	
5:11	338
1 Peter	
3:19-20	543
1 John	
3:10-12	319
Jude	156, 573
9	331, 543

Jude (cont.)
14–15 543

Revelation 43

Christian Writers and Literature

Augustine, *De civitate Dei*
6.11 83

Clement of Alexandria 282

Didascalia Apostolorum 342

Epistle of Barnabas 554

Eusebius, *Historia ecclesiastica*
4.6 36
4.26 261
6.12.1–4 259
25.1 386

Eusebius, *Praeparatio evangelica* 387
7.8 51

Gelasius, *Historia ecclesiastica*
2.21.7 332

Gospel of Thomas 422, 544

Jerome, *De viris illustribus*
11 289

Jerome, *Prologus Galeatus* 261

Justin Martyr 554

Origen, *Commentarium in evangelium Matthaei*
10.18 259

Origen, *Commentary on the Psalms* 261

Origen, *Letter to Africanus* 268

Pseudo-Clementine Homilies 535

Serapion 259

Shepherd of Hermas 258

Greco-Roman Writers and Literature

Antonius Julianus 386

Cassius Dio, *Historia romana*
57.18.5a 74
69.12 36–37

Cicero, *Epistulae ad Atticum*
1.19 385
2.1 385

Cicero, *De oratore*
2.18.80 384

Cicero, *Epistulae ad familiares*
5.12 385

Cicero, *Pro Flacco*
66–69 74

Cledemus Malchus 387

Demetrius of Samothrace 286, 386

Diodorus Siculus, *Bibliotheca historica*
40.2 23
40.3 82

Dionysius, *De Thucydide*
1–3 381
2 381
6–18 391
21 381
50–51 381

Eupolemus 381

Galen, *De Usu partium corporis humani*		Plutarch, *Alexander*	
2.630	95	1.2	386
Hecataeus of Abdera	82	Plutarch, *Lucullus*	
		1.3	385
Herodotus, *Historiae*			
1.8	355	Plutarch, *Quaestiones convivialum libri IX*	
		4.6.2	83
Homer, *Odyssey*	287		
		Plutarch, *Sulla*	
Horace, *Satirae*		23.2	385
1.9.70	83		
		Polybius, *Historiae*	
Juvenal, *Satirae*		1.1.2	381
3.296	51	12.25–25a.4f	391
6.159–160	83	12.25i–26b	391
		12.25i.9	391
Lucian	295, 381	36.1.1–7	391
		38.4	388
Macrobius, *Saturnalia*			
2.4.11	83	Polyhistor, *Periloudaion*	386–88
Manetho	386	Pseudo-Eupolemus	386
Martial	83	Pseudo-Hecataeus	387
Minucius Felix, *Octavius*		Pseudo-Plutarch, *De Herodot malignitate*	
33.4	386	381	
Petronius		Quintilian, *Institutio oratoria*	
frag. 37	83	1.8.18	384
		2.4.2–3	384
Philo of Byblos	386	4.2.1, 52–53	384
Plato, *Theaetetus*	289	Sallust, *Bellum catalinae*	
		4–5	386
Plato, *Timaeus*	290		
		Sallust, *Bellum jugurthinum*	386
Pliny the Elder, *Naturalis historia*			
1.3c	387	Seneca	75, 83, 292
1.4c	387		
1.5c	387	Sextus Empiricus, *Adversus mathematicos*	
1.6c	387	1.248	382
31.24	83	1.269	382

Strabo	391	b. Hagigah	
		14b	528
Suetonis, *Divus Claudius*			
25.4	74	b. Megillah	
		29a	220
Suetonis, *De rhetoribus*			
1	384	b. Ta'anit	
		68a	265
Suetonis, *Tib.*			
36	74	Demetrius	81, 282, 286
Tacitus, *Annales*		Eupolemus, *On the Kings of Judea*	81
1.1	381		
2.85	74	Ezekiel the Tragedian	81, 282
Tacitus, *Historiae*		Hekhalot Zutarti	530
1.4	381		
5.4.3	83	Ma'aseh Merakvah	529, 530
5.5.2	83		
5.5.5	83	Mekilta	498, 499
Thallus	387	Midrash Wayisa'u	340
Thucydides, *History of the Peloponnesian War*		m. Menahot	
		10:3	490
1.1	381		
1.22.1	391	m. Niddah	
		8:3	503
Valerius Maximus, *Factorum ac dictorum memorabilium libri IX*		m. Sanhedrin	
1.3.3	74	10:1	262, 497
Virgil, *Aeneid*	385	m. Ta'anit	
		4:2	265
Jewish Writers and Literature		m. Yad	
Aristobulus	282, 286, 438	3:5	261, 262, 263
		3:6–8	490
Artapanus	81, 282, 387	4:6	491
		4:6–8	501
b. Bava Batra			
14a	265	Pirke Avoth	459
b. Gittin		Seder Olam	498, 502
60b	149		

Sifra	497, 499
Sifre Numbers	498
Sifre Deuteronomy	498
344	501
t. Berakhot	
3:28	490
t. Kippurim	
10:8	490
t. Sotah	
13:2	268
13:3	269
15:11	490

Modern Scholars Index

Aarne, Antti 118
Abrams, Daniel 530
Adams, Samuel L. 440
Ackerman, Susan 51
Ackroyd, Peter 218
Adan-Bayewitz, David 228
Adelman, Rachel 576–77
Adler, William 259, 386–88, 571, 573–74, 576, 579–80
Adler, Yonatan 228
Afterman, Adam 527
Ahearne-Kroll, Patricia 8, 11
Aitken, James K. 450
Albeck, Hanoch 492–93, 495, 577
Albertz, Rainer 51
Albright, William F. 147
Alexander, Elizabeth Shanks 493–94
Alexander, Philip S. 153, 163, 167, 263, 266, 424, 472, 477, 522, 553
Alesse, Francesca 291
Allegro, John M. 310, 439
Allison, Dale C. 421
Ameling, Walter 76–77, 185, 188, 190
Amihai, Aryeh 161
Amir, Yehoshua 285
Anderson, Gary A. 105
Anderson, Janice Capel 106
Anderson, Matthew R. 101–2
Angel, Andrew 104
Angel, Joseph L. 165
Araujo, Magdalena Díaz 105
Arbel, Vita Daphna 105
Archer, Léonie 52, 97
Argall, Randall A. 452
Ariel, Donald T. 33

Arnold, Russell 129, 477
Arnould-Béhar, Caroline 33
Asale, Bruk Ayele 573
Assis, Moshe 500
Assmann, Jan 131–32
Atkinson, Kenneth 98, 332, 475
Attridge, Harold W. 245, 382, 388, 392–93
Auerbach, Erich 127
Aune, David E. 262
Avemarie, Friedrich 548
Aviam, Mordechai 49, 225, 229
Avigad, Nahman 49, 184
Ayali-Darshan, Noga 492

Baarda, Tijtze 342
Babota, Vasile 23
Bacher, Wilhelm 294
Bachmann, Michael 549
Bachmann, Veronika 105
Badalanova Geller, Florentina 573–74
Baer, Richard A. 101, 104
Bagatti, Bellarmino 184
Bahat, Dan 227
Bailey, Elizabeth 545, 573
Bailliet, Maurice 463
Bainbridge, William Sims 123
Bakhos, Carol 496, 501
Bakhtin, Mikhail 125, 360, 371, 426, 441
Balberg, Mira 503
Balentine, Samuel E. 462
Balla, Ibolya 99
Balla, Marta 153
Ballaban, Steven A. 577
Bar-Asher Siegal, Michal 501

Bar Ilan, Meir 122
Barclay, John M. G. 27, 59, 80–81, 286, 294, 549
Baron, Lori 555
Barth, Frederik 58
Barthélemy, Dominique 294, 543
Barthes, Roland 120
Bartlett, John R. 75, 385
Barton, Carlin A. 59, 383
Barton, John 119, 260, 263–65, 267, 319, 320
Barton, Stephen C. 131
Barzilai, Gabriel 317
Baskin, Judith 503
Bauckham, Richard J. 3, 259, 408, 542, 575–79, 581
Baumgarten, Albert I. 53, 122, 417, 490
Baumgarten, James M. 531
Baumgarten, Joseph 464
Bautch, Richard J. 463, 466
Becker, Adam H. 554, 578
Becking, Bob 306
Beckwith, Roger 260, 263–65, 267, 307
Beentjes, Pancratius C. 99, 450
Begg, Christopher T. 336, 393
Beiser, Frederick C. 381
Belkin, Samuel 289
Bell, Catherine 128–29
Ben-Dov, Jonathan 426
Ben Ze'ev, A. 127
Benjamin, Walter 443
Benoit, Pierre 212
Berger, Klaus 552
Berger, Peter 447
Bergmeier, Roland 392
Bergren, Theodore A. 571, 579
Berlin, Adele 355, 358, 360–61, 364
Berlin, Andrea 52, 60
Bernhardt, Johannes Christian 28
Bernstein, Moshe J. 9, 97, 155, 159, 313
Berquist, Jon L. 99, 123
Berthelot, Katell 157–58, 552
Bettiolo, Paolo 581
Betz, Hans Dieter 10
Biale, David 502
Biale, Rachel 97
Bickerman, Elias 84
Bieringer, Reimund 552
Bij de Vaate, Alice J. 186
Bilde, Per 292, 389–93
Binder, Donald D. 50–51, 79, 226
Birnbaum, Ellen 283
Blackwell, Ben C. 422
Bland, Kalman P. 225, 230
Blenkinsopp, Joseph 308, 447
Bloch, Marc 381, 390
Bloch, René S. 286
Bloedhorn, Hans-Wulf 76–77, 185
Bloomquist, L. Gregory 408
Boccaccini, Gabriele 451, 543, 551, 573
Bockmuehl, Markus 410, 552
Boda, Mark J. 463, 466–68
Boer, Martinus C. de 422
Boer, Roland 48, 441
Bogaert, Pierre-Maurice 576
Bohak, Gideon 340, 445, 502 523
Bohec, Yann le 184
Bolin, Thomas M. 380
Bons, Eberhard 475
Borchardt, Francis 575
Borg, Marcus 421
Borgen, Peder 286
Böttrich, Christfried 572, 574, 576, 579, 583
Bourdieu, Pierre 94, 130
Boustan, Ra'anan S. 424–25, 502, 524, 528, 531–32
Boyarin, Daniel 5, 59, 71, 292, 383, 498, 500–503, 551, 554
Boyd-Taylor, Cameron 362
Bradshaw, Paul F. 463
Brand, Miryam T. 169
Brandes, Yehudah 493
Breed, Brennan W. 569
Bregman, Marc 494
Bréhier, Emile 290
Brendin, Mark 370
Brenner, Athalya. 360–61, 363
Brettler, Marc Zvi 477
Brighton, Mark Andrew 36, 390

Brison, Ora 367
Brock, Sebastian P. 205, 572
Brooke, George J. 4, 120–22, 126, 132, 153, 155, 159, 169, 313, 448, 473, 477, 496, 542
Brooten, Bernadette J. 51, 100, 195
Broshi, Magan 153
Brown, Cheryl Anne 99
Brown, Dennis 258
Brown, Raymond E. 258–59
Bruin, Tom de 342
Brutti, Maria 23
Buhl, Frants 263
Buller, Bob 1
Bultmann, Rudolf 422, 547
Bundvad, Mette 426
Bundy, David 572
Burchard, Christoph 575
Burke, Kenneth 10, 126
Burke, Tony 568, 583
Burkes, Shanon 445, 450
Burn, A. R. 198
Burns, Joshua Ezra 495, 502, 552, 555
Burrell, Barbara 33
Burridge, Kenelm 122
Burrus, Sean P. 217
Burrus, Virginia 101
Burtchaell, James Turstead 195
Butler, Judith 93–94, 96

Cain, Carole 126
Calabi, Francesca 283, 389
Calduch-Benages, Núria 99
Camp, Claudia V. 104, 123–24
Campbell, Jonathan G. 119–20, 159
Cansdale, Lena 150
Caponigro, M. S. 365
Cappelletti, Silvia 75
Capponi, Livia 78
Caquot, André 444
Carey, Greg 408
Carr, David M. 122, 149, 307, 451
Carson, D. A. 548
Carter, Charles E. 220, 222
Carter, Warren 133

Cason, Thomas Scott 337, 338
Cataldo, Jeremiah W. 23
Cawthorn, Katrina 95
Ceriani, Antonio 331
Chancey, Mark A. 49, 191, 217, 221–23, 225–27, 230–31, 544
Chaney, Marvin L. 47
Chapman, Honora H. 390
Charles, Robert H. 259, 332, 568, 578
Charlesworth, James H. 3, 80, 117, 211, 406, 474, 542–43
Chazon, Esther G. 169, 463–65, 469
Chernus, Ira 528–29
Chesnutt, Randall D. 4–5, 337
Cheung, Simon Chi-Chung 441
Childs, Brevard 320
Chilton, Bruce 390
Christiansen, Ellen Juhl 128
Cioată, Maria 572, 575, 579, 583
Clarke, Katherine 382
Clarysse, Willy 208
Claußen, Carsten 195
Clements, Ruth 554
Clines, David J. A. 362
Coblentz Bautch, Kelley 124, 157, 426–27
Cockle, W. E. H. 192, 211
Cohen, Boaz 294, 495
Cohen, Jeffery Jerome 133
Cohen, Naomi 289
Cohen, Shaye J. D. 5, 37, 45–46, 59, 193, 261, 263, 267–68, 543, 555
Colautti, Federico M. 390
Collins, John J. 4–5, 7, 27, 53, 56, 80, 155, 162, 167, 270, 286, 329, 331, 333, 335, 339, 342, 355, 392, 405–10, 417–18, 424, 441–42, 444–45, 448, 477, 496, 542, 550–51, 574, 581
Collins, Nina L. 285
Colson, F. H. 281
Conte, Gian Biagio 381
Conway, Colleen 101, 103–4
Coogan, Jeremiah 571, 576
Coogan, Michael 220
Cook, Stephen L. 269

Corley, Jeremy   128, 365, 367–69, 463
Coşkun, Altay   32
Cotton, Hannah M.   29, 34, 186, 192, 211–12
Cover, Michael B.   294, 549
Cowey, James M. S.   30, 72, 210
Cowley, Roger W.   571
Craig, Kenneth   360–61
Craven, Toni   364–65
Crawford, Sidnie White   97, 152–53, 159, 169, 310–11, 360, 366, 406
Crenshaw, James   440–41
Crone, Patricia   570
Cross, Frank Moore   269, 319, 405
Crossan, John Dominic   48, 421, 544
Csordas, Thomas J.   130
Curran, John R.   388
Czajkowski, Kimberley   212

Dabrowa, Edward D.   32
Dalley, Stephanie   355
D'Angelo, Mary Rose   99, 102
Darshan, Guy   497
Daschke, Dereck   412
Daube, David   494
Davies, Philip R.   119, 122, 261, 307, 408, 413
Davies, W. D.   410, 547
Davila, James R.   3, 247, 259, 424, 464, 523, 529, 531, 542, 575, 577–78, 581–82
Davis, Kipp   269
Day, Linda M.   363
DeConick, April   524, 533
De Jonge, Marinus   339, 340, 342–43, 570–71, 575, 578, 580–82
De Lange, Nicholas   268
Dell, Katherine   441
DeSilva, David A.   340, 366, 384
De Vaux, Roland   212
De Vries, Johannes   552
Deines, Roland   55
Delamarter, Steve   149
Den Hollander, William   294, 390
Denis, Albert-Marie   572

Deutsch, Celia   57
Diamond, Eliezer   503
Dieleman, Jacco   357, 359
Dijkhuizen, Pieternella   106
Dillon, John   290
Dimant, Devorah   152, 312, 354, 369–71, 426
DiTommaso, Lorenzo   407, 415, 417, 427, 572, 575, 579–80, 583
Docherty, Susan   552
Doeker, Andrea   477
Doering, Lutz   162, 289, 546, 549, 552
Dohrmann, Natalie B.   281, 294, 494–96
Donaldson, Terence L.   550
Doran, Robert   118, 353–54, 357, 365, 385
Dorothy, Charles V.   360, 362, 364
Doudna, Gregory   150
Douglas, Mary   50, 129
Dozeman, Thomas   307
Drawnel, Henryk   340
Droysen, Johann Gustav   84
Duggan, Michael W.   127
Dumville, D. N.   571
Dunn, James D. G.   53–55, 545, 547–49, 553–54
Durkheim, Amile   131

Eagleton, Terry   120
Eck, Werner   34, 37, 383
Eckhardt, Benedikt   23, 29, 365, 367–68
Edmondson, Jonathan   389
Edrei, Arye   577
Edwards, Douglas R.   49
Egger, Rita   390
Egger Wenzel, Renate   127, 463, 475
Ego, Beate   127
Ehrenkrook, Jason von   102, 103
Ehrman, Bart   421, 422
Eilers, Claude   32
Eisen, Arnold M.   85
Ekstein, Arthur M.   391
Elgvin, Torleif   155
Eliade, Mircea   526
Elior, Rachel   522–23, 531, 532

Eliyahu, Eyal ben	489	Flint, Peter W.	156–57, 271, 470
Elizur, Shulamit	502	Flusser, David	461, 544
Elliot, John H.	53	Fonrobert, Charlotte	503
Ellis, Teresa Ann	101	Fontanille, Jean-Philippe	33
Elman, Yaakov	492–93, 501	Foucault, Michel	120, 125–26, 503
Engberg-Pedersen, Troels	56, 101	Fowler, Alastair	409
Engels, Donald	48	Fox, Michael V.	361–64
Enns, Peter	316	Foxhall, Lin	359
Epp, Jay	1	Fraade, Steven D.	162, 496, 498, 502–3
Epstein, Jacob N.	493, 495, 499	Frankel, Yonah	492, 499–500
Erho, Ted M.	571, 573	Frankfurter, David	572, 581
Erlich, Adi	224	Franzmann, Majella	474
Eshel, Esther	340, 365–66, 463, 472, 474	Fraser, M. P.	285
		Frazer, James	129
Eshel, Hanan	37, 150, 153, 212	Fredriksen, Paula	59, 550
Esler, Philip F.	47–48, 51, 53, 56, 58–60, 414	Freedman, David Noel	260
		Frei, Peter	266
Evans, Craig A.	546	Freudenthal, Jacob	387
Evenbauer, Peter	477	Frey, Jean-Baptiste	184–86, 191
Eybers, Ian H.	270–71	Frey, Jörg	418, 421, 423, 541–42, 549
Fabricius, Johann A.	568, 571, 573	Freyne, Sean	48–49, 222
Falk, Daniel K.	52, 117, 159, 169, 464–67	Fricke, Klaus Dietrich	257
Farrell, Joseph	381	Fried, Lisbeth	23
Fausto-Sterling, Anne	94	Friedländer, Moritz	519
Feder, Frank	8	Friedman, Shamma	501
Feldman, Louis H.	71, 83–84, 197, 260, 316, 380, 386, 389, 392–93	Fröhlich, Ida	577
		Frost, Samantha	94
Felsch, Dorit	552	Fuks, Alexander	72–73, 205
Ferrura, A.	184	Furstenberg, Ya'ir	294, 546
Fiensy, David A.	48–49, 544		
Fine, Steven	217, 224, 230, 281–82	Gabbay, Uri	492, 501
Finkbeiner, Douglas P.	390	Gadot, Yuval	219
Finkelstein, Israel	57, 218	Gafni, Chanan	492, 502
Finley, Moses	48	Gafni, Isaiah M.	71, 502
Fiorenza, Elizabeth Schüssler	97	Gager, John G.	84, 549
Fisch, Yael	496	Gallagher, Edmond	258, 268
Fischel, Henry Albert	494	Galor, Katharina	100
Fishbane, Michael	309, 313	Gambetti, Sandra	30, 73
Fisk, Bruce	342	García Martínez, Florentino	153, 416–18, 420, 446, 463, 472, 542
Fitzmyer, Joseph A.	368		
Flannery, Frances	131–32, 134	Garrett, Susan	336
Fletcher-Louis, Crispin H. T.	522, 532, 551	Garrison, Irene Peirano	6, 8–9
		Gaston, Lloyd	549
Fleischer, Ezra	465	Gathercole, Simon	548–49, 579

Gehrke, Hans-Joachim	359	Greenwood, Eamon	569
Geiger, Abraham	577	Gropp, Douglas	211
Geiger, Joseph	211	Grossman, Maxine L.	97–98, 119–20, 126, 134, 154, 162, 169
Geljon, Albert C.	283		
Gemunden, Petra von	342	Grosz, Elizabeth	94
Genette, Gérard	121	Gruen, Erich S.	21, 25, 27–30, 46, 71, 73–74, 80, 83–84, 86, 286, 291, 356, 358, 365, 383, 386, 388
Gera, Deborah L.	365–67, 574, 579		
Gera, Dov	29, 32		
Gerber, Christine	386	Gruen, William	335
Gereboff, Joel	127	Grüenfelder, Regula	390
Gerhards, Albert	477	Gruenwald, Ithamar	129, 424, 522, 528–29, 532
Geva, Hillel	218		
Ghiretti, Maurizio	34	Guffey, Andrew	336, 343
Gibson, E. Leigh	78, 185, 190, 196	Gunneweg, Jan	153
Ginzberg, Louis	574	Gunkel, Hermann	467
Goering, Greg Schmidt	448	Gurtner, Daniel M.	4, 7
Goff, Matthew J.	105, 165, 410, 439–42, 444, 446, 449, 452	Gussmann, Oliver	390
		Gutman, Ariel	572–73, 575, 578–79
Golb, Norman	150	Gvaryahu, Amit	499, 501
Goldberg, Abraham	493		
Goldberg, Shari	101	Haas, Cees	335
Goldberg, Sylvie-Anne	389	Haber, Susan	129
Goldstein, Jonathan	384	Hachlili, Rachel	185, 217, 225, 230–31
Goodblatt, David	25, 36	Hadas-Lebel, Mireille	283, 389
Goodenough, Erwin R.	521	Hadot, Piere	503
Goodman, Martin D.	26, 34–36, 79–80, 83, 194, 199, 258, 267, 294, 390–91, 502, 554	Hägg, Thomas	289
		Halbertal, Moshe	495, 498
		Halbwachs, Maurice	130–31
Goodrich, John K.	422	Halivni, David Weiss	501
Gordley, Matthew E.	476	Hall, Robert G.	380
Gordon, Benjamin D.	219, 227–28, 232	Hallet, Judith P.	95
Gorea, Maria	335	Halliday, Michael A. K.	121
Goshen-Gottstein, Alon	503	Halperin, David M.	95, 529–30
Goudriaan, Koen	30	Halpern, Baruch	318–19, 380
Grabbe, Lester L.	24, 70, 82, 223, 283, 408, 413–14, 489	Halpern-Amaru, Betsy	99, 333–34, 390, 393
Graetz, Heinrich	262, 519, 525, 535	Hammond, Martin	389
Graf, Georg	572	Hancock, Rebecca S.	99–100, 363
Granat, Yehoshua	574	Hanneken, Todd R.	4, 571
Grantham, Billy J.	228	Hanson, John S.	36, 132, 545
Gray, Patrick	338	Hanson, K. C.	47–48, 50
Gray, Rebecca	35, 393	Hanson, Paul	405–7, 412–13
Greenberg, Moshe	462	Haralambakis, Maria	335–36, 338
Greenfield, Jonas C.	340	Haran, Menachem	320
Greenspoon, Leonard	2, 360	Harker, Andrew	31, 73, 292

Harkins, Angela Kim   52, 117, 123–25, 128, 130, 158, 165, 169, 337, 471, 476–77
Harl, Marguerite   268
Harlow, Daniel J.   4, 7, 575, 581
Harness, Kelley   573
Harrill, Albert J.   295
Harrington, Daniel J.   165, 258, 385, 444
Harrington, Hannah K.   129, 161, 165
Harris, Jay Michael   495
Harris, William V.   122
Hartog, François   359
Hartog, Pieter B.   496, 499
Harvey, Charles D.   362
Hasan-Rokem, Galit   500
Hasselbach, Trine Bjørnung   121
Hata, Gohei   389
Hauptman, Judith   503
Hawkins, Ralph K.   48
Hayes, Christine E.   502, 550
Hayes, Christopher   498
Hazelrigg, Lawrence E.   123
Heckel, Ulrich   549
Heelas, Paul   126
Heemstra, Marius   554–55
Heger, Paul   97
Heinemann, Joseph   465
Hellholm, David   406–7, 412
Hempel, Charlotte   4, 121, 162–65, 472
Hengel, Martin   36, 118, 221, 549
Henshke, David   498
Henten, Jan Willem van   24, 98, 186, 333, 365–66, 581
Henze, Matthias   8, 12, 53, 158, 313, 355–56, 358, 426
Herholt, Volker   84
Herman, Geoffrey   501
Herr, David Moshe   495, 575
Heschel, Susannah   97
Hezser, Catherine   122, 281, 294, 495, 500, 543
Hicks-Keeton, Jill   555
Hidary, Richard   495
Hieke, Thomas   367
Hillel, Vered   340, 342

Himmelfarb, Martha   342, 425, 523, 527, 571, 576–78, 581
Hirschfeld, Yizhar   150
Hirshman, Marc   498–99, 501
Hjälm, Miriam   572
Hobsbawm, Eric   132
Hoek, Annewies van den   101, 294
Hoffman, Christhard   84
Hoffman, David   498
Hofmann, Norbert Johannes   332, 333
Hogan, Karina Martin   121, 451, 571
Holladay, Carl R.   80, 281, 283, 285, 387
Holland, Dorothy   126
Hollander, Harm   342–43
Holloway, Paul A.   295
Holm, Tawny L.   355
Holmén, Tom   545
Holmes, Brooke   95–96
Honigman, Sylvie   28–29, 31, 210, 266, 284, 286
Horbury, William   76–77, 131, 185, 195, 258, 551, 554
Horsley, Richard A.   36, 48, 49, 122, 132–33, 306–7, 410, 414, 451–52, 545
Horst, Pieter W. van der   30, 186, 190–91, 194, 198, 283, 292, 335–36, 386, 463
Hughes, Julie   468
Huizinga, Johan H.   380
Hultgren, Stephen   164
Humbert, Jean-Baptiste   150
Humphreys, W. Lee   353, 357
Hunt, Alice   24
Huss, Boaz   524, 532
Hutardo, Larry W.   551
Hutchinson, John   58–59
Hüttenmeister, Frowald G.   185

Idel, Moshe   526–27
Ilan, Tal   96–100, 169, 196, 211, 367, 390, 392, 502
Inowlocki, Sabrina   387
Inwood, Brad   503
Isaac, Benjamin H.   36, 83–84, 294
Israeli, Edna   332

Jacobi, Christine	545	Kister, Menachem	448–49, 452, 496, 499, 549, 576–78
Jacobson, Howard	81		
Jaffee, Martin	494	Klancher, Nancy	337
James, Montague R.	573–74	Klawans, Jonathan	6, 50, 129–30, 161
James, William	534	Klijn, Albertus F. J.	265
Janowitz, Naomi	2, 529	Kloner, Amos	223
Janzen, J. Gerald	308	Kloppenborg, John S.	51, 421
Japhet, Sara	306	Knibb, Michael A.	410, 581
Jassen, Alex	161	Knight, Douglas K.	1
Jensen, Morten Hørning	33, 49	Knoppers, Gary N.	58, 264, 311, 319
Jeremias, Joachim	545	Koch, Klaus	405, 421, 550–51
Jobes, Karen H.	364	Kokkinos, Kikos	33
Johnson, Mark	121, 130	Kolenkow, A. B.	330
Johnson, Sara Raup	284, 353, 356, 358	König, Alice	295
		Konradt, Matthias	553
Jokiranta, Jutta	56, 168, 475	Konstan, David	99
Jonquiere, Tessel	463	Kooij, Arie van der	22, 265
Junod, Éric	583	Koselleck, Reinhart	359
		Kosmin, Paul J.	415
Kahana, Menahem	497–98	Kraabel, A. Thomas	70, 217–18, 224–25
Kalman, Ya'akov	225	Kraemer, David	492
Kalmin, Richard	501–2	Kraemer, Ross S.	99–101, 186–87, 283, 293, 581
Kalms, Jürgen U.	389		
Kamesar, Adam	283, 286	Kraft, Robert A.	1–2, 6–7, 9–10, 12, 14, 45–46, 117, 147, 159, 183, 205, 252, 260–61, 281, 382–83, 389, 405–6, 437, 439, 451, 474–75, 477, 520, 541, 543, 567, 570, 574, 580–81
Kampen, John	165, 444, 446		
Kant, Lawrence H.	184, 190		
Karrer, Martin	552		
Kartveit, Magnar	57–58, 264, 311		
Käsemann, Ernst	544, 546	Kramer, Bärbel	209
Kasher, Aryeh	27, 210, 389	Kratz, Reinhard	162
Kattan Gribetz, Sarit	503	Kraus, Christina S.	380
Katz, Peter	285	Kraus, Wolfgang	552
Katz, Steven T.	489	Krause, Andrew	125
Katzoff, R.	495	Krieger, Klaus-Stefan	392
Kautsky, John H.	47	Kristeva, Julia	121
Kautzsch, Emil	568, 578	Kroll, John H.	185
Kazen, Thomas	546	Kruse, Thomas	210
Keddie, G. Anthony	283, 475	Kugel, James L.	158, 260, 314, 316–17, 319, 341, 496, 574
Kee, Howard Clark	51		
Keith, Chris	545	Kugler, Robert A.	128–29, 135, 210, 329, 334–36, 338, 340–43
Kerkeslager, Allen	31		
Keshet, Lia	500	Kuhn, Heinz-Wolfgang	542, 549
Kiel, Micah	370	Kulik, Alexander	572, 575
Kiel, Yishai	501	Kurowski, Philip	342
Kierkegaard, Bradford A.	335	Kynes, Will	440, 443

Labbé, Gilbert	34	Lewis, David M.	184
Labendz, Jenny R.	577	Lewis, Jack P.	262–63
Labow, Dagmar	389	Lewis, Naphtali	48, 212
Lackicotte Jr., William	126	Lichtenberger, Achim	33
Lacocque, André	361, 364	Lichtenberger, Hermann	165
Ladouceur, David J.	391	Lieber, Laura Suzanne	99–100, 476
Lakoff, George	121, 130	Lieberman, Saul	191–92, 493–94
Lambert, David A.	127, 496	Liebner, Uzi	500
Landau, Tamar	390	Liebowitz, Etka	98
Lange, Armin	152, 155–57, 165, 444	Lied, Liv Ingeborg	11, 124–25, 426, 569, 572, 575–76, 579, 581
Langer, Ruth	463, 465		
Langgut, Dafna	219	Lieu, Judith M.	554
Langlands, Rebecca	295	Lifshitz, Baruch	100, 184–85, 190, 192
Laniak, Timothy	361	Lim, Timothy H.	4, 56, 260–62, 264–68, 270–71, 307, 318, 568
Lapin, Hayim	193, 281, 495		
Lapp, Eric C.	228	Lincicum, David	552
Laqueur, Richard	388, 390, 392	Linski, Gerhard E.	132
Laqueur, Thomas	94–95, 96	Lipschits, Oded	218–19, 306
Lattke, Michael	474	Llewellyn-Jones, Lloyd	381
Laureys-Chachy, Rachel	225	Loader, William	97, 546
Lawlor, H. J.	573	Lock, Andrew	126
Lawrence, Louise J.	168	Long, A. A.	387
Le Donne, Anthony	545	Longenecker, Bruce W.	548
Lee, Kyong-Jin	266	Longenecker, Richard N.	496
Leeming, Henry	389	Lopez, Kathryn M.	124
Leeming, Katherine	389	Louvish, David	522
Lefebvre, Henri	123, 426	Lowenthal, David	381
Legaspi, Michael	337	Luckman, Thomas	447
Leicht, Reimund	577	Lüderitz, Gerd	30, 75, 78, 184, 210
Leiman, Sid	260, 265, 267, 269	Lundhaug, Hugo	427, 569
Lemaire, André	150, 380	Luraghi, Nino	359, 380
Lembi, Gaia	389	Luz, Menahem	391
Lemche, Neils P.	382	Luz, Ulrich	553
Lenski, Gerhard	46, 47, 54	Lyons, William John	119
Leon, Harry J.	75, 184, 190		
Leonhard, Clemens	552	Macaskill, Grant	569
Leonhardt-Balzer, Jutta	289, 463	Macatangay, Francis	356, 368–70
Lesses, Rebecca	337, 529	Macchi, Jean-Daniel	364
Levenson, Jon D.	355, 361–62	Machiela, Daniel A.	316, 371
Levine, Amy-Jill	3, 59, 99, 366, 370	Machinist, Peter	337
Levine, Lee I.	50–51, 79, 193, 195, 220, 225–26, 228, 230	Maciver, Culum	381
		Mack, Burton L.	437–39, 453, 544
Levison, John R.	105, 319, 386	MacLennan, Robert S.	70
Levinson, Joshua	500, 503	Mader, Gottfried	391
Lévy, Carlos	291	Magen, Yitzhak	57, 150, 219, 225, 228, 264

Magness, Jodi   49, 100, 150, 217, 230
Maier, Christl M.   99
Maier, Johann   474–75, 477
Malina, Bruce J.   47, 49, 128, 462
Mandel, Paul   496–97
Mannheim, Karl   413
Marböck, Johannes   448
Marcus, Joel   342–43, 502
Marcus, Ralph   281
Maresch, Klaus   30, 72, 210
Marincola, John   381, 383
Marshak, Adam Kolman   33
Marshall, John W.   421
Martola, Nils   385
Martone, Corrado   152
Maschmeier, Jens-Christian   549
Mason, Steve   5, 34–35, 56, 59, 71, 102, 268, 294, 383, 389–94, 552
Maston, Jason   549
Matlock, Michael D.   463
Matson, Jason   422
Mattila, Sharon L.   49, 101, 103–4
Mayer-Schärtel, Bärbel   390
Mazar, Benjamin   184
McConville, J. Gordon   319
McCraken, David   369
McCready, Wayne O.   261
McCullough, Patrick G.   424–25, 524
McDonald, Lee Martin   318
McDonnell, Myles A.   95
McDowell, Markus   463, 476
McGinn, Bernard   524, 534
McGrath, James   251
McKay, Heather   51
McLaren, James S.   390–91
McKechnie, Paul   27
McLaren, James   26, 35
McNamara, Patrick   126
McRae, George W.   1
Meeks, Wayne   122
Meier, John P.   545
Meiser, Martin   552
Mendels, Doron   50, 385, 577
Menken, Maarten J. J.   552
Merkur, Daniel   134
Merleau-Ponty, Maurice   130
Mermelstein, Ari   103, 127
Merz, Annette   544–47
Meshorer, Ya'akov   25
Metso, Sarianna   11, 155, 162–63
Mevorah, David   227
Meyer, Eduard   84
Meyers, Carol L.   100, 218–19, 227–28, 232
Meyers, Eric M.   49, 217–32
Migne, Jacques-Paul   573, 578
Milgram, Jonathan S.   492, 495
Milik, Józef Tadeusz   184, 212
Milikowsky, Chaim   498, 502, 574
Millar, Fergus G. B.   79–80, 192, 211, 383
Miller, Patrick D.   462
Miller, Robert J.   421
Miller, Stuart S.   228–29, 502
Milne, Pamela J.   354, 366
Miltenova, Anasava   572, 575–76
Minov, Sergey   572, 574
Miranda, Elena   185
Mirguet, Françoise   10–11, 51, 106, 127, 292, 342–43
Misgav, Haggai   188
Mittmann-Richert, Ulrike   155
Mizzi, Dennis   150
Mommsen, Theodor   84
Monaco, David Gregory   451
Monger, Matthew   571
Moore, Cary A.   365–69, 371
Moore, Stephen D.   106
Mor, Menahem   389
Morgan, Teresa   354, 357
Morray-Jones, Christopher   525
Moscovitz, Leib   495, 500
Most, Glenn W.   381
Mowinckel, Sigmund   467
Moyer, Ian S.   357, 359
Mroczek, Eva   157, 159, 261, 271, 470, 496–97, 575, 578
Muilenburg, James   10
Munk, Johannes   330
Munn, Mark   381
Munnich, Olivier   389

Muradyan, Gohar 316
Murdoch, Brian 571
Murphy, Frederick J. 421
Murphy, Roland E. 437–39, 453
Murphy-O'Connor, Jerome 439
Müz-Manor, Ophir 502
Myres, John L. 380

Naeh, Shlomo 493, 500
Najman, Hindy 6, 8–9, 155, 158–59, 312, 409, 412, 441, 443, 450, 496, 575
Nanos, Mark D. 549–50
Nasrallah, Laura 295
Naveh, Joseph 185, 193, 211
Neill, Stephen 544
Netzer, Ehud 33, 224–25, 227
Neuser, Wilhelm H. 257
Neusner, Jacob 54, 70, 71, 97, 261, 382, 390, 490, 492–93, 543
Neutel, Karin B. 101–2
Newman, Hillel 55, 573
Newman, Judith H. 121, 130, 158, 165, 306, 316, 367, 442–43, 452, 463, 468–69, 476
Newsom, Carol A. 10, 119, 125–26, 129, 162–63, 165, 168, 355, 357–58, 408, 427, 463, 477
Nicholls, Peter H. 335
Nichols, Stephen G. 569
Nickelsburg, George W. E. 1–2, 6–7, 10, 12, 14, 45–46, 117–19, 125, 147, 167, 183, 205, 252, 281, 316, 332, 369, 382–83, 389, 405–6, 410, 437, 439, 445–46, 451, 474–75, 520, 541, 543, 551, 567, 573–74
Niditch, Susan 118, 354, 357
Niebuhr, Karl-Wilhelm 549
Niehoff, Maren R. 99, 283–86, 288–89, 291–94, 499
Nikiprowetzky, Valentin 289
Nirenberg, David 84
Nisse, Ruth 342
Nitzan, Bilhah 161, 165, 464–65, 468, 472, 531
Noam, Vered 491, 495–96, 502

Nodet, Étienne 57, 389
Nogossek, Lena 545
Nolan, Patrick 46–47, 54
Nongbri, Brent 59, 383
Nordheim, Eckhard von 329, 334–35
Norelli, Enrico 581
Novak, Michael 474
Novenson, Matthew 551
Nowell, Irene 368
Noy, David 76–77, 185, 192
Nussbaum, Martha C. 127

Oakman, Douglas E. 47–50
O'Brien, Peter T. 548
O'Connor, M. John-Patrick 338
Oegema, Gerbern 25
Oesterley, W. O. E. 568
Olson, Ryan S. 390
Olsson, Birger 50–51, 79
Omerzu, Heike 337
Onn, Alexander 223
Oppenheim, A. Leo 306
Orlov, Andrei A. 527, 533, 572
Osterloh, Kevin Lee 25
Otto, Rudolph 526
Overman, J. Andrew 35, 70

Paganini, Simone M. 127
Paget, James Carleton 421
Pajunen, Mika 473
Panayotov, Alexander 3, 76–77, 185, 259, 542, 577–78, 581
Parente, Fausto 389
Park, Joseph S. 198
Parkes, James W. 552–53
Pastor, Jack 389
Patterson, Stephen 421
Patrich, Joseph 294
Paz, Yakir 282, 499
Pearce, Sarah J. 289
Pedley, Katharine Greenleaf 269
Peleg, Yuval 150
Perdue, Leo G. 440, 450–51
Perkins, Pheme 258–59
Perrin, Andrew B. 368–69, 371

MODERN SCHOLARS INDEX 641

Pestman, Pieter W. 206
Petterson, Christina 48
Peuch, Émile 474
Peursen, Wido van 572–73, 575, 578–79
Pierce, Laurie E. 220
Pietersen, Lloyd K. 119
Piovanelli, Pierluigi 568, 583
Pitkänen, Pekka 370
Plaskow, Judith 97
Poirier, John C. 546
Pomykala, Kenneth E. 167
Popović, Mladen 157, 159, 409, 441
Porten, Bezalel A. 72, 206
Porter, Stanley E. 545
Portier-Young, Anathea E. 28, 53, 122, 133, 336, 410, 415
Porton, Gary G. 54–55
Pouchelle, Patrick 343, 475
Pregill, Michael 570
Price, Jonathan J. 35–36, 186, 188, 390–91
Priest, John F. 333
Propp, Vladimir 118, 354
Pucci Ben Zeev, Miriam 29, 37, 73–74
Puech, Emile 167
Pummer, Reinhard 57–58, 60, 311, 390
Purvis, James D. 57
Pypers, Hugh 369

Rad, Gerhard von 444
Rahmani, L. Y. 185
Rajak, Tessa 25, 29, 190, 284–85, 389–91, 394
Rakel, Claudia 366, 368
Ramsby, Teresa R. 96
Rappaport, Uriel 29
Reed, Annette Yoshiko 5, 9, 247, 312, 335, 340, 343, 424, 427, 524, 532, 535, 554, 568–71, 573–75, 577–79
Reed, Jonathan L. 48–49, 544
Reeder, Caryn A. 102–3
Reeg, Gottfried 185
Reeves, John C. 427, 496, 570–71, 573, 575–78

Regev, Eyal 25, 55–56, 97, 122–23, 168, 224
Reich, Ronny 228
Reif, Stefan C. 127, 463–65, 475, 500
Reinhartz, Adele 5, 106, 129, 261
Reiterer, Fiedrich V. 44
Reventlow, Henning 462
Rey, Jean-Sébastien 166, 542, 549
Reydams-Schils, Gretchen 290
Reynolds, Joyce Marie 190
Richardson, Peter 227
Ritter, Bradley 73, 76
Rives, James B. 389
Rivkin, Ellis 490
Robert, Louis 184
Rocca, Samuel 32–33
Roddy, Nicolae 572
Rodgers, Zuleika, 389
Rohrbaugh, Richard 335–36, 338
Roitman, Adolfo 367
Roller, Duane W. 33
Rollston, Christopher 220
Römer, Cornelia 334
Romer, Thomas 319
Roncace, Mark 99
Rönsch, Hermann 571
Rooke, Deborah W. 22–23
Rosenfeld, Ben-Zion 193
Rosenthal, Yoav 500
Rosen-Zvi, Ishay 105, 281, 342, 491–92, 495, 499, 503
Rosner, B. 342
Roth-Gerson, Lea 185
Rozenberg, Silvia 227
Rowland, Christopher 134, 406, 422
Royse, James R. 386
Rubenstein, Jefferey L. 501
Runesson, Anders 50–51, 79
Runia, David T. 283, 289–90, 294
Runnalls, Donna 391
Rutgers, Leonard V. 70, 190
Ryle, Herbert E. 263–64

Safrai, Shemuel 489
Saldarini, Anthony J. 54–55, 258–59

Sanders, E. P.   51–52, 54, 71, 261, 382, 544–49
Sanders, Jack T.   447–48
Sanders, James A.   271, 318, 470, 473
Sanders, Seth L.   523
Sanderson, Judith   311
Sänger, Patrick   210, 283
Sanzo, Emanuel   532
Satlow, Michael L.   477, 496, 503
Satran, David   578, 581
Saulnier, Christiane   391
Schäfer, Peter   30, 83, 84, 424–25, 500, 521, 523, 529–30, 550–51
Schalit, Abraham   332
Schaller, Berndt   334–36, 581
Schams, Christine   122, 451
Schattner-Rieser, U.   311
Scheiber, Alexander   184
Schellenberg, Annette   440
Schenke, Gesa   334
Schiffman, Lawrence H.   160–61, 260, 522, 553
Schiffman, William   316
Schmid, Konrad   307
Schmidt, Francis   50
Schmidt, Rüdiger   51
Schmitz, Barbara   127, 365, 367
Schmitz, Thomas   295
Schnelle, Udo   553
Schneider, Michael   527
Schniedewind, William   307
Schofield, Alison   3, 24, 123–24, 153, 155, 159, 163, 167, 169, 224, 416, 541
Scholem, Gershom   423–25, 519–23, 525–30, 532–33, 535
Schott, Jermy M.   295
Schreckenberg, Heinz   389
Schremer, Adiel   212, 490, 492, 495, 501, 503
Schröter, Jens   545
Schuller, Eileen M.   97, 99, 169, 462–64, 471–73
Schuol, Monika   74
Schürer, Emil   79–80
Schwabe, Moshe   184
Schwartz, Barry   131
Schwartz, Baruch J.   307
Schwartz, Daniel R.   33, 71, 292, 384, 392, 489–90, 554
Schwartz, Seth   229, 389, 391–92, 495
Schweitzer, Albert   421–22, 544
Scott, James C.   70, 132–33
Scott, Joan Wallach   93
Secunda, Shai   501
Seely, David   473
Seeman, Chris   25, 28, 32
Segal, Alan F.   134, 533–34
Segal, Michael   159, 310–11
Segovia, Carlos A.   543
Seidman, Naomi   503
Seifrid, Mark A.   548
Sekki, Arthur   503
Seland, Torrey   283
Selden, Daniel   354, 362
Semenchenko, Lada   394
Septimus, Zvi   501
Severy-Hoven, Beth   96
Shahar, Yuval   382, 391
Shantz, Colleen   134
Sharon, Nadav   35
Shatzman, Israel   31
Shaw, Brent D.   105, 337
Shayegan, M. Rahim   501
Shemesh, Aharon   161, 169, 491, 496
Sheppard, Gerald T.   448
Shin'an, Avigdor   502
Siegert, Folker   82, 389
Sievers, Joseph   389
Siggelkow-Berner, Birke   390
Simmel, George   123
Simon-Shoshan, Moshe   492
Simonsohn, Shlomo   75
Sinding, Michael   442
Skemp, Vincent   369
Skinner, Debra   126
Skinner, Marilyn B.   95
Slingerland, Dixon   342
Sly, Dorothy   101, 292
Smallwood, E. Mary   292, 386

Smith, Anthony D. 58–59
Smith, Jonathan Z. 5–6
Smith, Morton 490
Smith, William Cantwell 59
Smith, William Robertson 129
Smith-Christopher, Daniel L. 53, 133
Sneed, Mark 440–41, 443
Soja, Edward W. 123–25, 426
Soll, William 354, 368
Sparks, H. F. D. 259, 578
Spencer, Richard A. 368–71
Spilsbury Paul 393
Spittler, Russell 335
Spolsky, Bernard 192
Stacey, David 150
Standhartinger, Angela 99, 103
Starcky, Jean 212
Stark, Rodney 123
Stegemann, Hartmut 269, 416, 463
Stein, Dina 500
Steinman, Andrew E. 260, 263, 267
Stemberger, Günter 55, 193, 543
Stendahl, Krister 547
Sterling, Gregory E. 80, 283, 285, 288, 294, 393
Stern, Ephraim 218
Stern, Menahem 187, 318
Stern, Pnina 389
Stern, Sacha 246
Steudel, Annette 166
Stocker, Margarita 99
Stökl ben Ezra, Daniel 153, 552, 555
Stone, Meredith J. 133
Stone, Michael E. 123, 134, 312, 340, 406, 408, 410–12, 417, 423, 427, 543, 568–70, 572, 575, 577–81, 583
Stowers, Stanley K. 549
Strange, James F. 218
Strange, James L. 49
Strange, James R. 544
Strugnell, John 444, 531
Stuckenbruck, Loren T. 4–5, 7, 131, 257–58, 368, 423, 471, 543, 551, 568, 571–76, 579, 581
Sundberg, Albert 260

Sussman, Yaakov 490, 493–94, 496, 500–501
Sutter, Rehmann 337
Swain, Simon 295
Swancutt, Diana M. 96
Swartz, Michael 476, 523, 529, 534–35
Szesnat, Holger 102

Tal, Oren 221
Talmon, Shemaryahu 121, 265–66
Tannenbaum, Robert F. 190
Tanner, Norman P. 263
Tanzer, Sarah 445–46
Taylor, Joan E. 56, 100, 153, 293
Tcherikover, Victor A. 29, 72–73, 187, 205, 208–9
Tervanotko, Hanna 99–100
Teugels, Lieve 496
Thackeray, Henry St.-John 390–91, 393
Theissen, Gerd 544–47
Thiessen, Matthew 550, 555
Thomas, Johannes 342
Thomas, Rosalind 380
Thomas, Samuel I. 156
Thompson, Dorothy 208
Thompson, Stith 118
Thompson, Thomas L. 382
Tigchelaar, Eibert J. C. 119, 149, 152, 155, 157, 159–60, 165, 167, 412, 444, 463
Tiller, Patrick 410
Tilly, Michael 423
Tiwald, Markus 549
Toher, Mark 390
Tomson, Peter J. 489, 549
Toorn, Karel van der 122, 307, 311, 312, 451
Topchyan, Aram 316
Tov, Emanuel 121, 147, 149–50, 157, 308, 310
Trebilco, Paul R. 74
Trenchard, Warren C. 97
Troeltsch, Ernst 413
Tromp, Johannes 331, 581
Tropper, Amram 380, 495

Trümper, Monica 225
Tucker, Gene M. 1
Tuval, Michael 392
Twelftree, Graham 342
Tzionit, Yoav 225

Uden, James 295
Udoh, Fabian E. 49, 382
Ulfgard, Håkan 552
Ullmann, Lisa 389–90
Ulrich, Eugene C. 152, 156–57, 159, 270, 310, 318
Ulrichsen, Jarl Henning 340
Unnik, Willem Cornelis van 70, 85
Urbach, Ephraim 495
Uusimäki, Elisa 166, 450

Van Seters, John 380
Vanderhooft, David S. 219
VanderKam, James C. 2, 23–24, 151–52, 156–57, 270, 310, 318, 410, 571, 573–74
Ventor, Pieter M. 124–25
Vermes, Géza 55–56, 79–80, 163, 310, 544
Vidas, Moulie 494, 501–2
Vielhauer, Philipp 406
Villalba i Verneda, Pere 384, 389, 391
Villiers, Pieter G. R. de 407
Vogel, Manuel 389
Voloshinov, Valentin 125

Wacker, Marie-Theres 99
Wahl, H.-M. 336
Wassen, Cecilia 97, 152, 161, 169
Wasserman, Emma 451
Wasserman, Mira 501
Wasserstrom, Steven M. 570
Watson, Francis 295, 548, 549
Waugh, Robin 337, 343
Weber, Max 413
Weber, Robert 258
Weber, Wilhelm 388
Wedderburn, A. J. M. 550
Weeks, Stuart 368, 439, 441, 443, 579

Wegner, Judith R. 97
Weinbender, Jack 157
Weinfeld, Moshe 464, 473
Weiss, Herold 552
Weiss, Johannes 421–22
Weiss, Richard 311
Weiss, Zeev 489, 554
Weissenberg, Hanne von 162
Weitzman, Steven 28, 128
Weksler-Bdolah, Shlomit 36–37, 223
Werline, Rodney A. 10, 126, 131, 133–34, 463, 466–68
Werman, Cana 161, 496
Werrett, Ian C. 152, 161
Wesselius, David S. 382, 385
Westerholm, Stephen 549
Westermann, Claus 467
Wheaton, Gerry 552
Whitaker, G. H. 281
White, L. Michael 51, 225, 283
White, Sidnie Ann 363, 366
Whitmarsh, Tim 295, 356, 359, 371
Whitters, Mark 332
Wick, Peter 463
Wildeboer, Gerrit 263
Willgren, David 470
Williams, Margert H. 186, 193–96, 198
Williamson, Robert, Jr. 442
Wills, Lawrence M. 118, 356, 358, 364, 369, 410, 445–46, 452
Wilson, Bryan 53, 123
Wilson, Gerald H. 470
Wilson, Walter T. 283, 451
Wimpfheimer, Barry 500–501
Winkler, John J. 95–96
Winston, David 503
Wise, Michael O. 191–92
Wiseman, T. P. 394
Wisse, Maarten 335
Witte, Markus 127
Wold, Benjamin G. 131, 166, 169
Wolfson, Elliot 523, 527
Wolfson, Harry A. 290
Wollenberg, Rebecca 577
Wolter, Michael 549, 553

Woodman, A. J.	384
Wörrle, Michael	29
Woude, A. S. van der	444, 464
Woyke, Johannes	549
Wright, Benjamin G., III	8, 81, 155, 283–84, 409–10, 441–42, 445, 446, 448, 450, 577
Wright, G. Ernest	218
Wright, J. Edward	574
Wright, N. T.	544–46, 548–49
Wyrick, Jed	311–12
Xeravits, Géza	370
Yadin, Yigael	12, 48, 211–12
Yadin-Israel, Azzan	499
Yarbro Collins, Adela	411, 421, 423
Yardeni, Ada	211–12
Yarrow, Liv M.	385
Yassif, Eli	500, 574, 577, 579
Yavetz, Zvi	84
Yellin, Joseph	153
Yuval, Israel Jacob	500, 555
Zahn, Molly M.	159, 309, 311
Zangenberg, Jürgen K.	150
Zeitlin, Froma I.	95
Zetterholm, Magnus	549–50
Zilm, Jennifer	337
Zissu, Boaz	37, 223
Zlotnick, Dov	492
Zlotnick, Helena	99–100
Zollschan, Linda	32
Zsengellér, József	362, 370
Zurawski, Jason	541

www.ingramcontent.com/pod-product-compliance
Lightning Source LLC
Chambersburg PA
CBHW021412300426
44114CB00010B/466